SHORT STORIES
for Students

Advisors

Jayne M. Burton is a teacher of English, a member of the Delta Kappa Gamma International Society for Key Women Educators, and currently a master's degree candidate in the Interdisciplinary Study of Curriculum and Instruction and English at Angelo State University.

Tom Shilts is the youth librarian at the Okemos branch of Capital Area District Library in Okemos, Michigan. He holds an MSLS degree from Clarion University of Pennsylvania and an MA in U.S. History from the University of North Dakota.

Amy Spade Silverman has taught at independent schools in California, Texas, Michigan, and New York. She holds a bachelor of arts degree from the University of Michigan and a master of fine arts degree from the University of Houston. She is a member of the National Council of Teachers of English and Teachers and Writers. She is an exam reader for Advanced Placement Literature and Composition. She is also a poet, published in *North American Review*, *Nimrod*, and *Michigan Quarterly Review*, among others.

SHORT STORIES
for Students

Presenting Analysis, Context, and Criticism on Commonly Studied Short Stories

VOLUME 42

Matthew Derda, Project Editor

Foreword by Thomas E. Barden

GALE
CENGAGE Learning·

Farmington Hills, Mich • San Francisco • New York • Waterville, Maine
Meriden, Conn • Mason, Ohio • Chicago

GALE
CENGAGE Learning®

Short Stories for Students, Volume 42

Project Editor: Matthew Derda

Rights Acquisition and Management: Moriam Aigoro

Composition: Evi Abou-El-Seoud

Manufacturing: Rhonda A. Dover

Imaging: John Watkins

Product Design: Pamela A. E. Galbreath, Jennifer Wahi

Digital Content Production: Edna Shy

Product Manager: Meggin Condino

For product information and technology assistance, contact us at
Gale Customer Support, 1-800-877-4253.
For permission to use material from this text or product,
submit all requests online at **www.cengage.com/permissions.**
Further permissions questions can be emailed to
permissionrequest@cengage.com

Gale
27500 Drake Rd.
Farmington Hills, MI, 48331-3535

ISBN-13: 978-1-4103-1591-5
ISSN 1092-7735

This title is also available as an e-book.
ISBN-13: 978-1-4103-1593-9
Contact your Gale, a part of Cengage Learning sales representative for ordering information.

Printed in Mexico
1 2 3 4 5 6 7 19 18 17 16 15

Table of Contents

Why Study Literature At All?

Short Stories for Students is designed to provide readers with information and discussion about a wide range of important contemporary and historical works of short fiction, and it does that job very well. However, I want to use this guest foreword to address a question that it does *not* take up. It is a fundamental question that is often ignored in high school and college English classes as well as research texts, and one that causes frustration among students at all levels, namely why study literature at all? Isn't it enough to read a story, enjoy it, and go about one's business? My answer (to be expected from a literary professional, I suppose) is no. It is not enough. It is a start; but it is not enough. Here's why.

First, literature is the only part of the educational curriculum that deals directly with the actual world of lived experience. The philosopher Edmund Husserl used the apt German term *die Lebenswelt*, "the living world, "to denote this realm. All the other content areas of the modern American educational system avoid the subjective, present reality of everyday life. Science (both the natural and the social varieties) objectifies, the fine arts create and/or perform, history reconstructs. Only literary study persists in posing those questions we all asked before our schooling taught us to give up on them. Only literature gives credibility to personal perceptions, feelings, dreams, and the "stream of consciousness "that is our inner voice. Literature wonders about infinity, wonders why God permits evil, wonders what will happen to us after we die. Literature admits that we get our hearts broken, that people sometimes cheat and get away with it, that the world is a strange and probably incomprehensible place. Literature, in other words, takes on all the big and small issues of what it means to be human. So my first answer is that of the humanist we should read literature and study it and take it seriously because it enriches us as human beings. We develop our moral imagination, our capacity to sympathize with other people, and our ability to understand our existence through the experience of fiction.

My second answer is more practical. By studying literature we can learn how to explore and analyze texts. Fiction may be about *die Lebenswelt*, but it is a construct of words put together in a certain order by an artist using the medium of language. By examining and studying those constructions, we can learn about language as a medium. We can become more sophisticated about word associations and connotations, about the manipulation of symbols, and about style and atmosphere. We can grasp how ambiguous language is and how important context and texture is to meaning. In our first encounter with a work of literature, of course, we are not supposed to catch all of these things. We are spellbound, just as the writer wanted us to be. It is as serious students of the writer's art that we begin to see how the tricks are done.

Seeing the tricks, which is another way of saying "developing analytical and close reading skills," is important above and beyond its intrinsic literary educational value. These skills transfer to other fields and enhance critical thinking of any kind. Understanding how language is used to construct texts is powerful knowledge. It makes engineers better problem solvers, lawyers better advocates and courtroom practitioners, politicians better rhetoricians, marketing and advertising agents better sellers, and citizens more aware consumers as well as better participants in democracy. This last point is especially important, because rhetorical skill works both ways when we learn how language is manipulated in the making of texts the result is that we become less susceptible when language is used to manipulate us.

My third reason is related to the second. When we begin to see literature as created artifacts of language, we become more sensitive to good writing in general. We get a stronger sense of the importance of individual words, even the sounds of words and word combinations. We begin to understand Mark Twain's delicious proverb "The difference between the right word and the almost right word is the difference between lightning and a lightning bug." Getting beyond the "enjoyment only" stage of literature gets us closer to becoming makers of word art ourselves. I am not saying that studying fiction will turn every student into a Faulkner or a Shakespeare. But it will make us more adaptable and effective writers, even if our art form ends up being the office memo or the corporate annual report.

Studying short stories, then, can help students become better readers, better writers, and even better human beings. But I want to close with a warning. If your study and exploration of the craft, history, context, symbolism, or anything else about a story starts to rob it of the magic you felt when you first read it, it is time to stop. Take a break, study another subject, shoot some hoops, or go for a run. Love of reading is too important to be ruined by school. The early twentieth century writer Willa Cather, in her novel *My Antonia*, has her narrator Jack Burden tell a story that he and Antonia heard from two old Russian immigrants when they were teenagers. These immigrants, Pavel and Peter, told about an incident from their youth back in Russia that the narrator could recall in vivid detail thirty years later. It was a harrowing story of a wedding party starting home in sleds and being chased by starving wolves. Hundreds of wolves attacked the group's sleds one by one as they sped across the snow trying to reach their village. In a horrible revelation, the old Russians revealed that the groom eventually threw his own bride to the wolves to save himself. There was even a hint that one of the old immigrants might have been the groom mentioned in the story. Cather has her narrator conclude with his feelings about the story. "We did not tell Pavel's secret to anyone, but guarded it jealously as if the wolves of the Ukraine had gathered that night long ago, and the wedding party had been sacrificed, just to give us a painful and peculiar pleasure." That feeling, that painful and peculiar pleasure, is the most important thing about literature. Study and research should enhance that feeling and never be allowed to overwhelm it.

Thomas E. Barden
Professor of English and Director of
Graduate English Studies, The
University of Toledo

Introduction

Purpose of the Book

The purpose of *Short Stories for Students* (*SSfS*) is to provide readers with a guide to understanding, enjoying, and studying short stories by giving them easy access to information about the work. Part of Gale's "For Students" Literature line, *SSfS* is specifically designed to meet the curricular needs of high school and undergraduate college students and their teachers, as well as the interests of general readers and researchers considering specific short fiction. While each volume contains entries on "classic" stories frequently studied in classrooms, there are also entries containing hard-to-find information on contemporary stories, including works by multicultural, international, and women writers.

The information covered in each entry includes an introduction to the story and the story's author; a plot summary, to help readers unravel and understand the events in the work; descriptions of important characters, including explanation of a given character's role in the narrative as well as discussion about that character's relationship to other characters in the story; analysis of important themes in the story; and an explanation of important literary techniques and movements as they are demonstrated in the work.

In addition to this material, which helps the readers analyze the story itself, students are also provided with important information on the literary and historical background informing each work. This includes a historical context essay, a box comparing the time or place the story was written to modern Western culture, a critical overview essay, and excerpts from critical essays on the story or author. A unique feature of *SSfS* is a specially commissioned critical essay on each story, targeted toward the student reader.

To further help today's student in studying and enjoying each story, information on audiobooks and other media adaptations is provided (if available), as well as reading suggestions for works of fiction and nonfiction on similar themes and topics. Classroom aids include ideas for research papers and lists of critical and reference sources that provide additional material on the work.

Selection Criteria

The titles for each volume of *SSfS* were selected by surveying numerous sources on teaching literature and analyzing course curricula for various school districts. Some of the sources surveyed include: literature anthologies, *Reading Lists for College-Bound Students: The Books Most Recommended by America's Top Colleges*; *Teaching the Short Story: A Guide to Using Stories from around the World*, by the National Council of Teachers of English (NCTE); and "A Study of High School Literature Anthologies," conducted by Arthur Applebee at the Center for the Learning and Teaching of Literature and sponsored by the National Endowment for the

Arts and the Office of Educational Research and Improvement.

Input was also solicited from our advisory board, as well as educators from various areas. From these discussions, it was determined that each volume should have a mix of "classic" stories (those works commonly taught in literature classes) and contemporary stories for which information is often hard to find. Because of the interest in expanding the canon of literature, an emphasis was also placed on including works by international, multicultural, and women authors. Our advisory board members—educational professionals—helped pare down the list for each volume. Works not selected for the present volume were noted as possibilities for future volumes. As always, the editor welcomes suggestions for titles to be included in future volumes.

How Each Entry Is Organized

Each entry, or chapter, in *SSfS* focuses on one story. Each entry heading lists the title of the story, the author's name, and the date of the story's publication. The following elements are contained in each entry:

Introduction: a brief overview of the story which provides information about its first appearance, its literary standing, any controversies surrounding the work, and major conflicts or themes within the work.

Author Biography: this section includes basic facts about the author's life, and focuses on events and times in the author's life that may have inspired the story in question.

Plot Summary: a description of the events in the story. Lengthy summaries are broken down with subheads.

Characters: an alphabetical listing of the characters who appear in the story. Each character name is followed by a brief to an extensive description of the character's role in the story, as well as discussion of the character's actions, relationships, and possible motivation.

Characters are listed alphabetically by last name. If a character is unnamed—for instance, the narrator in "The Eatonville Anthology"—the character is listed as "The Narrator" and alphabetized as "Narrator." If a character's first name is the only one given, the name will appear alphabetically by that name.

Themes: a thorough overview of how the topics, themes, and issues are addressed within the story. Each theme discussed appears in a separate subhead.

Style: this section addresses important style elements of the story, such as setting, point of view, and narration; important literary devices used, such as imagery, foreshadowing, symbolism; and, if applicable, genres to which the work might have belonged, such as Gothicism or Romanticism. Literary terms are explained within the entry, but can also be found in the Glossary.

Historical Context: this section outlines the social, political, and cultural climate in which the author lived and the work was created. This section may include descriptions of related historical events, pertinent aspects of daily life in the culture, and the artistic and literary sensibilities of the time in which the work was written. If the story is historical in nature, information regarding the time in which the story is set is also included. Long sections are broken down with helpful subheads.

Critical Overview: this section provides background on the critical reputation of the author and the story, including bannings or any other public controversies surrounding the work. For older works, this section may include a history of how the story was first received and how perceptions of it may have changed over the years; for more recent works, direct quotes from early reviews may also be included.

Criticism: an essay commissioned by *SSfS* which specifically deals with the story and is written specifically for the student audience, as well as excerpts from previously published criticism on the work (if available).

Sources: an alphabetical list of critical material used in compiling the entry, with bibliographical information.

Further Reading: an alphabetical list of other critical sources which may prove useful for the student. Includes full bibliographical information and a brief annotation.

Suggested Search Terms: a list of search terms and phrases to jumpstart students' further information seeking. Terms include not just titles and author names but also terms and topics related to the historical and literary context of the works.

In addition, each entry contains the following highlighted sections, set apart from the main text as sidebars:

Media Adaptations: if available, a list of audio-books and important film and television adaptations of the story, including source information. The list also includes stage adaptations, musical adaptations, etc.

Topics for Further Study: a list of potential study questions or research topics dealing with the story. This section includes questions related to other disciplines the student may be studying, such as American history, world history, science, math, government, business, geography, economics, psychology, etc.

Compare and Contrast: an "at-a-glance" comparison of the cultural and historical differences between the author's time and culture and late twentieth century or early twenty-first century Western culture. This box includes pertinent parallels between the major scientific, political, and cultural movements of the time or place the story was written, the time or place the story was set (if a historical work), and modern Western culture. Works written after 1990 may not have this box.

What Do I Read Next?: a list of works that might give a reader points of entry into a classic work (e.g., YA or multicultural titles) and/ or complement the featured story or serve as a contrast to it. This includes works by the same author and others, works from various genres, YA works, and works from various cultures and eras.

Other Features

SSfS includes "Why Study Literature At All?," a foreword by Thomas E. Barden, Professor of English and Director of Graduate English Studies at the University of Toledo. This essay provides a number of very fundamental reasons for studying literature and, therefore, reasons why a book such as *SSfS*, designed to facilitate the study of literature, is useful.

A Cumulative Author/Title Index lists the authors and titles covered in each volume of the *SSfS* series.

A Cumulative Nationality/Ethnicity Index breaks down the authors and titles covered in each volume of the *SSfS* series by nationality and ethnicity.

A Subject/Theme Index, specific to each volume, provides easy reference for users who may be studying a particular subject or theme rather than a single work. Significant subjects from events to broad themes are included.

Each entry may include illustrations, including photo of the author, stills from film adaptations (if available), maps, and/or photos of key historical events.

Citing Short Stories for Students

When writing papers, students who quote directly from any volume of *SSfS* may use the following general forms to document their source. These examples are based on MLA style; teachers may request that students adhere to a different style, thus, the following examples may be adapted as needed.

When citing text from *SSfS* that is not attributed to a particular author (for example, the Themes, Style, Historical Context sections, etc.), the following format may be used:

> "How I Met My Husband." *Short Stories for Students.* Ed. Sara Constantakis. Vol. 36. Detroit: Gale, Cengage Learning, 2013. 73–95. Print.

When quoting the specially commissioned essay from *SSfS* (usually the first essay under the Criticism subhead), the following format may be used:

> Dominic, Catherine. Critical Essay on "How I Met My Husband." *Short Stories for Students.* Ed. Sara Constantakis. Vol. 36. Detroit: Gale, Cengage Learning, 2013. 84–87. Print.

When quoting a journal or newspaper essay that is reprinted in a volume of *SSfS*, the following form may be used:

> Ditsky, John. "The Figure in the Linoleum: The Fictions of Alice Munro." *Hollins Critic* 22.3 (1985): 1–10. Rpt. in *Short Stories for Students.* Vol. 36. Ed. Sara Constantakis. Detroit: Gale, Cengage Learning, 2013. 92–94. Print.

When quoting material from a book that is reprinted in a volume of *SSfS,* the following form may be used:

> Cooke, John. "Alice Munro." *The Influence of Painting on Five Canadian Writers.* Lewiston, NY: Edwin Mellen Press, 1996. 69–85. Rpt. in *Short Stories for Students.* Vol. 36. Ed. Sara Constantakis. Detroit: Gale, Cengage Learning, 2013. 89–92. Print.

We Welcome Your Suggestions

The editorial staff of *Short Stories for Students* welcomes your comments and ideas. Readers who wish to suggest short stories to appear in future volumes, or who have other suggestions, are cordially invited to contact the editor. You may contact the editor via E-mail at: **ForStudentsEditors@cengage.com.** Or write to the editor at:

Editor, *Short Stories for Students*

Gale

27500 Drake Road

Farmington Hills, MI 48331-3535

Literary Chronology

1797: Mary Shelley is born on August 30 in London, England.

1804: Nathaniel Hawthorne is born on July 4 in Salem, Massachusetts.

1833: Mary Shelley's "The Mortal Immortal: A Tale" is published in *The Keepsake*.

1835: Mark Twain is born on November 30 in Florida, Missouri.

1844: Nathaniel Hawthorne's "Rappaccini's Daughter" is published in *United States Magazine and Democratic Review*.

1851: Mary Shelley dies of a brain tumor on February 1 in London, England.

1864: Nathaniel Hawthorne dies in his sleep of unspecified causes on May 19 in Plymouth, New Hampshire.

1869: Algernon Blackwood is born on March 14 in Shooters Hill, Kent, England.

1879: E. M. Forster is born on January 1 in Marylebone, England.

1891: Zora Neale Hurston is born on January 7 in Notasulga, Alabama.

1905: Mark Twain's "Eve's Diary" is published in *Harpers*.

1907: Algernon Blackwood's "The Willows" is published in *The Listener and Other Stories*.

1909: E. M. Forster's "The Machine Stops" is published in *Oxford and Cambridge Review*.

1910: Mark Twain dies of a heart attack on April 21 in Redding, Connecticut.

1912: John Cheever is born on May 27 in Quincy, Massachusetts.

1916: Roald Dahl is born on September 13 in Cardiff, Wales.

1921: Hisaye Yamamoto is born on August 23 in Redondo Beach, California.

1924: Zora Neale Hurston's "Drenched In Light" is published in *Opportunity*.

1933: Philip Roth is born on March 19 in Newark, New Jersey.

1939: Margaret Atwood is born on November 18 in Ottawa, Ontario, Canada.

1947: John Cheever's "The Enormous Radio" is published in *New Yorker*.

1949: Hisaye Yamamoto's "Seventeen Syllables" is published in *Partisan Review*.

1949: Le Minh Khue is born on December 6 in Thanh Hó Province, French Indochina.

1951: Algernon Blackwood dies of cerebral thrombosis and arteriosclerosis on December 10 in London, England.

1954: Andrea Barrett is born on November 16 in Boston, Massachusetts.

1959: Roald Dahl's "The Landlady" is published in *New Yorker* magazine.

1959: Philip Roth's "Defender of the Faith" is published in *New Yorker*.

1960: Zora Neale Hurston dies of hypertensive heart disease on January 28 in Fort Pierce, Florida.

1970: E. M. Forster dies of a stroke on June 7 in Coventry, England.

1971: Le Minh Khue's "Những ngôi sao xa xôi" is published. It is published in English as "The Distant Stars" in *North Việt Nam Now: Fiction and Essays from Hà Noi* in 1996.

1972: Yiyun Li is born on November 4 in Beijing, China.

1979: John Cheever is awarded the Pulitzer Prize for Fiction for *The Stories of John Cheever.*

1982: John Cheever dies of cancer on June 18 in Ossening, New York.

1989: Margaret Atwood's "The Age of Lead" is published in *Toronto Life* magazine.

1990: Roald Dahl dies of myelodysplastic syndrome on November 23 in Oxfordshire, England.

1997: Philip Roth is awarded the Pulitzer Prize for Fiction for *American Pastoral.*

2000: Margaret Atwood is awarded the Booker Prize for *The Blind Assassin.*

2004: Yiyun Li's "The Princess of Nebraska" is published in *Ploughshares.*

2011: Hisaye Yamamoto dies of natural causes on January 30 in Los Angeles, California.

2011: Philip Roth is awarded the Man Booker International Prize.

2012: Andrea Barrett's "The Particles" is published in *Tin House.*

Acknowledgements

The editors wish to thank the copyright holders of the excerpted criticism included in this volume and the permissions managers of many book and magazine publishing companies for assisting us in securing reproduction rights. We are also grateful to the staffs of the Detroit Public Library, the Library of Congress, the University of Detroit Mercy Library, Wayne State University Purdy/ Kresge Library Complex, and the University of Michigan Libraries for making their resources available to us. Following is a list of the copyright holders who have granted us permission to reproduce material in this volume of *SSfS*. Every effort has been made to trace copyright, but if omissions have been made, please let us know.

COPYRIGHTED EXCERPTS IN SSfS, VOLUME 42, WERE REPRODUCED FROM THE FOLLOWING SOURCES:

China, 47.2, Spring, 2008. Copyright © 2008 *China*. Reproduced by permission of the publisher.—***Christian Science Monitor***, August 30, 2013. Copyright © *Christian Science Monitor*. Reproduced by permission of the publisher.—Cooper, Alan. From ***Philip Roth and the Jews***. State University of New York Press, 1996. Copyright © State University of New York Press, 1996. Reproduced by permission of the publisher.—***Critical Survey***, 17.1, 2005. Copyright © 2005 *Critical Survey*. Reproduced by permission of the publisher.—***Economist***, February 9, 2002. Copyright © 2002 *Economist*. Reproduced by permission of the publisher.—Hofkosh, Sonia. From ***The Other Mary Shelley: Beyond "Frankenstein."*** Edited by Audrey A. Fisch, Anne K. Mellor, and Esther H. Schor. Oxford University Press, 1993. Copyright © 1993 Oxford University Press. Reproduced by permission of the publisher.—Hoeveler, Diane Long. From ***Iconoclastic Departures: Mary Shelley After "Frankenstein."*** Edited by Syndy M. Conger, Frederick S. Frank, and Gregory O'Dea. Fairleigh Dickinson University Press, 1997. Copyright © 1997 Fairleigh University Press. Reproduced by permission of the publisher.—Goho, James. From ***Journeys into Darkness: Critical Essays on Gothic Horror***. Rowman & Littlefield, 2014. Copyright © 2014 Rowman & Littlefield. Reproduced by permission of the publisher.—Howard, Lillie P. From ***Zora Neale Hurston***. Twayne, 1980. Copyright © 1980 Cengage Learning. Reproduced by permission of Gale, a part of Cengage Learning.—***January***, November, 2000. Copyright © 2000 *January*. Reproduced by permission of the publisher.—Johnson, Sarah Anne and Andrea Barrett. From ***Conversations with American Women Writers***. University Press of New England, 2004. Copyright © 2004 University Press of New England. Reproduced by permission of the publisher.—***Kirkus Reviews***, March 1, 1997. Copyright © 1997 *Kirkus Reviews*. Reproduced by permission of the publisher.—Littmann, Greg.

From *Roald Dahl and Philosophy: A Little Nonsense Now and Then*. Edited by Jacob M. Held. Rowman & Littlefield, 2014. Copyright © 2014 Rowman & Littlefield. Reproduced by permission of the publisher.—Mangione, Jerre and Philip Roth. From *Conversations with Philip Roth*. Edited by George J. Searless. University Press of Mississippi, 1992. Copyright © 1992 University Press of Mississippi. Reproduced by permission of the publisher.—*MELUS*, 24.4, Winter 1999. Copyright © 1999 *MELUS*. Reproduced by permission of the publisher.—*New Statesman*, November 1, 2010; December 20, 2011. Copyright © 2010, 2011 *New Statesman*. Reproduced by permission of the publisher.—Newman, Lea Bertani Vozar. From *A Reader's Guide to the Short Stories of Nathaniel Hawthorne*. G. K. Hall, 1979. Copyright © 1979 G. K. Hall. Reproduced by permission of the publisher.—Nischik, Reingard M. From *The Canadian Short Story: Interpretations*. Edited by Reingard M. Nischik. Camden House, 2007. Copyright © 2007 Camden House. Reproduced by permission of the publisher.—O'hara, James. From *John Cheever: A Study of the Short Fiction*. Twayne, 1989. Copyright © 1989 Cengage Learning. Reproduced by permission of Gale, a part of Cengage Learning.—*Outlook*, 1906. Public Domain.—*Philip Roth Studies*, 7.1, Spring 2011. Copyright © 2011 *Philip Roth Studies*. Reproduced by permission of the publisher.—*Publisher's Weekly*, 244.12, March 24, 1997. Copyright © 1997 *Publisher's Weekly*. Reproduced by permission of the publisher.—Samuels, Wilfred D. From *Critical Essays on Zora Neale Hurston*. Edited by Gloria L. Cronin. G. K. Hall, 1998. Copyright © 1998 G. K. Hall. Reproduced by permission of the publisher.—*Spectator*, 97, September 22, 1906. Public Domain.—Sullivan, Jack. From *Elegant Nightmares: The English Ghost Story from Le Fanu to Blackwood*. Ohio University Press, 1978. Copyright © 1978 Ohio University Press. Reproduced by permission of the publisher.—Waldeland, Lynne. From *John Cheever*. Twayne, 1979. Copyright © 1979 Cengage Learning. Reproduced by permission of Gale, a part of Cengage Learning.—West, Mark I. From *Roald Dahl*. Twayne, 1992. Copyright © 1992 Cengage Learning. Reproduced by permission of Gale, a part of Cengage Learning.—Wilson, James D. From *A Reader's Guide to the Short Stories of Mark Twain*. G. K. Hall, 1987. Copyright © 1987 G. K. Hall. Reproduced by permission of the publisher.—*Women's Review of Books*, 16.3, December 1998. Copyright © 1998 *Women's Review of Books*. Reproduced by permission of the publisher.—*World Literature Today*, 72.1, Winter 1998; July-August, 2006. Copyright © 1998, 2006 *World Literature Today*. Reproduced by permission of the publisher.—Worthington, Heather. From *Roald Dahl*. Edited by Ann Alston and Catherine Butler. Palgrave Macmillan, 2012. Copyright © 2012 Palgrave Macmillan. Reproduced by permission of the publisher.

Contributors

Susan K. Andersen: Andersen is a writer and teacher with a PhD in English literature. Entry on "Drenched in Light." Original essay on "Drenched in Light."

Bryan Aubrey: Aubrey holds a PhD in English. Entries on "The Machine Stops" and "The Willows." Original essays on "The Machine Stops" and "The Willows."

Rita M. Brown: Brown is an English professor. Entry on "The Mortal Immortal." Original essay on "The Mortal Immortal."

Klay Dyer: Dyer is a freelance writer and editor specializing in topics relating to literature, popular culture, and innovation. Entry on "The Landlady." Original essay on "The Landlady."

Kristen Sarlin Greenberg: Greenberg is a freelance writer and editor with a background in literature and philosophy. Entry on "Defender of the Faith." Original essay on "Defender of the Faith."

Michael Allen Holmes: Holmes is a writer with existential interests. Entries on "The Distant Stars" and "The Particles." Original essays on "The Distant Stars" and "The Particles."

David Kelly: Kelly is an instructor of creative writing and literature. Entry on "The Enormous Radio." Original essay on "The Enormous Radio."

Amy L. Miller: Miller is a graduate of the University of Cincinnati, and she currently resides in New Orleans, Louisiana. Entry on "Seventeen Syllables." Original essay on "Seventeen Syllables."

Michael J. O'Neal: O'Neal holds a PhD in English. Entry on "Rappaccini's Daughter." Original essay on "Rappaccini's Daughter."

Kathy Wilson Peacock: Wilson Peacock is a freelance writer who specializes in contemporary literature. Entry on "The Age of Lead." Original essay on "The Age of Lead."

Laura Pryor: Pryor has a master's degree in English literature and thirty years of experience as a professional writer. Entry on "The Princess of Nebraska." Original essay on "The Princess of Nebraska."

Bradley Skeen: Skeen is a classicist. Entry on "Eve's Diary." Original essay on "Eve's Diary.".

The Age of Lead

MARGARET ATWOOD

1989

"The Age of Lead" is a short story by Margaret Atwood that was first published in *Toronto Life* magazine in July 1989. It was included in her short-story collection *Wilderness Tips and Other Stories* in 1991 and in *Telling Tales*, an anthology of stories from world-renowned writers published as a fundraiser in conjunction with World AIDS Day in 2004. The story is a stream-of-consciousness recollection by Jane, a middle-aged woman living in Toronto, about her lifelong friend Vincent, who recently died. Jane's thoughts wander toward Vincent while she watches a television documentary about the exhumation of John Torrington, a British sailor who died in 1845 on a seafaring expedition to find a navigable passage through the Arctic. His preserved body has been recovered from the permafrost on a remote Canadian island and is being studied by a group of scientists. Vincent died of an unidentified virus, whereas Torrington, the scientists discover, died of lead poisoning. Jane realizes the deaths of both men were due to forces unknown at the time, a silent killer lurking in a poisoned environment. Critics have commended the story for Atwood's ability to meld a dispassionate look at modern urban life with a historical event that looms large in the Canadian imagination.

Canadian writer and activist Margaret Atwood
(© *Jeremy Sutton-Hibbert | Alamy*)

AUTHOR BIOGRAPHY

Atwood was born in Canada in 1939. Her father was an entomologist, which resulted in the family's living in remote rural areas for much of her childhood. This early experience fueled a lifelong love of the natural world, which has been a common theme in much of her work, including "The Age of Lead." Atwood graduated from the University of Toronto in 1961, received her master's degree from Radcliffe College in 1962, and attended Harvard University for several years after that. She has been married to the poet Graeme Gibson since the 1970s and has one daughter.

Atwood launched her writing career with her award-winning book of poetry *Double Persephone* in 1961. Her first novel, *The Edible Woman*, was published in 1969 and concerns a young woman who feels that her independence is threatened by her recent engagement. As a result she finds herself increasingly unable to eat while simultaneously feeling that she is being psychologically devoured by her fiancé.

Among Atwood's best-known and most popular novels are *The Handmaid's Tale* (1985) and *Oryx and Crake* (2003), both dystopian novels set in a totalitarian society in the near future. *The Handmaid's Tale* takes place in a conservative and repressive world where environmental degradation has rendered most women sterile. Those who are able to procreate are enslaved as handmaids and forced to bear children against their will. The postapocalyptic world of *Oryx and Crake* is told mostly in flashbacks by a character named Snowman, whose childhood friend, Crake, is responsible for a genetically engineered virus that has wiped out humanity but also has created a not-quite-human race known as Crakers. Oryx was the woman they both loved, a mysterious person who rose to fame as a victim of child prostitution. The book is the first in the MaddAddam Trilogy, which continues with *The Year of the Flood* (2009) and *MaddAddam* (2013). All three novels serve as a warning about genetic experimentation, environmental ruin, and social injustice.

Two other of Atwood's most well-known novels, *Alias Grace* (1996) and *The Blind Assassin* (2000), have a historical focus; the former novelizes the true story of Grace Marks, a young Irish immigrant in rural nineteenth-century Canada who was accused of murdering her employer and his housekeeper. The latter is a story of two sisters in Toronto between the world wars, told by the surviving sister after the other has died in a car accident. *The Blind Assassin* is the dead woman's posthumously published novel, which Atwood features as a novel within the novel. Atwood has published several well-received collections of short fiction over the years, including *Dancing Girls and Other Stories* (1977); *Bluebeard's Egg* (1983); *Wilderness Tips* (1991), which includes "The Age of Lead"; and *Stone Mattress* (2014).

Few writers have garnered as many awards as Atwood. She won the Booker Prize in 2000 for *The Blind Assassin* and was shortlisted for it three additional times; she received the Arthur C. Clarke Award for science fiction for *The Handmaid's Tale*, the Giller Prize for *Alias Grace*, and a Guggenheim fellowship, and she was named the Humanist of the Year in 1987 and *Ms.* magazine's Woman of the Year in 1986. Atwood has received dozens of other awards from both Canadian and international organizations for her poetry, novels, and contributions to literature in general.

Atwood is a popular and respected writer throughout the world for her unflinching exploration of environmental degradation, gender issues, and political dystopias. She is also regarded as a leading voice in Canadian letters because of her many works that examine Canadian life and her vocal support of Canadian writers. Her collection of essays *Survival: A Thematic Guide to Canadian Literature* (1972) and *Strange Things: The Malevolent North in Canadian Literature* (1995) both seek to identify the elements unique to Canadian literature and establish it as an independent discipline.

PLOT SUMMARY

Jane, the main character in "The Age of Lead," is a forty-three-year-old single woman who is watching a televised documentary about scientists recovering a frozen body from the permafrost of the Canadian arctic. The frozen man is John Torrington, a crew member of the Franklin Expedition, which in 1845 sailed from England to discover a Northwest Passage through the Arctic Circle to India. Everyone on the expedition's two ships, the HMS *Terror* and the HMS *Erebus* eventually died, and some of the last survivors resorted to cannibalism. The reason for their deaths and the location of the ships has been a mystery for over a century. Jane is amazed at how well preserved Torrington's body is. He has "an indecipherable gaze, innocent, ferocious, amazed, but contemplative."

The story is an interior monologue of Jane's thoughts as she watches the show. She rarely watches television, because she finds news shows' dedication to reality depressing and vaguely sinister. But this show brings back fond memories of her good friend Vincent, and she is fascinated by Torrington, a petty officer who was only twenty when he died. He was one of the first to die, and he was buried deep within the permafrost. He is dressed nicely, and his coffin has an engraved nameplate. Jane ruminates on the others' deaths; as time went by, the crew must have expended less energy on burials because they needed to keep themselves alive. Their prayers probably became less pious and more desperate. The last of the dead were left where they fell. No one had any clue what had happened to them for decades.

Although Jane is not much of a history buff, even she knows the broad facts of the Franklin Expedition, having learned about it in her suburban Toronto school in the early 1960s. The expedition appealed to Jane; she liked the idea of taking off in a boat and going somewhere new and uncharted. It was dangerous—like having unprotected sex.

As Torrington's body begins to emerge from the melting ice, Jane remembers Vincent as a teenager. They were best friends who bonded over their lack of seriousness about life. They loved to dress up and make fun of people and events; they were always joking. Vincent was popular—the class clown—appreciated by both boys and girls because he was nonthreatening and fearless.

Other boys had swaggering attitudes and slicked-back hair, but Vincent was just Vincent. Even Jane's mother liked him; she sensed that Vincent was safe—he would not hurt Jane, break her heart, or get her pregnant. Jane's mom called such things "consequences." Jane herself had been a consequence, and her mother drummed it into her daughter's head that a similar fate would inevitably befall her. Jane regards her mother as a sad woman, her body and soul sagging and exhausted by the daily grind of her job as a department store saleswoman. Nevertheless, Jane internalizes her mother's warnings; she distrusts all boys except for Vincent.

Jane fondly recalls drinking gin with Vincent in her backyard while they made fun of their mothers, imitating their shrewish voices and their warnings about the waywardness of men and their own impending doom. However, they were never a romantic couple; instead they parodied the idea. They wore crazy outfits in public or dressed as Chinese people and ordered Chinese food, just for fun. They went to prom together dressed in outré vintage outfits and danced the tango around the school gym, mocking the event itself. Ultimately, their friendship was based on the fact that they both "wanted a life without consequences."

The scientists on television are slowly thawing Torrington's body, revealing his bare feet. Jane thinks they should have left him with his socks. She remarks that parts of his body are tied together, presumably to make burial easier, but she thinks that it is because they were afraid he would get up and walk around. Jane is about to change the channel because "it is too reminiscent." The subject turns to Torrington's clothing. "An interest in the clothing of the present is frivolity, an interest in the clothing of the past is archaeology; a point Vincent would have appreciated," Jane muses.

After high school Jane and Vincent went to college together. Jane never dated other boys and thought that perhaps she was in love with Vincent. When they kissed, however, there was no passion, only friendship. Eventually, their lives diverged. Jane moved to Vancouver and then Montreal and took a series of arts-related jobs. Like other young women of the early 1970s, she shied away from commitment. She lived with several men, no strings attached, in nondescript apartments but never stayed for long.

Eventually, she returned to Toronto, and so did Vincent, who opened a design studio. They fell into their old roles, pleased with their own "outrageousness" and "air of conspiracy." Jane's life revolved around Vincent and his wide circle of friends in the art world; she started a small business managing their money. At some point during these years, she and Vincent tried to be a couple, but he never committed himself to the role. It occurred to her that he might be gay, but she was afraid to ask him.

The documentary shows etchings of the *Erebus* and the *Terror*, and Jane thinks of how lonely the men must have been without love to get them by while they were stranded. She wonders who comforted John Torrington as he lay dying and if he knew why he was dying.

Jane considers Toronto in the 1980s, when the good times suddenly did not seem so good anymore. In the din of construction "the air was full of windblown grit." People too young and healthy to die seemed to succumb suddenly to terrible diseases, including bone cancer, heart attack, emphysema, pneumonia, AIDS, suicide, hepatitis, and meningitis. Jane attributes these deaths to some insidious force that pervades the environment—"a thing like a colorless gas, scentless and invisible, so that any germ that happened along could invade their bodies, take them over." Everything in the environment is being slowly poisoned. The trees are dying, chemicals and pesticides have invaded the food supply, and the water is polluted. Breathing has become a dangerous activity. The countryside is no better, with its radioactive trash hidden in the trees.

Vincent has been dead for a number of months, Jane reveals. Torrington, she surmises, probably looks better than Vincent at the moment, who was only forty-two when he was admitted to the hospital "for a mutated virus that didn't even have a name yet." It was clear that he would die as soon as the virus reached his brain. In the hospital Vincent was "packed in ice," with his cold, white feet poking out the bottom of a sheet, just like Torrington's. Jane selfishly worried about herself while Vincent was dying. Even though Vincent could barely speak, he joked about his situation. Jane realized that her mother was right: life did have consequences.

The scientists on television reveal that Torrington died of lead poisoning. It turns out that the modern technology that was supposed to save the Franklin Expedition from the scourge of scurvy—canned food—was what did them in. The cans were sealed with lead solder, which seeped into the food and poisoned the men. They could not taste it, but as the lead coursed through their veins, it rendered them susceptible to the mildest germs. Eventually, it destroyed their brains and made them incapable of making sound decisions that would save them. The last survivors had set off on foot over the ice, pulling a sled of useless items with them.

Jane turns off the television and retreats to her sterile kitchen, recently renovated but without any touch of her personality. Her possessions will outlive her, as Vincent's had. She considers the street outside, littered with the detritus of modern life—disposable plates, empty cans. She tries to clean it up every day, but it's a losing battle. People jettison trash as if they are fleeing the city, casting off unnecessary objects as they go.

CHARACTERS

Jane

Jane is the protagonist of the story, which is a reminiscence of her friend Vincent that takes place while she is watching a documentary on the exhumation of John Torrington, whose frozen corpse is being thawed after nearly a century and a half in the Arctic permafrost.

Jane is in her mid-forties; she is single and lives alone in Toronto. She has been friends with Vincent since high school. Their friendship was built on a shared love of goofing around, wearing ridiculous costumes and making each other and their fellow students laugh. She recognizes that she is simply a prop for Vincent— he is usually the star of their antics and the popular one at school. She, like everyone else, adores him. Jane desires a life of adventure without consequences, which means taking care of herself and relying on no one else. In her youth this takes the form of never being serious about anything.

Because of her mother's constant warnings about men, Jane becomes very guarded and never forms a long-term, intimate romantic relationship with a man, although she lives with several boyfriends over the years. Instead, she relies on Vincent to be the center of her world when they both land back in Toronto in the early 1980s; she tries to fall in love with him, but he remains detached from the process. In the end, Vincent's death makes her realize that everything has consequences, no matter how hard a person tries to avoid them. This realization is the moment of her emotional growth.

Jane's Mother

Jane's mother looms large in the story. She was just a teenager when she became pregnant with Jane and married Jane's father, who left the family after five years. Thus, she is forever warning Jane of the "consequences" of dating, which entail being taken advantage of, getting pregnant, and then being forced to raise a child on her own. Jane's mother can see no other life for her daughter than for her to repeat her own mistakes, leading to a permanent downfall and a subsequent life of misery and drudgery. However, Jane's mother likes Vincent, probably because she senses that he is gay and recognizes that, for this reason, he is a "safe" choice for Jane. Jane's mother eventually retires to Florida, where she writes Jane long letters full of bitter admonitions that Jane often fails to respond to.

John Torrington

John Torrington is a corpse whose frozen body is slowly being thawed by scientists who hope to discover what killed him. He was one of the first crew members to die during the doomed 1845 Franklin Expedition, in which the *Erebus* and *Terror* set sail from England in search of a Northwest Passage through the Arctic Circle. He is carefully dressed in a cotton shirt and pants and buried in a coffin with an engraved nameplate. He is barefoot, as Vincent was when he was dying, and scraps of cloth tied around his head and legs keep his jaw shut and his legs together for ease of burial. Jane is entranced by Torrington's face, which seems perfectly preserved, with only his lips peeled back from his mouth, his eyes the color of "milky tea." Torrington died of pneumonia brought about by lead poisoning, which resulted from consuming food from tin cans soldered together with lead. Torrington's body serves as a symbol of the invisible consequences of modern technology. Thematically, he is compared to Vincent as he lay dying, suggesting that nothing can save us from our ultimate demise.

Vincent

Vincent was Jane's close friend, who dies young of a mysterious virus that slowly takes over his body. Even on his deathbed, he retains his characteristic good humor, joking with Jane that the pod people have finally come for him.

Vincent has always been popular with everyone because he is genuinely joyful, funny, and nonthreatening. As a teenager he loved dressing up in vintage clothing to garner attention. He accompanied Jane to their senior prom in white tails and a top hat and danced the tango around the gymnasium with her pearls in his teeth. He seems to sublimate his homosexuality by humor to deflect attention away from the topic. His relationship with Jane is one of mostly platonic friendship; at her insistence they try to become a couple, but it does not come naturally to him. Jane suspects that he is gay, but he never says so explicitly. It appears that he does not want to suffer the consequences of making such a public declaration at a time when AIDS is ravaging the gay community and gay rights are still in their infancy.

Vincent is compared to Torrington and the others who died during the Franklin Expedition. He is "laid out on ice like a salmon," just like Torrington, with his cold, white feet exposed. This comparison demonstrates that in every age, humankind introduces unintended consequences through technology.

THEMES

Death

"The Age of Lead," which compares the deaths of two men who died 150 years apart, is an exploration of death. Atwood contrasts the

TOPICS FOR FURTHER STUDY

- Watch the 1988 NOVA documentary *Buried in Ice*, which is likely what Jane is watching during the story. It is available on the Internet Archive at https://archive.org/details/BuriedInIce. Write a one-page description of what John Torrington's frozen body looks like to you, using as many adjectives, similes, and metaphors as you can (without repeating any that Atwood uses in "The Age of Lead"). What or who does he remind you of? Be as poetic as possible and try to relate it to something in your own life.

- Canada has the world's third-largest oil reserves, thanks to the 1.7 trillion barrels of crude oil in Alberta's Athabasca tar sands. Research the impact of increased mining and development in the region on the local and national environment since the mid-2000s. Create a PowerPoint presentation with statistics on oil production and environmental damage and how they relate to Atwood's "The Age of Lead."

- The Franklin Expedition looms large in the Canadian imagination, and many people over the years set out to find the ships and bodies of the crew before Owen Beattie unearthed John Torrington in 1984. Research the early search-and-rescue operations and the later expeditions to find the ships and create a detailed time line, ending with the Canadian expedition that located the *Erebus* in 2014.

- *Graves of Ice: The Lost Franklin Expedition* (2014) by John Wilson is a young-adult novel about a fourteen-year-old boy named George on the HMS *Erebus* during the Franklin Expedition. George and Commander James Fitzjames are the last survivors and have abandoned their ship in an effort to make their way to safety. Write a five-paragraph report in which you compare the events of the book with those that Atwood recounts in "The Age of Lead" and determine whether you feel that *Graves of Ice* is accurate in its retelling of the expedition and why or why not.

---

seemingly unrelated deaths of John Torrington and Vincent to demonstrate that despite the march of progress they have more in common than not. Both died too young, Torrington at twenty and Vincent at forty-two. Neither knew their cause of death; the Franklin crew had no clue about the lead poisoning that killed Torrington, and doctors were helpless against the unidentified virus that slowly killed Vincent.

The common link between these two deaths is Jane. She watches a documentary on Torrington and reflects on his death as well as the recent death of her best friend, Vincent. Jane had always sought to live her life without consequences (i.e., the responsibilities of being a spouse or mother), but it becomes clear to her at this moment that "there were consequences after all." The consequence of life, Atwood suggests, is death.

Atwood also suggests that "progress" itself has deadly consequences. The newfangled canned food was supposed to save the sailors, but it killed them. In 1980s Toronto, Vincent and his friends are flush with money in a booming city, yet many are dying too young—their prosperity cannot save them. Jane wonders what the sailors told Torrington about his illness; "If you are dying, you want to know why." Later, she asks Vincent why he is dying, and he jokingly responds that "it must have been something I ate." This is juxtaposed several paragraphs later when the scientists on the television discover that "it was what they'd been eating that had killed" the members of the Franklin Expedition.

When Jane and Vincent were kids, they were close, though he was not interested in her romantically.
(© auremar | ShutterStock.com)

Ultimately, "The Age of Lead" is a middle-aged woman's meditation on death as she becomes concerned about her own mortality. As the story ends, she is in her kitchen, contemplating her small appliances, which after her own death will become nothing more than "purposeless objects adrift in the physical world," just like the contents of Vincent's apartment and the useless items the dying crew of the *Terror* and *Erebus* dragged over the Arctic ice.

Ecology

"The Age of Lead" warns readers of the dangerous "consequences"—a term that both Jane and her mother use—of humans tinkering with the environment. In the 1840s, this hubris was manifested in the canned food that was hailed as a way for the Franklin Expedition to survive a years' long journey without contracting scurvy. Scurvy is a disease caused by a lack of vitamin C, which in its advanced stages can be fatal. Prior to the 1840s, many sailors suffered and died from it on long voyages because of

a lack of fresh fruits and vegetables in their diets. The Franklin Expedition believed it had solved this age-old problem with its new technology. But, Atwood suggests, for every action there is an equal and opposite reaction. The British were smart enough to build ships that could withstand the planet's most punishing climate and find a way to prevent scurvy, but their solution introduced a new problem—lead poisoning. This danger was invisible to them. The lead that leached into their food made them just as vulnerable to illness, madness, and death as scurvy had. Thus, as they traversed the pristine environment of the Arctic, untouched by the dirt and grime of Britain's Industrial Revolution, they managed to bring their own pollution with them.

Atwood also links Vincent's death from an unknown virus to Canada's environmental degradation in the 1980s. Jane enumerates the various afflictions that have killed her friends and acquaintances: bone cancer, AIDS, heart attack, emphysema, viral pneumonia, hepatitis, and spinal meningitis. She theorizes that they had been infected by a "mysterious agent . . . scentless and invisible" that rendered them unable to thwart everyday germs—just as lead poisoning that "nobody could taste" rendered Franklin's crew susceptible to pneumonia and impaired their thinking. Jane's litany of diseases is followed in the next paragraph by a similar litany of ecological disasters: acid rain; food laced with hormones, pesticides, and poisons; polluted drinking water; toxic waste dumps; and radioactive waste. These ecological disasters are largely out of sight, either invisible or "masked by the lush, deceitful green of waving trees." Meanwhile, the city streets are "clogged with fumes and cars," and "the air [is] full of windblown grit."

Finally, Jane connects the path of the expedition's last survivors, littered with useless, inessential items, with the steady stream of trash that she is constantly removing from her front sidewalk: "plastic drinking cups, crumpled softdrink cans, used take-out plates." These items pollute the environment, Atwood suggests, and may be harming us in ways that we do not yet fully understand.

STYLE

Interior Monologue

An interior monologue is a literary device in which a character's or narrator's thoughts are conveyed to the reader as they occur in his or her mind. In "The Age of Lead," the entire story is Jane's interior monologue. The action of the story is negligible: Jane is home alone watching a television documentary about the exhumation of John Torrington. At the end of the story, she turns off the television and goes into her kitchen. However, Atwood uses the technique of interior monologue to create a vivid outline of Jane's life from her days as a teenager up to the present, a span of roughly twenty-five years, complete with flashbacks and dialogue.

While Jane watches the documentary, her thoughts range widely as she compares the long-deceased Torrington to her best friend, the more recently deceased Vincent. The reader learns about Jane's youth, growing up fatherless with a bitter, weary mother who "inspired in almost everyone who encountered her a vicious desire for escape." Jane recalls the antics she and Vincent engaged in during their high school years—dressing up in old clothes and acting ridiculous. They drank gin in her backyard and made fun of their mothers.

Jane's thoughts about Vincent proceed fairly chronologically except for the fact that early on she notes that he is dead. This bit of context allows readers to understand why Jane is transfixed by the show. Vincent has been dead less than a year, so Jane is understandably still grieving. Her grieving process takes a familiar form; she remembers the good times they had together, she remembers the funny things he said and did. Readers see that Vincent's infectious joie de vivre contrasted with her mother's cynicism, and in embracing Vincent's desire for an adventurous life without consequences Jane was rejecting her mother. As the action on the television progresses, Jane thinks about their college years, her misguided thoughts of romance toward Vincent, and her inability as a young adult to form deep, lasting relationships with other men. They moved to different cities, they lived without consequences, and eventually both ended up back in Toronto. Their lives remained entwined.

The interior monologue presents the story from Jane's limited viewpoint. Vincent and Jane's mother say only what Jane remembers they said. Jane's memory may be selective; Vincent most likely had some solemn moments, even if he did utter bon mots on his deathbed, and her mother probably had moments of levity. Regardless of her possibly slanted take on people, the thoughts that cross Jane's mind while she watches television are her most honest interpretation of events. Because the story is simply a record of her passing thoughts, she has no reason to skew them. The interior monologue is an effective way to present a character study, and in "The Age of Lead" Atwood uses it to present the main character's slow realization that life has consequences, even if they are unintended.

Imagery

Imagery refers to the pictures an author's words create in the reader's mind. In its most simple form, imagery is conveyed through adjectives and adverbs. In a wider context it is evoked by descriptive passages, similes, and metaphors that help readers envision the characters and action of a scene. In "The Age of Lead" Atwood, whose language is direct and simple, uses numerous similes and metaphors to provide the story's imagery.

Interestingly, much of Atwood's imagery involves food (which is common in many of her other works as well, most notably *The Edible Woman*). Torrington's ice-encased body is "like those maraschino cherries you used to freeze in ice-cube trays for fancy tropical drinks." A couple of sentences later, his light brown skin is described as "like a gravy stain on linen" and his eyes as "the light brown of milky tea." Television news snippets are "thirty-second clips they call *bites*, as if they were chocolate bars." She describes the money of her newly wealthy clients as "like milk and cookies for them." According to Jane's mother, a woman's downfall after giving in to a man is akin to a plummeting "overripe apple." Later, the sailors' bones are scattered over the Arctic "like the trails in fairy tales, of bread crumbs or seeds." Vincent's teeth are "like the magazine ads for baby foods," and appreciating his sense of humor was "like appreciating an anchovy." Ultimately, as he lies on his hospital bed, Jane notes that he is "laid out on ice like a salmon."

This focus on food underscores the fact that what killed the members of the Franklin Expedition was what was meant to sustain them—their food. Conversely, Jane describes what is now killing the people she knows is "like a colorless gas, scentless and invisible." Just as the sailors did not know "it was what they'd been eating that had killed them," neither do Jane's friends in Toronto realize that an invisible agent will allow "any germ that happened along [to] invade their bodies."

The story's ultimate image is the one that compares Torrington's frozen body with Vincent's as he lies on his deathbed. Torrington's feet are "bare, and white rather than beige; they look like the feet of someone who's been walking on a cold floor, on a winter day . . . . His big toes are tied together with a strip of cloth." Vincent, 150 years later, "lay packed in ice, for the pain. A white sheet wrapped him, his white thin feet poked out the bottom of it. They were so pale and cold." The only difference is that Vincent jokingly surmises that his illness must be the result of something he ate; the irony is that Torrington's death really was because of something he ate.

The final image of the story compares the "lifeboat laden down with toothbrushes, soap, handkerchiefs, and slippers, useless pieces of junk" that the last doomed survivors of the expedition dragged across the ice to the "plastic drinking cups, crumpled soft-drink cans, used take-out plates . . . like a trail left by . . . the fleeing residents of a city under bombardment" that Jane clears from her front sidewalk. This last example compares the sailors, poisoned and dying from lead, with Toronto's residents, poisoned and dying from the aforementioned "invisible agent."

HISTORICAL CONTEXT

The Franklin Expedition Forensic Anthropology Project

The tragedy of the Franklin Expedition has loomed large in the Canadian imagination for over 150 years. Since the 1850s groups have periodically set out in search of evidence of what went wrong. While some of them originated in Great Britain, many were led by Canadians because it was almost certain that the ships had been lost in Canadian waters. The most successful of these was Owen Beattie's Franklin Expedition Forensic Anthropology Project, which began in 1981. He first traveled to King William Island in the Nunavut Territory, where a few human remains were found, some with cut marks indicating that they had been the victims of cannibalism. He had the bones analyzed and they were found to have extremely high levels of lead.

In 1984 Beattie and his crew reached Beechey Island, significantly farther north than King William Island, and found the graves of the first three crew members of the Franklin Expedition who had died. They exhumed the body of John Torrington first, took samples of his tissue and bone, and later determined that although the immediate cause of death was pneumonia, lead poisoning was a significant contributing factor. Video footage of the researchers lifting Torrington from the permafrost and examining his body inspired Atwood to write "The Age of Lead." The footage was part of a 1988 NOVA documentary *Buried in Ice*. Beattie also published his findings in the best-selling book *Frozen in Time: The Fate of the Franklin Expedition* (1987); Atwood provided

COMPARE & CONTRAST

- **1980s:** On February 5, 1981, the Toronto Police Service raid four establishments frequented by gay men and arrest 300 people. A mass protest ensues, which is considered the city's first Toronto Pride event. The event mobilizes the community to work together to end discrimination and prejudice.

  Today: Toronto's annual Pride Week is one of the largest gay pride festivals in the world, a ten-day affair featuring numerous parades and musical events that shut down twenty-two city blocks each June and attracts upward of 100,000 people for the main parade and between 500,000 and one million total over the course of the week.

- **1980s:** The wreck of the HMS *Breadalbane*, a ship that sank off the coast of Beechey Island in 1853 while searching for the Franklin Expedition, is designated a national historic site by the government of Canada. It is both the most northern shipwreck known as well as the most well preserved.

  Today: The wreck of the HMS *Erebus* is located on September 8, 2014, and the ship's bell recovered 169 years after it set sail for the Northwest Passage. The site,

along with that of its sister ship, the HMS *Terror* (yet to be found), are a National Historic Site of Canada.

- **1980s:** The Great Lakes Water Quality Agreement of 1972, designed to create a partnership between the United States and Canada to prevent ecological harm to the world's largest freshwater system, is revised in 1987 to add ecosystem-based management and remedial action plans to limit pollution in the Great Lakes.

  Today: The Great Lakes Water Quality Agreement is revised again in 2012, but Lake Ontario remains the most polluted of the lakes. Hardest hit is Hamilton Harbour, thirty-eight miles from Toronto, which contains dangerous levels of nitrogen, mercury, and PCBs. Invasive species such as the zebra mussel have damaged the lake's ecosystem and the water intake pipes for municipalities and power plants.

- **1980s:** Eight hundred people in Canada die of AIDS in 1989.

  Today: One thousand people in Canada die of AIDS in 2009.

---

the introduction for the revised edition of the book several years later.

Toronto in the 1980s: Urban Growth and Pollution

Toronto, Ontario, is a thriving metropolis that is as ethnically diverse as it is economically prosperous. It was not always this way. For much of its history Toronto was a modest working-class city, but its open immigration policies created a welcoming atmosphere that allowed many émigrés to find a foothold in North America. Toronto's population reached one million in 1951 and two million by 1971. By

the 1980s, it had become Canada's largest city and economic center, the hub of the finance industry and home to many multinational corporations. Some attribute this surge to the Quebecois sovereignty movement during this time, which prompted many companies to move their headquarters from Montreal to Toronto.

This sudden growth fueled a building boom that changed the skyline. In 1976 the CN Tower was completed, becoming the tallest freestanding structure in the world, a title it held until 2010. The population growth resulted in the construction of dozens of high-rise condominiums near the waterfront, replacing acres of

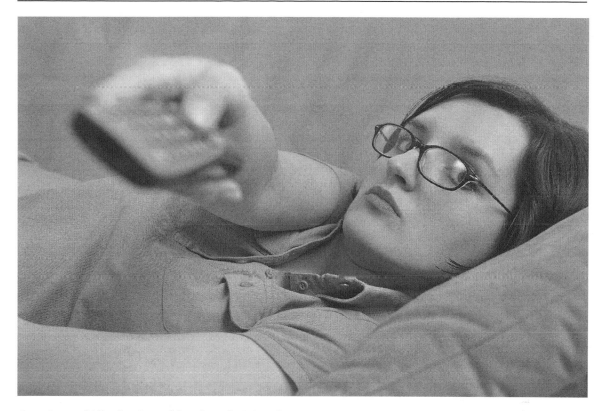

Jane is morbidly fascinated by the television documentary. (© *dotshock* / *ShutterStock.com*)

aging rail yards. With a higher population came many more vehicles on the road, which translated into air pollution. From 1985 through the end of the decade (and up to the present), levels of nitrogen oxide, sulfur dioxide, carbon dioxide, and other greenhouse gases impaired air quality in Toronto, leading to many illnesses and negative health effects, from bronchitis and asthma to cancer. The population growth also has had unintended social costs. A surge in drug use resulted in a rising crime rate through the late 1980s, much of which involved gang-related incidents. The murder rate, while low by US standards, rose dramatically.

Toronto's first environmental organization, Pollution Probe, began investigating Toronto's water supply in the early 1980s. It issued a statement urging pregnant women not to drink the city's water, based on tests that found benzene and other chemicals in it. Concurrently, much of Canada's environmental movement was focused on cleaning up the Niagara River, seventy-five miles away from Toronto, where chemicals from the New York neighborhood of Love Canal, which was built on a toxic waste

dump, were leaching into the water. Additionally, the Recycling Council of Ontario began to roll out a citywide recycling program in Toronto by the mid-1980s in an effort to address the growing trash problem.

The AIDS Crisis

Acquired immune deficiency syndrome (AIDS) was first observed in Canada in 1982, and by the following year it had claimed its first victim in the country. Initially, the disease was a death sentence, and many people watched their loved ones die agonizing deaths from this new virus that had spread through the gay community before anyone understood how to prevent it. In the 1980s gay rights were in their infancy, but the threat of AIDS mobilized the community to fund research and fight discrimination. In 1986 it was discovered that AIDS was caused by the human immunodeficiency virus (HIV). This virus weakens the body's immune system, rendering it unable to fight even minor infections and bacteria, just as the lead poisoning rendered Torrington unable to fight pneumonia and the "mysterious agent" in Jane's circle allowed "any germ that happened along [to] invade their bodies, take them over."

Although Vincent is dying of an unknown virus, both he and Jane are aware of AIDS and have had friends who died from it. Even though Vincent's sexual orientation is not explicitly stated, it seems likely that many of Vincent and Jane's friends in their social circle of artists were gay and had been affected by the disease. Concern over this new disease verged on hysteria in some places, including Toronto, and people who were HIV positive were actively discriminated against out of fear and misinformation about how the disease is transmitted. The AIDS Committee of Toronto was formed in 1983 with a goal of community education; one city councilman worried that AIDS was entering the city's water supply from hospital sewage. A Toronto AIDS activist compared the hysteria to that associated with cholera epidemics of the past, which actually were spread through tainted water.

CRITICAL OVERVIEW

Atwood's story "The Age of Lead" garnered significant critical attention when it was published in *Wilderness Tips* in 1991, a majority of it positive. *New York Times Book Review* critic Michiko Kakutani was impressed with the collection as a whole, particularly with how each story succinctly captures "how characters move from the insecurities of adolescence into the passions of young adulthood, into the sobering ambiguities of late middle age." Novelist Marianne Ackerman, reviewing *Wilderness Tips* for the *Montreal Gazette*, called "The Age of Lead" a "profoundly sad story" of "life-long friends who were never able to find their way beyond friendship." *Milwaukee Journal* reviewer Steven Blackwood called the story "apocalyptic" in its portrayal of "inattentively experienced lives" and "insidious" deaths and appreciated how Atwood conveyed this with her typical "cantankerous pessimism." William French, reviewing the story's original appearance in *Toronto Life* magazine, noted in the Toronto *Globe and Mail* that "The Age of Lead" was written with "Atwood's typical astringent flavor" and "cleverly links the flawed technology that helped destroy the Franklin

Arctic expedition with the chemical junk in our own environment."

Yet some critics accused Atwood of sameness in her themes and characters. In the London *Observer*, Nicci Gerrard called the stories in *Wilderness Tips* "burnt scrapings from longer works" but conceded that "The Age of Lead" demonstrated "the parallels between past and present, the traps in time that trip us into our deeper selves, or . . . between youthful dreams and ageing cynicism." However, novelist Claire Messud stated in the *Guardian* that "Atwood is not a natural short-story writer: most of the pieces in this collection strain for bigger things, squashing entire decades into flashy, occasionally sloppy, paragraphs." Bronwyn Drainie, writing in the Toronto *Globe and Mail*, noted that "betrayal is the overarching theme of these stories," which "are bitter pills swallowed in cramped rooms that make one long for a lungful of fresh air."

Later critical analysis of "The Age of Lead" focused on its theme of environmental poison. Ronald B. Hatch, in his essay "Margaret Atwood, the Land, and Ecology," commented on how Jane realized that in contrast to the Franklin Expedition's exposure to one poison, "in the late twentieth century, there are a multitude of poisons and they are everywhere." Furthermore, he stated that Atwood used the story to illustrate "how, in the midst of nature, the technological innovation which seems to be the expedition's salvation—canned food—is also what drives the men mad and eventually kills them . . . . Atwood implies that we are living in an age of lead, with spreading madness in the population and a civilization consumed by its own apparent mastery of the environment." Carol L. Beran, in her essay "Strangers within the Gates: Margaret Atwood's *Wilderness Tips*," drilled down a precise stance: "Because the mysterious disease killing Vincent is specifically not AIDS, we become aware that AIDS may only be a precursor to dreadful diseases yet to come; even as knowing and being able to prevent the mysterious disease that killed John Torrington does not end human suffering." In her essay "Scarlet Ibises and Frog Songs: Short Fiction," Karen F. Stein characterized all the stories in *Wilderness Tips* as focusing "on the dangers humans cause rather than the dangers posed by the landscape." Sherrill E. Grace, in "'Franklin Lives': Atwood's Northern Ghosts," summarized Atwood's point in "The Age of Lead" by saying that if Franklin's crew "could not read the signs connecting their destruction with the conveniences of their world in time to save themselves, why should we?"

CRITICISM

Kathy Wilson Peacock

Wilson Peacock is a freelance writer who specializes in contemporary literature. In the following essay, she explores how Atwood uses the image of John Torrington as a memento mori in "The Age of Lead."

Memento mori is a Latin phrase meaning *remember you have to die*. In Christian art it takes the form of a skull, which symbolizes the fleetingness of life and the permanence of death. This is both a reminder to enjoy the terrestrial world while one can and to appreciate its transient nature. The memento mori is featured in many famous works of art from the Renaissance through the modern era, including Hans Memling's *Earthly Vanity and Divine Salvation,* Frans Hal's *Youth with a Skull*, and Hans Holbein the Younger's *The Ambassadors*. In literature the memento mori is most famously represented in Shakespeare's *Hamlet* when the titular character holds the exhumed skull of his friend and states, "Alas, poor Yorick! I knew him, Horatio: a fellow of infinite jest." Much more recently, Atwood uses the frozen body of John Torrington as a memento mori in her short story "The Age of Lead" from her collection *Wilderness Tips*.

"The Age of Lead" is a short story about Jane, a forty-something woman living in Toronto who considers the consequences of her life while watching a television documentary on the autopsy of Torrington's body, which has been recovered from the Canadian permafrost in a state of remarkable preservation. Torrington was a member of the lost Franklin Expedition, which in 1845 sailed from Great Britain to find a Northwest Passage through the Arctic. The expedition's two ships, the HMS *Terror* and HMS *Erebus*, quickly became embedded in the ice and within several years all crew members had died, their bodies weakened by lead poisoning from improperly sealed canned food. Torrington was a young petty officer, about twenty years old, who died of pneumonia along with

> IT WAS PERHAPS INEVITABLE THAT TORRINGTON'S FROZEN BODY WOULD BECOME ATWOOD'S MEMENTO MORI. THE VERY IMAGE JANE DESCRIBES—THE EYES LIKE MILKY TEA, THE GRUESOME SHRIVELED LIPS EXPOSING HIS TEETH, THE CLOTH-WRAPPED HEAD—WAS A MEDIA PHENOMENON ITSELF IN CANADA IN THE 1980S, OWING TO THE WORK OF OWEN BEATTIE."

two other crew members very early in the expedition. They were carefully buried on Beechey Island, where their graves were discovered generations later and exhumed. Unlike a traditional memento mori—an eyeless skull—Torrington is a whole body, whose "tea-stained eyes" glare at Jane from her TV set with "an indecipherable gaze, innocent, ferocious, amazed, but contemplative." This vision from her television begins her reverie about Vincent, a lifelong friend who recently died from a mysterious virus. It had been their goal from the time they were teenagers to live a life without consequences. Now Jane realizes that everything has consequences.

Atwood fashions her story around this symbol of Torrington as memento mori. Jane's distrust of life's "consequences" were drummed into her head by her mother, a bitter woman who believed that life was nothing more than a moment of happiness, after which "you plummeted downwards like an overripe apple and hit the ground with a squash." A moment of carnal desire would forever be followed by struggle, depression, loneliness, and abandonment. Jane took her mother's lesson to heart, never forming lasting intimate relationships and flitting from city to city and job to job. This was her way of enjoying the terrestrial world—by never settling down. Instead, she remains close to Vincent, the perennial joker who cracks wise even on his deathbed, himself incapable of a lasting intimate relationship. They hope to escape the tragedy of life by ignoring it. The vision of Torrington's ghastly face makes her

WHAT DO I READ NEXT?

- Owen Beattie and John Geiger's *Frozen in Time: The Fate of the Franklin Expedition* (1987) has been revised several times, and recent versions contain a foreword by Atwood. The book recounts what is known about the Franklin Expedition and Beattie's mid-1980s exhumation of the bodies at the Beechey Island grave site. The original cover featured a haunting and famous image of John Torrington that inspired Atwood to write "The Age of Lead."

- "The Bog Man," another story from *Wilderness Tips* (1991), concerns the discovery of a mummified 2,000-year-old man in a Scottish bog (like Torrington, he is almost perfectly preserved) and the relationship between a young woman ending her affair with her married archaeology professor.

- "Concerning Franklin and His Gallant Crew," in Atwood's collection of speeches, *Strange Things: The Malevolent North in Canadian Literature* (1995), is a transcript of a lecture Atwood gave at Oxford University and summarizes the effect the Franklin Expedition has had on the development of a specifically Canadian literature.

- Canadian writer Mordecai Richler's comic novel *Solomon Gursky Was Here* (1990) concerns the antics of Ephraim Gursky and his descendants. Ephraim was the sole survivor of a failed 1845 British expedition to find a Northwest Passage that left him with first-hand experience of cannibalism and stranded with the Inuit.

- In the young-adult novel *A Love Story Starring My Dead Best Friend* (2010), by Emily Horner, introvert Cass deals with the sudden death of her best friend, Julia, by helping stage a musical Julia had written in secret. Along the way, she is forced to reexamine her relationship with her nemesis, Heather, which raises questions about her sexual orientation.

- *Survival: A Thematic Guide to Canadian Literature* (1972; reprint 2013) by Atwood features twelve chapters in which the author explores what is Canadian about Canadian literature. Above all, she states, Canadian literature is strongly associated with the theme of survival as it centers on the victim.

- *The Long Exile: A Tale of Inuit Betrayal and Survival in the High Arctic* (2008), by Melanie McGrath, is a nonfiction account of how in the 1950s the Canadian government relocated a small community of Inuit from their home on Hudson Bay to Ellesmere Island, the northernmost landmass on the planet and part of the same archipelago that doomed the Franklin Expedition.

- The award-winning novel *Consolation* (2007), by poet and novelist Michael Redhill, tells the history of Toronto from several viewpoints, including that of a photographer living in the frontier city in 1857, whose glass-plate photographs have been found in a shipwreck in the Toronto harbor, which is now a construction site for a new sports arena.

- The novel *Girls Fall Down* (2004), by Maggie Helweg, takes place in modern-day Toronto, where residents randomly succumb to mysterious illnesses, perhaps an airborne poison spread by terrorists. A photographer sets out to document the city before he loses his sight to diabetes and encounters a former girlfriend, a political activist, who broke his heart in the 1980s.

---

realize that "there were consequences after all; but they were the consequences to things you didn't even know you'd done."

Paintings depicting a memento mori became part of the tradition of *vanitas* painting that became established in the seventeenth century, as the country's rising economic tides generated an affluent class that spent much of their wealth on paintings as decoration for their homes. Such paintings helped these stoic Christians remember the "transience of life and the certainty of death through representations of mortality and ephemerality alongside signs of wealth and worldly possessions," according to Jonathan Koestle-Cate in an essay for *Art and Christianity*. Such is also the case with Jane in "The Age of Lead." Although she is not wealthy, Jane is associated with Vincent's circle of friends, who are "delighted" and "enchanted" with their money, which "was like milk and cookies for them." At the end of the story Jane regards her wealth and worldly possessions—her microwave, toaster oven, and espresso maker—as "purposeless objects adrift in the physical world." This contrast between her accumulated goods and the death skull staring at her from her television represent the literary counterpart of the memento mori that appears in those old paintings.

This symbolism becomes even more clear when one considers how large the Franklin Expedition looms in the Canadian imagination. Canadian writers, including novelists Mordecai Richler, John Wilson, and Dominique Fortier; poets David Solway and Gwendolyn MacEwen; and folk musician Stan Rogers, have all created works that revolve around this grim episode of nature's cruelty, calling upon their Canadian readers' familiarity with the topic to supply context. (The Franklin Expedition has been fodder for non-Canadian writers too, including Jules Verne, Mark Twain, William T. Vollmann, and Clive Cussler.) Atwood's contribution to the oeuvre of Franklin Expedition literature ties together the tragedy of the journey—fearless, adventurous souls who succumb to an invisible and unidentified killer in their midst (lead)—with latter-day Toronto, a gentrified urban playground that is being ravaged by an unidentified killer in its midst (an unnamed virus). Both tragedies, Atwood suggests, are the result of humans' hubris at not respecting the fragility and importance of the environment. This is the *vanitas* (i.e., vanity or excessive pride) portion of the memento mori concept, meaning humans' concern with worldly things. The worldly concern of the Franklin Expedition was to find the Northwest Passage that would create a more direct trade route between Great Britain and India than going around South America, which would "cost less and increase their profits." Jane's worldly concern was a life without consequences. In the end, Atwood demonstrates, these vanities are transient; only death is permanent.

Atwood was so taken with the tragic romance of the Franklin Expedition that it was the subject of her first Clarendon lecture at Oxford, "Concerning Franklin and His Gallant Crew," which was printed in *Strange Things: The Malevolent North in Canadian Literature* (1995). In this lecture Atwood demonstrates that the Franklin Expedition is a legend known to all Canadian children. (In "The Age of Lead," Jane mentions that she and Vincent learned of it in school and characteristically made fun of it.) Thus, it was perhaps inevitable that Torrington's frozen body would become Atwood's memento mori. The very image Jane describes—the eyes like milky tea, the gruesome shriveled lips exposing his teeth, the cloth-wrapped head—was a media phenomenon itself in Canada in the 1980s, owing to the work of Owen Beattie. It was Beattie, an archaeologist from the University of Alberta, who led the expedition to Beechey Island to exhume Torrington's body from the permafrost. He was accompanied by documentary filmmakers, who captured the indelible image of Torrington's blackened face emerging from his icy coffin. Jane is likely watching the resulting documentary, *Buried in Ice* (1988), which contains the startling footage as well as Beattie's theory that the crew had been poisoned by lead.

Torrington's mangled face was also featured on the cover of Beattie's best-selling book, *Frozen in Time: Unlocking the Secrets of the Franklin Expedition* (1989). The popularity of this book meant that many of Atwood's readers were already familiar with the image Jane describes; it was a ready-made symbol that suited the author's thematic purpose nicely. Atwood even wrote the introduction to the 2004 reprint of *Frozen in Time*, further solidifying her literary association with the topic. "Frozen Franklin," as she calls Torrington in her introduction, "gave me nightmares." The explanation of her fascination with him evokes the purpose of the memento mori without naming it explicitly: "Here is someone who has defied the general ashes-to-ashes, dust-to-dust rule, and who has remained recognizable as an individual human being long after most have

The story ends with Jane looking out at a bleak scene: the littered street outside her window.
(© Concept Photo | ShutterStock.com)

turned to bone and earth . . . . He has travelled through time, all the way from his age to our own, in order to tell us something we long to know." In "The Age of Lead," "Frozen Franklin" is traversing time to tell us of the dangers lurking in the environment. His danger, though he remained blithely unaware of it, was also environmental: lead in his food. Our danger, according to Jane, is also something that we remain blithely unaware of. Just as Jane states that "it was what they'd been eating that had killed them," Vincent jokes on his deathbed that the source of his illness, a mysterious unnamed and unidentified mutating virus, "must have been something I ate." Vincent's lighthearted statement perfectly captures the spirit of ars moriendi—the art of dying well— which is a companion concept to memento mori. According to Donald F. Duclow, writing in the *Macmillan Encyclopedia of Death and Dying*, the "'art of dying' [was placed] within a broader 'art of living,' which itself required a consistent memento mori, or awareness of and preparation for one's own death."

In *Strange Things* Atwood argues that while the unifying theme of American literature is the frontier, for Canada it is survival. Thus, "The Age of Lead," in which Jane questions the quality of her life after surviving her friend's death, uses the quintessential Canadian memento mori—a dead, frozen explorer—as a beacon honing in on Jane from her television to make her contemplate what survival means in a world without consequences. Ultimately, it means that she has a house full of objects that look "ownerless," as if they "might as well be pieces of an exploded spaceship orbiting the moon." Neither she nor Vincent had children: no one will survive them; their deaths will be final. Even Vincent, she realizes, has returned to dust and ashes over the course of a few months, while the well-preserved Torrington, the memento mori, glares back at her after 150 years in the ground. In the end, Atwood contrasts Jane's and Vincent's lighthearted mocking antics with Torrington's grisly image to underscore what Koestle-Cate called "the all-too-briefly-enjoyed pleasures of this world allied with intimations of the next."

Source: Kathy Wilson Peacock, Critical Essay on "The Age of Lead," in *Short Stories for Students*, Gale, Cengage Learning, 2016.

Reingard M. Nischik

In the following excerpt, Nischik highlights some of the common themes in Atwood's short stories.

. . . Atwood's short stories and shorter fiction have undergone significant developments (see Nischik 2006). Atwood's short-fiction oeuvre may be formally divided into short stories proper (published in *Dancing Girls*, *Bluebeard's Egg*, *Wilderness Tips*, and *Moral Disorders*) and short prose pieces—of variable forms and styles but mostly of very short length—which are hard to classify, being partly prose poems, sketches, dramatic monologues, short dialogues, mini-essays, or "reflections." These pieces of "short short fiction," which explore and extend the received generic borderlines of the short story, have made up three of her seven short-fiction collections published up to 2006 (*Murder in the Dark*, *Good Bones*, *The Tent*). With respect both to form, contents and theme, Atwood is indisputably the most variable, innovative, and challenging Canadian short-story writer. As part of this range, the stories of *Dancing Girls* (the individual stories of which were first published between 1964 and 1977) often show borderline characters on the brink of or having already entered the realm of madness ("Under Glass" and "Polarities," for example). Individuals and partnerships in crisis and relationships in their terminal stages are other important themes of her first short-story collection, which are also to be found in her second collection, *Bluebeard's Egg*. In these latter stories, written in the 1970s and early 1980s, there is a move away from individual psychological problems towards sociopsychological themes. Individual characters are now rather shown not as loners but as members of specific groups, often within their family context. The collection *Wilderness Tips*, in turn, leaves behind the family-oriented stories of *Bluebeard's Egg*, often placing its protagonists in a work context instead.

"Significant Moments in the Life of My Mother" is one of Atwood's formally more traditional short stories. It was first published in, and is the prominent opening to, her second collection *Bluebeard's Egg*. The story is indeed, as suggested above in connection with the entire volume *Bluebeard's Egg*, a "family story," but it

THE COLLECTION *WILDERNESS TIPS*, IN TURN, LEAVES BEHIND THE FAMILY-ORIENTED STORIES OF *BLUEBEARD'S EGG*, OFTEN PLACING ITS PROTAGONISTS IN A WORK CONTEXT INSTEAD."

is much more than that. The story has autobiographical generic traces, not the only reason why it may also be regarded as a disguised artist story. It is an ingenious fictional demonstration of what it takes to "translate the world into words," that is, to be artistically creative, to develop into or to be a writer. Last but not least, it shows Atwood's focus on female characters, on female influences and on the long-neglected "female tradition" in literature.

The story is rendered in a retrospective set-up by a female first-person narrator, who focuses mainly on the representation of her mother, either directly or, mostly, indirectly by what the mother transmits to her children and how. The mother's stories and remarks are either vividly rendered in direct speech, contextualized with comments by the narrator, or are summarized by the narrator. In either case, the narrator enters into a sort of indirect retrospective dialogue with her mother, whose apparently cheerful mentality colors the writing. The text, taking its cue from the mother's stories, is structured episodically and rather impressionistically, though in a largely chronological manner (starting with the mother as a child and ending with her daughter having grown into the role of the adult narrator). By telling stories to her children (to the narrator and to her brother and sister, usually referred to as "we") and others, the mother is characterized as a highly expressive and communicative person, observant, caring, mentally alert, not taking herself too seriously, and generally demonstrating a pronounced sense of humor.

The episodes, which are added to each other apparently at random, at first seem to belie their classification by the title as "significant moments" in the life of the mother. In fact, the "events" appear altogether rather insignificant; they mainly belong to the quotidian family and domestic sphere, and are thus all in the realm of the mother's personal experience: baby chickens dying because as a child she had unwittingly fondled them too much ("'I'd loved them to death,'"); her appendix operation ("'Never get sick,' she says,"); the mother tricking her father into allowing her to cut her hair; the preacher at Sunday service temporarily losing control over his false teeth; a cat transported in a car, "wet[ting] itself copiously" on the mother's lap; the family driving along in the car and barely escaping a collision with a hay wagon, and other episodes.

These events as such are perhaps not particularly remarkable. Nevertheless, they are obviously "worth a story"—and on different levels of reception—because of the manner in which the narrator's mother tells these episodes, and how their telling characterizes her; because of her daughter's interpretation of the stories (attaching further significance to them); and because of the effects and influence this particular mother may have had on the narrator—a budding writer, as the story as a whole and in particular the ending carefully suggest.

In several respects, the narrator's mother seems to be a born storyteller. To begin with, she obviously loves telling stories. She does so graphically and entertainingly, in a fluent, witty, colloquial style. And she does so with an eye towards the addressees, those who listen to her stories. Thus she consciously tells certain stories only to a female audience, as the narrator remarks. The narrator also suggests that the mother may have told her stories for an effect beyond a merely expressive, informative, or entertaining purpose, that is, with a particular "message," an educating intention, in mind. This is presumed right at the beginning of the story in the narrator's comments following upon the very first "significant moment," the chicken episode:

> Possibly this story is meant by my mother to illustrate her own stupidity, and also her sentimentality. We are to understand she wouldn't do such a thing now.

> Possibly it's a commentary on the nature of love; though, knowing my mother, this is unlikely.

This beginning—a story told by the mother, contextualized by the daughter's evaluating comments—sets the stage for what is to follow. The mother relates events she finds noteworthy and largely refrains from commenting upon them. Whether or not the mother pursues effects beyond informative, expressive, or entertaining ones remains open. In the perspective of the daughter/narrator who analyzes and evaluates these stories in retrospect and thereby draws her own conclusions (the most effective method of learning), the mother seems not only to have been an active oral storyteller, but at the same time an educator as well (the mother's profession in the story is indeed that of a school teacher).

The narrator's mother also exerts an influence on her daughter in the art of storytelling. That domestic storytelling in this text is related to artistic storytelling, to writing, is suggested by reflective passages such as the following (if here perhaps *ex negativo*): "There is, however, a difference between symbolism and anecdote. Listening to my mother, I sometimes remember this." In the framework of the short story, it is the narrator/daughter who attaches significance to the partly hilarious, always entertaining and apparently rather harmless "events" her mother tells the children in a cheerful, jaunty, even chatty manner. It is the meaningful characterization and contextualization by the daughter in hindsight that attach to the storytelling a weightier cognitive significance and that at the same time, in the writing process, transfer an aesthetic value to the stories, thereby transforming the episodes and anecdotes indeed into "significant moments." In this step from oral to written storytelling, from the mother as storyteller to the daughter as narrator/writer, lies the metafictional gist of "Significant Moments" and its Chinese-box-like set-up. The two types of storytelling—which share the sequencing of a meaningful series of events—are obviously related to each other. But whereas the mother's narrations, though nicely expressed for ready reception, stick factually and apparently as closely as possible to "real events," the daughter/narrator makes use of her imaginative (" . . . which I pictured as . . . ,"), analytical, and aesthetic capacities to make sense of these events not only as a daughter but also as a writer. By writing a short story about her mother's stories—and hereby we approach an autobiographical reading of the story—she "translates the world into words."

Atwood's short story is related in its poetological aspects to William Carlos Williams's equally deceptively simple poem "The Red Wheelbarrow." This imagist poem transforms everyday objects into art—through the perceiving, selecting, arranging, and representing perspective of the artist, on whom "so much depends" (as Williams's poem begins). In the Atwood story, this transforming power of art is suggested by a mise-en-abymic rendering of a mundane object turned into something marvelously extraordinary:

> It was in this house that I first saw a stalk of oats in a vase, each oat wrapped in the precious silver paper which had been carefully saved from a chocolate box. I thought it was the most wonderful thing I had ever seen, and began saving silver paper myself.

This fascinating image of the metamorphosing capacity of art links the story's involvement with storytelling, its metafictional impact, with its autobiographical aspects and the female line of influences which this story sketches. For the wonderful image of the wrapped stalk of oats—which results in the first-person narrator's beginning to save silver paper, too (in order to be able to effect such metamorphosis herself)—is, significantly, situated in her *mother's* family house, where "its secret life . . . was female." In connection with her mother's oral storytelling, we can see the coordinates of a female line of tradition . . . .

Source: Reingard M. Nischik, "'The Translation of the World into Words' and the Female Tradition: Margaret Atwood, 'Significant Moments in the Life of My Mother' (1983)," in *The Canadian Short Story: Interpretations*, edited by Reingard M. Nischik, Camden House, 2007, pp. 332–36.

Linda L. Richards and Margaret Atwood

In the following interview excerpt, Atwood discusses why she wanted to become a writer.

. . . You've been very fortunate and this has been a wonderful year, but seeing your CV made me think about something I always say: 90 per cent of good luck or good fortune is hard work. And you've really done the work in so many ways. That's part of it. It seems as though you really were setting up for this amazing career.

[Laughs] I think the hardest work as a student that I ever did was writing the grade 13 exams in Ontario in 1957. I don't think it's the same anymore, but at that time they were province-wide exams. They were marked blind. Nothing you had done during the year counted.

AT 16 I JUST STARTED WRITING. DON'T ASK ME WHY. I DON'T KNOW."

It was just make or break: one exam. And they were all held within a period of about two weeks in the high school gym which had no air conditioning and it was just unbelievable. On that depended whether you went to university, what university you went to: all of these things. I was so pressured. I kept a jar of Noxema in the freezer. I used to come home and take it out and rub this frozen Noxema all over my face to clear my mind and then get hard at it studying again. I wrote two more exams than the number actually needed because I didn't think my Latin marks were going to be that good.

Latin too?

Oh, you had to have Latin to get into Honors English then. That was just as well because my science marks were actually very good. [Laughs] The top of all of my marks were in botany and zoology. And in those days they took marks off for spelling. They took half a mark off for each spelling mistake and I was always a speller by ear.

So you're a good speller or you're not a good speller?

I was not a good speller. I'm a better speller now, but I'm still . . . [Shrugs]. A lot of writers are like that. They hear words but they don't necessarily see them. I wasn't an *atrocious* speller, but I made enough mistakes that it took my mark down.

It's funny, though, because people associate the whole spelling thing with writing so much. When I was a kid, my mom would say: How can you be a writer if your spelling is so bad? And she didn't really understand that the two weren't related.

My mother said: If you want to be a writer, maybe you should learn to spell. [Laughs] And I said: Others will do that for me. And they do. Either it's the real person editor, or it's the little man hiding in the computer who comes out and waves his hands at you and underlines your things with squiggly lines.

Did you always know you wanted to he a writer?

No, I didn't. I knew from the age of 16, but before that, no. I did write the way most children write. As quite a young child I wrote. But then I didn't. For years. I had no interest in it. I read a lot, but I never thought I would be a writer. From about the ages of, say, seven to 16. I had other interests. At 16 I just started writing. Don't ask me why. I don't know. Looking back, you could say I always read. I always read a lot. I read voraciously. But I did not in my mind translate that voracious reading into writing.

And you were attacked by the muse at 16?

[Laughs] My own version is that a big thumb came out of the sky and said: You. And everybody at that time, which was 1956 in Toronto, Ontario—which was not the multicultural metropolis that it is today, but was a rather provincial limited town. And I was at what was known as the most boring high school in the city. Although it was quite a good high school, but it was not pulsating with creative energy of that kind. Everyone thought I was a bit crazy.

For wanting to be a writer?

Well, apparently I was rash enough to actually say, in the high school cafeteria to my group of friends, that I was going to be a writer. Says one of my high school friends who told me this. I don't remember, but she said that we were all eating our little bag lunches with our packed sandwiches and apples and apparently I said this.

They all pictured you in a beret and . . . .

They all thought I was completely berserk. It wasn't even berets: nobody had a clue. We only took dead people. And usually dead English people. A few dead American people. So as far as anybody knew, there only was one Canadian writer and that was Stephen Leacock.

So it was an unusual thing for me to have decided to do and I still don't know why I did that.

And then you aligned your life for that.

Then I aligned my life to it. Once I was converted, once I'd had this conversion experience in the football field—there wasn't a game

going on at the time. [Laughs] It was just the way I used to walk home. Once that had happened, I did try to arrange my life to make that possible.

And you did.

And I did. But it wasn't always terrifically easy, because there was no obvious thing to do. There were no creative writing schools that I knew about at that time. It was very early days.

And role models?

Well, there were no living role models. Luckily, we did study the English curriculum and therefore I knew there were such people as Jane Austen and the Brontës and George Eliot. Then I got hold of modern short stories and there was Katherine Anne Porter. There were people and there were female poets that I knew about. We took Elizabeth Barrett Browning for instance. None of them were contemporary, but that was the way of the school curriculum most of the time.

Is that something you have an awareness of now? That there was such a dearth of role models then and the fact that you are a role model for many young writers now.

Yeah. It's a bit heavy. [Laughs] I never wanted to be a role model because role models, when I went to this very Radcliffe/Harvard of which you speak, that term had just come in. And what it really meant was that you had to dress in suits, with a little feminine touch [indicates perhaps a scarf at the throat] to show that you were a girl. You had to have nice manners and you had to have a service mentality. I mean, they're all very good things, but not very useful from writers, if you see what I mean.

Not very useful for living, maybe.

Well, I think they're fine for living if you wanted to be a dean in a university and be an example to young people. I didn't see what I was doing as necessarily what other people ought to do in order to live a proper sort of life.

And now?

I wouldn't necessarily tell people that they should pursue a career in writing if they want a pension and a guaranteed income. It's a risk. It's a risk for anybody who takes it up. It's not a job with a pension plan, a boss and a guaranteed income and raises. It doesn't go like that.

And your "overnight success" has come with considerable hard work.

My overnight success did not come over night! [Laughs] I wrote for 16 years before I could make a living out of it. So, day jobs and being a student and getting scholarships and being the cashier behind the coffee shop soda counter . . . .

Source: Linda L. Richards, "Margaret Atwood," in *January*, November 2000.

SOURCES

Ackerman, Marianne, "Why We Love to Hate Atwood," in *Montreal Gazette*, September 7, 1991, p. J1.

Air Pollution Burden of Illness from Traffic in Toronto—Problems and Solutions, November 2007, http://www.toronto.ca/legdocs/mmis/2007/hl/bgrd/background file-8046.pdf (accessed February 24, 2015).

Atwood, Margaret, "The Age of Lead," in *Wilderness Tips*, Doubleday, 1991.

———, "Concerning Franklin and His Gallant Crew," in *Strange Things: The Malevolent North in Canadian Literature*, Clarendon Press, 1995, pp. 7–34.

Beattie, Owen, and John Geiger, *Frozen in Time: The Fate of the Franklin Expedition*, rev. ed., Greystone Press, 2014.

Beran, Carol L., "Strangers within the Gates: Margaret Atwood's Wilderness Tips," in *Margaret Atwood's Textual Assassinations: Recent Poetry and Fiction*, edited by Sharon Rose Wilson, Ohio State University Press, 2003, pp. 74–87.

Blackwood, Steven, "Atwood's 'Wilderness' Has a Sense of Canada," in *Milwaukee Journal*, January 5, 1992, p. E9.

"Canada HIV & AIDS Statistics," AVERT website, http://www.avert.org/canada-hiv-aids-statistics.htm (accessed February 24, 2015).

Drainie, Bronwyn, "Atwood's Pen Is Also Her Sword," in *Globe and Mail*, September 7, 1991, p. C18.

Duclow, Donald F., "Ars Moriendi," in *Macmillan Encyclopedia of Death and Dying*, edited by Robert Kastenbaum, Macmillan, 2002, p. 92.

French, William, "Eclectic Supplement Comes to the Aid of Writers' Fund," in *Globe and Mail*, July 20, 1989, p. C7.

Gerrard, Nicci, "Beached on the First Tide," in *Observer*, September 15, 1991, p. 62.

Grace, Sherrill E., "'Franklin Lives': Atwood's Northern Ghosts," in *Various Atwoods*, edited by Lorraine M. York, Anansi, 1995, pp. 159–61.

Hatch, Ronald B., "Margaret Atwood, the Land, and Ecology," in *Margaret Atwood: Works and Impact*, edited by Reingard M. Nischik, Camden House, 2000, pp. 180–97.

"HIV/AIDS," http://healthycanadians.gc.ca/diseases-conditions-maladies-affections/disease-maladie/hiv-vih-eng.php (accessed February 13, 2015).

Kakutani, Michiko, Review of *Wilderness Tips*, in *New York Times*, November 26, 1991, p. C1.

Koestle-Cate, Jonathan, "Death: A Portrait," in *Art and Christianity*, Vol. 73, Spring 2013, p. 8.

Messud, Claire, "Tales from the Campfire," in *Guardian*, October 31, 1999, p. 28.

O'Connor, Ryan Ernest, "Toronto the Green: Pollution Probe and the Rise of the Canadian Environmental Movement," Ph.D. diss., University of Western Ontario, December 2010, http://ir.lib.uwo.ca/cgi/view content.cgi?article = 1114&context = etd&sei-redir = 1& referer = http%3A%2F%2Fwww.google.com%2Fsearch %3Fq%3Dhistory%2Bpollution%2BToronto%26client %3Dsafari%26rls%3Den%26oe%3DUTF-8%26oq%3D %26gs_l%3D#search = %22history%20pollution%20-Toronto%22 (accessed February 24, 2015).

Robertson, Mark L., "An Annotated Chronology of the History of AIDS in Toronto: The First Five Years, 1981–1986," in *Canadian Bulletin of Medical History*, 2005, http://yorkspace.library.yorku.ca/xmlui/handle/ 10315/2482 (accessed February 24, 2015).

"Sir John Franklin: Fabled Arctic Ship Found," in *BBC News*, September 9, 2014, http://www.bbc.com/news/ world-us-canada-29131757 (accessed February 24, 2015).

Stein, Karen F. "Scarelt Ibises and Short Fiction," in *Margaret Atwood Revisited*, Twayne Publishers, 1999, 125–44.

FURTHER READING

Atwood, Margaret, *Bluebeard's Egg and Other Stories*, McClellan and Stewart, 1983.

> This collection focuses on gender politics, a common concern in Atwood's writings, and takes place mostly in Toronto.

Atwood, Margaret, *Survival: A Thematic Guide to Canadian Literature*, Anasi, 1972.

> This volume has been reprinted several times and puts forth Atwood's argument to distinguish Canadian literature as a distinct subgenre of Western literature.

Gordimer, Nadine, ed., *Telling Tales*, Bloomsbury, 2004.

> The twenty-one stories in this anthology, including "The Age of Lead," were chosen by their authors for this volume, the proceeds of which were directed toward the fight against HIV/AIDS in southern Africa. While none of

the stories is directly about AIDS, many are somber and touch on the theme of death. Five are written by Nobel Prize winners.

Mowat, Farley, *High Latitudes: An Arctic Journey*, Steerforth, 2003.

Atwood wrote the introduction to this memoir, in which fellow Canadian writer Mowat recounts his 1966 trek through remote Canadian territories and the people and the truths about the environment his journey revealed.

Wynne-Davies, Marion, "The Mysteries of Time and Memory: 1988–1999," in *Margaret Atwood*, Writers and Their Work Series, Northcote House, 2010, pp. 42–67.

This book looks at Atwood's works critically and focuses on gender identity in her fiction. Wynne-Davies covers Atwood's novels, stories, poems, and children's books.

SUGGESTED SEARCH TERMS

Margaret Atwood

The Age of Lead AND Atwood

Wilderness Tips AND Atwood

Canada AND Literature

Franklin Expedition

lead poisoning

Toronto AND Margaret Atwood

environmentalism AND Canada

AIDS and Canadian Literature

Owen Beattie

Defender of the Faith

PHILIP ROTH
1959

In Philip Roth's short story "Defender of the Faith," Sergeant Nathan Marx, though not particularly devout, comes to be seen by his non-Jewish army superiors as somehow representative of all Jews. He also is taken advantage of by one particular Jewish soldier, Sheldon Grossbart, who tries to use their common faith as a bond so that he might ask for special treatment. When Marx resists, Grossbart accuses him of being ashamed of being Jewish, of taking the anger and embarrassment he feels about being Jewish out on the "rest of us."

When "Defender of the Faith" first appeared in the *New Yorker*, on March 14, 1959, many Jews were angered by the manipulative behavior of his Jewish characters, believing that Roth was reinforcing negative stereotypes. When the story was published in *Goodbye, Columbus: And Five Short Stories* (1959), however, the collection won the National Book Award. Roth sparked controversy yet again with his novel *Portnoy's Complaint* (1969), though the book became a best seller.

Roth faced similar accusations after the publication of his novel *Portnoy's Complaint*. Some critics, especially Jewish ones, accused Roth of being anti-Semitic—a self-hating Jew—because his work portrays Jewish characters who are flawed or even wild. However, "Defender of the Faith"—indeed all of Roth's work—is not just a story about what it is to be

Pulitzer Prize-winning author Philip Roth
(© Everett Collection Historical | Alamy)

a Jew. Roth creates for Marx a predicament that arises from his sharing a religious faith and a cultural background with Grossbart, but as Marx struggles with his moral dilemma, he must consider much wider, universally human issues: what it is to show mercy, the difficulty of trusting other people, and the shame of resorting to vindictiveness.

"Defender of the Faith" is readily available in multiauthor short-story collections, such as *The Best American Short Stories of the Century* (1999), and online.

AUTHOR BIOGRAPHY

Roth was born in Newark, New Jersey, on March 19, 1933. He and his brother, Sandy, grew up in a middle-class New Jersey suburb. After briefly enrolling at Rutgers University, Roth transferred to Bucknell University, where he started writing in earnest. He founded

a literary magazine, in which several of his early short stories appeared.

In 1954, after his graduation from college, Roth enlisted in the US Army but continued writing. Upon finishing his stint in the military, Roth went back to school, earning a master's degree in English literature at the University of Chicago. When "Defender of the Faith" was published in the *New Yorker* on March 14, 1959, it was the second of nine Roth stories to appear in the magazine.

Over the course of his career, Roth published more than thirty novels and received countless awards, including the 1987 National Book Critics Circle Award for *The Counterlife*, the 1991 National Book Critics Circle Award for *Patrimony*, the 1994 PEN/Faulkner Award for fiction for *Operation Shylock*, the 1995 National Book Award for fiction for *Sabbath's Theater*, and the 1998 Pulitzer Prize for fiction for *American Pastoral*. In 2011, he was awarded the Man Booker International Prize for his body of work. Other novels include *Everyman* (2006) and *Nemesis* (2010).

Roth has been married twice. His first marriage, to Margaret Martinson in 1959, ended in a separation. The pair were still legally married in 1968 when she was killed in a car accident. His second marriage, in 1990 to the actress Claire Bloom after a long relationship, ended in separation in its second year. After the couple's divorce was finalized in 1995, she wrote *Leaving a Doll's House*, a memoir that portrays Roth in unflattering terms.

As of 2015, Roth was living a somewhat reclusive life at his home in Warren, Connecticut. In 2012, he formally announced that he was retiring. In an interview for a French magazine that David Daley reported on in *Salon*, Roth explains:

> I decided that I was done with fiction. I do not want to read, to write more . . . . I have dedicated my life to the novel: I studied, I taught, I wrote and I read. With the exclusion of almost everything else. Enough is enough! I no longer feel this fanaticism to write that I have experienced in my life.

PLOT SUMMARY

Sergeant Nathan Marx, the first-person narrator, has returned from fighting in Europe in World War II and is now helping to train army

MEDIA ADAPTATIONS

- In 2009, Phoenix Books released an unabridged audiobook of *Goodbye, Columbus: And Five Short Stories*, which includes "Defender of the Faith." John Rubinstein narrates the recording, which has a total running time of eight hours and twenty-one minutes.

recruits at Camp Crowder in Missouri. He has trouble leaving the battlefront mentality behind. Captain Paul Barrett is Marx's commanding officer, and he holds Marx up to the trainees as a fine example of a soldier.

One of the enlisted men, Sheldon Grossbart, comes to Marx to complain that the other soldiers resent his missing the Friday night G.I. parties, during which the barracks are thoroughly cleaned, to go to religious services for the Jewish Sabbath. Marx can tell Grossbart is trying to figure out whether he is a fellow Jew and resents Grossbart's assumption that a common faith somehow connects them. He tells Grossbart to stop whining, that if he is not forbidden to go to services, he has no reason to complain, even if the other men grumble about it.

Marx goes to Captain Barrett to explain the situation, and Barrett has little patience with Grossbart's complaints. Marx asks Corporal LaHill, the charge of quarters, to tell the men they should line up at 1900 hours if they want to attend synagogue. When LaHill relays Marx's permission, it sounds like an order.

Grossbart and two other soldiers show up to go to shul (synagogue). Grossbart introduces Marx to Larry Fishbein and Mickey Halpern, and the three young men march off. Marx, waxing nostalgic about nights of his Bronx childhood, decides to follow them. He finds Halpern closely following the service, but Fishbein and Grossbart are not paying much attention to the rabbi, Major Leo Ben Ezra.

Ben Ezra, in his role as chaplain, expresses sympathy to the soldiers about the nonkosher food offered in the mess hall. He encourages them to eat what they must to stay healthy, even if it breaks religious laws. After the service is over, Marx speaks with the three young soldiers about the food situation.

A week later, Captain Barrett is frustrated by a letter, supposedly from Grossbart's father, complaining about the nonkosher food. Marx tries to explain Jewish dietary laws and the protectiveness of some Jewish parents, though he feels uncomfortable being put in such a defensive position. Barrett and Marx drive out to the training fields to speak with Grossbart. Barrett again holds up Marx as an example: a Jew who has served on the front who eats the food provided without complaint.

Once Barrett storms off in frustration, Marx realizes that Grossbart, not his father, has written the letter. Marx is disgusted with Grossbart's behavior, that he complains even though he "eat[s] like a hound at chow." Grossbart is unembarrassed at being discovered in the lie, saying he did it to help Halpern, who is made ill by eating the nonkosher foods.

A few days later, Marx sees another letter, again supposedly from Grossbart's father, explaining that Grossbart has decided he can eat like the other men and asking for recognition for Marx in helping him to reach this decision. Marx cannot guess Grossbart's motives in writing the second letter, but he is relieved that Grossbart leaves him alone for a while. Marx focuses on his work and starts to think about his future, writing to girls he knew before he shipped out and sending away for information about law school.

When Grossbart appears again, he asks Marx about where the unit may be deployed after training. When Marx explains that he has no real information but doubts they will be sent to Germany, Grossbart asks for another favor: he wants a pass so that he can visit his aunt in Saint Louis and share a seder to celebrate the Jewish holiday of Passover. When Marx points out that Passover was actually a month earlier and refuses to give the pass, Grossbart accuses him of being ashamed of being Jewish.

Grossbart attempts to leave the base without permission, and Marx breaks down and gives him the pass he wants. Grossbart promises to bring a piece of gefilte fish back from his aunt's seder. Though he has promised to tell no one about the pass, Grossbart is soon back with Halpern and Fishbein, hoping to get passes for them too. When Marx refuses, Grossbart gives his pass to Halpern. Marx gives in and writes passes for all three young men.

The next day, Marx is playing softball with some of the other noncommissioned officers and asks Sergeant Wright if he knows where his trainees will be sent. He is shocked by the news that they will be sent to the Pacific, where there is still fighting against Japan.

After his weekend in St. Louis, Grossbart comes to see Marx. He asks for any information Marx may have about where the unit will be sent after training because Halpern is upset from wondering about it. Marx resents Grossbart's bringing Halpern into it. Even if it is true that Halpern has been crying, it sounds like a lie because Grossbart is trying to manipulate the situation and get sympathy from Marx.

Marx tells Grossbart that they are indeed going to the Pacific and makes it clear that he cannot do anything to change the orders. Just before Grossbart leaves the room, Marx notices the paper bag in his hand. Marx asks for it, thinking the bag will contain the gefilte fish Grossbart promised, but instead it holds an egg roll. Marx is furious that Grossbart has lied to him about the seder. Grossbart explains that he simply got the date wrong, but Marx is finished with being fooled. He yells at Grossbart and throws the egg roll out the window.

A week later, Marx receives the orders for his unit. Every man is ordered to be sent to the Pacific except for Grossbart, who is slated for Fort Monmouth, New Jersey. Marx rereads the list in disbelief and then calls his softball buddy, Wright, asking to have Grossbart's assignment changed. Marx makes up a story—that Grossbart's brother has been killed in action, making him eager to go fight in the Pacific—and explains that he is trying to help a fellow Jew. Wright does not make any promises other than that he will do what he can.

The orders are changed, and Grossbart is headed for the Pacific. That night after dinner Grossbart confronts Marx. He is furious about having his plum stateside assignment given to another man. Marx reminds Grossbart of his own words: that they have to learn to watch out for each other. Marx truly seems to be believe that Grossbart is going to be all right—as will

Fishbein and Halpern, because Grossbart will watch out for them as long as there is a chance that they will be useful to him. However, Marx clearly feels guilty for acting vindictively. He has the "impulse to turn and seek pardon" but resists.

CHARACTERS

Captain Paul Barrett
Captain Barrett is in charge of the basic training division to which Marx is assigned and in which Grossbart, Fishbein, and Halpern are training. Barrett is frustrated by the complaints from Grossbart about being resented for not helping to clean the barracks on Friday nights because of services and about the food provided not being kosher. Roth manages to convey Barrett's frustration without turning him into a two-dimensional villain. The reader can understand Barrett's impatience with such issues when he has men to train for war.

Major Leo Ben Ezra
Ben Ezra is the chaplain who leads the Sabbath services for the Jewish soldiers. Because he is a rabbi, it is his job to help the enlisted men follow the rules of their religion. However, he also feels a responsibility to keep them strong and healthy, so he asks them to at least try to eat the nonkosher foods in the army mess hall.

Private Larry Fishbein
Fishbein is one of the three soldiers in training. He follows Grossbart's lead in trying to gain special privileges from Marx because of their common faith. Fishbein has a cadaverous face and bad teeth, suggesting that he is not completely healthy. He is also from New York, which he points out as another thing he has in common with Marx.

Private Sheldon Grossbart
Grossbart's actions drive the plot of the story. He is brazen in his attempts to manipulate Marx into granting him special treatment simply because they are both Jewish. Grossbart leads his friends Fishbein and Halpern into his schemes. Marx notices Grossbart's good teeth, which show that he had parents who could afford to take him to the dentist. Grossbart is personable, and Marx is fairly easily taken in by

his charm, but in the end, Marx concludes that almost everything Grossbart does is selfish and calculating. Sometimes Fishbein and Halpern call Grossbart by the nickname Shelly.

Private Mickey Halpern
Halpern is the quietest of the three young soldiers and the only one who seems truly devout. He follows the Sabbath service closely and becomes sick from eating at the mess hall, which serves nonkosher foods like sausage and ham (pork is forbidden for orthodox Jews). Although Halpern never directly asks Marx for a favor, he is willing to go along once Grossbart has secured a privilege, such as leaving the base for a contrived holiday meal.

Corporal Robert LaHill
LaHill is the C.Q., or charge of quarters, for the barracks to which Marx is assigned. The duties of the C.Q. in the army include monitoring who goes in and out of the barracks and some light cleaning. LaHill is asleep when Roth introduces him, although it is not clear whether he is supposed to be on duty at the time. LaHill is not bright, and he reminds Marx of a caveman. When he relays Marx's permission to attend Friday night religious services to the enlisted men, LaHill makes it sound like an order.

Sergeant Nathan Marx
Marx is the first-person narrator of the story. He has recently returned from fighting in Europe in World War II, and Captain Barrett respects him for his combat experience and points him out to the trainees as a war hero. Since his return to the United States, Marx is trying to figure out who he is now and how much the war has changed him. He tries to be kind to the enlisted men but resists granting privileges to them just because they are Jewish, like him. Marx feels forced into a position of defending himself and others of his faith from the assumptions and prejudices of others in the army. After Grossbart takes advantage of him several times, Marx acts vindictively, arranging to have Grossbart sent to the Pacific to fight, though he does seem to feel remorse for what he does.

Corporal Shulman
Shulman answers the telephone when Marx calls Wright to arrange to send Grossbart to the Pacific after basic training. When Shulman

lets out a surprised "*Oh!*" when Marx identifies himself, Marx suspects that Grossbart has manipulated Shulman into sending him to a fort in New Jersey, close to his family and away from the fighting.

Shelly
See Sheldon Grossbart

Sergeant Bob Wright
Marx calls Wright to ask him to send Grossbart to the Pacific after training. Wright asks Marx, "How's the pitching arm?" because they play softball together on the base. Marx uses his connection with Wright on the ball field the same way Grossbart use the connection of being Jewish.

THEMES

Deception
Deception is a central theme in "Defender of the Faith." Time and time again, Marx discovers that he has been fooled by Grossbart. First, Grossbart complains that he is not able to go to religious services because the other men resent the idea that he will not help with the cleaning during the Friday night G.I. parties. After Marx makes sure the Jewish soldiers are free to attend Sabbath services on Fridays, he sees Grossbart goofing around during the prayers, making it seem that Grossbart was more interested in avoiding chores than being devout.

Grossbart does not even pretend to be ashamed of his deceptions. When Marx learns that Grossbart himself, rather than his father, wrote the letter complaining about the nonkosher foods served to Jewish enlisted men, Grossbart at first jumps back, but "it took him only a second or two for his eyes to flash happy again." Later, Marx breaks the rules, giving Grossbart, Fishbein, and Halpern passes to attend a Passover seder with Grossbart's aunt in Saint Louis. When Grossbart presents a Chinese egg roll instead of the gefilte fish Marx has requested from the seder table, Marx knows he has been deceived again.

The repeated tricks prompt Marx, who understandably feels Grossbart has taken advantage of him, to perpetrate a deception of his own. Trying to put Grossbart off, he claims

TOPICS FOR FURTHER STUDY

- Many readers were incensed by "Defender of the Faith" when it was first published. Jon Michaud of the *New Yorker* quotes one letter the magazine received in protest of the story: "With . . . "Defender of the Faith," you have done as much harm as all the organized anti-Semitic organizations have done to make people believe that all Jews are cheats, liars, connivers. Your one story makes people—the general public—forget all the Jews who have lived, all the Jewish boys who served well in the armed services, all the Jews who live honest hard lives the world over." Think about whether "Defender of the Faith" reinforces negative stereotypes about Jews or whether Roth presents complex characters who have strengths as well as weaknesses? Discuss the issue with a group of classmates and then stage a debate on the subject. Ask the rest of the class to vote on the debate's winner.

- The narrator of "Defender of the Faith" explains that he "thought about the future more and more, and wrote letters to girls I'd known before the war." Imagine what Marx might say in his letters. What was his relationship like with the young women he knew before the war? Think about whether he tells them about his experiences fighting overseas or discusses his plans for the future. What does he hope to accomplish with his letters, such as looking for his future wife or a simple human connection? After carefully considering the character, his situation, and his motives, write a letter from Marx's perspective to one of the women from back home.

- Read *Wolf by the Ears* (1991), a young-adult historical novel by Ann Rinaldi that tells the story of Harriet Hemings, a slave who may be Thomas Jefferson's daughter, as she struggles with her biracial heritage. As you read, think about how Harriet approaches her search for personal identity. Write an essay comparing her journey with that of Nathan Marx in "Defender of the Faith."

- Using print and online resources, research the movement of Allied troops during World War II. Where were American soldiers trained? Where did fighting occur? How did the course of the war determine where the soldiers were sent? Create digital maps showing where troops were stationed throughout the war and displaying the sites of major battles. Combine your maps into a PowerPoint presentation, and share it with your class, explaining the significance of each slide.

he can do nothing in directing where the soldiers will be sent after training. Once he finds out that Grossbart has pulled strings and been assigned to a safe position in New Jersey, Marx uses what little pull he has to make sure Grossbart goes to the Pacific theater, where fighting against Japan still rages. Marx lies to his buddy, saying that he is doing a favor for Grossbart: "He's a Jewish kid, so he thought I could help him out. You know." However, Marx is acting out of vindictiveness, sending Grossbart into a war zone in retaliation for his constant dishonesty and manipulation.

Jewish Identity

Although Roth would prefer to be thought of simply as an American writer, he is most often identified as a Jewish American writer. Indeed, many of his characters are Jewish and face predicaments that arise specifically because they

The story takes place during basic training at Camp Crowder, Missouri. *(© Ken Wolter / ShutterStock.com)*

are Jewish. In "Defender of the Faith," Roth presents several Jewish characters, each of whom displays different levels of observance of their faith. First and foremost is Marx, who seems to be ignoring the religious part of himself. Even when he allows for the right of the Jewish soldiers to go to services on Friday evenings, it does not occur to him to go himself until a moment of nostalgia, "remembering the shrill sounds of a Bronx playground," pushes him to go, almost on a whim. Throughout the story, Marx tries to figure out who is. After spending a year in the European theater of World War II, he feels like a different person. His Jewish heritage and its familiar traditions are part of what he thinks about in trying to define this new self.

Other characters' Jewishness is also explored. For Grossbart, his faith seems to be a label he can apply to himself when it is convenient for him to do so, that is, when he can use it to forge a connection to someone who, like Marx, may be able to help him get what he wants. With Mickey Halpern, however, Roth seems to offer an example of a man with some measure of true devotion. He follows the rabbi's words in the prayer book and sips his wine at the proper time during Sabbath services while Grossbart and Fishbein goof around. The reader also learns that Halpern's religious faith presents problems: he repeatedly becomes ill after eating nonkosher food in the mess hall. With this detail, Roth adds another facet to the feelings of difference and alienation the Jewish soldiers must feel.

Although Roth frequently uses Jewish characters and focuses on uniquely Jewish issues, the discussion of these issues builds a bridge to examining the broader, universal topics of trust, deception, vindictiveness, and generosity. In "Defender of the Faith," Roth does not provide definitive answers about what it means to be Jewish, but he probes big issues all people must face, such as how to be kind to one another, while knowing that someone may take advantage of that kindness. Roth asks the right questions—questions that must be explored to learn what it means to be human.

STYLE

First-Person Narrative

"Defender of the Faith" is told in the first person. This means that the narrator, Nathan Marx, refers to himself as *I*, and the events of the story are told completely from his point of view. The story is particularly well suited to a first-person narrative because of the repeated deceptions. Readers learn the truth about Grossbart's manipulations exactly when Marx does, allowing readers to experience for themselves Marx's sense of being fooled by Grossbart.

Roth's choice of the first-person point of view also works well with the introspective nature of the story. As Marx questions how the war has changed him, as he struggles to please his commanding officer and remain kind to the young soldiers, and as he wonders about Grossbart's motives, the first-person narrative gives his thoughts and feelings an authenticity and an immediacy that might have been lacking with a more distant, third-person narrator.

Language

Throughout "Defender of the Faith," Roth is careful in his choice of words. Perhaps the most obvious feature of the language of the story is the use of Yiddish words, which provide realism. Young men raised in the first half of the twentieth century by Jewish parents, some of whom were immigrants who spoke only Yiddish, would likely incorporate some of that vocabulary even when they are speaking English, at least when communicating with others who share their background.

For example, Grossbart once calls Halpern *leben*, which literally means "life." Because it is an affectionate term, usually used by older people speaking to younger relatives, it gives the idea that Grossbart, though perhaps teasing a bit, also feels some protectiveness of and affection for Halpern. Marx recalls his own grandmother calling him *leben*, and it gives him a pang of nostalgia, as does the thought of the traditional foods of a seder meal to celebrate Passover, like *chrain* (a mixture of horseradish and chopped fish). The Yiddish terms sprinkled throughout the text give hints of the culture the characters grew up in, providing a rich background to the story.

Roth also uses words to more pointed effect, such as when Marx, rather than saying "church," as Captain Barrett does, or even "synagogue," uses the Yiddish term shul (school or synagogue). It is Marx's almost unconscious use of the Yiddish word that confirms Grossbart's suspicion that Marx is a fellow Jew, a suspicion that takes root the moment he hears Marx's surname. Roth clearly did not choose his characters' names randomly: many readers will recognize, as do the characters, that names like Marx, Grossbart, Fishbein, and Shulman are more likely to belong to Jewish families than are names like Barrett and Wright. With these surnames, Roth subtly reminds readers that they, like the characters, use names as clues to the background and heritage of the people they meet.

The specificity of language also becomes important in Marx's insistence on using proper military terms. He objects when Grossbart calls him "sir," because that address is not appropriate for a sergeant. When Fishbein refers to Major Ben Ezra as "the rabbi," Halpern corrects him, using the military term for clergy of any faith, "chaplain." Marx is careful to always use "chaplain" as well. Marx's being so particular about appropriate use of language, especially military terms, reflects the way he has immersed himself in the rules and order of the army.

HISTORICAL CONTEXT

The United States in the 1950s

In the 1950s, the United States continued to experience the booming economy that World War II sparked. Unemployment was low, and wages were good. Many soldiers returning from the front got married and soon had children, resulting in the baby boom. In 1946, the birth rate in the United States was 3.4 million, the highest recorded to that time. Throughout the 1950s, approximately four million children were born per year, and the birth rate did not begin to slow until the mid-1960s. The suburbs were expanding, providing affordable housing for these burgeoning new families. Paychecks were generous, and there was a huge variety of consumer goods to spend them on, including cars, appliances, and reasonably priced furnishings for new homes.

Although the 1950s were perhaps a golden age economically for the United States, the decade was also a time of great social change and

COMPARE
&
CONTRAST

- **1940s:** At the end of the fighting in Europe on May 8, 1945, the US Army has almost 1.9 million personnel in Europe. Within a year, that number falls to less than three hundred thousand. Some US soldiers are organized into constabularies to help maintain peace and order in war-torn countries.

   Today: The US Army continues to have a presence in Europe. United States Army Europe works with allies in the area. Its units and individual soldiers also are deployed to Afghanistan and Iraq.

- **1940s:** Jewish Americans have fought in every American war since the American Revolution, but anti-Semitism is common. More than half a million Jewish American men and women are in the armed forces during World War II, serving in both the Pacific and Europe. More than 4 percent of all soldiers are Jews. In the middle of the twentieth century, it is common for newly ordained rabbis to spend two years serving as chaplains in the military before finding a permanent position with a synagogue or school.

   Today: Anti-Semitism is not tolerated in the US Army. Dietary accommodations are made so that soldiers can keep kosher and properly celebrate religious holidays. However, as Ted Merwin explains in his article for *Veterans News Now*, the military's "culture of uniformity is very deeply entrenched," and many Jewish American soldiers still do not feel comfortable making their faith common knowledge. Statistics from the US Department of Defense show that although Jews account for approximately 2 percent of the overall US population, they account for less than one-third of 1 percent of those serving in the US military. Few rabbis start their career with a stint in the military, resulting in a shortage of chaplains to serve the needs of Jewish American soldiers.

- **1940s:** In the first half of the twentieth century, many Jewish immigrants to the United States speak only Yiddish, like Grossbart's parents in "Defender of the Faith." Before World War II, according to Jeffrey Shandler, an associate professor of Jewish studies at Rutgers University quoted by Sewell Chan in the *New York Times*, "Yiddish is the most widely spoken of any Jewish language in history." Before the war and the Holocaust, the language is spoken by an estimated eleven million people all over the world. Afterward, however, the number of Yiddish speakers dwindles to the point that the language is in danger of fading from use.

   Today: The number of Yiddish speakers is rising. Approximately a quarter of a million people in the United States speak Yiddish, along with another quarter of a million in Israel and another hundred thousand in other countries. The language seems to be experiencing a renaissance. Yiddish theater productions are performed in New York, Montreal, Tel Aviv, and Warsaw; Yiddish board games and novels are published; and dozens of colleges offer courses in Yiddish language and culture as part of their Jewish studies programs.

political tension. The civil rights movement got under way; the 1954 Supreme Court case *Brown v. Board of Education*, which legally proclaimed the unfairness of separate schools for African American children, was a huge victory. The United States and the Soviet Union faced off in the Cold War, and American fears about the stalemate led to paranoia and hearings to root out possible communists and so-called un-American activities. Women who experienced the freedom of earning a wage during the war were encouraged, if not forced, to leave the workforce and concentrate on being wives and mothers, causing deep resentment and dissatisfaction for many and leading to a resurgence of the feminist movement in the 1960s.

American Literature in the 1950s

Literature in United States in the 1950s experienced a period of change. From the mid-1910s and well into the 1940s, the ravages of two world wars caused many to reject traditional views of society and religion and to search for new meaning in life. This is reflected in the modernist period of literature, which was characterized both by realism in terms of characterization and dialogue and by new literary techniques, such as unreliable narrators, stream-of-consciousness narrative, and narratives fragmented by multiple points of view or by a skewed time line.

The end of World War II saw the beginning a more hopeful period in the United States, and postmodernism began to overtake modernism in American literature. Although they used many of the same narrative techniques as the modernists, postmodern writers often poked fun, through parody and black humor, at the modernist way of thinking. Where a modernist work may search for meaning, a postmodern work may cast doubt that there is any meaning to life at all.

Books like J. D. Salinger's *The Catcher in the Rye* (1951), Ralph Ellison's *Invisible Man* (1952), Vladimir Nabokov's *Lolita* (1955), and Ayn Rand's *Atlas Shrugged* (1957) challenged conservative midcentury social sensibilities. The writers of the Beat generation, such as Jack Kerouac and Allen Ginsberg, spoke out for individual freedoms and rejected the consumerism, materialism, and conformity that dominated most of American society at the time.

In genre fiction, science fiction was popular. The 1950s saw huge advances in technology, including the first satellites in space, and writers were inspired. Many new magazines published science-fiction stories, and publishers began giving new respect to science-fiction authors, publishing their work in hardcover form rather than just pulp paperbacks. Mystery novels also began to be more popular and gained respect from publishers, critics, and readers.

Angry because he feels taken advantage of, Sergeant Marx makes a call that sends Sheldon to fight in the Pacific.
(© Sergey Kamshylin / ShutterStock.com)

CRITICAL OVERVIEW

Early in his career, Roth was a controversial figure. When "Defender of the Faith" was first published in the *New Yorker*, many readers were angered by his less-than-flattering portrayal of his Jewish characters. His first financial success was *Portnoy's Complaint*, which was an instant best seller that made literary critics wild, according to Chris Cox in the *Guardian*. Many leaders in the Jewish community, however, were again not pleased. Cox explains that

> the pages of *Portnoy's Complaint* caused such uproar because they were the first to show "a Jew going wild in public," which according to Roth was "the last thing in the world a Jew was supposed to do."

Although *Portnoy's Complaint* is somewhat shocking, filled with sex and other mature themes, Cox did not believe that the book could be written off as "mere literary porn." He writes, "the novel transcends its own vulgarity . . . by using sex to explore pretty much everything else: history, culture, identity, religion, politics."

Although *Portnoy's Complaint* splashed onto the scene brashly, causing a stir, Roth was also able to ingeniously and delicately introduce issues important to Jewish culture. For example, Richard Brody, writing for the *New Yorker*, explained that although the first sentence of "Defender of the Faith" seems like a simple statement of fact, by setting the story during World War II, Roth was able to comment on the horrors of the Holocaust. "For Roth," Brody writes, "the contrast between Jewish life in Nazi Germany and Jewish life in the United States—even in the service of the U. S. Army—was incommensurably different." Grossbart raises the subject as part of his attempted manipulations. "That's what happened in Germany," Grossbart says pointedly, slyly accusing Marx of not supporting his fellow Jews. "They didn't stick together. They let themselves get pushed around." Brody asserts that "Roth never minimized the moral and historical gravity of the Holocaust; he resisted its being played like a card." Brody praises Roth's subtlety: Grossbart's tactic of bringing up the Holocaust to make Marx feel guilty is one of the ways Roth characterizes Grossbart as a person not to be respected or trusted.

Jan Dalley, writing in the *Financial Times*, describes how Carmen Callil, who was one of the judges considering Roth for the Man Booker International Prize, "thought Roth was 'no good' and would not prove a durable talent" and "said Roth 'writes the same thing over and over again.'" Dalley responds sarcastically, writing, "Well, yes, if you consider 'notions of nationhood, religion, love, death, belief, despair, destiny' [quoting an unnamed British critic who was an admirer of Roth's] . . . to be 'the same thing.'"

Although most readers and critics would likely think of him as a Jewish writer, Roth stated that he would rather be considered simply an American writer. He is quoted by James Duban in *Philip Roth Studies*, saying "America is first and foremost." Duban believed that Roth should not be pigeonholed: although many of Roth's protagonists are Jewish, his work extends to what is true for all people from all walks of life. Duban also scoffs at the accusations that Roth is a self-hating Jew:

> It is hardly the case that Roth here engages in the self-loathing or anti-Semitism with which he was charged within rabbinical circles in the 1950s; rather, he seems to imply that he is comfortable enough in his Judaism to use his characters, their religion, and their dilemmas as points of departure to arrive at universal truths about human nature and its dilemmas.

William Peden, who reviews *Goodbye, Columbus: And Five Short Stories* for the *New York Times*, agrees, describing the stories in the collection as being "concerned with universal, archetypal experiences." Peden praises the collection as a whole, calling it impressive, especially for a first book. He continues: "[Roth] is a good story-teller, a shrewd appraiser of character and a keen recorder of an indecisive generation." Writing for the *Wire*, Jen Doll also points out Roth's shrewdness as a writer. She discusses rereading *Goodbye, Columbus* years after her first experience with the book: "I'd forgotten how funny it is, and I'd only partly remembered the depth of Roth's keen eye, his descriptive talents, and the way he can turn any mundane phrase or action into something beautiful."

CRITICISM

Kristen Sarlin Greenberg

Greenberg is a freelance writer and editor with a background in literature and philosophy. In the following essay, she examines the changes that Sergeant Marx experiences in Philip Roth's "Defender of the Faith."

Upon its publication in the *New Yorker* in 1959, "Defender of the Faith" angered many Jews. One reader, quoted by Jon Michaud, sent a letter to the author in protest, writing "With your one story . . . you have done as much harm as all the organized anti-Semitic organizations have done to make people believe that all Jews are cheats, liars, connivers." The story does indeed center on the actions of Sheldon Grossbart, a young Jewish enlisted man in basic training who tries to garner special treatment from his sergeant, Nathan Marx, simply because they are both Jewish. The furious readers saw Grossbart as reinforcing many of the negative stereotypes of Jews, but a closer reading of the story shows that Grossbart is not the

WHAT DO I READ NEXT?

- *Dear Miss Breed: True Stories of the Japanese American Incarceration during World War II and a Librarian Who Made a Difference* (2006), by Joanne Oppenheim, focuses on the letters written between the children's librarian Clara Breed and her young Japanese American friends, who were held in internment camps in the United States during World War II. Breed provided a connection to the outside world for these children and teens and wrote articles protesting their treatment, a controversial stance at a time when America was at war with Japan and many Americans feared and hated anything associated with that country.

- Will Hobbs's 1991 young-adult novel *Downriver* and its sequel, *River Thunder* (1997), feature a group of teenagers and the mishaps they experience while on a wild white-water rafting trip. Like "Defender of the Faith," the books explore whether people have a responsibility to take care of one another.

- Roth won the Pulitzer Prize for *American Pastoral* (1997). This novel, the first in Roth's American trilogy, was followed by *I Married a Communist* (1998) and *The Human Stain* (2001). *American Pastoral* offers a glimpse into the political turmoil of the 1960s: a man's quiet life is shattered when his daughter plants a bomb to protest US involvement in Vietnam. The novel is controversial, like much of Roth's work, so it is more appropriate for older students.

- In *Whistling Vivaldi: How Stereotypes Affect Us and What We Can Do* (2010), Claude M. Steele gives a detailed report of his research into identity and stereotyping and offers a plan for lessening the damaging effects of stereotypes on American society.

- Robert Nusbaum's memoir, *Once in a Lifetime: The World War II Memoir of a Jewish-American Soldier* (2012), recounts the personal experiences of an enlisted man in the European theater in World War II.

- The graphic novel *Jerusalem: A Family Portrait* (2013) was written by Boaz Yakin and illustrated by Nick Bertozzi. The story, which takes place in the politically explosive setting of 1940s British-occupied Jerusalem, presents a difficult moral dilemma: Is it ethical to take advantage of political and social upset to make one's fortune?

---

true focus. Although his manipulations of Sergeant Marx drive the plot, the most important element of the story is the evolution of Marx and how he feels about himself and the world around him. A careful look at Marx's thoughts at the beginning and the end of the story hints at the kind of person he will become, now that the war is over.

Roth opens the story with a series of seemingly simple statements that provide the setting. World War II is coming to an end. Marx has been with Allied forces "racing across Germany," and he can hardly believe that task is finished. As the paragraph progresses, however, Roth offers the central issue of the story: Marx finds himself back in America, away from the front, and thinks about how two years in a war zone have affected him. He considers himself fortunate to have developed "an infantryman's heart, which, like his feet, at first aches and swells but finally grows horny enough for him to travel the weirdest paths without feeling a thing." The war has changed him: in order to withstand "the trembling of old people, the crying of the very young, the uncertainty and fear in the eyes of the once arrogant," he has hardened his heart, cutting off his softer side as a form of self-protection.

Marx immerses himself in the comfortable order of the army's schedules and regulations. For all that Marx is annoyed by Grossbart's complaints and machinations to get himself excused from the G.I. party to go to Sabbath services, the conversations the two men share spark something in Marx. Hearing Yiddish words and remembering going to synagogue himself "on long spring evenings such as this" when the "slant of the light" was just so prompt Marx to recall his own childhood and "the shrill sounds of a Bronx playground." He finds himself "in a reverie so strong that I felt as though a hand were reaching down inside me" and seems surprised that the feeling had to "reach so very far to touch me." The tender emotions had to find their way past all the horrors of war that he had "refused to weep over." Marx has had to "shut off all softness I might feel for my fellows" and be strong so that he can carry out his duties. Warm nostalgia seems alien to him.

Grossbart then causes another to-do by writing a letter—signing his father's name—complaining about the Jewish soldiers' being served nonkosher food in the mess hall. Marx is again disgusted by Grossbart's deception, but once the fuss dies down, Marx has time to think "about the future more and more." He sends "letters to girls I'd known before the war" and gathers information about law school. He is making plans for what he will do with his life once the war is over and he is out of the army, and he begins to be happy.

Grossbart disrupts Marx's quietly emerging contentment with another request: he wants a pass to leave the base to visit his aunt in Saint Louis for a Passover seder. Once again, Marx is coerced into helping Grossbart, and once again, Roth ties the softening of Marx's war-hardened shell with his Jewish background. When Marx gives in and lets Grossbart have his pass, Grossbart tells him "'You're a good Jew, Sergeant. You like to think you have a hard heart, but underneath you're a fine, decent man. I mean that.'"

Marx's kindness is met by yet more pushing from Grossbart. Not content with his own pass, he returns to ask Marx for passes for his friends as well. Marx is again angry and frustrated by Grossbart's presumption, yet he wonders "if perhaps the struggle with Grossbart wasn't as much my fault as his. What was I that I had to *muster* generous feelings? Who was I to have been feeling so grudging, so tight-hearted?" Marx thinks of times when he was a boy and would hurt himself "doing something I shouldn't have done." While Marx's mother was "busy bawling me out" for breaking the rules, his grandmother would say to her "What are you making a *tsimmes*?" ("Why are you making a fuss?") and instead comfort him. Marx recognizes that his grandmother knew mercy overrides justice and realizes that he also should have known it.

The idea of mercy overriding justice is important to the story. Marx concludes that perhaps he has been more concerned with the army's rules than with his higher duty of taking care of the men in his charge. He fears that he has become a penny pincher with kindness and thinks that "Surely . . . the Messiah himself—if He should ever come—won't niggle over nickels and dimes. God willing, he'll hug and kiss," showing mercy, like Marx's grandmother. Roth touches on this theme earlier in the story, when Marx jokingly calls Grossbart "a regular Messiah" when he claims to be taking care of his friends, Larry Fishbein and Mickey Halpern. Grossbart's response echoes Marx's thoughts: "What Mickey says is the Messiah is a collective idea. He went to Yeshiva, Mickey, for a while. He says together we're the Messiah. Me a little bit, you a little bit." This implies that every person bears some responsibility for taking care of others.

Sheldon asks to be excused from cleaning the barracks so that he can attend Sabbath services, but Mickey is the one who prays piously. *(© Boris Stroujko | ShutterStock.com)*

Almost against his will, Marx does seem to feel this responsibility. When he hears the news that his trainees will go to the Pacific, where there is still fighting between Allied forces and Japan, Marx finds that "the news shocked me, as though I were the father of Halpern, Fishbein, and Grossbart." He does identify with the young men, after all, and care for them. However, is this because they are all Jews, as Grossbart seems to think? Sharing a common faith does give them a certain connection, being a minority among the masses of soldiers. But perhaps, beyond that arbitrary connection, Marx also cares because they share circumstances: they are all people in a difficult time, facing a frightening war.

Roth seems to intend for readers to see the latter. For example, when Marx is trying to explain to Grossbart, Fishbein, and Halpern why he cannot give them all passes to go to Saint Louis, he says "'I don't want enemies. I'm just like you—I want to serve my time and go home. I miss the same things you miss.'" The men are discussing the seder, a specifically Jewish ritual, but this illustrates how Roth turns the specific—his Jewish characters' celebrating the holidays they grew up with—into the universal—all soldiers away from home missing their families and their own comforting traditions.

What is most important about "Defender of the Faith" is not the religion of the characters but the moral dilemma for Marx. Can he continue to be kind, giving, and merciful even after Grossbart takes advantage of him? War has changed Marx, and he must figure out who he is now. Just as a close reading of the story's first paragraph shows Marx's state of mind before he encounters Grossbart, an examination of the final paragraph hints at the kind of person Marx will become.

Marx watches the men in the barracks as they prepare to ship out to the Pacific: "With a kind of quiet nervousness, they polished shoes, shined belt buckles, squared away underwear, trying as best they could to accept their fate." Clearly Marx feels for them, perhaps remembering how he felt before being sent to the front in Europe, wondering if he would make it home again. Marx also clearly has sympathy for Grossbart, noticing how he swallows hard, accepting his fate as the other enlisted men do.

Finally, Marx explains how he faces his own fate, "resisting with all my will an impulse to turn and seek pardon for my vindictiveness" in having Grossbart sent to the Pacific. Marx feels remorse, and his fate will be to worry about Grossbart in the Pacific and to imagine the guilt he himself will feel if Grossbart dies. He wants Grossbart's forgiveness, recognizing that he may have shirked his responsibility to take care of his fellow man. Marx's heart, like his body, is no longer hardened by war, and he must be human again, with all the pain and joy that embodies.

Source: Kristen Sarlin Greenberg, Critical Essay on "Defender of the Faith," in *Short Stories for Students*, Gale, Cengage Learning, 2016.

James Duban

In the following excerpt, Duban discusses how Roth's characters sometimes deny their Jewishness.

... "Defender of the Faith" had much earlier dramatized Levin's account, in *In Search*, of how Jewish self-denial relates to the passage from Psalms 147, "If I Forget Thee, O Jerusalem, may my right hand forget its cunning." Moreover, in Roth's creation of Sergeant Nathan Marx as Camp Crowder autobiographer, "Defender of the Faith" anticipates the retrospective narration of the older narrator in *The Plot Against America* and is reminiscent of Levin's backward-looking narration and analysis—"It seems to me now"; "Many years later, it appeared to me"; "in my later interpretation, I was seeking" (*In Search*)—especially with regard to the loss of feeling in, or amputation of, hands or legs. In *In Search*, Levin records the most egregious instance self-amputation as that of the army general whom he interviewed (as part of his World War II service in the

SOMETHING RESEMBLING THAT TRANSMISSION OF SENTIMENT OCCURS WHEN GROSSBART CAUSES MARX TO FEEL GUILTY ABOUT HIS HAVING SACRIFICED JEWISH IDENTITY IN ORDER TO BLEND INTO ARMY LIFE."

Office of War Information) when accompanying troops pressing forward, ultimately to liberate German concentration camps. Levin's account of that most "troublesome" incident of amputation entails a "revelation of every malformation of the human spirit," including his own and that of countless other Jews. Moreover, this startling instance of shame over one's Judaism appears to have significant implications for the casting, narrative technique, and anguished inventiveness of Roth's "Defender of the Faith."

Anticipating a key part of that story, in which Sergeant Marx must deal with Privates Grossbart, Fishbein, and Halpern—three recruits who seem to use their Judaism to shirk responsibility—Levin, in *In Search*, wishes to dispel, in his capacity as war correspondent, "little wisecracks and legends about Jews finding soft spots behind the lines, Jews in the commissaries and in public relations jobs and in transport." Intent on interviewing "fighting Jews"—indeed, "Jews who had performed outstandingly," thereby "counteracting the myths upon which anti-Semitism is founded"—Levin tracks down a number of combat-seasoned kinsmen, but none more alluring than the heroic Jewish general, "the commander of a crack armored division" whose "tanks had been the first to pierce the Siegfried line and enter Germany." The general, however, "didn't want it mentioned that he was of Jewish origin"; he was, in fact, rumored to have feigned Christian worship. Thus, remaining "bold" and "vigorous" in "mechanical warfare," he fights a less courageous war with his core identity. He dies some days later when, following capture, he is machine-gunned after reaching for his pistol to surrender it to Nazis. Ironically, the obituaries concentrate on two points: the general's having been the son of an "aged Hebrew-school teacher in Denver" and the general's having met his death toward the end of Passover. For Levin, though, the general had already surrendered to the enemy within after suffering from one of those "psychic cancers, ugly secret growths that our people had so long buried in their souls." Anticipating Sergeant Marx's—and foreshadowing the related dilemma, in *The Plot Against America*, of narrator Philip's—quandary over balancing his Jewish and American identities, Levin adds, "It was only a ghastly wrestling that could have ended in a man's suppressing so much of himself." In that game of wrestling, Marx is the general's equal—and more.

I say "more" because, in "Defender of the Faith," Marx, beyond being a "goddam hero" who has done his fair share of "killing Germans" ("Defender"), survives, and then becomes his own retrospective narrator searching futilely to understand a psychological dismemberment somehow linked to what, in his narrative's concluding line, he admits to having been his vindictiveness in dispatching Grossbart to the Pacific. Stated otherwise, Roth's story picks up where Levin's *In Search* leaves off, through the metamorphosis of the general (as war hero) and Levin (as retrospective, self-searching narrator) into a mechanical sergeant who, seeking autobiographically to fathom incidents that continue to haunt him, has risen to military valor but who, trapped within the confines of his evasive narrative, falls short of the eventual insight and psychological wholeness that Levin claims for himself when narrating his own search. Still, in the process of reaching that goal, Levin anticipates Sergeant Marx's problematic outlook through the confession that the war "released me from the responsibility [. . .] to be a good Jew, to be anything but a man in motion" (*In Search*), just as Levin's duties as a war correspondent allowed him to achieve "for myself a sense of equality with a goy." Further anticipating the dilemma of Sergeant Marx, Levin adds that this "was the way for many Jews in the war. It was in a measure a healing experience for those who, like myself, had the Jewish complex overextended." That would include, of course, the conflicted general, whose behavior Levin sees as mirroring his own insecurity about Jewish identity, and that of many other Jews. Honest confessions, these, by Levin. Quite otherwise for Sergeant Marx in his

retrospective reflection: while teetering upon insight, Marx ultimately becomes self-justifying rather than self-educating as he ponders but never grasps how his aversion to the wiles of the Jewish conscripts reflects unsettlement over the religious part of himself that he has obliterated through military routine and heroism.

That process of evasion expresses itself in the transference of the biblical loss of "cunning" in one's right hand to an insensate feeling in Marx's feet that corresponds to the calcification of Jewish sentiment in his heart; indeed, he has developed "an infantryman's heart, which, like his feet, at first aches and swells but finally grows horny enough for him to travel the weirdest paths *without feeling a thing*" ("Defender", emphasis added). Marx thereby experiences his own loss of cunning and chances to conform to accounts, by Levin, in *In Search*, of the "Jewish soldier" who, "during periods of intense activity at the front," could "forget himself and become entirely one of a unit." Though perhaps justifiable with regard to the unity and uniformity expected of a soldier in combat, or of a war correspondent such as Levin, Marx wishes to prolong the evasion once he ends up at the aptly named Camp Crowder, in Missouri, too-close-for-comfort to Jewish recruits. Lacking Levin's capacity for fruitful self-analysis, Marx narrates events in a way that is disingenuous about his motives, relative to the negativity about his own Judaism that he projects onto Grossbart through an act of vengeance rationalized as military justice and impartiality. Still, Marx is no venal and non-reflective self-hater, for his being "in search of more of me" ("Defender") turns out to be rather Levin-like in an anguished, albeit unsustained, quest to balance one's Jewish and American identities.

Something resembling that transmission of sentiment occurs when Grossbart causes Marx to feel guilty about his having sacrificed Jewish identity in order to blend into army life. Unexpected references to "synagogue," "shul" (Yiddish for "synagogue" or "school"), "*leben*," (Yiddish term of endearment that conflates one's life with one's descendents [Budick, 59]), "gefilte fish" and "*chrain*" (chopped fish and horseradish, Passover fare) occasion in Marx, even amidst his resentment at having been exploited by the new recruits, nostalgia for the Jewish heritage he has suppressed. In fact, the associations of gefilte fish and *chrain* are especially suggestive, inasmuch as Marx allows Grossbart leave for a belated Passover meal with Grossbart's aunt, requesting, in return, only "'a piece of that gefilte fish'," even though Passover has occurred some weeks earlier. Levin's *In Search* provides a helpful context for appreciating Marx's psychological susceptibility to Grossbart's wiles, since "even the most unbelieving Jew, raised in a home where religious folk-customs were retained, still [. . .] feels a faint guilt [. . .] if he fails to participate in a feast on Passover," since "fundamental symbols, connected with eating, link us to our horde." Related sentiments of guilt cause Marx to straddle the worlds of contempt and indulgence in his dealings with Grossbart, Halpern, and Fishbein. He can say of the manipulative Grossbart, "Very simply, I didn't like him" ("Defender"), all the while indulging and abetting Grossbart's and Fishbein's duplicity. And whatever the conspicuous hypocrisy of the recruits, they nonetheless remind Marx of the institutional anti-Semitism and smugness—expressed all too vocally by Captain Paul Barrett: "'Jews have a tendency to be pushy'"—against which Marx has immured himself in military service. Amidst this jumble of confusion, Marx is an autobiographer who apprehends but fails to comprehend the haunting "hand"—one previously described in the parallel world of Meyer Levin—that reaches to the depth of Marx's perplexity as a repressed Jew.

If only momentarily, Marx feels thusly touched when, after granting Grossbart, Fishbein, and Halpern passes to attend Friday night "*shabbus*" (Sabbath) services, he is overwhelmed by a "deep memory" of his youth, as a Jew, in the Bronx. Growing "exceedingly tender about myself," Marx experiences "a reverie so strong that I felt as though a hand were reaching down inside me. It had to reach so very far to touch me!" The hand reminds Marx of his identity as Jew who has missed opportunities, even when marching through Germany, to take pride and satisfaction in being a Jew. The hand becomes one with the biblical hand of Psalms 147 evoked by Levin, for Marx is awakened, if only transiently, to the ethnic consciousness that had until then been anesthetized. With words that may carry added weight

for readers attentive to Levin's *In Search*, Marx says that "it was not altogether curious that, *in search of more of me*, I found myself following Grossbart's tracks to Chapel No. 3, where the Jewish services were being held" (emphasis added). There Grossbart and Fishbein exhibit "faked devotion" while Halpern wholeheartedly follows the service, with the "fingers of his right hand [. . .] spread wide across the cover of his open [prayer] book." Halpern's is the sensate right hand of Judaism, as evoked in Levin's *In Search*.

Beyond Marx's intimation of core Judaism resides his claim about having, on that occasion, possessed a fuller sense of "myself." That feeling, in turn, approaches the most significant insight of *In Search*:

> It is this, I believe, that is the subject of each man's search. He must, to begin with, identify what is within himself. He must know himself. [. . .] My whole story in this book [. . .] is the story of an element in *myself*—Jewishness—that strove and forced itself through every wall, to come out as a full part of my personality. (emphasis added)

Marx, however, despite momentary intimations of personal wholeness through alignment of his American and ethnic identities, ultimately remains insensate to his Judaism, validating Grossbart's claim that Marx is "Ashamed" ("Defender") . . . .

Source: James Duban, "Written, Unwritten, and Vastly Rewritten: Meyer Levin's *In Search* and Philip Roth's 'Defender of the Faith,' *The Plot Against America*, and *Indignation*," in *Philip Roth Studies*, Vol. 7, No. 1, Spring 2011, pp. 39–43.

Alan Cooper

In the following excerpt, Cooper discusses the accusation that Roth's work can be seen as anti-Semitic.

. . . Reviewing *Goodbye, Columbus* in *The Reconstructionist* (March 4, 1960), Harold Ribalow says of Roth that " . . . he writes out of hatred more often than not," that "his people are so unsympathetic that you find yourself not caring for them, their troubles and the ways in which they try to solve their problems," and that his stories are "open to the charge of anti-Semitism." Four years later Oscar Janowsky would say of Roth that

> . . . his rebellion against the Jewish world from which he springs is so extreme that the characters he describes are frequently

IT IS MARX'S STORY, TOLD IN MARX'S NARRATIVE VOICE, MUCH MORE THAN GROSSBART'S. OVER A GENERATION OF COLLEGE STUDENTS, MOST OF THEM GENTILE, HAVE NOT FAILED TO GRASP THAT POINT."

unconvincing and revolting . . . . The umbilical cord which ties the author to his Jewish past is torn with such violence that the clinical details of the rupture obscure every other element."

These condemnations, one by a partisan Jewish publicist and one by a respected scholar, are somewhat restrained compared to the views of countless rabbis expressed in pulpits and of letter writers to the review columns and magazines in which the various *Goodbye, Columbus* stories originally appeared. But they show how the insecurity of the times could color critical judgment. Of another *Goodbye, Columbus* story, "Defender of the Faith," Ribalow writes

> . . . I do not think anyone will deny that it is a vivid and, in a way, brilliant story about a Jew in the United States Army who spends all his time, energies and abilities in trying to fool everyone with whom he deals, to get away from every responsibility. It is a story about a perfect "goldbrick," a hateful, miserably phony type. Grossbart, the faker, is a Jew who exploits his Jewishness in every possible way to avoid work, to get off the Army base. Grossbart is constantly dealing with a fellow Jew, Sergeant Marx, and uses psychological pressure to get what he wants . . . you remember Grossbart as the meanest, most unsavory Jew you have come across in years, and you cannot help being revolted by him.

Grossbart is almost everything Ribalow says he is, and yet Ribalow is wrong in his most essential point: "Defender of the Faith" is not a "story about [this] perfect 'goldbrick'"; it is a story of conscience about the sergeant who has to deal with him. It is Marx's story, told in Marx's narrative voice, much more than Grossbart's. Over a generation of college students, most of them gentile, have not failed to grasp that point. Appearing in several— including the most widely read—freshman

English anthologies, the story has been presented—and elucidated in ample study notes—as a model of moral dilemma played out in the psyche of its protagonist, Sergeant Marx.

And, indeed, Marx moves from dilemma to dilemma, as he considers Jewish issues for perhaps the first time: whether he has not helped save Jewry from Hitler only to deliver it into bland assimilation, whether the army that fights for democracy should not consider the pluralism of its own citizenry and attempt to provide special sabbath observances and kosher food for Jewish soldiers, whether the pressures of war and army conformity have too easily severed Marx's own ties with his Jewish tradition. These are not new issues. During World War I, one of the improvised choruses of "Inky Dinky Parlez Vous" advised that "many a son of Abraham is eating ham for Uncle Sam," and the case of an army doctor who chose to wear a yarmulke during surgery would hold the headlines a generation after this story was published. Roth presents an issue so universal that it anticipates the very criticism that would be leveled at the narrative. At the end of the story Grossbart shouts, " . . . There's no limit to your anti-Semitism, is there! . . . " as earlier he had averred, "I've run into this before, but never from my own!"

In slowly succumbing to Grossbart's suggestion that his G.I. heart has hardened by disassociation from his Jewish roots, Marx lets guilt—and a dose of sentimental memory— color judgment.

> Out of the many recollections that had tumbled over me these past few days, I heard from some childhood moment my grandmother's voice: "What are you making a *tsimas*?" It was what she would ask my mother when, say, I had cut myself with a knife and her daughter was busy bawling me out. I would need a hug and a kiss and my mother would moralize! But my grandmother knew— mercy overrides justice. I should have known it, too. Who was Nathan Marx to be such a pennypincher with kindness? Surely, I thought, the Messiah himself—if he should ever come—won't niggle over nickels and dimes. God willing, he'll hug and kiss. (*GC*)

This self-examination comes after Marx has just written a weekend pass, against the rules of basic training, to allow Grossbart and his two Jewish fellow trainees to go to an aunt's home for a (as it later turns out) fictitious, month-late special seder. That Marx can derive Portia's "quality of mercy" scruples from the homey teachings of his Jewish grandmother or that Roth neatly distinguishes for his reader the Jewish idea of the messiah as separate from God and still anticipated—these gifts to a general readership could not move critics like Ribalow to modulate their attack. To them, fear that Gentiles would take all Jews to be like Grossbart overrode every other consideration.

A subtext of the story is the war itself and its background assimilation of Jews and Gentiles in the army. Marx has fought in the already concluded European phase of the war, which began as Germany's war against the Jews. His commanding officer, Captain Barrett, uses him as an example to answer Grossbart, flattering Marx with the status of hero. Grossbart wants to avoid the dangers of the remaining action in the Pacific by being shipped back to New Jersey. Both Grossbart and Barrett are using Marx.

Marx's redemption comes in a hard but fair act. Grossbart finally makes the move he has been building toward throughout the story and, deserting the two other recruits he has claimed to champion, finds another Jewish patsy to reverse his combat orders and keep him from being sent to the Pacific. But Marx has the orders restored. He alleges to the commanding officer that he is doing so at Grossbart's bidding, ironically explaining that the "boy" is indeed the patriot he has painted himself as being, one who wishes fervently to remain with his friends assigned to the remaining war zone. Roth makes Marx the titled "Defender of the Faith" by having him refuse to allow other characters in the story to perceive the Jews as seeking—or getting—special treatment. The resolution is finally of Marx's conflict. Having been forced to reconsider his Jewish difference, he lets his duty as soldier properly prevail. He is equally the sergeant of all his recruits.

> With a kind of quiet nervousness, they polished shoes, shined belt buckles, squared away underwear, trying as best they could to accept their fate. Behind me, Grossbart swallowed hard, accepting his. And then, resisting with all my will an impulse to turn and seek pardon for my vindictiveness, I accepted my own. (GC)

There is real anti-Semitism in the story, but it is not Roth's. Sergeant Marx is torn not only between two impulses but between

> I WAS VERY SURPRISED BY THE WAY IT WAS RECEIVED, AS A KIND OF REGIONAL BOOK, A BOOK ABOUT A PARTICULAR GROUP. NOW MAYBE I SHOULDN'T HAVE BEEN SO SURPRISED. TO ME THE STORIES WEREN'T SO MUCH ABOUT THE BREAKDOWN OF THE AMERICAN JEWISH COMMUNITY."

two representative characters. Grossbart is one. The other, Captain Barrett, is perhaps more sinister because totally unaware: like most of America, he sees no reason to know who Marx is. In one statement he both honors Marx's military record and erases his identity. Barrett's "native corn," as Roth would call it elsewhere, chills as much as Grossbart's weaseling enrages . . . .

Source: Alan Cooper, "Starting Out," in *Philip Roth and the Jews*, State University of New York Press, 1996, pp. 34–36.

Jerre Mangione
In the following interview excerpt, Roth discusses a bit of his Jewish heritage and talks about the themes in Goodbye, Columbus, *which contains "Defender of the Faith."*

Mangione: How much Yiddish was spoken at home by your parents?

Roth: Oh, very little Yiddish was spoken. When Yiddish was spoken, it was not spoken so that I would understand, but so that I *wouldn't* understand. That is, it was the language of secrecy, the language of surprises and chagrin. So I learned very little; I didn't pay much attention to it. What I heard, however, wasn't always English, at the other extreme. I heard a *kind* of English that I think was spoken by second-generation people in what was essentially a very tightly enclosed Jewish neighborhood in Newark. My knowledge of Yiddish is very slight. People say things and I don't know what they're talking about. Apparently I don't spell it right, either, when I do it in my books. I've been told that.

Mangione: But some of the critics give the impression that you know a great deal of Yiddish. For example, I remember one critic who attributed great meaning to the fact that you had called the main character in Goodbye, Columbus *Neil "Klugman."*

Roth: Yeah. That was Irving Howe. But *he* knows a lot of Yiddish . . . much more than I do. I wanted a kind of name that wasn't recognizably Jewish (like Cohen or Ginsberg or whatever), that wasn't ordinary, wasn't conventionally Jewish, but one that had a Jewish sound to it. Now, in the deepest reaches of my unconscious, I might have been aware of its Yiddish meaning; I don't believe I was.

Mangione: Did you read a fellow named Joseph Landis on the subject? He's written an article called "The Sadness of Philip Roth." He said that "Klugman" has two meanings: If you say "KLUGman" it means "clever fellow," but if you say "KLOOGman" it means "mourner" or "sad fellow." And he talks about the fact that you are struck with sadness when you see what is happening.

Roth: Landis is a Klugman, in the first sense. No, I don't know; that kind of speculation about the meanings of names or the derivations of names doesn't really concern me very much. When I wrote those stories I wasn't trying to be clever, particularly, and in many ways they weren't terribly "literary," as I think of them. They were kind of responses to my background, responses to my origins, and they were also written independently, one of the other. I had no sense they'd be brought together in a book, or that the book would have a kind of Yiddish or Jewish theme. In fact, when the book came out and received the kind of criticism it did and the kind of attention it did, I was very surprised. I was perhaps being too innocent. But nevertheless I was very surprised by the way it was received, as a kind of regional book, a book about a particular group. Now maybe I shouldn't have been so surprised. To me the stories weren't so much about the breakdown of the American Jewish community, as some of the critics said.

Mangione: Yes. They kept talking about the fact that you were portraying a people whose values were breaking down because they were joining the mainstream of middle-class America, which was in this "swampland of prosperity."

I think that was one of the expressions that [Saul] Bellow used.

Roth: Yeah, Bellow had a nice expression I remember it well—in his review, which appeared in *Commentary*. He talked about the Patimkins (the leading characters in *Goodbye, Columbus*) as living in "pig heaven." That was more the spirit in which the book had been written. I'm not a sociologist, and my categories weren't sociological. The *comedy* of the thing got me—the comedy of this particular kind of Jewish affluence, the comedy of certain Jewish predicaments. I think of the book, really, taken altogether, even though it has a kind of sad or melancholy edge to it, as a *comic* book, and the situation as funny, very often.

Mangione: When you say "the book," do you also include the short stories that go with Goodbye, Columbus, *or are you talking about specifically the novella* Goodbye, Columbus?

Roth: No, I mean the whole thing taken together. For instance, "The Conversion of the Jews" is a story about a kid who goes up on a roof and threatens to jump. It's not a grim story, it's comic—sometimes at the expense of this kid himself, sometimes at the expense of the other people. But the comedy really doesn't derive from any satire directed at the characters, but out of the bizarre nature of the experience. Also, I think a certain kind of comedy comes out of the fact that there's a bizarre experience in a kind of recognizable setting. There's something recognizable about what the people say in that story.

Mangione: I suppose it's hard to be comic without being serious at the same time. You can't help but base your comedy on serious things. I was thinking, for example, of the story "Eli, the Fanatic," which says some pretty serious things. One of the things it says, it seems to me, is something that you more or less keep saying in various ways throughout all your writing. And it's expressed by dialogue between Eli's wife and Eli. She says, "You won't do anything in moderation. That's how people destroy themselves." And he says, "I do everything in moderation. That's my trouble."

Roth: Yeah, that's a good bit of dialogue to point to . . . I didn't remember it. But that problem of how far to go—how far to go, especially when you have large personal ambitions, large moral aspirations . . . how far do you go with them? In a way, that's not so much the subject of the novella *Goodbye, Columbus* as it is, say, of "Eli, the Fanatic," about a man who's driven to sort of create right out of a situation, to create a kind of "good order," and of a story like "Defender of the Faith," where you get Sargeant Marx, who's appalled by the behavior of this soldier, and doesn't know how far to go to stop him. He's very hesitant to be savage, very hesitant to be openly cruel. He really can't deal with his cruelty. He doesn't know how necessary it is. And also, of course, what happens in that story is that it conflicts with his sense of being a civilized man. It may be that his sense of civilization is narrow, or mistaken. It's this theme that I picked up in *Letting Go*, the novel that followed *Goodbye, Columbus*. And in a way I see *Letting Go* coming out of—not directly, but in a hazy kind of way—"Defender of the Faith" and "Eli, the Fanatic." The central problem is, really, "How far do you go? How far do you penetrate into the suffering and the error and the mistakes," say, "in other lives?" And so both the hero, Gabe Wallach, and even the other hero, Paul Herz, are battling between maintaining some kind of authentic self, and some sense of detachment. Because, after all, there's only so much one can do. But the problem for them is to determine *how* much one can do, how much one ought to do, how much is necessary—to feel yourself not just fully human or fully civilized, but manly, to feel yourself altogether a man. And I think that's the kind of problem those two heroes face in *Letting Go*, and I think that if you look back you'll see it in those two stories we mentioned in *Goodbye, Columbus*. As for the novella, you don't see it, but you do get someone dealing with the question "What kind of man am I going to be?" More broadly, "What kind of *person* am I going to be? What kind of life am I going to live?" . . .

Source: Jerre Mangione and Philip Roth, "Philip Roth," in *Conversations with Philip Roth*, edited by George J. Searless, University Press of Mississippi, 1992, pp. 3–6.

SOURCES

"The American Novel: Mid-1950s–1960s Beat Generation," PBS website, http://www.pbs.org/wnet/american-novel/timeline/beatgeneration.html (accessed March 1, 2015).

"Books That Shaped America: 1950–2000," Library of Congress website, http://read.gov/btsa.html (accessed April 13, 2015).

Brody, Richard, "*Philip Roth: Unmasked* and the Birth of a Meme," in *New Yorker*, March 11, 2013, http://www.newyorker.com/culture/richard-brody/philip-roth-unmasked-and-the-birth-of-a-meme (accessed February 28, 2015).

Chan, Sewell, "Yiddish Revival, with New York Leading the Way," in *New York Times*, October 17, 2007, http://cityroom.blogs.nytimes.com/2007/10/17/a-yiddish-revival-with-new-york-leading-the-way (accessed March 1, 2015).

"Clara Breed," Japanese American National Museum website, http://www.janm.org/exhibits/breed/breed_t.htm (accessed March 1, 2015).

Cox, Chris, "Portnoy's Complaint: Still Shocking at 40," in *Guardian*, September 7, 2009, http://www.theguardian.com/books/booksblog/2009/sep/07/portnoys-complaint-shocking-49 (accessed February 28, 2015).

Daley, David, "Philip Roth: 'I'm Done,'" in *Salon*, http://www.salon.com/2012/11/09/philip_roth_im_done (accessed March 1, 2015).

Dalley, Jan, "At Home with Philip Roth," in *Financial Times*, June 26, 2011, http://www.slate.com/articles/life/ft/2011/06/at_home_with_philip_roth.html (accessed February 28, 2015).

Doll, Jen, "A Look at *Goodbye, Columbus* on Philip Roth's 80th Birthday," in *Wire*, http://www.thewire.com/entertainment/2013/03/philip-roth-80th-birthday/63274 (accessed February 28, 2015).

Duban, James, "Written, Unwritten, and Vastly Rewritten: Meyer Levin's *In Search* and Philip Roth's 'Defender of the Faith,' *The Plot Against America*, and *Indignation*," in *Philip Roth Studies*, Vol. 7, No. 1, Spring 2011, p. 41.

"History," United States Army Europe website, http://www.eur.army.mil/organization/history.htm (accessed March 1, 2015).

"The Holocaust: Combat and Resistance—Jewish Soldiers in the Allied Armies," Yad Vashem website, http://www.yadvashem.org/yv/en/holocaust/about/07/jewish_soldiers.asp (accessed March 1, 2015).

Merwin, Ted, "Jews Are Underrepresented in the U.S. Military and Its Leadership," *Veterans News Now*, December 1, 2011, http://www.veteransnewsnow.com/2011/12/01/jews-are-underrepresented-in-the-u-s-military-and-its-leadership (accessed March 1, 2015).

Michaud, Jon, "Eighty-five from the Archive: Philip Roth," in *New Yorker*, May 28, 2010, http://www.newyorker.com/books/double-take/eighty-five-from-the-archive-philip-roth (accessed March 1, 2015).

"The 1950s," History.com, http://www.history.com/topics/1950s (accessed March 1, 2015).

Peden, William, "In a Limbo between Past and Present," in *New York Times*, May 17, 1959, http://www.nytimes

.com/books/97/04/20/reviews/roth-goodbye.html (accessed February 28, 2015).

"Philip Roth," Houghton Mifflin Harcourt website, http://www.houghtonmifflinbooks.com/authors/roth (accessed March 1, 2015).

"Philip Roth Biography," *Biography.com*, http://www.biography.com/people/philip-roth-9465081#personal-life (accessed February 28, 2015).

"Postmodernism in Literature," study.com, http://education-portal.com/academy/lesson/postmodernism-in-literature-definition-lesson-quiz.html (accessed March 1, 2015).

Roth, Philip, "Defender of the Faith," in *The Best American Short Stories of the Century*, edited by John Updike and Katrina Kenison, Houghton Mifflin, 1999, pp. 384–410.

Silverberg, Robert, "Science Fiction in the Fifties: The Real Golden Age," Library of America website, http://www.loa.org/sciencefiction/why_silverberg.jsp (accessed February 28, 2015).

"World War II: Statistics on Jewish American Soldiers," in *Jewish Virtual Library*, http://www.jewishvirtual library.org/jsource/ww2/jewstats.html (accessed March 1, 2015).

"Yiddish FAQs," Rutgers School of Arts and Sciences, Department of Jewish Studies website, http://jewish studies.rutgers.edu/yiddish/102-department-of-jewish-studies/yiddish/159-yiddish-faqs (accessed March 1, 2015).

FURTHER READING

Farris, Joseph, *A Soldier's Sketchbook: From the Front Lines of World War II*, National Geographic, 2011.
> Like Nathan Marx, Farris fought in the European theater at the end of World War II. This volume combines passages from his letters with photos and drawings to provide a very real, in-depth picture of what life was like for a soldier on the front.

Fischman, Wendy, Becca Solomon, and Deborah Greenspan, *Making Good: How Young People Cope with Moral Dilemmas at Work*, Harvard University Press, 2004.
> Fischman, Solomon, and Greenspan performed a sociological study to learn young people's attitudes about moral dilemmas they may find in their everyday lives. The authors focused their study on competitive, high-pressure jobs—genetics research, theater, and journalism—to explore the challenges of the modern workplace and the ethical challenges workers face.

Schoen, Robert, *What I Wish My Christian Friends Knew about Judaism*, Loyola Press, 2004.
> Schoen offers an engaging introduction to Jewish traditions, explaining everything from holidays and ceremonies to kosher food and religious texts.

Trueman, Terry, *Inside Out*, HarperTempest, 2003.
> The themes of justice and fairness are central in this novel told from the point of view of teenager Zach Wahhsted, who is schizophrenic. The character's unique perspective sheds light on a moral crisis: two young men doing the wrong thing (robbing a store and holding hostages) for the right reason (hoping to get enough money to help their very sick mother).

SUGGESTED SEARCH TERMS

Philip Roth AND Defender of the Faith

Philip Roth AND Goodbye, Columbus

Philip Roth AND Jewish writer

US Army AND basic training

US army chain of command

theaters of World War II

Jews in the US military

Jewish dietary laws

The Distant Stars

LE MINH KHUE

1971

Vietnamese author Le Minh Khue's story "The Distant Stars" is a portrait of the life shared by three young women serving as military volunteers at a strategic site along the Ho Chi Minh Trail during what is known—from their nation's perspective—as the American War. Dinh, the narrator, is from Hanoi, which was the capital of North Vietnam prior to the unification of North and South Vietnam at the end of what is known elsewhere in the world as the Vietnam War. During the war, Khue herself volunteered for four years defusing and exploding stray bombs, much as the protagonists of her story do.

The Vietnam War has received literary treatment from an esteemed cohort of American soldier-authors, including Tim O'Brien, Yusef Komunyakaa, and W. D. Ehrhart. Khue offers a unique perspective to US readers not only in being a woman, a relative rarity among American writers treating the war, but also in being North Vietnamese, thus presenting the war as experienced by the opposing side. The story does not delve into either the war's political implications or American-Vietnamese interactions at the personal level, however; Khue has reported that she neither fired a shot nor even laid eyes on an American soldier during the war. As ensconced in the young women's daily activities, then, the story is a fairly timeless one of friendship, bravery, and the love at the heart of it all in the midst of great danger. It was

The story takes place in Vietnam during the war. (© *Keith Tarrier / ShutterStock.com*)

written when the author was nineteen and still volunteering and was first published in Vietnamese in 1971 as "Nhũng ngôi sao xa xôi." The story was published in English as "The Distant Stars" in *North Viêt Nam Now: Fiction and Essays from Hà Nôi* (1996) and then as the opening story in *The Stars, the Earth, the River: Short Fiction by Le Minh Khue* (1997).

AUTHOR BIOGRAPHY

Khue was born on December 6, 1949, in Thanh Hóa Province, south of Hanoi, which was then the capital of French Indochina. (Her name is represented without accents in her 1997 collection, but with accents is rendered as Lê Minh Khuê.) Independence led to the partition of Communist North Vietnam and nominally democratic—but later military-ruled—South Vietnam in 1954. Khue's paternal grandfather had served as a mandarin, a local official, in Khai Dinh's regime, and her parents were schoolteachers. Khue's parents died during

calamitous land reforms carried out in the 1950s, when class warfare was stoked by the North's Communist government, pitting the proletariat against the bourgeoisie and intelligentsia. After her parents' death, Khue and her younger sister were raised by an uncle and aunt who were passionate nationalists and also devoted to literature.

The horrors of the unfolding Vietnam War, the flames of which were rapidly fanned through the 1960s, reached Khue when she was sixteen and her village was bombed, leaving her to witness the burned and mutilated bodies left behind. She soon enlisted as a youth volunteer, serving with Unit 118N23 on Road 15 of the network of largely concealed roads called the Truong Son Trail, known to Americans as the Ho Chi Minh Trail. Serving for four years, Khue was active during major campaigns at Thanh Co and in Quang Tri Province and for a period was stationed close to the US base at Khe Sanh. Khue has spoken out about the trials of her wartime experiences, such as at the inaugural Conference of US and Vietnamese Veteran-Writers in June 1990. As quoted by

W. D. Ehrhart in his article "A Common Language," she then remarked of her service:

> We were many times the targets of US Air Force bombing . . . . We were subjected to acid showers produced by thousands and thousands of silver iodine crystals dropped into the clouds. We struggled against incendiaries, mines, bombs, and other killing devices. We endured many privations almost too horrible to speak of.

Khue added that she gained courage not only from her comrades—many of whom died while still teenagers—but also from books by American authors her aunt and uncle had pressed upon her, including works by Jack London and Ernest Hemingway. Their tales, marked by hardship, bravery, and love of life, hit close to home for Khue. After her volunteer service, Khue became a field journalist reporting on the war until its end in 1975. In the meantime, she published short stories, including "The Distant Stars," her first, in 1971; it would be the title story of her first collection, which was published in 1973.

Returning to Hanoi, Khue at last finished high school and found work as an editor with the Writers' Association Publishing House. She married a social science lecturer in 1980 and had a daughter in 1983. In 1986, when the Vietnamese government implemented a policy dubbed *doi moi*, meaning "renovation," whereby authors were encouraged to write with utter freedom—a sharp contrast to the Communist government's former insistence on the promotion of socialism—Khue was among those authors who took advantage. Having already published three books, she went on to write eight more over the next two decades, with many of her stories characterized by postwar disillusionment with the lost ideals of Vietnamese society. Khue would make academic stops at such locations as Moscow and Massachusetts, and she coedited *The Other Side of Heaven: Postwar Fiction by Vietnamese and American Writers* (1995), the first anthology to compile literature from opposing sides of any war. Through the early 2010s, Khue continued to write.

PLOT SUMMARY

"The Distant Stars" opens on three young women working as wartime bomb clearers, or sappers— they constitute a ground reconnaissance team— while living out of a cave at a strategic hill in Vietnam. They are attached to an army unit that passes frequently along the road that the women are charged with keeping in good repair. They work even through the hot days, sometimes get buried in dirt during explosions, and in times of rest listen to the radio in their cave.

The narrator, Dinh, ponders the attention she gets from men. While tending to their hobbies, the young women chat about future plans. Dinh is led to recall how Nho first received her—lukewarmly—when she started the volunteer work there at age seventeen. Thinking further back, she recalls life in her home city of Hanoi (North Vietnam's capital), where she often awoke a doctor neighbor at night with her boisterous singing. When it came to organizing her papers for schoolwork, she would always need help, which her mother would give grudgingly.

Nho alerts Dinh to a reconnaissance plane flying overhead, a signal that bombs will soon be dropped. Nho quickly dons her helmet while Thao nonchalantly eats a biscuit. After the bombs strike just three hundred meters away, smoke fills the cave's entrance. Thao instructs Dinh to remain inside as she and Nho take care of the few bombs dropped. While the two are outside, several more bombs are dropped. Stepping out into the smoke, Dinh hears that military construction workers have arrived at a neighboring hill, ensuring reinforcements if needed. She worries about her friends, but Thao returns in half an hour to report the overwhelming volume of dirt that they will need to haul to fill the holes. Dinh radios the company commander and assures him that they need no assistance. Nho returns after having bathed in the stream.

That night, the three young women go out together to work on four bombs. Imagining the distant antiaircraft gunners watching her through binoculars, Dinh boldly plants some dynamite next to her bomb, lights the fuse, runs for shelter, and waits until the explosion comes. Three others follow nearby. Thao emerges wide-eyed, and they find Nho buried; frantically digging her out, they find she has a serious but nonlethal wound in her arm. Dinh bandages Nho, and they return to the cave. Nho takes a nap, and Thao tells Dinh to sing. Dinh is not in the mood, so Thao sings instead—in a poor, squeaky voice.

Clouds rapidly darken the sky, and a hailstorm strikes—recalling for Dinh a midnight hailstorm in Hanoi several years ago, when she woke all her neighbors but only one was moved to join her watching the storm. In the wake of the present brief storm, bombers catch them off guard, and they rush into the cave to escape the explosions. Dinh has a thigh injury, but she goes out anyway to help measure the craters. In a surprise explosion, Dinh and Thao get buried together, and Dinh digs Thao out. Back at the cave, Dinh radios to relay their measurements and tell the liaison officer that they have stood their ground.

Despite Thao's haggard condition, she and Dinh spend all afternoon detonating bombs. At day's end, Dinh collapses in sleep. She wakes up in the night to find that troopers have climbed the hill to join them. The liaison officer good-naturedly fends off the young women's flirtations. Hearing activity outside, Dinh rises painfully and insists on going out despite the officer's objections. The troops have been exploding bombs while Dinh slept. Around midnight, the troops drive off. Nho expresses her defiance of advice to go to a hospital farther back from the front line. She sees a shooting star. When another convoy of trucks motors through, Dinh strikes a pose for them. Nho and Dinh are united in feeling an abundance of love for their countrymen and the world.

CHARACTERS

Company Commander

The company commander, who usually answers the young women's radio calls, appreciates their ability to function independently and demand so little additional manpower from the company.

Liaison Officer

Known for being a perfect gentleman who declines to smoke or flirt, the liaison officer has attracted the attention of the three young women. He is at their cave when, after a long day, Dinh wakes up; he has apparently come close enough for his hair to brush her face and his breath to warm her. As he prepares water (for tea), Dinh admires his fit and slender waist, which is like a ping-pong player's. A poor student as a child in Hanoi, the officer is now remembered for deeds like preserving a road by pushing away five bombs.

Nho

Nho, like Dinh "a Hanoi girl," was the first one stationed at the strategic hill, and she welcomed Dinh hesitantly at first but wholeheartedly at length. Nho takes her job seriously, duly donning her helmet in preparation for bombings. Nho is romantically attached to a machine-shop engineer back in Hanoi who sends long, affectionate letters, although, like Dinh, Nho has decided never to marry. She embroiders as a hobby, in an unconventional style that has earned her criticism—but she *wants* what she makes to look different. After the war, Nho intends to work as a welder at a hydroelectric plant and play volleyball for the plant's team. Like Dinh, Nho is fiercely proud of her self-sufficiency.

Phuong Dinh

The narrator of Khue's story, Dinh, largely paints the wartime life that she and her two friends share in idyllic hues. She makes the dangers of their occupation clear, but ultimately for them, the story suggests, the threat of the bombs represents the excitement of life more than the specter of death.

Dinh acknowledges herself to be beautiful and remarks on the extent to which men tend to be curious and inquire about her. Drivers are inspired to comment on the look in her eyes, although Dinh makes a point of (disingenuously) ignoring them when they visit; in truth, she believes military men to be "courageous and noble." Nevertheless, in light of her mother's warning that her husband would beat her if she could not take care of things for herself, Dinh has sworn never to marry. At the time of the story, Dinh, like Nho, is about twenty, having spent the last three years volunteering with the Ground Reconnaissance Team. She sings beautifully and can imagine herself working someday as a voice-over artist or choir singer (at a construction site, in some capacity), not to mention as a freight driver. Like Nho, Dinh apparently does not feel limited by gender stereotypes with regard to employment. She fully enjoys receiving and (sometimes) requiting male attention, but she also devotes intimate attentions to her female friends, all of which contributes to her overflowing sense of shared love at this time in her life.

Thang

When the visiting troops head out at midnight, a voice from one truck—Nho thinks it is Thang's—calls out to tease the Hanoi girls about missing their mothers.

Thao

The more pensive of Dinh's two companions, Thao enjoys spending her free time copying out song lyrics, including some composed by Dinh. She has her mind set on a career as a doctor, with a dream of a military-captain husband who would not always be around, since otherwise the marriage would grow boring. There is a contrast between Thao's medical aspirations and her aversion to injuries, blood, leeches, and the like. This might be seen to reflect a certain disconnect from reality on her part, or perhaps instead it speaks to one of the best qualities of youth, the ability to disregard current limitations and envision oneself attaining even improbable goals.

THEMES

Vietnam War (1959–1975)

"The Distant Stars" is noteworthy not only for being one of the most buoyant war stories one is likely to read but also for offering, in translation, a representation of life among the North Vietnamese during a war that has largely left English-speaking audiences with a one-sided picture. Well known are the deceptive guerrilla tactics used by the North during the war, which were condemned by some frustrated American authorities as dishonorable. Such commentators were inclined to blame US massacres of civilians, such as the infamous My Lai episode in which American soldiers killed over two hundred villagers, on the fact that North Vietnamese soldiers, both men and women, often wore no military outfits and blended in with village populations to prevent detection. However, because of the superior weaponry and financial resources of the allied United States and South Vietnam, the North had little choice but to employ such tactics in order to survive the war; the end—the victory of the North—arguably justified the means. What remains to be filled in, in this more sympathetic imagining of the North Vietnamese, is an image of citizens of the North not just as soldiers or wartime sufferers but as human beings. Where history can provide an abundance of facts, fiction may have the upper hand in such revelations of humanity.

Khue's story, then, does not make an issue of the precise wartime context—of where in Vietnam this strategic hill is located, of how far away battles or guerrilla engagements are occurring, or even of what the feeling about the course of the war is. This reflects the very limited military intelligence shared with the story's three young women in their voluntary posts as well as their more humanistic interests. They listen to their radio not for wartime news and reports but for music; they think about the soldiers not in terms of rank and status but in terms of heroism and romance. As the war goes on, so do these young women's lives.

Friendship

The situation in which Dinh, Nho, and Thao find themselves bonds them as much as any could. Together they must live straitened, ascetic lives, sleeping on the floor of a cave while eating little more than water and rice, with no other reliable company, as the soldiers come and go only as troop movements demand. Thus the young women are dependent on each other not only for daily emotional needs and fundamental companionship, but for the preservation of their lives. More than once in the story, one of the girls is dug out of a potential shallow grave by one or both of the others. Like a friend as much as like a commanding officer, Thao tells Dinh to stay behind in the cave if it is not necessary for all of them to risk their lives. Whenever they get hurt, they rely on each other to tend to their wounds. All of this mutual dependence makes for very powerful friendship, for a sense of unity in facing the world; in that they must care so much *for* each other, the young women naturally come to care as greatly *about* each other. The friendship they share goes a long way in helping them confront the harrowing facts of their lives.

Courage

The young women's friendship empowers them with courage. Their trust in each other while out defusing and exploding bombs is essential to their security, allowing them to navigate life-threatening circumstances with the assurance that help, if needed, will be there. The three indeed make the sharing of courage a point of honor. No matter how distraught the demands

TOPICS FOR FURTHER STUDY

- Think of a time when you had an interpersonal conflict, whether with a peer at school, a sibling, a parent, a teacher, or anyone else—ideally one in which you believed yourself to be squarely in the right. Then write a story about the conflict from the point of view of the other person, who may or may not have also felt him- or herself to be in the right. Think carefully about how to cast yourself in that person's narrative.

- Alternatively, write a story in which the climax is a moment of transcendent love, or some such emotion, in the midst of difficulty.

- Read two other stories in Khue's collection *The Stars, the Earth, the River* whose titles reflect a significance for nature, such as "The Blue Sky," "Fragile as a Sunray," "Rain," "The Last Rain of the Monsoon," or "The River." Write an essay in which you compare your two chosen stories with "The Distant Stars" with respect to ecological imagery and interactions between the characters and nature, drawing conclusions, if justified, regarding Khue's worldview.

- Read the story "Princess Lieu Hanh, Tea-Seller of Ngang Mountain," which can be found in the illustrated collection *Two Cakes Fit for a King: Folktales from Vietnam* (2003). Then write an essay in which you compare and contrast the mythic heroine Lieu Hanh and Dinh from "The Distant Stars."

- Watch a classic or more recent film whose plot revolves around the Vietnam War, such as *The Deer Hunter* (1978), *Apocalypse Now* (1979), *Good Morning, Vietnam* (1987), or *Dead Presidents* (1995). (Readers should be advised that most such films are rated R for war violence.) Post online a critical commentary deconstructing the film's depiction of North and/or South Vietnamese soldiers and citizens, including links to clips and/or still frames from the film, as well as to outside resources, to help illustrate and support your points.

- Research the roles that American women played in the Vietnam War effort and write a paper summarizing their roles and also comparing them to the wartime roles of Vietnamese women, using this entry—and an additional source or two if you choose—for points of comparison.

---

of the day might leave them, they do their utmost to refrain from crying, which is conceived of as a betrayal of friendship, a failure to project a positive attitude for the sake of the others: "Anyone who shed a tear while we needed strength from each other would be seen as guilty of self-debasement."

As far as facing their work is concerned, the women are furthermore lent courage by the presence of the nearby troops, who, one gathers, have received more extensive training and have more resources at their disposal than such volunteers as the young women. Dinh relates how knowing that distant soldiers would be watching her through binoculars emboldens her as she approaches a bomb to be carefully set off. She thus embodies courage as she can be seen "standing straight and calmly stepping forward." As for the soldiers' firepower, so crucial a resource in wartime, Dinh relates that there is "nothing more lonely and terrifying" than a bombing unanswered by armed resistance from their own side: "Even the sound of a single rifle can give you a feeling of some protection, an impression of solid self-defense." This remark speaks to the visceral nature of courage, the level of which can be affected by both emotional and physical experiences.

The three girls hide and wait until they have a job to do. (© Thor Jorgen Udvang | ShutterStock.com)

Independence

While the young women take heart from the presence of their comrades in arms, they leave no doubt about the extent to which they value their independence, both as a self-contained military unit and individually. The concept of self-sufficiency is first broached in a romantic context, as Dinh tells the reader, "Like me, Nho liked independence. We would say to each other, 'From now until we're old, we'll have romance but we'll never marry.'" In defense of this notion, she mentions how, as in any patriarchal society, "[m]arriage would mean too much work," with the domestic duties of cooking, cleaning, and child rearing traditionally falling to the woman. This feminist impulse toward independence extends to the women's envisioned careers in traditionally masculine employments such as welding and driving freight, and it more tangibly extends to their position as an all-female team of sappers. Dinh clearly takes pride in being able to report, "As always, we would do everything ourselves." Similarly, Thao instructs Dinh with regard to a radio communication about a difficult day,

"Tell them everything, but let them know that we've stood our ground." Nho is so protective of her independence that she has no interest in leaving her post to seek medical attention for a mere surface wound, largely because she is reluctant to be forced into dependency and coddled "like a spoiled brat lying in bed." Far from being children any more—despite Dinh's referring to them as "girls" throughout the story—these young women feel a sense of independence that is deeply allied with their courage.

Love

The theme of love plays a minor role early in the story, with hints at love, or perhaps merely attraction, offered at several points—in Dinh's mention of her appeal among men and the extent to which their heroism appeals to her, in the contents of the letter from Nho's significant other, and in the playful banter between the male soldiers and the female bomb squad. In addition, a degree of love is implicit in the intensity of the friendship between the young women, as suggested by a few of Dinh's descriptions of her feelings toward her companions, such as when she says of Nho, "I wanted to lift her in my arms."

The notion of love flourishes thematically only in the story's closing paragraphs, as Dinh finally makes explicit the feelings that have been underlying the worldview expressed in her story all along: she is simply overflowing with love. As witnessed in her irrepressible appreciation for life even in the midst of the constant jeopardy of their hazardous work, Dinh is overcome with "the love of the people in smoke and fire, the people of war. It was a selfless, passionate, and carefree love, only found in the hearts of soldiers." The themes of wartime life, friendship, and courage are thus united in what proves the story's governing emotion.

STYLE

First-Person Narration
Written when Khue was just nineteen, "The Distant Stars" shares a feature common with many debut stories and novels: the use of a first-person narrator who bears some resemblance to the author's self. Khue indeed volunteered during the Vietnam War in the capacity ascribed to Dinh, allowing her to draw on her firsthand understanding of what such work entailed to fill out the story's telling details. As Dana Sachs notes in her essay "Small Tragedies and Distant Stars," one effect of this firsthand narration is that the story is imbued with the emotional sense of the narrator, Dinh. As such, her buoyancy and optimism propel the story over the patches of existential uncertainty with verve to spare, and the lead-up to the closing paragraphs allows for her effusive declarations of universal love to be absorbed and appreciated as sincere. As Sachs points out, "It's not hard to imagine an authorial [third-person narrator's] voice which would cynically contradict such hopeful passion," but the exclusion of any voice but Dinh's allows for the unmediated and unadulterated sharing of her passion for life with the reader.

Vietnamese Literature in Translation
As the translators of "The Distant Stars" and the other stories in the specially compiled English-language collection *The Stars, the Earth, the River*, Bac Hoai Tran and Sachs were

obliged to be proactive in shaping the text to accord with English grammar and syntax. As their translators' note indicates, the task of translation to English from Vietnamese is more demanding than translation from, say, one of the Romance languages—French, Spanish, or Italian—because these languages share not only many etymological roots with English words but also syntactic patterns: aside from the reversed orientation of adjectives/nouns ("white house" versus *maison blanche*) and other variations, sentences in the Romance languages largely accord with the subject-verb-object patterns of English. Vietnamese, on the contrary, would confound the English reader if translated literally. For example, one sentence of Khue's with which they were confronted, about an exaggerated piece of journalism, would translate directly as "Finish reading know is stretch the truth"—a formulation that has both a specific and a universal sense. Sachs and Tran had little choice but to choose from "When I finished reading it, I knew it stretched the truth" and "Anyone who finishes reading it will know it stretched the truth." This example is taken from Khue's story "Blue Sky," but the translators faced such choices in all of her stories.

In addition, where Vietnamese largely features present-tense verbs, relying on context (instead of different tenses) to indicate time frames, Sachs and Tran changed the tense to what English readers would expect. Vietnamese pronouns are also more complicated, with speakers forgoing direct pronouns like *I* or *you* to instead refer to themselves and others in the context of their personal relationship. For example, in talking to Nho, Dinh might call Nho "big sister" while referring to herself as "little sister"; instead of saying, "Can I help you?" she might say what would translate as "Can little sister help big sister?" Sachs and Tran explain in their note that they changed pronoun usage to match English readers' expectations.

HISTORICAL CONTEXT

Along the Ho Chi Minh Trail
The strategic importance of the Truong Son Trail, called by Americans the Ho Chi Minh Trail, became evident early in the Vietnam War. The region had been volatile since the

COMPARE & CONTRAST

- **Early 1970s:** With Vietnam having been engaged in war or preparation for war almost continuously since the 1940s, conflict is part of the fabric of life for all those less than three decades old. Morale yet remains high among those determined to maintain the independence of their nation, accounting for the great numbers of civilians, including women, who volunteer in the North.

  Today: After achieving unification in 1975, Vietnam was militarily engaged with Cambodia from 1979—when they also fought with China—through the 1980s, as it saw fit to oust Cambodian dictator Pol Pot. Since then, Vietnam has retained its peace.

- **Early 1970s:** Sappers along the Ho Chi Minh Trail and elsewhere in Laos and Vietnam are given the unenviable job of clearing bombs from the roads, whether by defusing or detonating them, often risking exposure from above while working through daylight hours. Many lose their lives in the process, especially when new bomb technology must be figured out.

  Today: In the year 2000, when President Bill Clinton pays a reconciliatory visit to Vietnam, the Asian nation reports that

since the war's end, some forty thousand people have lost their lives from mines and munitions that had yet to be set off. The United States pledges additional help in clearing the mines. The similarly daunting cleanup of contamination from Agent Orange, again conducted with US assistance, does not take place until 2011.

- **Early 1970s:** After the Tet Offensive of January 1968, the American public, especially the burgeoning youth counterculture, increasingly believes the war is not worth the deaths of so many young soldiers. As the US effort wanes, fatalities drop from over sixteen thousand in 1968 to six thousand in 1969, to less than a thousand annually from 1972 on. A total of 58,193 American servicemen and women lose their lives in the war.

  Today: The United States has emerged from the Iraq War with under 4,500 deaths and is emerging from the Afghanistan War with fewer than 2,500—figures that pale in comparison with Vietnam but nonetheless, to many, represent lives lost in vain. Both nations remain highly volatile, while many terrorists, ostensible targets in both wars, are at large elsewhere.

Vietnamese, led by Communists, revolted against French colonial rule in the 1940s. It was in the 1950s that the North versus South dynamic shaped up, and in 1959, the North designated the trail—which goes through Laos to the South—as a military region coded Line 559. Little more than dirt footpaths along much of the way, the trail was widened, graveled, and rendered suitable for vehicles laden with heavy artillery beginning in March 1965, the year US regiments began landing en masse to support the South. The North's Major General Phan Trong Tue would proudly note in his memoirs

that it was in October 1965 that US news reports acknowledged that the trail had evolved into a "road." The trail in fact consisted of interlinked networks of roads, largely camouflaged from the sight of US aircraft with foliage, which allowed the North to transport soldiers and supplies effectively no matter how frequently the United States bombed portions of the route.

This is not to say that the North Vietnamese felt no effects from American air attacks. The pressure of bombing was constant, leading to overworked laborers, inadequate food rations, and high fatality rates. In late 1965, despite fore-boding American reports of its efficacy, the trail became bogged down in the rainy season. Bridges were washed out, portions of road were submerged (though some were intentionally constructed as submerged to avoid sighting from the air), explosive supplies were inadequate, and malaria rates among the road workers were sky high; sometimes entire twenty-person squads had to be hospitalized together and replaced. As food ran low, road workers were left to forage, fish, and hunt—meals of bat and squirrel were specialties—to sustain themselves.

In their history *Even the Women Must Fight: Memories of War from North Vietnam*, Karen Gottschang Turner and Phan Thanh Hao take particular note of the role that women played in sustaining the Ho Chi Minh Trail. Regarding the period when the trail was at last rejuvenated in 1966, the historians remark,

> Although we know . . . that thousands of women were in the field by then, they do not yet appear in the military reports. The reports do indicate, however, that work was getting done more efficiently and various labor forces were better coordinated than before.

In his memoirs, Major General Phan Trong Tue acknowledged that women accounted for up to 40 percent of volunteers in many units. Many of these women bore rifles as well as shovels, and some became renowned as war heroes—especially Nguyen Thi Lieu, a name that appears time and again in soldiers' memoirs and diaries. She volunteered at seventeen, was one of the first women to deactivate time bombs, and was known for surviving, with her workmates, being buried under half a dozen different bomb-triggered landslides and yet emerging to continue with the work. One comrade in arms, cited in Turner and Hao's book, praised her to a journalist after she had died in battle:

> And there was Lieu, whose death filled us not only with sorrow, but self-reproach . . . . [S]he sang very well . . . she could breathe life into any folk song. Not only in our regiment, but throughout the road, everyone loved her.

Various aspects of female soldiers' historical experiences from the war are reflected in Khue's story, such as the ability to appreciate humor even in dire circumstances. One woman related to Turner and Hao how her regiment had marched in pitch dark by holding onto each other's shirts, though if one in the front suddenly stopped, everyone's face would bump into the pot hung on the pack of the woman ahead. "When daylight came," the woman said, "we had black faces, and couldn't help but laugh." A male soldier told the historians about how the men "felt sorry for the women. It was harder for them." He specifically acknowledged health concerns related to long periods of moving stones while submerged in water. Publicly, Vietnamese journalists were moved to take note of "the women's courage and cheer in danger" as well as "their devotion to each other." Ho Chi Minh himself had issued military commanders a compassionate directive regarding all youth: "At the construction sites you and the other cadres must take care of them, on behalf of their families, and look after their smallest needs." One diarist said of youthful volunteers, "They are so young, but they all have a deep way of thinking." Noting how hard the young women worked and how determined they were, through rain or shine, he wrote, "These women volunteers laugh all the time and are very determined. I was so moved when talking to them."

Le Minh Khue herself was one of the women volunteers with whom Turner and Hao spoke. In contrast to the buoyancy of her short story "The Distant Stars," she made clear the deprivations and death that she and her comrades faced, such as in burying—and, after some bombings, reburying—the dead. She stated:

> We had no idea when we signed on how life would be. We had to encourage each other. Sometimes we would be so tired we would fall asleep on the march . . . . Sometimes as we walked we would come upon a skeleton, someone at the rear of a column who had died alone, of malaria or some other disease . . . . I kept going because I had to.

One seasoned military man's assessment of the significance of the famous trail, as related by the historians, resonates profoundly with Khue's story:

> If the Truong Son is a university, . . . for me it is first of all a school to teach me to love and believe in mankind. In my judgement this love and this belief is actually the source of revolutionary heroism.

While they wait for tasks to help the war effort, the girls live in a hidden cavern in a strategic location. (© choketot / ShutterStock.com)

CRITICAL OVERVIEW

Khue is an acknowledged standard bearer among the Vietnamese literary world, with her works accorded great critical respect both within her home country and internationally. This is due in part to the fact that, as phrased by Wayne Karlin in a *Dictionary of Literary Biography* essay, "her themes—the redemptive quality of love and the moral erosions of hatred, brutality, and greed—are universal." Her fiction, Karlin notes, has ranged from "the passion, sacrifice, and emotional intensity of wartime life" to "the disappointments, disillusionments, and more-complex realities that followed the euphoria of victory."

According to a review of *The Stars, the Earth, the River* in *Publishers Weekly*, "[t]hrough her stories, Khue exposes a Vietnam more vital and complex than the stereotypes that linger in the minds of many Westerners," as she "unearths secrets assiduously buried in the psyches of her characters." In "The Distant Stars,"

Khue is said to be "deft at evoking the bonds of sisterhood among three teenage girls working as North Vietnamese sappers during the war." Reviewing the collection for *World Literature Today*, James Banerian also comments on the opening story, stating that Khue effectively conveys "idealism, shared hardship, and the intimacy of trenchmates." Focusing then on the later stories, Banerian concludes that "the book offers a stark, unadorned look at some of the more tragic aspects of the postwar nation and the spiritual depression of its people," representing "a tentative step toward a broader understanding of Vietnam."

In her essay "Small Tragedies and Distant Stars: Le Minh Khue's Language of Lost Ideals," Sachs suggests that the story is marked by a "simple, naive exuberance" in a positive sense: "The images of beauty combine with the heroic characterizations of soldiers to imbue the story with a sense that something pure and good exists beyond the grueling struggles of war." Karlin, in the *Dictionary of Literary*

Biography, also offers appreciative commentary on "The Distant Stars":

> The juxtaposition of . . . normalcy against the deadly task to which the girls are assigned, and their matter-of-fact courage in performing it, startles and engages the reader. The story vividly depicts not only the grim details of the war but also the deep sense of purpose, the idealism and optimism, and the willing self-sacrifice and comradeship of the girls and the other soldiers.

In his introduction to *The Stars, the Earth, the River*, Karlin declares that

> the images and emotions in "The Distant Stars" form shining points of light far over the heads of Khue's characters in her other stories as well, lights that sometimes make them, and us, ache for lost dreams, that sometimes, still, act as beacons that suggest infinite possibilities.

He thus calls "The Distant Stars" a "touchstone" for her later works, "the ideal held in memory." As to Khue's body of work as a whole, Karlin aptly compares her modus operandi to her wartime work as a sapper:

> searching out and identifying the bombs that lay buried along the Trail along which we must move, bringing them out of the earth, . . . sometimes defusing them, and sometimes exploding them, and sometimes smoothing over the scars they leave in the earth. She never lets us forget what is buried and where; in doing so, she gently suggests the directions we must continue to travel.

In his *Dictionary of Literary Biography* essay, Karlin affirms that in addressing "the more complex struggles—physical, moral, emotional, and spiritual—of postwar life," Khue "remains one of the most influential contemporary writers in Vietnam."

CRITICISM

Michael Allen Holmes

Holmes is a writer with existential interests. In the following essay, he examines the significance of nature's four elements in "The Distant Stars."

War and nature are readily conceived of as mutually exclusive entities. The former is marked above all by destruction and death, as punctuated by the ear-splitting reports of guns and bombs and gut-wrenching images of wounded soldiers. The latter is characterized

DINH'S EXPERIENCE OF THE SUDDEN HAILSTORM ON THE STRATEGIC HILL SUGGESTS A RECKONING WITH THE ELEMENTS—IN THE FORM OF ICE (WATER) AND WIND (AIR)—TANTAMOUNT TO TRANSCENDENCE."

by slow growth over time, the beauty of living things, and mosaics of tranquil sights and sounds—at least, such is nature in the imagination of many readers. Indeed, war often entails the wholesale destruction of nature, as witnessed in the desolate no man's lands of blasted earth between the trenches of World War I. During the Vietnam War, the United States treated nature like an enemy, since the North Vietnamese so effectively used the cover of the jungles to stage guerrilla attacks and transport troops and supplies up and down the Ho Chi Minh Trail. Thus was Agent Orange sprayed by American aircraft to strip the flora of its foliage, amassing ecological casualties left largely untallied at war's end, not to mention the destruction of nature wrought by bombs, with napalm fueling many a fire.

All this led to the sort of characteristically barren wartime landscape found in Khue's moving short story "The Distant Stars," in which three young women strive to maintain the trail on a constantly bombed strategic hill:

> Neither side of the trail had any sign of vegetation. There were only stripped and burned tree trunks, uprooted trees, boulders, and a few empty gas cans and twisted parts of vehicles, rusting in the earth.

From such a beginning one hardly expects nature to play much of a role in what transpires, and yet Khue's narrator, Dinh, proves highly attuned to nature's four fundamental elements—earth, water, air, and fire—and the young women's relationship with nature is a thematic key to the story.

The opening paragraphs of "The Distant Stars" give ample indication that Dinh, the narrator, is not given to excessive intellectual abstraction but is instead highly attuned to her physical surroundings. The first mention of

WHAT DO I READ NEXT?

- Another Vietnamese writer who has approached the war from the perspective of common citizens of the North is Nguyen Quang Thieu, whose work can be found in English in the collection *The Women Carry River Water: Poems* (1997), edited and translated by Martha Collins and Nguyen Quang Thieu with Nguyen Ba Chung.

- Le Luu is one of the most popular novelists of modern Vietnam. He has published some twenty volumes in his native language. Appearing in English was his renowned 1986 novel *Thời xa váng*, translated by Ngo Vinh Hai as *A Time Far Past* (1997), about a North Vietnamese soldier's problematic return to his home village after the war.

- Nguyen Huy Thiep was among the authors who, like Khue, took advantage of the *doi moi* period of artistic freedom. His social realism is evident in the English-language collections *The General Retires and Other Stories* (1992), translated by Greg Lockhart, and *Crossing the River: Short Fiction* (2003), edited by Nguyen Nguyet Cam and Dana Sachs and translated by Bac Hoai Tran.

- Well known as one of the most significant Vietnamese treatments of the war is Bao Ninh's *Thân phân cua tình yêu* (1991), translated by Phan Thanh Hao as *The Sorrow of War: A Novel of North Vietnam* (1995).

- Walter Dean Myers treats the Vietnam War as experienced by a Harlem teenager in *Fallen Angels* (1998), which won the Coretta Scott King Award. In the face of the horror of warfare, protagonist Perry contemplates heavy philosophical questions, including race relations and the purpose of the war.

- One of the writers Khue has cited as an early influence is Nobel Prize winner Ernest Hemingway, whose wartime books include *A Farewell to Arms* (1929), about an ambulance driver's trials in Italy during World War I, and *For Whom the Bell Tolls* (1940), about an American munitions expert's role in the Spanish Civil War. Both revolve as much around interpersonal relations, including romance, as war itself.

- French author Gérard Chaliand offers a cultural exploration of life for the common people during wartime in North Vietnam in *Les paysans du Nord-Vietnam et la guerre*, translated by Peter Wiles as *The Peasants of North Vietnam* (1969).

- *Vietnamese Women at War: Fighting for Ho Chi Minh and the Revolution* (1999) is an in-depth history with chronologically arranged chapters highlighting the challenges of the terrain, women as warriors, the roles of youths, and other topics.

---

bombs leads not to any exposition of how and why bombs are being dropped there but to a description of their aesthetic effects, "mixing the red and white soil together." Throughout the story, in fact, Dinh declines to provide details (aside from an offhand mention of a Soviet Red Army song), about who is fighting, or where, or against whom—though the many mentions of Hanoi make clear that the protagonists are North Vietnamese and that the conflict is the Vietnam War. Even the leader of the North and namesake of the trail they are working, Ho Chi Minh, will be mentioned only later when Dinh awakes in the cave to *see* the "picture of Uncle Ho" hanging on the wall. For the time being, while Dinh's description of the landscape may be one of desolation, she remains focused on the physical, not the political, terrain.

Dinh and her friends and comrades Nho and Thao are almost immediately portrayed in unity with nature, specifically with the earth, as the bombs, Dinh relates, often left them "so covered in dirt that only our gleaming eyes showed through." At such times they call each other "Black-Eyed Demons," but the girls' high moral character makes clear that this reference holds no suggestion of evil; if anything, it may suggest a certain primeval impishness, a connection with the innermost self and its reserves of savage fortitude—reserves that come in handy in the young women's enduring their state of constant danger. This is reflected in their ability to effectively give death the cold shoulder; Dinh calls death "a serious guy," but the very formulation (not a *man* or *beast* but a "guy") diminishes Death's power, as does the suggestion that he resorts to *hiding*—no more than a trickster himself—in the bombs. Rather than dwell on mortality, Dinh quickly turns to the "pleasures" of their work, which are of a highly sensory character: "smoking earth, trembling air"—signaling two of nature's elements—"the roar of airplanes . . . taut nerves, an erratic heartbeat." Regarding the cave in which they live, many a writer might have been tempted to draw out a meaning-packed metaphor to describe it—as a prison, dungeon, or besieged rabbit hole, perhaps. Dinh, however, straightforwardly describes both the environs and the actual experience of being in the cave, from the chill that makes them shiver, to the sugared water they drink there, to the feel of the damp ground, to the sound of the music their radio gives out.

Dinh soon further hints at unity between the young women and the elements. She describes how when they first heard the bombs they would be coping with as volunteers, some of them, out of fright, "lay down and hugged the earth." Also, one of their primary tasks is carrying dirt to fill bomb craters. Meanwhile, Nho's totem element seems to be water, as suggested in Dinh's description of her arrival at the strategic hill: "Nho walked up from the stream. Her hair was wet. Drops of water remained on her forehead and her nose. The water in the stream must have been abundant." Uncompelled to wipe the stray drops from her face, Nho fairly embodies water's essential plenitude. Thao, too, is linked with water, when she drinks and "water fell continuously from her chin to her shirt, like raindrops." Nho is later again depicted by Dinh returning from the stream, in a passage that hints at a romantic appreciation for the fluidity of Nho's body:

> In her wet clothes, Nho sat down . . . . She put her arms behind her and leaned all the way back. Her neck was round and her shirt had delicate buttons on it. I wanted to lift her in my arms.

A flashback strengthens the reader's understanding of Dinh's relation to nature, where she praises their "green city," Hanoi. With her family's ancient house set "deep within an alleyway where many green trees grew," Dinh's joyous singing out her window again carries a sense of primeval engagement with the world, in a civilized version of a wolf howling at the moon. In declaring, "Only I can know the vastness and freshness of the city night"—a transcendental line reminiscent of modern American literature's bard of lived experience, Jack Kerouac—Dinh heralds the primacy of the self stretching out into space, imbibing the living, breathing world through the air. Dinh is sharply contrasted with the neighboring doctor and his formulaic responses to her singing, three polite taps on the wall, and to her celebration of the natural delight of the rare hailstorm, a grave warning about being "forced to take the necessary measures." The difficulty Dinh experienced in shuffling through her school papers is further evidence that—like the liaison officer who had "gotten bad grades"—she is inclined not to abstraction but to the real experience of existence, an inclination that serves her far better than book learning would in her capacity as a wartime volunteer. In this respect, she is also contrasted with Thao, who is intelligent enough to have dreams of practicing medicine but, unlike Dinh, impractically shies away from her comrades' wounds.

Dinh's reminiscence of singing out her window takes an interesting turn when she speaks of once almost falling out into the "bottomless abyss" of the darkness. With a hose left running overnight to fill a cistern, Dinh relates, "the gushing of the water gave me the feeling that it was about to rise to the windowsill"—as if foreshadowing the immersion in the elements she will experience as a war volunteer, with the cistern's sense of challenged containment to be replaced by the stream's sense of flowing openness.

Consciousness of the elements comes again to the fore when Dinh undergoes the intense experience of managing the controlled explosion of a dropped bomb. Taking shelter after lighting the dynamite's fuse, she presses herself "against the wall of earth." Though typically paying attention strictly to what *is* present, here Dinh sees fit to note, "There was no wind." Meanwhile, "over there, the fire burned along the fuse." Here Dinh makes a somewhat cryptic reference to "the eternal numbers" of her watch—the watch itself is not eternal, of course, but time itself may be, and the phrasing suggests that the powerful contraction of her consciousness into precisely the immediate present, a contraction that severe peril tends to promote, leads to infinite expansion on the other side, a felt sense of eternity. This is suggestive of the mind-expanding philosophy of Zen Buddhism, a highly significant tradition in Vietnamese history, which advocates immersion in the present as a means to a sense of immortality.

Interactions and comparisons between the young women and the elements recur through the story's end. The scene where Dinh neutralizes the bomb—which "was hot," due either to chemical processes already taking place within the bomb or maybe just to "heat from the sun"—suggests that the bombs, representing fire, are the girls' true enemy. And fittingly, they fight fire with fire, appropriating that destructive element in lighting the fuses of their dynamite. When Thao emerges after the ensuing explosions with a piece of parachute over her shoulders, "the wind tried to snatch the parachute, but couldn't do it"—another minor elemental victory for the young women. Beyond her unity with water, Nho is viscerally united with the soil when "blood gushed out of her arm and was absorbed into the earth." In turn, Dinh's experience of the sudden hailstorm on the strategic hill suggests a reckoning with the elements—in the form of ice (water) and wind (air)—tantamount to transcendence:

> Something sharp was pulverizing the air, tearing it into tiny fragments. The wind. I felt a pain and at the same time, my cheeks became wet . . . . I ran inside, and put a few small hailstones into Nho's open palm. Then, I ran back outside, extremely thrilled . . . . My childish joy had bloomed again.

The hailstorm is what leads Dinh to meditate on the stars, as the storm's end leaves her with the sense that she is missing something, perhaps "the big stars over the city"; even the electric lights of Hanoi "glowed like the stars in the stories about fairylands." Thus are stars linked with a mythical or magical experience of the world. Later, when she awakes from her nap, Dinh again ponders the stars, which "seemed to move overhead. They were very far away, but as clear as drops of blue water, and they were scattered all across the sky. How vast was the sky!" Here, then, the stars are thematically linked with water, which by association links the stars with the women. Cementing the association, Dinh recalls a passing poet who called the young women "the stars above the strategic hill." This further recalls Dinh's mention of how military drivers would comment to her, "You have such a distant look in your eyes."

To humankind, the stars are as distant as can be; they are unreachable. These young women are far from inaccessible to the young men who pass through—the women are not too shy to flirt and harbor romantic sentiments and yet for all the passing men who will meet their deaths in war without ever seeing again the women who so inspired them, the three indeed are unreachable. Moreover, they are fiercely independent women who are proud not to depend upon the enlisted soldiers for material support and whose unity with the elements of nature sets them on the boundary of human experience and thus makes them mediators between the civilized and natural worlds, living out of a cave and working explosive wonders like sorceresses. Figuratively, the story's title and the motif of stars together suggest that the young women act as beacons of light for their compatriots, burning with the fire of the "selfless, passionate, and carefree love" overflowing their hearts to keep the souls of their people warm on their way to victory.

Source: Michael Allen Holmes, Critical Essay on "The Distant Stars," in *Short Stories for Students*, Gale, Cengage Learning, 2016.

James Banerian

In the following review, Banerian asserts that Le Minh Khue's work will further the world's understanding of her home country.

It is a paradox of war that our enemies are just as human as we. Before this realization can lead to understanding and forgiveness, however, many bridges must be crossed and wounds must heal.

One of the sappers' jobs is to detonate unexploded bombs. (© Sinisa Botas / ShutterStock.com)

In an effort to forge reconciliation among the opposing sides of the Vietnam War, Curbstone Press has initiated *Voices from Vietnam*, a project designed to bring the "unheard voices" of contemporary Vietnamese literature to an English-reading public. This follow-up to its Vietnamese-American collaborative anthology *The Other Side of Heaven* (1995; see WLT 71:2, p. 468) begins with a collection of fourteen short stories by one of that volume's editors, Le Minh Khue, a former war correspondent, now an author and editor in Hanoi. Edited by Wayne Karlin and translated by Tran Bac Hoai and Dana Sachs, *The Stars, The Earth, The River* offers one writer's perspective on life in postwar Vietnam.

The collection opens with a war story, "The Distant Stars," describing a team of youth volunteers assigned to clear the Ho Chi Minh Trail for the heroes of the North Vietnamese Army. Through idealism, shared hardship, and the intimacy of trenchmates, the narrator is overwhelmed by "youthful joy" and "passionate love" that extends to everyone in her company. Contrast this with postwar reconstruction in the 1980s. Gone are the exuberance, collective spirit, and dreams for the future that characterized the revolutionary youth. Instead, the author finds her people have lost their ideals and given way to materialism and the desire for modern comforts. Of two friends from the front, one throws away her dreams to fulfill commonplace family responsibilities while her more fortunate comrade lacks the motivation to help her. A young woman correspondent relinquishes her infatuation with a war hero as she cynically adapts herself to the demands of her profession. In "The River" (placed at the end of the volume in the editor's interpretive arrangement) an urban professional leaves the noise and confusion of the city to discover quiet reminiscences of the village of his youth; the river is a wistful link to the past, yet it cannot impede the intrusion of modern life into the countryside.

The tales that follow leave a trail of tragedy and heartbreak. Greed justifies murderous impulses in "The Almighty Dollar" and "Scenes from an Alley." The ghost of a black American soldier haunts a man and his son trying to sell the soldier's bones in "Tony D." True love proves illusory for women with profound hopes. Even the apparently perfect match between young lovers in "A Small Tragedy" is spoiled when a father's secret from the Land Reform is revealed.

"To understand my stories," says Le Minh Khue, "you should try to understand the history of revolution, war, and struggle that my country has gone through and out of which they grow." These stories reveal a failed revolution, a war whose sacrifices have come to naught, and a struggle to survive that favors the lucky and the opportunistic. Raised in the mystique and idealism of the communist cause, the author matures to find that there is no global family and one should be grateful just to be alive. Like many American veterans, Le Minh Khue never fully adjusts to peacetime and yearns to return to a time of innocence and intensity, when all soldiers were heroes and life had a purpose (if only to repel the enemy in the "American War"). The harsh realities of existence have driven her to fatalism and the conclusion that "no one in this world is really happy."

For editor Karlin, a former Marine, the stories break down stereotypes about the North Vietnamese and display with compassion and hope "the Vietnamese genius for survival." That may be wishful thinking, and time will tell if books such as this will lead to true reconciliation between former enemies. Still, the book offers a stark, unadorned look at some of the more tragic aspects of the postwar nation and the spiritual depression of its people. With many strides yet to be made, *The Stars, The Earth, The River* takes a tentative step toward a broader understanding of Vietnam.

Source: James Banerian, Review of *The Stars, the Earth, the River*, in *World Literature Today*, Vol. 72, No. 1, Winter 1998, p. 214.

Publishers Weekly

In the following review, the anonymous reviewer praises Khue's complex and vibrant portrayal of Vietnam.

As a journalist who covered the Vietnam War and its aftermath, and later as a prominent writer in Vietnam, Khue has witnessed her compatriots at their noblest and most venal. Throughout this collection of 14 stories, she unearths secrets assiduously buried in the psyches of her characters. These may be a tenderness too fragile to reveal, emotions long forgotten or a passionate love too frightening to admit. Often, they are greedy manipulation, duplicity and selfishness so wantonly immoral it would wreak disaster were it known by others. Khue is fascinated by the odd contradictions in human nature, particularly those that are tragic and self-defeating. She is as deft at evoking the bonds of sisterhood among three teenage girls working as North Vietnamese sappers during the war ("The Distant Stars") as she is at portraying the fratricidal envy that erupts between the families of twin brothers ("The Almighty Dollar"). Measuring her culture against an alien and invasive Western one, she disfills both, able to see alike their uniqueness and commonality. The stories never blame savagery on poverty or deprivation, arguing instead that human character matters. There is a bleakness to this collection, a blasted feel that comes in war's wake, relieved by genuine but brief interjections of wonder. Through her stories, Khue exposes a Vietnam more vital and complex than the stereotypes that linger in the minds of many Westerners.

Source: Review of *The Stars, the Earth, the River*, in *Publishers Weekly*, Vol. 244, No. 12, March 24, 1997, p. 61.

Kirkus Reviews

In the following review, the anonymous reviewer calls Le Minh Khue's writing "a rare combination of compassion and objectivity.

Fourteen stories of life during and after the war in Vietnam, by an accomplished North Vietnamese writer experienced both in combat and as a war correspondent. Khue's passionate tales of her people's struggles are essentially divided between vigorous descriptions of transformative experiences in or near battle ("The Distant Stars," "The Blue Sky") and relentlessly frank portrayals of peacetime adjustment ("A Day on the Road," "Fragile as a Sunray"). Khue is often discursive, but virtually never doctrinaire, and her finest stories—such as the superb "A Small Tragedy"—convey with a rare combination of compassion and objectivity the dual nature of a grievously damaged country and its people's stoic resilience.

Source: Review of *The Stars, the Earth, the River*, in *Kirkus Review*, March 1, 1997.

SOURCES

Banerian, James, Review of *The Stars, the Earth, the River*, in *World Literature Today*, Vol. 72, No. 1, Winter 1998, pp. 214–15.

Borton, James, "Vietnam Exports Literature Lessons West," in *Asia Times Online*, December 4, 2003, http://www.atimes.com/atimes/Southeast_Asia/EL04Ae02.html (accessed February 17, 2014).

Ehrhart, W. D., "A Common Language," in *Virginia Quarterly Review*, Vol. 67, Summer 1991, pp. 377–96.

Karlin, Wayne, ed., Introduction to *The Stars, the Earth, the River*, Curbstone Press, 1997, pp. vii–xviii.

———, "Le Minh Khue," in *Dictionary of Literary Biography*, Vol. 348, *Southeast Asian Writers*, edited by David Smyth, Gale Group, 2009, pp. 132–36.

Le Minh Khue, "The Distant Stars," in *The Stars, the Earth, the River: Short Fiction by Le Minh Khue*, translated by Bac Hoai Tran and Dana Sachs, edited by Wayne Karlin, Curbstone Press, 1997, pp. 1–20.

"Operation Iraqi Freedom and Operation Enduring Freedom/Afghanistan," iCasualties, http://icasualties.org/ (accessed February 16, 2015).

Review of *The Stars, the Earth, the River*, in *Publishers Weekly*, Vol. 244, No. 12, March 24, 1997, p. 61.

Sachs, Dana, "Small Tragedies and Distant Stars: Le Minh Khue's Language of Lost Ideals," in *Crossroads: An Interdisciplinary Journal of Southeast Asian Studies*, Vol. 13, No. 1, 1999, pp. 1–10.

Sachs, Dana, and Bac Hoai Tran, Translators' Note to *The Stars, the Earth, the River*, Curbstone Press, 1997, pp. xix–xxi.

Turner, Karen Gottschang, with Phan Thanh Hao, *Even the Women Must Fight: Memories of War from North Vietnam*, John Wiley & Sons, 1998, pp. xiii–xvi, 93–116.

"Vietnam War: American Casualty Statistics," Military Factory, July 3, 2014, http://www.militaryfactory.com/vietnam/casualties.asp (accessed February 16, 2015).

"Vietnam War: History," BBC News website, http://news.bbc.co.uk/2/shared/spl/hi/asia_pac/05/vietnam_war/html/introduction.stm (accessed February 16, 2015).

FURTHER READING

Duong Thu Huong, *Paradise of the Blind*, translated by Phan Huy Duong and Nina McPherson, Morrow, 1993.
> Originally published as *Những thiên duòng mù* in 1988, this novel was the first Vietnamese novel to be translated into English. It focuses on the lives of three women who must struggle to sustain their family traditions in the shadow of Communism and the land reforms of the 1950s.

Mitchell, Margaret, *Gone with the Wind*, Macmillan, 1936.
> Well versed in American literature, Khue told Turner and Hao at the end of the twentieth century that "a favorite now of many Vietnamese women is your only war story with a woman hero, *Gone with the Wind*." Mitchell's classic, which won the Pulitzer Prize, was and remains hugely popular as a creative treatment of the Civil War and its aftermath from a woman's perspective.

Walker, Keith, *A Piece of My Heart: The Stories of 26 American Women Who Served in Vietnam*, Presidio Press, 1986.
> In this volume, Walker has collected autobiographical anecdotes from a couple dozen of the roughly 7,500 women who served with the military in Vietnam. With US military policy restricting women from life-threatening war zones, most served as nurses, while a few served with the Women's Army Corps, relief services, or the USO.

Zumwalt, James, *Bare Feet, Iron Will: Stories from the Other Side of Vietnam's Battlefields*, Fortis Publishing, 2010.
> Written by a US Marine Corps lieutenant whose father was an admiral who commanded the US Navy during the Vietnam War, this volume uses anecdotes from Communist soldiers to broaden sympathetic understanding among Americans with regard to what went on during the war from the other perspective.

SUGGESTED SEARCH TERMS

Le Minh Khue AND The Distant Stars

Le Minh Khue AND The Stars, the Earth, the River

Le Minh Khue AND Vietnam War

Vietnam War AND women AND fiction

Vietnam War AND Vietnamese women

Vietnamese women AND society

Vietnam War AND poetry

war AND short stories

war AND love

Drenched in Light

ZORA NEALE HURSTON

1924

Zora Neale Hurston is now considered a mainstream figure in American literature, but she was not always. Although she was well known from 1925 to 1945 as a leading African American author in the United States, she was forgotten after her death in poverty and obscurity in 1960. The novelist Alice Walker revived her reputation in the 1970s by putting a headstone on her unmarked grave in Florida and by writing articles and gathering her work. Today Hurston's work is taught in schools as a classic African American author alongside Langston Hughes, James Baldwin, and Richard Wright; this is particularly notable because Wright famously denounced her for not being militant enough against racism. Hurston is perhaps even more relevant today because her narratives combine issues of race, class, and gender, with the eye of both an artist and an anthropologist. She has preserved African American culture and history in her creative stories using southern black dialect as well as in her collections of folklore.

Hurston came to wider public attention with Oprah Winfrey's 2005 TV production of *Their Eyes Were Watching God*, Hurston's 1937 novel, starring Halle Berry as Janie Starks. Critical attention to Hurston's short fiction has been slow to catch up, but her short stories were collected in *The Complete Stories: Zora Neale Hurston* (1995) and announced as worthy of closer appreciation. One such story is "Drenched

American writer Zora Neale Hurston is best known for 1937's Their Eyes Were Watching God. *(Library of Congress)*

in Light" (1924), one of her early publications. It is based on Hurston's own childhood memory of an encounter with white people in her hometown of Eatonville, Florida. Today, many see it as a fable that exemplifies the Harlem Renaissance itself, with black artists being sought out by white audiences.

AUTHOR BIOGRAPHY

Hurston was born in Notasulga, Alabama, on January 7, 1891, to John Hurston and Lucy Potts Hurston. Both parents were the children of former slaves. They had eight children. John Hurston was one of the early founders of Eatonville, Florida, an all-black community where Hurston grew up. John Hurston became minister of the Baptist church and was the mayor of the town. Hurston thrived in Eatonville, where her imagination was free. She was

a precocious child, excelling in school. Hurston's mother had been a schoolteacher and encouraged her to learning and use her imagination. When her mother died in 1904, Hurston was traumatized, and her life became much harder.

Hurston's father remarried very quickly, and she did not get along with her stepmother. Hurston, according to her own account, attended a school in Jacksonville, Florida, where she first became aware of racial prejudice. Her father died in 1917, also a turning point for her, because now she had to invent her own life, without any financial support except what she could earn and gain from benefactors. She took jobs as a maid and a nanny and in a traveling musical company. In Baltimore, she earned a high school diploma from Morgan Academy in 1918. Later, she worked and went to Howard University in Washington, D.C., on a scholarship. Hurston realized at an early age that literature was her world and wrote poetry and stories. In 1921, she became a member of the literary society of Howard professor Alain Locke, whose anthology of black literature, *The New Negro* (1925), included work by Hurston. She published "Drenched in Light" (1924) in the Urban League's magazine, *Opportunity*.

Hurston moved to New York in 1925. She became part of the literary movement known as the Harlem Renaissance and met other notable writers, such as Langston Hughes and Claude McKay. Hurston was able to attend Barnard College on scholarship while working as a secretary for writer Fannie Hurst. After earning a bachelor's degree in 1928, Hurston did two years of graduate work at Columbia. In 1927, she was briefly wed to Herbert Sheen, a student from Howard. A wealthy white patron, Charlotte Osgood Mason, supported Hurston from 1928 to 1932 while she was studying anthropology under Franz Boas at Columbia. She did fieldwork in Florida on a fellowship in 1927 to collect African American folktales, which she published as *Mules and Men* (1935). Her anthropological travels also inspired her novels *Jonah's Gourd Vine* (1934) and *Their Eyes Were Watching God* (1937). Hurston worked on a play, *Mule Bone: A Comedy of Negro Life* (1931), with Langston Hughes, but they argued over the credit for it, and it caused a break in the friendship. Hurston worked for the WPA

Federal Theater Project in 1935 and the next year earned a Guggenheim fellowship to study the voodoo religion in Haiti, producing *Tell My Horse* (1938). *Moses, Man of the Mountain* (1939) is a fictional retelling of the biblical story about the deliverance of the Israelites from slavery.

Hurston married Albert Price in 1939 but divorced him in 1943. In 1941, she became a story consultant for Paramount in Los Angeles, where she began her autobiography, *Dust Tracks on a Road* (1942). Hurston was a teacher at Bethune-Coleman College in Daytona Beach in the 1930s and at North Carolina College for Negroes in Durham later in life. She published her novel *Seraph on the Suwanee* in 1948, the same year she was falsely arrested for molesting a child. The charges were dropped but had a devastating effect on her because she had been vilified by the black press. In the 1950s, she lived in poverty in Florida, still writing but ill and unable to publish. She had a stroke in 1959 and died on January 28, 1960, in Fort Pierce, Florida, of hypertensive heart disease. Hurston was largely forgotten until novelist Alice Walker revived her fame in the 1970s. The collection *Every Tongue Got to Confess* (2001) was published posthumously; it includes some of Hurston's folktales that were found in the Smithsonian archives.

MEDIA ADAPTATIONS

- *Speak, So You Can Speak Again: The Life of Zora Neale Hurston* by Lucy Anne Hurston, the niece of the author, is like a family album with facsimiles of letters and notes, photographs, and a CD including radio interviews and Hurston singing a southern railroad work song. The collection was published by Doubleday in 2004.

- *Zora Neale Hurston: Stories* is an audiobook of the short fiction narrated by Renee Joshua-Porter. The running time for this unabridged audiobook is three hours, nine minutes. It was released by AudioGO in 1995.

PLOT SUMMARY

Isis Watts is a little African American girl sitting on a gatepost watching traffic pass by, her favorite occupation. Her grandmother tells her to get down and begin to do her chore, raking the yard. Isis sees Jim and George Robinson, white cattlemen, on the road that passes north to Sanford and south to Orlando, Florida. She likes to call greetings to passersby. Everyone in the neighborhood, black and white, knows her.

Her insistence on waiting to greet the cattlemen angers her grandmother, who calls to Isis's brother, Joel, to fetch her a stick to beat the girl. Isis is upset because the Robinsons like her and usually invite her to sit on their horses and ride for a while down the road with them. Isis loves going up and down the road with travelers, talking to them. When Grandma Potts goes inside, Isis takes the stirrup offered her and rides behind Jim Robinson as he herds cattle down the road. He affectionately calls her "Snidlits." Grandma screams for Isis, and she slips off the horse and sneaks through the corn into the backyard. She does a cartwheel and lies to Grandma saying she was just playing in the yard. Grandma starts to cut switches from the trees to beat her.

Isis quickly rakes the yard and then starts romping with the coon dogs. Grandma tells her to sit on the porch quietly. Isis throws herself on the steps, and Grandma continues to lecture her for not being more ladylike. Isis sits on a chair and slides down on it while Grandma tells her to sit up straight and keep her knees together. As Isis sits up in the chair, she begins to whistle. Grandma goes to get the switch to beat her for being saucy, but it is noon, and John Watts, the widowed father, comes home for dinner. Isis is the only daughter and is expected to do kitchen work, like washing dishes. She takes the puppy and plays with him in the dishwater. When Grandma is asleep in the front room rocker in the afternoon, Isis plays make-believe under the center table with the fringed cloth.

Isis watches her grandmother snore and, seeing the whiskers on her chin, decides she needs a shave. When Joel comes to invite her to go fishing, she talks him into helping shave Grandma. Joel creates lather and Isis holds the razor over Grandma. When Joel puts the soap lather on Grandma, she wakes up and sees the razor held over her. She starts screaming and runs out of the house. Joel runs off to fish, and Isis hides under the house, afraid of a whipping.

Meanwhile, she sees and hears a band marching down the road. It is the Lodge of Odd Fellows band announcing the barbecue and log-rolling to raise money for a new hall. Isis is a gifted dancer and begins dancing around to the music. She runs after the band. However, she realizes she is not dressed appropriately for the carnival. She runs back to the house and gets Grandma's new red tablecloth that she can wear like a Spanish shawl. At the event, a speaker cannot be heard because the crowd is surrounding Isis, watching her dance barefoot with the tablecloth. They clap. When Grandma finds Isis missing, she tracks her to the carnival and sees she is wearing the new tablecloth and smelling of lemon extract that she had used for perfume. Isis sees her and runs away to the woods.

Isis follows the creek to a ford and lies on the grass in the April sunshine. She is worried about the whipping she will get. She works herself up and decides to drown herself in the creek. She wades into the water, splashing and singing, with a little alligator and a bullfrog. A car stops on the road near her with white people who saw her dance at the carnival. The man exclaims it is the little gypsy in the creek. He asks her what she is doing, and when she says she is killing herself so she can escape from a beating, the people laugh. They ask her the way to the Park Hotel in Maitland, and she is invited to get in the car and show them. During the ride, she explains her fantasy world to them, how she takes trips to the horizon with gold shoes that have blue bottoms, on a white horse. As they pass Isis's house, Grandma sees her tablecloth in the back of the car. She begins yelling at the girl.

The white woman named Helen offers to save Isis, holding her by the hand, while Grandma angrily tells all her crimes, especially spoiling the new tablecloth from Orlando. Isis says she was going to shave Grandma because she was too old to do it for herself. Helen thinks this is an act of selfless love, misunderstood by the grandmother. She offers her five dollars if

she will let Isis show them to the hotel and dance for them in the tablecloth. She says that she needs the child's joy, for Isis is full of light. Isis feels appreciated for the first time in her life, especially when the lady says she likes Isis as she is. As she gets in the car, Isis offers to stay with the white people. The lady hugs her as they drive off.

CHARACTERS

Harry

Harry is one of the white men in the car. He tells Helen she has been adopted by Isis, who clings to her for protection from her grandmother. He is amused by Isis but more indifferent than Helen.

Helen

Helen is the white tourist in the car staying at the hotel in Maitland for the carnival. She is the one who appreciates Isis's dancing and imagination, saying that she needs the light in the little girl for her soul. Helen seems to be in a state of sorrow about something that happened to her, probably a love affair gone wrong, possibly with one of the men in the car. She thinks Isis is loving and is misunderstood by her grandmother. Isis is unused to being interpreted in this way and is grateful. She wants to stay with Helen.

Grandma Potts

Grandma is severe with Isis, finding her high spirits a constant trouble around the house, where she is the only girl. She is an old woman and finds it difficult to deal with the young children of her widower son. She tries to make Isis behave as an older generation would have expected, believing that children should be obedient and quiet. Grandma scolds Isis to do her chores and behave in a ladylike manner and tries to make her behave through beatings. She has no understanding of the young girl's heart, as the white lady does. She is impressed, however, that the white lady will pay her for the tablecloth and feels proud of Isis's acceptance by the strangers.

Jim and George Robinson

The Robinson brothers are white cattlemen who ride horses and herd cattle down the road in front of Isis's house. They are fond of Isis, whom they call "Snidlits," and let her ride on their horses with them.

Sewell

Sewell is one of the white men in the car who drives to the hotel with Helen and Harry.

Isis Watts

Isis is the main character of the story, an African American child growing up in Florida. The story is similar to experiences Hurston describes during her own childhood in Eatonville, Florida. Isis is not really a bad girl, just wild and imaginative, living in her own world. She loves the traffic on the road outside her house because she wants adventure, especially to travel to the horizon that she believes is the end of the earth. She wants to know what is there. She imagines going there on a white horse.

Isis is uninhibited and a contrast to the white people, who are more restrained. It is Isis's freedom that Helen envies. Isis is too young to have had her innocence and love crushed out of her. The grandmother makes her feel fear but not enough to repress her spirits. The white woman sees Isis as a symbol of life and happiness, as she dances fearlessly before a crowd. It is implied that the white woman has had some sorrow in love or in her life and that Isis helps her forget it.

Isis does not behave like a lady, sitting with her knees together. She is not interested in status or propriety like adults. She is not even interested in race, seemingly unaffected by the privilege of whites in the South. Isis is interested only in her own imaginative world. When Helen praises Isis her for this quality, calling her a child of light, it changes her self-image. She feels appreciated for the first time. Her traits are seen by the white lady as gifts instead of evil habits.

Isis has strong emotions and independence. She is willing to take risks to fulfill her dreams. The visitors laugh at her in the pond, calling her a tragic actress as she plays at drowning herself, but she is never able to suppress her happiness for long. Within minutes, she is laughing at the alligator and frog who swim near her. Her main characteristic is her dynamism, for she cannot be still for a moment, always onto the next project—shaving Grandma or dancing for a crowd. Even at this early age, she feels the disapproval of those who only know practical life and conventional behavior, like Grandma. Isis does not mean to cause trouble or to be thoughtless; she simply cannot help being herself, drenched in light.

Joel Watts

Joel is the older brother of Isis. He likes to go fishing in Blue Sink Pond. Isis is able to involve him in her plot to shave Grandma. He feels like the man as he tells her she does not know how to shave, and he must show her how to do it. Grandma seems to excuse the behavior of boys but expects a lot of Isis as the girl in the family.

John Watts

John is Isis and Joel's father. He is a widower.

THEMES

Race Relations

In many ways, "Drenched in Light" mirrors the shift in race relations taking place in the United States in the early twentieth century, symbolized by the Harlem Renaissance. African American philosopher Alain Locke was explaining there was a "New Negro" to replace the old stereotype of the primitive and dependent former slave. The Harlem Renaissance showcased this New Negro to the public, with dazzling displays of creative genius in jazz, blues, drama, dance, and literature. Many educated blacks were professionals and took the opportunity not only to display creativity but also to document their own history, as Hurston's anthropological background allowed her to do.

Little Isis represents the New Negro to the whites in the story. She is not fearful around them and actually acts superior to them in some ways. She is self-confident she has the magic they want. She is the one with the light that they seek, and they line up to give her rides and money for her performances. The grandmother is representative of an older generation, conservatively staying in what she sees as her proper place, whereas the granddaughter acts in an outrageous and spontaneous manner. She sits on the fence post and hails the white passersby, who are invariably charmed by her stories and manner.

Helen represents the white attitude that idealized blacks as freer than whites in their

TOPICS FOR FURTHER STUDY

- Research the music that would have been heard in Harlem in the 1920s, for instance, jazz and blues, and how white audiences came to listen and dance at the Cotton Club, the Savoy, and the Apollo Theater. Create a PowerPoint presentation with photos or film clips showing dancers and music of various famous musicians, such as Duke Ellington and Louis Armstrong, and share your presentation with your class.

- Compare the poetry of Langston Hughes and Countee Cullen, two poets who write in different styles. Read aloud to the group "Po Boy Blues," "The Weary Blues," "Bound No'th Blues," and "Let America Be America Again" by Hughes and "A Brown Girl Dead," "Yet Do I Marvel," and "Heritage" by Cullen. Explicate the verses in terms of their importance in theme and style to the Harlem Renaissance writers. The issue of whether to use standard English or black vernacular was hotly debated. Find poems written in both styles and compare and contrast the effects in a short paper, using quotes from the poems to make your point.

- As a group, read the first section of Hurston's collected folktales *Mules and Men* (1935), in which the tales improvise on biblical characters like God, the devil, Saint Peter, and Noah. They also include animal stories and tall tales about Big John de Conquer, a slave who wins battles against his master. Have individuals present certain stories to the group, and then discuss how these folktales give insight into African American culture. Make a group website or a wikispace on world folktales with visuals and comments on the importance of keeping folklore alive from the oral traditions of various peoples. Find examples of the use of folktales in popular culture and songs, showing how they are transformed by various media.

- In class, discuss the lives of Phillis Wheatley and Zora Neale Hurston as artists dependent on white patronage. What advantages and disadvantages did they encounter? Are there minority artists who are dependent on white patronage today? Use a social bookmarking service such as Delicious.com, StumbleUpon, or Diigo.com with websites and materials online that answer these questions, and share with the class.

- Read the young-adult autobiography of Francisco Jiminez, *The Circuit* (1997), which describes his childhood as part of a migrant working family who moved constantly. Discuss how this upbringing compares with the life of Isis Watts as a child. How do the social circumstances shape the personality of the children? Or is there some innate quality in children (an inner "light") that goes beyond race and environment, as Hurston believed? Write a story of your own about a child who must confront difficulties growing up and how he or she deals with them.

---

expressive behavior. While the story does not symbolize an ideal race relationship, it has moved toward equality and away from the brutality of bigotry and racial conflict so widespread in the South at the time. The white tourists are charmed with Isis, but so too are her white neighbors, the Robinson brothers.

Hurston was often criticized for her depiction of amicable race relationships with whites, while other African American authors were expressing anger against racism. Hurston was interested in depicting African American life but less interested in politics and racial philosophy. She loved white literature as well as the voodoo religion of Haiti and the black

Grandma is startled when she wakes to find Isis and Joel playing with the straight razor and shaving soap. *(© addimage / ShutterStock.com)*

folktales of the South. For her, imagination was more powerful than race.

Imagination

What makes Isis drenched in light is her imagination. She does not see the world as her grandmother does, as a set schedule of daily chores. Isis lives in a world of her own making, a world of one spontaneous adventure after another—riding on the horse of Jim Robinson, playing make-believe under the table, shaving her grandmother, dancing at the carnival, drowning herself in the pond, and riding with the white people to their hotel. The ordinary world is secondary to her, and that gets her into trouble with authority figures. Hurston's own personality is reflected in Isis, for she had trouble holding down jobs and was thought to be irresponsible. Like Isis, she was restless and could hardly stay still or focused except on her own imaginative productions.

Isis never sees herself as inferior in any way. She imagines herself to be various people in robes and gold shoes, going on journeys to the horizon, being a Spanish dancer with lemon extract for perfume, or drowning herself dramatically so her family will miss her. She does not see the white people in a social light but as her audience or saviors. She decides she wants to be adopted by Helen, who appreciates her. The whites have cars, money, carnivals, hotels, and horses, but they do not have the joy and light of Isis, and she is more than willing to share it with anyone open enough to appreciate it.

STYLE

Short Story

The modern short story generally concerns the everyday world of realistic events and settings. James Joyce, Katherine Mansfield, and Joseph Conrad helped to make the twentieth-century short story a highly polished form, with surprise turns and philosophical depth, where the character has a revelation. In "Drenched in Light," the surprise turn and revelation comes when Isis discovers power over her grandmother by an alliance with a white tourist.

The American short story of the twentieth-century was largely modernist, compressed, symbolic, and focused on social and psychological issues, such as F. Scott Fitzgerald's "Babylon Revisited" (1931) about the alcoholic high life of the 1920s and Ernest Hemingway's "The Snows of Kilimanjaro" (1936) about the meaninglessness of life and death. Regional stories such as William Faulkner's fiction about race and class in the South and Willa Cather's short stories about settling the land in the West are other important contributions to this genre.

Short fiction is a popular multicultural form today, with authors from every ethnic group contributing their unique point of view, such as African American Toni Cade Bambara, Native American Sherman Alexie, and Indian American Jhumpa Lahiri. Hurston specializes in reproducing life in the rural South, especially in the use of African American vernacular speech and folklore.

African American Literature

Some early African American literature was a rendering of oral roots into written form that began even before the Revolutionary period but was most celebrated in the first famous slave poet, Phillis Wheatley (1754–1784). Wheatley was a child prodigy who used polished eighteenth-century verse to express herself and became famous in Europe and America. In the Reconstruction era, many nineteenth-century authors such as Frederick Douglass, William Wells Brown, James Weldon Johnson, Charles Waddell Chesnutt, and especially Paul Laurence Dunbar, paved the way for the Harlem Renaissance with their experiments in rhythm and form in English.

An important forerunner of Hurston's short fiction is Chesnutt, a nineteenth-century African American author whose short stories collected in *The Conjure Woman* (1899) involved a character called Uncle Julius telling African American folktales to a white couple. Famous short fiction by African American authors of the twentieth century includes Richard Wright's "Fire and Cloud" (1938) about white persecution and black solidarity that foretells the civil rights movement and Toni Morrison's postmodern story "Recitatif" (1983) about the ambiguity of race relations.

Hurston's stories are a contrast to the angry activist tone of authors like Wright and James Baldwin and closer in tone to Langston Hughes, who, while he could show anger, wrote to celebrate the joy and unique perspective of African American life. "Drenched in Light" shows the harmony of the races that Hurston experienced in Eatonville, Florida, growing up. It highlights the ability of the arts to make connections between the races, as happened when mainstream America began to appreciate the contributions of African Americans during the Harlem Renaissance.

Hurston got into trouble with other black authors of the time because they were trying to take African American literature in a direction they considered more serious and sophisticated. They felt the attitude of Hurston's fiction, as in this story, could be seen as primitive and condescending to the stereotype of the happy darky, instead of taking a militant stance against the social wrongs in race relations. Hurston felt this pressure but stuck to her guns, showing black folk life without rancor or judgment. She was, above all, an anthropologist recording life as she found it.

Use of Black Dialect

The poet Paul Laurence Dunbar (1872–1906) pioneered the use of black dialect in his poetry, as he performed it for white audiences on tours. These poems about life on the plantations, such as "When Malindy Sings" and "A Negro Love Song," were viewed by white audiences as an authentic and exotic display, but Dunbar grieved because he was not taken seriously when he wrote in standard English. He wrote at the turn of the century when racist stereotypes were even harder to overcome than they are today. Consequently, certain writers in the Harlem Renaissance refused to write in dialect, for fear of being branded as ignorant minstrels.

This shame about black vernacular speech was turned around in the 1920s when it became a matter of racial pride in the work of authors like Hurston and Hughes. They did not feel the dialect conveyed inferiority but instead reflected the abundance and richness of uniquely African American culture and language. These authors felt that the rhythms, words, and expressions that became famous in their literature and in black music like the blues could convey a lot more about the black experience in the vernacular than in standard English. Hurston became noted for the way she could integrate standard English and black idiom with rhythm and grace.

HISTORICAL CONTEXT

Eatonville, Florida

Hurston was so proud of the town she grew up in that she claimed to be born in Eatonville, Florida, north of Orlando, in her autobiography, *Dust on the Tracks* (1942). In reality, her family moved there later after living in Alabama. Her father, John Hurston, was one of the builders of this all-black community, founded in 1886 and said to be the first incorporated African American town in the United States. It is the setting for much of her fiction, including the novel *Their Eyes Were Watching God*, the play *Mule Bone*, and the story "Drenched in Light."

Hurston and her seven siblings grew up in a comfortable large house with a barn and fields around it, and she recounts many idyllic

COMPARE & CONTRAST

- **1924:** Race perceptions are starting to shift with the Harlem Renaissance. Black pride begins to replace the old stereotypes of African Americans as subservient.

  Today: It is understood that racial stereotypes are not founded on biological differences but on social prejudice. Barriers have come down for African Americans in education, housing, and careers.

- **1924:** Even after emancipation, former slaves like the grandmother in "Drenched in Light" are cautious around whites, while Isis represents a new generation that does not remember slavery and believes she can do what she likes, unafraid of the white-dominated world.

  Today: While racial integration is a fact of American life, many African Americans of the inner city still face violence, poverty, and disadvantage. They fear hate crimes by whites and overreaction by white police.

- **1924:** White audiences, particularly the young, are hungry for what they perceive to be the new exotic freedom of African American music, art, and dancing. White culture is felt to be too conservative in its public display of emotion and movement.

  Today: White audiences and artists have imbibed the idiom of black art for decades, resulting in a rich cultural exchange between mainstream art and African American art.

---

scenes with people and nature. Hurston's father, a Baptist preacher, was also the mayor. Hurston felt great freedom to be herself in Eatonville. Whites coming through the town were only visitors, and they were invariably impressed by Hurston's unquenchable spirits and bright nature. She explains she never felt the effects of racial prejudice until her teen years in Jacksonville.

From an early age, she engaged in her two passions: making up stories and collecting folktales. The porch of Joe Clarke's store in Eatonville, where men gathered to tell tales, was her first exposure to the African American oral tradition that she made her specialty as an anthropologist. One of her first works, "The Eatonville Anthology" (1926), contains short character sketches of people that she knew there and appeared in *The Messenger*, an important civil rights magazine.

Harlem Renaissance

Harlem, a culturally diverse area of New York City, was a creative hot spot for African American artists in the 1920s. The group of gifted writers, visual artists, dramatists, dancers, and musicians who lived and worked there from about 1920 to 1940 sparked a "renaissance" of black culture so compelling that people of all races flocked there to sample the trend-setting styles, especially in jazz music. The area was so magnetic that Langston Hughes, one of its stars, turned down a European education so he could live in Harlem, the center of the black universe, as far as he was concerned. This was where jazz and the blues entered mainstream culture.

Harlem began drawing African Americans from the South during the Great Migration of the early 1900s, after the Civil War and Reconstruction. Blacks sought jobs and fled persecution and Jim Crow discrimination in the south. The Harlem Renaissance made a great contribution to the finding of black identity through art. It was a blossoming of black pride. African American writers, including Hurston, published their work in prestigious black magazines, such as the *Stylus, Opportunity, Crisis*, the *Messenger*, and *FIRE!!*.

Isis sees the white shell road as a path to better things. (© *Daniel Novak | ShutterStock.com*)

Alain Locke, a philosopher working at Howard University, declared Harlem the center of the new African American identity in his anthology, *The New Negro* (1925). Hurston's work was included in the collection, and she moved to Harlem the year of its publication. Locke stressed that the old Negro was a stereotype of weakness and dependence, but the New Negro was independent and could speak for himself. Hurston fit the new definition, for she became known as incorrigibly her own person. Hurston met other authors and collaborators in Harlem such as Hughes, Jessie Fauset, Dorothy West, Wallace Thurman, Claude McKay, James Weldon Johnson, Countee Cullen, Alice Dunbar Nelson, and Arna Bontemps. The Harlem Renaissance gave Hurston the freedom to express her own experience, using African American dialect and vernacular speech.

Hurston's Patrons

Although Hurston's career was furthered by many black sponsors, such as Alain Locke, she also drew to her many white patrons inspired by her spontaneity and knowledge of black culture, such as Franz Boas, Charlotte Osgood Mason, Carl Van Vechten, Fannie Hurst, and Annie Nathan Meyer. Each of them showed up at a critical point in her life to usher her into higher opportunities for her talent. In her autobiography, Hurston tells a story about how one day in grade school she showed off for some white lady visitors by reading and explaining the Greek myth of Persephone. She consequently received gifts of money and books from them for her precocious performance and went on most of her life to attract similar support. This experience is reflected in the white tourist in "Drenched in Light" who is willing to pay for the company of little Isis and foreshadows the long string of patrons who helped forward Hurston's career.

Hurston took a class from famed anthropologist Franz Boas at Columbia, and he singled out Hurston and became her mentor as an anthropologist specializing in black folklore. Boas helped Hurston find a fellowship, projects, and funding. Charlotte Osgood Mason was a rich patron of the arts and supported various African American artists, such as Hurston,

McKay, and Hughes. Although she was generous, Mrs. Mason was controlling and believed in the primitive nature of black art. Hughes argued with her and dropped her so he could have freedom of expression. Hurston had an equally difficult time with "Godmother" as Mrs. Mason insisted on being called. Hurston claimed they had a psychic connection, but it is painful reading about when she argued with her patron about whether she should buy a new pair of shoes. Although Hurston endured many lectures from Mrs. Mason, she continued to follow her own creative urges.

Carl Van Vechten was a white critic and photographer who championed artists of the Harlem Renaissance, including Hurston. He photographed her several times and introduced her to other artists. Fannie Hurst was a famous white novelist who employed Hurston as a secretary. In Hurst's portrait of Hurston, she writes how she kept Hurston on as her secretary in spite of her irresponsibility and poor performance, because Hurston would chauffeur her around on amusing and strange adventures. She knew Hurston was brilliant and valued her company. Annie Nathan Meyer was an activist for higher education for women and sponsored Hurston to attend Barnard College by finding her a scholarship.

Hurston was a hard worker and had many jobs, from teaching and writing, to being a maid and nanny. Unfortunately, there were no patrons or publishers at the end of her life, and she died in poverty. The amazing thing is how she had so much support from others from her teen years to her sixties, enabling her to have a first-class education, career, and fame.

CRITICAL OVERVIEW

Today, Hurston is an established representative of the African American literary canon, with four novels, three books of folklore, an autobiography, and over fifty short stories, plays, and essays. It is widely acknowledged that she hit her stride in 1937 with her masterpiece, *Their Eyes Were Watching God*, which combines fiction and folklore. She was one of the most famous African American authors between 1925 and 1945 but lost favor after that until her revival in the 1970s.

Hurston published short stories in the 1920s, winning literary contests and making a place for herself among the Harlem Renaissance literati by sheer talent and audacity. "Drenched in Light" (1924) was published in the Urban League magazine, *Opportunity*, in which she also received a prize for "Spunk" (1925), reprinted in Alain Locke's anthology *The New Negro* (1925). As she published her books in the 1930s, she attracted mostly positive critical attention from mainstream readers and critics, culminating in her appearance on the cover of the *Saturday Review of Literature* in 1943 for winning the Anisfield-Wolf Book Award for *Dust Tracks on a Road*. Hurston's male black critics, however, made trouble for her as the civil rights era approached, making her look like a conservative Uncle Tom pandering to white audiences.

Chief among her critics was Richard Wright, whose own naturalistic style, communism, and radical political views are in direct contrast to Hurston's positive and apolitical depiction of African American life. His review for *New Masses* on October 5, 1937, insists that *Their Eyes Were Watching God* has no theme or message and instead continues "the minstrel technique that makes the 'white folks' laugh." He refers to her use of dialect and accuses her of addressing her writing to whites, not to blacks. Even Hurston's mentor, Alain Locke, in a review for *Opportunity*, criticizes the novel for its lack of social comment. Women reviewers, on the other hand, perhaps responding to the book's feminist point of view, are enchanted by it, such as Lucille Tompkins for the *New York Times Book Review*, who finds the book beautiful in its African American folklore and dialect but universal in theme. Sheila Hibben writes for the *New York Herald Tribune Weekly Book Review* that Hurston writes with both her head and her heart "vibrant Negro lingo with its guitar twang of poetry, and its deep, vivid humor."

Hurston hit her low point with critics and readers when she criticized the 1954 Supreme Court decision to uphold desegregation of schools. She was no longer able to get published in the last years of her life, having to work as a maid. After dying in poverty in 1960, she remained in oblivion until her work was revived by novelist Alice Walker in the 1970s. Walker wrote articles praising Hurston as an important writer, such as the groundbreaking 1975 piece for *Ms.* magazine, "In Search of Zora Neale Hurston." In her dedication to *A Zora Neale Hurston Reader*, which she edited in 1979, Walker puts the author in a class with Billie Holiday and Bessie Smith as a consummate black artist and icon. Similarly, Henry Louis Gates Jr., in the preface to *Zora Neale Hurston: Critical Perspectives Past and Present* (1993), describes Hurston as the most widely taught black woman author today "because of her command of a narrative voice that imitates the storytelling structures of the black vernacular tradition," thus vindicating her use of black idiom.

CRITICISM

Susan K. Andersen

Andersen is a writer and teacher with a PhD in English literature. In the following essay, she considers Hurston's story "Drenched in Light" in terms of Hurston's unique angle on race relations.

W. E. B. Du Bois defined the burden African Americans bear as having to live in two cultures at war with each other: black and white. African Americans never lose this sense of double consciousness, he explains in *The Souls of Black Folk* (1903), measuring themselves by two standards instead of seeing themselves whole. Many African American writers have delved deeply into the pain of this double consciousness in their works. The Harlem Renaissance represented a time of triumph when black artists felt free for the first time to celebrate their black heritage as a strength instead of a weakness, a trait that made these artists representatives of the "New Negro," a phrase coined by philosopher Alain Locke in his 1925 anthology.

Despite the civil freedoms won in the twentieth century, many African American authors still carry this double consciousness to some degree. Hurston has a unique perspective on the white/black divide in the African American psyche. While she had to struggle with racial prejudice and stereotypes, she came from a peculiar position of self-confidence in her black roots that opened doors for her. Like Isis Watts in "Drenched in Light," Hurston always acted as a queen in her own world, a world that she was willing to share. Paradoxically, it is a

> HURSTON HAS A UNIQUE PERSPECTIVE ON THE WHITE/BLACK DIVIDE IN THE AFRICAN AMERICAN PSYCHE. WHILE SHE HAD TO STRUGGLE WITH RACIAL PREJUDICE AND STEREOTYPES, SHE CAME FROM A PECULIAR POSITION OF SELF-CONFIDENCE IN HER BLACK ROOTS THAT OPENED DOORS FOR HER."

cross-fertilization of black and white cultures that led to her success. This delicate balance between black and white that Isis experiences in a positive fashion overturns racial stereotypes in a surprising way. The black grandmother becomes almost a villain, beating the girl and blocking Isis's artistic expression, while Helen, the white woman, is the savior who supports it. This simple fable celebrates Hurston's rich racial background that gave birth to her imagination, as it foresees the audience that will help her to express it: the white patron.

In "Drenched in Light," the white people are friends, not enemies. Isis never sees herself as poor or disadvantaged or limited because she is black. She is the archetypal joyful child, a Wordsworthian innocent, still close to the original source of light compared with the melancholy adult Helen. Hurston's autobiography, *Dust Tracks on a Road*, offers an elaboration of "Drenched in Light" in the early chapters where she describes her childhood in Eatonville, Florida. Hurston presents herself as a child with a strong imagination and a mystic streak. She played the games she gives to Isis in the story, for instance, her quest to travel to the horizon, where she imagined the world ended. She believed the moon was following her. Trees had personalities and talked to her, such as the one she named the "loving pine"; she played all day under its branches instead of with toys. She made up stories with corn cob dolls: "I was driven inward. I lived an exciting life unseen." As a child of seven, Hurston had a series of twelve visions, prophetic scenes of her own future that all came true. She describes how these visions changed her; she felt different from others.

WHAT DO I READ NEXT?

- William Faulkner's "That Evening Sun Go Down" (1931) is a different view of race relations in the South. Nancy is an African American washerwoman who works for the Compson family. They treat Nancy's fears of being killed by her husband for being pregnant with a white man's child as superstition. The title of the story was taken from a blues song sung by Bessie Smith.

- *The Best of Simple* (1961), by Langston Hughes, is a collection of the stories Hughes wrote about his comic character and folk philosopher, Jesse B. Semple, for the *Chicago Defender* beginning in the 1940s. Hughes's satire on black urban life has become a classic.

- Hurston's *Their Eyes Were Watching God* (1937), her masterpiece, is a narrative about Janie Crawford's search for love and happiness. Her life throughout three marriages is told in flashback to her friend Phoeby. Celebrated for its style, the novel incorporates African American folklore and dialect.

- Mare G. Lee's *Finding My Voice* (1992) is a young-adult novel about a Korean American high-school student, Ellen Sung, who has to find her identity combating racial prejudice in Minnesota. This theme of struggling to find a voice among those of a different race contrasts with Isis's easy confidence as a child in her own secure neighborhood in the South.

- Alain Locke's *The New Negro* (1925) is an anthology of the seminal voices of the Harlem Renaissance that launched a new definition of African American culture with poetry, short stories, and essays. Included among others are Countee Cullen, Langston Hughes, W. E. B. Du Bois, Alain Locke, Jean Toomer, and Hurston's story "Spunk."

- Eudora Welty's "A Worn Path" (1941) presents a white view of African American life in the South as an old woman, Phoenix Jackson, makes a painful and heroic journey to get medicine for her sick grandson. This view contrasts Hurston's depiction of blacks as contributing their strengths to whites.

- Dorothy West's "The Typewriter" (1926), written by another Harlem Renaissance author, tied for first prize in *Opportunity* magazine with a story by Hurston. The tale is about the fantasy of an old black man to be a businessman, as he dictates pretend letters to his daughter practicing her typing.

- *How I Found America: Collected Stories of Anzia Yezierska* (1991) is a collection of short stories by this Polish Jewish immigrant author, who wrote about the life of Jews on New York's Lower East Side during the Harlem Renaissance. She won the O. Henry Award for "The Fat of the Land" as the best short story of 1919. Her relationship with her mentor, Professor John Dewey, at Columbia parallels Hurston's with Professor Franz Boas.

As a girl, Hurston was encouraged by her mother, who told her children to "jump at de sun." She liked Hurston's stories, but her grandmother called her stories lying, and her father thought she had a sassy tongue. Her grandmother had known slavery and thought Hurston's ways were too forward when she sat on the fence hailing white travelers and neighbors, as Isis does. Like Isis, Hurston was not afraid of white people and gives several anecdotes about positive interactions with whites, even though she seems to be aware of racial subtleties and sees that whites do not fully understand the black world.

Hurston claims that one white neighbor was there when she was born, helping her mother through labor when her father was gone. This man delivered her and gave the family meat. Later, he taught her to stand up for herself. In school, Hurston impressed white visitors by knowing the Greek myth of Persephone. They gave her books that she loved, such as *Gulliver's Travels*, *Grimm's Fairy Tales*, Norse tales, and Greek myths. These stories taught her to soar in spirit: "My soul was with the gods and my body in the village." It was in high school when she heard Samuel Taylor Coleridge's "Kubla Khan" read aloud as the teacher "liquified the immortal brains of Coleridge" that she knew literature was her world. She loved John Milton's *Paradise Lost*, the Bible, and the stories of Hans Christian Andersen and Rudyard Kipling. She was equally stimulated by African American oral tales told on the porch of Joe Clarke's store in Eatonville, her first inspiration for becoming an anthropologist. Hurston thus presents a fortuitous mix of white and black influences on her budding author's imagination.

Hurston was proud of her hometown of Eatonville, and it became the stage for her artistic imagination. Her father had been a leader in the community, acting as both the Baptist minister and the mayor. Even though she points out that Florida had a dark and bloody history, Eatonville was a "pure Negro town," and the Hurstons were a respected family. They lived in a large house on a large piece of land with fish in the lakes and fruit trees in the yard. With African American life as the focus and white culture there to be enjoyed but not to interfere, Hurston paints a picture of racial harmony in her early years. She was later criticized by other blacks for her lack of racial militancy. She did not approve, for instance, of desegregation in the South, as mandated by a 1954 Supreme Court ruling; she insisted that blacks had their own educational system, not inferior to the whites. While she was always able to get along with whites, she did not want to sell out her culture or see it disappear into mainstream white-dominated culture.

Hurston admits to feeling pressure from expectations that she had to write about race problems. Her story "Gilded Six-Bits" (1933) turned her around to see she could write about race without making it into a problem. It is a story about a marriage and how the couple solve their problems amicably. There are no whites in the story, nor a white point of view. The story was not intended for a white audience. Hurston became famous for writing about the Southern black world on its own terms, without apologies and without political messages.

Some critics find her pronouncements on race evasive. In her autobiography, she mentions that she went through some soul searching as an adult about race, concluding finally,

> Light came to me when I realized that I did not have to consider any racial group as a whole. God made them duck by duck and that was the only way I could see them.

There is nothing but individuals, she asserts: "There is no *The Negro* here."

In some ways, Hurston's love of black culture and the use of black idiom mirrors that of Langston Hughes, her onetime creative partner. Hughes said of her in his autobiography, *The Big Sea*:

> She was always getting scholarships and things from wealthy white people, some of whom simply paid her just to sit around and represent the Negro race for them, she did it in such a racy fashion.

The question comes up whether Hurston was consciously playing to her white audience's expectations, giving them what they wanted to hear, as she once had to pacify her patroness, Mrs. Mason. The main impression from reading her works, however, is that her joy and understanding go beyond race. Fannie Hurst describes Hurston's "blazing zest for life." Harold Bloom says her art "exalts an exuberance that is beauty" and that she was "outrageous, heroically larger than life." Alice Walker, in an essay called "A Cautionary Tale and a Partisan View," feels Hurston shows blacks to be "complete, complex, *undiminished* human beings." She appreciates that Hurston was always herself, indifferent to the opinions of others and, in many ways, full of pity for the lack of soul in whites. Robert E. Hemenway, in his essay "That Which the Soul Lives By," calls Hurston's collection of black folklore "psychic savings banks" for African Americans and notes the absence of racial bitterness in her.

In her 1928 essay "How It Feels to Be Colored Me," Hurston recounts her happy childhood in Eatonville, claiming that only at

The woman in the car hopes to brighten her own life with Isis's joy. (© *Rob Marmion | ShutterStock.com*)

the age of thirteen when she went to Jacksonville did she become a colored girl. She asserts,

> I am not tragically colored. There is no great sorrow dammed up in my soul . . . . I belong to no race nor time. I am the eternal feminine with its string of beads . . . . I am merely a fragment of the Great Soul.

Yet in her later essays "Crazy for This Democracy" (1945), "My Most Humiliating Jim Crow Experience" (1944), and "What White Publishers Won't Print" (1950), Hurston is clearly aware of racial politics and the continuing stereotypes of African Americans. She found it increasingly hard to be published, claiming that the white publishers did not want to know the real internal lives of black people, only certain ideas they entertained.

Although Hurston was out of fashion for a time, today her place in the African American canon is solid. In the introduction to *The Complete Stories: Zora Neale Hurston*, edited by Henry Louis Gates Jr. and Sieglinde Lemke, they note that her mastery of the short story was recognized by the 1930s, with her skill in narrative voice, dialect, plot, character, and

themes of moral justice. According to Gates and Lemke, her fiction affirms that African Americans have "another kind of knowledge" that cannot be dismissed as superstition or inferiority. "Drenched in Light" illustrates the recognition by white audiences that black culture has something unique that is precious to life. While this idea is something of a commonplace today in the mainstream consumption of black music and art, "Drenched in Light" expresses that first acknowledgment of new respect for the "New Negro" of the Harlem Renaissance.

Source: Susan K. Andersen, Critical Essay on "Drenched in Light," in *Short Stories for Students*, Gale, Cengage Learning, 2016.

Wilfred D. Samuels

In the following excerpt, Samuels explains how Hurston shows stereotypical male and female behavior in "Drenched in Light."

. . . Hurston's narrator offers what the author takes to be conventional: a faithful representation of male and female behavior. The dreams of men, the narrator maintains, remain remote because men often complacently respond

> LIKE FREDERICK DOUGLASS, WHO RESOLVES NOT TO BE BROKEN BY THE WHIPPING FORCED ON HIM BY THE SLAVE BREAKER, MR. COVEY, ISIS IS EMPOWERED IN THE END BY HER REJECTION OF THE DEMEANING ABUSE SHE SUFFERS AT THE HANDS OF HER GRANDMOTHER."

to them; they even procrastinate. According to the narrator, men seldom journey to the horizon to explore the possibilities that may lie ahead. Consequently, on the one hand, men's lives are static, lacking ebullience, and are not infused with reality. Women, on the other hand, assume agency and existential responsibility for the outcome of their lives. They convert their dreams into "the truth," that is, into *their* reality, and consequently arrive at a greater sense of authentic existence.

More than a decade before Hurston's narrator offers this profound observation and unsettling pronouncement, the protagonists of her first two stories validate them. John Redding, the daydreaming protagonist of "John Redding Goes to Sea," and Isis Watts, the joyful protagonist of "Drenched in Light," both create, during their childhood, fantasy worlds in which they envision traveling to the horizon and beyond. However, John never gets beyond the borders of his vivid imagination, although he lives a mere three hundred feet from the St. John River. As a child, John "loved to wander down to the water's edge, and, casting in dry twigs, watch them sail away down stream to Jacksonville, the sea, the wide world and . . . [he] wanted to follow them." Like his twigs, which get tangled in the weeds, John does not go out to sea.

At first his mother forbids it, despite the support and encouragement he gets from his understanding father. He later marries, only to become "home-tied" to a wife who, like his mother, cannot support his desire to "go roving about the world for a spell." John is left to "saunter out to the gate to gaze wistfully down the white dusty road; or to wander again to the

river as he had done in childhood." In the end, he drowns while helping to fortify a bridge during a storm. When John's body is found, his distraught father refuses to have it retrieved from the river. He explains, "Leave my boy go on. Doan' stop 'im. Doan' bring 'im back . . . . He wants tuh go. Ah'm happy 'cause dis mawnin' mah boy is goin' to sea, *he's goin' to sea*." In his death, John finally realized his dream of going to sea.

Unlike John, and despite an overbearing grandmother who believes in not sparing the rod while spoiling the child, Isis epitomizes an untrammeled spirit that marches to the beat of her own drum. Her womanist behavior wins her such labels as "limb of Satan," "lil' hasion," and "hellion." At 11 years of age, she is a dancing banshee who must be reprimanded and reminded to "put yo' knees together" and behave like a lady. Like John Redding, however, Isis becomes various personages through her vivid imagination, which also takes her to the "horizon, for she still believed that to be [the] land's end."

Drawn by the sounding brass and tinkling cymbal of a carnival marching band, the fluid and joy-filled Isis instinctively bolts out of her grandmother's circumscribing gate, dancing, imitating the dignity and grace of a Spanish dancer and creatively costuming herself with her grandmother's new red-and-white tablecloth for her shawl, a daisy thrust behind her ear.

> The Grand Exalted Ruler [of the sponsoring Grand Order of Odd Fellows] rose to speak; the band was hushed, but Isis danced on, the crowd clapping their hands for her. No one listened to the Exalted one, for little by little the multitude had surrounded the brown dancer.

Not surprisingly, Isis's exhilaration is quelled only by her grandmother, whose appearance signifies yet another whipping to the gifted and life-filled child. Deciding to commit suicide rather than submit to her grandmother's abuse any longer, Isis is rescued by an older white couple who identify her as their "little gypsy." They invite her to travel with them to their destination, the Park Hotel, located a short distance up the road from her grandmother's house. Although Isis readily agrees, her grandmother thwarts her plans once again, describing her as "de wustest lil' limb dat ever drawed bref." However, the grandmother is easily muted by the white lady, who gives her five dollars to replace her now-ruined tablecloth, which is apparently more valuable to her than her granddaughter. The grandmother allows Isis to escort the couple, realizing a profit of four dollars for her shawl. The white woman explains, "I want brightness and this Isis is joy itself, why she is drenched in light! . . . I want a little of her sunshine to soak into my soul. I need it."

In "Drenched in Light," Isis, despite her grandmother's suppression, actively seeks to determine the outcome of the events in her life. Although cognizant of the punitive consequences her behavior will inadvertently elicit, she remains uninhibited. Even her decision to commit suicide rather than be whipped once again attests to the empowerment she desires. She yearns to validate her own voice and maintain and exercise control over her own body. Like Frederick Douglass, who resolves not to be broken by the whipping forced on him by the slave breaker, Mr. Covey, Isis is empowered in the end by her rejection of the demeaning abuse she suffers at the hands of her grandmother.

In contrast, John Redding submits to defeat, admitting to being beaten by both mother and wife. John remains a passive dreamer. He tells his father, "Oh, yes, I'm a dreamer . . . . I have such wonderfully complete dreams . . . . They never come true." Consequently, John remains "soil lying helpless to move" himself, like the unyielding soil in which Claudia and Frieda plant marigold seeds in Morrison's *The Bluest Eye*. Song-filled Isis, on the other hand, erupts with the energy released by fulfilled plowed lands in Jean Toomer's *Cane*. John's father, Alfred, concedes as he laments, "Oh, yes, my boy, some ships get tangled in the weeds."

However, Alfred takes a giant step beyond the sentimental, landing in the midst of the argument that will occupy Hurston's many narrators and characters, when he offers a different reason for John's quandary: the fundamental and complex issue of proprietorship. He tells his wife, Stella:

> Yas, dat's all you wimmen study 'bout—settlin' some man. You takes all de get-up out of 'em. Jes' let uh fellah mak uh motion lak gettin' somewhere, an' some 'oman'll begin tuh hollah, "Stop theah! where's you goin'? Don't fuhgit you b'longs tuh me."

Thus, in his near-misogynistic view Alfred sees and defines Stella, and all women, as emasculating agents who in attempting to own and stabilize men—making them homebodies—prevent them from exercising what he presumes to be an almost instinctive independent mobility. Hurston's reversal is indeed noteworthy. Ironically, Alfred, in claiming that "dat's all you wimmen study 'bout," accuses Stella of behaving like men. This bent toward ownership is generally associated with masculine behavior, as is ascertainable from the behavior of Logan Killicks and Jody Starks, Janie's first and second husbands respectively in *Their Eyes Were Watching God*. Whereas Logan tells Janie, "You ain't got no particular place. It's wherever Ah need yuh," Jody declares that Janie is "uh woman and her place is in . . . [the] home." Certainly these men claim the prerogative of owning "their" women like they own their land or dry-goods store. When Jody explains the role he envisions for Janie, he makes this quite clear: "[M]ah wife don't know nothin' 'bout speechmakin'. Ah never married her for nothin' lak dat." Jody appropriates Janie's voice as he relegates her to the domestic place he has determined she should occupy.

This is what makes Isis such a significant first character for Hurston. Isis, though a child, flaunts a "magic and feistiness" generally associated with untrammeled black male behavior. She yearns for what Morrison describes as a form of male prerogative and privilege of being "free"—"not free in the legal sense, but free in his head." Isis, like the Janie who eventually reclaims her voice, is not to be domesticated in the final analysis; each must adhere to the imperative of pulling in her own horizon—of calling in her soul to come and see. This feat is not only physically emancipatory but, perhaps more important, results in spiritual transformation. As argued by Lloyd Brown, who finds similarities between Hurston's ideas and the philosophical analysis Simone de Beauvior offers in *The Second Sex*, both Hurston and de Beauvior conclude that "it is a female trait . . . to use dreams as a means of transcending rather than resigning to reality." Dreams allow the "imprisoned woman to transform her prison into a heaven of glory, her servitude into sovereign liberty." What remains problematic, however, is yet another reversal. In "John Redding Goes to Sea" father and son are imprisoned by women; Isis's jailor, like Janie's guardian, is none other than her grandmother, a woman.

Robert Bone describes "Drenched in Light" as the story of "the portrait of the artist as a young girl." It clearly resonates with Hurston's own quest, which she seems to verify in *Dust Tracks*:

> I kept on probing to know . . . . I had a stifled longing. I used to climb to the top of one of the huge chinaberry trees which guarded our front gate, *and look over the world*. The most interesting thing I saw was the horizon . . . . It grew upon me that I ought to walk out to the horizon and see what the end of the world was like. (italics added)

Like Isis and Janie, Hurston had discovered, at an early age, the importance of not only exploring the horizon beyond one's gate but doing so in a manner that leads to personal liberation. She desires to "look *over* the world," to gaze above and beyond, to exceed the limited space with which she has been provided. Only then, it seems, can she become the art and the artist, the very clay she uses to mold and shape her own life . . . .

Source: Wilfred D. Samuels, "The Light at Daybreak: Heterosexual Relationships in Hurston's Short Stories," in *Critical Essays on Zora Neale Hurston*, edited by Gloria L. Cronin, G. K. Hall, 1998, pp. 241–244.

Lillie P. Howard

In the following excerpt, Howard characterizes "Drenched in Light" as partly autobiographical.

According to Robert Bone (*Down Home*, 1975), "the Afro-American short story entered an authentic local-color phase in the 1920's . . . . Abandoning their former hopes of cultural assimilation, black writers began to place a premium on being different . . . to celebrate those differences." Not only were "the lives of the black masses accepted as a legitimate subject for the first time," but more importantly, "their speech was perceived as a powerful expression of ethnicity" instead of "a badge of social inferiority." Zora Neale Hurston was very much a part of this movement to validate and authenticate the black folk experience.

Storytelling was an integral part of life in Hurston's Eatonville. The men—women were not allowed to participate—often held "lying" sessions, "straining against each other in telling folk tales. God, Devil, Brer Rabbit, Brer Fox, Sis Cat, Brer Bear, Lion, Tiger, Buzzard, and all the wood folk walked and talked like natural men." Zora imbibed this tradition, stored it in her memory banks and withdrew

> THOUGH CHILDREN APPEAR IN OTHER HURSTON WORKS, THIS IS THE ONLY WORK IN WHICH A CHILD FIGURES SIGNIFICANTLY IN THE PLOT. THE WORK IS FILLED WITH A CHILD'S LAUGHTER, IMAGINATION, AND ENERGY."

a bit at a time to entertain people and to start her own literary career.

Almost all of Hurston's writings reflect her immersion in black folk life which, as is apparent from *Dust Tracks on a Road* and *Mules and Men*, she both lived and studied. Her short works and most of her novels are all set in southern black communities, sometimes actually identified as Eatonville, in Florida—"the roosting place of Hurston's imagination." Anticipating Ralph Ellison's prescription for folklore, they reflect specific forms of humanity "found in those communities offering drawings of the group's character. [They] preserve mainly those situations which have repeated themselves again and again in the history of any given group; [they] describe those rites, manners, customs, and so forth, which insure the good life, or destroy it, and [they] describe those boundaries of feeling, thought and action which that particular group has found to be the limitation of the human condition. [They] project this wisdom in symbols which express the group's will to survive; [they] embody those values by which the group lives and dies. [And although sometimes] these drawings may be crude, they are nonetheless profound in that they represent the group's attempt to humanize the world."

In December 1924 Hurston launched her literary career with the publication of her first professional work, a short story, "Drenched in Light." She was in school at Howard University at the time and had submitted the story to the Urban League's magazine, *Opportunity: A Journal of Negro Life*, when the editor, Charles S. Johnson, requested material. Johnson was searching for material that would exemplify the "New Negro" philosophy that Locke would soon espouse in *The New Negro*. "New Negro" philosophy held that Blacks were full human beings (not three-quarters, as had been commonly argued), thinking persons filled with self-respect and self-dependence in contrast to the shuffling, "Old Negro" often caricatured and stereotyped in literature. Blacks now shared a common consciousness which would give rise to the black affirmation and exuberance of the Harlem Renaissance. Zora was a natural contributor, being the product of the nurturing, self-sufficient, racially proud, all-black community of Eatonville.

Johnson liked "Drenched in Light" because in expressing "New Negro" thoughts it celebrated blackness. Johnson was so effusive in his praise of the story that Hurston submitted "Spunk" which was published in June, 1925, and which Alain Locke included in *The New Negro* (1925); along with "Spunk," Zora sent a play, *Color Struck*, which was later reworked and published in Wallace Thurman's *Fire!!* By this time, Zora herself was in New York, having arrived the first week of January 1925 with "1.50 in her purse, no job, no friends, but a lot of hope."

II "DRENCHED IN LIGHT"

. . . "Drenched in Light," Hurston's first contribution to the black literary and cultural awakening called the Harlem Renaissance, is "a portrait of the artist as a young girl." The subject is Isis Watts, a free-spirited eleven-year-old black girl, filled with imagination, energy, love, and vitality. Secure in self, Isis bustles with pride, talent, and self-confidence as she searches for self-actualization. Unfortunately, she is stifled and limited by the restrictions imposed by her provincial grandmother.

The story is set in Florida, and focuses upon a day in the life of Isis. From sunup to sundown, the impish Isis romps with the dogs, turns somersaults, dances, perches upon the gatepost in front of her home, races up and down the road to Orlando "hailing gleefully all travelers," begging rides in cars and winning her way into the hearts of "everybody in the country." Typically, she gets into all kinds of mischief, even attempting at one point to shave her grandmother's beard ("No ladies don't weah no whiskers if they kin help it. But Gran'ma gittin' ole an' she doan know how to shave like me.") while the old lady sleeps. When the outside world fails to amuse, Isis turns inward to her vivid imagination for entertainment. She wears "trailing robes, golden slippers with blue bottons," rides "white horses with flaring pink nostrils to the horizon," pictures herself "gazing over the edge of the world into the abyss." She is busy making the most out of life, much to the chagrin of her grandmother.

The only conflict in the story is caused by Grandma Potts, an old, traditional parent who sanctions corporal punishment for anything which goes against her seasoned principles. She thus metes out punishment for such crimes as sitting with the knees separated ("settin' brazen" she called it), whistling, playing with boys, or crossing legs. Obviously there is no peace for Isis when Grandma is around.

Grandma Potts seems to be the natural product of the slavery tradition. When Helen, for instance, a white stranger who has been captivated by a gypsy dance Isis performed at a local barbeque, her grandma's new red tablecloth draped about her shoulder as a Spanish shawl, requests that Isis be allowed to accompany her to her hotel to dance for her, grandma, bowing and dissembling, happily turns her granddaughter over to the woman. Because the grandmother does not really know Helen, the reader at first assumes that she allows Isis to accompany her only because the woman is white, a member of that ruling class whom grandma has grown accustomed to obliging without question. When we are told that the grandmother is secretly bursting with pride, however, we begin to suspect that she understands and appreciates Isis's worth and only keeps up a stern front to keep the girl in line, to perhaps break her spirit (as Zora's father tried to do hers) so that she will not fall victim to a world which had little tolerance for spirited blacks. On the other hand, perhaps the grandmother was pleased because the "missus" was pleased. Isis, though ignorant of even the name of her patron, only knows that someone finally appreciates her talents, and she is happy to be rescued from a grandmother who stifles her.

Helen is sincere in her feelings for Isis; she longs for Isis's vitality. Since life has gone out of her own existence, she is determined—like the whites who hungrily flocked to Harlem during the 1920s to be liberated by the "exotic primitive"—to snatch excitement from other sources. She determines to absorb Isis's light, to live delightfully, vicariously, through Isis. When one of her male companions sarcastically suggests that Isis has adopted her as a surrogate mother, Helen is quick to reply: "Oh, I hope so, Harry . . . I want a little of her sunshine to soak into my soul. I need it."

The story is partly autobiographical and anticipates what is to come in the later works. Potts was Hurston's mother's maiden name; Isis's village seems to be Hurston's own Eatonville, and some of the events of the story are also found in autobiographical pieces written by Hurston. In a May 1928 article in the *World Tomorrow*, "How It Feels to Be Colored Me," for instance, Hurston says that as a child "my favorite place was atop the gate-post. Proscenium box for a born first-nighter. Not only did I enjoy the show, but I didn't mind the actors knowing that I liked it . . . . I'd wave at them and when they returned my salute, I would say something like this: 'Howdy-do-well-I-thank-you-where-you-goin'?'" Sometimes she would "go a piece of the way" with them. White travelers liked to hear her "speak pieces" and sing and dance and would pay her for doing those things, unaware that "I wanted to do them so much that I needed bribing to stop." And she wrote in her autobiography (1942) that, as a child, "I used to take a seat on the top of the gate-post and watch the world go by . . . . Often the white travelers would hail me, but more often I hailed them, and asked, 'Don't you want me to go a piece of the way with you?'" It never occurred to either Hurston or her fictional counterpart, Isis, that they were doing anything out of the ordinary. Proud and content in their blackness each wanted to improve others by bestowing themselves and their talents upon them. Robert Hemenway calls the story Hurston's "Manifesto of selfhood, an affirmation of her origins." Indeed it is that, and more. By cherishing and immortalizing her memories in fiction, Hurston was seeing to it that an important part of black tradition—the folkways of her people—was not lost. The Potts family again appears in *Jonah's Gourd Vine* (1934), and *Dust Tracks on a Road* (1942); Isis, as a character, appears in *Jonah's Gourd Vine*, another autobiographical piece, as the daughter of Lucy Ann Potts and John Pearson; Isis's yearning for a vital life at eleven anticipates Janie's yearning at sixteen in *Their Eyes Were Watching God*. Like Isis, Janie is a sensitive, poetic soul in a basically unfeeling prosaic world. The dialect, infused with striking metaphors and sayings, is used to advantage in all of Hurston's novels, and the white person as deliverer or benefactor appears in *Dust Tracks* (where Hurston herself often benefits from the largesse of whites), *Jonah*, and *Their Eyes Were Watching God*.

"Drenched in Light" is undeniably Isis Potts's story. She is the heroine and subject of most of the action. Though children appear in other Hurston works, this is the only work in which a child figures significantly in the plot. The work is filled with a child's laughter, imagination, and energy. It possesses a child's charm, though it discusses more adult themes—the lasting effects of slavery and the boredom and emptiness of white adult life—in passing . . . .

Source: Lillie P. Howard, "The Early Works," in *Zora Neale Hurston*, Twayne, 1980, pp. 56–57, 59–62.

SOURCES

Bloom, Harold, Introduction to *Modern Critical Views: Zora Neale Hurston*, edited by Harold Bloom, Chelsea House, 1986, pp. 3–4.

Gates, Henry Louis, Jr., Preface to *Zora Neale Hurston: Critical Perspectives Past and Present*, edited by Henry Louis Gates Jr. and K. A. Appiah, Amistad, 1993, p. xii.

Gates, Henry Louis, Jr., and Sieglinde Lemke, Introduction to *The Complete Stories: Zora Neale Hurston*, HarperCollins, 1995, x–xiii, xvii.

Hemenway, Robert E., "That Which the Soul Lives By," in *Modern Critical Views: Zora Neale Hurston*, edited by Harold Bloom, Chelsea House, 1986, p. 91; originally published in *Mules and Men*, by Zora Neale Hurston, Indiana University Press, 1978.

Hibben, Sheila, Review of *Their Eyes Were Watching God*, in *Zora Neale Hurston: Critical Perspectives Past and Present*, edited by Henry Louis Gates Jr. and K. A. Appiah, Amistad, 1993, p. 21; originally published in *New York Herald Tribune Weekly Book Review*, September 26, 1937.

Hughes, Langston, "A Perfect Book of Entertainment in Herself," in *Modern Critical Views: Zora Neale Hurston*, edited by Harold Bloom, Chelsea House, 1986, p. 14; originally published in *The Big Sea*, 1940.

Hurst, Fannie, "A Personality Sketch," in *Modern Critical Views: Zora Neale Hurston*, edited by Harold Bloom, Chelsea House, 1986, p. 23; originally published in *Yale University Library Gazette*, Vol. 35, No. 1, July 1960.

Hurston, Zora Neale, "Drenched in Light," in *The Complete Stories: Zora Neale Hurston*, HarperCollins, 1995, pp. 17–25.

————, *Dust Tracks on a Road: An Autobiography*, 2nd ed., edited by Robert E. Hemenway, University of Illinois Press, 1984, pp. 1, 21, 40, 56, 147, 235, 237.

————, "How It Feels to Be Colored Me," in *I Love Myself When I Am Laughing and Then Again When I Am Looking Mean and Impressive: A Zora Neale Hurston Reader*, edited by Alice Walker, Feminist Press, 1979, pp. 153, 155.

Jones, Sharon L., *Critical Companion to Zora Neale Hurston*, Facts on File, Infobase Publishing, 2009, pp. 3–13, 25–27, 225–31, 236–39, 241–42.

Locke, Alain, Review of *Their Eyes Were Watching God*, in *Zora Neale Hurston: Critical Perspectives Past and Present*, edited by Henry Louis Gates Jr. and K. A. Appiah, Amistad, 1993, p. 18; originally published in *Opportunity*, June 1, 1938.

Tompkins, Lucille, Review of *Their Eyes Were Watching God*, in *Zora Neale Hurston: Critical Perspectives Past and Present*, edited by Henry Louis Gates Jr. and K. A. Appiah, Amistad, 1993, p. 18; originally published in *New York Times Book Review*, September 26, 1937.

Walker, Alice, "A Cautionary Tale and a Partisan View," in *Modern Critical Views: Zora Neale Hurston*, edited by Harold Bloom, Chelsea House, 1986, p. 64; originally published in *Zora Neale Hurston: A Literary Biography*, by Robert E. Hemenway, University of Illinois Press, 1980.

Wintz, Cary D., "Introduction: A Historical Overview of the Harlem Renaissance," in *The Harlem Renaissance: An Anthology*, edited by Cary D. Wintz, Brandywine Press, 2003, p. 3.

Wright, Richard, Review of *Their Eyes Were Watching God*, in *Zora Neale Hurston: Critical Perspectives Past and Present*, edited by Henry Louis Gates Jr. and K. A. Appiah, Amistad, 1993, p. 16; originally published in *New Masses*, October 5, 1937.

FURTHER READING

Bernard, Emily, *Carl Van Vechten and the Harlem Renaissance: A Portrait in Black and White*, Yale University Press, 2012.

> White photographer and music critic Carl Van Vechten was an important impetus for the Harlem Renaissance. His photographs of the writers and musicians of that period are legendary. He photographed Hurston and furthered her career.

Hemenway, Robert E., *Zora Neale Hurston: A Literary Biography*, University of Illinois Press, 1980.

> This groundbreaking biography has historical background on the Harlem Renaissance with an extensive bibliography and foreword by Alice Walker.

Hurston, Zora Neal, *Zora Neale Hurston: Folklore, Memoirs and Other Writings*, The Library of America, 1995.

> This volume includes Hurston's nonfiction prose works. The first volume of this series includes her fiction.

Lewis, David L., *When Harlem Was in Vogue*, Knopf, 1981

> This Pulitzer Prize–winning historian gives an overview of the founders of the Harlem Renaissance.

Williams, Vernon J., Jr., *Rethinking Race: Franz Boas and His Contemporaries*, The University Press of Kentucky, 1996.

> The anthropological work of Franz Boas on race at Columbia during the Harlem Renaissance had a great influence on W. E. B. Du Bois and Booker T. Washington, as well as Hurston. Boas believed in the equality of the races and disproved the old ideas of white supremacy based on biological factors. Hurston measured skulls on the streets of Harlem as part of her field work for this important research.

SUGGESTED SEARCH TERMS

Zora Neale Hurston

Drenched in Light AND Hurston

Harlem Renaissance

Eatonville, Florida

African American literature

short story

black dialect

Alice Walker AND Zora Neale Hurston

Langston Hughes AND Zora Neale Hurston

The Enormous Radio

JOHN CHEEVER

1947

"The Enormous Radio" is an early work by John Cheever, who is recognized as a twentieth-century master of the American short story. The story concerns a middle-class couple with two children living in Manhattan in the prosperous years after World War II. Their comfortable but boring life is disrupted when their radio, their main source of entertainment (as it was for most people at the time), breaks down. The replacement they buy has a unique, unexplainable property: it lets them hear what is happening in their neighbors' apartments. As Irene Westcott finds herself hooked on the dramas of the sad, desperate lives other people hide from the outside world, she becomes increasingly withdrawn and depressed, while her husband, Jim, becomes more and more impatient with her. Page by page, the Westcotts become more like the unhappy people they initially tuned in to listen to for entertainment.

Cheever seldom used supernatural premises like this one in his writing. He is remembered as a writer who did the most to capture the uneasiness lying under the surface of America's prosperous years and who recognized that the suburban middle-class experience was more complex than people living it would ever admit. Like most of his stories, "The Enormous Radio" was first published in the *New Yorker*, one of the country's most prestigious magazines in the mid-twentieth century. After its debut on May 17, 1947, the story was republished in

American author John Cheever is sometimes called "the Chekhov of the suburbs."

The Enormous Radio and Other Stories, Cheever's 1953 collection, which was the version used in preparing this entry, and again in his hugely influential, career-spanning collection, *The Stories of John Cheever*, published in 1978.

AUTHOR BIOGRAPHY

Cheever was born in Quincy, Massachusetts, on May 27, 1912. His family lineage spanned back to Ezekiel Cheever, who arrived in New England in 1630. In 1927, his father left John, his mother, and his older brother, Frederick, forcing the family to scrape to get by. The older Cheever owned a shoe factory but lost it during the Great Depression and eventually died impoverished.

Cheever attended Thayer Academy in South Braintree, Massachusetts, but quit or was expelled before graduating. In 1930, his short story "Expelled" was published by the *New Republic*—it was his first published story. With the help of *New Republic* editor Malcolm Cowley, Cheever made a name for himself in the publishing world. He moved to New York City, where he lived in a cheap apartment in Greenwich Village for a time. In 1935, he published the story "Brooklyn Rooming House" in the *New Yorker*, beginning a working relationship with the magazine that would last four decades. He would eventually publish over a hundred and twenty stories there.

In 1938, Cheever moved to Washington, D.C., to work as a junior editor for the Federal Writers' Project, a government program to employ writers during the Depression, but he stayed for only six months before returning to New York. That year, Cheever met Mary Winternitz, who worked as a secretary at his agent's office. They married in 1942 and stayed wed for the rest of Cheever's life. Also in 1942, Cheever, then twenty-nine, enlisted in the army. He was trained as a rifleman but was given publicity work to capitalize on his writing talent.

Cheever's first collection of short stories, *The Way Some People Live*, was published to acclaim in 1943. By 1953, when *The Enormous Radio and Other Stories* was published, he had moved his family out of New York to suburban Scarborough, in Westchester County, just as the Westcotts in this story aspire to do. He continued publishing stories in the *New Yorker*, though in his later years he would go increasingly to publications like *Esquire* and *Playboy* that paid better. He also published novels, though infrequently: *The Wapshot Chronicles* in 1957 won the National Book Award and was followed by *The Wapshot Scandal* in 1964, *Bullet Park* in 1969, and *Falconer* in 1977. (The latter novel, set in a prison, was based on Cheever's time as a writing teacher in Ossening Prison—famous as "Sing Sing.")

Cheever's literary output was marred by excessive alcoholism throughout the 1960s and 1970s, though his reputation was cemented in 1978 with the publication of the career-spanning *The Stories of John Cheever*. It won him the Pulitzer Prize and the National Book Critics' Circle Award in 1979. He also won the National Book Award for its paperback edition in 1981.

Cheever died of cancer at home in Ossening on June 18, 1982, at four o'clock in the afternoon, surrounded by his wife and three children.

PLOT SUMMARY

"The Enormous Radio" begins with a description of the life and aspirations of Jim and Irene Westcott. They live comfortably on the prestigious Upper East Side of Manhattan, near (though, the story specifically points out, not in) the Sutton Place neighborhood. They are cultured, attending the theater often. They have two children and aspire to living in the affluent suburb of Westchester someday. They have been married for nine years.

The Westcotts live in a social situation that values conformity, but they have one trait that makes them stand out from their neighbors: they both love music. In the late 1940s, when this story was written, music appreciation often entailed listening to classical music concerts broadcast on the radio, which is something the Westcotts do often. When their radio breaks down during a Sunday afternoon concert broadcast, Jim tries to fix it, but nothing helps. The next day, he phones Irene to say that he has bought a new radio, but he does not give her any details about it, hoping for it to be a surprise.

The radio is delivered on Tuesday. Irene is disappointed, because she finds it too large and too ugly to fit into her tastefully decorated living room. The first time she turns it on, she is surprised and discomforted by how loud the radio is. In the evening, after Emma, the Westcotts' maid, has taken the children away to give them baths, Irene explores the radio a little more. At first, she is impressed with its tone, but after listening for a while she starts to hear other sounds in addition to the music being broadcast. She hears an elevator, then doorbells and mixers. She comes to realize that these are sounds of the building she lives in. Unable to control the radio's technical abilities, she turns it off.

Jim comes home that night and has a similar experience with the radio: the programs he wants to listen to are interrupted by sounds of electrical appliances being operated in other apartments. The next day, he arranges to have a repair man come and fix it.

The next afternoon, Irene returns home from lunch with friends and finds that the repairman has been there and worked on the radio. Now, the music the radio plays sounds faint and scratchy, but she hears background voices. She

turns the radio off when her children arrive home from school. During dinner, she and Jim listen to the radio and clearly hear a man and a woman having a conversation. At first, they think it must be a play being broadcast, as was common at the time, though they hear the man swearing in a way that broadcasters would never allow. When Jim turns the station, they pick up another conversation. On a third station, they hear a woman reciting a nursery rhyme; Irene recognizes the voice as belonging to Miss Armstrong, the nurse who watches the Sweeney children in apartment 17-B.

With the realization that they are listening to people in their own building, Irene fears that the radio will broadcast their conversations to other apartments as well. Jim goes to the speaker and talks into it, with no response.

With a turn of the dial, they hear a cocktail party in another apartment. Soon Irene, who views this ability to eavesdrop as a wonderful development, asks Jim to try finding specific apartments. The radio plays only random conversations. Some of the conversations are arguments, but some are just uninteresting discussions. They listen until midnight and then go to bed.

In the middle of the night, Irene gets up because her son wants a glass of water. She goes to the living room and turns on the radio. It plays a sad conversation between a man and a woman; the woman is depressed because her doctor's treatments do not help, but they cannot afford for her to see a new doctor.

The next morning, as soon as the children and Jim are off to school and work, Irene goes back to the radio to listen to the neighbors. She hears people's very private moments: "demonstrations of indigestion, carnal love, abysmal vanity, faith, and despair." She realizes that her own life is much simpler than the private lives of her neighbors. Later, when she goes to a lunch date, she looks at the women in the elevator of her building, wondering which woman was involved in which conversation she overheard. She thinks about the friend she is lunching with, wondering what secrets this woman is hiding. Instead of going shopping, as planned, she makes up an excuse and races home to listen to the radio again, eavesdropping on other lunch conversations after abandoning her own. As the afternoon passes and evening approaches, she listens in on cocktail parties and arguments and financial schemes by people who appear respectable in public.

The Westcotts go to dinner at the home of friends that night. Jim notices that Irene is acting oddly. On the walk over, she gives money to a Salvation Army collector with a strangely blissful look on her face. She is rude to their hostess. She stares silently at other guests. That night, after Jim has fallen asleep, she goes to the living room to listen to the radio again.

When Jim comes home the following evening, Irene meets him at the door, frantic. She insists that he must go up to apartment 16-C, where Mr. Osborn is beating Mrs. Osborn. Jim tells her to quit listening to the radio if it makes her feel so bad. He becomes upset that she is spending so much time listening in on the neighbors, but his anger panics Irene, who has been listening to angry people arguing all day. "Life is too terrible, too sordid and awful," she tells him. "But we've never been like that, have we, darling? Have we?" He tries to assure her, but he is tired and impatient with her.

The next day, Jim has another repair man come to work on the radio. After he leaves, it plays music and not sounds from the neighboring apartments.

When Jim comes home, he mentions the huge price he paid for the radio, four hundred dollars. He also says that he has seen overdue bills for clothes that Irene bought. His business is not doing well, and he is concerned that she is spending too freely. He admits that he is not doing as well in life as he had hoped he would, and he does not think that things will be getting any better.

As Jim describes his dissatisfaction with his life, Irene interrupts him. She is afraid that people will hear them through the radio. Her fear makes Jim angry and impatient. He thinks she is being hypocritical by acting good, and he lists bad things she has done in her life, from taking the jewelry from her mother's estate, which she did not share with her sister, to some vague terrible thing she did to someone named Grace Howland to an abortion she once had.

Irene goes to the radio, planning to shut it off before people can hear what Jim is saying, but she pauses. She wants to hear pleasant, calming things from the radio. It gives no sign of broadcasting the conversation from their apartment, and it does not play anything being discussed in any other apartment either. Instead, it plays only the news and weather broadcast.

CHARACTERS

Miss Armstrong

Miss Armstrong is the nursemaid for the Sweeneys, another couple in the Westcotts' building. She is from England and has a distinctive accent. Of all voices that the Westcotts hear through their radio, it is hers that they hear most often. In several scenes, they hear her reciting or singing English nursery rhymes between the sounds of couples like themselves arguing; her calm voice casts an eerie tone over the entire situation.

Emma

Emma is the Westcotts' maid. She also cares for their children, feeding them, bathing them, and putting them to bed before Jim comes home on some nights. She has a room in the basement of the building that she goes to when she is off duty.

Mr. and Mrs. Osborn

After listening to the radio for some time, Irene Westcott becomes emotionally involved in the lives of some of her neighbors. The Osborns are one couple she knows by name. When she hears Mr. Osborn abusing his wife, she tells Jim to go to their apartment, 16-C, four floors above their own, to intercede. Jim, however, refuses to become involved in the neighbors' stories. Instead of helping Mrs. Osborn, he suggests that Irene stop listening to the radio.

Irene Westcott

Irene is the main character in the story. She is a housewife who has a maid to do the household chores and to watch over her two children, feeding and bathing them. Irene has a lot of time on her hands, which she uses to focus on the lives of her neighbors while Jim, her husband, is off to work.

Irene is a perfectionist about her home and is therefore disappointed when she sees the new radio. It is big and ugly, and she finds it an intrusion into her decor. The same perfectionism extends to her taste in music, and when she hears the quality of the sound produced by the radio, she is impressed enough to accept it into her home.

Listening to the neighbors affects Irene's personality. At first, she is delighted at this newfound ability. "Isn't this too divine?" she asks Jim as she comes to accept the new reality of her situation. She becomes addicted to eavesdropping, cancelling social engagements in order to get home and listen.

Quickly, though, she finds the sadness of other people's hidden lives weighing her down. When she does go out, she finds a Salvation Army band soliciting donations on a street corner to be emotionally uplifting. At a party among her peers she is withdrawn, knowing that they might all have secret lives that they hide from her. Eventually, she is frightened when she hears a neighbor physically abusing his wife and she can do nothing to help. She

becomes so self-conscious that an argument with Jim terrifies her: she worries that they are as bad as the people she hears over the radio seem to be. She begs Jim for assurance that they are happy together, and he gives it, though half-heartedly.

Later, Irene and Jim have an argument about money, which the story indicates might simply be the kind of discussion they would commonly have. Irene worries that the radio can hear them arguing, and Jim turns on her, pointing out the bad things she has done in her life, from cheating her sister over their mother's estate to an illegal abortion she once had. Irene's casual handling of money and the way it upsets Jim indicates that the radio is not the cause of the problems in their marriage but is rather a catalyst that makes them admit their problems.

Jim Westcott

Jim Westcott is a thirty-seven-year-old businessman with a wife and two children, living in a twelfth-floor apartment on Manhattan's Upper East Side. He works hard, arriving home late each night, after his children are already in bed. He gives his wife a weekly allowance to pay for household needs and personal items. He tries to keep quiet about his money troubles, but by the end of the story, he is just too infuriated by Irene's behavior to keep silent.

Jim tries to be a good husband. He and Irene both enjoy classical music, and so they go to concerts and listen to music on the radio. When their radio breaks, Jim goes out the very next day and buys a new one. Irene thinks the new radio is big and ugly, but Jim was not looking at its style when he bought it; he was listening to its sound. When Irene notices problems with the radio, Jim makes arrangements for a repair man to come and fix it.

Jim does notice the sounds of the neighbors' apartments being played through the Westcotts' new radio, but he does not pay much attention to it: he is busy every day at his job and comes home tired. He does not have time to focus on what other people are doing, the way Irene does.

He is protective of his wife. When he notices that listening to the radio is upsetting Irene, he advises her to turn it off rather than worrying herself about it. Later, he admits the pressure mounting on him from trying to keep the family living the life they are used to. His concerns about finances lead Jim to an even greater confession: he feels as if he has become a failure, as if he has not accomplished what he wanted to do in his life and he never will succeed.

In the end, Jim's insecurity about himself drives him to lash out at Irene. Her concerns about what people will think of them have now come into the privacy of the Westcotts' home; Jim takes this to be a sign of insincerity. He calls her out for the bad things she has done in the past. He may be shouting at her to shock her back into reality, but he may also be letting out anger that he has bottled up within himself.

The Westcott Children

The Westcotts have two young children. They are never mentioned by name or even by gender. They are often in the care of the maid when their parents are dining together or going out or when Irene is out in the afternoon for social engagements.

THEMES

Materialism

In the first paragraph of this story, Cheever establishes that Jim and Irene Westcott are average but aspire to more. They want to move to an affluent suburb, and Irene wears a coat that is not an expensive mink fur but looks like one. They think of themselves as being set apart from their friends and neighbors by their interest in music.

When their radio breaks down, Jim arranges to replace it with one that is big and expensive. Making such an extravagant purchase is a sign of their love of music, but also of his materialistic worldview. Several times he mentions the radio's cost—four hundred dollars. His keen awareness of its cost indicates that the radio is one aspect of the Westcotts' materialistic view of the world.

Social Class

The Westcotts are very conscious of their social position. They live in a society where different social classes interact, with maids and nannies and elevator men on hand to serve men and women who work for people who, in turn, are even wealthier. They do not talk about social class, but they think about it constantly. For

Irene, with her refined tastes, the stranger whistling "The Missouri Waltz" is a reminder of the poverty surrounding them, since Missouri, a rural state, is considered much poorer and less cultured than their Manhattan world: this popular music is the opposite of the social status of the Westcotts' aspirations.

When they hear a woman telling her maid to be careful about doling out the expensive liquor or a couple deciding to not tell a houseguest that she has lost a precious jewel so that they can make a profit selling it, the Westcotts laugh at these signs of hidden selfishness. By the end of the story, however, readers find out that the Westcotts are no better than the people they look down upon, having stolen from their family while settling Irene's mother's estate. They look at the handyman's drunkenness and Mr. Osborn's violence toward his wife as being low class, but in the end, they are drinking and fighting themselves. This story is all about the gradual chipping away of their social pretension.

Repression

One of the central themes of this story is that the Westcotts have repressed their awareness of their lives in order to remain calm and comfortable. At the beginning of the story, they think of themselves as being a cultured, upwardly mobile, happy couple. Their love of what the story calls "serious music" makes them feel a little smarter than their neighbors. In order to maintain that illusion, Jim spends more on a new radio than he can comfortably afford.

When the Westcotts start hearing what the lives of their neighbors are really like, the repressed self-awareness continues. Irene becomes so distracted by what is going on in other apartments that she cannot think of anything else. At first, she, and most likely the readers as well, think that what is upsetting her is her deep sense of humanity, which makes her sympathetic toward people like Mrs. Osborn, the victim of domestic violence; Mrs. Melville, who has heart trouble; Mr. Hendricks, who is faced with unemployment; and the unnamed girl who plays "The Missouri Waltz," who is promiscuous. In the end, though, Jim Westcott loses patience with his wife's sadness, and in his frustration, he ends up shouting at Irene, listing some of the terrible things she has done in her life.

TOPICS FOR FURTHER STUDY

- Some people say that social media and surveillance cameras have made the very concept of privacy a thing of the past. Rewrite this story with the main characters finding out about their neighbors through contemporary means of wireless communication. Make the shock that the central characters feel about their look into others' lives believable.

- Any response to Mr. Osborn's violence against his wife in this story carries risk: ignoring it endangers Mrs. Osborn, confronting Mr. Osborn might put the person speaking to him in danger, calling the authorities risks exposure of the radio or charges of violation of privacy, and so on In small groups, discuss with other members of your class the right way to deal with this unexpected and unwanted information. Compare each group's decision with the others' and, through discussion, determine the best response.

- As a fiction writer, Cheever is allowed to make up any circumstances he can think of, as long as he can make them believable in the context of his story. Would wireless technology such as WiFi or Bluetooth make it any easier for a contemporary writer to convince readers that someone might snoop into a neighbor's life without meaning to? Research how wireless technology works and present a multimedia explanation to your class using PowerPoint or your own videos to show why such a situation is or is not credible.

- Early in their adventure, and then frequently throughout it, Irene and Jim hear a nanny singing nursery rhymes to the children she is watching. Go online to find recordings of a few nursery rhymes or children's songs from at least three cultures around the world that are different than your own. Write an essay describing the defining qualities of each and an explanation of which one you think would be most comforting to a child who is not from that culture.

- The mood that Cheever captures in this book, contrasting external normalcy with the shame one hides behind closed doors, is similar to that in Lauren Baratz-Logsted's young-adult novel *Secrets of My Suburban Life*. Read this serio-comic novel, first published in 2008, about a teen girl whose father moves her out of New York after her mother is crushed by a pallet full of *Harry Potter* books, only to find danger and conspiracy in the suburbs of Connecticut. Present your observations as a dual-column chart, listing the aspects of Irene Westcott from Cheever's story that you think could help the novel's protagonist, Ren, with her situation, and the aspects of Ren's personality that you think Irene could use to face her circumstances. Explain each element you identify.

- J. D. Salinger was a famous literary figure who, like Cheever, published short stories in the *New Yorker* in the 1940s and 1950s. While Cheever's characters were almost always adults, Salinger often wrote about intelligent young people living in Manhattan. Read Salinger's story "Just Before the War with the Eskimos," published in the *New Yorker* the year after "The Enormous Radio." Keep track of the ways in which the teens of the story struggle to be honest and authentic in circumstances similar to those that Cheever's characters live in. Write a one-act radio play with characters from Salinger's story reacting to the same situation Cheever presents, of a radio that lets people know other people's business. Include a paragraph that explains why the perspectives of young people and middle-aged people would be different in the postwar years from those held now.

Although at first excited by what she hears over the radio, Irene quickly becomes upset by the sordid things her neighbors are doing.

(© Stokkete / ShutterStock.com)

It turns out that her life is just as sordid as the lives that she has been listening to: the only significant difference is that she allowed her mind to block out all of the sadness and criminality and promiscuity that she herself has engaged in. Repression has played a big role in her view of herself, but the radio's magic properties have made her see her true self.

Insight

The high point of the story is when Irene Westcott comes to see herself as she truly is. The radio is not a window into the lives of other people; it is a mirror that lets her see her own life in a way that she has not been able to see it up to that point. In the last scene, it is Jim who shouts at her to remind her of the terrible things she has done in the past, but his rage alone is not what leads her to her particular insight.

His shouting is just a continuation of the sad dramas of humanity that the radio has been presenting to Irene all along. When Jim raises his voice and tries to hurt her feelings, Irene can see that their marriage is clearly just as bad as the marriages of the hateful, arguing people that surround them.

Irene's insight is not spelled out explicitly in the story. Instead, it is implied in the way that she turns to the radio for comfort. She cannot argue against Jim's accusations because she knows that they are true, so she tries to forget about herself and her own past behavior. Listening to the lives of others has given her a way to stop thinking about her own life, but now that the radio is "fixed" and will not bring her the lives of others, she is left with an unpleasant awareness of who she really is. In the story's final paragraph, she listens numbly to random news announcements that have little to do with her, unable to find any interest in them because she cannot stop thinking about the terrible person she now knows herself to be.

STYLE

Third-Person Limited Point of View

Most fiction is told either from the first-person point of view, with the narrator speaking of him- or herself as "I," or from the third-person point of view, with the narrator referring to all of the characters as "she" or "he." When the story is told in the third person, it is frequently told from the third-person "limited" perspective. This means that the third-person narrator cannot wander from one character's view of the world to another but is instead limited to the insights and experiences that a single character would have.

In "The Enormous Radio," the first two paragraphs set the situation in the Westcott home with information that could be experienced by either Jim or Irene. After that, however, most of the action is filtered to readers through Irene's point of view. She is the one who listens to the radio when Jim is not home, and the story follows her when she goes out to lunch. The story reports on what she is doing throughout the days that the radio is there. For the most part, readers experience this strange phenomenon in the way that Irene experiences it, and they follow her emotions about what is going on.

In a few places, the story drifts over to Jim's point of view. When Jim comes home tired, the narrator tells us that this is how he feels, instead of saying that Irene thinks he looks tired. When the Westcotts go to a dinner party, it is Jim's opinion, not Irene's, that Irene has been rude to the hostess. These few passes into Jim's mind are infrequent, though: overall, the narrative is limited specifically to Irene's point of view.

Magical Realism

Magical realism is a style of fiction that reached the height of its popularity in the late 1960s and is frequently associated with Nobel Prize winner Gabriel García Márquez. As its name implies, it combines two contrasting elements: realism, indicating a focus on objective reality, and magic, which is usually thought to describe things that are beyond reality. Because fiction writers have the ability to bend reality with the ways they describe the world, they are able to present situations that are both realistic and magical at the same time.

The world of "The Enormous Radio" is realistic in its setting and characters. In the years after World War II, there were hundreds of thousands, if not millions, of families like the Westcotts: young executives and their wives who were raising children with the hope of social advancement. Into this realistic scenario, Cheever has added the magical element of a radio that can broadcast people's private lives. He does not offer his readers any explanation for why the radio can do this. Readers are simply expected to believe that the radio can do this in the same way that they are asked to believe that it is made of gumwood or that the women who ride the elevator with Irene wear furs and hats with flowers in them: these details are just as made up as a radio with supernatural powers is made up, but readers of fiction are used to imagining a world from the details the author has given them. Magical realism exploits the readers' willingness to believe in made-up details by slipping in a few details that are not generally believed possible in our common understanding of reality.

HISTORICAL CONTEXT

The New Yorker *Style*

Throughout his long writing career, Cheever was usually associated in the public's mind with the *New Yorker*, the magazine where he published the overwhelming majority of his short stories. His elevated grammar and his witty observations about behavior in and around New York were considered a perfect fit for the magazine's urbane style.

The *New Yorker* was founded in 1925 by Harold Ross, a veteran newspaper writer who had reported for over twenty-three newspapers over the course of his long career, and Raoul Fleischmann, a millionaire related to the Fleischmann's yeast empire. Both men were affiliated, through their participation in a weekly poker game, with members of the Algonquin Round Table, a legendary gathering of writers who lunched together at the Algonquin Hotel in New York. Membership in the Algonquin Round Table was not formal, and at various times such literary giants as Franklin P. Adams, Dorothy Parker, Ring Lardner, Robert Benchley, Edna Ferber, Robert Sherwood, and George S. Kaufman might show up to swap stories and jokes with their peers. From his association with them, Ross had the idea to start a publication that would reflect their kind of sophistication and cleverness in print. The first edition of the *New Yorker* hit the stands on February 21, 1925.

The magazine's distinctive fiction style was developed under its longtime fiction editor, William Maxwell, who served in that post from 1936 to 1975. Maxwell, a novelist and short-story writer himself, created bonds with some of the country's greatest writers, whose works he edited and published. In addition to Cheever, whom he counted as a close friend, he is also considered instrumental in the careers of such midcentury literary juggernauts as Vladimir Nabakov, John Updike, J. D. Salinger, Mavis Gallant, and Shirley Hazzard.

The distinctive *New Yorker* style of fiction, beginning in the 1930s, was a response to the types of plot- and sentiment-heavy stories that were common in popular magazine fiction of the time. *New Yorker* stories were driven by character, not plot. They made heavy use of dialogue and focused on scenarios of daily life. The *New Yorker* was aimed at an educated audience: the ideal reader was not necessarily

COMPARE
&
CONTRAST

- **1947:** Married women most often stay at home, tending house while their husbands go off to earn enough money to support the entire family. Only 31.5 percent of American women are in the workforce, according to the National Bureau of Economic Research.

  Today: Most families depend on two incomes. Married couples with children supported by only the husband's income account for only 7 percent of the population.

- **1947:** Radio is the dominant form of in-home entertainment. Television is just becoming familiar to Americans; there are not even television broadcasts that go out to the whole country yet.

  Today: Many people do not rely on broadcast programs for entertainment. We can pick what shows we want to watch via the Internet and watch them when we want to watch them.

- **1947:** Having lived through the Great Depression, which lasted from 1929 to around the time World War II started in 1939, many businessmen feel financially insecure, knowing that losing their jobs could drive their families into poverty.

  Today: Many Americans are still recovering financially from the Great Recession of 2007–2009, which led to a long-lasting downward shift in employment opportunities and recession across the globe following decades of prosperity.

- **1947:** Radios are run by large glass tubes, requiring them to be big pieces of furniture, like the one described in the story. The transistor is developed this year, which will allow the invention and production of portable radios in the mid-1950s.

  Today: Microchips allow for radio receivers as small as a pen or a postage stamp. They are usually included with more popular portable devices like MP3 players or phones.

- **1947:** Fans of classical music can often find a symphony or opera on their radios.

  Today: The number of over-the-air classical music stations has dwindled, but satellite radio and subscription services like Spotify and Pandora cater to enthusiasts of all styles of music.

- **1947:** For much of the country, life in New York City reflects the ideal of wealth, elegance, and culture.

  Today: New York and its surrounding areas still serve as a magnet for the arts, but the ease of air travel and movement of goods, as well as the information accessible through the Internet, make it possible to live a rich cultural life from anywhere in the world.

- **1947:** Many middle-class families have domestic servants, such as maids or cooks. A driving force for this is the racial segregation legally enforced in the South and often upheld in the North, driving down wages for minorities.

  Today: Only the rich can afford full-time domestic workers, but corporate cleaning services make maid services available to many American households for a few hours a week.

---

a college graduate but rather someone who appreciated intellect over cheap thrills. In addition, there were several elements that Maxwell and Ross would not permit in the magazine, including lagging pace, ambiguity, and sexual situations.

Irene sees the light from the radio dial as "malevolent." (© Denise Lett | ShutterStock.com)

The strong hand the editors asserted over their writers, as well as the magazine's prestige, meant that many authors with clear, distinctive artistic voices came out sounding similar to all of the other authors the magazine printed. For Cheever, this was not a problem, since time has shown his style and sensibilities to be those that the magazine favored anyway.

Postwar New York

When World War II ended in 1945, the United States was poised for tremendous economic growth. It had finally rebounded from the Great Depression with the boom in manufacturing required by the war effort, starting before America's entry into the war in 1941 and continuing all throughout the fighting. America was the biggest developed economic power in the world to not endure fighting on its soil, leaving the country's growing economic structure intact.

New York City was the center of this economic boom. It was the base for over forty thousand factories in the area that were responsible for millions of jobs, but, even more important, it was the base of much of the country's commerce: over a fifth of all American commercial transactions were run through New York. It was also the world's largest and busiest port city, handling 40 percent of the country's water freight, and the home city to many of the nation's largest companies, including IBM, General Electric, RCA, Standard Oil, and U.S. Steel, all companies that were viewed during the postwar years as the backbone of the American economy.

New York's status as an international economic center was reinforced in 1946 when the United Nations chose the city for the site of their new world headquarters. Although New York had always been one of America's most ethnically diverse cities, being the port that millions of immigrants came through when entering the country, the new UN headquarters confirmed that it was not just a city of families seeking new lives but of diplomats as well, working toward world peace and cooperation just months after the most wide-reaching global confrontation in history.

With the money and rich mix of cultures enforcing the city's cosmopolitan traditions, New York became, in the later 1940s, a center for the arts. Most of the country's publishing houses were there, as were the magazines, important galleries, radio networks, and networks for television, which grew at a tremendous rate once the war ended. Artists of all kinds came to New York for national and international attention. For people like the Westcotts, who were not in the arts but were affluent and upwardly mobile, the richness of culture around them was sure to affect the way they viewed themselves.

CRITICAL OVERVIEW

In the late 1940s and early 1950s, when this story was published (first in the *New Yorker* and then in the collection of stories bearing its title), Cheever's literary reputation was not yet clear. This was only his second collection of stories, and he had not yet published a novel. His style fit the *New Yorker* well, a fact that tended to polarize critics: those who looked at the magazine as one of the country's standard-bearers of artistic integrity tended to view Cheever's writing as being superb, while those who saw the magazine as being rigid and old-fashioned and formulaic saw those elements in his fiction as well.

In an essay titled "John Cheever: Critical Reception" published in a 2012 collection called *Critical Insights: John Cheever*, Francis J. Bosha noted that when *The Enormous Radio and Other Stories* was published "critics gave it a lukewarm reception." He quoted a range of critical observations, from one who found that he captured the *New Yorker*'s "brilliant, bitter essence" to the author who dismissed Cheever as "not a writer of any great talent." Taliaferro Boatwright's review of *The Enormous Radio and Other Stories* in the *New York Herald Tribune Book Review*, quoted in *The Critical Response to John Cheever*, was not at all shy about praising his talent, ending with the notation that "John Cheever's competence and craftsmanship are a constant delight."

As Cheever's career continued throughout the decades, from one story collection to the next, critics came to see him as the quintessential American writer, capturing a particular mood of upper-middle-class postwar America.

By the time *The Stories of John Cheever* was published in 1978, it was praised as a major literary achievement, a crowning achievement by one of the great artists of the late twentieth century. At that time, critics frequently included the story "The Enormous Radio" as one of Cheever's best, though there were still varying opinions.

Bruce Bawer, in an overview called "Underachiever?" in the *Hudson Review*, listed "The Enormous Radio" among six stories that he called Cheever's best: "They give the impression of being genuinely inspired, alive, deeply felt; they are pithy, subtle, rich." He contrasts them with the majority of Cheever's stories, which, Bawer believes, "feel contrived and quickly blend together in one's mind." On the other hand, Keith Cushman's review of *The Stories of John Cheever* for the *Library Journal* notes that some of the works in it—"even so famous a story as the 'Enormous Radio'—are rather contrived."

Though there is still contention about the merit of this story, critics tend to tilt toward the opinion posed by Patrick Meanor, who, in his 1995 study *John Cheever Revisited*, cited it as one of two early stories that "proved that his work merited comparison with the very greatest short-story writers in modern American literature, such as Fitzgerald, Hemingway, Faulkner, and Sherwood Anderson." Meanor also quotes critic James O'Hara as identifying "The Enormous Radio" as "perhaps the most imaginative story Cheever ever wrote."

CRITICISM

David Kelly

Kelly is an instructor of creative writing and literature. In the following essay, he examines the way that Cheever used the two main characters in "The Enormous Radio" to represent the conflicting values of society and the individual.

Throughout his long career, Cheever wrote frequently and beautifully about the vanity that plagued the upwardly mobile—not those born to wealth and not those who could never hope be financially or socially successful, but smart young executives and their fashion-conscious wives (following the rigid gender roles of the day) who came bursting out of World War II with jobs and opportunities for even greater jobs

WHAT DO I READ NEXT?

- Although Cheever was best known for his short stories, he did write a few novels. His first novel, *The Wapshot Chronicle*, published in 1957, won the National Book Award. It portrays an eccentric Massachusetts family and shows Cheever's gift for sly humor and his thorough understanding of life in New England in the mid-twentieth century. This book has never been out of print and is available now in a 2011 Harper Perennial Classic edition.

- First-time novelist Mark Haddon's best-selling young-adult novel *The Curious Incident of the Dog in the Night-Time* (2004) is a detective story at heart, about a fifteen-year-old with autism who can memorize an unbelievable number of facts and statistics but has little understanding of human emotion. After being initially considered a suspect, he takes it upon himself to investigate the death of a neighbor's dog and, like the people in "The Enormous Radio," he learns more about the people he lives among than he knows how to handle. This book was published by Vintage.

- Author Irwin Shaw was another writer who, like Cheever, published short fiction regularly in the *New Yorker*. Shaw's short story "The Girls in Their Summer Dresses," published in the magazine on February 4, 1939, captures the mood of big-city life at that time. The story is about a young married couple: the man frequently comments on the beautiful women in the city as the woman slowly realizes that he will never be able to remain fully faithful to her. This story is considered a modern classic and is available in many anthologies as well as the Shaw collection *Short Stories:*

Five Decades, published by University of Chicago Press in 2000.

- James Alan McPherson is an African American author whose skill as a short-story writer is often compared to Cheever's. One of his best stories is "The Story of a Scar"—it starts out with two patients, one black and one white, sitting in a doctor's waiting room holding an idle discussion to kill time, but, like "The Enormous Radio," McPherson's story meticulously peels away the coating of self-esteem a person wraps around himself. This story is included in McPherson's collection *Elbow Room*, winner of the 1978 Pulitzer Prize for Fiction.

- As a writer, Cheever was meticulous with his word choices, and the lives of his characters were frequently similar to his own. Readers can learn much about his thought process by looking at his correspondence with friends and family, collected in *The Letters of John Cheever*, a 1988 book published by Simon and Schuster. It was compiled and edited by the author's son, Benjamin Cheever.

- Cheever talked quite candidly about life and art and his ideas about how the two fit together in his interview with Annette Grant for the *Paris Review*. The interview was originally published in *Writers at Work: The Paris Review Interviews* in 1981, which is now out of print, but it has been reprinted in several places, including *Critical Essays on John Cheever*, edited by R. G. Collins, and *Conversations with John Cheever*, edited by Cheever biographer Scott Donaldson.

---

and who fooled themselves into thinking that they deserved their success. Their mistake was to assume that their affluent lifestyles were not just based on luck, connections, and a willingness to go along with the pretense that the constraints of social order are all fair and good.

> " THE STORY IS IRENE'S BUT WOULD HAVE MUCH LESS OF AN EFFECT IF JIM WERE NOT A STRONG PRESENCE. CHEEVER USES THE COUPLE LIKE A PAIR OF LAND SURVEYORS—ONE HOLDS STILL WHILE THE OTHER WALKS BACKWARD, AWAY FROM THE STARTING POINT, TO MEASURE THE CONTOURS OF THE LAND BETWEEN THEM."

In story after story, Cheever characters try and fail to grow as humans, stopped in their tracks because they take their social positions for granted. In "The Country Husband," for instance, a man survives a plane crash, and his new thirst for life puts him on a path of behaviors that offend his suburbanite friends and relatives: he ends up seeing a therapist, looking for a way to make himself ordinary once more. Neddy Merrill in "The Swimmer," one of Cheever's most famous stories, goes on an epic odyssey to swim across his county, from one neighbor's in-ground pool to another, only to find out that epic odysseys are for fools: he ends up shivering in his swimming trunks, stripped of pretensions and vulnerable to the truth that he is not a great, or even a good, man. In "The Five-Forty-Eight" a man who has had an affair with a worker in his office has tried to shake her and return to his stable suburban life as if they had never met, but she follows him onto the train home and holds a gun on him until, groveling in the parking lot of his suburban stop, he realizes the impact of what he has done to her by treating her like something disposable.

These and other Cheever stories all share a similar worldview, though they are not, in any sense, redundant. Each conveys a familiar sadness while dealing with its own situation. A fine example of this is how Cheever treats the idea of being faced with one's own pettiness in "The Enormous Radio," an earlier story from the 1940s. In this story, it is a couple, not just a man, whose delusions crumble. The woman, Irene Westcott, is actually the one to see through her own pretensions by the end of the story, while her husband, Jim Westcott, holds

fast to the idea of sticking with the status quo in spite of the misery it causes them.

The way that Jim's and Irene's perspectives pull apart over the course of this story allows Cheever the opportunity to look at the conflict between the individual and contemporary society in a much richer, more three-dimensional way than he could with just one protagonist. In doing this, the story captures one of the most prevalent issues bothering artists throughout the first half of the twentieth century: the question of conformity.

At the start of the story, in the introductory paragraphs, the Westcotts are of one mind. They aspire to the same social advancement; though likely neither would admit so out loud, they both feel slightly superior to their friends and neighbors because of their shared appreciation of classical music. The future looks bright for Jim and Irene. Cheever implies that the reason for this is that, like most couples, they support each other's ambitions.

However, this couple is made of individuals. They are bound to have different experiences, and those experiences are bound to shape their different ways of looking at the world. It does not take long for the story to focus on Irene. She is the one left at home with only the radio to keep her company—the breakdown of their old radio and the arrival of the replacement affect her life more deeply than they do Jim's.

Cheever does not explain that the radio's breakdown is a bigger disappointment to Irene than to Jim. He does not have to. The circumstances speak for themselves. Jim leaves the house each morning to go to his job: it is Irene who counts on the radio for company when her children are at school and her husband is at work. If their reliance on it were equal, Cheever would say that Jim promised to buy a new radio for "them"—instead, he says Jim is buying it for Irene.

Assuming that she relies on radio listening for company, the magic of the new radio, which plays conversations from other apartments in her building, serves that function almost too well. Like the soap operas that filled up daytime radio programming when this story was published and that were beginning to offer companionship to isolated housewives via the television, the lives of her neighbors give Irene a chance to participate in the drama of the human race in a way that she cannot do while passively listening to music. This involvement comes at a price, however. At first, she hears the soothing tones of a young woman singing nursery rhymes, which, once she gets over the weirdness of what is happening, proves to be a pleasant experience. Eventually, though, she is exposed to the depravity of her neighbors—the drinking, the lies, the sexual infidelity, and the petty crimes. This culminates in the need to act, to break down the invisible walls between them, when Irene hears a man hitting his wife.

At this point, she tries to draw Jim into her experience—a violent man could not be confronted by a woman at that time, but only by another man—but Jim is not having any of it. He stands back from her stories about the neighbors, even in this case of a man beating a woman. Attempting to draw Irene back into the cocoon of smug aloofness they had to themselves at the beginning of the story, Jim pelts her with a list of all of the dirty secrets she herself has hidden from the world.

The story is Irene's but would have much less of an effect if Jim were not a strong presence. Cheever uses the couple like a pair of land surveyors—one holds still while the other walks backward, away from the starting point, to measure the contours of the land between them. Jim is the one who stands still.

Readers are given very little direct insight into Jim Westcott's thoughts. Indeed, he does not really appear to have any thoughts. The one idea associated with him that is repeated in the story is that he is tired when he gets home. This makes sense at first. When he comes home one day, his wife is complaining that the expensive radio he bought does not work right. Wearily he realizes that, even though she has not asked him to, it is his job to arrange to have the radio fixed, a day after paying an uncomfortable amount for it. After that, Irene's reports on the neighbors' lives become, for Jim, a tedious mixture of a woman repeating the thrilling plot twists of her favorite soap opera and a nosy woman reporting neighborhood gossip. Saying that Jim is tired is actually a nearly polite way of telling Irene that he believes he has more important things to worry about. He is not flinging the relative value of his job versus her home tending in Irene's face, but it is clearly

what makes Jim so uninterested in the radio's amazing power.

The proof of this is in the story's climax, in which Jim hits Irene with two lines of attack. One is a personal assault, a list of horrible things that he knows she has done, which were apparently never talked about—an abortion, cheating her own sister on an inheritance, and so on. In Jim's mind, this assault is intended as shock therapy, to make Irene agree that even good people like her have sins that they would prefer nobody, especially not some stranger, discuss. Forcing someone to see reality by offending her is a suspicious move, however, and readers have to wonder what else is motivating Jim. It could be resentment at Irene because she has the luxury of worrying about things that he has no time for.

Despite what he himself might believe, though, Jim's behavior toward his wife turns out to be driven not by world-weariness but by fear. He explains at the end of the story the sort of existential dread that frequently propels Cheever's characters, particularly the ones in the stories mentioned earlier: he had assumed that he would advance socially, but time's passage has forced him to face the opposite—social stagnation or even dwindling prestige. One gets the sense that anything Irene would do from this point forward would scare Jim, making him think that she is endangering his social position. In Jim's mind, her concern about the neighbors is erratic behavior, which makes the Westcotts socially vulnerable.

A story with just one main character has to rely on readers' assumptions about what the world thinks of that character. In a story like that, the author has to present the main character's battling desires: to escape from social constraints or to curl up in the security of social constraints. Cheever's stories often reflect this dynamic, but in "The Enormous Radio" he has the luxury of splitting the attraction and repulsion toward conformity into two different people, Jim and Irene.

It might be the story's conceit that gives Cheever this luxury: he does not have to explain that the characters somehow developed curiosity about their world because Irene and Jim do not choose to look into their neighbors' lives—instead, they have the outside world forced on them. The magical radio forces them each to react, to redefine how they feel about the social

At the end of the story, Irene and Jim have an argument that is just as bad as the things she has overheard on the radio.

(© Darren Baker / ShutterStock.com)

world they have tried to build around themselves. Jim panics about losing his position while Irene panics about having to keep hers. Cheever often poked holes in the fabric of society, and the Westcotts' opposing reactions to their situation reflect the ambivalence that is common in his fiction.

Source: David Kelly, Critical Essay on "The Enormous Radio," in *Short Stories for Students*, Gale, Cengage Learning, 2016.

James E. O'Hara

In the following excerpt, O'Hara characterizes "The Enormous Radio" as a story without precedent in Cheever's earlier stories.

In the late thirties and early forties, the world edged closer to war, and Cheever's short stories increasingly reflected the gradual shift in national mood from malaise to apprehensiveness. His work also continued to display an

uncanny ability to discover the hidden significance in seemingly unpromising material—everything from childhood dancing class to racetrack romance. In the two years before the United States entered the war, he published twenty-seven stories, making this his most prolific period in terms of number of stories produced. His marriage to Mary Winternitz in March of 1941 may have had something to do with this, and with his turning out to be more self-assured as a writer after he entered the service.

With few exceptions, the stories Cheever published between 1935 and early 1942 are coldly detached in tone, as if the teller were curious about his characters and their problems—but nothing more. They are essentially naturalistic reports on biological specimens responding to various stimuli, rather than stories about people told by someone with a human interest in their human spirits. As such they are technically impressive, and magazines like the *New Yorker* were quick to realize that young Cheever's eye for revealing details was as sharp as that of any of its more established writers. Still, readers familiar with his work of the late forties onward, starting with "The Enormous Radio," will sense that something is missing in these earlier stories. The passionate voice of "Expelled" had been muffled, or at least toughened into a flat monotone.

The war would give that voice a deeper modulation and make it more assertive. About three weeks before Cheever was inducted into the army, the *New Yorker* (18 April 1942) published "The Shape of a Night," a story that marks a clear transition from the Depression into the war period for Cheever.

. . . But there is virtually no precedent for the most widely read of Cheever's short stories, a fantastic tale set in a Manhattan apartment. It would be only a slight exaggeration, in fact, to claim that the apartment building in "The Enormous Radio" (1947) is a central character in the story; it is as alive as any of the "real" people in the narrative. The animation of inanimate structures is an ancient literary device, and such writers as Emile Zola had fully explored the thematic possibilities inherent in the technique long before Cheever tried it. Few writers, however, have been able to achieve the intensity of effect that Cheever creates with seeming ease in "The Enormous Radio" by

> "HAVING DRAWN THEM IN THIS FAR, HE COULD NOW COMPEL THEM TO OVERHEAR AN ECLECTIC CATALOG OF HUMAN FOLLY, BY TURNS HUMOROUS AND FRIGHTENING."

blending realism, fantasy, comedy, and pathos. By carefully manipulating these elements into a structure that is larger than the sum of its parts, Cheever first hypnotizes the reader and then illuminates some of the darker regions of the human psyche.

The story's two main characters, Jim and Irene Westcott, are described in the opening lines as "the kind of people who seem to strike that satisfactory average of income, endeavor, and respectability that is reached by the statistical reports in college alumni bulletins." They are outwardly as normal as can be: productive, law-abiding, the parents of two young children. The teller of the story merely hints at a skeptical view of their life-style (Cheever may even be parodying himself) when he records that the Westcotts go to the theater "on an average of 10.3 times a year."

The only significant difference between the Westcotts and other young couples in their set is their interest in serious music. When their old radio suddenly dies in the middle of a Schubert quartet, Jim decides to buy a replacement. This could serve as the stuff of comedy pure and simple, and in fact Cheever would work on scripts for the *Life with Father* television series only a few years later. A less experienced writer might have succumbed to the comic potential of his narrative premise, but Cheever had other intentions.

The Westcotts soon discover that their new radio can garner sounds and conversations from every corner of their building. At first the narrator suggests that this is due to some technical oddity in the radio or the building itself, but it quickly becomes apparent that no "logical" explanation will suffice. The radio tunes in quite accurately on the private lives of the building's tenants. The Westcotts eavesdrop on "a monologue on salmon fishing in Canada,

a bridge game, running comments on home movies of what had apparently been a fortnight at Sea Island, and a bitter family quarrel about an overdraft at the bank." For awhile this incredible addition to their home strikes the Westcotts as funny, a source of free entertainment beyond their wildest imagining. But the reference to a family quarrel should warn the reader that the story is not simply a comic sketch. The radio takes on tremendous symbolic importance when we realize that the particular form of voyeurism the Westcotts have succumbed to is essentially no different from the "normal" reader's own, supposedly more respectable vice: looking over the narrator's shoulder into the turmoil of his characters' lives. In this light Cheever, or any good storyteller, is our enormous radio, and by extension we are the Westcotts.

Thus "The Enormous Radio" converts a comic premise into a powerfully enlightening narrative engine. In one brilliant stroke, Cheever had both fully exploited and utterly transcended his own cleverness. More than forty years later the idea seems so obvious, and the writing so effortless, that it is easy for us to make the same mistake that some of Cheever's contemporaries made by overlooking the great advance this story represents for its writer and, I think, for the short story as a narrative form. It is an amazingly compact blend of fantasy and stark realism. In the following excerpt, for example, Cheever manages to move Irene from a restaurant back to her apartment, establish the almost magnetic hold of the radio on her consciousness, reinforce the terrible truthfulness of the radio, and advance the theme of pervasive, inescapable duplicity:

> Irene had two Martinis at lunch, and she looked searchingly at her friend and wondered what her secrets were. They had intended to go shopping after lunch, but Irene excused herself and went home. She told the maid she was not to be disturbed; then she went into the living room, closed the doors, and switched on the radio. She heard, in the course of the afternoon, the halting conversation of a woman entertaining her aunt, the hysterical conclusion of a luncheon party, and a hostess briefing her maid about some cocktail guests. "Don't give the best Scotch to anyone who hasn't white hair," the hostess said. "See if you can get rid of that liver paste before you pass those hot things, and could you lend me five dollars? I want to tip the elevator man."

T. S. Eliot has noted that humankind cannot bear too much reality, but Cheever seems determined to give us a strong dose of it; not the least disturbing aspect of "reality" in this case is the obsessive need of the Westcotts to hear it in such a sneaky fashion.

Cheever had achieved economy of style after his first few stories, but he had rarely demonstrated this kind of smooth, assured balance even in his army stories. Having released himself from his addiction to realism, he was clearly enjoying the full exercise of his talent. How many of his readers had at some time or other wanted to spy on their neighbors? Having drawn them in this far, he could now compel them to overhear an eclectic catalog of human folly, by turns humorous and frightening. We finally share in the psychic pain of the Westcotts when, too late, they realize they have heard too much:

> "Of course we're happy," he said tiredly. He began to surrender his resentment. "Of course we're happy. I'll have that damned radio fixed or taken away tomorrow." He stroked her soft hair. "My poor girl," he said.
>
> "You love me, don't you?" she asked. "And we're not hypercritical or worried about money or dishonest, are we?"
>
> "No, darling," he said.

But the following day, after the radio has been "fixed" and dutifully tunes in classical music, the Westcotts have a terrible argument—about their own problems with money and dishonesty—as the radio news reports disasters from around the globe. In a masterful demonstration of his storytelling art, Cheever has quietly yanked us out of our fascination with his clever story into an awareness of what we should have known all along: all those Westcotts parading up and down the supermarket aisles of America are every bit as normal and abnormal as we are. The story needs no explicitly stated moral; awareness is the beginning of understanding and sympathy for our fellow humans, and in that direction, Cheever knew, lies salvation . . . .

Source: James E. O'Hara, "Breakthroughs," in *John Cheever: A Study of the Short Fiction*, Twayne, 1989, pp. 13, 18–21.

Lynne Waldeland

In the following excerpt, Waldeland praises Cheever's storytelling.

. . . "The Enormous Radio" is probably the best story in the collection. It, too, is based on a fantastic premise, this one that a radio can mysteriously tune in the goings-on in other apartments in the building where the protagonists, Jim and Irene Westcott, live. The couple is portrayed as average in aspiration and achievement: "They were the parents of two young children, they had been married nine years, they lived on the twelfth floor of an apartment house near Sutton Place, they went to the theatre on an average of 10.3 times a year, and they hoped someday to live in Westchester." The only difference in their lives from those around them—and they conceal this difference—is that they are passionately interested in classical music. Ironically, it is their one unique trait that leads to the point of the story; Jim buys Irene a fancy new radio when their old one breaks during a Schubert quartet. The new radio is depicted ominously—much as Joan Harris was in "Torch Song"; it has an ugly cabinet and stands among Irene's other furnishings "like an intruder." When turned on, the complex dials glow with "a malevolent green light"; it comes to life with a violent roar of sound. Irene is made uneasy by this acquisition. As the couple listens to the new radio, it not only plays music but picks up a variety of discordant sounds—telephones, electric razors, cooking appliances. Finally, it transmits conversations in other apartments; Jim and Irene overhear marital quarrels, nurses reading bedtime stories, tales of financial woes, revelations of dishonesty. After prudently ascertaining that *they* cannot be heard, Jim and Irene settle down for a fascinating evening of eavesdropping. Irene even gets up in the middle of the night to listen some more. But in a twist which is reminiscent of Hawthorne, Irene comes to be haunted by all she has heard and begins to scan the faces of people she meets in the elevator for signs of the dishevelment she has learned exists in their private lives. Finally, distraught at these revelations of hidden secrets, she begs her husband to assure her that *their* lives are not like those around them. The radio, however, which brought the knowledge of discord into their lives, has the effect of stripping away the veneer that kept the same sort of discord at bay in their lives. Jim, worried about money, accuses his wife of improvidence and then, in an angry

> THE RADIO, HOWEVER, WHICH BROUGHT THE KNOWLEDGE OF DISCORD INTO THEIR LIVES, HAS THE EFFECT OF STRIPPING AWAY THE VENEER THAT KEPT THE SAME SORT OF DISCORD AT BAY IN THEIR LIVES."

outburst, reveals the hidden secrets of their lives just as the radio has done for the neighbors':

> Why are you so Christly all of a sudden? What's turned you overnight into a convent girl? You stole your mother's jewelry before they probated her will. You never gave your sister a cent of that money that was intended for her—not even when she needed it. You made Grace Howland's life miserable, and where was all your piety and your virtue when you went to that abortionist? . . .

Desperately trying to shut out his words, Irene turns on the radio, hoping to hear the Sweeneys' nurse crooning a comforting lullaby. But, as her husband continues to shout, the voice on the radio, "suave and noncommittal," announces railroad disasters, a fire in a hospital for blind children, the temperature and the humidity. Irene has to face her own moment of self-awareness and guilt with no comfort— only a sense of the giddy motions of the world between the cataclysmic and the mundane.

This story, with the radio droning on into the distance at the end, has an effective climax and is one of Cheever's most memorable. It has been viewed as a modern version of the Edenic myth with the radio acting as the serpent to Irene's Eve. More helpfully, in my view, the story has been compared to Hawthorne's "Young Goodman Brown." In this story, the plausibility of the radio's strange power is as insignificant in the end as is the issue in "Young Goodman Brown" of whether or not there really was a devil's bonfire in the forest. What is important is the effect upon the characters of what *they* believe has happened. Irene's preternatural sense of evil and unhappiness, following the radio's revelations, reminds us not only of Young Goodman Brown sensing evil everywhere in his community after his traumatic

night but also of Hester Prynne, through her own suffering, becoming sensitive to the signs of hidden guilt and suffering in the faces she meets in *The Scarlet Letter*. One critic observes that "in Cheever's darker tales objects often seem to overwhelm the characters' sense of well-being, as if these people were living in a strange and alien world of obstacles and mysteriously laid traps." Such a situation certainly informs "The Enormous Radio"; the effects of the radio overwhelm the characters' carefully constructed sense that they are not like other people, that they are more loving, less guilty. The story's narrative pace is fast, allowing for little slippage in the necessary suspension of disbelief that must take place in the reader for this story to work. And the abruptness of the ending is perfect, leaving us with the image of Irene standing, self-esteem in shreds, before the mysterious radio which, having destroyed her illusions, now perversely gives the news.

Most of the other stories in this collection are in some way concerned with people who do not quite belong in the world in which they are trying to live. In "The Pot of Gold" Ralph and Laura Whittemore are innocents in pursuit of wealth and success in the business world whose quest is doomed to repeated failure because of their incredibly bad luck and a degree of naiveté. In "O City of Broken Dreams" the cause of the characters' dislocation is more obvious. Evarts Malloy and his family have come from an Indiana small town to Manhattan on the strength of one act of a folksy play which Evarts has written and in which a down-on-his-luck producer has shown some interest. Duped during their stay by everyone from the hotel bellboy to several shyster agents and producers, they finally leave town, but, Cheever hints, probably not to return home where their stories might not be believed, but perhaps to remain on the train all the way to California, made permanent wanderers by their disillusionment. In "The Children" a couple, Victor and Theresa MacKenzie, spend their entire lives being surrogate children to a series of lonely but often cruel rich people. They are the sort of persons whom one automatically asks to mix the drinks or run errands; they do not, however, feel put upon but, rather, fulfilled by such exploitation and at home whenever they find themselves taken in by people who will use them in this way. "The Hartleys" are a couple who seem happy on the surface as they arrive at a ski resort with their daughter. However, we learn that they have been separated and that now, together again, they are engaged in frantically revisiting places where they had been happy in the past to try to recapture the feelings of that other time. The futility of this search turns to tragedy; their daughter is killed in an accident on the ski tow, a hostage to their ill-fated attempt to reestablish a meaningful relationship by reliving the past. "The Summer Farmer" involves a man who commutes on the weekends from his job in the city to a small farm, a place he loves immoderately. The story revolves around a conflict between this man, Paul Hollis, and Kasiak, a local farmer whom Paul hires to help with heavy chores and who taunts Paul about his outsider status by predicting that he will not return the following year. The tension between them is great enough so that when Paul's children's pet rabbits are poisoned, he accuses Kasiak of having left poison in the rabbit hutch with an eye toward hurting the children. It turns out that Paul's wife left the poison there the previous summer. Paul has to rush to catch the train back to the city after this trying weekend.

> No harm had been done, he thought. "No harm," he said under his breath as he swung his suitcase onto the rack—a man of forty with signs of mortality in a tremor of his right hand, signs of obsoleteness in his confused frown, a summer farmer with blistered hands, a sunburn, and lame shoulders, so visibly shaken by some recent loss of principle that it would have been noticed by a stranger across the aisle.

The point of the story seems to be the difficulty of understanding and participating in an alternative way of life, a difficulty underlined by Paul's hypersensitivity to the hired man's prediction that he won't be back and by his sense of dislocation at the end of the story.

One story in the volume foreshadows the suburban stories which will dominate Cheever's next collection. "The Cure," set in an unnamed suburb, involves a couple whose marriage is rocky. The narrator's wife has just left him for what may be the final time; their previous separations have been serious, one ending in divorce and then remarriage. The narrator, accepting the finality of this last break, prepares himself for living alone, the loss of his house, and other disruptions while his wife and children are away at a summer place. One night a

Peeping Tom comes and watches the narrator through the picture window, a visitation which is repeated several times even after the narrator recognizes the prowler as one of his neighbors. He becomes jumpy alone in the house, a state of mind compounded when a woman who claims to be clairvoyant tells him at a party that she sees a rope around his neck. That night, when the Peeping Tom returns, the narrator concludes that it's because he has some mysterious awareness that he is to witness a hanging. The narrator searches house and garage, finds the only piece of rope on the premises, and burns it. Caught up in visions of ropes, the narrator has an irrational urge the next day in the city to embrace a strange woman he sees on the street, believing that only such an act can save his life. That night, his wife calls, they are reconciled, and, we are told, they've been happy ever since. The Peeping Tom never returns, so that we are tempted to conclude that he was a sort of fortunate visitant, sent in to shock the narrator back to his senses so that he would put forth the effort necessary to make his marriage work. This mixture of everyday details with supernatural occurrences—or at least ominously weighty coincidences—plus the fortuitousness of the ending are qualities that will characterize the stories in Cheever's next collection, *The Housebreaker of Shady Hill*.

The Enormous Radio received mostly favorable reviews when it appeared and set a standard by which Cheever's later stories have often been judged. William Peden in his book on the American short story since 1940 calls it "unquestionably one of the major collections of the period." He identifies the special impact of the stories in these terms: "Beneath the often placid, impeccably drawn surfaces of his stories there is a reservoir of excitement or unrest that is capable of erupting into violence; his well-mannered characters walk a tightrope that at any minute may break; the vast, shining city masks cruelty, injustice, and evil." This explains the effect of stories like "The Enormous Radio," in which the pleasant exterior of a marriage is stripped away, or "The Cure," in which a man who faces a divorce with seeming equanimity suddenly finds himself in a suicidal despair precipitated by random external events. In many of these stories the characters start from a sense of well-being only to have the order of their lives shattered by the sudden intervention of mysterious events over which they have no control; afterwards, they are never again quite as they were. The only area of critical complaint has had to do with the very well-made-ness of some of the stories. Paul Pickrel, in a predominantly favorable review, said: "If one has any criticism of this volume it is that the stories are too uniformly excellent, and of the same kind of excellence—the writing highly finished, the emotions carefully weighted and cunningly deployed, the point carefully made without calling attention to itself." Pickrel and a few other reviewers expressed concern that Cheever might have been developing, through his great mastery of style, into a writer who was more flash than fire, a danger that several of them connect with his association with the *New Yorker*. However, most critics, now and in retrospect, have been impressed with the successful combination of moral thrust and storytelling skill that emerges in this volume and that will continue to dominate Cheever's writing in his first novel, *The Wapshot Chronicle*.

Source: Lynne Waldeland, "'The Enormous Radio': Cheever's Short-Story Craft," in *John Cheever*, Twayne, 1979, pp. 31–36.

SOURCES

Bawer, Bruce, "Underachiever?," in *Hudson Review*, 2010, p. 597.

Boatwright, Taliaferro, "Snapshots in the East Fifties," in *The Critical Response to John Cheever*, edited by Francis J. Bosha, Greenwood Press, 1994, p. 10.

Bosha, Francis J., "John Cheever: Critical Reception," in *Critical Insights: John Cheever*, edited by Robert A. Morace, Salem Press, 2012, p. 90.

Cheever, John, "The Enormous Radio," in *The Enormous Radio and Other Stories*, Funk & Wagnalls, 1953, pp. 169–81.

Collins, R. G., "Cheever, the Man," in *Critical Essays on John Cheever*, G. K. Hall, 1982, pp. 6–8.

Cushman, Keith, Review of *The Stories of John Cheever*, in *Library Journal*, September 15, 1978, p. 1766.

Francis, David R., "Changing Work Behavior of Married Women," National Bureau of Economic Research website, http://www.nber.org/digest/nov05/w11230.html (accessed February 23, 2015).

Kunkel, Thomas, *Genius in Disguise: Harold Ross of the New Yorker*, Random House, 1995, pp. 308–11.

Mahon, Gigi, *The Last Days of the New Yorker*, McGraw Hill Publishing, 1988, pp. 7–17.

Meanor, Patrick, "'Fiction Is Never Crypto-autobiography': The Life of John Cheever," in *John Cheever Revisited*, 1995, Twayne Publishers, pp. 1–27.

———, *John Cheever Revisited*, 1995, Twayne Publishers, p. 52.

"New York after WWII," American Experience: TVs Most Watched History Series, Corporation for Public Broadcasting, http://www.pbs.org/wgbh/americanexperience/features/general-article/newyork-postwar/ (accessed February 20, 2015)

"Traditional Families Account for Only 7 Percent of U.S. Households," Population Reference Bureau, 2015, http://www.prb.org/Publications/Articles/2003/TraditionalFamiliesAccountforOnly7PercentofUSHouseholds.aspx (accessed February 23, 2015).

FURTHER READING

Bailey, Blake, *Cheever: A Life*, Vintage Press, 2009.
> This huge book is considered the definitive biography of the author: it is carefully, exhaustively researched and is forthright about many aspects of Cheever's life, such as his alcoholism and his homosexuality, that he tried to keep hidden from the public.

Boddy, Kasia, "The *New Yorker* Short Story at Midcentury," in *The American Short Story Since 1950*, Edinburgh University Press, 2010, pp. 37–54.
> Nestled into the middle of Boddy's literary history of that specific, short time period, this chapter recognizes the importance of Cheever's place in literature and also the passing, temporary nature of a style that once seemed like the apex of literary fiction.

Josyph, Peter, "The John Cheever Story: A Talk with Richard Selzer," in *Twentieth Century Literature*, Fall 1993, pp. 335–38.
> Selzer, himself a noted novelist, gives a close observer's perspective of Cheever, telling the interviewer of a time when he saved Cheever's life and the cold, almost bitter reaction he received for it.

"The Metamorphosis of John Cheever," in *Time*, March 27, 1964, pp. 89–90.
> As an unsigned article in a popular magazine, this short work is not worth much for academic research, but it does provide readers a sense of what those outside the literary world thought of Cheever at a time when he was respected and frequently published but was not the literary giant he is considered today.

Morace, Robert A., "From Parallels to Paradise: The Lyrical Structure of Cheever's Fiction," in *Twentieth Century Literature*, Winter 1989, pp. 502–28.
> This long scholarly article barely mentions "The Enormous Radio." Instead, it provides

a look at Cheever's writing style as it evolved over the course of his life, offering readers who are new to Cheever a good idea of what was so special about his unique talent.

Yagoda, Bill, *About Town: The New Yorker and the World It Made*, Scribner, 2000.

Cheever naturally has a significant role in the story of the *New Yorker*'s rise to prominence, because he was such a valued writer for them and presented a clear example of what came to be called "the *New Yorker* style." In this book, Yagoda looks down at that style and its writers, casting them as boring, but his explanation of the history and the evolution of the style is clear.

SUGGESTED SEARCH TERMS

John Cheever

Cheever AND The Enormous Radio

Cheever AND literary fiction

Cheever AND New Yorker

Cheever AND 1940s

Cheever AND magical realism

American literature AND subject AND radio

The Enormous Radio AND classic short fiction

John Cheever AND Manhattan

The Enormous Radio AND secrets

Eve's Diary

MARK TWAIN

1905

Mark Twain, considered among the greatest American authors, is famous for his trenchant and satirical examination of American culture. In "Eve's Diary" (1905), Twain turns his wit onto the disconnect between modern science and fundamentalist religion that emerged in his lifetime and has since become an increasingly active fault line in American society. He also stakes out his position as a feminist against the misogynist culture of his day. Twain delighted in the hypocrisy displayed in a censorship controversy over the illustrations to the original edition of the story, which scrupulously followed the biblical text in portraying Adam and Eve nude in the Garden of Eden. "Eve's Diary" is available with its companion work, "Extracts from Adam's Diary" (1904), in *The Diaries of Adam and Eve*, published by Fair Oaks Press in 2002.

AUTHOR BIOGRAPHY

Samuel Langhorne Clemens was born on November 30, 1835, in Florida, Missouri. He is better known by his pen name, Mark Twain. He grew up in Hannibal, Missouri, on the Mississippi River, where his father was a judge. After his father died, when Twain was eleven years old, Twain worked at a variety of jobs, including typesetter, and wrote for the *Hannibal*

American writer and humorist Mark Twain
(© Everett Historical | ShutterStock.com)

Western Union, the newspaper edited by his brother Orion Clemens. Twain educated himself during this period of his life by reading in public lending libraries. His first great ambition in life was to work as a steamboat pilot on the Mississippi. He reached this goal, and the experience inspired the name Mark Twain. A crewman on a riverboat would measure the river's depth with a rope marked in fathoms (lengths of six feet) and call back the information to the pilot. *Mark twain* meant "two fathoms," the depth necessary for navigation.

Twain's career as a pilot was cut short in 1861 when the Civil War curtailed commercial navigation on the Mississippi. Perhaps because of an early manifestation of a pacifism that became pronounced later in Twain's life, he avoided the war by going with his brother Orion to the Nevada Territory, where he tried and failed to make a fortune as a miner. This period of his life is the subject of his semiautobiographical novel *Roughing It* (1872) and provided material for his so-called California stories, including "The Celebrated Jumping Frog of Calaveras County" (1865). Twain was working as a journalist in San Francisco when

his stories made him a national success. For the rest of his life, Twain made his living writing and lecturing. Some of his best-known works are *The Adventures of Tom Sawyer* (1876), *The Prince and the Pauper* (1882), *Life on the Mississippi* (1883), and *A Connecticut Yankee in King Arthur's Court* (1889).

In 1884, Twain published *The Adventures of Huckleberry Finn*, acknowledged as one of the greatest American novels. It is perhaps the most effective satire against racism ever written but is ironically the most frequent subject of censorship in contemporary America because its racist characters use the colloquial slurs against blacks common in the antebellum period.

Twain enjoyed unprecedented success as a writer and proved equally popular in England and the United States. His humorous style, biting satire and skepticism, and ear for the American language helped Twain create the very structure of modern American literature. He used his celebrity to champion the progressive causes of women's suffrage, racial equality, and pacifism and to criticize imperialism. He received honorary degrees from Yale University in 1901, the University of Missouri in 1902, and Oxford University in 1907.

Twain valued inventiveness as a cornerstone of the American character and reveled in living in an age of scientific advancement. He became close friends with Nikola Tesla, the greatest inventor of his age. Twain obtained many patents for inventions of his own, but none ever proved profitable. He invested much of his considerable earnings in a newly invented typesetting machine, which eventually proved unworkable, leaving him bankrupt in 1894. Instead of peacefully retiring, in the 1890s Twain had to work more furiously than ever. He continued writing and lecturing, first to prop up his faltering business scheme and then to pay his creditors. He was scrupulous about paying his debts, even those that had been canceled by the courts.

By the end of the first decade of the twentieth century, Twain's wife (Olivia Langdon, whom he had married in 1870) and most of his children had died, and Twain turned his skeptical eye to conventional religion, producing "Eve's Diary." The story was published in the 1905 Christmas issue of *Harper's Magazine* and reprinted the next year in a lavishly illustrated booklet. The work became the subject of a famous case of censorship because the illustrations showed Adam and Eve nude, exactly according to the biblical text.

At the end of his life, Twain mused wistfully that the return of Halley's comet, which had been in the sky at this birth, would usher him out of this life, and his prediction came true. He died of heart failure on April 21, 1910, in Redding, Connecticut.

PLOT SUMMARY

Saturday
Although he takes some satirical liberty with the story, in "Eve's Diary" Twain follows the plot outline of the first few chapters of Genesis. Thus the first day of the diary is also the day after Eve's creation (according to the usual reconciliation of the texts of Genesis chapters 1 and 2), when she comes to self-awareness with a fully formed adult mind and knows how to read, presumably in Hebrew (hence the need for translating the original manuscript). Twain would probably be pleased if the reader were to ask where Eve obtains the pen and paper she uses to write the diary.

Eve believes that she and the whole world are an experiment. She thinks, too, that the world is not quite finished, because the mountains are still a bit too jagged and there is a good deal of rubbish lying around. She is more concerned that the stars are clumped together (that is, in the constellations) rather than evenly distributed. She also interprets the motion of the moon relative to the stars as disorderly and thinks its setting is its falling out of the sky. She fears someone must have gotten hold of it and hidden it, because that is what she would do with such a beautiful object. She concludes that the essential part of her nature, of human nature, is love of the beautiful, an idea that goes back to Plato.

Eve wants some stars with which to adorn her hair. She first tries to knock some down by throwing clods of earth at them and then determines to walk to the edge of the world and pick out some that are closer to the ground. It is too far to walk, however, and she spends the night sleeping with tigers, which are quite friendly because they live by eating strawberries.

The next day she starts to study the other experiment—Adam—whom she concludes to be a reptile. He climbs a tree to avoid her.

Sunday
Adam is still in the tree. He comes down to get some fish from a pond, which Eve thinks is horrid, so she pelts him with clods of earth until he ascends again into the tree. She concludes that he must be a man and so determines to refer to him as *he* rather than *it*.

Next Week Sunday
By this time, Adam allows Eve to follow him around. Eve, at least, does a good deal of talking, which Adam tolerates.

Wednesday
Adam more easily tolerates Eve, and she is his constant companion. She is always trying to make herself useful to him and does this chiefly by naming the animals (a task assigned to Adam in Genesis). The names come to her through a kind of inspiration. For instance, when they first see a dodo, Eve can tell by the look in Adam's eye that he is going to call it a wildcat, so before he can speak, she says, "Well, I do declare if there isn't the dodo!" so that it seems a natural thing to say and without usurping his authority.

Thursday
Unaccountably, Adam goes back to shunning Eve and shuts her out in the rain from the shelter he has built. Eve so loves to be with him now that it breaks her heart: "But now it was a mournful place and every little thing spoke of him, and my heart was very sore."

Sunday
Adam again admits Eve to his company, dispelling her sadness. She tries to knock some apples off the tree for him by throwing clods of earth at them but fails. He warns her that the apples are forbidden, but her attitude is that if she can get them to please Adam, she does not care what harm may come of it: "But so I come to harm through pleasing him, why shall I care for that harm?"

Monday
Adam takes disappointingly little interest in learning Eve's name, and he has not so far told her his own. When he saddens her in this way,

she consoles herself by looking at her reflection in a pool, which she childishly thinks is another being.

Tuesday

Eve makes garlands of flowers for decorating herself and first thinks of showing them off to Adam. She decides not to, however, when she realizes he will only criticize her for doing something useless. She then eats her lunch of apples, which have no disastrous effect. She accidentally starts a fire while trying to drill a hole in a piece of wood and thinks the fire a marvelous and beautiful invention, even when the whole forest starts to burn. Adam also dismisses fire as something useless. But when she finds the fire has cooked her remaining apples, Eve thinks that it may have a use one day.

Friday

Eve is again disappointed that Adam takes no interest in her efforts at gardening. He also cannot understand the fear she discovers after she invents fire. Her admonition that he stop his sport of going over a waterfall falls on deaf ears.

Extract from Adam's Diary

This section, culled from Twain's 1893 short story of the same title, did not appear in the story as originally published in *Harper's Magazine*. The magazine was published by Harper and Brothers, and the company had already contracted to publish both diaries in book form and did not want to mix them in the magazine. Twain persuaded them to add Adam's entries to the book publication. The text is printed in italics.

Adam gives a general assessment of the difference between his and Eve's characters that echoes Eve's. She is all girlish enthusiasm over the color of the sunset and similar phenomena, which he finds quite useless. But he is reduced to the prose-poem type of description she gives to the dawn and sunset in regard to her beauty.

In an entry dated Monday noon, Adam describes in some detail Eve's failed attempts to domesticate a brontosaurus, or at least to train it to act as a bridge. She at first thinks they can milk it, but it turns out not only to be not a mammal but also to be a male.

Tuesday—Wednesday—Thursday—and To-day

When Eve's diary resumes, the heading is not offset as the others are. Eve has gone four days without seeing Adam. She concludes, "It is a long time to be alone; still, it is better to be alone than unwelcome."

Friday

Abandoned again by Adam, Eve consoles herself with all of the animals in Eden. She considers them intellectually and morally superior to human beings; they are perfectly at peace with each other. She sets out, over the course of a few days, to explore the entirety of the world, riding on a tiger or an elephant. She learns a great deal about the world through scientific investigation; for example, she has never observed water flowing uphill, so she thinks it must do so only while she is asleep at night. Similarly, probably having seen comets or meteors, she thinks the stars will one day vanish because she has seen some of them fall.

After the Fall

With the Garden lost to her, Eve ponders why she loves Adam. She concludes there is nothing rational about it, but it is something she must do, "merely because he is *mine* and is *masculine*."

Forty Years Later

Eve wishes that she and Adam may die together or, if that is not possible, that she die first, because Adam has a greater strength than she does to bear the separation.

At Eve's Grave

The narrative ends with Adam's own statement: "Wheresoever she was, *there* was Eden."

CHARACTERS

Adam

If Eve is taken to be a sentimental tribute to Twain's wife, Olivia (or Livy, as she was known), then it follows that Adam's character is to a degree Twain's satirical self-representation. Accordingly, Eve says of him, "It has low tastes, and is not kind," a type of Twain's irascible nature. The low habits in question are probably drinking and smoking cigars, for which Twain was famous. When she hits Adam with a clod of earth, he speaks for the first time, but in a language Eve does not understand. Presumably this means he swears, as when people who swear say "excuse my French," pretending the oaths are in a foreign language.

As their relationship progresses, Eve is the one who pursues Adam, doing all of the talking. If this reflects Twains' courtship with Livy, it may seem unexpected in light of Twain's voluble writing style. However, a withdrawn, inexpressive character would be in keeping with Twain's misanthropy and could well find its form of expression in the very different context of writing. Adam is touchy, so that he will not take offense, Eve cunningly makes it appear as if, for example, she just happens to be mentioning the names of the animals he cannot properly name himself. Nevertheless, Adam is moody and sullen and longs for solitude and cannot help but hurt Eve by shunning her from time to time. Again, this rings true as a reflection of Twain's own temperament.

Eve criticizes Adam for being too concerned with his own cleverness. This perhaps also applies to Twain, who was probably defensive about his lack of formal education (Eve mentions of Adam, "He is self-educated, and does really know a multitude of things, but they are not so."). She also wishes he would not worry about wealth. Adam and Eve in the Garden would have had no use for wealth, so this must be a reflection of Livy and Twain. Although Twain made a fortune from his writing, in 1891 he had to declare bankruptcy and sell the house they had built for themselves after losing money on poor investments. Eve's advice to Adam, "I wish I could make him understand that a loving good heart is riches, and riches enough," rings true as Livy's consolation of her husband through that crisis.

Eve is concerned that Adam may be judgmental of the trivial. She makes garlands of flowers and supposes that Adam will not care for them. She writes, "He calls them rubbishy and cannot tell one from another, and thinks it is superior to feel like that." One wonders whether Twain treated Livy the same way, considering it human vanity, for example, if she were to show him a new dress. Similarly, Adam takes no interest in Eve's gardening, which she calls trying to improve the estate, a phrase more apt for the Twains' Connecticut home than for Eden.

What Adam does care for is checking fruit to see if it is ripe. If he had ever gone shopping together with his wife, Twain must have delighted at discovering even the small human mendacity of a grocer selling unripe fruit as if it were ready to be eaten. One can compare the story of Twain's switching the bands on cheap and expensive cigars and the pleasure he took in hearing his guests praise the quality of the cheap ones thinking they were the expensive ones. Commerce has a wonderful way of playing up to human vanity.

Toward the end of "Eve's Diary," Eve gives a general assessment of their relationship: "He loves me as well as he can; I love him with all the strength of my passionate nature." She does not love him because of any of his virtues (all of which she undercuts even as she praises them) but because he is masculine. She probably means gender, but it is still a daring revelation of Twain and Livy's private life.

Brontosaurus

Aside from the strawberry-eating tigers, the only animal described in any detail in "Eve's Diary" is the brontosaurus that invades Adam and Eve's camp. Eve wants to turn it into a pet and even to start milking it, to which Adam objects because it is a male and because they have no ladder to reach its belly. Being eighty feet long, it is entirely out of the human scale. The point, as in so much of the narrative, is to have the world revealed by modern science come crashing into the world of Iron Age mythology presented by Genesis. There is no place in the biblical narrative for an entire world populated by dinosaurs, yet the evidence that they existed is inarguable.

Eve

"Eve's Diary" is generally thought to be Twain's loving memoir of his relationship with his wife, Livy. An element of the story that reflects Livy is her naming of the animals when Adam proves unequal to the task. In reality, Livy was the first editor of all of Twain's writings, and according to Twain a very effective one. When Eve complains in her diary that Adam has a habit of favoring new words he has learned, it has the ring of correcting a manuscript.

Although she is slow to fully realize it, Eve is in love with Adam. She first tells herself that she loves only to be with him because she recognizes him as another person different from the animals or her reflection (which she mistakes for a creature of its own) and is the only one who can talk to her (although she loves to talk far more than he does). In the relationship between Twain and Livy, it would seem that Twain was the pursuer because she turned down his first marriage proposal, but there are many details of a romantic relationship that the outside world does not have access to.

When she complains that her life is constant hardship, Eve means that Adam makes it a hardship by his sullenness, silence, and rejection. If the story reflects Twain's relationship with Livy, he is looking back with regret on what he must have considered his mistreatment of her. He had periods of depression that must have taken a toll on his wife. Eve has the habit of consoling herself by visiting her reflection in a pool when Adam sullenly rejects her. While this is presented as charmingly childish in the story, Twain must have realized that his desire for isolation imposed an unfair burden on his wife, throwing her back on her inner resources. There must have been times when Twain realized he had gone too far even though he could not change himself to help her. This is perhaps reflected in Eve's second heartbreak whenever her reflection abandons her (because the sky is too overcast or the surface too rough to see the image). Eve's wish to die first because Adam has more strength to bear the solitude may be Twain's trying to find some sense in his wife's death.

In the extract from Adam's diary, Adam gives a general assessment of Eve's character: "Perhaps I ought to remember that she is very young, a mere girl, and make allowances." She has a girlish enthusiasm for everything in nature and delights in finding poetic names for the colors and phenomena of nature, such as "the purple shadows on the mountains, the golden islands floating in the crimson seas at sunset," reflecting perhaps, for all that he considers such things useless, a girlish enthusiasm that Twain found charming in Livy. Adam slowly realizes that he finds Eve beautiful and creates his own equally poetic praises: "She was standing marble-white and sun-drenched on a bowlder."

Eve has a habit of coining apothegms, which are pithy sayings that seem to sum up briefly some wise idea. Usually Twain uses them for a trenchantly satirical purpose, so this need not reflect a habit of Livy's. The first of them, for example, is "Eternal vigilance is the price of supremacy." This is an inversion of Thomas Jefferson's phrase "Eternal vigilance is the price of liberty." The meaning is opposite, since supremacy implies social control, which works against liberty. Eve praises, or perhaps from the reader's perspective excuses, herself by adding, "That is a good phrase, I think, for one so young," by which Twain suggests that there is something immature in a personality more concerned with supremacy than with liberty.

THEMES

Morality

Twain is famous for his misanthropy. This attitude is a central feature of "Eve's Diary." When Eve first encounters Adam and gives what is to be taken as a subjective assessment of him, she concludes he is a reptile. The implication is that people are somewhat less exalted than they consider themselves to be. In private, however, Twain thought that human beings fell short even of the reptile in the department of morals. In a letter to his friend J. Howard Moore written on February 2, 1907, at the height of the controversy over "Eve's Diary," Twain writes:

> As inheritors of the mentality of our reptile ancestors we have improved the inheritance by a thousand grades; but in the matter of the morals which they left us we have gone backwards as many grades. That evolution is strange, and to me unaccountable and unnatural. Necessarily we started equipped with their perfect and blemishless morals; now we are wholly destitute; we have no real morals, but only artificial ones—morals created and preserved by the forced suppression of natural and hellish instincts. Yet we are dull enough to be vain of them. Certainly we are a sufficiently comical invention, we humans.

Reviewers of "Eve's Diary" charged Twain with irreverence, supposedly a moral failing. He sharply responds to the charge in his autobiography:

> As to my irreverence, I am sure I was never irreverent in my life; I am also sure that no irreverent person has ever existed in the earth. It is not the privilege of governments, or laws, or churches, or even editors, to tell us what we must revere. In this matter we may choose for ourselves, and we always do.

TOPICS FOR FURTHER STUDY

- World mythologies are often presented in a summarized form for young-adult readers, such as *D'Aulaire's Book of Greek Myths* (originally published in 1962), by Edgar Parin and Ingri d'Aulaire, and Charles Phillips and Michael Kerrigan's *Realm of the Rising Sun: Japanese Myth* (1999). Rewrite one of the myths, particularly a creation myth, from a satirical perspective.

- Create a poster for your class outlining the divergences in "Eve's Diary" from Genesis. Use an online resource such as http://www.easel.ly as an aid in preparing your poster.

- Interview a local Christian clergy person about "Eve's Diary" and make a presentation to your class about what you learn. Ask your subject to discuss whether his or her tradition includes a conflict between science and scripture. How does your subject reply to the conflicts that Twain perceives and makes clear in the story? Ask your subject about the matter of freedom of conscience that Twain perceived. Alternatively, interview a librarian and solicit his or her opinion about the history of censorship concerning the story. What criteria does the librarian use in selecting books for the collection. Would the original published form of the story meet these criteria?

- Many of Twain's works are frequently censored, often on the ground of racism. Interview members of the English faculty at your school about Twain and the issue of censorship. Ask them especially how their views are influenced by their racial or religious identities. Write a paper summarizing your findings.

Twain espouses a dialectic in which so-called immorality arises from the attempt of people to force their own view of morality upon others:

All our fellow-citizens forgive us for it and concede that we are merely exercising an indisputable right. Then those fellow-citizens face the other way, and naively require us to revere *their* sacred things and personages. They even pass laws exacting this reverence of us—laws which punish us if we decline to obey them. These fine intelligences talk about freedom of conscience, and then tell our consciences how to act, under pain of penalties!

The true immorality is the hypocritical desire to coerce. Those who have fallen below the moral level of a reptile must try to cover over the moral failing that they know is inside themselves by calling immoral anyone who exercises the freedom that is their right as human beings. Twain continues in the autobiography:

Properly, no such thing as irreverence is possible. No man can be irreverent toward the things which *he* holds sacred in his heart—the thing is impossible; but he is free to say disagreeable things about any other's person's gods and Bibles.

Twain considers religion to be only one example of this immoral coercion and so is happy to hold it up to ridicule in a work like "Eve's Diary." Twain's satire could not be more timely a century later, as Steven Pinker, in a January 27, 2015, editorial in the *Boston Globe*, points out when he still has to ask, "Was Pope Francis right when he said that 'you cannot make fun of the faith of others'?" The answer Pinker gave is the same as Twain's: institutions of religious coercion do not hold any fundamental truth. Pinker writes: "History tells us that this is not the world we live in. Self-proclaimed truthers have repeatedly been shown to be mistaken—often comically so—by history, science, and common sense." Twain was quick to seize on the comedy of Adam and Eve living in the Garden of Eden with dinosaurs. The ideas come from what Stephen Jay Gould called two different magesteria, and something must give when one makes them coexist. Twain's humor lies in that gap.

Science

Near the beginning of "Eve's Diary," Eve writes that she and the whole world are part of an experiment. Twain introduces here the theme of the conflict between science and religion. Eve also justifies the diary by saying that what she will record will be of interest to historians. Even at the beginning of the twentieth century, Twain was well aware that the Genesis

Some critics believe Twain wrote "Eve's Diary" as a tribute to his late wife, Olivia Langdon Clemens. (© *AP Images / Eric Risberg*)

creation myths were incompatible with science and that the patriarchal narratives have no support in historical evidence. In the extract from Adam's diary, Adam writes of Eve,

> Nothing ever satisfies her but demonstration; untested theories are not in her line, and she won't have them. It is the right spirit, I concede it, it attracts me; I feel the influence of it; if I were with her more I think I should take it up myself.

This goes to the concept, apparent to Twain, that the human mind naturally partakes of the magical worldview of the Stone Age, where evolution left it, and can acquire a scientific worldview only through education. Even if she reaches the conclusion that water must run uphill only at night while she cannot observe it (Twain is not above satirizing the certainties of science), Eve makes the point even more explicitly: "It is best [to] prove things by actual experiment; then you *know*; whereas if you depend on guessing and conjecturing, you will never get educated."

STYLE

Pseudepigraphy

Pseudepigraphy is the practice of attributing a written work to a figure of the remote past. It is mostly done in the case of religious texts. For example, probably the most important religious work in the Judeo-Christian tradition written between the Hebrew Bible and the New Testament is the Book of Enoch. Composed no earlier than the third century BCE, the work is attributed by its author to Enoch, a mythical figure whose period was thousands of years in the past. The reason is not deception but to pay tribute to a traditional figure revered by the actual author. It was common in all religious traditions in antiquity and is exemplified in the Greco-Egyptian Hermetica, works of philosophy and alchemy composed after 200 CE but attributed to a mythical figure associated with the earliest period of pharaonic Egypt, Hermes Trismegistus.

"Eve's Diary" is a pseudepigraphic work written by the biblical matriarch Eve and evidently edited by Adam. Twain's purpose, however, is satirical, playing on the impossibility of a mythical figure's composing a document. The subtitle of the story, "Translated from the Original Ms.," is also of interest in this regard. "Ms." is the standard abbreviation for manuscript, and Twain is introducing the fiction that he was working from an actual ancient document written by Eve and Adam. As a fictional device, this would tend to create verisimilitude, but because Twain's story is so obviously fictional and modern, his purpose is ironic. The inspiration for this device is probably the periodic archaeological discovery and publication of ancient documents trumpeted in the popular press for their relevance to the Bible. An example Twain may have had in mind is the Babylonian *Epic of Gilgamesh* which was first translated in the 1870s and widely promoted as proving the biblical Flood narrative.

Twain's stories often have an uncanny way of applying to later events. "Eve's Diary" was probably a satire of the popular commotion surrounding the publication of Pierre Louÿs's *The Songs of Bilitis* (1894). Louÿs perpetrated a hoax, credulously accepted by the press, after the excavation at Oxyrhynchus in Egypt of real manuscripts of the Greek poet Sappho. The hoax was that he was offering translations of

COMPARE
&
CONTRAST

- **1900–1910:** Evangelical fundamentalism is in the process of becoming organized in reaction to what is perceived as challenges to biblical authority from the results of scientific investigation.

  Today: Evangelical fundamentalism is a powerful cultural and political force in American life and constantly brings pressure to exclude the teaching of science in schools.

- **1900–1910:** Artistic nudity is a commonly accepted convention but is sometimes subjected to censorship efforts.

  Today: Artistic nudity continues to stir little controversy, but censorship efforts are more likely to focus on racially charged material. Twain's works remain among the most often censored.

- **1900–1910:** Women have second-class status and lack even basic political rights, such as the right to vote.

  Today: Women have legal equality, but cultural equality is not yet fully achieved. For example, fewer women than men enter scientific and technical fields or are executives of major corporations, but the numbers are increasing.

a series of recently rediscovered poems by a student of Sappho's. Robert Graves used the technique in *I, Claudius* (1934), which was represented as a translation of a recently discovered manuscript of the memoirs of the Roman emperor Claudius. Press furor also occurred over the publication of the Gospel of Judas—a pseudepigraphon—by *National Geographic* in 2007.

Epistolary Fiction

The writing of fictional prose, though today the most common literary form, was a relatively late development in literature, coming after the Hellenistic period. University-level training at that time consisted mainly of writing letters and reports of the kind the aristocratic young students would later have to produce in their professional careers in government. The subject matter of these documents was necessarily hypothetical and therefore fictional. Professors would publish examples of these kinds of texts both for classroom use and as advertisements of their literary skill. This practice eventually evolved into short stories and novels. The text known as the Seventh Epistle of Plato is one of the earliest surviving examples of this kind of fiction writing. That

the work was accepted into the manuscript tradition of genuinely Platonic works shows the sense of vivid realism the technique can achieve. Even early English novels often took the form of journals (*Robinson Crusoe*) or letters (*Pamela*, *Frankenstein*). Twain uses the form in "Eve's Diary," which is presented as a series of journal entries written by Eve and one by Adam.

HISTORICAL CONTEXT

Censorship

"Eve's Diary" was originally published in the Christmas 1905 issue of *Harper's Magazine*. The following year, it was published in a slightly expanded form in a generously illustrated booklet. The illustrations were by Lester Ralph and done in the art nouveau style typical of the period. Arthur Rackham and Frank Papé were other illustrators who worked in the style. Like much serious artwork, the illustrations treated the nude figure, a decision that seems unavoidable because according to the biblical narrative Adam and Eve did not need clothing before the Fall. In a memo to his

Adam sees a dodo and seems to think it might be dangerous, but Eve corrects him without wounding his pride. (© *Morphart Creation | ShutterStock.com*)

editor Frederick Duneka (quoted in *The Bible according to Mark Twain*), Twain highly approves of the art: "We all think Mr. Ralph's pictures delightful—full of grace, charm, variety of invention, humor, pathos, poetry."

Harper's evidently had doubts about the nude figures, and Twain deflects them: "Do you think draperies indis[pens]ible to picture women? . . . Clothes would vulgarize her." He further observes, "Do you note how charged with childlike wonder and interest" Eve is in the illustrations? He meant that Eve has child-like innocence that would be cheapened by covering her with clothes like an adult, a view entirely in keeping with the theology of Genesis.

In 1907, the Charlton Public Library in Worcester County, Massachusetts, acquired a copy of "Eve's Diary." The head librarian, H. L. Carpenter, in consultation with the trustee Frank O. Wakefield decided to ban the book because of its illustrations. In an interview about the banning given to the *New York Times* (also quoted in *The Bible according to Mark Twain*). Twain describes the illustrations with his typical wit:

> On every left-handed page is a picture, fifty
> of which represent Eve in Summer costume.
> Her dresses are all cut Garden of Eden style.
> In one of them Eve is seen skipping through
> the bushes unrestrained and not at all afraid.
> The bushes do not seriously cut off the view
> of Eve.

Twain comments in particular on the decision to ban the book: "After looking long and earnestly at one picture depicting Eve pensively reclining on a rock, Mr. Wakefield decided to act." Although he could not have had any special insight into Wakefield's mental process, Twain was suggesting that Wakefield was projecting his own prurient interest in the pictures onto the images themselves, which Twain considered innocent. Twain expands on this theme in testimony before Congress about the matter (also quoted in *The Bible according to Mark Twain*):

> It appears that the pictures in Eve's Diary were first discovered by a lady librarian . . . . It took her some time to examine them all, but she did her hateful duty! I don't blame her for this careful examination; the time she spent was, I am sure, enjoyable, for I found considerable fascination in them myself.

Moving on to Wakefield, Twain adds: "He, also, took a long time to examine the unclothed ladies. He must have found something of the same sort of fascination in them that I found." For Twain the impulse to censor, to control other's people's access to art, came from the censor's abnormal self-revulsion at a natural human impulse. Art is full of nudes because human beings naturally find the human figure among the most beautiful objects in nature. Twain is far more scathing in a letter to his neighbor Mrs. Whitmore dated February 7, 1907 (she had informed him of a public lecture by the Yale professor William Lyon Phelps, who defended the book):

> The truth is, that when a Library expels a book of mine and leaves an unexpurgated Bible lying around where unprotected youth and age can get hold of it, the deep unconscious irony of it delights me and doesn't anger me.

During Banned Books Week in 2011, the Charlton Library officially placed a copy of "Eve's Diary" in its collection.

CRITICAL OVERVIEW

One of the earliest reviews of "Eve's Diary" ran in the *Westminster Gazette* soon after publication of the story. The anonymous review would probably have been forgotten except that Twain pasted a clipping of the notice in his autobiography. Its single point is that "'Mark Twain,' in his somewhat irreverent 'Diary of Eve' [sic] (Harper's), is guilty of an amusing error." The reviewer means that according to the text of Genesis, Eve was created only after Adam had completed naming the animals: "And Adam gave names to all cattle, and to the fowl of the air, and to every beast of the field; but for Adam there was not found an help meet for him." It is as well for the sake of the reviewer's sensibilities that Twain did not scandalize him by responding that according to the Talmudic interpretation of this text, Adam cohabited with every animal species. Twain replies, "This depresses me. It always saddens the professional lightning-bug when he flares up under the mole's nose and finds that the mole doesn't know that anything has happened." He held it as his right as a satirist to treat or mistreat a text as he wished. He wrote that satirists were as likely to distort the multiplication table as they were to distort Genesis.

"Eve's Diary" is part of a massive pastiche Twain wrote of the book of Genesis. He published several items from it in individual short stories like "Eve's Diary" and "Extracts from Adam's Diary," but most of it was unpublished at the time of Twain's death. Much, but not all, of this material has been published in various collections of Twain's papers, and large extracts were collected by Howard G. Baetzhold and Joseph B. McCullough, in *The Bible according to Mark Twain*. In their introduction to "Eve's Diary," they cover the censorship controversy over the illustrations and conclude "Looking at the pictures, it is difficult to see why anyone would object." They also repeat the most common analysis of the story, that is, "As many readers have noted, 'Eve's Diary' constitutes the author's moving eulogy to his wife, Livy, who had died a year earlier." They substantiated this by quoting a letter from Twain to his brother-in-law, Charles Langdon, soon after Livy's death. In that letter, Twain notes, "Wherever Livy was, that was my country." They consider that Twain reworked this apothegm into the final line of "Eve's Diary" in Adam's pronouncement over Eve's grave: "Wheresoever she was, *there* was Eden." Baetzhold and McCullough also relate "Eve's Diary" and "Excerpts from Adam's Diary" to the larger corpus: "Both of these published diaries lack the darker implications of the other biblical pieces (largely unfinished) that Mark Twain wrote but did not publish during his lifetime."

Baetzhold and McCullough, together with Donald Malcolm, in a 1991 article in *American Literary Realism*, revisited the original manuscripts to establish the chronological relationship between the various documents that Twain wrote over the last fifteen years of his life, which they demonstrate that earlier editors did not fully understand. For Ann M. Ryan, in "The Voice of Her Laughter" (2009), the feminist utopia of Eden in "Eve's Diary" is important evidence in her construction of Twain as a radical feminist. David Surrey, in "Mark Twain's Weapon of Mass Destruction" (2013), recounts his classroom use of "Eve's Diary."

CRITICISM

Bradley A. Skeen

Skeen is a classicist. In the following essay, he explores the theological satire in "Eve's Diary."

In "Eve's Diary," Twain engages with the biblical book of Genesis, one of the most familiar texts of the Western canon. In the strictest sense he satirizes it, throwing light on implications in the text that play out into self-evident absurdities. Twain and his readership, which is to say any modern person, have access to two worldviews, the mythical and the scientific. Where myth and science conflict, Twain finds his humor.

In popular understanding, the word *myth* often means something like a story that is not true. But a historian of religion defines a myth as a traditional story that provides meaning for the identity of the community that holds the myth. Myth is very much true, indeed extraordinarily true, in the sense that it is a defining characteristic of group identity. But in terms of incidental or extraneous matters, those that do not relate to self-definition, a mythical narrative simply embraces the common beliefs of the time in which the narrative was composed. During the Enlightenment, especially by the beginning of the twentieth century, the Judeo-Christian myth was being challenged, not in its essence but in its incidentals, by another worldview: science.

Although science has nothing to say about many core concepts of myth, it has a great deal to say about nature and the world. And what it says is often startlingly different from the incidental material in the mythical narratives of

WHERE MYTH AND SCIENCE CONFLICT, TWAIN FINDS HIS HUMOR."

Genesis that embrace a worldview that is three thousand years old. The scientific method, moreover, is used to investigate natural phenomena, form hypotheses about their operations and relationships, and test the hypotheses with experiments. The results of the experiments either confirm or disprove the initial hypothesis and in turn provide material for new hypotheses. In this way, science is self-correcting and can move toward an ever closer description of conditions as they really are while acknowledging that absolute knowledge is impossible.

Twain is very much alive to the nature of science in "Eve's Diary" and presents its experimental, investigative method in some detail (though not without some satire of science). He recognizes that scientific knowledge is different from mythical knowledge in that scientific methods produce testable results that can be either confirmed or disproved. He is also aware of the limited application of science, which he considers one of its greatest strengths:

> Some things you *can't* find out; but you will never know you can't by guessing and supposing: no, you have to be patient and go on experimenting until you find out that you can't find out.

Twain also considers science to be a natural expression of curiosity, for him the defining characteristic of human beings. His Eve thinks, "If there wasn't anything to find out, it would be dull." She eventually comes to recognize that scientific investigation is the true purpose of her existence:

> At first I couldn't make out what I was made for, but now I think it was to search out the secrets of this wonderful world and be happy and thank the Giver of it all for devising it.

Here Twain yields to myth its proper place as giving meaning to identity, binding the Christian community together.

The real problem for Twain is that the mythical narratives in Genesis present a picture of the physical world that simply does not relate

WHAT DO I READ NEXT?

- *Inventing Mark Twain: The Lives of Samuel Langhorne Clemens* (1997), by Andrew Hoffman, is a respected biography of Twain and especially useful regarding Twain's relationship with his wife, Livy.

- Ronald L. Numbers, in *The Creationists: From Scientific Creationism to Intelligent Design* (2006), provides a history of creationism and its origin in the religious fundamentalist reaction to the theory of evolution.

- *The Adventures of Tom Sawyer* (1876) is a classic novel by Twain. It is often used as young-adult literature in schools. It deals with inequalities of race and class, but less stridently than in some of Twain's other works.

- In *African Myths and Folktales* (1928), Carter Charles Woodson, often called the father of black history, retells African myths of creation and other subjects for a young-adult audience.

- David N. Livingstone, in *Adam's Ancestors: Race, Religion, and the Politics of Human Origins* (2011), traces the history of a radical theological idea, namely, that not all human beings are descended from Adam and Eve but that other human populations existed before and alongside them. This theology originated in the Middle Ages but was quickly adopted as one religious response to the theory of evolution. The idea entails the inferiority (in lacking a soul or other supposedly human characteristics) of the non-Adamic humans and was originally used to justify slavery and later racism and white supremacy.

- In *The Duplicating Imagination: Twain and the Twain Papers* (1990), Maria Marotti shines the light of modern literary theory on the mass of literary papers Twain left unpublished at the time of his death.

to reality. His Eve imagines that the stars are just out of her reach, a few meters above the ground, and that the world is a place one can walk across or ride a tiger across in a few days, and it simply is not. This is reductio ad absurdum (carrying something to an absurd extreme) that the reader may find charming in its childlike simplicity, but it is not very far removed from the mythical Babylonian conception of the world that is reflected in the creation narratives in the first two chapters of Genesis.

The universe created in Genesis is made in a preexistent expanse of water. The creator fashions a flat disk (the earth) and closes it over with a dome (the sky) to shut out the water. One may think of it as a snow globe floating in a vast ocean. The disk itself is no more than a few hundred, or at most a few thousand, miles across, and the stars, suspended on the interior surface of the dome, can be no farther than half that distance, the radius of the disk. One could indeed walk to the edge of that world and find the seam where the sky joins to the earth and discover stars within one's reach.

This is not the universe that science has unveiled (though in Twain's day the extent of the universe was believed to be the Milky Way galaxy: science is self-correcting and constantly making new discoveries). The conflict between the mythical and the scientific worldviews became acute in the mid-nineteenth century (in Twain's lifetime) when Charles Darwin published *On the Origin of Species* (1859). Darwin proposed that human beings, as animals, are descended through evolution from other animals. If one were to trace back the ancestry of a particular human being, one would find not a single pair of humans but a large population of ancestral individuals. Moreover, as one traveled back through time, the creatures that were one's ancestors would become more ape-like in appearance. Even further back, human ancestors would be fish and, still earlier, single-celled organisms. From the point of view of biblical myth, this might seem to pass incidental matters and attack human identity as a special creation uniquely bearing god's image.

By and large, however, Christians, both Christian denominations and individual Christian believers, accepted the new scientific findings. It became more difficult to not do so as confirmation of Darwin's hypothesis was strengthened by the ever better populated fossil record and by the science of genetics, a field that was in its infancy when Darwin and Twain were writing. Another response to science and to evolution, however, became the basis of fundamentalism. In this essentially postmodern reaction, the results of scientific investigation are simply denied, and the absolute truth of every detail of the biblical creation accounts (which are not acknowledged to be mutually contradictory, even though, for example, in Genesis 1 human beings are created as a pair, whereas in Genesis 2 Adam is created first and Eve is made from Adam later) is insisted upon. Proponents of this view call it creationism, in distinction to the theory of evolution. Theory in this case does not have its common meaning of an unsubstantiated guess but its scientific meaning of a hypothesis whose predictions have been confirmed through experiment and observation.

Although fundamentalism was only becoming established in Twain's day—through the work of the theological faculties at Princeton University and the Northwestern Bible and Missionary Training School in Minneapolis—and publication of the series of tracts called *The Fundamentals* would not begin until 1910, Twain identified where the fault lines between myth and science lie in Genesis and exploited the comic potential in the clash of ideologies.

An example of the clash between science and myth whose implications Twain found especially absurd follows from the discovery of dinosaurs through paleontological investigation. According to Genesis, during the creation week, God made "every living creature that moveth" (1:21 Authorized [King James] Version) which would logically include dinosaurs, even though the animals were unknown to the biblical authors. Fundamentalists have reacted to this disconnect in various ways, for instance by claiming that dinosaurs never existed and that all the gigantic skeletons on display in natural history museums throughout the world are counterfeits created by Satan for the purpose of deceiving humankind (or, with more sinister implications, fakes made by scientists). A more common fundamentalist response has been to insist that dinosaurs lived in the Garden of Eden along with Adam and Eve, although one might think that the authors of Genesis would have seen fit to mention that the Garden was filled with these extraordinary and gigantic creatures unlike any animals that existed in the world they knew. Twain sees the absurdity of this and has a brontosaurus smash into his narrative, wreaking havoc on the first human pair's encampment.

In another place in Genesis, God says, "And to every beast of the earth, and to every fowl of the air, and to every thing that creepeth upon the earth, wherein there is life, I have given every green herb for meat" (1:30 Authorized [King James] Version). Fundamentalists take this passage to mean that there was no predation in the Garden of Eden. This brings up the problem of obligate predators, whose bodies are evidence that they are adapted to eating meat, both in their digestive organs, which cannot process plant material, and in their sharp teeth and claws. Twain immediately sees the absurdity—and along with it the only suitable solution to the problem—and portrays the tigers in Eden as subsisting on a diet of strawberries.

Twain cannot outdo actual creationists, however. Ken Ham, the director of Answers in Genesis and a leading contemporary creationist apologist, made a similar deduction and considered that the teeth of *Tyrannosaurus rex*, which resemble steak knives, were designed by God not to rend the flesh of other dinosaurs but to crack open watermelons and coconuts. In *The Complete Creation Museum Adventure*, Ham states, "T-rex's knife-like teeth and massive jaws would be perfect for gobbling up all sorts of melons."

But Twain identifies a more serious disconnect between myth and modernity. In *The Second Sex*, Simone de Beauvoir wrote that the biblical worldview, and the dominate ideology of Western civilization as a whole, has kept women in a subordinate role by identifying them as other, an inferior copy of the male prototype, a representative of passivity rather than activity, of chaos rather than order, of evil rather than good. Genesis plays a prominent part in this stereotyping, presenting Eve as the agent of humankind's Fall in accepting the devil's temptation to eat of the forbidden fruit and seducing Adam into the same sin. Twain will have none of this. His Eve eats apples and even discovers how to bake them with no ill effect. It is a measure of how ridiculous Twain found his own culture's marginalization of women in the face of the fact that they are intellectually and in every way fitted to be the equals of men.

Several times in the story, Eve eats apples, which recalls the biblical story of the Tree of Knowledge.
(© Artur Synenko / ShutterStock.com)

Twain underscored what he considered the vicious absurdity of sexism by making Eve herself the inventor of science, the very system of knowledge that most clearly exposes the vapidity of sexism. Here too, anthropology and paleontology have marked Twain as a prophet. Women have been discovered to be the inventors of the first tool, the primitive sling women tens of thousands of years ago devised for carrying their infants.

Source: Bradley A. Skeen, Critical Essay on "Eve's Diary," in *Short Stories for Students*, Gale, Cengage Learning, 2016.

James D. Wilson

In the following excerpt, Wilson sums up critical reception to the story.

. . . The romantic emphasis of the diaries, their scenes of comic domestic bickering and adjustment, and the gentle liberties taken with the biblical source did not please all readers. An anonymous reviewer for the *Spectator* complained in 1897 that "Extracts from Adam's Diary" shows a lack of both taste and skill, "is

too far-fetched, grotesque in fact, and the humor by no means rich," and admonished the author "to leave such subjects alone" (89). Most readers, however, are moved by what Harris sees as Mark Twain's "delineation of the ideal woman" (123).

Certainly Mark Twain emends his biblical source. Central episodes in Genesis receive little attention in these two stories. God's command not to eat the fruit of the Tree of Knowledge, the temptation scene, the Fall itself, Cain's murder of Abel—all are neglected. "Adam's Diary" makes no mention of God at all; Eve refers to God on two or three occasions, but simply as "the Giver of it all." The extract form of the diaries enables Mark Twain to gloss over matters of theological import and to focus instead on the developing relationship of the protagonists. "Extracts from Adam's Diary" opens shortly after the arrival of Eve—she is "the new creature"—and continues through the Fall to a time some ten years after the birth of Abel. "Eve's Diary" follows essentially the same time frame; indeed Eve uses "Adam's diary as her unwitting text" (Ensor 49). The first man and woman are, Macnaughton writes, "scientists whose major pleasure in life comes from exploring their magnificent environment" (220).

And, one might add, exploring each other, for the diaries chart their discovery of the redemptive power of human love. For Adam, the Fall proves fortunate because it occasions his full discovery of Eve. Convinced by his mate that it was the chestnut—one of his jokes—that led to the Fall, Adam blesses that "chestnut that brought us near together and taught me to know the goodness of her heart and the sweetness of her spirit!" His final comment—"Wheresoever she was, *there* was Eden"—suggests that Eve, or the human love she manifests, is the indispensable component of any paradise. As Hill points out, Eve too is "willing to sacrifice her prelapsarian innocence for her love of her husband" (113–14). "The Garden is lost," she muses, "but I have found *him*, and am content." Eve prays that she and Adam might die together or, if that is impossible, that she die first; life without her mate, she realizes, is no life at all. Mark Twain, Brodwin writes, transmutes "Eve into the Eternal Feminine, all love derived from her" (57). "I am the First Wife," Eve reflects, "and in the last wife I shall be repeated."

The humanization of Adam through his discovery of Eve is according to Harris the central theme of the two stories. At the outset Adam is totally self-absorbed, and his primitive control of language testifies to an under-developed aesthetic imagination. To him the created universe is merely a collection of objects designed for his own practical benefit. Eve too is an object, an "it," until she teaches him the words "she" and "we"—and the concepts those words represent; she is an annoyance Adam wishes "would but go by herself and not talk" (*Complete Short Stories*). In short, Harris writes, Adam's Eden is "a solipsistic universe in which any voice from outside offends the privacy of his dream" (126). But Eve, whose greatest horror is utter loneliness, shatters Adam's solipsistic dream, forces him to "cease imagining that he is alone and include her in his psychic landscape." The destruction of Adam's self-absorbed dream coincides with the Fall; the loss of Eden makes him human. Adam's increasing sophistication with language reflects his broadened vision of the world occasioned by Eve's devotion and love, the "truly human emotions" that free him from the edenic "paralysis of solitude" (Harris 127). The objects of this world appear intrinsically beautiful to his awakened aesthetic imagination, and the loss of

his solipsistic dream—Eden—becomes inconsequential. Far more devastating is the loss of Eve.

In his penetrating study of the humor in the Adamic diaries, Brodwin focuses not on the relationship of Adam and Eve but on the Fall as the "central event" in Mark Twain's "theology of the comic." Humor in the diaries, Brodwin writes, derives from "contradiction, absurdity, and incongruity, the principle of irony triumphant"; it "functions as a theological sign of man's fall but at the same time enables him to deal with that pathetic state" (49). In Mark Twain's version of Genesis, the Fall results from Eve's compassion and Adam's humor. Eve willingly brings death into the world not because she is motivated by vanity or pride but because in her naive sympathy for God's creatures she believes death necessary to provide appropriate food for carnivores. When subsequently Eve blames Adam for the Fall, he realizes that his "chestnut" "meaning an aged and moldy joke"—was likewise responsible: "Alas, I am indeed to blame." But if the "chestnut" caused the Fall, it is also the agent of redemption, for it is the "blessed" chestnut, Adam confesses later, "that has brought us together." Hence, Brodwin concludes, "Eve's compassion and Adam's humor, twin ideas that at best reflect man's celebratory, healing qualities, have caused the fall, caused the exile and at the same time created the means by which man is able to face that exile" (55). The ironic absurdity of life is that human values such as compassion, love, humor "would find no place in the 'real' world if they were not needed to cope with a Divine Nature which has no place for them; indeed, makes them the very causes of the fall" (57).

Source: James D. Wilson, "Extracts from *Adam's Diary*: 'Eve's Diary,'" in *A Reader's Guide to the Short Stories of Mark Twain*, G. K. Hall, 1987, pp. 96–98.

Spectator

In the following review, the anonymous reviewer describes the characters in "Eve's Diary" as materialistic.

Mark Twain has been writing about the first woman, and thinking about the last. The modern American girl belonging to the moneyed class is the youngest, and perhaps the prettiest, of Eve's daughters. The American humourist thinks her like her prototype in the Garden of Eden. Accordingly he sets his heroine in the most primitive circumstances which the imagination—with the help of the Book of Genesis—can conjure up, and draws a picture, not of her twentieth-century surroundings, but of her very self. Eve, in Mark Twain's parable, becomes suddenly conscious of her own existence and finds herself in Paradise. A woman has been created,—that is, a little American has grown up. She is self-conscious and self-absorbed; she is in love with her own reflection in the water; yet she hardly knows what to make of herself. "I feel like an experiment," she says; but "if I am an experiment, am I the whole of it? No, I think not; I think the rest of it is part of it." She is, she does not doubt, "the main part of it." Yet she has some suspicions that her exalted position is precarious. "Some instinct tells me that eternal vigilance is the price of supremacy." "The core and centre of my nature," she writes in her diary, "is love of the beautiful, a passion for the beautiful." Herein lies, we gather from her self-revelations, the key to her strength and her weakness, together with the explanation of her strange superficiality. She is endowed with an inexhaustible capacity for enjoyment. She is marvellously happy and diffuses happiness round her. On the other hand, to gain pleasure she will make most serious sacrifices, and even put up with a good deal of pain. All the great realities of life for her are only splendid appearances. "The moon," she writes, "got loose last night, and slid down and fell out of the scheme—a very great loss," for "there isn't another thing among the ornaments and decorations that is comparable to it for beauty and finish." The worst of it is, she comments, "whoever gets it will hide it; I know it because I would do it myself." She could, she believes, "be honest in all other matters," but "it would not be safe to trust me with a moon that belonged to another person and that person didn't know I had it." At first her eagerness for pleasure is checked by her want of experience. She makes long and fruitless journeys to get stars to put in her hair. She plays with fire because it is beautiful, burns her fingers, and learns the meaning of fear,—a terrible sensation, as she observes, the only one, perhaps, of which she would have desired to remain ignorant. Worldly wisdom is not slow to come to her,—for she is intensely receptive. "To-day," we read, "I am getting better ideas about distances." At first "I was so eager to get hold of every pretty thing that I giddily grabbed for it, sometimes when it was too far off." All is grist which comes to her mill. If she longs for the moon and the stars, she yet does not disdain the simplest pleasures. The love and companionship of animals delight her, especially when "the other experiment" is grumpy and will not talk. To be alone is misery to her. The beasts occupy her time. "Animals," she says, "have the kindest disposition and the politest ways; they never look sour, they never let you feel that you are intruding, they smile at you and wag their tail, if they've got one, and they are always ready for a romp or an excursion or anything else you want to propose .... They all talk, and they all talk to me; but it must be a foreign language, for I cannot make out a word they say." Adam, on the other hand, feels himself far more divided from the brute creation, and altogether much less at home in the world. His spirits are lower, his greed is greater. "It has low tastes and is not kind," she writes on the early leaves of her diary while Adam is still a stranger to her, still nothing but another experiment. "Yesterday evening in the gloaming it had crept down and was trying to catch the little speckled fishes that play in the pool, and I had to clod it to make it go up the tree again and let them alone."

Adam, she gives us to understand, does not climb up trees because his habits are arboreal, but because he wants to get away from her. Eve always wants to talk, and insists upon pursuing him. He does not like her at first because she interrupts his calculations about the crops. "He does not care for me," she laments; "he does not care for flowers, he does not care for the painted sky at eventide—is there anything he does care for, except building shacks to coop himself up in from the good clean rain, and thumping the melons, and sampling the grapes, and fingering the fruit on the trees, to see how those properties are coming along?" Adam, on his side (the author interpolates a page or two out of his diary), is amazed at her versatility, and cannot imagine why any one should be interested in anything which is unproductive. He tries to remember that she is young, and to make allowances. The world to her, he says, is "a charm, a wonder, a mystery, a joy; she can't speak for delight when she finds a new flower." She raves about the shadows on the mountains, the colours in the sunset; but "none of them is of any practical value, so far as I see." Then her restlessness fatigues him. "If she could quiet down and keep still a couple of minutes at a time, it would be a reposeful spectacle. In that case I think I could enjoy looking at her; indeed

I am sure I could, for I am coming to realize that she is a quite remarkably comely creature."

It is a curious society which is represented by Mark Twain's Adam and Eve; and though he seems to think otherwise, we see very little that is primitive about them but their names. Tom Tiddler's Ground would be a better description of their birthplace than the Garden of Eden. That a man should be absorbed in thoughts of gain is no new thing. The greater proportion of the world must always think chiefly of how to get its bread. What is new is that he should prefer to think of nothing but gainful labour, and should use all the advantages of civilisation to help him to return to the mental state of the man coerced by hunger. All the higher occupations of the mind he puts deliberately aside,—turns them over to the woman. She has heart and she has imagination; she is romantic and she makes love; but the taint of the commercial spirit rests upon her also. Her love of beauty is half of it love of possession: her genuine delight in Nature teaches her much; but a large portion of that which passes for a passion for the beautiful is cupidity *plus* discrimination. She dreams of getting stars for her personal adornment, and admits that where the shining object of her desire is concerned she would not be deterred by any scruple of honesty. Without a thought for the morrow, she sets the wood on fire to see the blaze. The love of money lies at the root of both their characters. It is the foundation of her aesthetic distraction, as of his materialistic concentration. They are both the offspring of their surroundings, the children of a Pecuniary Paradise,—a lawless pair, whose ultimate fate may be prophesied from precedent.

Source: "Review of 'Eve's Diary,'" in *Spectator*, Vol. 97, September 22, 1906, pp. 393–94.

Outlook

In the following review, the anonymous reviewer writes that Twain strikes a "peculiar note" with "Eve's Diary."

Eve's Diary is a very characteristic book. The peculiar note of its quiet farce has been simply touched off in a little-known critical dissertation by Mark Twain, where it is laid down that the American development of humour has its basis in the humourist's "doing his best to conceal the fact that he even suspects that there is anything funny about it." "Another feature," it is added, "is the slurring of the point." This is contrasted rather pungently with the comic method, which is treated as characteristically English. "The teller of the comic story does not slur the point; he shouts it at you—every time. And when he prints it he italicises it, puts some whooping exclamation points after it, and sometimes explains it in a parenthesis." This is probably true of us as a nation. All that can be urged in our defence is that we strain every nerve to understand and live up to the American ideal. Not only do we buy its books furiously; we sit at the feet of American professors of humour in all our many music-halls, and quite enjoy being told by them, when the laughs do not come with instant reaction, to "think it over" and "go home and sleep on it." In our theatres, too, such perfect practitioners of the method described by Mark Twain as Mr. Gillette and Mr. William Collier have their successful seasons. But the English sense of humour, it seems true, still pants at the heels of that which owns its greatest master in Mark Twain. Certainly, there are not a few of our race who would see little to amuse them in *Eve's Diary*. Great numbers would regard it as profanity, and be interested in it on that account, while missing most of the fun. But to all who share in the divine gift—if divine it be, and not quite otherwise—of a full sense of humour, this fragment will be very welcome.

Mark Twain has probably been read by multitudes of us who have never really come within range of the author's personality, that strange mingling of misanthropy and charity, coolness and enthusiasm, which makes the man cynic and crusader by turns, so that he stands out as the most eminent scoffer in a scoffing nation, and, at the same time, as the supreme American example of the kind of disposition which provides us here with pro-Boers, pro-Zulus, and other much abused and earnest children of the race of Barebone. *Eve's Diary* might be called some harsh names by different kinds of mental invalid; but nobody who used words correctly could call it frivolous on laying it down. Its writer is one of the least frivolous men living. The morals and religion of this iconoclast are tougher plants than will readily grow in the minds of a later generation. They were sown in the heroic age of the United States, before the discovery of the West and before the vast invasions from Europe, days when there seemed to be something stirring within the nation that meant greatness as well as size and wealth; when the American problem, of which the bare conditions are now seen to be scarcely yet laid down, seemed already to be visibly working itself out on the lines ordained. Those hardy spiritual qualities are more or less visible in every extravaganza from Mark Twain's pen, and not least so in this short piece and in the *Extracts from Adam's Diary*, published some years ago. He has despaired of men but never of Christian morals, democratic principles or women.

There is much of the spirit of Heine in this quaint summing-up of a keen mind's observations of the feminine. The inquisitive characteristic is often referred to:

> At first I couldn't make out what I was made for, but now think it was to search out the secrets of this wonderful world and be happy, and thank the Giver of it all for devising it. I think there are many things to learn yet—I hope so; and by economising and not hurrying too fast I think they will last weeks and weeks. I hope so . . . . If there wasn't anything to find out it would be dull.

Another alleged quality of woman's mind is touched upon in this among several passages:

> I have learned a number of things, and am educated, now, but I wasn't at first. I was ignorant at first. At first it used to vex me because, with all my watching, I was never smart enough to be around when the water was running up-hill; but now I do not mind it. I have experimented and experimented until now I know that it never does run up-hill, except in the dark. I know it does in the dark, because the pool never goes dry; which it would, of course, if the water didn't come back in the night.

Adam does not show to any great advantage in *Eve's Diary*. The determination to idealise woman at the expense of man has always been one of the most American things about Mark Twain. The conception, present all through this little book, of man as the gross materialist, with no sense of beauty and no faintest stirring of the artistic impulse, both of which are regarded as in the nature of woman, is an American conception. It probably corresponds to the facts of American life, but it would be hard to make out a case for it from the general history of our species. Eve's long deliberation as to why she loves Adam is the most characteristic part of a characteristic book. She decides, for reasons detailed with grave precision, that it is not on account of his singing, his education, his "brightness," his gracious and considerate ways, or his chivalry. Finally:

> It is not on account of his industry that I love him—no, it is not that. I think he has it in him, and I do not know why he conceals it from me. It is my only pain. I am sure he keeps nothing from me but this. It grieves me that he should have a secret from me, and sometimes it spoils my sleep, thinking of it, but I will put it out of my mind.

Adam's meditation at the woman's grave, at the end, is the philosophy of this delightful fragment: "Wheresoever she was, there was Eden." Mr. Lester Ralph's quaintly clever illustrations are altogether in the spirit of the writer.

SOURCES

Baetzhold, Howard G., Joseph B. McCullough, and Donald Malcolm, "Mark Twain's Eden/Flood Parable: 'The Autobiography of Eve,'" in *American Literary Realism, 1879–1910*, Vol. 24, No. 1, 1991, pp. 23–38.

de Beauvoir, Simone, *The Second Sex*, translated by H. M. Parshley, Vintage, 1980, pp. 78–80.

Goodnough, Abby, "Century after It Was Banned, Place of Honor for Twain Tale," in *New York Times*, September 21, 2011, http://www.nytimes.com/2011/09/22/us/eves-diary-banned-twain-book-back-at-charlton-mass-library.html?_r=0.

Ham, Ken, ed., *The Complete Creation Museum Adventure*, New Leaf, 2008, p. 45.

Pinker, Steven, "Why Free Speech Is Fundamental," in *Boston Globe*, January 27, 2015, http://www.bostonglobe.com/opinion/2015/01/26/why-free-speech-fundamental/aaAWVYFscrhFCC4ye9FVjN/story.html (accessed January 24, 2015).

Ryan, Ann M., "The Voice of Her Laughter: Mark Twain's Tragic Feminism," in *American Literary Realism*, Vol. 41, No. 3, 2009, pp. 192–213.

Surrey, David, "Mark Twain's Weapon of Mass Destruction: 'The Human Race Has Only One Really Effective Weapon and That Is Laughter,'" in *Novel Approaches to Anthropology: Contributions to Literary Anthropology*, edited by Marilyn Cohen, Lexington, 2013, pp. 139–70.

Twain, Mark, *Autobiography of Mark Twain*, edited by Benjamin Griffin and Harriet Elinor Smith, University of California Press, 2013, Vol. 2, pp. 167–68.

———, *The Bible according to Mark Twain*, edited by Howard G. Baetzhold and Joseph B. McCullough, Touchstone, 1996, pp. 17–19.

———, *Eve's Diary: Translated from the Original Ms.*, Harper and Brothers, 1906, https://archive.org/details/EvesDiary (accessed January 24, 2015).

———, *Mark Twain's Letters*, edited by Albert Bigelow Paine, Harper and Brothers, 1917, Vol. 2, pp. 804–806.

FURTHER READING

Camfield, Gregg, ed., *The Oxford Companion to Mark Twain*, Oxford University Press, 2003.
  This Oxford companion gives an overview of Twain scholarship and has an especially useful section on the history of attempts to censor Twain's works.

Twain, Mark, *The Adventures of Huckleberry Finn*, Chatto & Windus, 1884.
  The Adventures of Huckleberry Finn is Twain's masterwork and ranks alongside Herman Melville's *Moby-Dick* as greatest American novels. It is a satire of race relations in America and was difficult to publish in America because of its trenchant social criticism. The American edition was published a year after the publication and success of the novel in Britain. It is still frequently censored because it uses the racial slurs against blacks common in the South before the Civil War.

———, *Europe and Elsewhere*, edited by Brander Matthews and Albert Bigelow Paine, Harper & Brothers, 1923.
  This volume published for the first time some of Twain's massive amount of material satirically rewriting the Book of Genesis.

———, *Letters from the Earth*, Bernard DeVoto, Harper, 1960.
  In this volume, DeVoto publishes material that Twain left in a manuscript that is closely related to "Eve's Diary," including diary excerpts attributed to Eve, Adam, Cain, and the devil. This material is different from the similar matter published earlier in *Europe and Elsewhere*. There are other unpublished materials that make up part of this cycle.

SUGGESTED SEARCH TERMS

Mark Twain OR Samuel Clemens

Eve's Diary AND Twain

American literary realism

Genesis

creationism

science

censorship

feminism

The Landlady

ROALD DAHL

1959

Appearing initially in the *New Yorker* magazine in November 1959, "The Landlady" remains one of Roald Dahl's most frequently anthologized short stories. A story that exemplifies Dahl's skill at foreshadowing and his focus on creating a conclusion loaded with impact, this is a tale that places the optimism of an era of prosperity (represented by Billy Weaver) next to the dark undertones associated with an uncritical ambition (represented by the landlady). One part horror story, one part social commentary, and one part compelling read, "The Landlady" sounds a warning about the dangers of self-confidence and the fatal risks involved in not paying attention to the cues the world gives us, both professionally and personally. "The Landlady" appears in *The Umbrella Man and Other Stories* (1998).

AUTHOR BIOGRAPHY

Roald Dahl was born on September 13, 1916, in Cardiff, Wales, to parents of Norwegian descent: Harald Dahl, co-owner of a business that helped international shipments find shipping partners, and Sofie Magdalene Hesselberg Dahl. The only son in a family of four children, Roald was named after the polar explorer Roald Amundsen, a national hero in Norway. As a young child, Dahl endured the death of an

Roald Dahl is best known for his humorous, and often dark, children's books.

older sister from appendicitis as well as the death of his father from pneumonia while on a fishing trip in the Antarctic.

Following his education at a number of English boarding schools, Dahl worked briefly with the Shell Petroleum Company before joining the Royal Air Force in 1939, where he was trained as a fighter pilot. Hospitalized following a crash landing in the fall of 1940, Dahl returned to action in World War II early in 1941 and saw aerial battle action. However, severe headaches caused him to be sent back to England, where he eventually was appointed to a post as assistant air attaché at the British Embassy in Washington, DC.

After the war, Dahl married American actress Patricia Neal in 1953. The couple remained together for thirty years and had five children: Olivia Twenty (born in 1955; she died at age seven from measles-related encephalitis), Chantal Tessa Sophia (1957), Theo Matthew (1960), Ophelia Magdalena (1964), and Lucy Neal (1965). The couple divorced in 1983, and Dahl married a much younger woman, Felicity Ann d'Abreau Crosland.

A prolific writer by any standard, Dahl published his first short story in 1942, a story about his wartime adventures for which he was paid relatively handsomely by the *Saturday Evening Post*. His first children's book, *The Gremlins*, was published in 1943 and launched a string of remarkable successes that included *James and the Giant Peach* (1961), *Charlie and the Chocolate Factory* (1964), and *Matilda* (1988). He also adapted as screenplays two novels by his friend Ian Fleming, both of which became popular films: the James Bond movie *You Only Live Twice* (1967) and *Chitty Chitty Bang Bang* (1968). Often overlooked is the fact that Dahl is also the author of a smaller but still very distinct body of fiction for adults, including "The Landlady," which was originally published in 1959. His book-length adult titles include *Over to You* (1946), *Someone Like You* (1953), *Kiss Kiss* (1960), and *Switch Bitch* (1974).

Most critics agree that by the mid-1960s and throughout the 1970s, Dahl reached a financial stability that coincided with a marked decline in the quality of his adult fiction, due in part to the spectacular success of his books for children. Some would suggest, too, that his "misanthropic sneer" (in the words of Stephen Amidon, writing in the *Nation*) was distinctly out of sync with the increasingly explicit and open sexuality of the 1960s.

Among the numerous awards and recognitions that Dahl received during his life are the World Fantasy Award for Life Achievement (1983) and the Children's Author of the Year (British Book Awards, 1990). He died from the blood disease myelodysplastic syndrome on November 23, 1990, in Oxfordshire, England. He was seventy-four years old.

PLOT SUMMARY

The story opens with seventeen-year-old Billy Weaver relocating from London to the city of Bath via train, arriving late one evening. The night is clear and very cold. Upon departing the train, Billy asks a porter for directions to some inexpensive accommodations. He is directed to a pub (which also offers lodging) called the Bell and Dragon, which is about a quarter mile from the station.

MEDIA ADAPTATIONS

- An adaption of "The Landlady" appeared on season six of *Alfred Hitchcock Presents* in February 1961. The adaptation was directed by Paul Henreid. Dean Stockwell was cast as Billy Weaver and Patricia Collinge as the landlady.

- A later television adaptation of the story appeared in 1979 as part of the first season of the *Tales of the Unexpected* series. Directed by Herbert Wise, this episode starred Leonard Preston as Billy Weaver and Siobhan McKenna as the landlady. Roald Dahl himself introduced this episode to viewers.

- BBC Worldwide released an audiobook of Dahl's stories under the title *More Tales of the Unexpected* in 2001. The collection includes a reading of "The Landlady."

- A reading of "The Landlady" was included in the 2006 Alfred A. Knopf audiobook of Dahl's *Collected Stories*.

- An adaptation of this story, renamed "Come into My Parlor: The Landlady," was included as part of the 2008 audiobook *Murderous Schemes: An Anthology of Classic Detective Stories* published by Recordings for the Blind & Dyslexic.

- Katherine Maxwell directed a nine-minute film adaptation in 2011, with Jay Renshaw in the role of Billy and Catherine Lydon as the landlady.

- A reading by Tamsin Greig is included on Penguin's audiobook release of Dahl's *Kiss Kiss* in 2012.

Setting off on foot, Billy initially realizes that he knows no one in Bath, but then remembers the reassurances of his boss, Mr. Greenslade, who promised Billy that it is "a splendid city." More important, Billy remembers his direct instructions to find lodging and then report to the local branch manager. Billy is focused on moving briskly, which he believes will mark him as a success in the world of business.

As he walks through the streets of Bath, he notices that what were once relatively expensive city homes have fallen into obvious disrepair and are suffering from neglect. He notices a sign in a window advertising a bed and breakfast, or boarding house, and he looks in at the window. He is drawn to the hominess of the place, with its pleasant furniture, bright fire burning in the hearth, and the small dachshund that he can see curled in front of the fire.

Billy enters into a debate with himself over his two options: to check into the bed and breakfast or continue to the pub farther down the street. He feels comfortable in a pub environment, with its built-in promise of pleasant company in the evenings; never having stayed in a bed and breakfast, he is a bit nervous about what the experience would be like. After a few moments he decides to continue on his way and visit the Bell and Dragon before making his decision.

Billy is suddenly compelled to turn back to the bed and breakfast, as though by a force that he can neither understand nor resist. Before he realizes what is happening, he is climbing the front steps of the house and ringing the doorbell.

Almost instantaneously, a middle-aged woman opens the door, startling Billy. She invites him into the house, and, as before, Billy is compelled to follow her inside. The landlady's "very gentle blue eyes" are at once comforting and disconcerting. She seems to have known already that he was coming, and she has a room prepared for him. The price she quotes for the room is "fantastically cheap," and Billy leaps at the offer.

Stepping into the house, he notices that the place is empty except for him, which the landlady confirms while noting that she does not get many guests. She attributes this to her pickiness about the clients she accepts.

Showing him to his third-floor room, she mistakenly calls him Mr. Perkins, but Billy shrugs it off, supposing that she had lost a loved one, perhaps in the war. He does sense that she is "slightly off her rocker," but nothing about her actions or personality bother him at all. Leaving him to unpack, the landlady tells him that before turning in for the night, he must return to the ground floor and sign the guest book in order to be compliant with all laws.

With his unpacking complete, Billy returns to the ground floor to sign in. There he sees the names of the only other guests to have been registered in the house: Christopher Mulholland from Cardiff, Wales, and Gregory W. Temple from Bristol, England. As Billy mulls over why the names sound familiar to him, the landlady appears suddenly with a large silver tea tray.

As the landlady tries to change the subject of the names of the previous guests (the only two guests in three years), Billy continues to push himself to remember the names and the connection that he feels exists between them. As the landlady serves him tea and cookies, Billy grows more certain that he saw the two names connected via a newspaper article at some point in the past. At the same time, he occasionally notices an odd smell that emanates from the landlady as she sits, watching him drink his tea.

The story turns more ominous when Billy mentions to the landlady that the other two lodgers must have left recently. Her response leaves Billy stunned, as she states calmly that neither young man has ever left the bed and breakfast. "They're on the third flood," she says, "both of them together." As Billy stares at her in confusion, the landlady continues with a series of statements and questions about Billy's age, the condition of his teeth, and, very oddly, the condition of Mr. Temple's skin.

Taking another sip of his tea, Billy tries to change the subject by commenting on the parrot that was sitting in a cage in the corner of the room. He had just realized that it was not alive but stuffed. He asks the landlady who had done such fine work of taxidermy. She answers that she had done it herself, as well as the small dachshund, Basil, that had remained motionless by the fire throughout the evening.

Billy is fascinated with the craftsmanship of the landlady's work, but turns down her offer of more tea; it has an odd bitterness to it—a taste of "bitter almonds"—that he does not find appealing. The landlady asks him again if he has signed the guest book, saying that she will need it to remind her of his name once he has gone. The story ends with the implication that Billy is to join Mr. Temple and Mr. Mulholland on the third floor of the house, part of

the landlady's taxidermy collection. He has yet to realize that the bitter almond taste in the tea comes from cyanide, and the strange odor that he senses from the landlady herself is probably formaldehyde. which is commonly used as an embalming agent for dead bodies.

CHARACTERS

Mr. Greenslade

Mr. Greenslade is Billy's boss at the head office in London, who has sent his young employee to Bath. He is one of a group of men who represent, for Billy, success in the business world; his example inspires Billy to work with briskness and focus as he settles himself in Bath.

The Landlady

The unnamed landlady owns the bed and breakfast that draws Billy Weaver in as though by some unknown but undeniable force. Described as a pleasant woman with "a round pink face and very gentle blue eyes," she reminds Billy of "the mother of one's best school-friend welcoming one into the house to stay for the Christmas holidays." She claims to be particularly selective about the guests she welcomes into her house, and she is excited to have Billy as a potential lodger. However, there is an air of oddness about her that hints to the reader of something unusual about her interest in Billy. She is unusually concerned, for instance, that Billy sign the guest registry, and fusses around making him tea despite the fact he has not asked her to do so.

As the story unfolds, the sense of threat attached to her oddness intensifies. She reveals her fascination with taxidermy, which is followed immediately by a direct reference to the fact that the two previous lodgers never left the house but stay together on the third floor of the house. This tidbit of information is disconcerting, given that she earlier said to Billy that there is no one in the house except the two of them, and Billy has seen no evidence of Mulholland or Temple in the house. The reader can gradually put the clues together: this seemingly pleasant woman is, in fact, a murderer who keeps her victims' bodies as trophies, and Billy is drinking a cyanide-laced tea that will ensure that he is her next victim.

Christopher Mulholland

Christopher Mulholland, from Cardiff, Wales, was a guest in the bed and breakfast prior to the arrival of Billy Weaver. He came to the house as a seventeen-year-old Cambridge undergraduate. Billy thinks he remembers the name Mulholland name from an infamous newspaper case about an Eton schoolboy, but he is distracted from thinking more about this when the landlady changes the topic of conversation. Mulholland is one of the two previous victims whose body is kept on the third floor of the bed and breakfast.

Gregory W. Temple

Twenty-eight-year-old Gregory W. Temple, from Bristol, England, was a guest in the bed and breakfast prior to the arrival of Billy Weaver. The landlady comments that he had perfect skin, like that of a baby. Temple is one of the two previous victims whose body is kept on the third floor of the bed and breakfast.

Billy Weaver

Billy Weaver is a seventeen-year-old Londoner who travels to Bath to take up a new position in the company for which he works. Dedicated to what he sees as the ideal of success in the business world, Billy is a model of innocence who is drawn by some mysterious force and who remains oblivious to the clues that build up around him as his evening with the landlady unfolds. He does not find the landlady's oddness the least bit worrisome, nor does he connect the various sensory cues (her strange odor, a bitter taste to the tea) to a need for concern. Although he does struggle to connect the Mulholland and Temple names to a past event that was covered in the newspapers, he remains seemingly unaware of the imminent threat to his life as the story concludes.

THEMES

Ambition

Billy Weaver is a model of ambition, a young man with a strong desire to achieve success through determination and hard work. As the story begins, he is on his way to a new position with his company, in a new town, and he is inspired by the mantra of "briskness," that he equates with business success and worldly wisdom. His ambition compels him forward until he meets an equally compelling force in the landlady. She feeds off the ambition of young men like Billy, offering them spectacular deals on room and board as a lure into her murderous plan. Billy's youthful confidence and ambition combine with his naiveté (inexperience and lack of judgment) to blind Billy to the clues that something is wrong. By moving too quickly, Billy makes himself vulnerable to the wiles of the landlady, who distracts him from thinking too deeply about what he knows, for instance, about the previous lodgers, Mulholland and Temple, or about his own sense that she is "slightly off her rocker."

Innocence

Despite his determination to succeed in business, Billy Weaver is first and foremost an innocent seventeen-year-old whose naiveté ultimately proves fatal. At various moments in the story, he misjudges both the landlady and the environment in which he finds himself. At times, he rationalizes the oddness he feels as the cost of getting such a great deal on the room: "The old girl is slightly dotty, Billy told himself. But at five and sixpence a night, who [cares] about that?" At other times, such as when she tells him that both the parrot and dachshund are products of her taxidermy, he is simply distracted by the novelty of the hobby and sits in admiring fascination at the landlady's talent. In the end, it is Billy's youthful innocence that might be his biggest downfall when trying to negotiate the very dangerous world of the landlady.

Billy's lack of awareness is not unusual given his age. Scientists have found that the brain's prefrontal cortex, which is the home to higher-order cognitive functions such as judgment and reasoning, does not fully develop until late adolescence and into the early twenties. One of the crucial attributes that reaches maturity during this period is a speeding up of the signals that move within the brain, and which allow various parts of the brain to determine, among other things, whether an action or situation is dangerous. At seventeen, Billy might well be unable to process the information that is being presented to him (the strange odors, the odd taste to the tea) as quickly as an older person would be able to, making his innocence as much a neurophysiological condition as it is an emotional one.

TOPICS FOR FURTHER STUDY

- Critic David Burmester notes that Dahl had a definite opinion on the craft of story writing as it relates to the experience of reading and listening. He quotes Dahl as saying: "Very few ordinary readers are conscious of the care with which a real short story writer writes his stories, or of the work that goes into them. They are written primarily to be read aloud, which the novel is not. And if they are not read aloud, they should anyway be read slowly." Interpret "The Landlady" by reading it aloud (with or without sound effects) and capture your performance in an audio recording. If you need examples of powerful readings of classic horror stories, listen to any of the various story readings from *Closed on Account of Rabies: Poems and Tales of Edgar Allan Poe* (1997), many of which are available on YouTube.

- Critics William G. Brozo and Ronald V. Schmelzer, in "Wildmen, Warriors, and Lovers: Reaching Boys through Archetypal Literature," argue for an archetypal reading of literature, which suggests that most major characters fall into one of a number of constantly recurring patterns of imagery and theme (archetypes) that extend across generations. The magician, for instance, is an archetypal character that evokes amazement while displaying qualities of intuition and cleverness; Harry Potter is an example of this character type. They go on to suggest that Dahl's "The Landlady" contains a classic example of the archetype of the wildman, that is, a male character who is lusty, unpredictable, and independent. Write a well-structured and thoughtful essay in which you either agree or disagree with this assessment of the young Billy Weaver.

- Construct a visual representation of the moments of foreshadowing in "The Landlady," illustrating the connections between the moments and how they accumulate to point the reader to the implications captured in the final sentence of the story. The illustration may take the form of a cluster map (also known as a concept map or a mind map), or you may use a program like Prezi to create the illustration.

- A number of television adaptations of Dahl's "The Landlady" have appeared over the years, including one that starred Dean Stockwell as Billy Weaver. (Stockwell would go on to gain cult status for his portrayal of Admiral Al Calavicci in the television series *Quantum Leap*.) Write a thoughtful and well-structured multimedia proposal (pictures and text, for instance) in which you argue for your choices of current actors for each of the two key roles. Who would you choose to play Billy Weaver and why? Who would you choose to play the landlady and why?

- Taxidermy is not often used as a central theme in popular culture, despite the fact that it has been a cultural practice in many parts of the world for centuries. Create a multimedia time line tracing the appearances of taxidermy as a key element in works of literature, art, or film. Be prepared to share this time line with your class and to explain any patterns that you see emerging from these representations.

- Maria Snyder's young-adult novel *Poison Study* (2004) is an action-packed fantasy novel whose main character, Yelena, is an ex-acrobat, convicted of murder, who saves her own life by taking on the role of the commander's new food taster. But staying alive is not an easy task when faced with the possibility of dying with each meal, so Yelena becomes skilled at identifying poisons by smell and her other senses. In an essay, contrast either Snyder and Dahl's use of poison as a key plot element or Yelena and Billy's ability to learn how to deal with potentially fatal environments.

The landlady is friendly and welcoming to Billy.
(© Nika Art | ShutterStock.com)

Madness

Like many great works of fiction, Dahl's story explores madness and its ability to hide (and even flourish) in the everyday world. In many ways, Dahl's landlady is a particularly disturbing portrait of madness. Hiding behind a relatively convincing facade of normalcy and even pleasantness, she appears to Billy as nothing more than a "slightly dotty" middle-aged woman, the type he has seen often in his young life.

At the same time, however, the landlady does begin to seem more unstable; "dotty" gives way to "slightly off her rocker." But Billy remains comfortable in her presence, a tribute to the fact that society (and British society notably) has long accepted eccentricity as within acceptable limits of behavior. One has only to think of other Dahl characters such as Willie Wonka (*Charlie and the Chocolate Factory*) or Matilda Wormwood (*Matilda*) to understand the acceptance and even appeal of the eccentric within mainstream culture.

But eccentricity crosses into madness when the reader comes to understand that she has not only killed the previous two lodgers (most likely with poisoned tea) but also has prepared and stuffed their bodies to be kept as mementos or trophies on the third floor of her home. The harmlessness of the eccentric shifts dramatically into the dangerous threat of madness that has lured Billy to his death.

STYLE

Contrasting Characters

As David Propson notes,

> the true perversity of Dahl's tales lies not in their high-concept conceits, but in the characters. Dahl clearly enjoyed creating genuinely clever characters, particularly ones that prove too clever for their own good. These practical folk encounter a fantastical situation and see not the cruel caprice of an absurd universe, but an angle.

Dahl establishes Billy as the protagonist in "The Landlady," a young man with a very determined focus on a specific goal: to become the most successful businessman he can. His personal mantra is based on approaching life and work with briskness, on making quick judgments and executing them with urgency. Billy's emphasis on briskness guides him to make decisions based on casual rather than detailed observations and, in turn, to miss clues that things might not be as they appear in the bed and breakfast. For example, when he looks into the house from the street, Billy notices "a pretty little dachshund . . . curled up asleep with its nose tucked into its belly." He even notes to himself that "animals [are] usually a good sign in a place like this." But he never asks himself why the dog remains motionless when he rings the bell, enters the house, and moves his bags upstairs. Only later, when the landlady directs his attention in its direction, does Billy realize that the dog is not alive at all, but a stuffed version of its former self.

Dahl's antagonist, the landlady, is, in this sense, the opposite of what Billy stands for. Much older than Billy, she is a skilled at taxidermy, an art that requires slow, painstaking effort to execute properly. Whereas his world is defined by briskness and cursory views, hers is one of slow poison, the lengthy process of embalming, and paying careful attention to detail when skinning and reconstructing the object itself.

Denouement

A French word meaning "the unknotting," *denouement* refers to the point of resolution of the conflict or plot complexities that have accumulated throughout a novel or film. The term rose to prominence in the world of short stories thanks largely to Edgar Allan Poe, whose 1846 essay "The Philosophy of Composition" emphasizes the importance of the denouement in any composition. It is only through an acute awareness of where a story or poem will end, Poe argued, that a writer can build emotion and create a unified effect in any work. Poe's own stories remain, to this day, exemplars of this careful and strategic use of an ending to deliver a powerful, and in his case often horrifying, final punch.

In the tradition of Poe, Dahl's "The Landlady" leads readers to what Amidon calls "the twist, the sting in the tail, the comeuppance" when many of the complexities and ambiguities of the story are made clear. The landlady's initially cryptic comment that the previous lodgers, Mulholland and Temple, are still in the house, together on the third floor, is a classic example of such a sting. The reader recognizes that Billy's fate has been sealed: the almond taste of this tea signals the presence of a poison, the landlady's skill in taxidermy would soon be used as part of a gruesome ritual, and Billy will soon be adding his name to the list of lodgers who entered this bed and breakfast but never left.

Foreshadowing

Foreshadowing, which has also been described as guessing ahead, refers to an author's strategic use of words or phrases as hints to a reader that something is going to happen without revealing the story or diminishing the suspense or mood that is being created. Dahl uses this device extensively in "The Landlady," beginning with the suggestion that Billy is almost supernaturally compelled to ring the doorbell despite his intention of continuing onward to check out the Bell and Dragon. The landlady's comments are also peppered with phrases that suggest that there is more to what Billy is experiencing in the house than meets the eye. She is adamant, for instance, that he sign into the register, in part, because "it's the law of the land" and, more ominously, "because we don't want to go breaking any laws at *this* stage in the proceedings." The italicized "this" lingers in the reader's mind with its implication that at some other point in the "proceedings," laws might indeed be broken. Similarly, the landlady's emphasis on the physical similarities between Billy and the previous lodgers ("They were tall and young and handsome, my dear, just exactly like you"), the strange odor that she exudes, and the strange taste to the tea all begin to accumulate across the pages as a sign to the reader that things are not going to end well for young Billy.

HISTORICAL CONTEXT

Initially published in November of 1959, "The Landlady" captures in the character of Billy a sense of the overwhelming optimism within England that came from a decade of impressive economic growth, historically low unemployment, and general prosperity for a country that had been ravaged by sustained bombing by Nazi Germany during World War II. Interestingly, Dahl has his three victims come from cities that had been specifically targeted for heavy bombing during the war: London (Weaver), Cardiff (Mulholland), and Bristol (Temple).

The 1950s was also a decade that saw the spirit of business (what Billy calls "briskness") define much of English culture, sparked most dramatically by a postwar shift from a manufacturing and resource-based economy to a new focus on the service and knowledge sectors, particularly finance and education. Modernization of the economy was a primary driver of this new focus, marked most obviously by the first major highway construction project and replacement of aging neighborhoods with both private and public housing developments. Family and leisure activities became more accessible to a broader portion of the population, and both cars and televisions became increasingly common in households across the country.

With such prosperity come changes, both subtle and not-so-subtle, to longstanding

COMPARE
&
CONTRAST

- **1959:** The yearly unemployment rate in the United Kingdom is 2.3 percent, which combined with low inflation and sustained growth for most of the decade makes this a period of sustained economic optimism. This spirit is captured neatly in Dahl's characterization of Billy Weaver as a young man determined to succeed in the thriving world of business.

  Today: The unemployment rate in the United Kingdom hovers around 6 percent in early 2015, which is low relative to previous years but still translates to almost two million people unemployed. Britain is optimistic about an economic resurgence after years of sluggishness in the face of an increasingly complicated global economic climate.

- **1959:** The bed and breakfast that Billy Weaver selects has no television set, which is not unusual given that televisions are just starting to becoming commonplace in British homes.

  Today: In 2014, the BBC reports that the average British home has two televisions in it and that 95 percent of homes have some type of digital television service. Daily viewing averages almost four hours a day.

- **1959:** The British tradition of pubs can be traced back for centuries. Around the reign of King Henry VII, alehouses, inns, and taverns collectively became known as public houses (shortened to "pubs"), which became fully licensed institutions in about 1522. In 1959, pub culture is still a substantial part of British life, so it would not be surprising that Billy would be more comfortable checking into the Bell and Dragon than into the bed and breakfast.

  Today: The traditional, independent British pub is in decline as rezoning of prime real estate creates market pressure on urban space, niche marketing redefines what a public house does, and long-time independents consolidate under corporate structures.

geographic and cultural traditions. Small neighborhood stores were increasingly replaced by national and multinational chains and shopping centers. The historic retailer House of Fraser, for instance, won a heated and much-publicized bidding war for the prestigious Harrod's department store chain in August of 1959, with a final offer of more than thirty-seven million British pounds (almost fifty-seven million US dollars in 1959).

The silver lining of this period of prosperity was tinged with shadows of discontent, to be sure. On March 30, 1959, more than twenty thousand people attended a demonstration in Trafalgar Square, in London, in support of the Campaign for Nuclear Disarmament. Concern over nuclear energy and weaponry only intensified with each subsequent power station opening.

A number of industrial disasters were grim reminders, too, that not all citizens were realizing the benefits of what was being characterized as a new age of prosperity. In September 1959, for instance, forty-seven men were killed in a coal mine near the village of Auchengeich, Scotland, when an electrical fire created dense smoke that trapped them a few hundred yards from the surface.

Globally, 1959 was a year that saw Fidel Castro rise to power in the island nation of Cuba following the end of the reign of Fulgencio Batista. What was seen generally as a positive change was quickly tainted by the reality of the political executions of hundreds of former Batista supporters. The increasing brutality on the island led to the beginning of a mass exodus of Cuban nationals to the United States.

Billy is startled to realize that both the parrot in a cage and the dog by the fire are stuffed.
(© CHAINFOTO24 | ShutterStock.com)

In Vietnam, Ho Chi Minh declared a people's war to unite a divided Vietnam, thereby setting the political stage for the controversial and bloody Vietnam War, in which the United States became increasingly involved throughout the early 1960s.

Culturally, 1959 was the year that saw the release of the Disney classic *Sleeping Beauty*, the debut of the iconic (and now controversial) Barbie doll, and the introduction of both the British Mini and the transformative Cadillac that introduced the distinctive tail fins to the automotive world. At the movies, *Ben Hur* dominated the awards season. Tragically, 1959 was also the year that saw the brutal murder of the Clutter family of Holcomb, Kansas (inspiring Truman Capote's classic book *In Cold Blood*), as well as the plane crash that took the lives of singers Buddy Holly, J. P. Richardson (the Big Bopper), and Richie Valens.

CRITICAL OVERVIEW

Erica Wagner of the *New York Times* observes that readers and critics most often

> think of Roald Dahl as a writer for children, the magical creator of James, Charlie, Matilda and the BFG, who worked in a shed in his

English garden with a silver ball of chocolate-wrappers by his side. That he was, but only after he had established a reputation as a writer of clever, often savage, stories for adults.

As Joyce Carol Oates observes, Dahl's "reputation is that of a writer of macabre, blackly jocose tales that read, at their strongest, like artful variants of Grimm's fairy tales." He "exhibits the flair of a natural storyteller," she continues, "for whom no bizarre leap of the imagination is unlikely." His seemingly natural inclination, she suggests, is toward a fiction in which "intimacy is rejected for distance, sympathy for an Olympian detachment."

Howard Lachtman is more specific, arguing that Dahl's short fictions "are not great stories, but great plots—expertly contrived, told with charming ingenuity and perfect plausibility, and enlivened with a deliciously nasty wit that borders on wickedness." Written with a power that, as Wagner puts it, "derives, in large part, from the reader's simple desire to know what happens next," Dahl's stories are noted for often culminating in dramatic, surprising endings.

Wagner points out that Dahl tends to enlist the reader as an active participant, even by sometimes having the narrator refer to a reader, or listener. The "sensation" of being so called out "is never entirely comfortable," as Wagner admits. "This is not simply because so many of these tales have endings that depend on cruelty or vengeance," but because of "the deep vein of misogyny that runs through them." It is a discomfort shared by such critics as Oates, who noted that "it must be that such misogynist female portraits are self-portraits of the misogynist's malformed soul, since they draw forth such quivering, barely containable loathing." This loathing extends, Amidon suggests, to traditional values as well. "In Dahl's stories," he notes, "the core family values are not respect and love but torment and retribution. Intimacy doesn't just breed contempt; it breeds contempt in action."

Winner of the Edgar Allan Poe Award for the Best Short Story Mystery in 1960, "The Landlady" is, as Burmester notes, "a beautifully subtle horror story." Jacques Sohier suggests that it is an exemplar of the Freudian concept of the uncanny, or a deeply "disquieting strangeness."

CRITICISM

Klay Dyer

Dyer is a freelance writer and editor specializing in topics relating to literature, popular culture, and innovation. In the following essay, he explores Dahl's "The Landlady" as a commentary on Billy Weaver's ambition and the risk that he faces when his brisk, businesslike persona is confronted with a situation that he is unable to understand or defend himself against.

Ambition is both a common and elusive theme in literature, in part because it is so much a part of the human story, from William Shakespeare's play *Othello* (written around 1603) and John Milton's long poem *Paradise Lost* (1608–1674), through to the modern era, with F. Scott Fitzgerald's *The Great Gatsby* (1925) and Chuck Palahniuk's anti-ambition novel *Fight Club* (1996). Based on a relatively neutral term in Latin that referred to the practice of canvassing, or going from family to family to collect votes, the term *ambition* quickly became associated with people who focused intently on accumulating money, honor, popularity, or power.

Ambition appeals to what pioneering psychiatrist Sigmund Freud called the *Id*, the unconscious desire to satisfy individual needs, such as for food or power. The Id is a fundamental driver of human behavior that must always adjust in order to allow an individual to enjoy a balanced, healthy interaction with the world. Too much ambition, as readers see in everything from the Bible to the works of Shakespeare, leads inevitably to bad things happening to all involved (and in many cases even to those not involved). Too little ambition leads to a life of complacency, or "settling," and disappointment, as might be seen in Arthur Miller's 1949 play *Death of a Salesman*, in which Willie Loman fails to realize his ambition and dies deeply disillusioned with the American dream.

Dahl's "The Landlady" falls neatly into this tradition of literature that explores both the risk and the reward of ambition. Billy Weaver represents the next generation of ambition. Only seventeen, he is venturing forth in the world to realize his own dreams of making it big in business, and he is taking full advantage of the opportunities that lie before him. As Sohier notes, Billy is an enthusiastic student

> WHAT BILLY BELIEVES TO BE A STABLE TRUTH IN THE WORLD—THAT BRISKNESS EQUALS SUCCESS—WILL PROVE, IN FACT, TO BE AN UNSTABLE AND ULTIMATELY FATAL ASSUMPTION ABOUT A WORLD HE WILL NEVER UNDERSTAND."

who "identifies with the men that make up his working environment" and who sets out to internalize both their "logic of purposefulness" and the speed with which they move through their days. "He walked briskly down the street" upon his arrival in Bath, determined to fulfill his boss's order to find lodging and report to his new office. Billy's emphasis on pacing is both crucial and self-aware, given that "he was trying to do everything briskly these days. Briskness, he had decided, was *the* one common characteristic of all successful businessmen." Observant and eager, Billy sees his new dedication to speed as the precursor to greater things: "The big shots up at Head Office were absolutely fantastically brisk all the time. They were amazing."

However, this overly simplified expression of youthful ambition is, as Sohier notes, little more than an affectation in Billy's case, a taking on of appearance without the depth of maturity or wisdom to sustain it in a meaningful way. "Success is closely connected with outward speed," Sohier comments. "Success becomes the equivalent of speed, and speed, so goes the logic of youthful ambition, brings success, since the character adopts an exterior attitude, a mere empty outward form."

And herein lies the risk for Billy, for with ambition and this devotion to briskness comes a vulnerability to a world that does not always function as he might hope or wish for. Dahl, in fact, signals in his opening paragraph that the world into which Billy steps as he disembarks from the train from London is not a simple one. Rather, it is a world in which even the weather can be presented in a way that is at once familiar and beautiful and dangerous and deadly: "The moon was coming up out of a clear starry sky over the houses opposite the station entrance.

WHAT DO I READ NEXT?

- "Skin," another of Dahl's adult stories, is a disturbing satire on the world of art and art dealers. In it, a starving old man is forced to literally sell the skin off his back in order to survive in war-torn Paris of 1946.

- No list of recommended readings would be complete without reference to the works for which Dahl is best remembered: *James and the Giant Peach* (1961), *Charlie and the Chocolate Factory* (1964), and *Matilda* (1988). When reread with the experience of such classic Dahl stories as "The Landlady," "The Man from the South," or "Skin" in place, these modern classics of children's literature reveal a dark undertone that many readers overlook in early readings.

- Dahl's nonfiction work *Going Solo* (1986) is an autobiographical recounting of his adventures working in Africa as well as his trials as an ace fighter pilot during World War II.

- O. Henry (a pen name for William Sydney Porter) was a strong influence on Dahl's story writing, as can be seen by reading any of the selections collected in *The Best Short Stories of O. Henry* (1994). Dahl was an open admirer of the subtle yet complex plot development, the detailed characterization, and the clever endings of his fellow story writer.

- Canadian Yann Martel's *Beatrice and Virgil* (2010) is an allegorical novel that tells the story of a novelist, Henry, who traces a discovered letter to a taxidermist who, in turn, has been writing a play focused on two taxidermy animals: Beatrice, a donkey, and Virgil, a monkey. The animals, it becomes apparent, are stand-ins for the victims of Nazi persecution.

- Any number of stories by Edgar Allan Poe are similar to those of Dahl in their alignment of horror elements as well as their emphasis on building tension toward a shocking denouement. The 1965 collection *18 Best Stories by Edgar Allan Poe* or any similar collection will provide opportunities to explore the mastery of such stories as "The Cask of Amontillado," "The Tell-Tale Heart," and "The Pit and the Pendulum."

- Given that Dahl was asked specifically to work on the film adaptations of two novels written by his friend Ian Fleming, a reading of Fleming's *Chitty-Chitty-Bang-Bang: The Magical Car* (1964) provides an interesting context for readings of both Dahl's adult stories and his children's books.

But the air was deadly cold and the wind was like a flat blade of ice on his cheeks." As he walks down the street toward the pub, he sees, but does not understand, that the once "very swanky residences" (themselves symbols of ambition realized) had fallen into a state of disrepair. "Even in the darkness, he could see that the paint was peeling from the woodwork on their doors and windows, and that the handsome white facades were cracked and blotchy from neglect."

Dahl's word choice here is critical. Just as the houses are exposed through the crumbling of their facades, Billy's ambition and devotion to briskness will prove vulnerable to the forces of the landlady. What Billy believes to be a stable truth in the world—that briskness equals success—will prove, in fact, to be an unstable and ultimately fatal assumption about a world he will never understand.

Drawn almost supernaturally to the bed and breakfast, Billy enters a world in which the signs and objects of the real world are destabilized. The rent he is asked to pay is "fantastically cheap," for instance, and is much more a

The unusual flavor in Billy's tea hints at his grim end. (© *Olga Sapegina* / *ShutterStock.com*)

reflection of a world of fantasy than a world of real business and economy. In a twist of cosmic irony within a world defined by ambition, it is this same cheap rent that persuades Billy to overlook his growing awareness that the landlady is "slightly dotty" or even "slightly off her rocker." In a business world defined by the bottom line and ambition, no deal is ever too good to be true—but in the surreal world of the landlady, to believe that can (and does) prove fatal.

As Billy speeds through his assessment of his new situation, he misses clues that become increasingly obvious to the reader and dismisses his slight fear of bed and breakfasts as places of "watery cabbage, rapacious landladies, and a powerful smell of kippers in the living room." The fact that the house is empty of guests and has been for some years is shunted aside by the flimsy explanation from the landlady that she is especially picky about whom she takes in, as is the fact that she surveys him slowly from head to toe when he enters the foyer. In his haste to get unpacked and settled (per his boss's instructions), he overlooks the fact that she calls him by the wrong name. Moreover, he goes so far as to create a story that validates his own sense of her as a risk-free part of his journey toward success: "She was not only harmless—there was no question about that—but she was also quite obviously a kind and generous soul. He guessed that she had probably lost a son in the war, or something like that, and had never got over it."

Not surprisingly, Billy's settling into the house is undertaken with an appropriate attention to briskness. He unpacks in "a few minutes," and then trots (not walks) downstairs to the living room. Too busy to notice that the small dachshund by the fire has not moved a muscle since his arrival, he takes pride in the efficiency with which he has fulfilled his first important business task in Bath: "I'm a lucky fellow, he thought, rubbing his hands. This is a bit of all right."

Ironically, when Billy does begin to pay attention to the details around him, his attempts to remember the significance of the names in the register (Mulholland and Temple) makes him preoccupied and distracted, and thus even less likely to pay attention to further clues. He pays only passing attention, for instance, to the "peculiar smell that seemed to emanate directly from her person." In a wonderful layering of foreshadowing, Dahl has Billy recognize the scent as close to that of "pickled walnuts," newly cured leather, or "the corridors of a hospital." Individually, these smells should be disconcerting, but taken collectively they should raise some questions or concerns for Billy.

Billy, however, has already sped to his conclusion that there is "no question" that the landlady is harmless, so he does not make the connection when she reveals her love of taxidermy and the strange fact that the two previous lodgers are still in the house, despite there being no evidence of it and despite the obvious contradiction of her previous statement that she and Billy have the house to themselves.

Spurred forward in his life by ambition, and fueled by an untested confidence in the power of briskness, Billy falls victim to a sort of blindness. As he drinks more of the cyanide-laced tea offered to him by the pleasant, gentle, and unquestionably harmless woman on the couch beside him, Billy remains wholly unaware of the fate that awaits him. Fearless and naive to a fault, Billy is given over to the blinding ambition of youth and, symbolically, of a country that imagines the future as a seamless continuation of its current prosperity.

Seduced by the promises that flow freely from the shadowy Home Office of his company, Billy is a lamb wandering innocently into a world of wolves. Unable to perceive the danger that surrounds him, he will never have the chance to learn the important lesson that ambition, once uncoupled from such near cousins as pride, avarice, and unquestioning faith, can, indeed, generate great success.

Source: Klay Dyer, Critical Essay on "The Landlady," in *Short Stories for Students*, Gale, Cengage Learning, 2016.

Greg Littmann

In the following excerpt, Littmann characterizes Dahl as a writer of children's horror fiction.

A boy swims desperately against the current, but is not strong enough; he is sucked under the surface and into the pipes, swept along toward the mechanical knives. Meanwhile, a wild animal breaks free in the city, killing and devouring two young parents, leaving their orphaned son to be abused by his two demented aunts. In space, the

> PERHAPS MOST POWERFULLY, DAHL MAKES THE DANGER IN HIS TALES SEEM REAL BECAUSE THE WORLDS HE PORTRAYS ARE WORLDS IN WHICH TERRIBLE THINGS HAPPEN TO PEOPLE."

Vermicious Knids amass, leathery and terrible, ready to exterminate the humans as they have exterminated so many races before. All across the world, monstrous giants invade to butcher and consume human children in the night, while at a luxury hotel in Bournemouth, hideous child-hating witches plot the death of every child in England. Am I describing events from horror novels? Yes. They're from Roald Dahl's children's fiction.

Roald Dahl is perhaps the greatest writer of children's horror fiction who has ever lived. Of course, you won't find his work for children in the horror section of a bookstore or listed under "horror" on Amazon. Obviously, there are good, practical reasons for such businesses to clearly distinguish books suitable for adults from books suitable for children in this way. Yet to deny that Dahl's children's books constitute horror fiction, at least some of the time, is to fail to appreciate the way that he makes horror a primary tool for engaging the reader.

Charlie and the Chocolate Factory, one of the finest works in children's literature, is a surreal nightmare in which a group of children are picked off one by one in ways that suggest agonizing death or permanent disfigurement. All it needs to fit snugly in the horror section are fewer lucky escapes—Augustus Gloop is carved to pieces in the fudge machine as "a hundred knives go slice, slice, slice," and Veruca Salt tumbles screaming into the fires of the rubbish incinerator.

But if Dahl's children's books are horror fiction, what the devil are we doing giving them to children? Granted, Dahl's works are *children's* horror fiction, more restrained in many ways than adult horror. All the same, we might well wonder whether any works that focus so much on evil, fear, and the prospect of grizzly death are appropriate for impressionable kids.

As it happens, I badly want children to read Roald Dahl. Far from wanting to keep his work from their hands, I would like to see every kid have the opportunity to thrill at the mysterious Willy Wonka's chocolate factory, to laugh at the rude giant centipede from *James and the Giant Peach*, and yes, to get a little bit scared by those cruel witches from *The Witches*, the ones who hide among us, waiting to . . . *phwisst!* . . . "disappear" children. I'm so eager to pass on these stories that I'm even willing to "do the voices" when reading aloud, although I'm pretty bad at it—except for my evil giants.

Here you'll find a defense of the value of Roald Dahl's children's literature, in all its gruesome, violent, and disturbing glory. But before I go on to defend it, let's first establish beyond any doubt that Roald Dahl's children's literature really is horror for kids.

ROALD DAHL: THE MASTER OF CHILDREN'S HORROR

Most fiction features danger of one sort or another. However, fiction edges toward the horror genre in accordance with the potential degree of harm, especially bodily harm, suffered by characters, the amount of detail lavished on the potential for harm, and the apparent likelihood that characters, especially main characters, will actually be harmed. That's not a definition of "horror art," but these are three good rules of thumb that will usually distinguish horror art from other genres. And by all three standards, Dahl's work leans to the horrific.

In Dahl's stories, children face potential death all the time. Willy Wonka's factory is filled with ways for naughty children to die. Augustus Gloop, once he has tumbled into the lake of chocolate, is first in danger of drowning, then of being cut up and made into fudge. Veruca Salt is in danger of being burned to death, Violet Beauregarde of being squeezed to death, and Mike Teavee of suffering perhaps the most gruesome death possible—partial materialization. Good children are not much safer. Every wild ride Charlie takes in Wonka's hurtling glass elevator is a gamble with his life, all the more so when carnivorous Knids or infectious Gnoolies await his arrival. Likewise, James Henry Trotter of *James and the Giant Peach* lives in danger of being drowned, eaten by sharks, murdered by the monstrous Cloud-Men, and falling hundreds of feet to his death

in a spray of peach juice on the streets of New York. In *The BFG* it is revealed that hideous giants regularly raid our cities under the cover of night to eat "human beans," especially children, while the unnamed child protagonist of *The Witches* faces the possible extermination of every child in England.

The detail Dahl lavishes on the threats in his stories is striking, especially for children's literature. The threats in *Charlie and the Chocolate Factory* may mostly be conveyed by suggestion, but the Oompa-Loompas never let an opportunity pass to ghoulishly elaborate in song about what each vanished child may be suffering: the predicted slicing, boiling, and transformation into fudge of Augustus Gloop, the possible death of Violet Beauregarde from being squeezed in the juicing room, the disgusting filth into which Veruca Salt is plunged as she hurtles into the rubbish furnace, and the possibility that Mike Teavee will remain inches tall for the rest of his life. The Oompa-Loompas may sometimes be lying (as may Wonka when he casually remarks on the likelihood of one of the children dying in some horrible way), but for all the reader can tell, they are speaking the truth. Their songs provide particularly dark little horror stories within the main narrative. If you took the Oompa-Loompas' song about Augustus Gloop out of the novel and included it instead in *Revolting Rhymes* as an independent poem, it would become a straightforward story of a human being getting cut up and turned into food.

Likewise, in *James and the Giant Peach*, Dahl delights in giving frightening descriptions of encounters with alien life. When James first enters the peach, we're told, "Every one of these 'creatures' was at least as big as James himself, and in the strange greenish light that shone down from somewhere in the ceiling, they were absolutely terrifying to behold. 'I'm hungry!' the Spider announced suddenly, staring hard at James." And upon first seeing the Cloud-Men, "it became obvious that these 'things' were actually living creatures—tall, wispy, wraithlike, shadowy, white creatures who looked as though they were made out of a mixture of cotton-wool and candyfloss and thin white hairs." On further inspection, "James Henry Trotter, glancing up quickly, saw the faces of a thousand furious Cloud-Men peering down at him over the edge of the cloud. The faces had almost no shape at all because of the long white hairs that covered them. There were no noses, no mouths, no ears, no chins—only the eyes were visible in each face, two small black eyes glinting malevolently through the hairs."

Similarly horrible descriptions are given of Vermicious Knids and the intangible Gnoolies in *Charlie and the Great Glass Elevator*; evil human-eating giants like the Bloodbottler, Childchewer, and Fleshlumpeater in *The BFG*; and the haggish witches in *The Witches*. Dahl relates in loving detail the rashy pimpliness of the witches' bald, scabby heads, their clawed hands and square, toeless feet, and the pale blue spittle clinging to their pointed teeth, set in gums that are "like raw meat."

Perhaps most powerfully, Dahl makes the danger in his tales seem real because the worlds he portrays are worlds in which terrible things happen to people. We already know that Charlie Bucket is vulnerable long before he steps into the chocolate factory, because of just how hard a life the author has already given him. Charlie is not just our eyes and ears in the novel but also our mouths and tummies, and we have been feeling him starve. Giving credibility to the danger of Wonka's factory, it is made clear that Oompa-Loompas can and do suffer awful industrial accidents, being turned into blueberries, tumbling down the fudge mountain, or even floating away forever because they drank experimental "fizzy lifting drink" but failed to "do a great big long rude burp." The Oompa-Loompas know how dangerous conditions are in Wonka's factory: "Watching them, Charlie experienced a queer sense of danger. There was something dangerous about this whole business, and the Oompa-Loompas knew it. There was no chattering or singing among them here, and they moved about over the huge black camera slowly and carefully in their scarlet space suits." Things only grow worse for them in *Charlie and the Great Glass Elevator*, in which Wonka's reckless experiments turn 131 Oompa-Loompas into minuses, to face the prospect of painful subtraction and long division in Minusland. They were probably safer back in the jungles of Loompaland, hiding in trees to escape the wangdoodles.

It is knowing that terrible things happen to people in Charlie's universe that gives the danger an edge. The reader can believe that Augustus really might be slaughtered by the knives of the fudge machine and boiled into "Augustus-flavoured chocolate-coated Gloop," that Veruca Salt really might be burned alive in the bowels of the rubbish furnace, that Mike Teavee really might stumble forth as half a person after being sent by television, spraying gore in all directions from his ruined body. In *The Great Glass Elevator*, Charlie listens as the Knids devour the passengers of a commuter shuttle in space: "The screams continued. They were so loud the President had to put his fingers in his ears. Every house in the world that had a television or radio receiver heard those awful screams. There were other noises, too. Loud grunts and snortings and crunching sounds. Then there was silence."

In *James and the Giant Peach*, the horrible and meaningless death of innocent people is a recurring theme. James's parents are snatched away from him when "Both of them suddenly got eaten up (in full daylight, mind you, and on a crowded street) by an enormous angry rhinoceros which had escaped from the London Zoo." The fact that rhinos don't eat meat just underlines the arbitrariness of their deaths. For no good reason and without warning, James's parents are suddenly lost forever: "They were dead and gone in thirty-five seconds flat." Twice on the journey of the flying peach, Miss Spider breaks the narrative to tell a story of her own about the horrible death of a beloved relation, each a sentient spider like herself, at the hands of Aunt Sponge. Her father drowned when Sponge flushed him down the plughole of the bathtub, while her grandmother survived for six months stuck in paint upside down on the ceiling until she was crushed by Sponge's mop.

In *The BFG*, the BFG assures Sophie, "Giants is all cannybully and murderful! And they *does* gobble up human beans! . . . Bone-crunching Giant crunches up two wopsey whiffling human beans for supper every night! Noise is earbursting! Noise of crunching bones goes crackety-crack for miles around!" Children are particularly likely to be eaten. The Queen notes regarding one massacre, "Eighteen girls vanish mysteriously from their beds at Roedean school! Fourteen boys disappear from Eton! Bones are found underneath dormitory windows!"

Even when reading the book of poetry *Dirty Beasts*, we soon realize that a child introduced at the start of a poem is very likely to be dead by the end of it, often through no fault of their own. In *The Witches*, the child protagonist, by being transformed into a mouse, is cursed to die within nine years. The book ends with the curse unlifted and with the implication that it is unliftable. In Dahl's worlds, sometimes even heroic children die.

Of course, death isn't the only horrible thing that can happen to a child in Dahl's children's fiction. In *Matilda*, we know that the evil headmistress, Miss Trunchbull, might break Matilda's arm because she broke Miss Honey's arm when she was a little girl. In *Charlie and the Chocolate Factory*, Charlie's poverty and the way that he suffers because of it turn his search for the Golden Ticket into something desperate. Every time it fails to turn up in a Whipple-Scrumptious Fudgemallow Delight or a Nutty Crunch Surprise, it is an assurance that the universe does not automatically help children to prevent them from starving. The way that James from *James and the Giant Peach* is abused by his Aunts Spiker and Sponge is so vicious that it is unfilmable. In particular, capturing the violence visually requires making it too concrete to be appropriate for children. In the 1996 Disney film of *James and the Giant Peach*, the two aunts, for all their unkindness, are never shown physically *hurting* James. The difference between children's horror like Dahl's and adult horror is likewise often not a matter of the events depicted but of the detail given. In a poem in *Dirty Beasts*, Chocky-Wock the Crocodile eats multiple children at every meal. If this were depicted in visceral detail on the page or the screen, the result would be too horrible for a kid. . . .

Source: Greg Littmann, "Charlie and the Nightmare Factory: The Art of Children's Horror Fiction," in *Roald Dahl and Philosophy: A Little Nonsense Now and Then*, edited by Jacob M. Held, Rowman & Littlefield, 2014, pp. 173–78.

Heather Worthington

In the following excerpt, Worthington counters criticism that Dahl's work is not appropriate for children.

"VULGAR, VIOLENT, SEXIST, RACIST, CRIMINAL": CHILDREN'S LITERATURE?

In the oft-quoted words of Arthur Ransome, "You write not for children but for yourself, and if, by good fortune, children enjoy what you enjoy, why then you are a writer of children's books." These words could have been written with Roald Dahl in mind; he wrote about what he knew and enjoyed, and although in his writing for children he generally adopted a different narrative voice from that of his fiction for adults, the themes of and the humour in the two formats are uncannily similar. But, as Peter Hunt has noted, Dahl had a worldwide reputation as a writer of sinister short stories "that dealt with the very dark corners of human nature before he became a writer for children." Hunt goes on to query whether Dahl's "zestful exploitation of childish instincts for hate and revenge, prejudice and violence, [can] be as innocent as it appears." In the developed world, societies tend to define the child precisely as that which is not adult, endeavouring thus to set up clear demarcations between the two states of being, a position evident in children's literature. In this context, given the thematic similarities in his writing for children and for adults, particularly the pervasive presence of violence and the frequent representation of crime, can Dahl's juvenile fiction be considered to constitute a "suitable" read for a child?

Of course, the very concept of "suitability" is problematic; decisions as to what is "suitable" or indeed "unsuitable" for children are inescapably subjective and temporally and culturally contingent, as critical analyses of Dahl's fiction demonstrate. In 1991, Jonathan Culley offered a defence of Dahl's fiction, noting that while his texts had "been heavily criticised for . . . vulgarity, fascism, violence, sexism, racism, . . . promotion of criminal behaviour," because they are located in the folklore and fairy tale tradition they escape these charges. The child reader, Culley suggests, implicitly already familiar with the conservative patterns of such narratives (good triumphing over evil, virtuous characters rewarded and wicked ones punished, the triumph of the underdog), understands the imaginary status of the stories and so is unaffected by their content. In his 2010 biography of Dahl, Donald Sturrock devotes five pages to the adverse critical reception of Dahl's fiction for children. And yes. Dahl's juvenile texts wrap their violence and other potentially controversial aspects in a tissue of fantasy and they make the representation of crime acceptable either by moral justification or by ensuring its containment and punishment. Twenty years after Dahl's death and Culley's defence, in a world that in its reliance on television and electronic media would undoubtedly have horrified Dahl and which exposes children to actual violence and crime in unprecedented ways, his children's fiction seems less controversial and, I suggest, might now have more positive functions that outweigh the often negative adult perceptions of its suitability in moral terms of its content for their imagined child reader.

My contention here is that for the child of the twenty-first century and in the context of the contemporary emphasis on representing the "real" in literature for children, Dahl's juvenile canon affords escapist reading par excellence. As in crime fiction, Dahl's writing for adults offers its readers a variety of potentially cathartic reading positions—protagonist, antagonist, victim—and this is equally true, I suggest, of his stories for children. These allow child readers a safe space in which to explore their personal and social anxieties and to vent, in their imagination and/or unconsciously, their own feelings of anger and resentment towards the adults who control their world. In many ways, modern children are given unprecedented and often unmediated access to the trappings of the adult world, particularly in terms of clothing and popular culture: they are less imitation adults than simulacra, having the appearance of—but without the substance or properties of—adulthood. More visibly perhaps than ever before, adult power is revealed to but denied the child. In Dahl's narratives, adult and juvenile, a constant theme is the reversal or circumvention of normative power relations and the revenge taken by the disempowered upon the empowered, but where in the adult stories the social and narrative status quo is, disturbingly, not necessarily restored, the children's fiction mostly adheres to the normative conservatism of happy, if quirky, endings.

The stories which Dahl produced specifically for children are, for the most part, clearly marked out as fantasy. They accord with Rosemary Jackson's concept of narratives, which "assert that what they are telling is real—relying upon all the conventions of realist fiction to do so—and then they proceed to

break the assumption of realism by introducing what—within those terms—is manifestly unreal." Jackson is speaking of adult fiction, but Dahl's writing for a juvenile audience conforms to her description, presenting to the child reader a recognisable and often familiar world, peopled with everyday figures and events, and then introducing the patently unreal—animals and insects that can speak, children with magic fingers and kinetic powers, witches, giants. In Jackson's model, fantasy literature is precisely a literature of subversion, and the empowerment of the child and the (temporary) reversal of normative social structures in children's literature are subversive. In Dahl's texts the representation of adults is equally subversive; frequently they are depicted as at best thoughtless and at worst actively and intentionally cruel. Furthermore, this cruelty is always punished by a means that is directly or indirectly orchestrated by the child—or animal—victim. Once this has occurred, however, the subversion of the narrative is curtailed and conservative values and the proper status quo are restored, if in unconventional or reconfigured forms.

This containment of temporary subversion within conservatism, the veiling of violence in fantasy and the essentially restorative closures of the narratives are, in part, what make the majority of Dahl's fiction for children unthreatening and construct it as acceptable and morally appropriate, so making it "suitable" reading for a child. They are also what make it escapist literature: for the space of their reading, child readers can live in their imagination and can possess the control over their lives and circumstances that reality does not afford. This is a space in which the child can be naughty, scatological, empowered and, perhaps most importantly, be metaphorically revenged on the adults who control children's lives. From the child's perspective, the methods of control are not always pleasant and the rationale behind them unclear; from the adult perspective this control is conventionally seen to be part of the process of civilising the child. For Dahl and perhaps for other adults, "children . . . are only semi-civilised" and need training to become good (conformist) adult subjects. What Dahl's writing for children recognises is the child's perspective, particularly when adult behaviour is inconsistent or evidently unfair. Consequently, justice is often implicit in the revenge

"

**FOR HER THESE CORPSES ARE BETTER
COMPANY THAN LIVE MEN, IN PART BECAUSE SHE
CAN EXERCISE TOTAL CONTROL OVER THEM."**

that is at the centre of much of Dahl's fiction. In *Matilda* the eponymous heroine decides to revenge herself on her parents every time they mistreat her: "A small victory or two would help her tolerate their idiocies and stop her from going crazy." . . .

Source: Heather Worthington, "An Unsuitable Read for a Child?: Reconsidering Crime and Violence in Roald Dahl's Fiction for Children," in *Roald Dahl*, edited by Ann Alston and Catherine Butler, Palgrave Macmillan, 2012, pp. 123–26.

Mark I. West

In the following excerpt, West highlights some of the major themes in Kiss Kiss, *the collection in which "The Landlady" appears.*

In the late 1940s Dahl began writing macabre short stories. Although he always came up with new and unusual plot lines, these carefully contructed stories soon began to follow a discernible pattern: seemingly respectable characters are confronted with peculiar problems or opportunities and respond by committing, or at least contemplating, cruel or self-destructive acts. In most of these stories Dahl used sardonic humor, implied violence, and surprise endings. Often he incorporated material that related to his own recreational pursuits, such as collecting paintings and fine wines.

As he had done with his war stories, he submitted his macabre stories to American magazines, which quickly accepted them. The *New Yorker*, often seen as the most prestigious magazine in America, published eight of these stories between 1949 and 1959. This impressive record helped establish Dahl as a major figure on the American literary scene.

KISS KISS

. . . In February 1960 Knopf published *Kiss Kiss*, a collection of 11 of Dahl's stories. Four of these stories had never before been published. Of the remaining stories, four had

originally appeared in the *New Yorker*, while the others had first seen print in either *Esquire*, *Nugget*, or *Playboy*. Like the stories in *Someone Like You*, those in *Kiss Kiss* have tightly woven plots, macabre elements, and surprise endings. Also, many of the characters in *Kiss Kiss* have much in common with the quirky characters from Dahl's earlier stories. In fact, two of the *Kiss Kiss* stories feature Claud, the same character who figures in several of the stories in *Someone Like You*. There is, however, a major difference between the two collections. Most of the stories in *Kiss Kiss* focus on tense and unhappy relationships between men and women, whereas just a few of the stories in *Someone Like You* treat this theme.

Among the stories in *Kiss Kiss*, only three do not involve conflicts between the sexes. Two of these—"Parson's Pleasure" and "The Champion of the World"—are about the experiences of Claud and his rustic friends. In "Parson's Pleasure" Claud and his neighbors are the target of a wealthy antique dealer who tries to con them into selling a rare Chippendale commode that Claud's neighbors happen to own. Claud and his neighbors are drawn in by this fast-talking con artist, but because they believe his lies and act accordingly, they unwittingly foil his scheme. The underlying class conflict in "Parson's Pleasure" is even more evident in "The Champion of the World." In this story Claud introduces a friend to the art of poaching pheasants. Together they set out to capture nearly all of the pheasants that live on a vast tract of land owned by a wealthy sausage manufacturer. They want to accomplish this feat before the sausage manufacturer has his pheasant-hunting party, an annual event to which only the rich and the titled are invited. In both of these stories arrogant members of the upper class discover that they do not have total control over the country folk whom they so despise.

The other story in this collection that does not involve a conflict between the sexes is "Pig." This strange parable is about a boy who lives with his aunt on an isolated farm in the mountains of Virginia. The aunt is determined to preserve the boy's innocence, so she shelters him from the evils of the world. She keeps him out of school, raises him to be a vegetarian, and never takes him to town. When the boy is 17 his aunt dies, and he is suddenly forced to enter society. He does not, however, have the survival skills necessary to cope with life away from the farm, and he quickly meets a grisly end. In some ways this character is similar to Claud: they both have rural roots, limited educations, and pleasant dispositions. But Claud at least knows how society works. The boy in "Pig" is so naive and trusting that he cannot distinguish between good and bad advice. His innocence, in a sense, prevents him from taking control over his own life.

In the other stories a member of one sex is usually trying to control a member of the opposite sex. This pattern is first seen in the collection's lead story, a haunting tale entitled "The Landlady." Modeled after traditional ghost stories, "The Landlady" features a mysterious bed-and-breakfast establishment, a peculiar woman who owns the place, and a young man who decides to spend the night there. Shortly after entering the house, the young man learns that only two people have ever signed the guest book and that several years have elapsed since the last guest signed in. When he asks the landlady about the men whose names are in the guest book, she informs him that "they're on the fourth floor, both of them together." She also informs him that she has a passionate interest in taxidermy. The young man begins to suspect that something is not quite right, but his fate is already sealed.

What sets the landlady apart from many other murderers is her attitude toward her victims. She does not really think of them as being dead. By preserving their bodies, she is able to transform her victims into lifelike dolls. She visits them, provides them with a room, and takes pleasure in examining their physiques. For her these corpses are better company than live men, in part because she can exercise total control over them. The landlady, in other words, controls the men in her life by literally reducing them to possessions.

Mary Pearl, one of the central characters in "William and Mary," also gains control over the man in her life, but only after a most extraordinary turn of events. For most of her adult life Mary's stodgy and domineering husband had dictated her every move. He had not let her smoke, watch television, or participate in decision making. As the story opens she is under the impression that her husband has recently died, and she is beginning to enjoy her newfound freedom. She learns, however, that shortly before her husband's body had failed, he had agreed to participate in a medical experiment. As a result of this experiment his brain and one of his eyes continue to function normally, although they are detached from the rest of his body. At first she is quite taken aback by this strange news, but after seeing him in his altered state she realizes that she prefers him this way and decides to take him home with her. "From now on," she tells her bodiless husband, "you are going to do just exactly what Mary tells you" (*Kiss*).

Mary's desire to bring her husband home is partially motivated by revenge. This becomes obvious when she deliberately smokes a cigarette within his sight, even though she knows that he disapproves of smoking. Revenge, however, is not the only reason she wants to take control over her husband's life. She feels that the scientist who conducted the experiment does not know how to care for her husband. She points out, for example, that the newspaper that the scientist had placed before her husband's eye is not the one that her husband likes to read, and she insists that it be replaced with his favorite newspaper. It is not that she wants to make her husband miserable; it is just that she wants to be in charge. Mary and her husband both care for each other, but neither is capable of treating the other as an equal.

Unlike Mary and her husband, Mr. and Mrs. Foster, the central characters in "The Way Up to Heaven," care little about each other's welfare. These elderly and extremely well-to-do Americans live in a mansion in New York City. The mansion is so big that they are able to avoid each other most of the time, but when they are together they become tense. Mr. Foster exacerbates this tension by playing upon his wife's fear of arriving late to appointments. He seems to take a perverse pleasure in delaying their departures from the mansion until the last possible minute, knowing full well that this behavior makes his wife extremely agitated. During the course of the story Mr. Foster nearly succeeds in making his wife miss her long-planned flight to Paris. In the end, though, she not only catches the flight; she also wins the undeclared war that they have been quietly waging. Her victory proves that she is more than a match for her husband when it comes to the cunning use of passive aggression. For Mr. and Mrs. Foster the impulse to control the other is rooted in aggression and is not associated with possessive or protective feelings.

The other couples in the *Kiss Kiss* stories are not quite as combative as Mr. and Mrs. Foster, but they certainly do not have ideal marriages. Mr. and Mrs. Bixby in "Mrs. Bixby and the Colonel's Coat" treat each other in a civil manner, but both are hiding extramarital affairs. Edward and Louisa in "Edward the Conqueror" seem to have a good marriage at first, but it is undermined by Edward's jealousy and narrow-mindedness. In "Genesis and Catastrophe: A True Story," Alois and Klara Hitler (the parents of Adolf Hitler) have a rocky marriage that has been strained to its limits by the deaths of their first three children. Albert and Mabel Taylor, the major characters in "Royal Jelly," have a loving relationship, but even they are pulled apart when their newborn daughter refuses to eat. Without exception, the couples in these stories do not have open and honest relationships. At least one member of each couple uses intimidation, deception, or outright violence in an attempt to control his or her spouse.

"Georgy Porgy," the remaining story in the collection, focuses on a young clergyman named George. Although this story is not about marital dynamics, it does deal with male-female relationships. In part because of a traumatic childhood experience, George has an inordinate fear of sexuality. He is uncomfortable when women touch him, and the idea of being kissed by a woman repulses him. Not knowing how disturbed George is, some of the single women in his parish occasionally flirt with him in a playful way, and this drives George to the verge of insanity. Toward the end of the story an attractive woman propositions George, precipitating his psychological breakdown and subsequent institutionalization.

The issue of control plays a major role in "Georgy Porgy," just as it does in most of the other stories in *Kiss Kiss*. In this story, however, the major character is not trying to control other characters; he is simply trying to control himself. Unable to understand or tolerate his sexual impulses, he tries to repress them at all times. It is clear that he is a clergyman largely because it is an occupation that is often associated with celibacy. But try as he might, he cannot gain total control over this part of his personality. His refusal to accept his sexuality eventually causes him to lose control over all the other aspects of his life. In a way George's struggle to control his sexuality is similar to the experiences that many Dahl characters have when they attempt to control the lives of other people. The drive to be in control not only makes it difficult for all of these characters to accept other people and care for their welfare; it also often results in their isolation and self-destruction.

Like the critics who reviewed *Someone Like You*, most of the reviewers who wrote about *Kiss Kiss* praised Dahl for his ingenious plots and his careful use of details, but they paid little attention to the ideas and themes that underlie his stories. Some of the more thoughtful reviewers, however, did comment on Dahl's characters. The reviewer for *Time* made special note of "Dahl's gallery of females." Intrigued by the deceptiveness of these characters' gentle demeanors, this reviewer described them as "lovely ladies, indeed, but heaven help the poor man who falls into their clutches." In a review published in the *New York Times Book Review* Malcolm Bradbury commended Dahl for knowing "his characters inside out." Dahl's characters, Bradbury observed, "are usually ignoble: he knows the dog beneath the skin, or works hard to find it." Picking up on this point, the reviewer for the *Times Literary Supplement* wrote, "Where Mr. Dahl differs from the common run of spine-chillers is in the verisimiltude of his caricature of human weakness, . . . revealing a social satirist and moralist at work behind the entertaining fantast."

The suggestion that Dahl's characters should be seen as caricatures of human frailty is certainly valid. Although the reviewer for the *Times Literary Supplement* did not elaborate on this point, it lies at the core of Dahl's stories. Like any good caricaturist, Dahl exaggerates particular aspects of his characters' personalities in order to focus the reader's attention on traits and behavior patterns that might otherwise go unnoticed. In most of the *Kiss Kiss* stories these traits and behavior patterns are associated with the tensions between men and women. Although exaggerated, these tensions are present in many marriages and other male-female relationships. Thus, even though Dahl's characters may not be realistic, they are still drawn from real life. . . .

Source: Mark I. West, "Mastering the Macabre," in *Roald Dahl*, Twayne, 1992, pp. 36, 44–49.

SOURCES

Amidon, Stephen, "Getting Even," Review of *The Collected Stories of Roald Dahl*, in *Nation*, Vol. 283, No. 20, December 11, 2006, pp. 21–22.

Brozo, William G., and Schmelzer, Ronald V., "Wildmen, Warriors, and Lovers: Reaching Boys through Archetypal Literature," in *Journal of Adolescent & Adult Literacy*, Vol. 41, No. 1, September 1997, pp. 4–11.

Burmester, David, Review of *Teaching Literature to Adolescents: Short Stories*, in *English Journal*, Vol. 58, No. 4, April 1969, pp. 602–603.

Dahl, Roald, "The Landlady," in *The Umbrella Man and Other Stories*, Viking, 1998, pp. 54–68.

Lachtman, Howard, Review of *Tales of the Unexpected*, in *Studies in Short Fiction*, Vol. 17, No. 2, Spring 1980, pp. 189–90.

Oates, Joyce Carol, "The Art of Vengeance," in *New York Review of Books*, April 26, 2007, http://www.nybooks.com/articles/archives/2007/apr/26/the-art-of-vengeance/ (accessed January 11, 2014.)

Propson, David, "Guys & Dahls," Review of *The Collected Stories of Roald Dahl*, in *New Criterion*, Vol. 25. No. 6, February 2007, pp. 75–77.

Sohier, Jacques, "Metamorphoses of the Uncanny in the Short-Story 'The Landlady' by Roald Dahl," in *Miranda*, Vol. 5, 2011, http://miranda.revues.org/2515 (accessed January 11, 2015).

Wagner, Erica, "Cruel World," in *New York Times*, December 3, 2006, http://www.nytimes.com/2006/12/03/books/review/Wagner.t.html?_r=0 (accessed January 11, 2014).

that guides readers through discussions of Dahl's early childhood and his time spent learning the craft of writing. Sections are also included on creative writing tips, information for fans, and a quiz.

Kelley, True, *Who Was Roald Dahl?*, Grosset & Dunlap, 2012.
    Part of the popular Who Was series, this introduction for young readers is complete with eighty black-and-white illustrations.

Sturrock, Donald, *Storyteller: The Authorized Biography of Roald Dahl*, McClelland & Stewart, 2010.
    Despite his astonishing life as an ace fighter pilot, British intelligence agent, and husband for a while to one of Hollywood's top stars, Dahl nonetheless persistently embroidered the truth about himself. Facts bored him, as this fascinating read reveals, so he openly rewrote history, ignored reality, and reshaped his vulnerabilities with great skill. This biography is a carefully researched and gently nuanced work that draws on a wealth of sources to construct a rich and compassionate biography of one of the most beloved storytellers of the twentieth century.

Treglown, Jeremy, *Roald Dahl: A Biography*, Faber and Faber, 1994.
    The first full biography of Dahl. Treglown's work is an intimate psychological study of the man behind the stories. It also illuminates some of the more subtle intricacies of the publishing industry that affected Dahl throughout his career.

FURTHER READING

Bingham, Jane, *Roald Dahl*, Raintree, 2010
    Part of the Culture in Action series, this book provides young readers with interesting facts, imaginative activities, and fascinating photographs that explain both the life and creative force of Roald Dahl.

Craats, Rennay, *Roald Dahl*, Weigl, 2003
    A biography series for young readers, the volumes of the My Favorite Writer series follow an accessible and easy-to-follow format

SUGGESTED SEARCH TERMS

The Landlady AND Dahl

Roald Dahl

macabre AND short fiction

madness AND short fiction

cruelty AND short fiction

horror AND short fiction

taxidermy AND fiction

naiveté AND short fiction

The Machine Stops

E. M. FORSTER

1909

"The Machine Stops" is a science-fiction story by Edward Morgan (E. M.) Forster that was first published in the *Oxford and Cambridge Review* in 1909. The story was reprinted in Forster's collection of short stories *The Eternal Moment and Other Stories* in 1928 and *The Collected Tales of E. M. Forster* in 1947. It is also available in book form as *The Machine Stops*, published by Wildside Press in 2013, and in Forster's *Selected Stories*, published in 2001 in the Penguin Twentieth-Century Classics series. Forster is known primarily as a novelist, and this is the only science-fiction story he wrote.

The story is set in a distant future when humans live underground because the surface of the earth, it is believed, is no longer habitable. People live in identical small rooms and are under the control of a world government. The civilization is technologically advanced in the sense that all people's needs are met—or so they believe—by an all-encompassing machine. It is left to a rebel named Kuno to point out how the machine is destroying authentic human life by disallowing direct interaction with nature. When the machine stops working, a crisis ensues.

AUTHOR BIOGRAPHY

Forster was born on January 1, 1879, in London, England, to Edward Morgan Llewellyn Forster, an architect, and Alice Whichelo

British writer E. M. Forster (© *Pictorial Press / Alamy*)

Forster. His father died the following year, and Forster was raised by his mother and his paternal aunts. Forster attended Tonbridge School, Kent. Thanks to a legacy from his father's sister, he then attended King's College, Cambridge. There he was a member of the prestigious society The Apostles, which had previously counted Alfred Tennyson, the great Victorian poet, as one of its members. Forster graduated in 1901 and had sufficient wealth to travel and pursue a career as a writer. Over the next two years, he traveled extensively in Europe. His first novel was *Where Angels Fear to Tread*, published in 1905. This was followed by *The Longest Journey* in 1907 and *A Room with a View* the following year. His fourth novel was *Howard's End* (1910), which brought him widespread recognition for the first time. His first collection of short stories was *The Celestial Omnibus* (1911).

During World War I, Forster spent three years in Alexandria, Egypt. He also visited India twice, from 1912 to 1913 and again in 1921. It was this experience that led him to write what became his best-known novel, *A Passage to India*, in 1924. The novel is set in India, then under British rule. Forster published a second

collection of short stories, *The Eternal Moment and Other Stories*, in 1928. This collection contained "The Machine Stops," which had first been published in a journal in 1909. In 1946, King's College awarded Forster a fellowship, and he lived in Cambridge most of the time until his death.

In addition to his novels and short stories, Forster wrote two plays, travel books, biographies, literary criticism (notably *Aspects of the Novel* in 1927), and essays. He was awarded the Order of Companions of Honor in 1953 and Queen Elizabeth's Order of Merit in 1969. He died of a stroke at the age of ninety-one on June 7, 1970, in Coventry, England. A third collection of short stories, *The Life to Come and Other Stories*, was published posthumously, in 1972. Another posthumous publication was a sixth novel, *Maurice*, the theme of which is homosexual love. It was written sometime between 1913 and 1914 and published in 1971.

PLOT SUMMARY

Part 1: The Airship

"The Machine Stops" is set in a distant future when all human life is pleasantly regulated and controlled by something known as the Machine. As the story begins, a small, pale woman named Vashti sits in a small, hexagonal room underground on an island somewhere in the Southern Hemisphere. All humans live underground. The Machine ensures that the room is lighted, even though there are neither windows nor lamps. The Machine also ensures fresh air, even though there are no vents to let air in. The room is filled with music, even though there are no musical instruments in it. Furnishings are spare, just an armchair and a reading desk.

Vashti's listening to the music is interrupted by the sound of a bell. She touches a switch, and the music stops; then she rolls her chair, which is also controlled by the Machine, to the other side of the room, where she listens to a receiver. It is her son Kuno calling, and she receives a video image of him, even though he lives on the other side of the world. He says he wants her to come and see him, but Vashti is not interested. She thinks that meeting in person is a rather shocking thing to do. Kuno tells her that interacting via the Machine is not the

MEDIA ADAPTATIONS

- "The Machine Stops" was dramatized for the British Broadcasting Company (BBC) anthology television series *Out of the Unknown* in 1966.
- An audio recording of the story has been published by LibriVox. It is available at https://www.youtube.com/watch?v=ZOr-vjb6 ElzE via YouTube.

same as doing it in person, and he tells her not to make a god of the Machine.

Vashti replies that she does not really have time to visit, and anyway, she dislikes airships. She does not like seeing the earth, the sea, and the stars. Kuno says he wants to see the stars, but not from an airship. He actually wants to step on the surface of the earth, which few people do. Vashti does not like that idea. She says that because the earth no longer has any life on it, the cold air will kill him unless he uses a respirator. Kuno is aware of this and is no longer interested in the conversation, and his image disappears. Vashti, whose room contains various buttons that she can push to supply her every need, pushes the button that enables her to speak to her friends through a speaking tube. Then she prepares to give a ten-minute lecture on Australian music, which people can hear and see remotely. After that she listens to a lecture on the sea and then goes to bed.

On the bedside table lies the Book of the Machine, which contains all the information she needs to know about how to use the Machine. She leafs through it reverently. It even gives timetables for the airships. In a day or so, Kuno again asks her to come visit him. But she is nervous at the prospect. She does not like to go beyond her room and experience things directly. Kuno tries to persuade her, saying something tremendous may happen.

Vashti eventually decides to visit her son. She arrives at an airship, which is part of a transportation system that survives from the old days but is scarcely needed now, because people do not move around much. She feels uncomfortable about the presence of other people in the airship but is comforted by the presence of the Book, which she carries with her.

The airship takes off for the Northern Hemisphere. It is night, and Vashti can see the stars, but she does not like them. Neither do the other passengers, and the attendant pulls down the blinds. In the morning, Vashti tries to adjust the blind, which is letting in some light, but instead it flies upward, and she catches sight of some clouds and a patch of blue sky. She recoils from it, and the attendant touches her, just to steady her. Vashti is enraged. People do not normally touch one another.

The attendant tells Vashti they are over what used to be called Asia. She shows her the Himalayan mountains. Vashti wants the blind pulled down again. She says the mountains give her no ideas, and that appears to be what she enjoys most in life. At midday, however, she takes a second peek at the earth. Again she sees a mountain range, but it is mostly covered by clouds. It is in fact the Caucasus, but she quickly pulls the blind down again. In the evening she looks again and sees many islands and a sea (they are passing over Greece), but again it gives her no ideas and she pulls the blind down one more time.

Part 2: The Mending Apparatus

Vashti arrives at Kuno's room, which is exactly the same as her own. She says she has had a difficult journey and can stay only a few minutes. Kuno says that the central committee has threatened him with Homelessness, which is a euphemism for death. His infraction has been to go outside, onto the surface of the earth, without an official permit, and by a way of his own, not the officially approved way. While out, he walks through a railway tunnel and finds an old abandoned ventilation shaft through a gap in the tiles. He gets a respirator and climbs a ladder in the shaft until he gets close to the surface. He manages to turn the handle of a large stopper, about eight feet across, that keeps the cold outer air from penetrating underground. (The Machine creates its own air underground.) The stopper is pushed up by the force of air from below, and Kuno is on the surface, facing the sunlight. Kuno lies on the grass and looks around him. He knows he is in Wessex because he has heard a lecture about it. (Wessex was an independent kingdom in present-day southern England that existed from the sixth to tenth centuries.) He is in a hollow and climbs the slope to explore, looking at the hills and feeling that they are full of life. It is early evening, and the sun is about to set. Kuno has become separated from his respirator but is able to breathe by taking gulps of the air coming up through the open ventilator shaft. He cannot comfortably breathe the natural air.

Kuno breaks off his story to tell his mother that he believes the Machine is slowly killing them. Humans have created it, but now it controls them and has turned them into shadows of their real selves.

Kuno continues his story: he decides to put on his respirator and continue walking, but he cannot find it. The respirator has vanished. Kuno also realizes that what he calls the Mending Apparatus has been at work repairing the gap in the tunnel where he has found the ventilator shaft. He decides it would be better to die above ground than to go back underground. But then a long white worm appears, coming Kuno's way over the grass. The worm is part of the Mending Apparatus. It tangles Kuno up and drags him back below, the stopper closing above his head. Kuno hits his head against the ladder and loses consciousness, waking in his room.

Vashti is not sympathetic to Kuno. She says his experimenting will end in Homelessness, that is, death. Kuno, however, thinks he can live in the outer, natural air, even though his mother says that the earth can no longer support life. Kuno says that he has seen life on the earth, in the form of a female being who came to his help when he called, but he does not explain further. Vashti decides that her son is mad, and she leaves him.

Part 3: The Homeless

Over the next few years, respirators are abolished on the reasoning that no one needs to go to the surface of the earth. People applaud this new development. Another new development was the reestablishment of religion. The Machine becomes the object of worship and is regarded for all intents and purposes as divine.

The Machine becomes more essential to people's lives, and more efficient. People understand how to use it for themselves, but no one is left in the world who understands it completely. The more decadent humans become, the more powerful the machine becomes, and people call this progress.

One day Vashti receives a message from Kuno, who has been transferred from the Northern Hemisphere to the Southern Hemisphere and now lives not far from her. He tells her that the Machine is stopping. She does not believe him, even though she has noticed that the music she is receiving is defective and has complained to the authorities about it. The Committee of the Mending Apparatus tells her it will be fixed soon. The music gets no better, however, and Vashti becomes resigned to it. Other things go wrong with the Machine, and these are soon accepted as well.

One day all over the world, beds fail to appear when called up. Discontent grows among the people. The Committee of the Mending Apparatus admits that the Mending Apparatus needs repair. The situation worsens: the atmosphere darkens, making reading difficult, and the air becomes foul. The situation improves slightly, but the Machine never returns to its former efficiency. People pray to it in vain. But one day the communication system breaks down completely. Not being able to communicate, people are left in silence. Vashti is in distress. She goes out to the railway tunnel, where desperate people are crawling about or screaming, trying to summon the trains.

Vashti goes back to her room, which starts to collapse. Light begins to fade, and Vashti realizes the end of the world has come. She goes out to the tunnel again, where she sees many people dying. She weeps and crawls toward Kuno, whose voice she hears in the darkness. He says there is no hope for anyone. He kisses her and says that there are still humans alive on the surface of the earth. He calls them the Homeless, and says he has spoken to them; they are in hiding, waiting for the end of civilization. He adds that humanity has learned its lesson and will not try to start up the Machine again. An airship crashes over the city, killing Vashti and Kuno.

CHARACTERS

Kuno

Kuno is Vashti's son. He lives in an underground cell below what used to be Wessex, England. Unlike everyone else, he is an independent spirit and likes to explore. He wants to set foot on the surface of the earth so that he can reestablish a relationship with nature rather than having his life governed by the Machine. He is the stuff of which revolutionaries are made because he does not accept the status quo; he does not think like everyone else. He believes the Machine is gradually destroying human life rather than enhancing it, and he wants to tell Vashti in person what he has found out and what he believes. Kuno is curious about real life, that is, life that is not mediated through the Machine, and he has the courage to act on his curiosity, defying the central committee in the process. He finds a gap in a railway tunnel and manages to make his way to the surface of the earth, where he experiences for a while the beauty of nature until the Moving Apparatus drags him back. After this incident, the authorities perceive Kuno as a troublemaker, and he is moved to the Southern Hemisphere, where he lives near his mother.

Kuno realizes sooner than anyone else that the Machine is failing them and is coming to a stop. He knows that this means the end of the world as humans have created it through the Machine. Before he dies in the disaster that engulfs everyone, he takes consolation in the fact that he and his mother are communicating directly and touching each other, outside the confines of the Machine. He also is consoled by the fact that he has known, even briefly, what human life is really like in all its ancient glory, and he looks forward to a renaissance of the human race after the Machine is gone.

The Machine

Although it is not a character in the usual sense of the word, the Machine acquires the status of a god, and people pray to it. The ways of the Machine are embodied in the Book of the Machine, which acquires a sacred quality, like a bible. Although it is inanimate, the Machine seems to have certain qualities that mimic life itself, especially when it sends out the tentacles of the Mending Apparatus, which Kuno perceives as a living worm that does the bidding of the Machine.

Vashti

Vashti is Kuno's mother. She is a woman who is content with life as it is delivered to her via the Machine. The Machine satisfies all her wants and needs, or so she thinks, and she all but worships it. But the description of her physical appearance in the first paragraph shows that she is hardly an example of humanity at its finest. She is a "swaddled lump of flesh . . . with a face as white as a fungus." Vashti is an expert on music and gives lectures on it. She also likes to listen to lectures on many topics and prides herself on being open to ideas. She thinks that ideas are what feed her mind, but in reality she deals only with secondhand ideas, because no one in this society prizes original thinking. Her emphasis on ideas also shows someone who is used to over-intellectualization and using the rational mind only, at the expense of other faculties.

As is the practice in this civilization, Vashti has given up her son at birth, and he has been raised mostly in a public nursery, but they do spend some time together when he is a boy. She gives him his first lessons on the Book and shows him how to work the buttons and switches of the Machine. As a result, some affection remains between them, and she thinks there is something special about him, although they can hardly be considered close.

Vashti does not want to visit her son in person because she does not like to leave her underground cell or interact with anyone directly, let alone touch anyone. But the bonds between mother and son are such that she forces herself to make the trip across the world to visit him. The visit does not go well. When Kuno relates his story of how he has gone to the surface of the earth, she at first feels pity for him because she knows he will soon die. But she also finds herself filled with disgust and is ashamed of having given birth to him. She thinks he is reverting to a previous, savage form of human being. She ends up thinking that Kuno, with his unorthodox ideas and his adventurous nature, is mad. She has one more meeting with him, after the Machine has collapsed, but she has little understanding of what is happening around her. She dies along with Kuno.

THEMES

Technology and Civilization

The story takes place in a world in which technology has grown to the point at which it seems to provide humans with everything they wish for. This turns out to be a fond illusion, but it needs a rebel to point out that the Machine (i.e., technology) controls people, not the other way around. In this civilization, everyone lives underground because the surface of the earth is no longer habitable. One clue to how this happened is that all of the forests have been destroyed in the making of paper. (Deforestation was well under way at the time Forster wrote this story, although few people then were concerned about its environmental effects.) In the story, people live in small rooms stacked on top of each other, tier by tier.

Thanks to the Machine, people do not have to exert themselves physically or even walk. Vashti's chair just rolls to the other side of the room when necessary, and she has all kinds of other comforts, courtesy of the Machine. By operating various buttons and switches, she can make the room light or dark as desired. She can receive food and clothing and listen to music. If she wants a bath, she can press a button, and a marble basin will rise from the floor. She can summon a bed the same way. If the Book of the Machine is dropped, the floor raises it up automatically. The Machine even provides instant medical services. When Vashti tells Kuno she feels unwell, Kuno, via Vashti's doctor, orders up medical equipment, which descends from the ceiling to treat her.

Vashti can also communicate with her friends remotely by a form of video conferencing and give lectures that way too. This technology has put an end to public gatherings, because they are no longer necessary. The Machine has the power to bring everything to people, rather than the people having to go somewhere to get what they need. People in this civilization, which they like to think of as advanced, chatter in an intellectual way about ideas. Their life is reduced to that of the dry, rational mind, and they deal only with received ideas, envisioning nothing new. They neglect their bodies and their senses. Vashti, for example, can barely walk. When she finally has to travel, she totters.

Technology has reduced everything to sameness. There is no variety or diversity: the rooms and the beds are all the same size. To have different sizes of beds would involve huge changes in how the Machine is set up. Also, people no longer bother to travel much because "the earth was exactly alike all over. . . . What was the good of going to Pekin when it was just like Shrewsbury?" This triumph of uniformity through the Machine has involved the conquest of nature. Nature's rhythms are no longer of concern to people. It does not matter whether it is night or day, and storms at sea and earthquakes no longer affect humanity, because everyone lives underground. If people do have to travel, the airships can take them safely where they need to go without regard to weather-related events. Because no one has to interact directly with nature, people have become averse to doing so and even incapable of it.

As for the kind of government that presides over this civilization, it is clearly a world government. Different countries and national governments appear to have been abolished. The government is totalitarian. It has vast power and does not tolerate dissent, although there seems to be little of the latter. People like the way the Machine operates and seem largely content, if fundamentally passive. In this society, babies are taken from their parents at birth and raised in public nurseries. Parents have no responsibilities toward them after the moment of birth. Babies are examined at birth, and if they look as if they will develop unnecessary strength, they are killed. Physical strength is not required in this civilization. It is a disadvantage, because someone who is athletic will not be happy sitting in a room all day. An athlete "would have yearned for trees to climb, rivers to bathe in, meadows and hills against which he might measure his body." If people want children, they need official permission. Kuno applied and was turned down. He is not the sort of man the Machine wants to reproduce.

The government can tell people where to go and what to do. To go onto the surface of the earth requires a special permit. In the airship that Vashti travels in, one young man has been sent to Sumatra to propagate the race. Families no longer exist in the old sense of the word, and neither does love, although an attachment between mother and son exists in the case of Vashti and Kuno. Like families,

TOPICS FOR FURTHER STUDY

- Write a science-fiction short story in which there are two characters who, like Vashti and Kuno, are on opposite sides in terms of acceptance of or rebellion against the society in which they live. What are the distinguishing features of the society? How and why does one of the characters break out of this pocket universe into something different? Is your story going to be optimistic or pessimistic? To get your imagination working, visit the web page http://www.washington post.com/blogs/the-switch/wp/2015/01/28/bill-gates-on-dangers-of-artificial-intelligence-dont-understand-why-some-people-are-not-concerned and read the *Washington Post* article by Peter Holley, published on January 29, 2015, about how some people see the rapid development of artificial intelligence as an existential threat to human life. This may be an idea for the premise of your story, set, perhaps, several generations in the future.

- Write an essay in which you argue for or against the idea of a world government. How would such a government operate in principle? Discuss some of the thinkers of the past who have advocated the establishment of a world government. Why is the United Nations not considered a world government, and why are people today resistant to the idea of a world government?

Discuss whether such a proposition will ever be practical.

- Give a class presentation about the advantages and disadvantages of using social media sites such as Facebook. Research, for example, some of the studies that have been conducted about Facebook use. Discuss whether frequent use of Facebook makes people feel happier and more connected to friends and family and whether use of Facebook and other social media sites has negative effects. How does interacting online affect one's personal relationships? Discuss whether online interaction leads to spending less or more time with other people.

- Read *Kaleidoscope: Diverse YA Science Fiction and Fantasy Stories* (2014), edited by Alisa Krasnostein and Julia Rios, a collection of twenty stories for young-adult readers. What is the difference between science fiction and fantasy? Identify which stories belong in which category and also stories in which a hero like Kuno refuses to accept the premises on which his society is based and breaks free of them or stories that deal, like "The Machine Stops," with future technology. Discuss whether these stories can be classified as utopian or dystopian. Write a review of *Kaleidoscope* and post it to your blog for others to comment on.

---

religion is a thing of the past, or so it seems until people start to worship the Machine as a quasi-god. They also think that fears and superstition are things of the past. Euphemisms are used for unpleasant practices, which is characteristic of totalitarian regimes. Homelessness, for example, is a euphemism for death, because the victims are ejected from underground and exposed to the air, which they can no longer tolerate. Everything is run by an impersonal bureaucracy, presided over by a central committee. Like so many bureaucracies, however, it cannot cope with anything out of the ordinary or that does not fit the way things are supposed to be. This is one reason that the entire system eventually collapses.

Rebellion

By means of Kuno's exploits, as he relates them to Vashti, the story contrasts the artificiality of the world created by the Machine to the lost but natural mode of human life, which is to live in

Vashti owns only one book: the instructions for the Machine. (© Skylines | ShutterStock.com)

direct interaction with and appreciation of nature, drinking in all that nature offers through all the senses. Kuno exposes the limitations of the Machine and the fact that it is actually harming rather than helping people. He is aware of this well before the Machine collapses. Kuno is the rebel, the explorer who dares to seek life beyond the confines of how the government and everyone else tell him it should be lived. Although he has not received official permission to do so, Kuno dares to find his own way to the surface of the earth, showing courage, ingenuity, and physical strength. Through this journey and his ability to think for himself, he breaks free of his social conditioning and experiences life in a new way, even if it is just for a few minutes before the Machine drags him back despite his fierce resistance. During these few minutes, he finds out a great deal and intuitively senses much more. Vashti has told him that the surface of the earth is just dust and mud, but she does not really know, because she has never been there. Kuno, however, is able to sense the beauty of the earth. Although the only growing things he sees are ferns, he is struck by the mist between the hills because of its color—the color of pearl.

Kuno also keenly senses the presence of past human civilizations and believes that the earth itself is a living thing. He tells Vashti that although the hills may be colorless, to him

> they were living and the turf that covered them was a skin, under which their muscles rippled, and I felt that those hills had called with incalculable force to men in the past, and that men had loved them.

As the rebel, Kuno is buoyed by a sense of optimism about the future. Even when disaster strikes and it appears that everyone is about to die, Kuno insists that human life continues somewhere on the surface of the earth and will regenerate itself when the Machine finally stops and their current civilization ends.

STYLE

Dystopia

"The Machine Stops" is classified as dystopian, which describes a work that depicts a future society in which people are oppressed in some form or another. They may be enslaved by a tyrannical government or otherwise be forced to live restricted or distorted lives. In some way, human life has become degraded. A dystopian story is the opposite of a utopian story, which depicts an ideal human society in the future. Both utopias and dystopias are often related to science fiction. For example, utopian stories may explore how science and technology will eventually solve all human problems. Dystopian stories, on the other hand, may show what happens when science and technology, often promoted with the best of intentions (as in "The Machine Stops"), end up oppressing or damaging people and societies rather than liberating and improving them. Such works often draw out trends that are apparent in the society of the day and thus can appear as warnings of what may eventually happen if society does not change course.

Irony

The irony of "The Machine Stops" is that people in the civilization pride themselves on being highly advanced and are proud of the achievements of their technology, but they are unable to see in ways that really matter that they have regressed rather than progressed. They like to discuss ideas and accumulate knowledge, but they do not prize original thought; instead, they recycle old ideas or receive information second-hand in a way that is far removed from direct observation and experience, which they avoid completely. They do not want their ideas spoiled by facts.

The irony of a society that supposedly values ideas but in reality is stuck in an endless recycling of received opinions is brought out tellingly when Vashti passes over the Greek islands in the airship. The islands exist in a golden sea, but Vashti pulls the blind down over the window; the islands give her no ideas. The culture of ancient Greece, of course, is the cradle of modern civilization, especially in terms of philosophy, literature, drama, art, architecture, mathematics, and mythology. Vashti's reaction is another way of showing that the civilization in the story has turned its back on so much that is valuable in Western culture. The same applies when Vashti is completely unmoved by the sight of the Himalayas. The sight of mountains has thrilled travelers for centuries and inspired poets, artists, and religious thinkers, but the Himalayas do not stimulate Vashti in any way. They do not inspire in her any feelings of awe because she has no imagination and is unable to appreciate any input that comes to her directly from the senses.

HISTORICAL CONTEXT

The Development of Science Fiction

When Forster decided to make his one and only contribution to science fiction, he was entering a fast-developing genre. In the early nineteenth century, the stories of Mary Wollstonecraft Shelley and Edgar Allan Poe contained elements of science fiction, but the genre began to take serious hold with the work of the French writer Jules Verne (1828–1905), who wrote novels such as *Journey to the Center of the Earth* (1864), *Twenty Thousand Leagues under the Sea* (1869), and *Around the World in Eighty Days* (1872). Contemporary with or immediately after those of Verne, notable science-fiction novels included *Erewhon* (1872) by Samuel Butler, *Strange Case of Dr. Jekyll and Mr. Hyde* (1886) by Robert Louis Stevenson, *Looking Backward, 2000–1887* (1888) by Edward Bellamy, *A Connecticut Yankee in King Arthur's Court* (1889) by Mark Twain, and *News from Nowhere* (1890) by William Morris.

The most important writer of science fiction in the late nineteenth and early twentieth centuries was H. G. Wells, who is famous for novels such as *The Time Machine* (1895), *The Invisible Man* (1897), and *The War of the Worlds* (1898). It is likely that Wells's *A Modern Utopia* (1905) was what prompted Forster to respond with "The Machine Stops." Forster himself wrote that his story was "a counterblast to one of the heavens of H. G. Wells" (as quoted by Alan Wilde in *Art and Order: A Study of E. M. Forster*). *A Modern Utopia* is set on a planet like Earth but one that differs from Earth in that all of the problems humans experience have been solved. Thanks to science and technology, an ideal society exists that is able to satisfy all human needs. The state has a ruling class, the samurai, which reflected Wells's belief in and advocacy for a world state under a single government. *A Modern Utopia* represents the optimism Wells felt regarding the development of science and technology. On the evidence of "The Machine Stops," Forster did not share this optimism.

COMPARE & CONTRAST

- **1909:** Air travel is in its infancy. In 1900, the first zeppelin airship is launched in Germany and covers three and a half miles in a flight that lasts eighteen minutes. The ship, which is fueled by hydrogen gas, is named after Count Ferdinand von Zeppelin. During the decade, the technology develops, and in July 1908 a zeppelin flies for twelve hours over Switzerland. A month later, a zeppelin crashes and is destroyed in an explosion. However, development of the airships continues.

  Today: Airships no longer exist. Airplanes are fueled not by hydrogen or helium but by a refined form of gasoline. Unlike the airship depicted in "The Machine Stops," which takes nearly two days to go from the Southern to the Northern Hemisphere, airplanes cover the same distance in a fraction of that time.

- **1909:** Direct, instant voice communication between people at a distance is accomplished by the telephone, which is a relatively new technology. In England in 1906, the first coin-operated telephone call box is installed by Western Electric Company in London. The development of wireless telegraphy allows messages to be sent across large distances.

  Today: Although the telephone is still in use, instant messaging across computer networks is also a popular form of communication, as is video conferencing, through which any number of people in different places can see and talk to each other in real time.

- **1909:** Some writers and thinkers propose the establishment of a world government. The idea seems attractive to some, such as H. G. Wells, because of the rapid growth of technology and communication that is leading to the globalization of the world economy. Proponents of world government also believe it is a way to prevent war.

  Today: The idea of a world government has little support, although some theorists of international relations still debate the issue, offering different models of world government ranging from those with centralized power and authority to more decentralized models that rely more on mutual cooperation.

The role of technology in human life has been a key element in science fiction from its beginnings. According to Peter Nicholls and Brian M. Stableford, in their article on technology in *The Encyclopedia of Science Fiction*,

> it was the perception of the power which the new machines of the Industrial Revolution had to transform the world which gave birth to sf itself, inspiring Jules Verne's imaginary voyages . . . H. G. Wells's scientific romances, the hi-tech Utopian fantasies of Edward Bellamy and others, and the mechanized Dystopian nightmares which dissented from them.

As this quotation shows, attitudes to technology in early science fiction differed widely (as they have continued to do). Some writers, the article notes, thought technology would lead not only to material progress for humanity but also to moral progress. Others were aware of the possible dangers of technology and how it could represent a threat to human progress. As Nicolls and Stableford state, "Sf is, of course, the natural medium of antitechnological fantasies as well as of serious extrapolations of technological possibility." In "The Machine Stops," Forster clearly aligned himself with the former category.

The buttons and switches of the Machine meet every need. *(© Bejim | ShutterStock.com)*

CRITICAL OVERVIEW

In general, literary critics have not reacted to "The Machine Stops" quite as favorably as they have to much of Forster's other work. For Frederick P. W. McDowell, in *E. M. Forster*, Forster "fails to dramatize conclusively his complex and original concepts," and the result is that the story "lack[s] substance and weight." For Alan Wilde, the story is overly long and "too schematic, too fanciful (rather than fantastic), too didactic." Wilde also notes, however, that the story does convey "a feeling that man's condition is not inevitable. It is possible, in other words, to imagine a change in the social context that would allow Kuno or others like him to realize their ideals."

Writing in 1975, John Colmer, in *E. M. Forster: The Personal Voice*, took a more positive view of the story, expressing appreciation for Forster's original insight that people would become so dependent on their technology that they would not notice its deterioration and would accept "the jarring sounds as part of the harmony, the foul air and diminished light as natural. The relevance of this to modern-day world-pollution and the break-down in basic social services is obvious." Two decades later, however, in 1996, Carroll Viera, writing in

Dictionary of Literary Biography, offers a different view, stating that "despite its uncanny Orwellian prophecy of human dependence on technology and its frequent inclusion in anthologies earlier in the century, the story now seems dated." But such a view is not universal. Mordecai Roshwald, in *Dreams and Nightmares: Science and Technology in Myth and Fiction*, sees the relevance of the story for the twenty-first century:

> The octagonal room in a human beehive is not such a distant idea in an age when people sit in an armchair watching television . . . looking for information on the Internet, or interacting through electronic devices, while enjoying thermostatically controlled environments, and having supplies of food in refrigerators and freezers, and so forth. The image of automated living conditions . . . reveals a prophetic perception of a Zeitgeist which was far from the reality of [Forster's] world.

Roshwald also points to the occurrences of technological failure—from computers to electrical grids and nuclear power meltdowns—in contemporary society, and notes that too much reliance on technology can have negative consequences, as "The Machine Stops" demonstrates: "Forster's warning, though clearly exaggerated, as any literary caution is likely to be, is more relevant today than it was in the time of his writing."

CRITICISM

Bryan Aubrey

Aubrey holds a PhD in English. In the following essay, he discusses the relevance of the "The Machine Stops" for twenty-first-century readers and how the story reveals Forster's humanistic vision.

Some critics have viewed "The Machine Stops," first published more than one hundred years ago, as being somewhat dated. In respect to the picture it presents of a world government that issues edicts through a faceless central committee, that may be so. Forster was reacting to the idealism of H. G. Wells, who enthusiastically promoted the notion of a world government. But such ideas have little credence in the twenty-first century, when individual nations throughout the world are reluctant to give up their authority in favor of any supranational organization, let alone a world government.

WHAT DO I READ NEXT?

- Forster's short story "The Story of a Panic," first published in 1904, features a fourteen-year-old protagonist named Eustace. The story is set in Italy and includes a mythological or supernatural dimension because the local people have a fear of the god Pan and his perceived manifestations in natural phenomena. Eustace, an English boy who is not well adjusted to the human world, has no fear of Pan, however, and after experiencing the god on a hillside, he becomes illumined in some way, full of praise for nature and behaving in a manner that the locals find incomprehensible. In his appreciation of a mystical element in nature, Eustace has some resemblance to Kuno in "The Machine Stops." "The Story of a Panic" can be found in Forster's *Selected Stories* (2001).

- *Anthem* is a novella by the American writer Ayn Rand, first published in the United Kingdom in 1938 and in the United States in 1946. Rand was strongly anticommunist, and *Anthem* is set in a future, collectivist society in which individual identity has been erased. As the main character sets out to restore what has been lost, the novel develops its themes of the importance of the individual and the need for creativity and political freedom.

- In *Among the Hidden* (1998), a young-adult novel by Margaret Peterson Haddix, people in the near future live under an oppressive government that does not allow families to have more than two children. Some families, however, have illegal third children who have to stay hidden, and two such children, Luke and Jen, decide to emerge from the shadows and challenge the system.

- Isaac Asimov was one of the leading twentieth-century writers of science fiction. His short story "Nightfall," first published in 1941, has been immensely popular and is regarded as one of the greatest of all science-fiction stories. It is set on a world that is constantly in the light because it orbits six suns. But once every two thousand years there is a total eclipse, and people fear what may happen when darkness descends. However, it is not darkness that most affects people but the fact that they can now see many thousands of previously invisible stars. This sudden knowledge of how vast the universe is drives them insane. The story is available in *Isaac Asimov: The Complete Stories*, Vol. 1 (1990).

- *Science Fiction Stories* (2003) edited by Edward Blishen and illustrated by Karin Littlewood, is an anthology of twenty science-fiction stories aimed at young readers. It includes stories by some of the great writers in the genre, such as Asimov, Arthur C. Clarke, Wells, and Ray Bradbury, as well as some less well-known names.

- Octavia Butler (1947–2006) was an African American writer of mostly dystopian science fiction, perhaps best known for her Patternist and Parable series of novels. She also published a volume of short stories, *Bloodchild and Other Stories* (1995), which was issued in a second edition, with additional stories, in 2006.

- The use of technology, for good or ill, is fundamental to many a science-fiction story. In *The Second Machine Age: Work, Progress, and Prosperity in a Time of Brilliant Technologies* (2014), Erik Brynjolfsson and Andrew McAfee present an optimistic account of emerging technologies that will profoundly alter human life over the next few decades as digital technologies start to perform an array of functions that formerly could be done only by humans—rather like the way the Machine functions in Forster's story but, it is to be hoped, without the negative consequences.

> ONE CANNOT HELP BUT BE IMPRESSED BY THE PRESCIENCE OF FORSTER, WRITING IN 1909, IN INVENTING A FICTIONAL WORLD THAT ANTICIPATES SOME OF THE TECHNOLOGY AND SOCIAL TRENDS THAT ONLY BECAME APPARENT IN THE 1990S AND HAVE SINCE ACCELERATED AT LIGHTNING PACE."

When it comes to the scientific rather than political element of the story, however, it is a different matter.

The pre–World War I world Forster lived in when he wrote "The Machine Stops" has long since vanished, but the march of technology has not. The Machine (to use Forster's term) has kept on growing, its tentacles reaching into almost every corner of human life. It is not difficult to see how Western society has become ever more dependent on its version of the Machine, through computers and other electronic systems, than it was in Forster's day. Life in the twenty-first century provides enough examples for one to appreciate the prescience of Forster's imagined world. What happens when the Machine stops is a central part of the story, and the immediate result is unmitigated disaster, because people have become so dependent on the Machine that they cannot function without it. A couple of interesting contemporary parallels to this systemic failure show how such an event might play out in real life.

Toward the end of the twentieth century, the Y2K bug created widespread fears that as soon as the clock ticked over to the year 2000, there would be massive disruption of a wide range of computer-based systems. This was because computers had been programmed with only two digits representing the date (69 was read as 1969, for example), so when 99 rolled over to 00 (to represent the year 2000), the computer would not recognize that this meant 2000 and might register it as 1900. People feared that this would cause chaos in banking, insurance, and utility systems. There were even

dire predictions that cars would not start on January 1, 2000. Because the problem was anticipated, a great deal of time and money was put into fixing the problem before it occurred (though without an overarching Committee of the Mending Apparatus to supervise it). In the end, there was little disruption as 2000 dawned, but the flap did show how vital computer-related systems were to the smooth running of society and how damaging the disruption would be should this modern version of Forster's Machine stop running.

The Y2K bug receded into memory, but in the 2010s some people brought attention to the incredibly destructive effects that a solar flare would have on the world's electrical systems. In an article in *USA Today*, Glenn Harlan Reynolds, a professor of law at the University of Tennessee, warned that a solar flare—a sudden release of energy from the sun—"could wipe out the communications and electrical grids while frying a wide variety of electronics, quickly sending us back to the 19th Century." He pointed out that such an event did happen in 1859, before the widespread use of electricity. Should a similar event occur in the twenty-first century, it

> would fry computers, cell phones, new cars and more. More worryingly, it would probably melt major transformers in the power net, transformers that take months or years to replace. . . . Big chunks of the planet—all of North America, for example—might be without electricity for a year or longer.

Reynolds argues that many people would die because of disruption of medical systems and food and water supplies: "Without electricity, pretty much everything in our civilization comes to a stop. The economic damage would be incalculable."

In its effects, this is the kind of scenario that Forster envisioned in his story. From the point of view of the rebel Kuno, going back to the kind of lifestyle last seen in the nineteenth century might be regarded as a desirable outcome, because it would restore humanity to an age in which it lived in closer contact with nature rather than being propped up by an elaborate web of mechanized artificiality.

Other dimensions of Forster's story are likely to have resonance for contemporary readers. In "The Machine Stops," people connect with each other at a distance; few feel the need to leave their underground cells and actually interact directly with others. There are no public meetings, for example, because any number of people can interact at a distance through the agency of the Machine. Vashti is able to give and listen to lectures without leaving her cell, and she can interact with her friends in similar way. A similar phenomenon in the 2010s is online college classes, which make it possible to earn a degree without ever stepping onto a brick-and-mortar campus.

The lack of human contact also calls to mind the social media that are so popular in the early twenty-first century. In the story, Vashti considers that she knows several thousand people, because she has had contact with them remotely. The situation puts one in mind of the way people accumulate friends on the social media site Facebook and consider that to be knowing them, even though they may never have met in person. The Machine in the story has the effect of making people dislike face-to-face interaction. They prefer interacting at a distance, electronically. Vashti feels uncomfortable on the airship when she is close to other people, and she does not like to touch or be touched by others.

In the early twenty-first century, there is much discussion about the effects on people of the use of social media as a form of interaction with others. Many people prefer to interact online rather than in person in a variety of contexts, both business and social. In 2005 researchers at the Stanford Institute for the Quantitative Study of Society (SIQSS) found that people in the United States who used the Internet frequently spent seventy minutes less every day interacting with their families. The SIQSS had also reported in 2000 that there was a connection between frequent Internet use and social isolation. According to Professor Norman H. Nie, director of SIQSS, the growth of technology, going back to the eighteenth and nineteenth centuries, has steadily eroded the amount of time people spend interacting directly with each other. "It's a history that began with the Industrial Revolution, when the male started to leave the house to earn a living and was not teaching his son how to carry on his craft," Nie says in an interview with Kenneth M. Dixon, "Now we have very few remaining institutions that are face to face."

One cannot help but be impressed by the prescience of Forster, writing in 1909, in inventing a fictional world that anticipates some of the technology and social trends that only became apparent in the 1990s and have since accelerated at lightning pace. The world in which Vashti and Kuno live is more extreme than anything in twenty-first-century reality. Because they live underground and take part in little physical activity, humans seem to have lost their sense that they have a physical body that needs to be cared for. Vashti is pale and sickly looking; her face is as white as a fungus because she has almost never been exposed to natural sunlight, and she can barely totter from one place to another. In this society of the future, physical strength is discouraged; infants who look as if they may develop into strong adults are killed, because it is assumed that they would be ill-suited to an entirely sedentary life devoid of physical exertion and adventure.

It is left to Kuno to see the extent to which human beings have deteriorated in terms of their physical capabilities and the sharpness of their senses and to seek to recapture a more authentic way of life. It is he who breaks out of what is sometimes referred to in science-fiction studies as a pocket universe—a restricted, confined, often oppressive world from which the hero must escape into something that is larger, freer, and more complete or satisfying. In "The Machine Stops," the pocket universe is the entire underground civilization, and the escape made by the hero Kuno is through a narrow, dark passage—the ventilation shaft that he climbs. The shaft offers a route from the confined, artificial world that is slowly destroying human life—even as the Machine provides beguiling creature comforts—into a more expansive and natural world, the surface of the earth. Devastated by neglect and human exploitation the earth may be, but the life-giving sun still shines on it.

It is through Kuno and comments made by the narrator that Forster reveals his humanistic vision, which stands in contrast to the mechanistic world he sees as a threat to human survival. Against the merely rational, intellectual approach to life (as embodied in Vashti), Forster posits the intuitive, the sensual, the physical, and the imaginative life. As Kuno climbs in the darkness up the ventilation shaft, for example, he feels comforted by the spirits of the

Vashti struggles to decide whether to leave her cell. *(© Ruslan Guzov / ShutterStock.com)*

dead, and he tells Vashti, "I don't know what I mean by that. I just say what I felt." When he emerges into the light of day, Kuno feels a deep connection to the human past and its future and also to the earth itself, to nature, and to the entire cosmos. Humans cannot sever this connection however hard they try.

In the story, the human connection to the cosmos is symbolized by the constellation Orion, which Kuno sees. Kuno describes the pattern formed by the stars as resembling a man. He says to Vashti: "The four big stars are the man's shoulders and his knees. The three stars in the middle are like the belts that men wore once, and the three stars hanging are like a sword." This is the traditional identification of Orion as the hunter, which goes back in Western literature and mythology as far as

Homer's *Odyssey.* In "The Machine Stops," Orion symbolizes not only the connection of people to the cosmos but also human strength as opposed to the current weakness. Orion has similar significance in another story by Forster. In that story, "The Point of It," also published in *The Eternal Moment and Other Stories*, the thoughts of the character Michael are described as follows:

> He cared for the universe, for the tiny tangle in it that we call civilisation, for his fellow-men who had made the tangle and who transcended it. Love, the love of humanity, warmed him; and even when he was thinking of other matters, was looking at Orion perhaps in the cold winter evenings, a pang of joy, too sweet for description, would thrill him, and he would feel sure that our highest impulses have some eternal value.

This could almost be Kuno speaking. For Kuno, nature itself is alive. When he looks at the colorless hills he sees them as a living being: "the turf that covered them was a skin, under which their muscles rippled." Even Vashti, observing the fantastic shapes of the Caucasus Mountains as she flies over them in the airship, sees that one such peak "resembled a prostrate man," a symbol that the reader grasps the significance of—the weakened, slumberous state into which humanity has fallen while still possessing a mighty potential—even if Vashti does not.

"The Machine Stops" has rightly been referred to as dystopian, a vision of a future at odds with true human happiness and fulfillment, and yet even in the bleakness, there is hope. At the last, before their deaths, Vashti is finally converted into seeing the truth of Kuno's vision, and Kuno himself, although disaster is now upon them, cherishes the belief that there are others who still live somewhere on the face of the earth and who will build a new civilization when the present stunted, underground one finally collapses. The story ends on an almost positive note, or at least with a positive image, as Vashti and Kuno, chaos and destruction all around them, manage to look up and see scraps of the untainted sky, that is, an aspect of the natural world unmediated by the Machine.

Source: Bryan Aubrey, Critical Essay on "The Machine Stops," in *Short Stories for Students*, Gale, Cengage Learning, 2016.

Paul March-Russell

In the following excerpt, March-Russell discusses the characters' search for knowledge in "The Machine Stops."

. . . The citizens of Forster's world-state see themselves as members of a realised utopia: "How we have advanced, thanks to the Machine!" They define themselves in relation to what they regard as reactionary or inefficient. Forster portrays this kind of binary thinking as the unconscious effect of ideology, while the attendant lack of critical self-awareness is symbolised in the populace's retreat underground. While this metaphor alludes to Plato's parable of "the Cave," the self-deluding confidence of rationality also refers to Hegel. Vashti's comment that Kuno's behaviour "is contrary to the spirit of the age" indicates that the state mantra of historical

> " TO REFUSE TO BE ON TIME BUT TO ENJOY ITS PASSING, AS KUNO DOES, IS TO BE AUTOMATICALLY CONSIDERED AS DEGENERATE."

progress is Hegelian in character. Hegel's philosophy of Spirit, summarised in the claim that "Reason is Spirit when its certainty of being all reality has been raised to truth, and it is conscious of itself as its own world, and of the world as itself," is arguably motivated by a fear of the Other and a need to transcend difference. The subject's search for knowledge is generated both by the very otherness of the object—its resistance to comprehension—and by the realisation that the subject is itself an object within the gaze of the Other. In the most famous passage from Hegel's *Phenomenology*, that of the dialectic between master and slave, this conflict leads inexorably to violence where both participants assert their subjectivity:

> This presentation is a twofold action: action on the part of the other, and action on its own part. In so far as it is the action of the *other*, each seeks the death of the other. But in doing so, the second kind of action, action on its own part, is also involved; for the former involves the staking of its own life. Thus the relation of the two self-conscious individuals is such that they prove themselves and each other through a life-and-death struggle. They must engage in this struggle, for they must raise their certainty of being *for themselves* to truth.

In "The Machine Stops" this contest is played-out in terms of the mother-son relationship, home and homelessness, advancement and barbarism. By dramatising this struggle throughout the narrative rather than in the form of a single allegorical battle, Forster foregrounds and questions its rational basis. At its most visceral, the fear of the Other is experienced as a revulsion of physical contact:

> People were almost exactly alike all over the world, but the attendant of the air-ship, perhaps owing to her exceptional duties, had grown a little out of the common. She had often to address passengers with direct

speech, and this had given her a certain roughness and originality of manner. When Vashti swerved away from the sunbeams with a cry, she behaved barbarically—she put out her hand to steady her.

"How dare you!" exclaimed the passenger. "You forget yourself!"

The attendant's invasion of Vashti's physical space, in contravention of social custom, confirms her degenerate appearance in Vashti's eyes. Yet, this alleged degeneration has been produced by the attendant's adaptation to her environment: the same pseudo-Darwinist principle that Vashti and her neighbours take to be the basis for their own advancement over their predecessors. Here, then, Forster makes a distinction between history and ideology. Whereas the world-state harnesses social Darwinist precepts of natural selection to its own model of historical progress in order to ensure the perfectibility of its citizens (very much in keeping with the views of Forster's contemporaries such as Wells and Karl Pearson), Forster emphasises that this misuse of evolutionary theory is purely ideological. In acknowledging the more general Darwinist notion of constant change and adaptation, Forster asserts that the rationalisation of evolutionary theory will founder upon its own impossibility. Instead of ensuring perfection, the world-state will itself be subject to historical forces of change and decay. What turns the utopia of "The Machine Stops" into a dystopia is its failure to allow for the necessity of change and its abolition of personal and cultural difference. In equating stasis with utopia and uniformity with perfection, the world-state precipitates its own perfectibility. The story's wondrous technology is, nevertheless, insidiously ideological insofar as it appears to suggest that utopia is already now rather than in a continual state of evolution. In that sense, Forster's world-state is prematurely utopian or, in short, dystopian.

Whereas, in *The Secret Agent* (1907), Joseph Conrad satirises his anarchists' eugenic beliefs by emphasising their own degenerate characteristics, Forster undermines the social Darwinism of his world-state by accentuating the relative distinctions between sophistication and barbarism. These distinctions often take place in the context of efficiency and time-management. Forster offers no explanation for the emergence of his world-state—no war or famine or disease—but

he does briefly mention the civilisation that preceded it:

> To "keep pace with the sun," or even to outstrip it, had been the aim of the civilisation preceding this. Racing aeroplanes had been built for the purpose, capable of enormous speed, and steered by the greatest intellects of the epoch. Round the globe they went, round and round, westward, westward, round and round, amidst humanity's applause. In vain. The globe went eastward quicker still, horrible accidents occurred, and the Committee of the Machine, at that time rising into prominence, declared the pursuit illegal, unmechanical and punishable by Homelessness.

Whereas the previous society had, however foolishly, pursued the goal of speed with the sun as its creative inspiration, the movement underground and the replacement of the sun with artificial light constitute a management of time and nature, including that of human nature, by their very abolition. Science retreats "to concentrate herself upon problems that she was certain of solving" whilst "dawn, midday, twilight, the zodiacal path, touched neither men's lives nor their hearts." The romantic opposition between science and nature, and the gendering of this debate in terms of the domestication of masculine impulses, are given more nuanced expression in the relationship between Vashti and Kuno. For the moment, though, I want to pursue further the interaction between time-management and state ideology in Forster's imagined community.

The quantification of time and the rationalisation of human contact are highlighted early on in the story. Vashti knows "several thousand people; in certain directions human intercourse had advanced enormously," but she can only give Kuno "fully five minutes." The cultural orthodoxy of efficiency and advancement—that is to say, of *being seen to be* efficient and advanced—is predicated upon a notion of temporality: of being on time and in command of one's time-keeping. Vashti urges Kuno to "be quick" and reprimands him: "how slow you are." Kuno's deliberate "dawdling" marks him out as a dissident element even before the reader learns of his attempts to escape overground or of his abnormal physicality: "On atavism the Machine can have no mercy." To refuse to be on time but to enjoy its passing, as Kuno does, is to be automatically considered as degenerate. Only by the effective management of one's time can an individual ensure their true citizen status and, by extension, the organisation of the state. The penalty of Homelessness—of being exposed upon the upper earth—confirms the subject's descent into atavism by forcibly returning them to nature. The notion of Home, therefore, is based not only upon what it opposes (nature, wastage and change) but also by being more temporally advanced than its opponent; of being on time and calibrated to the instant.

The extensive study of the relationship between speed, time and politics by the philosopher, Paul Virilio, offers a useful illustration of this temporal disjuncture between those included within and those excluded from the locus of Home. Virilio's meditation upon the conduct of war and the evolution of the city-state turns upon a consideration of time and speed:

> The rudimentary hillock, the elevated observatory, already give the pastoral assembly quicker information on the surroundings, and thus the time to choose between the various military attitudes at their disposal. They avoid the uncalculated spontaneity of primitive struggle (a situation which would immediately be imposed upon them by the aggressor), and thus find themselves confronted with a *new freedom* since they can choose the solution they deem the most advantageous, depending on the size of the enemy group: i.e., either flee with all their goods and flocks, taking advantage of their head start; or face the enemy.

The conversion of the landscape into an armed fortress with ramparts, moats and other defensive strategies is intended to preserve and strengthen that original "head start" by slowing the antagonist down and giving the protagonists more time in which to act. By extension, the transition of the city-state from armed fortress is motivated by both the effective management of time and the speedy processing of information in order to stay ahead of enemies and competitors alike. The state's acquisition of new freedoms, including, in time, democratic and economic systems, is determined by the advantageous growth of time and speed at the expense of those outside the state or, increasingly, those marginalized from within. Virilio's reminder that civic existence is not an inevitable historical goal, but a product that is both mutable and discriminatory, illuminates Forster's

story in a couple of ways. Firstly, it helps to illustrate why time-management is deemed to be essential for the preservation of good citizenship and the running of the state. Vashti's lament for her son's poor time-keeping is tantamount to her pitying his ostracism. Secondly, Virilio indicates that, however advanced the state is in terms of its time-management, it will always be in a condition of crisis because of the paramount need to manage a quality that is, by its very nature, mutable and elusive. St Augustine describes this uncertainty in his consideration of the fleeting moment:

> In fact the only time that can be called present is an instant, if we can conceive of such, that cannot be divided even into the most minute fractions, and a point of time as small as this passes so rapidly from the future to the past that its duration is without length. For if its duration were prolonged, it could be divided into past and future. When it is present it has no duration.

While the calibration of time effectively conceals its elusiveness, the need for political self-preservation is also stimulated by an anxious awareness of time's ineffability. In "The Machine Stops" this anxiety takes the form of a revitalised, quasi-religious devotion to the Machine and a superstitious regard towards its Book (or user's manual). . . .

Source: Paul March-Russell, "'Imagine, If You Can': Love, Time and the Impossibility of Utopia in E.M. Forster's 'The Machine Stops,'" in *Critical Survey*, 2005, pp. 58–62.

SOURCES

Bryant, Gregory K. H., "A Very Brief History of Airships," in *LightSpeed*, July 2010, http://www.lightspeed magazine.com/nonfiction/a-very-brief-history-of-airships (accessed January 23, 2015).

Clute, John, and David Langford, "Pocket Universe," in *The Encyclopedia of Science Fiction*, September 29, 2013, http://www.sf-encyclopedia.com/entry/pocket_universe (accessed January 23, 2015).

Colmer, John, *E. M. Forster: The Personal Voice*, Routledge & Kegan Paul, 1975, p. 39.

Dixon, Kenneth M., "Researchers Link Use of Internet, Social Isolation," in *Stanford News*, February 23, 2005, http://news.stanford.edu/news/2005/february23/internet-022305.html (accessed January 23, 2015).

"The First Zeppelins: LZ-1 through LZ-4," Airships. net, http://www.airships.net/zeppelins (accessed January 23, 2015).

Forster, E. M., "The Machine Stops," in *The Eternal Moment and Other Stories*, Harcourt, Brace, Jovanovich, 1956, pp. 3–37.

———, "The Point of It," in *The Eternal Moment and Other Stories*, Harcourt, Brace, Jovanovich, 1956, p. 43.

Lu, Catherine, "World Government," in *The Stanford Encyclopedia of Philosophy*, edited by Edward N. Zalta, Fall 2012, http://plato.stanford.edu/archives/fall2012/entries/world-government (accessed January 24, 2015).

McDowell, Frederick, P. W., *E. M. Forster*, Twayne Publishers, 1969, p. 59.

Nicholls, Peter, and Brian M. Stableford, "Technology," in *The Encyclopedia of Science Fiction*, September 29, 2013, http://www.sf-encyclopedia.com/entry/technology (accessed January 23, 2015).

Reynolds, Glenn Harlan, "Solar Flare Poses Huge Threat," in *USA Today*, June 28, 2013, http://www.usatoday.com/story/opinion/2013/06/26/solar-flare-electrical-threat-column/2461313 (accessed January 23, 2015).

Roshwald, Mordecai, *Dreams and Nightmares: Science and Technology in Myth and Fiction*, McFarland, 2008, pp. 150, 152.

Rothman, Lilly, "Remember Y2K? Here's How We Prepped for the Non-Disaster," in *Time*, December 31, 2014, http://time.com/3645828/y2k-look-back (accessed January 25, 2015).

"UK Telephone History," http://www.britishtelephones.com/histuk.htm (accessed January 23, 2015).

Viera, Carroll, "E. M. Forster," in *Dictionary of Literary Biography*, Vol. 162: *British Short-Fiction Writers, 1915–1945*, edited by John H. Rogers, Gale Research, 1996, pp. 106–116.

Wilde, Alan, *Art and Order: A Study of E. M. Forster*, Peter Owen, 1965, pp. 86–87.

FURTHER READING

Beauman, Nicola, *E. M. Forster: A Biography*, Knopf, 1994.
>This biography of Forster elucidates the connections between his life and his novels.

Bradshaw, David, ed., *The Cambridge Companion to E. M. Forster*, Cambridge University Press, 2007.
>This collection of sixteen essays covers all aspects of Forster's work. Of particular interest is the essay by Dominic Head titled "Forster and the Short Story."

Luckhurst, Roger, *Science Fiction*, Polity, 2005.
>Luckhurst traces the history of science fiction from the nineteenth century to the present. He mentions "The Machine Stops" in the context of Forster's negative reaction to the utopian work of H. G. Wells.

Seed, David, *Science Fiction, A Very Short Introduction*, Oxford University Press, 2011.
>In this short introduction to the genre, Seed covers such topics as voyages into space, alien encounters, science and technology, and utopias and dystopias.

SUGGESTED SEARCH TERMS

E M Forster

E M Forster AND short stories

The Machine Stops AND E M Forster

E M Forster AND science fiction

H G Wells AND A Modern Utopia

utopia

dystopia

world government

pocket universe AND science fiction

The Mortal Immortal

MARY SHELLEY

1833

Mary Shelley's "The Mortal Immortal" (1833) is an example of popular, rather than serious, literature. It was published in *The Keepsake*, a series of books specially marketed to be given as Christmas presents. It represents the kind of work Shelley had to do to support herself as a writer rather than the creation of literature for its own sake. It is highly satirical, treating the humorous potential of many themes she had dealt with more seriously in her famous novel *Frankenstein*. The story concerns a sorcerer's apprentice who inadvertently becomes immortal and his alienation from the ordinary mortal world; he is suspected of witchcraft as his wife ages and dies. The tale appears in *The Mary Shelley Reader* (1990).

AUTHOR BIOGRAPHY

Shelley, née Godwin, was born in London on August 30, 1797. Her mother, Mary Wollstonecraft Godwin, died ten days later of an infection contracted during the birth. Mary Wollstonecraft had been one of the first recognizable feminists in history and was the author of *A Vindication of the Rights of Woman* (1792), which called for full equality between the sexes. Mary Shelley's father, William Godwin, was an equally notable intellectual, a journalist and a novelist, devoted to radical political causes.

Mary Shelley is best known for her 1818 novel Frankenstein. *(© GL Archive / Alamy)*

He educated his daughter unconventionally, giving her a classical, philosophical education, which he closely supervised himself. She was also exposed to a wide range of intellectuals in her father's circle, ranging from the romantic poet Samuel Taylor Coleridge to the scientist Erasmus Darwin, the grandfather of Charles Darwin.

By 1814, the poet Percy Bysshe Shelley had become part of Godwin's circle. The heir to a large estate from his aristocratic family, Shelley promised that when he came into his inheritance he would clear up Godwin's massive debt, which had come from a failed publishing house for children's books. It quickly became clear that this would not come in time to be useful to Godwin, who aggressively turned on the young poet, himself a political radical and atheist. However, Shelley soon ran off to France and Switzerland with two of Godwin's daughters, Mary and her half-sister Claire. Shelley intended to marry Mary but could not because of his estranged wife, Harriet. Shelley carried on affairs with both sisters, which Mary did not object to, following her mother's doctrine of free love. However, this enraged Godwin, who

refused to see any of them when they returned to London. Mary had been a prodigious writer even as a child, but a mass of her juvenilia was destroyed at this time. Mary's illegitimate child by Shelley (Claire would also bear one of his children) died shortly after birth, as would two of her other children.

In 1816, Shelley, along with Mary and Claire, returned to Switzerland, where they spent the summer with the more prominent poet Lord Byron (who fathered a daughter with Claire at this time). During this visit, Mary wrote *Frankenstein*, by far her most famous work and the most important romantic novel. Percy Shelley edited the novel and rewrote it to an unknown degree to prepare it for publication in 1818, which was highly successful. By this time, Shelley's wife had killed herself, allowing him and Mary to wed. This smoothed over relations with Godwin to a degree. Later that year, the Shelleys moved to Italy, at least in part because Shelley risked arrest in Britain over his political radicalism.

In 1822, Percy Shelley died in a boating accident. Mary returned to England with her only surviving child, Percy Florence Shelley, living initially on a small income provided by the boy's paternal grandfather. Mary determined to support herself by writing and eventually produced several more novels, including *The Last Man* (1826), and did a great deal of hack work, writing encyclopedia entries and short stories in well-paying but poorly respected publications like *The Keepsake*, including "The Mortal Immortal: A Tale" in 1833. She also profited by republishing collections of Percy Bysshe Shelley's writings, carefully expurgated to remove politically radical material. She continued to associate with leading intellectuals, such as the American poet Washington Irving. Her father became increasingly emotionally and eventually financially dependent upon her. She died on February 1, 1851, of what was at the time diagnosed as a brain tumor.

PLOT SUMMARY

"The Mortal Immortal" takes the form of a dated letter or journal entry (July 16, 1833) in which the narrator, Winzy, tells part of his life's story. He immediately reveals that he is over three hundred years old (but is not, therefore,

MEDIA ADAPTATIONS

- The 1986 science-fiction film *Highlander*, directed by Russell Mulcahy, concerns a sixteenth-century Scottish peasant who becomes immortal. A large story arc within the film concerns the difficulties he faces as his wife ages and dies, the inability of immortals to father children, and his education by an alchemist in the employ of the emperor Charles V (though he is not called Agrippa), themes that may have been suggested by "The Mortal Immortal."

to be confused with the Wandering Jew who is far older). He does not know if he is immortal. His appearance is youthful. He has a few gray hairs, but then so do many young men. In any case, he finds his long life a burden: "Oh! the weight of never-ending time—the tedious passage of the still-succeeding hours!" He wishes he were like Nourjahad (a character in a novel and play by Frances Sheridan) who slept through eternity.

In his youth, Winzy was an apprentice of Cornelius Agrippa, the famous philosopher and magician. Agrippa's apprentices deserted him after an episode in which one of their colleagues, following one of the master's rituals, supposedly summoned the devil and was destroyed by him. Even Winzy is scared off by this rumor and, poor as he is, refuses to go on working for the philosopher at any price. He turns his attentions to Bertha, the girl he is in love with. Her family had been poor farmers on land near that of his own parents, but they had died in an epidemic, and she was adopted by a rich but childless woman in the area. While her parents had encouraged Winzy as a suitor, Bertha's unnamed protectress views him as unsuitable because of his poverty. Nevertheless, he and Bertha continue to meet in secret. Bertha eventually comes around to her protectress's way of thinking and increasingly belittles Winzy for his poverty, preventing their marriage. When

she discovers he could gain a large income from going back to work as Agrippa's apprentice, she forces him to do so against his better judgment. Over the next year, Bertha increasingly puts passive-aggressive pressure on Winzy to become suddenly rich enough to marry her, and when his work attending Agrippa's alchemical furnace (in which he is carrying out a "mighty work," the *magnum opus* of alchemy) causes him to be late for one of their meetings, she as good as tells him that she will accept the hand of Albert Hoffer, a rich young man her protectress has settled upon for her.

At this news, Winzy is overcome with jealousy and despair. When he returns to Agrippa's laboratory, the philosopher has been tending a vessel in his furnace for three straight days. He turns the task over to Winzy, with strict instructions to watch the color change in the vessel and to get him at the crucial moment. He is anxious that Winzy should not even touch and especially not drink the elixir in the furnace and tells him that it will cure love, thinking that the young man would never want to extinguish his love for Bertha. In his new circumstances, that is exactly what he does want, so when the elixir's transformation is complete, Winzy in fact drinks it, or half of it, since Agrippa returns and startles his apprentice into dropping the half-empty vessel of elixir. He lets Agrippa think, however, that he did not succeed in drinking any of it.

After many hours of work, Winzy goes off to sleep and is overcome by a superhuman sense of well-being. The next day, he goes to confront Bertha with the fact, as he thinks, that he is now free of her charms and meets her with her protectress and her page; he is no longer afraid to confront the rich old woman herself and reproach her regarding her manipulation of Bertha. He finds that he is just as much in love with Bertha as ever, however, and that her own feelings for him have been rekindled, despite the loss of status and wealth that breaking with her protectress will mean.

Bertha and Winzy are married and live by working his family's farm. His emotional transformation from the elixir continues, and Bertha notices that Winzy no longer suffers from the brooding melancholy he once had. Five years later, Winzy attends Agrippa on his deathbed to discover that Agrippa has prepared a second elixir. Agrippa reveals that the substance is the elixir of life, an alchemical preparation that will confer immortality, but the vessel holding it explodes before Agrippa can drink it. Thinking back on the spiritual intoxication he experienced when he drank the first elixir, Winzy concludes that he is now immortal (he convinces himself that he looks no older than he did five years earlier). A few days later he dismisses his credulity. He cannot imagine that Agrippa, whom he knew to be an ordinary man, could command such supernatural powers and still less that he could have become an immortal being. He likens his disbelief to an old proverb, "A prophet is least regarded in his own country," meaning that the familiar cannot be regarded as mysterious and superhuman. In fact, this is a paraphrase of a saying of Jesus, when the people in Nazareth who knew him as a child refuse to hear his message: "But Jesus said unto them, A prophet is not without honour, but in his own country, and among his own kin, and in his own house" (Mark 6:4 KJV; cf. Matthew 13:57). But as the years go on, Winzy does not age at all. He begins to look more like Bertha's son than her husband, exciting comment from the neighbors and jealousy from Bertha. Significantly, they have no children. It is unclear if this is a side effect of the elixir.

Imagining that Winzy is under a demonic spell, Bertha urges him to somehow break free of it and show his true age. She is afraid he will be burned as a witch. At the same time, she is also jealous that he has not stopped her aging, not that her gray hairs would stop her being stoned to death in that case. So he tells her what happened, presenting himself as gaining a long life rather than immortality. He suggests that the only thing he can do is to leave her and take up the life of a wanderer, but Bertha cannot stand to be parted from him. Instead they sell the farm—at a great loss because of Winzy's suspicious reputation—and go off to live in a foreign country, where Bertha uses makeup and every other technique she can to try to match Winzy's youth. Even so, she becomes increasingly jealous of every young woman as a rival. Winzy must watch as Bertha becomes decrepit with age and finally dies. Cut off from human society, he longs for salvation through death, but he does not know if he can die. He drank only half of the elixir, so is he immortal or only long-lived, a mortal immortal? Even in the latter case, he might be doomed to live for thousands of years. He has often thought of

suicide. He has thought also of fighting in war, but he is horrified by the idea of dying at the hands of a mortal human being, since that is now something different from himself. Finally he decides to go on "an expedition, which mortal frame can never survive, even endued with the youth and strength that inhabits mine." This recalls the polar expedition in *Frankenstein* as well as the apparently immortal creatures living on mountaintop glaciers. He has left the document readers have before them as a record of his intention.

CHARACTERS

Cornelius Agrippa

Shelley's Agrippa in "The Mortal Immortal" is seen principally as an alchemist engaged in the great work of creating the philosopher's stone. He succeeds, but the fruit of his labor is lost to him when Winzy drinks the elixir of life, which is the practical outcome of his alchemical experiments. He succeeds a second time and has the elixir on his deathbed but is unable to drink it before expiring. In the course of the story, he leaves his assistant, Winzy, to tend the final transformation of the elixir in the alchemical furnace, warning him off drinking it by saying, "Winzy, my boy . . . do not touch the vessel—do not put it to your lips; it is a philter [magical drug]—a philter to cure love; you would not cease to love your Bertha—beware to drink." Counteracting love is not a traditional property of the elixir of life, nor does it have that effect in the story. Agrippa is probably telling his apprentice what he thinks will most likely keep him from drinking it. (Obviously anyone would be tempted to drink an elixir that he believed would result in immortality.) Through a comedy of errors, however, ceasing to love Bertha is precisely what Winzy, unknown to his master, wishes to do, so the instruction impels him to drink it, forming part of the satirical structure of Shelley's story.

Agrippa was a historical personage, one of the leading intellectuals in Germany in the early sixteenth century. Winzy himself says, "All the world has heard of Cornelius Agrippa." He was the author of *De occulta philosophia* (*Of Occult Philosophy*), one of the most important works in the tradition of Renaissance magic, as well as *De incertitudine et vanitate scientiarum atque artium declamation invectiva* (Declamation attacking the uncertainty and vanity of the sciences and the arts; Shelley refers to this work in the story, when on his deathbed she has Agrippa cry out against "the vanity of human wishes!"). He apparently practiced alchemy as part of a secret society in his youth but grew disappointed with the lack of positive results in his experiments. In *De vanitate* he attacks alchemy as for the most part a confidence game in which alchemists extract money from wealthy patrons with the promise that they will learn the secret of turning base metals into gold, though he leaves open the possibility that a true spiritual alchemy may be possible. However, Agrippa was far more concerned with ceremonial magic, the summoning of angels and demons. Shelley alludes to this when she has Winzy report, "In spite of the most painful vigilance, I had never detected the trace of a cloven foot; nor was the studious silence of our abode ever disturbed by the demonic howls." Agrippa taught at the University of Cologne and was employed by the emperor Charles V, though probably in a diplomatic capacity. Agrippa was apocryphally credited with having raised the ghost of Helen of Troy for Charles V, an item that became part of the Faust legend. Indeed, although Faust was also a historical magician and a contemporary of Agrippa, the Faust tradition is more closely based on Agrippa than Faust himself.

Bertha

Bertha is a caricature of the kind of woman who is completely untouched by the feminism espoused by Shelley and her mother, Mary Wollstonecraft. When Winzy describes Bertha as living next to "a gently bubbling spring of pure living waters," this is meant to be a concrete metaphor, an objective correlative, referring to Bertha herself. This satirizes the conventional belief of the time that a woman has worth only in respect of her virginity, and that worth is only as a potential wife. While Bertha fell in love with Winzy as a youth, under the tutelage of her protectress, she comes to see herself as a property on the marriage market and has no concern other than making the most advantageous match possible. This eventually begins to work against Winzy's interests: "Bertha fancied that love and security were enemies, and her pleasure was to divide them in my bosom." She brings pressure on Winzy to make

himself more attractive by increasing his income. This attitude is entrenched in her by her protectress, who enhances her youthful beauty with the promise of a dowry to lure advantageous suitors, and she finally overcomes any genuine romantic feelings she had for Winzy to accept as a husband a candidate proposed by her protectress. She had hoped at one time that Winzy would become wealthy and influential as Agrippa's disciple, perhaps even gaining wealth through alchemy. She is seemingly overcome by genuine affection at the last minute, after Winzy drinks the elixir. However, this change is meant to convey an important point of the plot with some subtlety.

Although Shelley does not say so directly, and perhaps Winzy is meant to be unconscious of it, the elixir has obviously done more for Winzy than make him immortal. It is apparent that, after drinking it, he thinks more boldly and philosophically. Anyone knowledgeable of alchemy would indeed expect the elixir to make him an intellectually and spiritually superior person compared with what he was before. No doubt it made him better in other ways as well, changing him into a sort of alpha male, irresistibly attractive to women. This is what Bertha responds to, immediately finding him a more attractive match than the financially superior husband her protectress had selected for her. Bertha herself remains unchanged, true to her original stereotyped character. She is jealous of other women and tries to remain competitive with them by laying on prodigious amounts of makeup to cover her aging. All of Winzy's difficulties about the relative aging of himself and his wife come from Bertha's self-consciousness that their apparent ages set them apart from the socially acceptable model of a prosperous older husband with a beautiful young wife. Winzy's apparent youth makes her "jealous and peevish." As he grows older, Bertha's jealousy becomes more intense and ridiculous. Winzy says, "I never dared address another woman: on one occasion, fancying that the belle of the village regarded me with favoring eyes, she bought me a gray wig." Through this satire, Shelley is addressing the plight of aristocratic women in her time. Their only hold on their husband's affection is their beauty, which is short-lived. On the other hand, a man's attractiveness to young women could increase with age in proportion to his wealth and status, leaving his wife in constant anxiety because of their unequal position. Immortality in this case is only a comic screen for the privileged position of men in a patriarchal society.

Albert Hoffer

Hoffer is a rich "silk-clad youth" whom Bertha's protectress intends for her to marry.

Nourjahad

Winzy mentions Nourjahad as being in a better condition than he with respect to immortality. Nourjahad is a character in *The History of Nourjahad* (1767), a tale by Frances Sheridan (mother of the Irish playwright Richard Brinsley Sheridan). Nourjahad is deceived into thinking that he is immortal and that he sleeps for decades at a time. Frances Sheridan reworked the novel into a play, *Illusion; or, The Trances of Nourjahad* in 1813, which was well known in Shelley's youthful circle. Winzy wishes that his immortal life also passed in sleep.

Page

The protectress's page briefly accompanies his mistress in the scene based on the illustration provided to Shelley by *The Keepsake* editors. Inasmuch as the image originally illustrated William Shakespeare's play *Romeo and Juliet*, he would correspond to the character called Peter in that play.

The Protectress

Bertha's unnamed protectress is a wealthy widow who adopts the poor orphan in compensation for her own childishness. Although she is a woman, she has completely internalized her patriarchal culture and acts toward Bertha like a manipulative, controlling father. She treats Bertha as a commodity to be bought and sold to increase her own prestige among other aristocrats, and she uses her economic power over Bertha to keep her away from her beloved Winzy.

The Wandering Jew

The Wandering Jew is a figure of medieval legend. It seems to have been created in response to a statement of Jesus in the Gospel of Matthew, "Verily I say unto you, There be some standing here, which shall not taste of death, till they see the Son of Man coming in his kingdom" (16:28 KJV). While the text probably indicates the author's belief that Jesus's return was imminent in the late first century, the Wandering Jew is supposedly a member of Jesus's audience who has gone on living until the present day and will do so until Jesus's eventual apocalyptic return, fulfilling the prophecy. The story was usually elaborated by naming the Jew Ahasuerus and making him a mocker of Jesus during the Passion. His eternal existence is a punishment because he is denied the possibility of salvation. He is doomed to wander the earth pursued by tormenting demons. He became a type of the immortal alchemist doomed to wander the earth alienated from humanity in the romantic Rosicrucian novel. His wretched existence is the subject of an epic poem by Percy Shelley, *The Wandering Jew*, written in 1822 but not published until 1887, though, of course, well known to Mary Shelley. Winzy mentions the Wandering Jew at the very beginning of "The Mortal Immortal." After claiming to be 323 years old, he rhetorically asks: "The Wandering Jew?—certainly not. More than eighteen centuries have passed over his head. In comparison with him, I am a very young Immortal." The idea that the reader might confuse Winzy with such a fantastic figure of legend is in keeping with Shelley's satirical approach to the literary themes and traditions she employs.

Winzy

The name Winzy (presumably short for Wenceslaus) would have seemed as ridiculous in 1833 as today and helps to set the satirical tone of "The Mortal Immortal." The story that Winzy tells as narrator is one of transformation. His ultimate transformation is from mortal to immortal, but long before that, his ambition has transformed him from a simple peasant to the apprentice or scholar of Cornelius Agrippa, in other words the equivalent of a modern graduate student. This places him in a position where he unknowingly drinks the elixir of life, making him immortal and transforming himself into something superhuman, or, as he sees, it, something inhuman. Besides his supposed or possible immortality, the elixir causes Winzy to undergo other transformations, as the reader should expect since the goal of alchemy is the spiritual rebirth of the alchemist, of which immortality is only a part. After Agrippa reveals to him that what he drank was the elixir of life, Winzy reminisces:

> I remembered the glorious drunkenness that had followed my stolen draught. I reflected on the change I had felt in my frame—in my soul. The bounding elasticity of the one—the buoyant lightness of the other.

Winzy undergoes still another kind of transformation. At the beginning of the story, the reader is told that he was voluntarily working for the magician Agrippa. It was not for extraordinary pay (the offer of that came only later), so he must have wanted to learn Agrippa's occult secrets for himself. Particularly in light of Shelley's *Frankenstein*, this desire can be described as a wish to fulfill some inner lack in Winzy, which a century later would be called a neurosis. After drinking the elixir, though, Winzy has no desire to associate with Agrippa either for money or for his secrets. Instead, he is better integrated and so perfectly happy working as a farmer and enjoying his married life. The elixir seems to have made his character more whole and mentally healthy. Even Winzy's deathbed visit to Agrippa is out of simple human decency (significantly, he makes no effort to seize the new dose of elixir as he could easily have done).

However, as the years pass and it becomes clear that Winzy is either immortal or aging so slowly (because he drank only half of the dose of elixir) that he will live for centuries, he becomes alienated from human society. He and Bertha have no children. If this is caused by the elixir, then it has left him unable to achieve the normal kind of human immortality by having offspring. His lack of aging makes him suspect to his neighbors and causes jealousy in Bertha. He is horrified by watching his wife age and then by tending her on her deathbed and burying her. His position ultimately leaves him cut off from human society because he has stepped out of the ordinary human life cycle:

> How many have been my cares and woes, how few and empty my enjoyments! . . . A sailor without rudder or compass, tossed on a stormy sea—a traveller lost on a wide-spread heath, without landmark or star to guide him . . . more lost, more hopeless than either.

Winzy longs that his "heart beat no more with emotions varied only by new forms of sadness!" This is the type of the Rosicrucian wanderer (that is, an alchemist), cut off from human society, of which he is no longer a part. He feels that the only salvation he can have is death, which has been denied him. He determines finally, back at the time in which the story begins, in 1833, to set off to some uninhabitable part of the world to see if the extremes of nature can end his life. Even if he returns, he is confident that he will finally be able to end his life and, "by scattering and annihilating the atoms that compose my frame, set at liberty the life imprisoned within." It is unclear if he means an ordinary suicide or if he will have finally gained a spiritual maturity from the elixir that would let him destroy his body through an act of will.

THEMES

Romanticism

Romanticism was a major cultural reaction to the Enlightenment, the scientific revolution, and especially the first stages of the Industrial Revolution, in the late eighteenth and early nineteenth centuries. While the Enlightenment had been quick to abandon traditions, including traditional religion, that seemed irrational, the romantics wondered if some important part of the human condition was not being lost. A life of industrial work, tending machines, which was becoming the lot of more and more people, seemed inhuman. Romanticism took a dialectical view of history. If traditional human culture represented a thesis, the Enlightenment and science offered an antithesis. The romantics hoped to achieve some synthesis that would preserve the best of both positions in a new whole synthesis. Shelley herself championed a form of romanticism in which the ancient tradition of magic is queried to determine if it has something to offer science. This is a main theme of her novel *Frankenstein*, and it occurs in "The Mortal Immortal" also through its validation of alchemy. The romantics recognized that tradition had been smashed and left as a heap of broken ruins. Accordingly, romantic literary works often take the form of a fragment of a larger text. This is the case with the "The Mortal Immortal," which is a fragment in relation to its form. It begins with a date, "July 16, 1833," which could be the heading of a journal entry but is more likely the date at the head of a letter. In either case, it implies a further text to which the reader has no access, either the rest of the journal or the series of correspondence to which the letter belongs. Documents such as letters or journals were often used in early novels (including Shelley's *Frankenstein*, which is entirely a series of letters), owing to the novel's origin in the school exercises of ancient Greece, where classwork often consisted of composing

TOPICS FOR FURTHER STUDY

- *Harry Potter and the Philosopher's Stone* (1997) is a young-adult novel by J. K Rowling. Much of the plot concerns the theft and recovery of a philosopher's stone owned by a 665-year-old alchemist. The original American edition was given the title *Harry Potter and the Sorcerer's Stone* because its publisher Scholastic did not believe that its potential readership would understand the Rosicrucian reference of the actual title. Write a fan fiction in which Winzy from "The Mortal Immortal" turns up at Hogwarts.

- In "The Mortal Immortal" Shelley interacts with her mother's ideas of feminism, expressed in her *Vindication of the Rights of Woman* and her novel *Maria; or, The Wrongs of Woman*. She satirically presents women's lives as they existed in the 1830s, inviting criticism from a viewpoint like her mother's. Write a paper comparing the two authors' presentations of women. Are they truly at odds or merely using different strategies or tones?

- Heinrich Cornelius Agrippa von Netessheim, a character in "The Mortal Immortal," was a historical person. Research his biography and create a poster illustrating his life for your classroom. Websites like http://www.easel.ly have tools for this purpose.

- *Alchemy, Medicine and Religion in the China of A.D. 320: The Nei P'ien of Ko Hung* (translated by James R. Ware in 1966) presents to English readers an early and important work of Chinese alchemy. In China, alchemy was created at the order of the First Emperor (in the second century), who directed the scholars at his court to find a way to make him immortal. Use this text and any references on the Internet to the First Emperor to prepare a talk for your class discussing the techniques of gaining immortality found in Chinese alchemy.

- Victor Frankenstein and his creature in *Frankenstein* both have points of similarity with Winzy in "The Mortal Immortal." These include alienation from society and the urge to escape the human world by going to the limits of the physical environment, as well as the theme of alchemy. Write a paper comparing the two works along these lines.

---

fictitious documents of the kind the students would later have to compose in their public careers.

Magic

Science is antithetical to magic and entails a rejection of magic as a valid means of understanding and controlling the universe. However, a theme of romanticism is the idea that the two could somehow be combined into a new synthesis that would exceed the power of either. The *locus classicus* of this idea is in Shelley's novel *Frankenstein*. In that work, the young Victor Frankenstein happens to read Agrippa's *De occulta philosophia*, and when he asks his father about Agrippa, he is told, "Ah! Cornelius Agrippa! My dear Victor, do not waste your time upon this; it is sad trash." This abrupt dismissal does not satisfy Victor, and reflecting upon it later, he wishes that his father had made a more formal refutation, as any scientist of the era would have done:

> If instead of this remark, my father had taken the pains to explain to me, that the principles of Agrippa had been entirely exploded, and that a modern system of science had been introduced, which possessed much greater powers than the ancient, because the powers of the latter were chimerical, while those of the former were real and practical; under such circumstances I should certainly have thrown Agrippa aside.

Though an orphan, Bertha is taken in by a wealthy old woman who lives in a castle.
(© Carlos Caetano / ShutterStock.com)

Instead, Victor spends his teenage years intensively studying magic, not only in the works of Agrippa but also in those of Paracelsus and Albertus Magnus (undoubtedly meaning the Renaissance magical books that were apocryphally attributed to this medieval scholastic). Once Victor receives a modern scientific education at university, he is able to combine the two theses—magic and science—into something greater than either, of which the practical outcome is the creation of the famous monster (called a creature in the novel), reviving the dead and hence creating a sort of immortality. Naturally, Shelley is vague about the details of this new form of philosophy since it must remain conjectural. The final development of this romantic hope came in the works of Frances Yates, who, in her *Giordano Bruno and the Hermetic Tradition* (1964) and a series of later books, argued that science developed out of Renaissance occultism, a thesis that has not been taken seriously since the 1960s.

In "The Mortal Immortal," the efficacy of magic, in the specific form of alchemy, is simply presented as a fact. This treatment is more nearly gothic than romantic, with the reality of the traditional world erupting disjointedly into modern reality. Shelley is here in line with the Rosicrucian literature that bridged the romantic and the gothic, whose heroes were typically alchemists who gained immortality, only to find themselves alienated from the rest of humanity, as in her father's novel *St. Leon: A Tale of the Sixteenth Century* (1799). Shelley derived the title "The Mortal Immortal" from John Keats's 1818 poem, *Endymion* (book 1, line 844). There the alchemical elixir of life stands as a symbol for love, and only by participating in love does a mortal have the ability to become immortal. In this context, Winzy's mistaking the elixir for a medicine to cure him of love must be taken as satirical of Keats, an in-joke for those well read in romantic poetry (probably not regular readers of *The Keepsake*).

Alchemy is an occult pseudoscience that took form in the Hellenistic era, probably though the Greek reception of Egyptian priestly tradition. The earliest proto-alchemical texts contain recipes that would allow the alchemist to make a favorable impression in Graeco-Roman society, centered on the institution of the *symposium*, or dinner party. These range from aid in striking up a conversation by feeding bread to fish in a fountain to making a dinner service manufactured of base metal appear to be made of gold. It quickly developed, however, into a spiritual science. The Greeks believed that metallic ores in the ground went through a life cycle, with iron changing into copper and eventually into gold, like the metamorphoses of a caterpillar into a butterfly. The aim of the alchemist was to stimulate these transformations through quasi-chemical experiments. The goal was to create an entirely spiritual material, the philosopher's stone, which, while it would have the power to transform base metals into gold, would have the more important result of spiritually transforming the alchemist, so that his soul would become like a god's. The elixir of life, derived from the stone, would confer divine immortality on the alchemist, which is the goal of Agrippa's experiment in "The Mortal Immortal." Shelley is far more explicit in her description of the alchemical processes than is the case in most other Rosicrucian literature, and she describes the preparation of the elixir in some detail: "The liquid it [the vessel] contains is of a soft rose-colour. . . . First it will turn white, and then emit golden flashes." This is an accurate description of an alchemical experiment, reflecting the actual transformation of various chemical compounds (though, of course, not of elements, as the alchemists believed). Shelley probably derived her knowledge of alchemy firsthand, through her contact with her father's intellectual circle, some of whom were practicing alchemists.

STYLE

The Gothic

The gothic was a genre of literature that had close contacts with romanticism. The term gothic acts as a specialized synonym for the Middle Ages. It derives from the Goths and other Germanic tribes that invaded and destroyed the Western Roman Empire at the end of antiquity in the fifth century. It does not refer so much to the actual Middle Ages as to a middle ages of the imagination, which can suddenly and disastrously erupt into the present. Gothic literature can therefore be set either in the medieval period or in the author's present at the time of writing. This is seen in the setting of "The Mortal Immortal" in the sixteenth century (although Shelley does nothing to explore the setting of her story in a remote historical period, instead describing a world that to all appearances is her own contemporary society) and particularly in its portrayal of the reality of alchemy. The story is particularly part of a subset of the gothic, Rosicrucian fiction, in which the main character is an alchemist who achieves immortality, setting him apart from ordinary human society. One of the main concerns of the gothic is the social control, conceived of as exploitative and repressive, of women and women's sexuality. In "The Mortal Immortal," Shelley satirizes this theme, presenting Bertha as a willing participant in the control of her protectress and her husband, and exposes that it is, in certain respects at least, just as limiting to men as to women.

Illustration

The inspiration for "The Mortal Immoral" was somewhat unusual. Shelley had been writing regularly for *The Keepsake* for several years by 1833, so when the editors solicited a new story from her, they sent her an engraving and asked her to write a story for which the image could serve as an illustration. She was meant, in other words, to take her inspiration from the picture. The engraving reproduced a painting by Henry Perronet Briggs, a member of the Royal Academy who was a well-known painter of the time, though he is obscure today. The painting itself, executed in 1827, was meant to illustrate a literary text, namely Shakespeare's play *Romeo and Juliet*. Titled *Juliet and Her Nurse*, it refers to act 2, scene 5 of the play, in which Juliet's nurse returns to her after having taken a communication to Romeo. The engraving was reprinted in *The Keepsake* as an illustration to Shelley's text and there bore the tile *Bertha*, referring to the character in the story. (It is not clear whether Shelley or her editors named this character.) In this context, the image illustrates this passage:

> I know not what sudden impulse animated
> her bosom but at the sight, she sprung with
> a light fawn-like bound down the marble

COMPARE & CONTRAST

- **1830s:** Women in Britain lack basic civil rights, such as the right to own property and the right to vote.

  Today: Women in Britain enjoy the same legal and civil rights as men.

- **1830s:** Although the principles of alchemy have already been disproved by chemistry, alchemy is still a serious theme in literature and is pursued by intellectually respectable persons, including some in the circle of William Godwin.

  Today: Alchemy has been further disproved. Scientists can, in fact, transmute elements, including turning lead into gold, by natural rather than alchemical means, although it is not a cost-effective process. Alchemy is generally limited to small fringe groups and to genre literature.

- **1830s:** The average human life span in the West is about forty years.

  Today: The average human life span in the developed world is approaching eighty years, especially because of the prevention of infant mortality through vaccines and other medical, rather than alchemical, interventions.

---

steps, and was hastening towards me. But I had been perceived by another person. The old high-born hag, who called herself her protectress, and was her tyrant, has seen me also; she hobbled, panting, to the terrace; a page, as ugly as herself, held up her train and fanned her as she hurried along and stopped my fair girl.

Thus in the original story that the image illustrated, the old woman is aiding the younger woman's love affair, but in Shelley's version she is trying to prevent it. Shelley characteristically inverts the meaning of her source material, as she does also, for example, with the title "The Mortal Immortal," drawn from Keats's *Endymion*, where the elixir of life is a symbol of love, while Shelley makes it a symbol of lovelessness.

This technique of using an illustration to inspire a literary work could be used in a more serious fashion. For example, Percy Shelley's sonnet "Ozymandias" was written in competition with the poet Horace Smith, both producing a work inspired by an engraving of the Colossi of Memnon, a famous Egyptian ruin.

HISTORICAL CONTEXT

Publishing in the Nineteenth Century

In antiquity and the Middle Ages, writers, if they were not independently wealthy, found financial support from rich patrons. The Roman poet Martial, one of the few ancient writers who made any attempt to support himself through his pen, wrote a number of poems in which he lamented that his works were known from one end of the empire to the other, but in pirated copies from which he did not derive any royalties.

In the eighteenth century however, conditions began to change drastically. Printing was probably a necessary condition, since a printing press, rather than a bookshop with a few copyists writing books out by hand, was required to achieve the scale necessary to profit from writing. The copyright laws that were enacted as part of the transformation to a capitalist economy were just as important a factor in deriving an income from writing. Authors like Jane Austen and Shelley's mother, Mary Wollstonecraft, significantly both women (middle-class women were barred from other professions), were able to barely secure a middle-class income for themselves. A more popular author like Lord Byron, a friend of the Shelley family, made a very handsome living from writing. Capitalism also transformed publishing in other ways. A book became a commodity to be marketed and sold like anything else. Marketing determined sales volume rather any intrinsic merit of what was sold. The first best sellers, for example, were gothic novels, frequently written by women but which were attacked as trash by serious literary authors. Austen's *Northanger Abbey* is a satire against the genre. Shelley's *Frankenstein*, in contrast, used the gothic genre as a form for legitimate artistic expression.

An even more extreme case of commercialization was a publication like *The Keepsake*, for which Shelley wrote "The Mortal Immortal" and fourteen other stories in the 1820s and 1830s. *The Keepsake* (as well as other competing publications like *The Forget-Me-Not* and *Heath's Book of Beauty*) was published once a year and was specifically intended to be given as a Christmas present. It was lavishly produced in terms of the quality of the printing, bookbinding, and illustrations and boasted short contributions from many of the most prominent writers of the day (even the austere William Wordsworth condescended to publish in it). It also paid more than any other publication to its writers. The quality of writing was irrelevant to *The Keepsake*'s purpose, as its authors understood, and it was filled with what is called hack work, writing of little literary quality that was produced merely as a job rather than for any artistic purpose. In his article "'Perhaps a Tale You'll Make It,'" Gregory O'Dea comments that *The Keepsake* was "enormously popular with the buying public but just as widely reviled in precisely the literary circles to which Shelley by rights belonged" and that its volumes were "little more than pretty baubles, handsomely designed and illustrated but notoriously devoid of serious literary merit." The first thing the editors of *The Keepsake* did was choose a selection of illustrations, and these were sent to authors like Shelley who were asked to write a text that incorporated a description of the picture, quite the reverse of the usual procedure. Writers were also instructed to introduce popular themes like romantic love, which Shelley subverted in the tragic relationship in "The Mortal Immortal."

Winzy falls in love with Bertha, his childhood friend. (© *Darja Vorontsova | ShutterStock.com*)

CRITICAL OVERVIEW

Thanks to her novel *Frankenstein*, Shelley is probably the best-known female writer in history, and she is consequently the subject of a large volume of scholarly literature. Even her least significant works have been analyzed and reanalyzed. "The Mortal Immortal" is no exception and is part of the basis for the blunt judgment of Gregory O'Dea, a leading Mary Shelley scholar, in his article, "'Perhaps a Tale You'll Make It,'" that, "For much of her later literary career, Shelley was a hack writer." O'Dea, is just as quick, though, to justify her descent to this level of popular writing. After the death of her husband, Percy Bysshe Shelley, Shelley had a child to support on her own with little help from her husband's family, in a world in which women were essentially debarred from employment. Writing was one of the few careers women could follow, and Mary Shelley was fortunate to be a prominent writer. However, her financial necessities required her to spend much of her time on high-paying commissioned work from publications like *The Keepsake*, rather than pursue more aesthetically important work. O'Dea also makes a great deal out of the fact that Shelley subtitles "The Mortal Immortal" as a tale rather than a story. He explains that "the 'tale' is an ancient and amorphous form, but it seems always to have been considered a genre of narrative fragmentation. Unlike the novel and the short story, which are the major narrative genres that came to supplant it, the tale is rendered as a part rather than a whole, insufficient to stand without an external, supporting context." The *tale*'s fragmentary character is part of the romantic program, which necessarily saw literature as inherently incomplete, in accord with its conception of the incompleteness of the modern world.

Diane Long Hoeveler, in her article "Mary Shelley and Gothic Feminism," sees Shelley as abandoning the radical feminism of her mother, with its call for true equality between the sexes, with a specifically gothic feminism in which women empower themselves through exploiting their victim status. Marie Roberts, in her *Gothic Immortals*, situates "The Mortal Immortal" in the tradition of what she calls Rosicrucian literature, a genre in which the main character becomes immortal through the use of alchemy and is doomed to become a lone wanderer over the earth for the rest of time. This literary theme extends from Shelley's father's *St. Leon: A Tale of the Sixteenth Century* (1799) down to Martin Amis's *Einstein's Monsters* (1987). Richard Garnett, in his 1891 introduction to his edition of *Tales and Stories by Mary Wollstonecraft Shelley*, finds "The Mortal Immortal" to be entirely derivative of *St. Leon*, but A. A. Markley, writing in the *Keats-Shelley Journal* in 1997, counters that Shelley transforms her source material through satire and parody and also transforms the Godwinian Rosicrucian wanderer by increasing his alienation from humanity in the fashion of the Byronic hero. Markley finds the story as much a humorous inversion of Shelley's own *Frankenstein* as of *St. Leon*. Markley suggests an ironic deconstruction of the Bertha illustration from which Shelley worked in "The Mortal Immortal," as a meeting between the young and the old Bertha, and finds the tragic death of Bertha a satire of the romantic theme required by *The Keepsake*'s editors.

CRITICISM

Rita M. Brown

Brown is an English professor. In the following essay, she explores the role of feminism in the gothic and romantic themes of "The Mortal Immortal."

Shelley's mother, Mary Wollstonecraft, is often cited as being among the first feminists. She advocated complete equality between the sexes, meaning that women should have the same opportunities for education and employment and the freedom to exercise political rights as men, and consequently endorsed the idea of *free love*. This term was coined in so-called Jacobin circles in England at the time of the French Revolution, which included thinkers such as Wollstonecraft, William Godwin, and the romantic poet William Blake. The idea of free love held that English law and social practice treated women as property and their husbands as little better than slave masters and that instead men and women should both be free to determine their own romantic relationships as they saw fit, without any legal proscription. (Nevertheless, Wollstonecraft would eventually marry Godwin.) In that she was heir to the feminism of her parents, Shelley's works and life are often analyzed from a feminist perspective and taken to show a more compromised version of feminism. "The Mortal Immortal," which analyzes the institution of marriage from a fairly objective perspective, that of its main character, Winzy, who can stand outside of the institution, is often used as important evidence in this discussion. It is clear also that the short story is in conversation with the critique of marriage offered by gothic literature.

A common element of gothic literature is a young female heroine who is sexually threatened or violated by a powerful male antagonist. This figure is sometimes the heroine's husband, who may have obtained that status by the practice of bride-rape, that is, kidnapping the girl and forcing her to marry him, but may also be the heroine's father or guardian, a male figure that is supposedly meant to protect her. Gothic literature had a primarily female authorship and readership. It is therefore not hard today to read the gothic heroines' threatened sexual status as a critique of marriage as it actually existed in eighteenth- and early-nineteenth-century England, even if some pains are taken

THE FATHER COULD GIVE OR WITHHOLD

HIS DAUGHTER JUST AS IF SHE WERE

ANOTHER CLASS OF PROPERTY."

to keep this equivalence from rising to the threshold of conscious perception. In theory, English women at that time were free to marry whom they chose, but the reality in law, and especially in social practice among the middle class, was often quite different. Middle-class status depended on owning land or other income-producing property. Women could not generally own property outright, as men could. In particular, in order to succeed, a middle-class marriage usually required a dowry, a grant of property from the bride's father to the control of the husband in order to help provide an income for the new family. Thus marriage for a middle-class woman was virtually impossible without her father's consent. The father could give or withhold his daughter just as if she were another class of property. Even within the marriage, while the dowry technically belonged to the wife, the husband had sole control over the income it produced and its disposition. Along with the legal and financial considerations, the father supposedly had a duty to *protect* his daughter from the depredations of men not of his choosing who would otherwise be assumed to want to abuse her (that is, engage her in a romantic relationship that did not include marriage). In practice, this meant that the father could take steps to prevent his daughter from even contacting any men of whom he did not approve, even if this meant shipping off her to Italy away from a troublesome suitor, physically confining her to his own house, or even confining her to a lunatic asylum if she proved she was of unsound mind by insisting on not following his orders.

Shelley exposes this quite plainly in "The Mortal Immortal." Bertha's protectress, though herself a woman, has completely internalized the patriarchal character of her culture and acts in a male role as Bertha's guardian. Since she is an orphan, Bertha is entirely dependent on her protectress, especially for a dowry, the sine qua

non for entering the middle class, while, as a widow, the protectress has more control over her own property than most women and so is free to play an essentially male role. Long after the protectress decided that Winzy would make an unsuitable husband for Bertha and succeeded in convincing the girl of the same, Bertha suddenly shows an interest in the young man. At that moment, the protectress says, "Whither so fast? Back to your cage—hawks are abroad!" The meaning of this highly metaphorical passage would have been clear to Shelley's readers. Bertha is following her own inclinations by rushing toward Winzy. The protectress intervenes and orders her back to the house, where she can be effectively confined like a songbird in a cage. It is taken for granted that men will prey upon defenseless young women. While the protectress does not quite have the legal power to keep her in what would effectively be a prison, she can threaten her with destitution, cutting her off from the property she promised the girl as a dowry if she marries a man of the protectress's choosing. In the protectress's version of things this is *protecting* Bertha; she sees Winzy as a hawk ready to prey on the girl the moment her protection is lifted. Protection in this case is a euphemism for control. From Bertha's perspective, or from the perspective of any young woman under the control of her father or guardian, it is the guardian who poses a threat to her freedom to choose her own husband.

Shelley's mother, Mary Wollstonecraft, was among the first to analyze the social role of marriage in English society. She realized that the so-called *protection* it offered women was actually oppressive and exploitative social control. The problem was that women were economically dependent on their male controllers. If women had the same rights as men to control their own property and the same right to earn their own living by, for example, practicing law or opening a business, they would also be in a position to make their own decisions about marriage and other romantic relationships. Wollstonecraft exemplified this in her own life by following practically the only profession open to women, that of an author, to guarantee her independence. If men and women were equal, they would then be free to enter into romantic relationships with each other on the basis of equality rather than of patriarchal control and subjugation. Women in that case

WHAT DO I READ NEXT?

- Andrew Smith's *Gothic Literature* (2007) is a general introduction to the genre for students.

- Barbara Johnson was a professional psychoanalyst rather than a literacy critic, but she devoted a number of essays and talks to using psychoanalysis to illuminate the works of Mary Shelley, especially from a feminist perspective. These are collected for the first time in *A Life with Mary Shelley* (2014), edited by Shoshana Felman and Judith Butler.

- "The Mortal Immortal" was written during the period when Shelley's main literary endeavor was her novel *Lodore* (1835). The novel follows an aristocratic mother and daughter who must make their own way in the world after Lord Lodore, the woman's husband and the girl's father, is killed in a duel. It criticizes the enforced dependency of women on men in a patriarchal culture and explores the possibilities inherent in Shelley's own egalitarian and unorthodox education.

- *Proserpine* is a drama for children by Shelley and her husband, Percy Bysshe Shelley. They wrote it in 1820, but it was not published until 1832, in *The Winter's Wreath*, a publication similar to *The Keepsake*. It retells the Greek myth of Persephone (Proserpine in Latin) and Hades in a feminist interpretation. This can be found on the Project Gutenberg website at http://www.gutenberg.org/ebooks/6447.

- *Maria; or, The Wrongs of Woman* (1798) is a novel by Shelley's mother, Mary Wollstonecraft. The heroine is condemned to an insane asylum by her husband after he collects her dowry, but she is able to find personal satisfaction through romantic relationships with a fellow inmate and one of her doctors. The novel is meant to illustrate Wollstonecraft's feminist idea that marriage as it existed in eighteenth-century Britain was oppressive of women.

- William Godwin's *St. Leon: A Tale of the Sixteenth Century* (1799) is a Rosicrucian novel that concerns an alchemist who gains immortality but, becoming alienated from merely mortal human beings, is forced to live in melancholy solitude. It was one of the main inspirations for "The Mortal Immortal."

- Pu Songling (1640–1715) wrote over a hundred satirical short stories, almost all of which concern alchemy or other occult sciences. A selection of 104 of his stories has been translated by John Minford as *Strange Tales from a Chinese Studio* (2006).

---

would not be stigmatized (*ruined* in the language of the day) if they entered into any kind of romantic relationship other than marriage, as men were free to do in practice. Wollstonecraft dramatized the situation of women in her novel *Maria; or, The Wrongs of a Woman* (1792). The heroine of this work is cast aside by both her father and husband when they wish to pursue sexual relationships outside of marriage, and she ends up locked away in a lunatic asylum. These are standard tropes of gothic literature. Once she is confined, Maria finds that she paradoxically has the freedom to pursue romantic and other types of relationships with men as she chooses. Wollstonecraft presents this as a caricature of the position of all middle-class women. It follows that men's actions are constrained by convention as well, since under the prevailing paradigm of marriage they also cannot pursue their own desires without social stigma, although the stress of normative forces on them is much less. Shelley also

Winzy drinks the potion thinking it will cure his love for Bertha, but instead he becomes immortal.
(© David Dewhirst / ShutterStock.com)

put her mother's principles into practice, becoming Percy Bysshe Shelley's mistress while he still had a wife and allowing him, both then and after they were married, to contract romantic relationships with other women. Later, she guaranteed her own independence by working as a writer, which allowed her to turn down marriage proposals she might have had to otherwise accept from economic necessity.

In "The Mortal Immortal" Shelley advances her feminist arguments through satire. As already noted, Bertha's protectress plays an essentially male role in the social control of Bertha, which would have seemed faintly ridiculous to her readers even as it calls endless abuse upon her from Winzy, since she is, strictly speaking, violating social norms. Winzy realizes that, while he has the upper hand in his patriarchal society, the power of his own feelings controls him just as effectively as any guardian could control a young woman, and he seeks to be free of them through magic. No doubt Shelley expected that her female readers would wish to be free of the control enforced on them

by the same miraculous means. Bertha gives up wealth and social position to marry, but within marriage she is just as controlled and infantilized as any other prefeminist woman. She is consumed by jealousy, since the only hope she has of equality within the marriage is enforcing her husband's faithfulness. Bertha's powerlessness within the marriage is emphasized through her concerns over her unequal aging compared with Winzy. In a real marriage, the only power a woman had over her husband was her attractiveness, and like many in real life, Bertha goes to ridiculous lengths to preserve her beauty against the effects of aging through the excessive use of makeup. Even mortal husbands in Shelley's day needed to have no such concern over their appearance; their attractiveness consisted in their wealth and position, not their youth. Because she lacks true freedom and independence, Bertha is reduced to becoming a "mincing, simpering, jealous old woman."

Because Shelley's technique in "The Mortal Immortal" is satirical, she does not have to speak positively for the ideals of feminism espoused by her mother and which she herself embodied. Rather, she presents the current situation of women as ridiculous, allowing her readers to draw their own conclusions about the changes that are necessary in society.

Source: Rita M. Brown, Critical Essay on "The Mortal Immortal," in *Short Stories for Students*, Gale, Cengage Learning, 2016.

Diane Long Hoeveler

In the following excerpt, Hoeveler gives a feminist reading of "The Mortal Immortal."

During the month of May 1794, the most popular drama in London, playing nightly to packed houses at Covent Garden, was Henry Siddons's *The Sicilian Romance; or The Apparition of the Cliff[s]*, loosely based on Ann Radcliffe's second novel, published in 1790. One of the more interesting changes in the play concerns the villain of the Siddons piece, who keeps his inconvenient wife chained to solid stone in a rocky cave in the forest, a place he visits only to feed her and blame her for inflicting wounds of guilt on his heart. Although the Gothic villain would later metamorphose into the Byronic hero consumed by unspeakable guilt over illicit sins, the villain of the Siddons drama is a bit more prosaic. He simply desires to marry a younger and more beautiful woman, one who will further improve his social and political status, because his first wife, the mother of his children, has become redundant. The young woman he desires, whom we would recognize as a future trophy wife, is pursued from castle to convent to cavern, aided by the hero, the villain's son-turned-outlaw. As the above synopsis makes obvious, female Gothic novels like Radcliffe's *Sicilian Romance* provided the subject matter, techniques, and melodramatic formulae that, first on the stage in England, later on the French stage, and much later in the Hollywood "women in jeopardy" films such as *The Silence of the Lambs*, have continued to promulgate the primal Gothic tradition of "good" or femininity triumphing over "evil" or masculinity.

The typical female Gothic novel presents a blameless female victim triumphing through a variety of passive-aggressive strategies over a male-created system of oppression and corruption. The melodrama that suffuses these works is explicable only if we understand that, as Paula Backscheider has recently demonstrated,

ONCE AGAIN, HER MALE NARRATOR EXPRESSES MARY SHELLEY'S OWN AMBIVALENCE AND REPUGNANCE TOWARD NOT ONLY THE FEMALE BODY BUT FEMALE SEXUALITY AND THE CHAINS OF LOVE."

a generally hyperbolic sentimentalism was saturating the British literary scene at the time, informing the Gothic melodramas that were such standard fare during the popular theater season. But melodrama, as Peter Brooks has demonstrated, is also characterized by a series of moves or postures that made it particularly attractive to middle-class women. Specifically, Brooks lists as crucial to melodrama the tendency toward depicting intense, excessive representations of life that tend to strip away the facade of manners to reveal the primal conflicts at work, leading to moments of intense confrontation. These symbolic dramatizations rely on what Brooks lists as the standard features of melodrama: hyperbolic figures, lurid and grandiose events, masked relationships and disguised identities, abductions, slow-acting poisons, secret societies, and mysterious parentage. In short, melodrama is a version of the female Gothic, while the female Gothic provides the undergirding for feminism as an ideology bent on depicting women as the innocent victims of a corrupt and evil patriarchal system.

If husbands can routinely chain their wives to stone walls and feed them the way one feeds a forsaken pet that will not die, then what sort of action is required from women to protect and defend themselves against such abuse? Demure, docile behavior is hardly adequate protection against a lustful, raving patriarch gone berserk. According to Brooks, the Gothic novel can be understood as standing most clearly in reaction to desacralization and the pretensions of rationalism. Like melodrama, the female Gothic text represents both the urge toward resacralization and the impossibility of conceiving sacralization other than in personal terms. For the Enlightenment mentality, there was no longer a clear transcendent value to which one could be reconciled. There was, rather, a social order to be purged, a set of ethical imperatives to be made clear. And who was in a better position to purge the new bourgeois world of all traces of aristocratic corruption than the female Gothic heroine? Such a woman—professionally virginal, innocent, and good—assumed virtual religious significance because, within the discourse system, so much was at stake. Making the world safe for the middle class was not without its perils. Gothic feminism was born when women realized that they had a formidable external enemy—the lustful, greedy patriarch—in addition to their own worst internal enemy—their consciousness of their own sexual difference, perceived as a weakness.

A dangerous species of thought for women developed at this time and in concert with the sentimentality of Samuel Richardson and the hyperbolic Gothic and melodramatic stage productions of the era. This ideology graphically educated its audience in the lessons of victimization. According to this powerful and socially coded formula, victims earned their special status and rights through no action of their own but through their sufferings and persecutions at the hands of a patriarchal oppressor and tyrant. One would be rewarded not for anything one did but for what one passively suffered. According to this paradigm, women developed a type of behavior now recognized as passive aggression; they were almost willing victims not because they were masochists but because they expected a substantial return on their investment in suffering. Whereas Richardson's Clarissa found herself earning a crown in heaven for suffering rape by Lovelace, the women in female Gothic texts were interested in more earthly rewards. The lesson that Gothic feminism teaches is that the meek shall inherit the Gothic earth; the female Gothic heroine always triumphs in the end because melodramas are constructed to suit this version of poetic justice. The God we call Justice always intervenes and justice always rectifies, validates, and rewards suffering. Terrible events can occur, but the day of reckoning invariably arrives for Gothic villains. This ideology fostered a form of passivity in women, a fatalism that the mainstream feminist would be loathe to recognize today. Yet Gothic feminism undergirds the special pleading of contemporary women who see themselves even today as victims of an amorphous

and transhistorical patriarchy. When the contemporary feminist theorist Naomi Wolf identifies what she calls "victim feminism"—characterized by a loathing of the female body and a reification of victimization as the only route to power—we can hardly be faulted for hearing the echo of Mary Shelley's literary visions.

As the daughter of Mary Wollstonecraft and William Godwin, Mary Wollstonecraft Godwin Shelley was destined to be an overdetermined personality. A heavy intellectual burden rested on her slight shoulders, and for the most part she fulfilled that expectation not only by marrying extravagantly but by writing well. In fact, her union with Percy Shelley may have been her greatest literary performance—her real and imagined victimization on his account, first as wife, then as widow, being only slightly less painful than the sufferings experienced by her fictional heroines. And although her husband's presence haunts all of her works, the real heroes or hero-villains of Mary's life were always her parents, who also recur obsessively in various mutated forms in everything she wrote. Mary Wollstonecraft may have left us only two inadequately realized fictions and two vindications, but she also left us Mary Shelley, in many ways destined to complete and fulfill her mother's aborted philosophical and literary visions. If Wollstonecraft failed to understand the full implications of her suggestions for women— that they effectively "masculinize" themselves and shun "feminine" values as weak and debilitating—her daughter understood all too well the consequences of such behavior for both men and women. Mary's major work, *Frankenstein* (1818), stands paradoxically as the Gothic embodiment of the critique of Gothic feminism. If Wollstonecraft could barely imagine a brave new world for women inhabited by sensitive Henrys, Mary Shelley puts her fictional women into that world and reveals that the sensitive male hero is a mad egotist intent on usurping feminine values and destroying all forms of life in his despotic quest for phallic mastery. Her other two works most clearly in the Gothic mode, *Mathilda* (1819) and the short story "The Mortal Immortal" (1833), also critique the female Gothic formulae as they had evolved by the time she was writing. For instance, *Mathilda* rewrites *Frankenstein*, turning the prior text inside out, revealing the incestuous core of the Gothic feminist fantasy as she experienced it. Everyone in Mary Shelley's corpus is a victim, but her female characters are the victims of victims and thus doubly pathetic and weak.

We do not think of Mary Shelley as a feminist by contemporary standards, nor did she think of herself as one. She once stated: "If I have never written to vindicate the rights of women, I have ever befriended women when oppressed—at every risk I have defended and supported victims to the social system. But I do not make a boast." But she understood all too well what her mother failed to grasp—that woman's protection was in her studied pose of difference and weakness. In fact, she went so far as to observe that "the sex of our [woman's] material mechanism makes us quite different creatures [from men]—better though weaker." But Mary's notion of the social system—the legal, financial, class, religious, and educational superstructure that undergirded nineteenth-century British culture—was finally codified and symbolized by her in the patriarchal bourgeois family. Her fathers are not simply demigods of the family hearth, they are representatives of a larger, oppressive, patriarchal system. They inherit and bequeath wealth because they represent and embody that lucre themselves, in their very persons. The body of the male in Mary Shelley's fiction is always a commodity of worth, an object to be valued, reconstructed, reassembled, and salvaged, while the bodies of the women in her texts are always devalued, compromised, flawed, and inherently worthless.

At the core of all of Mary Shelley's works, however, is the residue of what Freud has labeled in "A Child Is Being Beaten" (1919) as variations on the beating fantasy that children generally experience between the ages of five and fifteen. In these repeated scenarios of desire and repression a girl will typically move through three psychological positions. In the first and third positions, her stance is sadistic and voyeuristic—"another child is being beaten and I am observing the act"—but in the second psychic position her posture is masochistic, erotic, and deeply repressed: "I am the child being beaten by my father." For the boy, the psychic transformation is less complex due to the elimination of one stage. For him, the first position, "I am loved (or beaten) by my father," is transformed into the conscious fantasy "I am being beaten by my mother." According to Freud, the roots of the phallic

mother (the all-powerful mother in possession of the father's phallus) can be located precisely in this early fantasy, but for Mary Shelley, the psychic terrain is complicated by the fact that she, as a woman writer, typically seeks to elide gender by assuming the position of a male protagonist. The basic beating fantasies we see throughout her works—the attacks the "creature" makes on various members of Victor Frankenstein's family, the incestuous attack on Mathilda by her father, the attack on the body of the idealized female icon in "The Mortal Immortal"—all represent variations on the beating fantasy, expressing the child's ambivalence and impotence when confronted with the power and mystery of the parental figures.

Why does incest hover so blatantly over Mary (not to mention Percy) Shelley's Gothic works in ways that do not occur quite so self-consciously in the works of other female Gothic writers? Why are her heroines always defined and self-identified as daughters first, wives second, mothers only briefly? Why would she send the text of *Mathilda*, a shockingly graphic (for its time) portrayal of a father's incestuous love for his daughter, to her own father? And why would she then be surprised when he failed to arrange for its publication? Writing on the very margins of her unconscious obsessions, Mary Shelley played the role of dutiful daughter to the end, leaving the ashes of Percy in Rome and having herself buried with her parents and son in England. In many ways, Percy was as ephemeral a presence in her life as she was in his. It would appear from a reading of their letters and journals that both of them were playacting at love with ideal objects of their own imaginary creation. Unfortunately, as Mary learned too late, the real loves in both their lives were their parents, both real and imagined.

"The Mortal Immortal: A Tale" (1833), one of the many short stories Mary wrote for money in her later life, plays in its oxymoronic title with ambiguity and impossibility, suggesting that there may be a way to make mortals immortal, just as Mary desperately wanted to believe that there may be a way to equalize women with men. Note, however, that the fear and loathing of the female body that activated *Frankenstein* and *Mathilda* recur as dominant motifs in a majority of Mary's short stories, not simply in this one. *Frankenstein* punished every female body in that text, scarring and disfiguring all female attempts to rewrite the generative body as sacred and whole. It replaced the maternal womb with chemical and alchemical artifice, only to blast masculine attempts at procreation as futile and destructive. In *Mathilda*, the male principle once again would appear to be the only effectual parent; but, as in the earlier work, the father produces his progeny only to consume it, feeding on his daughter as a vampire feeds on victims in order to sustain a perverse form of death-in-life.

"The Mortal Immortal" situates the reader within the same psychic terrain, and, like the other works, it plays with variations of beating fantasies, with sometimes the male protagonist as victim, sometimes the female. But we begin this narrative initially within the frame of legendary discourse, this time of the Wandering Jew. We learn early in the text that the narrator defines himself in negative terms, in terms of what he is not. He tells us that he is not the Jew because he is infinitely younger, being only 323 years old (TMI). "The Mortal Immortal" actually reads as if it were inspired not by that particular old legend but by E. T. A. Hoffmann's "The Sandman" or "The Devil's Elixirs," the latter reviewed in *Blackwood's* in 1824 (16:55–67). Mary Shelley does not record in her journal having read "The Sandman" in either a French or Italian translation, and her knowledge of German was certainly not strong enough for her to have read it in the original, but the tale was well-known in England by 1833, the year she wrote and published "The Mortal Immortal."

Like the Hoffmann tale, "The Mortal Immortal" is told by a naive narrator attempting to decode the scientific experiments of a quasi crank and supposed quack, Cornelius Agrippa, the famous German alchemist whose assistant supposedly "raised the foul fiend during his master's absence, and was destroyed by him" (TMI). A deep fear of death and its association with the father's phallic power motivate Hoffmann's "Sandman," while they occur in more muted form in the Shelley tale. The invocation of the name of Cornelius Agrippa, the association of Agrippa and Satan, both of whom figured so prominently in *Frankenstein* as the inspiration of Victor's dabbling in reanimating the base metal of the human body, suggest that masculine, scientific, and phallic powers are as dangerous as they are crucial to

the development of human civilization. Once again, the human body is the obsessive focus of this tale, as it was in the two earlier Gothic works by Mary Shelley. Now, however, the issues are not only clear but very clearly delineated: the female body is decayed and fraudulent; it is a pale and inadequate copy of the prior and superior male body. The tale is predicated on the decline of the body of the beauteous Bertha, whose fading is contrasted to the continuing phallic power of the immortal Winzy, her body rotting while his flourishes over the course of their marriage.

Mary Shelley constructs her tale over the body of Bertha, but before she gets to Bertha, the narrator, Winzy, introduces the reader to his own desperate state of mind. He is a man who has lived for 323 years and fears that he may indeed be immortal. He is a man who feels "the weight of never-ending time—the tedious passage of the still-succeeding hours" (TMI). Traditionally read as a slightly veiled autobiographical statement expressing Mary Shelley's own repugnance at having survived her husband, parents, and three of her children, the fear of time in this text actually expresses a fear of death, a terror about the nonexistence of an afterlife. Life at least prolongs the uncertainty that there may indeed be an afterlife where one will be reunited with the souls of one's beloveds. Death will bring the final and unequivocal answer, and that is something that Mary Shelley was as unprepared to face in 1833 as she was in 1818.

Like a fairy tale, this short fiction begins with the poor, young assistant—"very much in love"—working for the notorious "alchymist" Cornelius Agrippa, who keeps killing all of his assistants because of the inhuman demands he makes on them. One need not search far to see Winzy as the victim of a beating fantasy at the hands of this father substitute. Thwarted in his efforts to persuade his recently orphaned childhood sweetheart Bertha to live "beneath [his] paternal roof," Winzy suffers greatly when Bertha goes off to live with "the old lady of the near castle, rich, childless, and solitary" (TMI). Rather than have a child herself, this wealthy woman "buys" (or, as we might more euphemistically say, "adopts") a beautiful adult woman and then tries to barter her off to the highest bidder. Bertha is dramatic and self-dramatizing. She begins to dress in "silk," pose in her "marble palace" (TMI), and generally amuse herself by taunting and tormenting the frustrated Winzy. Bertha wants Winzy to prove his love by accepting the risky job of working for Agrippa: "'You pretend to love, and you fear to face the Devil for my sake!'" (TMI). Accepting a "purse of gold" from Agrippa makes Winzy feel "as if Satan himself tempted me" (TMI). Bertha wants to put her would-be lover through a test, and she can think of no better one than to subject him to the ultimate evil father, the ultimate beater. No simple coquette, Bertha specializes rather in psychic and emotional abuse of her lover, continually subjecting him to anxiety and jealousy: "Bertha fancied that love and security were enemies, and her pleasure was to divide them in my bosom" (TMI). Notice, however, that everything Bertha metes out to Winzy is later delivered to her. She plays the role of Gothic villainess and later Gothic victim in this work.

If Cornelius Agrippa as the masculine and phallic aspect of the narrator is identified with the fires of Satan, Bertha as the feminine principle is associated with water and the fountain, "a gently bubbling spring of pure living waters" (TMI). While ordered to work overtime stoking the furnaces of Agrippa, Winzy loses the favor of Bertha, who rejects him in favor of the rich suitor Albert Hoffer. Consumed with frustrated jealousy, Winzy decides to drink the magical elixir that Agrippa is preparing because he has been told that the brew is "'a philter to cure love; [if] you would not cease to love your Bertha—beware to drink!'" (TMI). But that is precisely what Winzy wants—he wants to be free of his attachment to the feminine, or to put it another way, Mary Shelley wants to be free of her tie to the female body. Once again, her male narrator expresses Mary Shelley's own ambivalence and repugnance toward not only the female body but female sexuality and the chains of love. Listen to these revealing words from Winzy about his state of mind and motivations:

> False girl!—false and cruel! . . . Worthless, detested woman! I would not remain unrevenged—she should see Albert expire at her feet—she should die beneath my vengeance. She had smiled in disdain and triumph—she knew my wretchedness and her power. Yet what power had she?—the power of exciting my hate—my utter scorn—my—oh, all but indifference! Could I attain that—could I regard her with careless eyes, transferring my rejected love to one fairer and more true, that were indeed a victory! (TMI)

What power had she indeed? Questioning the source and the power of the female body stands as the central query of Mary Shelley's corpus. The answer she discovers suggests that the female body has only as much power as the male chooses to allot to it. But the focus in this passage is on the male response to the female body, running the gamut from hate to scorn to indifference. Notice the progression of emotions. Only when one reaches indifference is one free of the obsessive hold of the other on one's consciousness. Mary Shelley throughout her works strives to escape just exactly this—the corrosive effect of the passions on her heart and body, seeking the cool indifference, the frigidity, the stark embrace of reason that she represented in the climactic presentation of the Arctic Circle in *Frankenstein*.

Grabbing the elixir and drinking, Winzy declares his intention to be cured "of love—of torture!" He finds himself sinking instead into a "sleep of glory and bliss which bathed [his] soul in paradise during the remaining hours of that memorable night," only to awake and find his appearance "wonderfully improved" (TMI). When he ventures out to Bertha's neighborhood, he finds himself the amorous object not only of Bertha but also of her rich old protectress, the "old high-born hag," "the old crone." The ugly old woman represents a standard feminine archetype, the double-faced goddess motif that Mary and Percy would have been familiar with through their readings in classical mythology. Blake (in "The Mental Traveller"), Keats (in "Lamia" and "La Belle Dame Sans Merci"), and Percy himself (in "Prince Athanase") had used the duplicitous female figure. The old hag in this text represents not simply what Bertha will become, a sort of humanized foreshadowing element, but also a version of the phallic mother as class avenger. Now conceiving a lecherous attraction to Winzy, the old hag aggressively pursues him, sending Bertha back to the castle with the peremptory command, "Back to your cage—hawks are abroad!" (TMI). Ironically, the only hawk is the old hag, seeking to feast on her prey, the masculine flesh of Winzy.

But Winzy is now free of the earlier "respect" he had for the old hag's "rank." Now he boldly runs after Bertha, only to discover that he is as much in love with her as ever: "I no longer loved—Oh! no, I adored—worshipped—idolized her!" (TMI). The two triangles operating here—Winzy/Bertha/old hag and Winzy/Bertha/ false suitor—place the young lovers in the two varieties of oedipal rivalry that recur throughout Mary Shelley's fiction. The prior and more powerful association for her heroes and heroines is always the paternal and maternal home. The old hag represents the child-consciousness's (re)construction of the father and mother as one potent figure, all-powerful and all-consuming. This father/mother monad has been traditionally understood within psychoanalytical discourse as the phallic mother, the mother with the father's phallus, the fearful composite of maternity with power. If Ann Radcliffe was finally able by the conclusion of her novels to kill the phallic mother, Mary Shelley is able to flee only temporarily from her. Rather, Bertha decides to reject the old hag's wealth and power and to run away to an alternate maternal abode: "'O Winzy!' she exclaimed, 'take me to your mother's cot.'" But not only does Bertha gain a new mother-figure, Winzy's father also "loved her" and "welcomed her heartily" (TMI). Winzy is not so much gaining a wife as Bertha is gaining new parents. Or, to put it another way, Winzy is not so much gaining a wife as a new sibling.

Five years of bliss pass quickly, and one day Winzy is called to the bed of the dying Cornelius, who finally explains that his elixir had been not simply "a cure for love" but a cure "for all things—the Elixir of Immortality" (TMI). Love is here presented as another form of disease, a weakening and debilitating condition that leaves one prey to the ravages of mortality. To be "cured of love" is to be made immortal, impregnable, godlike, because to be human is to embody all the opposite qualities (TMI). Love here is also presented as something that feminizes or weakens the masculine self, but the narrator is hardly a realistic presentation of a male character. His consciousness, his sensibility is feminine. He loves; therefore, he is as vulnerable as Mary Shelley found herself. He seeks to escape the ravages to which the flesh is prone, the never-ending pregnancies that Mary endured for six years, the repeated processions to the cemetery to bury babies. Winzy is the idealized masculine component of Mary Shelley—her reason and her intellect— that she desperately wants to believe will provide a means of escape for her. If she can be like a man—free from the biological curse—she would be like a god, immortal, inhabiting a world of the mind.

But the feminine aspect of Mary Shelley lives in the figure of Bertha, the female body that rots and decays before the saddened eyes of Winzy. Years pass and Bertha is now fifty, while Winzy appears to be her son. The two are "universally shunned" (TMI) by their neighbors, largely because they embody the most pernicious incestuous dream of all—the tabooed love of a mother and son. Winzy has finally married the old crone, much to his dismay. Fleeing to a new country, the two decide to "wear masks," although Bertha's mask is infinitely less successful than Winzy's. Resorting to "rouge, youthful dress, and assumed juvenility of manner," Bertha is a parody of her former self. A desperate caricature of femininity, she has become a "mincing, simpering, jealous old woman." In other words, she has become another phallic mother, guarding her son Winzy with a "jealousy [that] never slept" (TMI). The female body—once so beautiful and perfect—has become, a flawed and diseased artifice, a shell fitted over a mass of stinking corruption. The male body, in stark contrast, continues to exist as statuesque and youthful, a perfect emblem of the triumph of masculinity and masculine values over the feminine. The female body has become the target and object of the beating given to it by the ultimate Nobodaddy—life, time, and mortality.

The years pass until Bertha is finally bedridden and paralytic and Winzy functions as her nurse: "I nursed her as a mother might a child" (TMI). The wheel has come full circle. The mother is the child, while the husband/son has become a "mother." All gradations in the family romance have been tried in much the same way that Blake depicted them in "The Mental Traveller." Confined within the bourgeois domicile, the sexes feed on each other parasitically until they have consumed themselves in the process of playing all their gendered and ungendering roles to a limited audience. When Bertha finally dies, Winzy decides to escape the family romance. He lives alone in melancholy depression, contemplating suicide, until he decides to "put [his] immortality" to the test by journeying to the Arctic Circle. Like Victor Frankenstein, he decides to seek his destruction in the embrace of the "elements of air and water" (TMI). This desire to reconcile opposites, to bathe and immerse himself in mutually exclusive physical elements, represents Mary Shelley's attempt to depict the catastrophic merging of masculine and feminine elements in the human psyche. If men are associated with the realm of air, the intellect, reason, and the mind, then women are identified with water, the physical, and the body and its fluids. Winzy's seeking oblivion in the extremely gender-coded landscape of the Arctic Circle suggests that the apocalypse Mary Shelley imagined for herself and her characters involved an escape from all polarities, or rather a freezing and holding of the two elements in a static situation. We do not know what becomes of Winzy, just as we never know what becomes of the creature at the conclusion of *Frankenstein*.

But the dream of desire is the same at the end of all of Mary Shelley's texts: to escape the body and live in the realm of pure mind. Like her mother, Mary Shelley was a reluctant sensualist. She needed, philosophically, to embrace free love and open marriage, but her disappointments in her philandering husband could not be concealed. Claiming to support free love is easy as long as one does not have a husband who has a history of collecting pretty young things and bringing them home. Finally a deep revulsion toward the female body emerges as clearly in Mary Shelley's works as it does in Wollstonecraft's.

Gothic feminism for Mary Shelley entailed the realization that women would always be life's victims, not simply because social, political, economic, and religious conventions placed them in inferior and infanticizing postures, but because their own bodies cursed them to forever serve the wheel of physical corruption. Being a mother, bringing to life a child who would die, and perhaps would die soon, condemned women to serve a merciless god—the cycle of generation, birth, and death—in a way that men did not. The nightmare haunting Mary Shelley's life was not simply that she caused the death of her mother but that she recapitulated a reversed version of the same tragedy with three of her own children. She experienced her life as a sort of curse to herself and the ones she loved, and why? She understood that her life, her very physical being, fed on her mother's body parasitically, cannibalistically consuming it. Later she watched her children wither, unable to be sustained by her. These recurring nightmares fed her fictions, but they also spoke to a deeper fear that has continually plagued women.

Gothic feminism seeks to escape the female body through a dream of turning weakness into strength. By pretending that one is weak or a passive victim, one camouflages oneself in a hostile terrain, diverting attention from one's real identity. Mary Shelley knew that on some level she was no victim; she knew her strength and intelligence were more than a match for anyone's. But she also sensed danger in that strength, or at least experienced it ambivalently, fearing that it caused the deaths of others. The grotesque freakishness of the creature in *Frankenstein*, made material in the description of "his" oddly assembled body and his continual rejection by everyone he seeks to love, trope Mary Shelley's own sense of herself and all women as diseased, aberrant, and freakish composites of the hopes and dreams of other people. Gothic feminism for Mary Shelley is embodied in the sense of herself and the female body as a void, an empty signifier, a lure into the cycle of painful birth and disappointing death. Railing against the female body—sometimes disguised as male and sometimes blatantly presented as female—is finally the only position that Mary Shelley can take. She can laud the bourgeois family, she can valorize community and what we now label "family values," but she ultimately cannot escape the mortality that gives the lie to everything she seeks to praise. She inhabits a female body, she bleeds and causes bleeding in others, and those unfortunate facts define for her and her fiction the Gothic feminist nightmare in its starkest terms.

Source: Diane Long Hoeveler, "Mary Shelley and Gothic Feminism: The Case of 'The Mortal Immortal,'" in *Iconoclastic Departures: Mary Shelley after "Frankenstein,"* edited by Syndy M. Conger, Frederick S. Frank, and Gregory O'Dea, Fairleigh Dickinson University Press, 1997, pp. 150–61.

Sonia Hofkosh

In the following excerpt, Hofkosh discusses the illustrations that appeared in the original publication of "The Mortal Immortal."

ONE PICTURE IS WORTH A THOUSAND WORDS

. . . The line engraving that illustrates Shelley's tale "The False Rhyme," written for *The Keepsake* in 1829, shows a man, Francis I, king of France, sitting with pen in hand, dagger, sheathed, across his lap, a woman leaning over him as she pulls aside a curtain and looks, with him, out the window. But appearances can

WRITING BEYOND THE FRAME OF THE ENGRAVING, SHELLEY REDRAWS THE LINES OF THE CONTRAST IN ORDER TO ILLUSTRATE WHAT IS AT STAKE IN THE FORM OF TRUTH BERTHA EMBODIES."

be misleading. In Shelley's story, created in response to the plate supplied by the editor, the gaze we follow does not lead through the window to some object or event situated transparently outside it, beyond the frame, as the picture might suggest; rather, the gaze stops at the window, at its surface, regarding this surface as the opaque site of representation. The dynamics of looking, of attributing meaning to the seen/ scene, itself becomes the subject of observation in Shelley's narrative.

As Shelley describes it, the king has written, or, more precisely, inscribed a couplet about female inconstancy on the window with a diamond. Francis uses neither the masculinized pen nor the dagger on his lap that the engraving depicts. In the story, his tool is instead a jewel, the first in a series of jewels that figure female beauty and truth—that figure the ideal of femininity itself—in the tale. As such, the diamond points to Shelley's interest in the way beauty and truth, taken to be at issue in the very essence of women—their integrity, value, their "very being"—get etched on surfaces, like women's bodies, as the sign of their dispossession. This authorial shift in the instrument of inscription from engraving to tale allows Shelley to contest the authority of appearance even as she demonstrates its tyrannical, transformative powers.

Objecting to the couplet that she calls high treason ("lèse majesté"), the king's sister Margaret proposes a bet. She will prove the integrity of Emilie de Lagny, "the most beautiful and the most virtuous of her maids of honour," who reputedly disappeared from France with her "pretty" page, "bearing her jewels with her," and leaving her husband, the Sire de Lagny, languishing in prison as a traitor. If she loses, says the Queen of Navarre, "I will

bear this vile rhyme of thine as a motto to my shame to my grave." If she wins, the king her brother will break the window and grant her any boon.

On the eve of losing her wager ("Margaret would have given many bright jewels to redeem her word"), the imprisoned de Lagny appears to offer proof of Emilie's fidelity and attain his pardon as Margaret's boon. When he kneels at the king's feet, "his frame attenuated by privation," "the sunken cheeks and pallid brow" of Emilie are revealed in his place. The king cries "treason," but the faithful Emilie explains that "wiser men than [the jailor] have been deceived by woman" and that she has assumed the chains of her husband, he her "attire," so that the Sire de Lagny could join the king's army and gather "testimonials of his innocence." Francis breaks "the false-speaking window" and at the celebration of "this 'Triumph of Ladies'" that follows, "there was more loveliness in Emilie's faded cheek—more grace in her emaciated form" than in "the most brilliant beauty."

But appearances can be misleading, as the tale truly tells. Mary Shelley's story turns on the potential of appearances at once to mask and to manufacture the truth. Deception, falsehood, inconstancy are treason, but they are also the means by which the integrity and authority of the sire—father, husband, brother, king—can be redeemed. The story also reveals that the tools of such redemption perpetuate its fiction, and that the stakes in such a transaction are high. With his diamond, Francis cuts the false rhyme that his sister, losing her bet, will have to "bear" as "a motto to [her] shame"; Emilie, "bearing her jewels with her," effects the exchange that restores her husband to honor and reward while it attenuates her own frame. In both cases, the body, particularly the woman's body, bears the mark, the "blemish" of transgression and of the truth it ultimately authorizes. The king smashes the rhyme that has been proven false by the fidelity of a deceptive woman, but it is really Emilie who is wrecked by representation that chains truth together with falsehood and makes her body the site of such productive, destructive coupling. In the triumph of Emilie's "faded cheek" and "emaciated form," Shelley inscribes her own motto: this "one true tale of woman's fidelity," "this lady's truth," tells of her own diminishment.

"I am worried to death to make my things shorter & shorter—till I fancy people think ideas can be conveyed by intuition—and that it is a superstition to consider words necessary for their expression" (11 June 1835). As a writer of attenuated stories, Shelley explains her own authorial project as an economical one: "Never was poor body so worried as I have been . . . money of course is the Alpha and Omega of my tale" (16 Jan. 1833). And if her authorship—being a worried body—reproduces the "mutilated lives" of women in patriarchal culture generally, as Anne Mellor argues, her gift annual stories also unsuperstitiously express that profit and loss are both risks of the market, and that for women, especially, that investment is often at great cost. Shelley's worries, then, are those of the working woman struggling to earn her living in an economy that wrecks as it rewards. Working within the limitations imposed on her—by the conditions of Sir Timothy's loans (no biography of Percy; no edition of his works) and by the generic constraints of the gift annuals ("make my things shorter & shorter")—her struggle as a writer is a struggle to survive and to prosper by telling tales of her own disempowerment. It is thus a struggle to tell her own tale, which is not simply a tale of submission or compromise; it is a tale that in its telling, from beginning to end, bespeaks the truth of her intuition, of her insight into what she gives up and what she gains through the fictions these economies share.

Shelley depicts in "The False Rhyme" how one woman's loss may be another's (a man's) gain, and how the losses women sustain uphold ideals of (intrinsic) beauty and truth, of authority, even as they imply the precarious foundation of those ideals. As an index of value, beauty fluctuates with the market. "The Mortal Immortal" (*The Keepsake*, 1833) also traces the revaluation of the ideal through the disintegration of the female body. In that tale, the narrator, Winzy, inadvertently becomes immortal by drinking the alchemist's potion ("admirable beauty, more bright than . . . the diamond") he thinks will cure him of love and thus render him independent, invulnerable; consequently, he also gains another "inestimable treasure" in finally winning the beautiful Bertha, whom he has loved since childhood. Bertha with her beauty personifies Winzy's transcendent achievement of complete self-sufficiency. She also naturalizes it: she is his rightful "inheritance," leaving her

aristocratic patroness to enrich Winzy in his "natal cottage," under his "paternal roof." But this redemptive "good fortune"—in which, through Bertha, Winzy drinks his value and has it too—is precisely the treasured ideal that the story is designed to interrogate. Such an interrogation takes place in Shelley's implicit dialogue with the engraving that "embellishes" her tale.

The engraving depicts the moment Bertha crosses her imperious patroness to marry her humble lover, renouncing the "detested luxuries" of aristocracy for the real "happiness" of an alternative economy—as Winzy puts it, "I am honest, if I am poor!" Here, aristocracy stands revealed as an artificial paradise in the person of the elaborately draped, shaded figure of "the old highborn hag" whose walking stick, held in front of her as a sign of her masculinized authority, foregrounds the picture. Centering the opposition between this bloated, enshadowed figure and the clear, light form of the beautiful Bertha, the walking stick both blocks Bertha's path and, visually, reinforces the true contours of her body, outlined through the folds of her dress as she gracefully moves down the stair. The engraving highlights this opposition in order to reveal Bertha's beauty in its true feminine form and, indeed, as the feminine form of the "honest" truth itself.

But rather than simply adhere to the contrast at the center of the engraving, Shelley's narrative takes its cue from it and departs, following Bertha out of the picture to see her turn into a "hag" herself and belie the truth of the vision immortalized in the engraving. Shelley's story says that we, watching Bertha, must also change the way we look: look at the way the engraving employs tricks of light and shade to make up the truth we would accept at face value; look at the way faces and bodies create truths they appear merely to discover. Writing beyond the frame of the engraving, Shelley redraws the lines of the contrast in order to illustrate what is at stake in the form of truth Bertha embodies.

Like the "old crone" she trades for "nature and liberty," Bertha inevitably grows old and ugly too, "antiquated" as a piece of dysfunctional machinery; the mechanism of inherent ("honest") value incarnate in her "very look" does not work in the world she must inhabit. Apparently transcending this world, the immortal Winzy in comparison retains his "good looks":

> I was laughed at for my vanity in consulting the mirror so often, but I consulted it in vain— my brow was untrenched—my cheeks—my eyes—my whole person continued as untarnished as in my twentieth year.

The tarnish that is thus invisible on the man is rendered in exaggerated form on Bertha's female body. He loses nothing, while she becomes a "mincing, simpering, jealous old woman" who recognizes her own loss in his perfect person. The story indeed turns on this disjunction in their appearances. Winzy's immortality, his wholeness, *counts* (as "good" or bad "fortune," for him or for her) exactly insofar as it is measured against Bertha's disintegrating body. Opposites, they reflect (on) one another. Winzy may be laughed at for his self-love, but Bertha looks all the more pathetic as she vainly tries to mask the signs of her inevitable vulnerability. "Her beauty sadly diminished,"

> she sought to decrease the apparent disparity of our ages by a thousand feminine arts— rouge, youthful dress, and assumed juvenility of manner . . . I should have revered her gray locks and withered cheeks; but thus!

Her vanity is a grotesque and painful deflection of his.

Winzy's ideal is thus both realized and ruined in Bertha; he sees in her "feminine arts"—makeup, clothes, affectation—the measure at once of his ultimate success and his ultimate failure. Initially a mirror for his achievement, Bertha discloses in the vulnerabilities of her body and her anxious efforts to hide them both the power and the tenuousness of the ideal (beauty, truth, wholeness) he has apparently accomplished, risk-free. She manifests what cannot be seen on Winzy; the price of his self-regenerating economy is displaced onto her. "Did not I myself wear a mask? Why quarrel with hers, because it was less successful?" But being "less successful," Bertha and her wrinkles (those "tell-tale chroniclers") expose the limitations to which, in his very transcendence, Winzy is nonetheless subject; her wrinkles tell the tale of the distortions and inequalities upon which his seemingly immutable power depends.

These limitations are finally represented, for Winzy as for Bertha, as bodily constraints:

> I yield this body, too tenacious a cage for a soul which thirsts for freedom, to the destructive elements of air and water—or, if I survive, my name shall be recorded as one of the most famous among the sons of men.

The disappearance of his body may yield a kind of freedom, but here it is survival within the limits of and on the body that constitutes individual presence. Understood as mutually exclusive, "sour" and "name" alternate as the content of identity. The body forms the site of these trade-offs. Bertha escapes from the "gilt cage" of aristocratic design—silk dresses and marble mansions—into "nature and liberty," but her liberation is purchased at the cost of a heightened sense of what she has got to lose. Similarly, Winzy has to die to be free, survive, caged, to be recognized; either way, his story records the exchanges—the losses and gains—necessitated and masked "among the sons of men" by the logic of a patrilinear economy. . . .

Source: Sonia Hofkosh, "Disfiguring Economies: Mary Shelley's Short Stories," in *The Other Mary Shelley: Beyond "Frankenstein,"* edited by Audrey A. Fisch, Anne K. Mellor, Esther H. Schor, Oxford University Press, 1993, pp. 208–13.

SOURCES

Garnett, Richard, ed., Introduction to *Tales and Stories by Mary Wollstonecraft Shelley*, William Peterson, 1891, pp. viii–xi.

Hoeveler, Diane Long, "Mary Shelley and Gothic Feminism: The Case of 'The Mortal Immortal,'" in *Iconoclastic Departures: Mary Shelley after* Frankenstein, edited by Syndy M. Conger, Frederick S. Frank, and Gregory O'Dea, Fairleigh Dickinson University Press, 1997, pp. 150–78.

Lehrich, Christopher I., *The Language of Demons and Angels: Cornelius Agrippa's Occult Philosophy*, Brill's Studies in Intellectual History 119, Brill, 2003, pp. 76–91.

Markley, A. A., "'Laughing That I May Not Weep': Mary Shelley's Short Fiction and Her Novels," in *Keats-Shelley Journal*, Vol. 46, 1997, pp. 97–124.

Nauert, Charles G., *Agrippa and the Crisis of Renaissance Thought*, Illinois Studies in the Social Sciences 155, University of Illinois Press, 1965, pp. 222–91.

———, "Heinrich Cornelius Agrippa von Nettesheim," in *Stanford Encyclopedia of Philosophy*, 2007, http://plato.stanford.edu/entries/agrippa-nettesheim/ (accessed January 20, 2015).

O'Dea, Gregory, "'Perhaps a Tale You'll Make It': Mary Shelley's Tales for *The Keepsake*," in *Iconoclastic Departures: Mary Shelley after* Frankenstein, edited by

Syndy M. Conger, Frederick S. Frank, and Gregory O'Dea, Fairleigh Dickinson University Press, 1997, pp. 62–78.

Potter, Franz J., *The History of Gothic Publishing, 1800–1835: Exhuming the Trade*, Palgrave, 2005, pp. 77–79, 146–51.

Roberts, Marie, *Gothic Immortals: The Fiction of the Brotherhood of the Rosy Cross*, Routledge, 1990, pp. 14–21, 72–92.

Shelley, Mary, *The Annotated Frankenstein*, edited by Leonard Wolf, New York, 1977, pp. 39–46.

———, "The Mortal Immortal: A Tale," in *The Mary Shelley Reader*, edited by Betty T. Bennett and Charles E. Robinson, Oxford University Press, 1990, pp. 314–26.

Shelley, Percy Bysshe, *The Wandering Jew*, edited by Bertram Dobell, Reeves and Turner, 1887, pp. 1–66.

Yates, Frances A., *Giordano Bruno and the Hermetic Tradition*, University of Chicago Press, 1964, pp. 130–43.

FURTHER READING

Clemit, Pamela, *The Godwinian Novel: Rational Fictions of Godwin, Brockden Brown, Mary Shelley*, Clarendon Press, 1993.

> In this study Clemit leaves behind merely thematic similarities, such as the gothic, between the authors he examines and concentrates on an analysis of subjective experience in light of Godwin's political radicalism. He also explores the same technique in Brown's and Mary Shelley's works.

Hill-Miller, Katherine, *My Hideous Progeny: Mary Shelley, William Godwin, and the Father-Daughter Relationship*, University of Delaware Press, 1995.

> Hill-Miller explores the overwhelming aesthetic and educational influence of Mary Shelley's father on her. He examines the psychodynamics of their relationship, which began with years of his personal supervision

of a masculine education, followed by a complete physical and emotional withdrawal from her as she approached adulthood, especially after her marriage to Percy Bysshe Shelley, and his reconciliation with and economic dependence on her after her husband's death.

Shelley, Mary, *The Journals of Mary Shelley, 1814–1844*, edited by Paula R. Feldman and Diana Scott-Kilvert, Oxford University Press, 1987.

> Shelley's journals throw light on her writing, especially concerning the overwhelming influence of her father, William Godwin.

———, *The Last Man*, 3 vols., Henry Colburn, 1826; reprinted in *The Novels and Selected Works of Mary Shelley*, Vol. 4, edited by Nora Crook, Pickering and Chatto, 1996.

> *The Last Man* is a science-fiction novel set at the end of the twenty-first century. During its course most of humanity is wiped out by a plague, but this dramatic theme provides a backdrop for Shelley's exploration of the failure of radical romantic-era politics, including the suppression of the French Revolution and the suppression of the political extremism represented by her father. William Godwin, and her husband. Percy Shelley.

SUGGESTED SEARCH TERMS

Mary Shelley

The Mortal Immortal AND Shelley

gothic

romanticism

alchemy

Cornelius Agrippa

Wandering Jew

Rosicrucian

The Particles

ANDREA BARRETT

2012

"The Particles" is a story by award-winning American author Andrea Fuller Barrett that blends a dramatic event from the earliest hours of World War II, an investigation into the state of the study of inheritance and genetics at the time, and a portrait of one scientist striving to bring new concepts to the fore of his field. Having won the National Book Award for her 1996 collection *Ship Fever*, her fifth volume of fiction, interweaving science, history, and human relationships, Barrett went on to write several more volumes advancing her themes around these topics. Her third collection of shorter fiction is *Archangel* (2013), whose five stories revolve around various moments in scientific and cultural history. "The Particles," the fourth and longest story, was originally published in *Tin House*, No. 51, in the spring of 2012.

AUTHOR BIOGRAPHY

Barrett was born on November 16, 1954, in Boston, Massachusetts, to a real-estate broker and his wife and grew up on Cape Cod. Their home was close enough to the seawater for the young Barrett to be able to usually see it, always smell it, and walk to it virtually every day. By late in high school Barrett decided, in the free spirit of the era, that she wanted to

National Book Award-winning novelist Andrea Barrett (© Andrew Harrer | Bloomberg | Getty Images)

move on before gaining a diploma, and so she applied to Union College, in Schenectady, New York, and attended following her junior year. She earned a degree in biology in 1974 and went on to graduate school at the University of Massachusetts to study zoology, but then she switched her line of study to history, and finally she realized that she wanted to be a writer. In 1979 she married Barry Goldstein, a biochemist.

Barrett spent the next decade writing, finally publishing her first novel, *Lucid Stars*, in 1988. She published three more novels over the next five years, including *Secret Harmonies* (1989), about a quirky, musically inclined family in Massachusetts, and *The Forms of Water* (1993), about an octogenarian's dramatic escape from a nursing home. With her fifth volume of fiction, the short-story collection *Ship Fever* (1996), Barrett won the National Book Award and was subsequently awarded a Guggenheim Fellowship. It was this volume

that marked Barrett's return to her earlier academic focus, science, as she brings historical scientific figures into narratives treating the process of discovery, especially on the fringes of the academic world, as well as the relationships behind that process. Over the next twenty years, Barrett came out with two more novels and two more story collections, including *Servants of the Map* (2002), which was a finalist for the Pulitzer Prize, and *Archangel* (2013), which includes "The Particles." She won a MacArthur Foundation Fellowship in 2001. Barrett has taught for a low-residency master of fine arts program at Warren Wilson College, in North Carolina, and has most recently been teaching at Williams College, in western Massachusetts.

PLOT SUMMARY

"The Particles," for which the date of 1939 is the parenthetical subtitle, opens on Sam surveying the scene around a ship that was struck by a torpedo—from a German U-boat, it is believed. The *Athenia* is now sinking, and Sam is manning an oar on a packed lifeboat. A few hours later, rescue boats reach the scene. One lifeboat unwisely approaches too near a tanker's rear propellers, and the boat itself is destroyed, the passengers' fates untold. Sam's lifeboat heads toward a yacht, but the passengers watch another boat get tipped over by the yacht's bow. They wait until morning, for better light, when they at last board a US merchant ship, the *City of Flint*—and, in being hauled on deck, Sam recognizes a rival, Duncan. They both just left a genetics conference in Edinburgh, Scotland. Sam tells Duncan that Axel, their mutual mentor, had not stayed behind as planned because of the onset of international conflict. (This is early September 1939, the start of World War II.) Duncan goes looking for Axel among the survivors and eventually returns with him.

Giving his berth to Axel, who has a head wound, Duncan moves to the floor; Harold and George also share the room, but Sam is left out. Supplies are collected and routines established to accommodate the 200 or so survivors aboard, along with the vessel's thirty original passengers. Unlike the other rescue ships, theirs is continuing to North America.

MEDIA ADAPTATIONS

- An Audible audio edition of *Archangel* (2013), which includes "The Particles," narrated by Jeff Woodman and with a running time of seven hours and forty-eight minutes, is available for download.

At dinner, the conference where Sam and Duncan scientifically quarreled is discussed with some college girls—also original passengers of the *City of Flint*—who have befriended them. After dinner, Laurel engages Sam in conversation, but mentally he stews over his rivalry with Duncan.

In 1921, sixteen-year-old Sam is going to college in upstate New York. In high school, ready for a challenge after skipping a couple of grades, he was introduced to the field of heredity and fruit-fly experimentation by Mr. Spacek, a biology teacher. Arriving at college, he meets his roommate, Avery. Mr. Spacek has helped secure Sam an academic relationship with young biology instructor Axel Olssen, who hires Sam to work in his lab. During the fall, Sam graduates from washing bottles to mashing up fruit-fly food. He loves working with the flies and returns to school early to help Axel during Christmas vacation—when he envisions supplanting Axel's prized senior student, Duncan. Axel discusses with Sam an exciting paper presented in Toronto by Hermann Muller, first conceptualizing *genes*—"the particles of heredity," as the story calls them—as units of biological inheritance. When Duncan returns the next week, Axel designs new experiments with Duncan, while Sam sterilizes forceps. In the spring, Duncan graduates.

On the *City of Flint*, Sam laments a lack of private time with Axel. He remembers enduring the night at sea. He shies away from Bessie, with whom he had shared space on the lifeboat. At dinners, Harold, George, and Duncan trade in academic gossip; Sam preferred the weightier

conversation he recently had with Avery, whom he visited in Cambridge, England. Back in Edinburgh, the Russian geneticists he knew missed the conference because of the political situation. The various nations' representatives left incrementally during the conference as the international situation worsened. After Sam lectured on Saturday, Duncan used his own lecture to discredit Sam's experiments. At present, Sam is loathing Duncan. He more specifically recalls the miserable night at sea as experienced intimately with Bessie and her son, Aaron. A doctor sets up a clinic on the ship; one ten-year-old girl (Margaret) is in a coma. The college girls organize fashion and talent shows; Duncan sings, reminding Sam of their summer at Woods Hole (in Massachusetts), after Sam's junior year.

Passing on the social scene at Woods Hole to focus on genetics, Sam marvels over the publication of Viennese biologist Paul Kammerer's fairly heretic paper suggesting that organisms, toads and salamanders in his study, can adapt to their environments *and* pass their adaptation to their offspring—findings reminiscent of Jean-Baptiste Lamarck's long-discounted, pre-Darwinian contentions that such acquired heritability is possible. While Ellen, a fellow student, is as fascinated by Kammerer's claims as Sam, Duncan's adviser narrow-mindedly dismisses them. Sam begins designing experiments inspired by Kammerer, but using fruit flies. He seems to find evidence that a redness caused by the application of a heated needle is inheritable, and at the program director's invitation, he gives a presentation to the group—a rare opportunity for an undergraduate. Duncan listens closely. Returning to college in New York in the fall, Sam shares his experience with Axel, who would have counseled him against sharing his research while still in process. Sam might have gotten further in his experiments, but he became involved with Ellen. Though she wants to, she has not yet become pregnant. Some six months later, Duncan publishes a paper disproving Sam's preliminary conclusions from Woods Hole, demonstrating that the red pigment in question was spread through larvae's ingestion of dead red-eyed flies. Sam's nascent academic reputation is upended. Instead of following Axel and Duncan to Columbia University for graduate study, he proceeds to a small school in Wisconsin. By Thanksgiving, Ellen, still without child, has left him. Some seven years later, Sam meets Duncan and Ellen's three-child family in Washington when Duncan is receiving an award.

On the *City of Flint*, Sam has little appetite; on the lifeboat, Bessie patted his neck when he was seasick. By the eighth day, Margaret has died. Sam tries to console Aaron, who played with her. When Bessie asks Sam if he has children, he says no and thinks of his presumed sterility. After Duncan and friends crowd around, Bessie makes a last sad comment and leads Aaron away. Realizing that those two and Sam shared a lifeboat, Duncan offers Sam an ear if he wants to talk about the experience.

In graduate school in Wisconsin, Sam persists in experimenting, with Hermann Muller serving as professional inspiration. In 1930, Sam gains work in Missouri. Duncan has a better position in California. In 1933, Sam loses his job. Getting no help from either Duncan or Axel in his hunt for a new post, Sam writes to Muller, now in Leningrad (modern-day Saint Petersburg), who finds Sam a position at the Soviet Union's Institute of Genetics. The living conditions are substandard, but Sam is happily absorbed in the work. Sam moves with the institute to Moscow. The Soviets start to favor Lamarckian inheritance as a potential windfall for Communism, in terms of improving both crops and humanity, but one zealous proponent, Lysenko, goes so far as to discredit formal genetics entirely. When mainstream geneticists' lives are in danger, Elizaveta leaves and gives Sam her flies. Muller leaves Russia in 1937, as does Sam, who returns home to Philadelphia, then gets a small-college post in Illinois. He begins experimenting further with mutations. In Edinburgh, he presents his incubating conception of genes not as "beads on a string" but something "more like spiderwebs." He also suggests that the timing of activation of genes may be as important as the genes themselves. Duncan, Axel, and Muller all seem baffled.

Two US Coast Guard cutters meet the *City of Flint* a few hundred miles from Halifax, Nova Scotia, bringing needed supplies. Doctors examine everyone and transfer those in need of better care to one of the cutters. People drink whiskey and relax. The college girls speak to a young art student who lost a friend when the second lifeboat was overturned. Sam finally gets a chance to hear Axel share his own experience—he was on that same lifeboat. Axel is surprised that Duncan had not relayed his story to Sam. Consoling Sam, Axel reports that he seems to favor Duncan only to support Duncan's ego. He sees Sam as more independent.

A day and a half from Halifax, Axel and others are transferred to a cutter. Upon arriving, the passengers are greeted by the Red Cross, officials, families, and journalists. The survivors answer reporters' questions in a disorganized mass, until Duncan steps up to amalgamate a story line about the incident—despite not having experienced it himself. Sam remembers how Axel had wanted to stay aboard the *City of Flint* with his friends, Duncan and Sam.

CHARACTERS

Aaron

Bessie's son is comforted by Sam during the night in the lifeboat and also after the death of Margaret, a recent playmate. Bessie says that the whole experience, especially the nearness of mortality, has left Aaron worried about his father back home.

Bessie

Bessie's knees irritated Sam during the night in the crowded lifeboat, but he proved to appreciate her shivering warmth and the consolation of her patting his neck while he was seasick. They seem to seal their circumstantial bond when they finally converse for a while on the *City of Flint*.

Sam Cornelius

The character who provides the narrative perspective in "The Particles" is Sam, presently a thirty-four-year-old geneticist with a tendency toward ambitious experimenting and theorizing. Sam's father, a Smithsonian astronomer, died when he was four, while his mother writes astronomy books and articles and lives in Philadelphia. The story goes back and forth between Sam's present circumstances aboard the *City of Flint*, after the sinking of the *Athenia*, and his past experiences, including his introduction to fruit-fly breeding experiments in high school, his time at college in New York and attending a summer program at Woods Hole, his graduate school studies in Wisconsin, his professional development in the Soviet

Union, and his attendance at the Edinburgh conference. Sam is utterly devoted to his genetic studies, but he cannot escape the irony of his apparently being unable to pass on his own genetic materials owing to sterility. He lost Ellen for precisely that reason, though he is presently seeing an unnamed woman. Sam cannot swim well, which led him to find the experience of lessons in college embarrassing and that of the night in the lifeboat without a life jacket harrowing. After the tragedy, he is desperate to connect with his old college instructor, Axel—his aching sentiments are suggestive of romantic desire—but cannot manage to do so until just before they reach North America, when Axel affirms their friendship.

Ellen Eliasberg

A tanned young instructor at Smith College, in Massachusetts, Ellen unites with Sam at Woods Hole. She is described as having taken up eugenics, suggesting that she favors the selective breeding of the human population. When, over the course of a year, Sam fails to impregnate her with the intelligent children she desires, she abandons him—and ends up having an attractive family with Duncan.

Elizaveta

A Soviet geneticist specializing in producing mutant fruit flies, Elizaveta has a lab that leaves Sam enraptured.

Duncan Finch

Sam's avowed rival in the field of genetics is Duncan Finch, who hogs Axel's academic affections when Sam is a college freshman; who takes the trouble to scientifically thrash the preliminary findings Sam shares at Woods Hole; who marries Ellen, the woman Sam lost when he failed to get her pregnant; and who upends Sam's findings-in-progress once again in Edinburgh in 1939. Duncan has a substantial belly and a flap of thinning hair that consistently draws Sam's attention. Sam is gratified when Axel acknowledges Duncan's social shortcomings, but, significantly, Axel still claims Duncan and Sam equally as friends.

George

George is a clean-shaven, space-filling geneticist from a small Massachusetts college who was at the Edinburgh conference and, in departing, boards the *City of Flint*.

Harold

Harold is a clean-shaven, space-filling geneticist from the same small Massachusetts college who was also at the Edinburgh conference and is going home on the *City of Flint*.

Avery Hayes

Avery, Sam's freshman-year roommate in upstate New York, apparently skis but, indoors, is sensitive to drafts. He and Sam stay in touch over the years. Avery's devotion to physics is analogous to Sam's devotion to genetics, and he supplies Sam with state-of-the-art equipment for his work in Wisconsin.

Laurel

One of the college girls aboard the *City of Flint*, Laurel seems to take an interest in Sam; yet, despite her having "solid hips" and being "pleasant," Sam finds her "unremarkable-looking."

Lucinda

Sam finds Lucinda, one of the college girls on the *City of Flint*, to be garrulous.

Trofim Lysenko

Sam attends a meeting in the Soviet Union in 1936 when Lysenko, a Lamarckian Communist, ridicules the formal scientific field of genetics.

Margaret

Margaret is the ten-year-old Canadian girl who is struck by a beam when the torpedo hits the *Athenia*. Despite being conscious during the night in the lifeboat and the first day on the *City of Flint*, she falls into a coma. In that span of time she becomes a sort of big sister to Aaron, who mourns her death eight days later.

Maud

Maud is one of the several college girls returning from an abbreviated European tour on the *City of Flint*.

Thomas Morgan

Having been Axel's teacher at Columbia University, Morgan also teaches Duncan in graduate school there.

Hermann Muller

Sam admires the biologist Hermann Muller professionally and sends him experimental results confirming or extending Muller's own results beginning in graduate school. Sam is approached by Muller at a conference, and they continue corresponding. Muller responds to Sam's appeal for help by securing him a post in Leningrad, where the Communist-leaning Muller ended up after being ousted from his post in Austin, Texas.

Axel Olssen

The latest in a vaunted chain of geneticists, Axel instructs both Duncan and Sam as undergraduates. Axel expresses disappointment when Sam reports having publicly shared some very preliminary findings at Woods Hole, and his disappointment is justified when Duncan's nullification of Sam's study sabotages Sam's career. As if to taunt Sam in his subsequent solitude, Axel gets married (to a Texas mathematician) right around the time that Duncan and Ellen marry. Axel again expresses disappointment with Sam's later career risk, the one taken at the Edinburgh conference, but he remains very close with Sam, and they are intimately interested in each other as colleagues and friends.

Pansy

Pansy is one of the college girls aboard the *City of Flint*.

Mr. Spacek

Sam's biology teacher, Mr. Spacek, first encourages and promotes Sam's interest in fruit flies and heredity.

THEMES

Trauma

"The Particles" is centered on the aftermath of the sinking of a passenger ship, the SS *Athenia*, at the start of World War II in 1939. The harrowing nature of the incident is made clear in the scenes where, though Sam's awareness is incomplete, lives are certainly lost—the original torpedo strike, the destruction of one lifeboat by a propeller, the overturning of another by the yacht—as well as in briefer moments where individuals' fates are left unknown, such as when an elderly woman plunges into the water while trying to board a rescue ship. In the course of the *City of Flint*'s subsequent passage across the Atlantic, the experience is dealt with in different ways depending on the degree to which the different characters have been traumatized. Sam, for one, wants to process the traumatic event and its significance in their lives. He sees it as an "enormous thing" that bonds him and Axel, who were in different lifeboats but experienced "the same sky, the same rain, the same flares and fears and darkness and dawn." Yet he never quite gets the discussion he desires, as Duncan and the others who were not present for the tragedy are content to talk about relatively trivial matters from the world of academia; the college girls are at least attentive to the proceedings of the war, but they as well cannot help Sam process the *Athenia*'s sinking in the way he desires. Sam's personal attention to trauma is highlighted when he makes a point of comforting Aaron, who has been traumatized by the sight of bodies in the water as well as by Margaret's death. Sam's finally interacting with Bessie helps him toward posttraumatic closure, but even this conversation is cut short when Sam's colleagues crowd around. Sam's difficulties in trying to interpersonally process the trauma are analogous to the difficulties he experiences in the scientific world, with countervailing forces making his quest for resolution uncertain.

Science

As a character, Sam's interests revolve in every way around his love of learning and especially science. He vaults through high school by age sixteen, enrolls in college buoyed by the explicit desire to continue work in genetics, and proceeds to live a life inundated in scientific experimentation and theorization. The pursuit of science is common to much of Barrett's fiction, and here, as in other stories, she demonstrates the inherent uncertainty of scientific exploration as well as the roles that malleable human emotions and relationships can play in the course of scientific history.

While science is often conceived as being hard and fast, a realm of abstract truths, by and large these truths are gradually and haltingly arrived at after much speculation in different directions. Lamarck's theories about adaptive inheritance may have been ill founded, but they were a stepping stone on the way to Charles Darwin's theory of evolution based on the variation of inherited traits and natural selection. As with many theories, Darwin's led to further practical progress, specifically the

TOPICS FOR FURTHER STUDY

- Write a short story in which a major component is the exploration, in some form, of an academic subject that you find absorbing. Your story might be historically grounded, like Barrett's, or grounded strictly in a protagonist's modern existence (like your own), with reference perhaps to revelations gleaned from a class or the impact of a powerful teacher.

- Compared with people of the present day, people in the mid-twentieth century were significantly more likely to suppress homosexual feelings or inclinations in light of the stigmatizing they could expect from broader society. Write a paper providing a reading of "The Particles" in line with queer theory, addressing such questions as where Sam might be positioned on a sexuality spectrum; what thoughts, comments, and behaviors speak to this; and how sexual repression might be a factor in Sam's personality, vocation, and relationships. Use at least one critical source to support your contentions.

- Read the young-adult novel *Origin* (2012), by Jessica Khoury, which portrays Pia, who through genetic manipulation has been rendered a virtually perfect human being by

her scientist parents. Then write a paper in which you analyze the significance of the science in this fiction, with regard to its proximity to reality, its metaphorical power, and its exploration of possible consequences. Include a discussion of how the science relates to that in "The Particles."

- In addition to epigenetics, another realm of science intertwined with recent history is hinted at in "The Particles" through the character of Ellen, namely, the improvement of humanity through breeding, or *eugenics*—a program whose problematic nature became glaringly apparent when it was taken up by Adolf Hitler during the Third Reich. Write a research paper on the history of eugenics, including its applications in the United States.

- Set up a website on which you present a visual map of the topics and people in "The Particles" drawn from real life. For each topic or person identified, include original text about the topic or person, appropriate pictures, and one or more links to further information on other sites. Be as extensive as possible, rooting out everything in the text that directly corresponds to real life.

discovery of the cellular mechanics of genetic transfer, and to more diverse theorization and experimentation, as exemplified in the story by such characters as Muller and the passionate, if misguided, Lysenko. In the story's present, Sam is a scientist whose interest in forging new conceptualizations contrasts with Duncan's conservative stance, whereby established precepts are assumed to be perfectly true and are defended at all costs. Such a rigorous stance might serve a scientist adequately as far as professional advancement goes, but the dreamers like Sam, Barrett suggests, are the ones who tend to turn the pages of scientific history.

Rivalry

Given their contrasting scientific roles, it is no surprise that Sam conceives of Duncan as his bitter rival—though Sam, rather, appears to be the bitter one, and with adequate cause in the realms of science and romance alike. Sam first conceived of a sense of rivalry as an undergraduate, when he realized that Duncan held the very position he desired, that of Axel's right-hand man in the laboratory. This inchoate rivalry takes on more serious proportions when Duncan refutes the findings that Sam shares at Woods Hole. Sam seems to imagine that Duncan is personally interested in quashing him

Sam struggles against the influence of his mother, a popular science writer.
(© Hasloo Group Production Studio / ShutterStock.com)

professionally: "What kind of a person would, in utter secrecy, interrupt his own project to replicate a fellow worker's experiments and double-check his results?" One answer to this question is, a true scientist—that is, someone whose scientific interest lies precisely in discerning the truth; Duncan suspected that Sam's findings strayed from the truth, and so he sought to identify where Sam was going wrong. Another answer to the question might be, someone who enjoys benefiting from another's misfortune—a rival. It is difficult to tell the extent to which Sam has concocted this sense of rivalry; Duncan does make a point of forwarding all of his recent publications upon Sam's return from Moscow to America, as if to flourish his accomplishments—or as if to kindly keep Sam abreast of the latest developments in their field. Regardless, Sam does seem to benefit from the sense of rivalry: despite occupying positions less prestigious than Duncan's throughout his career, Sam remains devoted to scientific progress and new conceptualizations. Even Duncan's last rebuking of Sam, at the

Edinburgh conference, may well serve a positive purpose, as Sam appears to be on the brink of a revolutionary understanding of the importance of timing in the activation of genes. With his rival spurring him forward and even keeping him on course, Sam may very well attain that understanding.

Community

In the end, regardless of whatever sense of rivalry there may be between them, Duncan and Sam remain part of—or, to put it more scientifically, particles within—the same vibrant academic community, and the support of this community is essential to their ability to continue with their work. Findings are freely shared between the likes of Duncan, Sam, and Muller, among others, and instructors like Morgan and Axel remain important counselors in the careers of their former students. As in any scientific field, there may be rivalry and competition between individuals or factions with different theories on the workings of the world, but this competition ultimately allows the most truthful theories to come to light. Sam resents that Axel fails to publicly or even privately take his side upon the eruption of the Edinburgh dispute, yet Axel's dual support of both Duncan and Sam represents not a contradiction but the objectivity of a mentor with a vested interest in the professional success of both of his protégés. They are all part of one community, and differences of opinion will be worked out in the end; meanwhile they can all care about one another as human beings, as Duncan expresses toward a dubious Sam, as Sam expresses toward Axel, and as Axel expresses toward Sam and Duncan alike.

STYLE

Frame Narrative

As with the scientific themes, the framing narrative is a literary approach that Barrett has favored in her collections of fiction. The ongoing drama of the sinking of the *Athenia* and its aftermath offers sustained narrative tension in the present, while the flashbacks scattered throughout fill in details that enlighten the reader with regard to the personalities and relationships shaping the events as they unfold. Barrett has implemented this framework in a complex way. To begin with, she has begun the story not before but just after the firing of the torpedo, leaving that pivotal action to appear in sharp moments of remembrance over the course of the story. Also, personal details of the events of the night at sea are left out of the introductory section, thus sustaining tension over the precise nature of Sam and Bessie's interactions on the lifeboat. Going back further, another pivotal moment occurred not long before the torpedoing, namely, Sam and Duncan's scientific dispute in Edinburgh, which weighs heavily on Sam's mind. In this way, tension is also sustained over just what happened at the conference—tension that is only partly resolved when the nature of Sam's talk is explained, since the nature of Duncan's refutation is never revealed. While descriptions of these very recent occurrences are scattered throughout the framing narrative, the deeper flashbacks offer a firmer structure, proceeding regularly from Sam's youth through his time in Russia and up to the present. Overall, the complex approach keeps the reader's mind busy patching together an understanding of the full extent of what is transpiring in each scene.

Scientific Fiction

Barrett's story is science fiction not in the sense of being a fantasized representation of a future world but in the sense of being fiction that is largely about science. Broadly assessing Barrett's fiction for the *Dictionary of Literary Biography*, Geoffrey Stacks is led to conclude that a "preoccupation with a literature of science" characterizes her later titles, which especially feature "the struggle of scientists at the margins of their fields." In this way she deftly figures science as both "pure and objective pursuit" and "imperfect art." Speaking with a *Salon* interviewer who suggested that science in her work comes across as an "adventure," Barrett responded:

> I perceive it that way. Maybe that's a false and romantic perception on my part, but I just conceive of it that way, in the same way that writing is an adventure. You know, that sense of starting out with a question and the haziest of ideas and just giving yourself over to the exploration and being willing to follow where that leads you and build something from what you find.

With "The Particles," Barrett fairly obliges the reader to do some scientific exploring of one's own, or else she assumes familiarity with modern developments in the field of genetics. That is, the reader is left to rely on background scientific knowledge or a trip to the (virtual) library to understand the extent to which Sam's sets of refuted preliminary findings actually prefigure modern developments in epigenetics, or the science of the varying expression of genes in accord with certain biological mechanisms. While his first experiment proves misguided, his direction of study is sound, and his second set of findings prefigures the modern epigenetic understanding of how the timing of genes' activation is indeed a crucial component of their expression and the healthy development of the individual. His conception of genes as arranged like "spiderwebs" seems to stray from the actual double-helix structure of DNA—which is indeed rather like the "beads on a string" model he bypasses; however, in terms of the complex ways that genes are manipulated and activated, Sam's spiderweb vision may remain a useful conceptual model.

HISTORICAL CONTEXT

In "The Particles," Barrett merges two major strands of history, with the sinking of the *Athenia* providing the context of the onset of World War II, while the scientific content speaks to the development of the field of epigenetics. Virtually all of the factual aspects of the story—the sequences of historical events, names of ships, the routes they took, names of scientists—are loyal to what occurred in real life.

The Sinking of the SS Athenia

A majority of Americans became directly engaged with World War II (1939–1945) only when the Japanese attacked Pearl Harbor in December 1941. But over 300 Americans were affected by the war almost as soon as it officially began with France and Great Britain's declaration of war against Germany on September 3. Germany had invaded Poland two days earlier, accounting for the awareness of the members of the Seventh International Congress of Genetics, held in Edinburgh, that the time to leave Europe had come. Britain's SS *Athenia*, however, carrying some 1,100 passengers and 300 crew members, proved an ill-fated getaway vehicle. Just hours after open war had been declared, it was mistaken by the commander of Germany's *U-30* for an armed cruiser—based, he reported, on its zigzagging course and its lights being out (plywood had been used to cover all the portholes)—and was thus promptly torpedoed. Only upon intercepting the distress call did the commander realize his mistake; he fled the scene, leaving other ships—the Norwegian merchant, Swedish yacht, and American merchant named in Barrett's story, along with three British destroyers—to come to the survivors' rescue. The commander never reported the incident to his superiors, and German leaders denied that they had committed the atrocity of sinking a passenger ship without heeding the rules of engagement. They feared an echo of the *Lusitania* incident of World War I, when the sinking of that passenger liner in 1915 brought the United States into the war.

The *Athenia* was struck at 7:39 on the evening of September 3, and it sank at 10 a.m. the following day. A total of 112 people died as a result of the attack, including most of those aboard the lifeboat that, in the darkness, was capsized by the propeller of the *Knute Nelson*; only eight of those fifty-five survived. One of the victims was Margaret Hayworth, a ten-year-old girl from Ontario who was struck by debris and later died in her mother's arms from the concussion. President Franklin D. Roosevelt, having delivered a radio address on US neutrality in the war that same evening, would not usher the United States into the war until over two years later.

The Development of Epigenetics

Following the propagation of Charles Darwin's theory of evolution throughout the scientific as well as civilian worlds, the theories of Jean-Baptiste Lamarck were widely discredited. In the eighteenth century, Lamarck had envisioned creatures being able to make fundamental changes to their bodies through daily use and to pass these changes on to their offspring. In this model, the giraffe as a species could have achieved its long neck simply through early giraffes constantly stretching their necks upward, making them longer and longer over time, with the achieved length passed on to descendants. As Darwin's theory has it, such changes would need to take longer, with baby giraffes having natural variations in the lengths of their necks and gradually, owing to ecological pressures, only the ones with the longest necks surviving to perpetuate the species. By the mid-twentieth century, Lamarckian inheritance was scientific anathema to a majority of biologists.

Yet it was around this time that the field of *epigenetics*—a term coined by Conrad H. Waddington in 1942—was just getting under way. As defined on the What Is Epigenetics website, the term refers to the study of "heritable changes in gene expression (active versus inactive genes) that does not involve changes to the underlying DNA sequence; a change in *phenotype* without a change in *genotype*." In other words, it is "the study of mechanisms that switch genes on or off." DNA has long been thought of as the *code* of a human being, suggesting that everything about the execution of the growth and development of the person is contained within that code. However, scientists came to realize that environmental factors, the physiological stimuli that people are subject to over the course of their lives, can influence the expression of various genes, determining whether or not certain genes are made active—such as those whose activation signals the onset of inheritable diseases. And in fact, genes can be

COMPARE & CONTRAST

- **1939:** Great Britain's passenger liner SS *Athenia* is attacked by a German U-boat and sunk in the opening hours of World War II on the night of September 3, killing 112. The Germans long deny responsibility.

  Today: When conflict erupts between the Ukrainian government and separatists allied with Russia in 2014, Malaysia Airlines Flight 17, flying over contested air space, is mistaken for a military transport and shot down, killing 298. Both sides deny responsibility, but intercepted radio communications indicate the separatists are to blame.

- **1939:** With scientists like Ernst Hadorn and Conrad Waddington in the process of combining the studies of genetics and developmental biology, the stage is set for Waddington to coin the term *epigenetics* in 1942 to refer to the study of how genes are expressed and adapted over the course of an individual's life.

  Today: With decades of research backing up claims regarding how genetic material can be altered and passed on in the course of an individual's life, epigenetics, far from being a fringe branch dismissed as neo-Lamarckian, is one of the fastest-expanding scientific fields, with vast room for further discovery of epigenetic processes and applications in the treatment of physiological development and diseases.

- **1939:** Homosexuality, being both criminalized and stigmatized as a mental illness, is generally condemned by a largely religious American society. As such, many individuals go through repressed, frustrating lives unable to acknowledge—perhaps even to themselves—that they have natural romantic feelings for members of the same sex.

  Today: The religious right is maintaining its stance against homosexuality, but beyond evangelicals, a majority of Americans, both religious and nonreligious, are now in favor of equality among people regardless of sexual orientation, making the ongoing state-by-state battles for same-sex marriage one of the most consistently noteworthy topics of the 2010s. Increasing numbers of gay celebrities with high profiles help encourage ordinary people to find fulfillment by being honest about and proud of their sexuality.

switched on or off in one generation in such a way that the switch is thrown, so to speak, for ensuing generations as well. Thus, DNA is now rather conceived as equivalent to the *script* for an individual's life, while epigenetic processes are equivalent to the director who actualizes that script, which can be done in myriad ways. Epigenetic processes were first linked to cancer in 1983, with intellectual disabilities, immunity disorders, and other physiological conditions demonstrably affected by what goes on at the epigenetic level.

From a modern scientific perspective, Sam's first wayward experiments in "The Particles," suggesting the inheritance of redness caused by injury to fruit flies, are fairly naive. Actual epigenetic processes are much more complex and typically involve prolonged exposure to certain conditions, such as famine, or chemical/biological agents, such as carcinogens. But his suggestion of the importance of timing in the expression of genes seems to hit the nail on the head. As the What Is Epigenetics website reports,

> Certain circumstances in life can cause genes to be silenced or expressed over time. . . . What you eat, where you live, who you interact with, when you sleep, how you exercise, even aging—all of these can eventually cause chemical modifications around the genes that will turn those genes on or off over time.

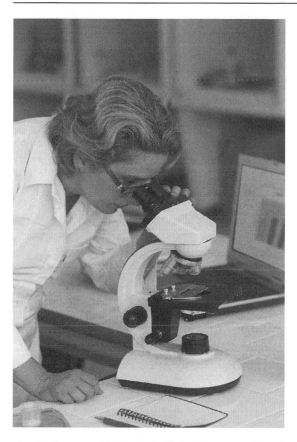

Axel tries to guide Sam, both in his research and in how he thinks about his own inherited traits.

The questions that Sam asks in Edinburgh, leaving his colleagues baffled—"When, in the course of development, might a tiny change cause massive later effects? Might inheritance not be far more complex than we'd guessed?"—are precisely the sorts of questions epigeneticists have been seeking to answer into the twenty-first century.

CRITICAL OVERVIEW

Having gained an enthusiastic critical consensus regarding the quality of her work with her receipt of the National Book Award for *Ship Fever* (1996), Barrett earned warm reviews for her second story collection since then and third overall, *Archangel*. A *Kirkus Reviews* writer notes that the book's stories have "uncommon scope and depth" and affirms that since *Ship Fever*, "Barrett has continued to command fictional territory all her own." The contributor characterizes the collection's first story, "The Investigators," a "masterwork of misdirection," while Donna Seaman, in *Booklist*, terms that story "dazzling." Seaman calls *Archangel*'s concluding title story "staggering," while in between Barrett writes "incisively" about the realm of science. The reviewer concludes, "Barrett's consummate historical stories of family, ambition, science, and war are intellectually stimulating, lushly emotional, and altogether pleasurable." In *Library Journal*, Susanne Wells declares that Barrett "has a remarkable ability to capture the essence of the natural world, as if describing a perfect snowflake." She calls *Archangel* "a delight for informed readers of challenging literary fiction."

Other reviewers were more ambivalent. A writer for *Publishers Weekly* suggests, "At times, Barrett's exercises . . . falter, leaving us with a barrage of historic-scientific details." Still, the writer says that "these few missteps don't counter the overall power of the book; there is indeed a sense of expansion as one travels onward in Barrett's world, and pleasure in watching it fill out."*All Things Considered* reviewer Alan Cheuse suggests that the opening story, for example, is "earnest" but "bland." In the end, according to Cheuse, the final story "achieves a fusion of life and wonder which the other pieces strove to reach but never seemed to grasp."

Critically assessing Barrett's literary modus operandi for the *New York Times Book Review*, Jess Row reached a more complex opinion of *Archangel*'s content and significance. Row observes that humble scientific achievements, like the observation of a leaping cricket, constitute "the essence of Barrett's method: where we expect a moment of high drama or a forceful resolution, we get a tiny, resonant detail, a shade of melancholy, a small satisfaction." Wondering what the stories might suggest about the broader social issues that peek out through the cracks of the science—like, for example, Ellen's support of eugenics—Row conjectures,

> It's difficult to say, because the scope of these stories is so small: there are the experiments themselves, which Barrett describes in rich and nuanced detail, and, likewise, the feelings of the characters. But the characters themselves are bit players, whose insights seem almost intentionally modest and limited.

Finding that Barrett's stories are too neatly celebratory of science while bypassing science's oft-tumultuous impact on culture, Row concludes, "Barrett is a consummate literary artist, but in *Archangel* she's trying to superimpose order and decorum on an era that tolerated neither."

In the *Dictionary of Literary Biography*, Stacks acknowledges Barrett's "widespread critical and commercial success" while pointing out that she "does not shy away from serious treatments of difficult material and presents intellectual fiction." In her stories and novels alike, Stacks finds, Barrett "expresses a wonder at the abilities of humans as they have helped to shape the world." The *Kirkus Reviews* contributor concludes of *Archangel* that "Barrett's stories rank with the best."

CRITICISM

Michael Allen Holmes

Holmes is a writer with existential interests. In the following essay, he considers how Sam serves as the antagonist of his own story in Andrea Barrett's "The Particles."

"The Particles" is a story that Andrea Barrett is tangibly presenting from protagonist Sam Cornelius's perspective, to the extent that the narration often blends with Sam's thoughts, in what is sometimes called a *free indirect* style. For example, shortly after Sam's being rescued by the *City of Flint*, the narrative reads, "Where was Axel, where was Axel? Maybe he'd been on that yacht, or maybe . . . he tried not to think about the huge propeller." In the question there, Sam's role as thinker of the repeated phrase is only implied—such repetition is not reflective of an objective third-person narrator—with indication of this role not coming until after the ellipsis (included in the original) with the word "think." And the fact that Sam's consciousness is assumed is emphasized by the fact that the "he'd" meaning Axel shifts to the "he" meaning Sam without any mention of Sam's name. It is no surprise, given the closeness between the narration and Sam's train of thought, that the reader is by and large, indeed almost exclusively, led to sympathize with Sam's position. He is the overlooked scientist hero, Axel is the wise guru, and Duncan is, cue the boos, the villain. Yet a close interrogation

THE NARRATIVE CENSURE OF DUNCAN CONTINUES THROUGHOUT THE STORY, REGARDLESS OF HOW LITTLE GROUND FOR CENSURE THE STORY PROVIDES."

of Sam's thought processes and conceptions of relationships suggests that Sam is perhaps as much the antagonist as Duncan is.

The tension inherent in the relationship between the two scientists is made clear from the moment they first interact, when Duncan happens to be the one to pull Sam aboard the *City of Flint* after his exhausting night at sea. The narration has made clear Sam's exposure to tragedy and trauma, such that the statement that "part of him wanted to jump back in the water" upon seeing Duncan hits the reader with some force. The presumption encouraged in the reader is that Duncan has wronged Sam or at least somehow earned his antagonism. That Sam feels the rescue ship's name to be "mocking" him further establishes his position as victim, someone being harassed or bullied. As far as the present circumstances are concerned, the implied characterization of Duncan is somewhat ironic, since he is in the middle of providing humanitarian assistance to the survivors of the *Athenia*'s sinking. However he has behaved in the past, he is behaving nobly enough at present, and he seems sincere in exclaiming "You're all right!" in finding Sam alive and kicking. Indeed, after the reader later learns that Sam spent much of the night on the lifeboat cramped, shivering, and vomiting, with death floating in the water, it is almost impossible to believe that at the sight of anyone short of the devil he would have wanted to "jump back in the water"—even more so given that he "could barely swim." Sam's animosity toward Duncan must truly be great to inspire that comment, or perhaps it is merely meant to be an exaggeration.

Duncan's character is undercut further when, after Sam cannot confirm that any other geneticists have survived, Duncan is said to remark "with apparent enthusiasm, 'But at least

WHAT DO I READ NEXT?

- *Ship Fever* (1996), which won Barrett the National Book Award, is her first story collection and features numerous historical treatments revolving around science. The life story of Gregor Mendel, whose nineteenth-century experiments laid the groundwork for the future field of genetics, figures prominently in "The Behavior of the Hawkweeds."

- One writer of a more popular nature whose novels frequently revolve around science is Michael Crichton. He brings genetics to a fantastic futuristic level—an approach that would become a widespread trend in science fiction—in his adventure novel *Jurassic Park* (1990), in which the coding provided by DNA preserved in amber is used to breed present-day dinosaurs.

- *Leviathan* (2009), by Scott Westerfeld, is a young-adult steampunk novel that, like "The Particles," mixes genetics with world war–era history. In this alternate history of World War I, the Central Powers and their steam-powered machines are set against British Darwinists who have genetically modified animals for warfare.

- John Wyndham's young-adult novel *The Chrysalids* (2008) takes a look at a future, post-nuclear-warfare society in which religious/genetic fundamentalists, who persecute and exile those considered mutants, are in control of a dystopian society.

- One of history's most famous science writers is the cosmological Carl Sagan, who is brought to mind in "The Particles" by Sam's mother, who writes about astronomy. Sagan once worked in the laboratory of real-life geneticist Hermann Muller. One would not be surprised if Barrett has read Sagan's essay collection *Broca's Brain: Reflections on the Romance of Science* (1979).

- One woman who played an outsized role in the development of genetic theories and medical solutions regarding the vaccine for polio, gene mapping, cloning, in vitro fertilization, and other practical matters actually had no conscious involvement: African American tobacco farmer Henrietta Lacks, who died of cervical cancer in the 1950s, had cells from a tumor removed and secretly cultivated, and for some reason those cells never died and proved phenomenally useful. Rebecca Skloot brings Lacks's story to light in *The Immortal Life of Henrietta Lacks* (2010).

---

you're here. You're safe.'" That the enthusiasm is *apparent* goes without saying, since enthusiasm is not enthusiasm if it is not apparent; the term can only be interpreted as undermining Duncan's supposed enthusiasm as potentially superficial. Yet there are no *apparent* grounds for Sam's doubting the other's present enthusiasm, no identifiable traces of duplicity, other than the past circumstances that Sam recalls after Duncan makes those remarks: how Duncan only "grudgingly" invited Sam to join the other geneticists aboard the American freighter *City of Flint* on their last day in Edinburgh, at which point Sam had already secured passage on the British liner *Athenia*. The import of this resentful recollection is ambiguous. The suggestion in the word "grudgingly" is that Duncan did not truly want Sam to join them, such that Sam, not feeling welcome, had (glumly, one imagines) adhered to his booked passage on the ill-fated *Athenia*. Thus, Sam has hazy grounds for resentment on two counts: first, because Duncan supposedly did not want Sam to join them and, second, if Duncan is to blame for Sam's being on the ship that got torpedoed. On the first count, Sam himself later notes how crowded the *City of Flint* was, a point that alone would have given Duncan cause to be reluctant to invite Sam along. Yet Duncan indeed invited Sam to join those boarding the *City of Flint*, and the ensuing paragraph makes clear that Duncan even urged Sam to join them because a British ship was more likely to prove a German target. As such, regarding the second count, reasonably one must conclude that Sam has only his own petty resentment of Duncan's belated invitation to blame for putting his own life in greater danger on the British ship.

Duncan certainly feels this way and is thus led to chide Sam—somewhat in the manner of elder brother, it seems—for failing to heed his warning. Duncan delivers his harping comments, the narrative reports, "after eighteen years of annoying Sam, unable to rein in his red-faced, bullying self." The suggestion that Duncan has been annoying Sam for eighteen years is clearly hyperbolic, or exaggerated beyond reason—again, perhaps simply for dramatic effect on Barrett's part or perhaps to reflect how Sam irrationally feels. (The two characters spent the vast bulk of this period in separate locations.) And while Duncan's face may be red from the exertion of helping Sam and others aboard the ship, he does nothing that can be accurately described as "bullying" in this scene. This twenty-first-century buzzword for labeling those who oppress their peers may quickly summon a ready-made image of amorality in the modern reader's mind, but Duncan is forcing Sam neither to do anything nor to say anything, and he is not injuring Sam or belittling him through name-calling or public embarrassment. Duncan is merely pointing out that he had, accurately, it turns out, warned Sam that taking passage on a British ship was unwise. This concern for Sam's welfare is far closer to *caretaking* than to *bullying*. The narrative misdirection continues when Sam derogatorily notes regarding Duncan and the question of booking passage home, "Anyone else would have understood how few choices existed." Again, the text implies fault on Duncan's part, specifically narrow-mindedness; yet in the circumstances only two choices are relevant, both of which were certainly understood by Duncan and available to Sam: either he could have boarded the *Athenia* as planned or, more safely if perhaps more expensively (presuming he had already bought a ticket for the *Athenia*), he could have boarded the *City of Flint*. Despite

its being brought up to imply a flaw or failure of Duncan's, the notion that there were "few" other choices in the matter is irrelevant. In fact, at one point Sam seems to have reveled in the choice he consciously made, experiencing "a twinge of pleasure" at the thought that his ship was actually "less crowded than Duncan's."

Sam's antipathy toward Duncan grows downright morbid when Axel is discussed. Once Duncan realizes that Axel was aboard the *Athenia* and remains unaccounted for, he grows suddenly pallid, and the narration states of Sam: "In another situation he would have enjoyed seeing the color drain from Duncan's cheeks." What is meant by *another situation* is unclear. For another situation to be equivalent to this one, the shock of Duncan's realization would have to be serious enough to literally drain the color from his face. Does this mean Sam would have enjoyed the sight if the acquaintance of Duncan's who is possibly dead were someone Sam cares nothing about? One hopes that this is not what Sam has in mind, but regardless, the fact that he is dwelling on vindictive thoughts in a time of tragedy demonstrates that his priorities are misplaced. He seems to care more about Duncan suffering than about others being free of suffering. (Perhaps this morbidity should come as little surprise, considering that Sam is the sort who identifies "the smells of ether . . . and flies fried on lightbulbs" as "the atmosphere of delight.") Sam's resentment of Duncan lingers even when he puts Sam's mind at ease by finding Axel, "proving himself astonishingly useful just when he was at his most annoying." Once again, the text second-guesses itself; if Duncan "always had this way of proving . . . useful" as such, why would it still be astonishing? One might conclude that Duncan's usefulness remains astonishing to Sam precisely because Sam is narrow-mindedly clinging to an inaccurate conception of Duncan as a villain. This must be the case if Duncan is found to be "at his most annoying" simply in being there where Sam now finds himself.

With the narrative's take on Duncan's character established, even what might be considered positive descriptions of Duncan and his behavior come off as ironic at best. He is referred to as "modestly" moving from his bunk to the floor to allow the injured Axel a bed, but the term rather implies that Sam thinks

Duncan is hardly modest enough; Sam would presumably approve of Duncan's level of social decorum only if he were to give his spot on the floor by Axel's side—where Sam has always wanted to be—to Sam. Indeed, Duncan is later conceived by the narrator/Sam as having been able to hear Axel's account of the night of the sinking while he "lay on the floor in the place where Sam should have been."

The narrative censure of Duncan continues throughout the story, regardless of how little ground for censure the story provides. Sam conceives of Duncan as having "attacked" his work at the conference, though a more objective term like *refuted* might better characterize what took place; since Duncan's refutation is never presented to the reader, the narrative perspective, which is Sam's perspective, must be taken at face value—and yet Sam's reliability in the judgment of Duncan's character has already been thrown into question. Similarly, it is difficult to give credence to a judgment of Duncan from Sam's freshman year of college: "he was shallow, Sam thought even then, and prone to leap to easy conclusions." There is little if any narrative evidence of Duncan's shallowness, other than his participation with George, Harold, and even the hallowed Axel in academic gossip. Given that Sam's judgment is inspired by Duncan's discovery of a new mutant, a legitimate scientific accomplishment, the grounds for Sam's judging his intellectual acumen are unclear. When Duncan graduates, it is conceived that he finally, if temporarily, "got out of Sam's way"—as if Sam's path is the only one that matters and Duncan is merely an obstacle, as opposed to a human being with his own path. Sam's villainous characterization of Duncan verges on the comical when he sees this middle-aged man with floppy hair and a potbelly pushing through the crowd on the deck of the *City of Flint* "like a fox through a field of wheat." Is this metaphorical fox chasing a mouse or escaping from bloodhounds or simply being stereotypically wily and untrustworthy, as foxes metaphorically are?—though how this would be evident in Duncan's walking through a crowd is, again, unclear.

Sam, it seems, is utterly determined to conceptualize Duncan as his antagonist; yet as far as the reader can tell, Sam is the one with the antagonistic attitude. He nearly acknowledges as much when, in speaking to Laurel, he insinuates that scientists in general— but really he can speak only for himself—are indeed "petty" and "as childish as everyone else." It is true that Duncan has antagonized Sam professionally, but Sam is the one who takes their professional differences personally; he assumes, or wants to assume, that because Duncan disapproves of his studies, he must harbor disdain for Sam as a person. Yet for one thing, Duncan's disapproval of Sam's studies has, for all the reader can tell, simply stemmed from the errors Sam is committing and potentially propagating in the scientific community— since one wrongheaded study might easily be cited by a follow-up to produce results that are further inaccurate, and so on and so forth. Duncan, in addressing Sam's errors as rapidly as possible, is arguably doing science a favor by limiting the potential damage caused by any erroneous study. He is also saving Sam a great deal of time and possibly even greater professional embarrassment than he experiences anyway. If Sam's reputation was compromised because his *preliminary* findings were discredited, how much more would it have been compromised if a published academic paper, disseminated among a far greater audience, were discredited? Similarly, if Duncan sees errors in Sam's Edinburgh presentation, from a certain moral perspective he might feel literally compelled to point them out, for the sake of science as well as Sam as he continues his research, hopefully, along accurate lines.

Once Sam's antagonistic attitude is clear even to Duncan, Duncan tries to assure Sam that he has no vendetta against him:

> What went on at the congress—that's work. I don't agree with your work; I want it buried. Doesn't mean I want *you* buried. Until you came over the side of this ship, when I thought you might have drowned, I felt—

Duncan is at last trying to open up to Sam, to share his feelings, but all Sam can say, still clinging to his fantasy of Duncan as villain, is "Oh, please." The reader might be forgiven for agreeing with Duncan's retort, "You're impossible." Affirmation of Sam's perspective of Duncan does finally come, however, in the form not of narrative evidence but of interpersonal judgment on the part of another: Axel. Sam almost worships Axel, and it would not be difficult to conclude that Sam's feelings for Axel amount to romantic ones. In this light, Sam's resentment of Duncan may stem as much from

Sam's interpretation of the results of the fruit-fly experiment seem far-fetched to his peers.
(© Roblan / ShutterStock.com)

professional antagonisms as from his jealousy of Duncan's apparent intimacy with Axel; Sam may (subconsciously) perceive Duncan as a romantic rival. Or perhaps the nature of his affection for Axel is strictly filial and platonic, in which case jealousy could still come into play.

One way or another, the reader realizes, Axel must on some level be aware of Sam's feelings for him—he even affirms for Sam "how attached we are"—and must be conscious of how Sam will interpret whatever he says. Thus, while on the surface he seems to confirm Sam's judgment of Duncan's character in the long-delayed heart-to-heart that they finally have, framing Duncan as ignorant and emotionally dependent, on a deeper level Axel may be (subconsciously) catering to Sam's own emotional needs—the need to be dredged up from the psychic swamp that self-comparison with Duncan inevitably leaves him in and the need to have the intimacy of his own relationship with Axel confirmed. Axel meets these needs of Sam's in a masterful way—that is, in a way befitting a master or mentor—and it is perhaps only Axel's persuasions that can draw Sam

down from the role of antagonist in his own life story. Duncan seems set to rile Sam one last time when he takes charge of telling the story of the *Athenia*, but for once Sam is at least able to register the experience without resorting to mental name-calling and disdain. Almost charitably, Sam finds himself thinking that "what Duncan recounted wasn't untrue," leading him to the realization that however skewed he might imagine Duncan's perspective to be, as far as Sam's own professional life is concerned, "who knew him better than Duncan?" The answer is Axel, but Duncan and Sam's participation in what is actually a symbiotic scientific relationship helps make them both Axel's true "friends," one on either side of him—like the wheels at either end of an axle, both of which are needed for the vehicle to roll—and whether Sam's antagonistic nature will be perpetuated further or at last overcome, his story, at least, is moving forward.

Source: Michael Allen Holmes, Critical Essay on "The Particles," in *Short Stories for Students*, Gale, Cengage Learning, 2016.

Katherine A. Powers

In the following review, Powers calls "The Particles" the "most fully realized story" in the collection Archangel.

Andrea Barrett has established her own little demesne in the world of fiction, one pervaded by science and metaphors drawn from its concepts. Here, she has cultivated a multigenerational, intertwined strain of characters, shoots of which have popped up from story to story since *The Voyage of the Narwhal.*

Evolutionary biology has been an informing presence behind these narratives, and it is again in *Archangel*, Barrett's new collection of stories, all five of which concern the tribulations of toilers and aspirants in the field of science.

In the first, "The Investigators," we find a twelve-year-old Constantine Boyd in 1908, sent from Detroit to work for the summer on an uncle's farm in western New York State, where he develops a lasting interest in doctoring animals. Here he meets Henrietta Atkins, a high school teacher in her mid-fifties who, with his uncle, is conducting experiments with cave fish, the object of which is to determine how they lost their eyes in the course of their evolution. Excited by this research and the enthusiasm for scientific and technological investigation he finds in the community, Constantine would like to stay on, but that course is blocked. Indeed, stymied ambition and confounded development play a large part in these tales, reflecting (perhaps) the waste that is nature's own way of going about its business. We encounter Constantine again, eleven years later, in the last story, "Archangel"—where we also discover Eudora MacEachern from Barrett's last novel, *The Air We Breathe*—and find that his intention to become a vet has been thwarted by the Great War and the subsequent military campaign in Russia. We leave him up in the air—literally—but the student of Andrea Barrett's work will not be surprised to find him at large again.

Taken in order as they come to us in the book, the stories touch down hither and yon chronologically. And so, a couple of stories later, we find Henrietta thirty-five years earlier, in "The Island." She is now a young woman embarked on a summer's course in marine biology under the tutelage of a pseudonymous Louis Agassiz. Failing in health, the great natural historian is in his last year of life, still insisting, though now with an old man's poignant intransigence, that species are immutable, ideal emanations from God's mind, and that nature reflects divine design and purpose. Henrietta is handed a copy of Darwin's *On the Origin of Species* by a fellow student; she reads it and is stunned, disenchanted, and eventually inspired. Darwin's vision of nature breaks on her as a form of epiphany as she sits in a rowboat surrounded by buckets of sea creatures, "lumps of protoplasm."

The appeal of these stories lies in their material detail, in the flicker of metaphor, and in their incidental links, the way characters, or their scions or progenitors, appear in another frame. There is in that last aspect something that is both random and orderly, just as it is in nature and, at another level, in a human life. In life, however, we look for what is necessarily absent in evolutionary biology: That is meaning, or, put another way, a reason for living. In most fiction, that comes down to love, power, freedom, or peace, but for the main characters in these stories, what gives purpose to their lives is an urgent desire to discover the workings of nature. Their characters and personal relations are subsidiary to this and as their predicaments echo scientific concepts, their lives seem, for the most part, theoretical and posited, rather than lived.

"The Particles" is the book's most fully realized story; it brings individual predicament and character together with a welter of metaphors drawn from evolutionary theory—the problem of biological variation, adaptation, natural selection, and developmental timing. It begins in September 1939, with Sam Cornelius (son of Phoebe, the central figure in an earlier story, "The Ether of Space") adrift in a foundering lifeboat, a survivor of the British ship Athenia, the first vessel to be torpedoed by German U-boats. He is a geneticist in his mid-thirties returning to the U.S. from a conference in Edinburgh, where, for the second time in his life, he has aired a theory of genetic change obnoxious to prevailing conventions.

Years earlier, he had committed the solecism of arguing, on the basis of a series of experiments, that acquired traits can be inherited. As it happened, his findings were shown by a rival-turned-nemesis to be the result of inadequately controlled experimental conditions. Though Sam did acknowledge his error,

I WANT THE HISTORY TO BE CORRECT INSOFAR AS IT CAN BE, BUT I ALSO, ULTIMATELY, WANT IT TO BE SUBORDINATE IN THE SENSE THAT I AM WRITING A NOVEL AND NOT WRITING HISTORY."

he quickly discovered that, in practice, scientific discourse is not in fact a matter of freely exchanged views and hypotheses among disinterested people whose primary goal is unlocking nature's secrets. Instead, he finds a world as red in tooth and claw as the natural one, an arena of power relationships and ad hominem arguments in which jobs and funding take priority over free inquiry.

Sam's second foray into heterodoxy—heresy, really—which he has just set before his fellow geneticists at the Edinburgh conference, is far more sophisticated than the last, but it gives rise to the same scandalized opprobrium. This theory stresses timing as the key element in change, and, in fact, reflects his own life's trajectory as shown with immense subtlety by Barrett as she traces his story from boyhood to survivor. Here, at last, Barrett truly does break out of the theoretical, transforming several linked metaphors into a complex rendering of character and plot.

Source: Katherine A. Powers, Review of *Archangel*, in *Christian Science Monitor*, August 30, 2013.

Sarah Anne Johnson

In the following interview excerpt, Barrett talks about her writing process and how she incorporates science into her fiction.

I know that you were a biology student. How did you go from science to writing fiction?

By a long, confused road. I initially went to graduate school in zoology, which didn't work out at all. Later on I studied medieval history for a couple of years in graduate school, but I didn't stick with that either. In and around those two things I had about thirteen jobs in ten years, none of them related to each other, and none but the last two related to writing. It

took me a long time to figure out what I wanted to do. It really wasn't clear to me. I kept trying awful jobs and fumbling around. I did finally just start writing, and I can't actually account for that, except that I've always been such a passionate reader. I loved reading and loved books and wanted to write, but I didn't understand how anyone became a writer. I didn't know any writers, and I didn't know about graduate programs in writing. But one day I started writing a novel. I worked on that for about six years and eventually had to throw it out, but in the process I learned something about writing and I began to meet other writers, and all that was helpful. It was a long road, though.

What did you do to develop your craft of fiction?

Mostly I wrote. I wrote and I read and I wrote and I read, which is still a way that a person can learn to be a writer. It's faster if you go to school. I teach now in the M.F.A. program at Warren Wilson College, and I visit other M.F.A. programs. I can see how much time it's possible to save if you have help and companions, but you can learn the same things by yourself. For a while, I did. As I got older, I began to go to writers' conferences and writers' groups and to make friends with other writers who I shared my work with and whose work I read. That was an enormous help to me.

It also helped me when I started teaching, for the obvious reason that before you teach something, you have to hurriedly go out and learn it yourself. I never felt more than a half hour ahead of my students. I've had wonderful students. They were often better read or farther along some paths than I was and I learned a great deal from them.

How did you decide to explore the possibilities offered in the world of science?

That's something that evolved gradually in me. Now, when I look back—at my early training as a biologist, all my friends who are biologists and doctors, and my husband, who's a scientist—it seems obvious that this is the world I know. It seems obvious to everyone now, including me, that I should write about that world, but in fact it wasn't obvious. It took me a while to find my way there. With my earlier books, it was so difficult for me just to do the basics of handling characters and trying to tell a story that I couldn't see my way into incorporating a lot of outside material into the work. By my third novel, *The Middle Kingdom*, I was able to begin to use some of that material. One of the chief characters is a freshwater biologist, but the book is not very much about his work. The work is in the background, more incidental. The work is not present in the book the way it is in my later books, but that's when it first crept in. In *The Forms of Water*, the fourth book, I began to use some historical material for the first time as background for a very elderly character. That's when I first started using a lot of research to build characters and to build material in the books.

Finally, in *Ship Fever*, something released in me. I think because I started trying to learn to write stories and left novel writing for a while, it suddenly seemed possible to reach into that older natural history material and see what I could make of it. Once I did, I felt really at home there. I loved it. I had that "Aha!" moment. I wondered why I wasn't always writing about this. I don't know what took me so long.

Were there any challenges you faced in incorporating science into your work?

Yes, and I still do. The truth is that I don't know science very well. I learned it as an undergraduate twenty-five years ago now, and I didn't learn it very well the first time. People often assume, and I'm grateful that they do assume, that I know a fair bit of science, because what I get on the page in the end is convincing, but the truth is that I don't know it very well. I do a lot of research to get it on the page, and I worry all the time that I've gotten things wrong. I have a flimsy understanding of it, and I'm always walking on eggs with it. Not so much with the older natural history material—that was written for a lay audience and anyone is capable of understanding it, even me. But when I'm working with contemporary science, I'm sometimes nervous.

Do you have readers who review your work for accuracy?

With certain stories I do. With "The Mysteries of Ubiquitin" in *Servants of the Map*—I got the idea for that particular field of research from a dear friend of mine who does research on ubiquitin. I asked her, when the story was finished, to read those sections for me and make sure that I hadn't done anything stupid. It was a great help.

Your work is often labeled as fiction about science, but it really strikes a balance between the science and the human story you're exploring. Is it difficult to strike that balance?

I'd propose that it's not really fiction about science, although it gets labeled that way and I often talk about it that way. It's fiction. Fiction is about people. Fiction is about stories. Those remain my primary interests. I use the subject matter of science as my "stuff." Any writer needs something to write about, and this is *my* stuff. But stuff is not what fiction is about. Stuff is what fiction is founded in and in part built by. But it isn't what it's *about*. Scientists are terrifically interesting people, and so the characters and the dilemmas that arise from people who are passionate about doing science can make for really interesting fiction. That's not exactly the same as fiction about science.

How do you go about conducting your research? What types of resources do you consult, and where do you find them?

I go to the library, nothing esoteric. I do read an enormous amount, but I'm not a great rummager in archives and lost papers and crumbling things, although I have friends who do that and I admire them enormously. I'm a reader of books, and of memoirs, and of diaries, and of collections of letters. I also look at a lot of visual material. If it's from a period when photography existed, I look at old photographs, which I find enormously helpful. I look at paintings. I look both at things about the time and things made *at* the time. It's interesting in one way to look at an etching made in 1857 of the things on Charles Darwin's desk, and it's interesting in another way to look at a painting or an etching made in 1930 about the things someone thought were on Charles Darwin's desk. They say two different things. Some of the things are about 1857 and some are about 1930, but it's all interesting. If there's music that I know from the period, I listen to the music. If I can, if the languages are available to me, I also look at novels and poems written in the period. Even though they may not be about what I'm researching, they tell me something about the tonality of the culture then, about what people are thinking, what things seemed important to them.

How concerned were you with getting the historical facts accurate?

I am pretty concerned. There are people who purposely bend historical fact in their fiction, but while that can make for interesting fiction, I'm not one of them. Because I spent a brief time formally studying history, it makes me nervous to bend what seems to be a known fact. There are people who would argue that there are no known facts, but again, I'm not one of them. If there's a historical person passing through a story or a novel, I won't have had him or her grow up in a place where they didn't grow up. I won't send a person to the Arctic when I know he went to the Antarctic. I won't have a woman living in Philadelphia when I know that during those years she was living in France. Those very basic things I will stick to.

Can you talk about how your research kindles your imagination and gets you writing?

Oh, in all sorts of ways. Sometimes things really do grow from the reading and the research, but it's always in such odd ways. Often it's a picture, a visual image. Sometimes it's an image in words, a sense of somebody on a dock or in a room holding a bandage. Sometimes a whole area of subject matter will seem interesting to me. That's what happened with "The Cure" in *Servants of the Map*. I used to drive through Saranac Lake a lot on my way to someplace else. I never stopped to look around, but it imprinted itself on me. I got curious about the porches, and then curious about the people who would've been on the porches, and then curious about the state of society that would've led everybody to be clumped in one place on the porches.

At what point do you stop your research and start writing?

Usually after the initial subject matter has suggested itself, I'll have to read pretty hard for a while just to get my feet under me. It's hard to write something about Gregor Mendel if you don't know what decades he lived in and you don't know what city his monastery was in. You have to get a sense of the period and the place in the most general way. But often I can start when I have only that general sense, because the research is very specific for the story or the sections of the novel. When I get to a part in *The Voyage of the Narwhal* where the men sail off on a ship, suddenly I realize that I don't know anything about how ships are built or where the stove is. I have to stop everything, and go learn about ships. As the ship comes up past Newfoundland to the edge of Greenland, I realize I don't know anything about Greenland. I don't know when the Danes went there or who administered what or what the Inuit peoples were doing or what the weather was like or what the coastline was like. The research lurches along stepwise.

It takes you on a journey of your own.

So much so. There's a hidden map of each story and each novel which exists beneath the story and which is the map of my own path through all these different areas of inquiry and exploration and learning.

How do you manage all of this historical information in a narrative, and what is the effect you want the history to achieve in the narrative?

I want the history to be correct insofar as it can be, but I also, ultimately, want it to be subordinate in the sense that I am writing a novel and not writing history. After the first draft or two, a lot of my efforts in further drafts and revisions are to take out much of the factual material I earlier worked so hard to learn and put in. I always put in too much. There are always long digressions and long ponderous passages and things that no person would actually say to another person.

Do you hate cutting them?

I do initially. I'm always glad in the end that I did. I always get used to it. I tend not to miss them soon after I've cut them, even though, each time, I think, "Oh, that was so interesting. I wish I didn't have to take that out."

But you asked how I managed all the information, and maybe you meant that in a more literal sense. It's evolved over time, and it's still evolving, and I don't have a perfect system. I keep thinking I'll find one, and I never do. For various books and sets of stories I've used various cumbersome, not very well organized combinations of three-ring binders full of notes, index cards, hanging files, smaller files, larger files, boxes, tubs, tins, maps on the wall. There's always a ton of paper around. It's hard sometimes to remember what's where and be able to get my hands on the stuff I need about, say, a ship's berth. I used to take notes on yellow pads, so there would be heaps and heaps and heaps of yellow sheets piled in folders all over. I'm trying to do some of this on the computer now, but I'm just learning to do that.

What's your process like when you're working on a story or a novel? What goes on through each draft or revision?

I do a great many drafts, no matter what it is. I'm a very clumsy writer. I've given up apologizing for it. It's the way I work, so it's the way I work. My first drafts tend to be unspeakably bad. I don't know how to express it: astonishingly bad, much worse than most student work. I'd never get into graduate school if I applied with those drafts.

I think all of you established writers should let us read your first drafts to renew our faith, to let us know that everyone starts at the beginning with each piece.

I gave a talk at the University of Michigan several years ago to the graduating students, the Hopwood Lecture. I was talking about exploration and discovery, but I talked some about *The Voyage of the Narwhal*, and I did actually read them the first three-quarters of a page of the first draft of that book.

Was it horrible?

Oh, it's amazing. Wrong in every way. It diverges from the final book in every way that it could. It's first person, not third. It's set thirty years before the time I actually started the book. They went to the Antarctic instead of the Arctic. Reading the draft was fun; it gave the students some sense of how messy the process always is. It always is, no matter how long you do it.

So how do you get from those early drafts to the final, beautiful piece?

I write a lot of drafts. I draft and I draft and I draft. Some people can do more of this in their heads and not have to write it out so many times, but I seem to think largely on the page. This means doing it and letting it sit for a few days before looking at it, then doing it again and letting it sit, and doing it again. I let my friends read drafts after the first ten or twelve, when it's starting to get faintly coherent and you can faintly see the direction. My closest friend is Margot Livesey, a wonderful writer. Margot and I have shared our work for about a decade now. I let Margot look at it at various points along the way, although I try not to hammer her more than two or three times. Often she'll look at something like the tenth, the twentieth, and the thirtieth iterations: it's a huge help, to have a wonderful brilliant reader

asking great questions. I cut a lot. It isn't as if I write very long the first time and cut in all the successive drafts, nor is it as if I write very sketchily the first time and add through all the successive drafts. Strangely, it's both. My early drafts are sketchy in the most important ways—everything vital is left out—and they're wordy in other ways—there's all this extraneous material that doesn't matter. So the revisions are in both directions. It's like building a house, if you don't know how to build a house and you're not very smart. You run around and you throw up some walls where you think the rooms should go, and then you come back in a week and you realize there's no bathroom and two kitchens, so you have to tear down some of those walls and put up others, and then in a week you come back and realize the attic is half the size it's supposed to be. The walls go up, the walls go down, the walls go up. Somehow a house gets built, but I don't exactly understand it. But that's what it feels like, putting up walls and tearing down walls until you get it right.

The more interesting question is, How do you know when you get it right? But I can't answer that one. I don't think anyone can truthfully. We all have feelings about that, but most writers, if we're honest, admit that that's what those things are—they're feelings, they're intuitions. Things *feel* right at a certain point. They assume a proportion or a shape that feels right. It's not an intellectual decision. It's an emotional or an intuitive decision.

At what point do you know if what you're writing is a short story or a novel? Do you know when you set out, or is it revealed in the writing?

Usually when things announce themselves to me, they announce themselves roughly in their form. Although I've made huge mistakes: I thought *The Voyage of the Narwhal* was a novella initially, but within thirty pages or so, I saw that I was wrong. I didn't persist in that very long. Again, I don't know what that is. It's a feeling thing, not a thinking thing. Some things *feel* like novels or novellas or stories. I've had stories get a good deal longer than I thought they'd be. I've thought I had a normal-size story on my hands and had it turn into fifty or sixty pages. But usually they arrive in their approximate shape.

Your most recent three books are concerned with the quest for scientific discovery during the nineteenth century and the complications, both difficulties and joys, that quest can bring to relationships. What draws you to this theme and this period?

It was such an interesting period both scientifically and in terms of exploration. It's an easy time and an easy place to make metaphoric sense from. If you're drawn to the shape of the journey anyways, and I am—the journey through our lives, the journeys we all make all the time—then that particular time and place is very rich in interesting examples. People made astonishing physical journeys for such complex reasons, some of which we now deplore, some of which we now admire.

How do your story ideas come to you?

All different ways. Sometimes I wake up in the middle of the night with an idea, but that doesn't happen often. Often they come to me through my reading. I see some little picture or some phrase that captures my fancy. I've been working with some of the same characters now through the last three books—you've probably noticed, in *Servants of the Map*, that there are things that hark back to previous books. Often these days, as I'm working on one story or novella or novel, I'll get a glimmer of somebody else in this gigantic family and what might have happened to them in some other time. Actually all the people are related, but you can't see it yet. . . .

Source: Sarah Anne Johnson and Andrea Barrett, "The Hidden Map of the Story," in *Conversations with American Women Writers*, University Press of New England, 2004, pp. 2–8.

Economist

In the following review, the anonymous reviewer praises Barrett's precise writing style.

Andrea Barrett grew up by the ocean on Cape Cod. When she realised she would never be Linnaeus or Mendel, or even an ocean-going naturalist like Darwin, she turned her back on biology and became a storyteller instead. But biology's loss was literature's gain, as her latest collection of six stories proves.

Ms Barrett has made the waters that swirl between a love of science and the science of love her special domain. In a previous collection, *Ship Fever*, two Englishwomen set out to prove that, contrary to the great Linnaeus's belief, swallows do not hibernate underwater. The year is 1764, and the women must experiment in secret if they are not to be dismissed by the scientific establishment. When, at the end of the story, the two women disappear, you are left hoping against hope that they have been stolen away by love.

In *Servants of the Map* Ms Barrett continues to explore loneliness and isolation, but with an eye on the comic discrepancies among different people's perceptions. In "The Forest," the inevitable gap of perspectives between an illustrious Polish scientist grown nostalgic with age and an uncertain young woman who yearns to break free from her past leads to a walk in the woods that ends with a twisted ankle and a hilarious escape for both heroes.

But it is the title story, selected for inclusion in last year's *Best American Short Stories*, which confirms how deserving Ms Barrett is to be ranked with Alice Munro and the other great North American storytellers of the moment. An English mapmaker, Max Vigne, leaves behind his wife and a child he has never seen to work as a topographical surveyor in 1860s India. In the western Himalayas he struggles to assuage his guilt and loneliness, writing letters home that serve only to chronicle the distance that is growing between man and wife. While he avoids the crude comforts sought by the other Englishmen around him, he comes to realise that in his unquenchable desire to be a botanist he must put off his return home, thus exposing himself to yet more guilt and his poor family to a still deeper loneliness.

It is the precision of Ms Barrett's words that makes her stories so rewarding, and the intelligence with which she creates bonds between characters from an age so different from our own that makes reading her such a joy.

Source: "Stories from Science: New Fiction," in *Economist*, February 9, 2002.

Carol Anshaw

In the following review, Anshaw raves about the subtlety of Barrett's writing.

At first blush, *The Voyage of the Narwhal* might seem an odd book for consideration in the *Women's Review*, concerning itself as it does mainly with men—moreover, men in acutely manly postures, engaged in the rugged heroics and privations of Arctic exploration. But Andrea Barrett is up to quite a bit more than an adventure saga. Like an iceberg, the bulk of her story lies in the vast dark stillness beneath its surface. Ultimately, the novel emerges into

BARRETT (WHOSE PREVIOUS BOOK, THE STORY COLLECTION *SHIP FEVER*, WON THE NATIONAL BOOK AWARD) HAS CREATED A FICTION THAT CONTAINS, LIKE THE HOLD OF A SHIP, MANY TRUTHS, BOTH LARGE AND SMALL."

a tale of the vainglorious beginnings of the modern, the Western, the scientific—traditions we now so comfortably inhabit that we seldom give thought to what might have gotten pushed aside in the process of obtaining this questionably higher ground.

The novel's protagonist, Erasmus Wells, is a quiet, modest man, a scholar and naturalist, his profitless vocation fostered by family money.

He was forty years old and had a history of failure; he'd sailed, when hardly more than a boy, on a voyage so thwarted it became a national joke. Since then his life's work had come to almost nothing. No wife, no children, no truly close friends; a sister in a difficult situation. What he had now was this pile of goods, and a second chance.

The pile of goods are all the supplies that will fit into a small ship, the chance is a new voyage, led by Zeke Voorhees, a friend who is now also engaged to Erasmus' sister, Lavinia. Zeke's ship, the Narwhal, with fifteen men aboard, sets sail from Philadelphia in June of 1855. Its ostensible mission is to find who- or whatever might remain of an ill-fated expedition launched ten years earlier to chart the seas off Greenland. Led by an Englishman, John Franklin (a real historical figure, as are many peppering the backdrop of the story), two ships with full crews and equipment that included—in the whimsical manner of the day—a library of 1,200 books and a hand organ that played fifty tunes had left in the spring, then disappeared by the end of that summer.

Tracking Franklin is only one part of the Narwhal's business; there are other agendas among those on board. Erasmus hopes to gather more specimens of wildlife to catalogue later at the Repository on his father's estate.

Zeke longs for the fame that has greeted other explorers upon their return. By now, exploration has become a lively sideshow, providing entertainment for a vast audience of armchair travelers. Erasmus sorrowfully notes that his sister Lavinia has friends like this, "for whom Darwin's Tierra del Fuego and Cook's Tahiti had merged with Parry's lgioolik and d'Urville's Antarctica until a place arose in which ice cliffs coexisted with acres of pampas, through which Tongan savages chased ostriches chasing camels." Zeke also has the primal male urge to mark, in his case to put his name on land and water still unnamed (at least by white men).

The voyage, of course, goes terribly wrong. Minor ailments give over to more serious ones. Personalities begin to abrade one other. Supplies dwindle. Zeke turns out to be a young man possessed by a demon of ego. Determined to prove the existence of an open polar sea that he might put his name on, and to do so before another expedition beats him there, he forces the remaining crew to stay over through an arctic winter, huddled within the hold of their ship, through days when the only semblance of light is a red glow at noon. Crew members start dying off, morale is nil. When the weather becomes more clement, instead of taking his men and ship back, Zeke—unable to muster any volunteers to accompany him—disappears into the short polar summer to scout for his open sea.

When the others can wait for him no longer lest they be forced through a second winter, which they will surely not survive, Erasmus abandons the Narwhal, still stuck in ice, and brings back what's left of the crew—"ten men in a whaleboat made for six." Along their impossibly hard way out, they lose valuable specimens and proofs of all they've found. Also lost to the elements are the young cook's nose and all of Erasmus' toes.

While these explorers have been discovering what has already been discovered—by competing explorers, by whalers before them and by the "Esquimaux" before that—while they are losing their ships and shipmates, their noses and toes, losing and becoming lost, all this while their women wait at home. Waiting is what women of this class and time do. Back in Philadelphia, Lavinia has waited agitatedly for her brother, and for Zeke. Waiting with her has been a paid companion, Alexandra Copeland, who, to while away the long hours, also to make money, takes up botanical drawing, an interest that shapes a hesitant connection between her and Erasmus—who has returned to an angry sister, an indifferent scientific community, a press critical of him for abandoning Zeke, and a public absorbed in the fabulous findings of Dr. Kane, whose expedition to the same area returned while the Narwhal was still away.

Then, a few months later, Zeke, all but given up for dead, returns, bringing with him an Esquimaux woman and her son, whose people guided him out of the arctic. In Zeke fashion, he has "named" them Annie and Tom. Quickly shifted from friends to actors in Zeke's roadshow, prompted to demonstrate native crafts and games, their humanity disappears in the transition. They become ill with a treacherous fever and are left to languish while Zeke is preoccupied with marrying Lavinia and being famous and insinuating himself into the new Smithsonian. Erasmus has been shut out, can do little to save them. When Annie dies, Erasmus inquires about her burial. His brother tells him:

There was no burial. . . . No body, even. There are men at the Smithsonian who—who do this sort of thing. I don't know how, I don't want to know how. I think the man Zeke was staying with gave him his permission and he, they, someone prepared and mounted her skeleton for the museum. Zeke stayed to oversee it.

In the end, Erasmus and Alexandra, who have become lovers, steal away to the great North, their mission not to explore, but simply to bring Tom home. Here and there, Barrett softly passes the narration to the boy, whose angle of vision on the white man's folly is quietly chilling. "His people had a name for Zeke," we are told, "a chain of soft syllables that meant The One Who Is Trouble."

For all involved, this journey shapes itself as release and freedom. For Tom, who belongs to the North. For Erasmus, who, out of his failure to capture the arctic, finds that he doesn't need to own or discover or name it, only to experience it. For Alexandra, who has been sitting on a sofa in front of a fire most of her adulthood. For her now, "every moment she felt as if she were inventing her life."

Although this is a book of larger ideas and reverberating themes, it is also a delight in its thousand details—the supplies of ships (plum puddings, brandy, heaps of hand-knitted socks, hundreds of pounds of pemmican, knives and needles to barter with the Esquimaux), the hospitality of the Esquimaux women, who reach out with tattooed hands to offer musk-ox horn tea and boiled caribou, the medical treatments for maladies of the day (tartar emetic, mercurous chloride, syrup of squill, tincture of opium). Barrett's vast research yields up quite astonishing moments, such as the one in which Erasmus and Dr. Boerhaave, the great friend he makes on the voyage, deprived for too long of fresh meat, retrieve stored caribou skins and squeeze small scars on their surface to bring forth larval grubs of the warble flies that stung the caribou while they lived; the two friends pop the grubs into their mouths and agree— not bad at all.

Barrett (whose previous book, the story collection *Ship Fever*, won the National Book Award) has created a fiction that contains, like the hold of a ship, many truths, both large and small. Perhaps the most central is couched in an entry in the journal of Dr. Boerhaave:

. . . there are continents and seas in the moral world, to which every man is an isthmus or an inlet, yet unexplored by him, but that it is easier to sail many thousand miles through cold and storm and cannibals . . . than it is to explore the private sea, the Atlantic and Pacific Ocean of one's being alone.

Source: Carol Anshaw, Review of *The Voyage of the Narwhal*, in *Women's Review of Books*, Vol. 16, No. 3, December 1998, p. 8.

SOURCES

Allen, Tonya, "The Sinking of the S.S. Athenia," uboat.net, March 21, 1999, http://uboat.net/history/athenia.htm (accessed March 1, 2015).

"Athenia: British Steam Passenger Ship," uboat.net, http://uboat.net/allies/merchants/ships/1.html (accessed March 1, 2015).

Barajas, Joshua, "Ukraine: Intercepted Audio Shows Separatist Rebels Shot Down Malaysia Airlines Plane," PBS website, July 18, 2014, http://www.pbs.org/news hour/rundown/ukraine-intercepted-audio-shows-separatist-rebels-shot-malaysia-airlines-plane/ (accessed March 4, 2014).

Barrett, Andrea, "The Particles," in *Archangel*, W. W. Norton, 2013, pp. 129–86.

Cheuse, Alan, Review of *Archangel*, in *All Things Considered*, NPR, August 26, 2013.

"Epigenetics: Fundamentals," What Is Epigenetics?, http://www.whatisepigenetics.com/fundamentals/ (accessed March 1, 2015).

Hustak, Alan, "The Sinking of the Athenia," in *Something about Everything Military*, http://www.jcs-group.com/military/war1941allies/athenia.html (accessed March 1, 2015); originally published in *History*, February/March 2013.

Kurth, Peter, "The Salon Interview: Andrea Barrett," in *Salon*, December 2, 1998, http://www.salon.com/1998/12/02/cov_02inta/ (accessed March 1, 2015).

Review of *Archangel*, in *Kirkus Reviews*, June 1, 2013.

Review of *Archangel*, in *Publishers Weekly*, Vol. 260, No. 24, June 17, 2013, p. 38.

Row, Jess, "Scientific Americans," in *New York Times Book Review*, September 29, 2013, p. 24.

Seaman, Donna, Review of *Archangel*, in *Booklist*, Vol. 109, No. 21, July 1, 2013, p. 43.

Stacks, Geoffrey, "Andrea Barrett," in *Dictionary of Literary Biography*, Vol. 335, *American Short-Story Writers since World War II, Fifth Series*, edited by Richard E. Lee and Patrick Meanor, Thomson Gale, 2007, pp. 10–18.

"A Super Brief and Basic Explanation of Epigenetics for Total Beginners," in *What Is Epigenetics?*, July 30, 2013, http://www.whatisepigenetics.com/what-is-epigenetics/ (accessed March 1, 2015).

"Timeline of World War II," PBS website, http://www.pbs.org/thewar/at_war_timeline_1939.htm (accessed March 1, 2015).

Wells, Susanne, Review of *Archangel*, in *Library Journal*, Vol. 138, No. 10, June 1, 2013, p. 104.

FURTHER READING

Carey, Nessa, *The Epigenetics Revolution: How Modern Biology Is Rewriting Our Understanding of Genetics, Disease, and Inheritance*, Columbia University Press, 2012.

Carey's volume, written to be accessible to popular audiences, provides an up-to-date treatment of the field of epigenetics and its scientific importance.

Carroll, Francis M., Athenia *Torpedoed: The U-Boat Attack That Ignited the Battle of the Atlantic*, Naval Institute Press, 2012.

Perhaps no fuller treatment of the sinking of the *Athenia* can be found than the one in Carroll's recent volume, which delivers the details of the incident, stories of those on board the ship, and the event's profound historical relevance.

Francis, Richard C., *Epigenetics: The Ultimate Mystery of Inheritance*, W. W. Norton, 2011.

Predating Carey's volume by a year, Francis's is touted as the first treatment of the science of epigenetics for general readers. The volume was published in paperback as *Epigenetics: How Environment Shapes Our Genes*.

Schwartzkroin, Philip A., *So You Want to Be a Scientist?*, Oxford University Press, 2009.

This volume is a comprehensive guide to the education, practices, thought processes, and ideals befitting those interested in scientific study as a lifetime pursuit.

SUGGESTED SEARCH TERMS

Andrea Barrett AND The Particles

Andrea Barrett AND Archangel

science AND literature

genetics AND literature

genetics AND science fiction

epigenetics AND fiction

epigenetics AND Lamarck OR Darwin

World War II AND Athenia

World War I AND Lusitania

The Princess of Nebraska

YIYUN LI

2004

Yiyun Li's short story "The Princess of Nebraska" first appeared in the literary journal *Ploughshares* in 2004, and it was later included in her 2005 debut short-story collection *A Thousand Years of Good Prayers*. It is the story of Sasha, a Chinese immigrant who has come to the United States to attend graduate school, only to discover that she is pregnant by a boy back in China, whom she slept with once before leaving. The boy, eighteen-year-old Yang, was once a member of the Peking Opera and has been trained to perform women's roles on stage. Boshen, a thirty-eight-year-old gay man and Chinese immigrant living in Chicago, also had an affair with Yang and is still in love with him. Together, Sasha and Boshen are in Chicago to end Sasha's pregnancy, though Boshen tries to persuade her to keep the baby.

Li is also a Chinese immigrant who, like her character Sasha, came to America to attend graduate school. In describing Sasha and Boshen's meeting in Chicago, Li explores themes of gender, the importance of human rights and personal freedoms, and how the main characters' identities have been shaped by their past in China.

The story brings up some controversial subject matter, such as abortion, male prostitution, and homosexuality.

Chinese American writer, editor, and teacher Yiyun Li (© *Geraint Lewis / Alamy*)

AUTHOR BIOGRAPHY

Li was born in Beijing, China, on November 4, 1972. Her father was a nuclear scientist, and her mother worked as a teacher. Her childhood was shaped by the Cultural Revolution of Communist leader Mao Zedong, who ruled China from 1949 to 1976 (the Cultural Revolution itself began in 1972). As in many Communist regimes, self-expression and nonconformity were discouraged in Mao's China, and Li learned to censor her thoughts and opinions early in life. In a National Public Radio interview, Li said that her parents thought writing was dangerous; having been through so many revolutions and political upheavals, they "did not trust words, did not trust language." All of Li's works were written in English, after she came to the United States.

In 1989, a government massacre of student protesters in Beijing's Tiananmen Square made headlines worldwide. Li was at home and did not see it in person, but she heard many stories of the incident from friends. In the early 1990s, Li was a recruit in the Chinese Army, where she

was forbidden to speak of subjects like the massacre. Later, an essay about the massacre was one of the first pieces of her writing that drew notice from literary critics in America.

Li attended Peking University in Beijing, where she met her future husband, Dapeng Li. After graduating, she came to the United States in 1996 to attend graduate school at the University of Iowa, intending to get a doctorate in immunology. However, she soon discovered a love of writing that prompted her to leave the immunology program and apply to the prestigious Iowa Writers' Workshop in 2000. She received a master of fine arts degree, and her work began to get published in impressive publications such as the *New Yorker* and the *Paris Review*. In 2005, ten of Li's stories (including "The Princess of Nebraska") were collected into a book titled *A Thousand Years of Good Prayers*. Critical reviews of the book were overwhelmingly positive; the collection garnered several awards, including a Guardian First Book Award and the PEN/Hemingway Award. One of the stories ("Immortality") also won a Pushcart Prize (a prestigious award for short stories).

In 2009, Li's first novel was published. Titled *The Vagrants*, it begins with the gruesome execution of a woman denounced for her counterrevolutionary writings. The story follows the effect that the execution has on the people of the small industrial town where it occurs. As with her first book, critical reviews were positive, and the novel won a California Book Award gold medal. Li followed *The Vagrants* with another collection of short stories, *Gold Boy, Emerald Girl* (2010), and a second critically praised novel, *Kinder Than Solitude*, released in 2014. Her short stories have appeared in many anthologies as well.

Li is a professor of writing at the University of California, Davis, and lives in Oakland, California, with her husband, Dapeng Li, who is a software engineer, and their two sons.

PLOT SUMMARY

As the story opens, Sasha and Boshen are at a McDonald's in Chicago, Illinois, getting lunch. They have come to Chicago for Sasha to get an abortion; she is four months pregnant, which is too far into pregnancy for a legal abortion in Nebraska, where she lives. Sasha, originally from Inner Mongolia, has come to America for graduate school. Boshen, a thirty-eight-year-old gay man, had to leave China and come to the United States after the Chinese government was displeased with his activities as an AIDS activist.

When they were still in China, both Sasha and Boshen had had affairs with the same eighteen-year-old boy, Yang, the father of Sasha's baby. Yang was a performer in the Peking Opera; he was a *Nan Dan*, a boy trained to perform women's roles in the opera. However, he was expelled from the opera after being discovered with a male lover, and he fell into prostitution. Hoping to save him from this life, Boshen took him in and attempted to get him reinstated into the opera. While living with Boshen, Yang met Sasha at a party, and they became friends; they slept together just once and conceived their child. Though Sasha was never really in love with Yang, she does care for him. Boshen, on the other hand, is still passionately in love with Yang and is pained when

MEDIA ADAPTATIONS

- A movie based on "The Princess of Nebraska" was released in 2007, directed by Wayne Wang. The movie starred Li Ling as Sasha and Brian Danforth as Boshen.

Sasha tells him that Yang has fallen back into prostitution.

As they eat their lunch, Boshen gently tries to persuade Sasha to consider keeping Yang's baby, but she is determined to get the abortion. Boshen thinks that if Sasha would tell Yang about the baby, he would want to come to America, and together they could help him. Sasha dislikes Boshen, however, and finds him "as fussy as an old hen." This did not stop her from calling Boshen for help when she learned she was pregnant; Boshen used to be a doctor in China before his hospital dismissed him for establishing a counseling hotline for homosexuals.

In flashbacks, the reader learns that Yang is a beautiful, elegant, and graceful boy with whom many men have fallen in love. However, it seems that neither Boshen nor Sasha really know him well; he reveals very little about himself, other than a careless, apathetic view of life. The only thing that seems to rouse his interest is the idea of returning to the stage, a promise that Boshen made and then was unable to fulfill.

The reader also learns that Sasha's mother was from Beijing and had married a Mongolian herdsman (Sasha's father). They had two daughters. Even though Sasha's mother later divorced her husband, she was not allowed to leave Mongolia, because her daughters were born there. Sasha has not seen her father in fifteen years.

In the present day of the story, Sasha and Boshen notice that outside the McDonald's, people are gathering for a holiday parade. Sasha wants to see it, so they find a spot where they can see the floats go by. The reader learns from her musings as she watches the parade that she did try to contact Yang about the baby, but he never responded. She feels resentful and bitter toward Yang and the baby. For the first time, she tells Boshen about these feelings, and then she begins to cry. Boshen puts his arm around her to comfort her, and when he does, Sasha feels the baby move for the first time. Though she is still conflicted, she begins to have some hopeful thoughts about the baby. She remembers that her mother, despite all her hardships, never regretted having her two daughters. "Being a mother must be the saddest yet the most hopeful thing in the world," Sasha thinks.

CHARACTERS

Boshen

In many ways, Boshen is the opposite of Sasha, the story's protagonist. Where Sasha is closed off, suspicious of emotion and sentiment, Boshen is almost too unguarded and passionate. His desire to help others results in his exile from China. The author tells us that Boshen lived an "openly gay life" in China; given the attitude of the government toward homosexuals, this was probably unwise, especially given Boshen's desire to stay in China with Yang. Unlike the pragmatic Sasha, Boshen has idealistic visions of how things should be, without practical ideas for making them a reality. Though he tells Yang that he will get him back on the stage, he makes little progress toward this goal. Both Yang and Sasha see his promises for what they are: dreams. When Boshen tells Yang that he will get him back to performing, Yang replies, "An empty promise of a man keeps a woman's heart full." Sasha puts it more bluntly: "You speak like the worst kind of politician," she tells him.

Though Sasha is carrying Yang's child, Boshen is far more maternal in nature. He frets about Yang's well-being and cares more about Yang's health and safety than about having his passion reciprocated. He sends Yang money via checks that remain uncashed; he cherishes hopes of adopting Sasha's baby and caring for it, of bringing Yang to the United States and caring for him. His dreamy outlook causes him to romanticize Yang, who cares little for anyone but himself. He tells Sasha that Yang might want to come to America if he hears about the baby, but Sasha knows this is not true, because she has already attempted to contact Yang about the baby.

Sasha

Sasha is a complicated, contradictory character. Her manner is uncaring, brutally blunt, even hostile, especially toward Boshen, whom she dislikes. However, there are signs throughout the story that this may be just a defensive posture to protect herself from pain. At the age of twenty-one, Sasha has left her home in China and come to the United States alone to attend graduate school in Nebraska. Her mother, forbidden to leave Inner Mongolia (a region of China) because her children were born there, remained behind.

Sasha has not seen her father in fifteen years, since her parents' divorce. She has already learned the lesson that Boshen took much longer to learn: in China, being too open with one's opinions and passions can lead to persecution and exile. Sasha has internalized this lesson; she sees Boshen's open and emotional nature as weakness and finds his devotion to Yang "pitiful." Despite her scorn, however, a part of Sasha longs for closeness, for connection, and for the freedom to be unguarded. As she watches the Americans at the holiday parade, she envies them: "They were born to be themselves, naive and contented with their naivety." And when Yang becomes distant after some earlier moments of intimacy, Sasha is simultaneously relieved and disappointed. She craves intimacy, but at the same time, it frightens her.

Though there is little physical description of Sasha, the author hints that she is plain. After Sasha calls Boshen to tell him she is pregnant, he imagines the perfect girl for Yang, someone mature, understanding and beautiful, "but Sasha had disappointed him." Next to the graceful and beautiful Yang, Sasha feels "like a mass-produced rubber doll."

Sasha's Mother

Sasha's mother was a high school student in Beijing when she was sent to Mongolia for "labor reeducation." In order to join the Communist Party, she married a Mongolian herdsman. Because her two daughters were born in Inner Mongolia, she was then forbidden to leave there. At one point in the story, Sasha wishes that she herself would be bound to the

TOPICS FOR FURTHER STUDY

- Li ends her story ambiguously, without revealing the fate of Sasha and Yang's baby. Do you think Sasha will continue with the abortion, or choose to keep the baby instead? Write an epilogue (a short ending) for the story, explaining what happens to Sasha and her baby in the coming months. Include Boshen and Yang. Are either or both of them a part of Sasha's life in the future?

- Sasha grew up in the region of China known as Inner Mongolia. Research the region and write a short one- to two-page report. Include a map showing the location of Inner Mongolia in China. How is this region unique compared with other regions of China?

- Actor and martial artist Jackie Chan was a student of the Peking Opera school. Research Jackie Chan online and read what he has to say about his experiences at the school. According to Chan, what were the benefits of attending the school? What were the drawbacks? Create a PowerPoint or Prezi presentation on Chan's experience.

- Read the biography *Mao's Last Dancer* by Li Cunxin. After growing up in extreme poverty, at age eleven the author was chosen to join Madame Mao's Beijing Dance Academy. Through his involvement with the academy he traveled to America, and eventually (with much difficulty) he defected to the United States. How is Li Cunxin's experience similar to that of Yang in "The Princess of Nebraska"? How is it different? Write a one-page comparison of the two stories.

- Because self-expression was a dangerous thing in China, Li never wrote creatively until she came to the United States in her twenties, and then she began writing in English. Do you study another language, such as Spanish or French? Try writing a very short story in that language. How could writing in another language make your writing more creative?

United States by her baby (as her mother had been bound), because she admires the carefree and optimistic nature of the Americans she sees.

Yang

Yang is an eighteen-year-old Chinese boy trained as a *Nan Dan*—a boy who plays women's roles—in the Peking Opera. He spent most of his childhood in the opera school, training to play roles, and now his whole life is a performance; he has no real identity of his own. Both Sasha and Boshen are fascinated with him, for different reasons; for each of them he plays a different role. When Yang speaks, he either speaks very briefly or quotes plays or songs. The few times Yang shows any real emotion are when someone refers to the Peking Opera. When Boshen shows him a stack of paperwork he has gathered to further Yang's return to the stage, Boshen sees "unmistakable hope" in his eyes. And when Sasha tells Yang that the organization is dead, Yang snaps, "Who are you to say that about the Peking Opera?" Yang was expelled from the Opera when he was caught with a male lover. Now he has fallen into prostitution, performing yet more roles for the men who are willing to pay his asking price.

THEMES

Gender Roles

Gender roles in "The Princess of Nebraska" are fluid and interchangeable. Yang is both woman and man; born male, he has been trained since childhood to portray women on stage. When Sasha tells him they could go to America and be the "prince and princess of Nebraska," Yang

Sasha's first year of school in Nebraska is disrupted when she discovers she is pregnant.
(© Diego Cervo / ShutterStock.com)

points out, "I was not trained to play a prince." For the gay men he sleeps with, he portrays a boy, albeit a delicate, beautiful one. Though traditionally a man is the sexual aggressor in a relationship, in Sasha's relationship with Yang, she is initially the aggressor; it is her idea to get a hotel room and spend the night together. Yang sleeps with both Boshen and Sasha; his sexuality is ambiguous. Boshen, a gay man, marries a lesbian friend in order to stay in America. Although Yang and Sasha, and Boshen and his "wife," are male-female couples, the feelings they have for each other are in no way conventional. The outward expression of gender in the story depends more upon the character than on their actual physical sex.

Human Rights

All of the characters in the story have had their rights restricted in one way or another. Yang was trained in a very disciplined, restricted school (the Peking Opera school was known for its harsh, restrictive discipline). His childhood was sacrificed, and now he knows little of life beyond performing; his identity is restricted

to that one function. Boshen's desire to help others was condemned and punished by the Chinese government, forcing him into a false marriage, exile from his home and separation from Yang. Sasha's existence was used as a reason to restrict her mother's rights; because she was born in Mongolia, her mother cannot leave there, and Sasha's going to the United States to attend school means she cannot see her mother. Basic rights that Americans take for granted—to speak one's mind, to choose whom to love and where to live—are not guaranteed to Sasha, Boshen, or Yang as Chinese citizens. Seeing the carefree Americans watching the holiday parade in Chicago, Sasha says, "I would trade my place with any one of them."

Identity

All three characters struggle with identity within the story. Yang's identity shifts constantly, depending on whom he is with and what he is doing. He has been trained since childhood to play roles, to take on new identities but not to discover his own. When he speaks, he often quotes plays, songs, poems, or the words of famous people, rather than put things into his own words. He has two names, one given by his parents and one by the Peking Opera school. Sasha feels that neither name fits him, but she is unable to think of one that does. When they try to get a room, they have difficulty because Yang has no identification card and symbolically no identity. Sasha lies and makes up identities for him—at one hotel she says he is her cousin, and at the next he is her brother.

Sasha's identity issues are different; she has an identity but wants to discard it, to invent a new self and leave her past behind in China. Anything can happen in America, she believes; identities can transform in an instant. "A prostitute becomes a princess; a crow turns into a swan overnight," she tells Yang. She is fascinated by the American concept of "moving on," and she imagines her Chinese life as a book whose pages she is stapling together so that no one can ever open it again. This desire is thwarted by the baby growing within her, a baby conceived in China and part of Yang, a creature invented by the Peking Opera, an old and nearly obsolete Chinese institution.

Boshen's identity issues are more subtle. His desire to help others often results in sacrificing himself. He tries to help homosexuals and loses his job as a doctor. He tries to help those with AIDS and ends up leaving the country. He tries to help Yang, though the boy does not return his feelings and treats Boshen carelessly. Boshen seems to have no desires or plans for himself, only for others. Formerly a physician, he now works in a Chinese restaurant, and he is married to a lesbian friend in order to stay in the United States. He never speaks of any plans to regain his license to practice medicine. He is focused only on Yang and on Sasha's baby. Boshen's entire identity is based on caring for others; now alone, he is adrift.

STYLE

Minimalism

In literature, minimalism refers to a sparse, stripped-down style of writing; stories are told directly, without long passages of description or flowery writing. Li's writing has a minimalist feel. Emotion is conveyed subtly, through dialogue and straightforward descriptions of the character's actions. Li's vocabulary is simple and easily understood; there are few words that send the reader to the dictionary. Her sentence structure is simple, and there are none of the lengthy, paragraph-long sentences that one might find in some other works. Most sentences are relatively short and to the point, as in the following excerpt:

> She called him "my little *Nan Dan*," and that was what he was to her, a boy destined to play a woman's part. She paged him often, and invited him to movies and walks in the park. She made decisions for them both, and he let her.

Third-Person Omniscient Point of View

"The Princess of Nebraska" is mostly written in the third-person omniscient point of view, meaning that characters are referred to as "he" and "she" (rather than "I"), and that the reader learns both Sasha's and Boshen's thoughts and feelings about their experiences. The viewpoint is not entirely omniscient (all-knowing), however; the reader does not have access to the thoughts and feelings of Yang. One possible reason for this omission is to maintain the air of mystery that surrounds Yang. Another possibility is that Yang functions as a mirror for others, performing the roles that they want him to play. In this case, Yang has no real point of view of his own.

Because the reader visits both Sasha's and Boshen's inner worlds, it is possible to see how they are incorrectly perceiving each other. Sasha sees Boshen as weak, but the reader learns of Boshen's caring nature and his disappointment in his own lack of achievement. Boshen sees Sasha as hard and unfeeling, but through her inner thoughts, the reader glimpses moments of vulnerability.

HISTORICAL CONTEXT

The Cultural Revolution in China

In 1966, Mao Zedong, leader of the Chinese Communist Party, was looking for a way to reassert control over the party after his disastrous economic experiment ironically titled the "Great Leap Forward," in which he attempted to rapidly industrialize the Chinese economy. The Great Leap Forward resulted in the

COMPARE & CONTRAST

- **Early 2000s:** Since opening up the economy in 1979, China is enjoying tremendous economic growth.

  Today: Though China is still prospering, the rate of economic growth has slowed. The growth rate of China's gross domestic product for the past thirty years has averaged about 10 percent, but the rate of growth in 2014 is only 7.4 percent.

- **Early 2000s:** Until 2002, condom manufacturers are banned from advertising their products in China. Clinical expertise in treating HIV and AIDS is limited, and the poor have little access to drug treatments. As late as 2007, only 19 percent of those in need of HIV treatment have access to it.

  Today: Condoms are now promoted in China as a medical device to avoid the transmission of HIV and AIDS. In 2011, 76 percent of those in need have access to HIV treatment.

- **Early 2000s:** It has been fifty years since Mao first established "labor reeducation," a system that sent millions to labor camps, often because of their opposition to the Communist regime or criticism of it. However, labor reeducation still exists, and it operates outside the formal Chinese prison system.

  Today: Near the end of 2013, the Chinese Communist Party announces the official termination of labor reeducation camps. However, critics of the system say that labor reeducation still exists under different names.

---

starvation of millions of Chinese people and weakened confidence in Mao.

To begin the Cultural Revolution, Mao called upon the nation's youth. He enlisted high school and college students as members of the Red Guards, encouraging them to return to the ideals of Communism and revolt against those in the party who had become complacent (in other words, Mao's opponents). He even closed schools so that China's youth could dedicate themselves completely to the revolution. Members of the Red Guards became violent, inventing reasons to attack people they felt were not supporting the cause of the revolution, usually those older than they. Anyone remotely suspected of counterrevolutionary opinions was at risk; children even turned in their parents and other older relatives. While Mao did not officially endorse all their actions, the Red Guards were given few guidelines or restrictions on their activities, and there was no clear definition of what officially constituted counterrevolutionary behavior. Violence and persecution

escalated to chaotic levels, and millions of urban Chinese were sent to rural areas for "labor reeducation," supposedly to learn what life was like as a peasant worker. Intellectuals were targeted for persecution, beaten, and often imprisoned. Many committed suicide.

By 1967, even Mao and other party leaders felt that the situation was out of control. They attempted to tame the violence by stressing Mao's philosophies and teachings over violent activities. However, in the end it was violence itself that calmed the chaos, when troops were called in to stop an uprising at a university in Beijing. Five people were killed, and 149 were wounded.

The Cultural Revolution was not over, however. It continued, in a less frenzied form, until Mao Zedong's death in 1976. Millions more were persecuted and sent away for labor reeducation. After Mao's death, the new head of the Chinese Communist Party arrested the four surviving leaders of the Cultural Revolution, using them as scapegoats for much of

Sasha goes to Chicago to figure out what to do next with her life. (© *Pigprox* / *ShutterStock.com*)

Mao's wrongdoing, to leave Mao's image clean. In 1979, Deng Xiaoping became the new leader of China, ushering in a new era of more international cooperation and moving away from hard-line Communism toward more capitalist policies. Still, the ghosts of Mao's revolution continued to haunt China's people for decades to come.

Tiananmen Square Massacre

In April and May of 1989, student protesters across China began staging demonstrations, mourning the loss of former Communist Party leader Hu Yaobang, who had worked for a more open political system in China and for democratic reforms. The crowds of students became larger as more and more joined them to call for a more democratic government. In May, thousands of students began a hunger strike in Tiananmen Square in Beijing. By late May, Chinese premier Li Peng had imposed martial law. Western journalists reported the events, although the government banned filming or photographing the protests. On June 4, Chinese troops entered Tiananmen Square and

began firing on protesters. The official death toll, according to the Chinese government, was 246, but there is great skepticism about this number. Most believe the count to be much higher.

Today the Chinese Communist Party has gone to great lengths to erase the incident from public memory. Many young people born after 1989 are not even aware of the massacre or the events surrounding it. It is not taught in the schools or memorialized anywhere. Some parents of students killed in the massacre, who attempted to get more information about their children's deaths, are still regularly monitored by the government. Louisa Lim, a correspondent for the US news organization National Public Radio, wrote a book about China's suppression of the event, titled *The People's Republic of Amnesia: Tiananmen Revisited* (2014). Today, China is more prosperous than ever, and there are more personal freedoms than before; however, the party is quick to suppress those freedoms if suppression is thought to be in the party's best interest.

CRITICAL OVERVIEW

"The Princess of Nebraska" is one of ten stories in Li's debut short story collection, *A Thousand Years of Good Prayers*. The critical response to the collection was overwhelmingly positive. The book won a host of awards, including the Guardian First Book Award, the PEN/Hemingway Award, and the California Book Award for first fiction. One of the stories in the collection, "Immortality," also won a Pushcart Prize and the Plimpton Prize for New Writers from the *Paris Review*.

Critics were impressed with Li's deft use of English, her second language. In a review for the *San Francisco Chronicle*, Alan Cheuse states, "Li writes as though English were her native tongue" and calls the collection "an extraordinary feat of intelligence and style." Li's spare, minimalistic style was also singled out for praise by more than one critic. Rodney Welch, reviewing the collection for the *Washington Post*, says that Li writes with a "brisk clarity" and "gets down to business quickly."

Coming from a country where government and politics invade every corner of one's life, Li often incorporates political issues into her work. Critics noted Li's ability to blend the political with the personal in her writing. In a review for the *New York Times*, Fatema Ahmed praises her "light touch" that "saves her stories from turning into consciousness-raising exercises." A review in *Publishers Weekly* agrees, saying that Li "deftly weaves a political message into her human portraits."

Negative comments were few and usually included as footnotes to otherwise positive reviews. A reviewer in *Kirkus Reviews* writes that the collection includes "some ungainly plotting," and Fatema Ahmed, though mostly impressed with Li's writing, admits that "Li's sentences occasionally creak under the weight of the information they convey, as if the didactic urge to explain the China she knows pushes aesthetics out of the way." Despite these criticisms, the overall critical response to Li's first book echoed that of the *Publishers Weekly* reviewer, who calls it "a beautifully executed debut collection."

CRITICISM

Laura B. Pryor

Pryor has a master's degree in English literature and thirty years of experience as a professional writer. In the following essay, she examines Judith Butler's concept of the performance of gender in "The Princess of Nebraska" as well as the concept of performance in general.

Literary critic Judith Butler theorizes that the behaviors we associate with gender—that women are more emotional, for example, or that men prefer not to talk about their feelings—are not natural, innate qualities, but rather a performance, passed on from generation to generation. These roles are taught to us gradually, over time, and the very act of the performance shapes our identities and reinforces the "truth" of the role. As evidence of Butler's theory, we need only to look toward "truths" that society once believed about gender: that women were fragile, irrational creatures dominated by emotion and that men, as the more rational and logical gender, were better equipped to run businesses and governments. Likewise, it was believed that men's logical, thought-based nature made them less nurturing and ill-equipped for the care of children. In the eighteenth century, it was believed that women had the more powerful sex drive, since they were at the mercy of their uncontrolled emotions, and so wives had to be carefully watched in social situations. Over time this belief turned on its head, with men portrayed as "wolves" who coerced women into sex by their charm and persistence.

The character of Yang in "The Princess of Nebraska" is an exaggerated example of Butler's theories. Trained to perform as a woman from a young age, Yang embodies qualities we normally associate with women: delicacy, grace, beauty. Sasha describes Yang as "an exquisite china doll" with a "delicate nose and mouth." His voice reminds her of "a satin dress," and she teases him for being vain and taking too long to fix his hair. Using Butler's logic, we might theorize that Yang became graceful and delicate as a response to his expected performance, rather than possessing those qualities from birth.

Yang has two names. Yang is the name given to him by his parents at birth, when he

WHAT DO I READ NEXT?

- In the novel *Girl in Translation* (2010), by Jean Kwok, main character Kimberly Chang and her mother emigrate from Hong Kong to Brooklyn, where Kimberly must work at a factory in Chinatown to help support herself and her mother. At the same time, she works hard to excel at school, hiding her secret life and her extreme poverty.

- *Baby Girl* (2007), by Lenora Adams, tells the story of Sheree, an African American girl who runs away from home. She is pregnant, in love with a twenty-five-year-old drug dealer who treats her poorly, and fed up with her mother's promiscuity. The book is written as a long letter from Sheree to her mother, telling her why she has left home.

- Louisa Lim's nonfiction book *The People's Republic of Amnesia* (2014) uses a wide range of interviews with eyewitnesses to the Tiananmen Square massacre to show the effect of the incident on the people of China and the lengths to which the Communist Party has gone to erase the event from Chinese history.

- Li's second novel, *Kinder Than Solitude* (2014), tells the story of four friends, all teenagers at the time of Tiananmen Square massacre. One of them is poisoned and brain-damaged as a result. The other three move on with their lives, two moving to America and one prospering in the new Chinese economy. The mystery of who poisoned their friend remains: Was it one of the three friends?

- *Red Scarf Girl: A Memoir of the Cultural Revolution* (1998) is the autobiography of Ji-Li Jiang, who was a teenager during Mao's Cultural Revolution. She tells her firsthand account of the atrocities committed in the name of the Communist Party. People she considered friends turn on her and her family, and they are imprisoned. Eventually, she emigrates to the United States.

- In *The Joy Luck Club* (1989), author Amy Tan tells the story of four mothers and their daughters, Chinese immigrants living in San Francisco, who meet each week to play mah-jongg. Each character takes a turn telling her story.

---

was born a boy. The word *yang* refers to the masculine half of the yin-yang symbol. The name given to him by the opera school, however, is Sumeng, which means "a serene and pure dreamer." Sasha says it sounds like "a weepy name from a romance novel." In other words, it is a feminine name, given to him by the school that wants him to portray women's roles. Naming a child is what Butler and another critic, John Searle, would term a "speech act." The act of naming something or someone affects the perception of that something or someone. Yang became Sumeng, became feminine; the name was one more part of his transformation.

However, now that Sumeng is no longer in the opera school, he is Yang, and he is exploring new roles. Still delicate and feminine, Yang nevertheless performs the ultimate act of masculinity: he impregnates a woman. Though Sasha initially takes the man's traditional role in the relationship ("She made decisions for them both, and he let her"), in the end, it is Yang who initiates the sexual act that conceives the child. It is Yang's idea to not use condoms, giving Sasha a line that, like much of Yang's dialogue, sounds like a quotation from a play or poem. He tells her that condoms are for "people who [touch] without loving each other." Later, when Yang objects to the idea of coming to America with Sasha and being "kept" by her, he spouts another line that sounds borrowed from a book or a movie: "Nothing humiliates a man more than living as a parasite on his woman." Given Yang's limited experience with women, this bit of philosophy must certainly come from someone else. As he has for his entire life, Yang is playing a role—the role of a masculine seducer, romancing Sasha with talk of love and then avoiding further commitment afterward.

Butler's theory is that there is no fixed self who performs the expectations of gender; rather, the self constantly shifts in response to the performance. With Yang's life being entirely focused on performance, a life spent for the stage, his "self" is pieced together from scripts and songs. His constant quoting of lyrics and philosophers may make him sound artificial, but we all are quoting, in our own way, the other characters in our lives: our mothers, fathers, siblings, friends, favorite books, the dialogue we are surrounded by day in and day out. Yang has been surrounded every day by songs, actors, and plays, and so he expresses himself using this language.

While Yang's performances are more overt, Sasha, too, is taking on a new role. Sasha wants to reinvent her life, to play the role of an American, yet she is as unfamiliar with the realty of that role as Yang is with seducing a woman. Just as Yang's perception of seduction seems to come from a movie or novel, Sasha's idea of what it means to be American comes from watching Julia Roberts in *Pretty Woman* (a movie in which a prostitute is whisked away into a glamorous life with a loving partner) and from observing people at a parade. The one place in America she has more experience with—Nebraska—does not fit into her ideal. As she watches the parade in Chicago, she is "saddened by memories of Nebraska and Inner Mongolia, the night skies of both places black with lonely, lifeless stars." To Sasha, America is bright lights, prosperity, and opportunity, not farms and cornfields. But most prostitutes do not become princesses, just as most gloves do not have four fingers, as Sasha points out to Boshen when Mickey Mouse passes by in the parade. The reality does not always fit the ideal.

Sasha imagines stapling the pages of her Chinese life together until they cannot be opened. Later in the story, she tells Yang that

if he comes with her to America, they can be "the prince and princess of Nebraska." When Yang tells her he was not trained to play the role of a prince, Sasha answers, "The script is changed . . . from today on." Her future life in America spreads out before her, a fresh new script, her own version of *Pretty Woman*. However, given her description of Nebraska's lifeless stars just a few months later, it seems that Sasha has discovered there are no princes or princesses in Nebraska. As Yang says, "Every place is a good place. Only time goes wrong."

Just as we perform gender without realizing it, we perform ideology and nationality as well. As Americans we take as a given that individuality is important and that the rights of the individual should not be sacrificed for the collective good. But this is a part of American ideology. In Communist philosophy, the collective good is the most important thing. As Americans, we look upon this as a flawed or unnatural viewpoint, in the same way people in 1950 would have looked upon a man who stayed home with his children and kept house while his wife went to work. But like gender roles, ideologies are challenged when they become oppressive or when change forces us to reexamine them. Revolutions can change ideologies.

Yang is the catalyst that causes Sasha and Boshen to veer from their usual course, to reexamine their personal ideologies. Sasha decides that this is Yang's value: "He made people fall in love with him, and the love led them astray, willingly, from their otherwise tedious paths." From his cameo performance as Sasha and Boshen's lover, he has created a child and given Sasha someone to help her care for it. Their lives will never be the same.

Source: Laura B. Pryor, Critical Essay on "The Princess of Nebraska," in *Short Stories for Students*, Gale, Cengage Learning, 2016.

Yiyun Li

In the following essay, Li explains how decreasing her time spent with technology increased her connection with literature.

A little over a year ago I disconnected myself from the internet, a technology-unfriendly decision for someone whose husband works in the IT industry. The reason for this decision: as a mother of two young children who teaches full-time and writes books, I don't have much time

Boshen tries to convince Sasha to keep the baby so that they can create a family and tempt Yang to join them. (© Rommel Canlas / ShutterStock.com)

left for reading. I decided to give up web-surfing to stay a better, calmer bookworm.

I couldn't possibly be entirely internet-free, but I started by limiting my connection time to 30 minutes a day, reducing it two weeks later to 15 minutes. And those precious minutes included all the business emails with agents, editors and publishers.

At the beginning it required much discipline. There were the Facebook friends who beckoned me with their updates; there were the Twitterings that had functioned as the soundtrack of my days; there were various websites, relevant or not so much, which somehow I had led myself to believe to be essential for my daily maintenance. Above all, there was the habit of mindlessly opening a website, looking for something that was not there, and, unfulfilled, looking elsewhere, one page after another.

Research has been done on how the internet affects us, but because I don't use the internet much now, I can't google those experts' opinions and reproduce their wisdom here. What I can report is how being disconnected has changed the pattern of my day and my life. Take my morning: I used to turn on the computer when I got up; with two children to get ready for school, what else could one squeeze into the craze of breakfast-cooking, lunch-packing, tooth-brushing, homework-hunting, but a few minutes of surfing the internet over a becalming cup of coffee? How happily surprised I was when I was proved wrong. The five or seven minutes spent reading some publishing gossip or an acquaintance's acquaintance retweeting a joke turned out to be just the right amount of time for a chapter of *War and Peace* or an intense battle in the *Iliad*.

Since my disconnection, I have reacquainted myself—and in some cases have gone from being a mere acquaintance to a close friend—with those too outdated to catch up with the trend for twittering or facebooking: Homer, Montaigne, Shakespeare, Tolstoy, Dostoevsky, Turgenev, Dickens, George Eliot, Elizabeth Bowen, Elizabeth Bishop—the list goes on. I am aware that my attachment to these new friends is one-sided and unrequited: they neither know nor care about my existence. On the other hand, they are much more interesting to listen to, and fun to argue with. As my afternoon friend, Montaigne—I call him that because I read him

mostly after 4pm for half an hour before I pick up my children from school, the same half-hour I used to fritter away on the internet—said of reading the ancients:

> I am pleased at this, that my opinions have the honour of often coinciding with theirs, and that at least I go the same way, though far behind them, saying, "How true!" Also . . . that I know the vast difference between them and me. And nonetheless I let my thoughts run on, weak and lowly as they are, as I have produced them, without plastering and sewing up the flaws that this comparison has revealed to me.

When I first read these words I wanted to agree loudly with Montaigne. It's the same pleasure for me to discover this or that thought of my own, no bigger than a tiny drop of water, in the vast ocean of Tolstoy's thinking; the same pleasure to eavesdrop, next to Turgenev on a summer night, a group of young boys speaking of death and fate. Even better is when you can disagree with a great mind, which I have often done, too, with some secret and unabashed joy, as in the case of my yelling at Iris Murdoch or shaking my head at Graham Greene.

There is a downside of staying disconnected— I have accumulated too many emails, unread and unreturned; I have neglected people from time to time. I have relaxed my schedule a little, though if the internet functioned before as an addictive distraction, I now have the opposite problem: more than ever, I am addicted to reading, and the moment I have to get on to the internet I become impatient. But these symptoms, at least in my case, are happily relished.

Source: Yiyun Li, "My Afternoons with Montaigne," in *New Statesman*, December 20, 2011, p. 81.

Clarissa Sebag-Montefiore and Yiyun Li

In the following interview, Li talks about the influence that her youth in China had on her writing.

Your mother tongue is Chinese, but you write in English. Why is that?

I've never written in Chinese and I don't write in Chinese now. I was going to become a scientist, so the possibility of writing fiction in Chinese just never occurred to me. When I first started writing, it was in English—so, very naturally, English became my first language in writing.

Your debut novel, The Vagrants *(2009), explores the brutality of the Cultural Revolution. Are your books banned in China?*

I don't think they are banned. It's interesting to be in America and to see all these Chinese writers saying their books are banned. To me, that's ridiculous. Calling your book banned in China will make the book appealing to some [readers] in the west. But actually a lot of books are banned—*Harry Potter* was banned, too, in certain places.

The Vagrants *begins with the execution of a young female "counter-revolutionary." Was this episode inspired by real life?*

[As a child] I didn't actually see an execution, but I did witness the denouncing ceremony beforehand. People would gather together to catch the last moments of the criminal before the execution. They were always very festive. I don't think guilt was something that would enter into people's emotions at those moments.

When you were growing up, your grandfather called Mao Zedong the "king of hell." Was that dangerous for the family?

In retrospect, I think it was a little risky to have him around. But as a child I didn't understand that; I just admired his outspokenness. There was nothing really unusual about him— he was just not as cautious as many. That stayed with me.

Did he influence your writing?

Temperament-wise, I am very far from him—the way I write is the opposite to how he talked. He was loud and straightforward, which is certainly not the way my writing is. But he would tell stories: folk tales, or stories he had read in books, or news stories. He didn't differentiate his storytelling, he just told anything that interested him to entertain himself. He did not censor himself in any way.

You were in high school in 1989 when the Tiananmen Square massacre happened. Can you remember anything about that day?

My parents locked me in my bedroom at home, so I did not see or hear anything. It was obvious what was going to happen, so they were just protecting us. My mother went into the street and saw lots of people running around.

How things were reviewed was what was interesting for me. Everybody was relying on somebody else for information and news. People would say, "That person got shot, and this person died," and you wouldn't be able to see that on the official news.

Were you surprised that there were no reports of the massacre in the Chinese media?

Nobody—not even teenagers—accepted that willingly, but you just had to make do.

Why did you compare Tiananmen to the 11 September 2001 attacks?

What I meant is that everybody has a story about it. Like 9/11, it was a historical event— and if something really important happens in history, everyone has a version.

*Your new book—*Gold Boy, Emerald Girl— *is a collection of short stories. You clearly think the short form is still commercially viable.*

The publishing world would argue that short stories are less important than novels, or don't sell as well. I don't ever participate in that conversation, because I love writing stories, I love reading stories, and I know that other people do, too. That conversation is driven by profit, not by the pursuit of art.

And the characters in the stories are all ordinary, flawed people.

Heroism is not interesting to me. It's just a simplified way of looking at life, which is not what fiction is about.

People often ask me why I write sad stories, and why I don't write about happy people. Those things just don't concern me. As a writer, you strip surfaces away and explore what is the real story, what [characters] are really feeling, who they really are. I want to cut open the situation and cut open the characters and see through them.

Source: Clarissa Sebag-Montefiore and Yiyun Li, "The Books Interview: Yiyun Li," in *New Statesman*, November 1, 2010, p. 41.

Vivian Chen and Yiyun Li

In the following interview, Li discusses some of the purposes behind her writing.

After growing up in Beijing, Yiyun Li left China in 1996 in order to study medicine at the University of Iowa. Four years later, Li determined that instead of pursuing a career in science, she wanted to become a writer. She shifted gears and earned an M.F.A. from the Iowa Writers' Workshop and an M.F.A. in creative nonfiction writing from the University of Iowa.

> POLITICS DO ENTER MY WORK, BECAUSE ESPECIALLY IF YOU'RE WRITING ABOUT CHINA IN THE PAST CENTURY, THERE'S NO WAY YOU CAN RUN AWAY FROM POLITICS. IT'S A VERY POLITICAL COUNTRY, IT'S NEVER BEEN UNPOLITICAL."

Her stories and essays were soon published in such well-respected venues as the *New Yorker*, the *Paris Review*, *Zoetrope: All-Story*, *Ploughshares*, the *Gettysburg Review*, *Glimmer Train*, and *Prospect*. In 2006, a volume of ten short stories, *A Thousand Years of Good Prayers*, was published by Random House to much acclaim. Her work has brought her a prodigious number of prestigious grants and prizes, including a grant from the Lannan Foundation, the Frank O'Connor International Short Story Award, the Whiting Writers' Award, the Guardian First Book Award, the California Book Award for First Fiction, the Plimpton Prize from the *Paris Review*, a Pushcart Prize, and the PEN/Hemingway Award. Li's book was also shortlisted for the Kiriyama Prize and the Orange Prize. Despite strong evidence that her talents are clearly exceptional, if not phenomenal, Yiyun Li has experienced difficulties in being approved for permanent residency by the U.S. Citizenship and Immigration Services as an applicant with "exceptional ability." She currently teaches in the M.F.A. program at Mills College and lives in Oakland, California, with her husband and two children. Li is at work on a novel, due to be completed in 2008.

Very informally, and with much laughter, this interview took place in the winter of 2007.

VC: Is there a question that you wish you had been asked in an interview that you haven't yet been asked?

YL: That's a clever question! I wish people would ask me about the importance of the imagination. I really believe that one should be able to imagine being somebody else. This is important for writers, but it's also important for readers, and for all human beings to be able to imagine being somebody else.

VC: Who do you consider your literary influences and why?

YL: I always love to talk about William Trevor. He's my biggest influence because he imagines the world; he has a very compassionate imagination, which is very rare. I remember in an interview, and when I met him, he said he likes to write about women because he doesn't know what it is like to be a woman. How beautiful that is because that's a real understanding of human nature—to be able to imagine what it's like to be a seventeen-year-old maid in a big mansion.

He doesn't carry a message in his writing, he's an observer, and I like that because I know so many writers who are not observers but who have an agenda. He doesn't have an agenda, he's just very curious about human beings. I share that curiosity and I share his interest in the mysteries of human nature. That's exactly why I write fiction—because you can't always understand human nature. He says that by nature he's very pessimistic, but that writing is a very optimistic thing. [We spin off into an extended discussion of William Trevor.]

VC: Let's switch tracks here. For whom do you write?

YL: I never know how to answer that question. At different times I answer that differently . . .

VC: If you were to imagine someone, who would you imagine?

YL: I would imagine someone who loves William Trevor. [laughs] I also imagine people who are curious about everything.

VC: People who are not so much curious about what life is like in China, but curious about what it is to be human? But I don't think your work is about what it means to be human in a universal sense, but what it is to be human in a specific context.

YL: Right, my characters just happen to be Chinese because I know Chinese people better. Also, the situations are very Chinese, and there's no running away from that, there's no denying that.

VC: In a way your imagination is grounded in what you know, as a starting point—

YL: I could write about American situations. Someone I knew told me the story of two older people falling in love. [Explains story at length.] This story could happen anywhere. There's something really interesting about older people. So I could write this story, and it could be set anywhere. On the other hand, I still have so many Chinese stories to tell.

VC: An Asian American literary critic, David Palumbo-Liu, has claimed that many works of fiction produced by Asian American writers include themes and characters that we can read as "depoliticized narratives of self-healing"—in other words, they tend to ignore politics or resist political grounding and instead focus on the personal, as if the personal were completely separate from the political. So there's a character who believes that her problem is this: My mother is Chinese and traditional and therefore she's less than me, but I'm American, and modern and superior, and this is what constitutes our conflict, period. How might you or your work respond to this charge?

YL: What you just described, this conflict, is a simplified version of life, and it doesn't work in fiction to simplify life—it doesn't work.

VC: Your purpose in writing fiction is not to simplify, but to look at the complexities, and if you removed politics, then it wouldn't be complex. So, do you feel that politics enter your work?

YL: Politics do enter my work, because especially if you're writing about China in the past century, there's no way you can run away from politics. It's a very political country, it's never been unpolitical. I remember this beautiful quote from Bernard Malamud—he grew up in New York, he never had direct involvement in the Holocaust, but he wrote a beautiful novel that is often read as an allegory of the Holocaust—probably there were criticisms that he didn't know anything about it—but he said that as a writer, you cannot turn your eye away from history or politics. I'm not going to turn away from politics, but I'm not going to use politics as something that I could cash in on.

VC: Do you believe your work engages with an Orientalist, invented, or imaginary notion of China? Do you think your work encounters or has any relationships to ideas that consider China exotic, foreign, or beyond the understanding of a person who is unfamiliar with China? Say there's a reader who sees your book and sees that it's written by a writer who's Chinese and thinks, "Oh, when I finish reading this book I'll know all about China, such a mysterious, exotic place."

YL: In the ideal world, I don't want to deal with that, [laughter] because I'm not writing for that reader, but realistically, you have no control, you have many readers. I'm very aware that many readers may read this way. When I've given readings, people have come up to me to say something like, "Oh I love your story so much because I can see how these poor women suffer." As a writer you really can't control how someone reads your work.

VC: How do you respond to that? Do you just say thank you or—

YL: I just say thank you. Once the book is done, I separate the book from myself.

VC: I really like your work because it avoids that attitude of let's slam China and say that China is a terrible place that has all this terrible history. So I would be less generous with certain kinds of readers.

YL: As a fiction writer I just accept people, my readers, as they are. I don't want to change anything, or change my readers . . .

VC: But you do want them to imagine more!

YL: I do, but I'm very pessimistic, I'm not hoping for better. The writer Lu Xun is interesting because he believes that literature is a way of changing the world, to make it a better world, and that's very heroic and admirable, but I don't share that.

VC: That seems to be contradictory! [laughter] Maybe you don't want to have an agenda, to be dogmatic, to be a dictatorial kind of writer.

YL: I did an interview in Chinese, and the interviewer kept asking me, "How do you think people react to your work, because ideologically, your work represents China?" But for me, I'm a little person, and writing is very private. It has nothing to do with ideology.

VC: And yet . . .

YL: And yet, as a writer, you just accept anything and everything from life.

VC: So let's talk a little about your stories. It seems that sexuality has a connection to the unclean. In "Immortality" there's the euphemism for castration, and in "Love in the Marketplace," there's something about how a character should keep herself "clean" for her husband. Does this connection seem important to you?

YL: These characters are probably more conscious of this than I am!

VC: So you really want to be like a blank slate, an empty vessel for your characters, and to try to take your own being out of your writing.

YL. That's the goal of my writing . . .

VC: So these characters who are living in China have an idea about sex being unclean, and this is part of their world, and it makes sense in that world.

YL: Right. That's how they would think about it. If you have sex before you're married then you're not keeping yourself clean or pure for your husband.

VC: So can we generalize and say that Chinese people have this sense that sex is unclean, would that be fair or not?

YL: I probably would not want to generalize. [laughter] It depends on which character or which person we're talking about.

VC: How has America entered your imagination, when you were living in China, and once you settled here?

YL: When I was in China, America seemed like a solution to many problems. Of course I was very naïve. It wasn't America that I was so much imagining. You know how a young person believes, college is the solution to all of my worries, or after college all my juvenile worries and pain will be gone, I will become independent? America was like that in a way, it was like adulthood, a future. But once I settled here, well, America is just another place.

VC: How does America enter the lives and imaginations of your characters?

YL: A lot of my characters do live in China, and America represents something, not only a future, because they can't go to America, so it's just something different. There are possibilities—like in "Love in the Marketplace" a husband disappeared, vanished in America! For some of my characters America is in their imagination as the present and as something different.

VC: Not better, just different . . .

YL: For instance, the boy, Yang, in "The Princess of Nebraska," he's such an egotistic person, but he recognizes that America is not a fairy tale, and he criticizes American—he says that the Julia Roberts movie *Pretty Woman* is only a fairy tale, an American fairy tale—and he didn't buy it. But it really varies from character to character. And I hope my characters don't represent me.

VC: And it's not a generalizable thing?

YL: Right.

VC: My last, my second to last question is, what are you reading now? I saw on your desk . . .

YL: Nabokov's book of lectures on literature. I'm also reading Graham Greene—he's a fabulous writer.

VC: Your work has been translated into film by Wayne Wang—he made two films of your work. What kind of an experience was it to see your characters on screen?

YL: It was very interesting. With *One Thousand Years* I wrote the screenplay, so I knew the story really well, and I knew what I wanted, and it was just amazing to see these characters from my imagination. "The Princess of Nebraska" takes place about ten years ago in Chicago, and Wang moved it to San Francisco today. I was actually very happy with it. I feel less attached to the work, and I loved the recreation of it, its not being completely loyal to the original story. . . .

Source: Vivian Chen and Yiyun Li, "'I Still Have So Many Chinese Stories to Tell': An Interview with Yiyun Li," in *China*, Vol. 47, No. 2, Spring 2008.

Alan Cheuse

In the following review, Cheuse calls "The Princess of Nebraska" the "best and most memorable fiction" in the collection.

Chinese emigre (and current Oakland, California, resident) Yiyun Li has just published her first book of stories, called *A Thousand Years of Good Prayers*. Several of these fine stories—there are ten in all—stay exclusively in China, treating us to dramas about homicidal peasants in the countryside; comedy about Mao impersonators in the big city; and bittersweet depictions of marriage under the reign of Mao and after. But however interesting the depiction of life in China, the best and most memorable fiction in this outstanding first book merges the worlds of modern China and the United States. The central characters in the story titled "The Princess of Nebraska," for example, dramatically straddle both worlds. Twenty-one-year-old Sasha, born and raised in Inner Mongolia and a recently arrived graduate student in Nebraska, has studied in Beijing. There she had a brief affair with a promiscuous eighteen-year-old male former opera star, the mad passion of their mutual pal Boshen. As the story opens, we find both Sasha and Boshen in the United States, in Chicago, where Sasha has an appointment at a Planned Parenthood clinic. She's determined to abort the fetus conceived during her brief affair with the beautiful male opera star. "Now it will be over soon." she says to Boshen. "She looked forward to the moment when she was ready to move on. 'Moving on' was a phrase she had just learned, an American concept that suited her well. It was such a wonderful phrase that Sasha could almost see herself stapling her Chinese life, one staple after another around the pages until they became one solid block that nobody would be able to open and read. She would have a fresh page then, for her American life." Her creator, Yiyun Li, couldn't have created fresher pages than those in this wonderful collection.

Source: Alan Cheuse, Review of *A Thousand Years of Good Prayers*, in *World Literature Today*, July–August 2006, pp. 35–36.

SOURCES

Ahmed, Fatema, "*A Thousand Years of Good Prayers*: Double Agent," in *New York Times*, October 21, 2005, http://www.nytimes.com/2005/10/23/books/review/23 ahmed.html?pagewanted=print&_r=0 (accessed March 1, 2015).

Cheuse, Alan, "Modernity Can Be Hard to Swallow," in *San Francisco Chronicle*, September 18, 2005, http:// www.sfgate.com/books/article/Modernity-can-be-hard-to-swallow-2607472.php (accessed March 1, 2015).

"HIV and AIDS in China," Avert website, http://www. avert.org/hiv-aids-china.htm (accessed March 1, 2015).

"Introduction to the Cultural Revolution," in *SPICE Digest*, Fall 2007, http://iis-db.stanford.edu/docs/115/ CRintro.pdf (accessed March 1, 2015).

Li, Yiyun, "The Princess of Nebraska," in *A Thousand Years of Good Prayers*, Random House, 2005, pp. 68–91.

Magnier, Mark, Lingling Wei, and Ian Talley, "China Economic Growth Is Slowest in Decades," in *Wall Street Journal*, January 19, 2015, http://www.wsj.com/articles/ china-gdp-growth-is-slowest-in-24-years-1421719453 (accessed March 1, 2015).

Martin, Michel, "MacArthur Fellow Pens Stories of Struggle," National Public Radio website, October 13, 2010, http://www.npr.org/templates/story/story.php?story Id=130538242 (accessed March 1, 2015).

Park, Madison, "China Eases One-Child Policy, Ends Re-education Through Labor Camps," CNN website,

December 28, 2013, http://www.cnn.com/2013/12/28/ world/asia/china-one-child-policy-official/ (accessed March 1, 2015).

Review of *A Thousand Years of Good Prayers*, in *Kirkus Reviews*, September 27, 2005, https://www.kirkusre views.com/book-reviews/yiyun-li/a-thousand-years-of-good-prayers/ (accessed March 1, 2015).

Review of *A Thousand Years of Good Prayers*, in *Publishers Weekly*, September 2005, http://www.publishersweekly .com/978-1-4000-6312-3 (accessed March 1, 2015).

Schroeder, Katharine, "Jackie's Story," Jackie's Kids Corner, 2002, http://www.jackiechankids.com/files/ Jackie_Bio.htm (accessed March 1, 2015).

"Tiananmen Square Fast Facts," CNN website, June 3, 2014, http://www.cnn.com/2013/09/15/world/asia/tianan men-square-fast-facts/ (accessed March 1, 2015)

Welch, Rodney, "Cultural Revolutions," in *Washington Post*, November 27, 2005, http://www.washingtonpost. com/wp-dyn/content/article/2005/11/23/AR2005112302 098.html (accessed March 1, 2015).

Zixuan, Zhang, "Male Parts, Female Roles," in *China Daily*, October 26, 2011, http://usa.chinadaily.com.cn/ china/2011-10/26/content_13977852.htm (accessed March 1, 2015).

FURTHER READING

Chan, Jackie, *I Am Jackie Chan: My Life in Action*, Ballantine Books, 1998.

Martial arts star and actor Jackie Chan tells his life story, including the ten years he spent at the China Drama Academy, a Peking Opera school. After leaving the school, Chan worked as a stunt man before becoming a popular actor, and he shares with readers a long catalog of the dozens of injuries he sustained in his career.

Chengbei, Xu, *Peking Opera*, Cambridge University Press, 2012.

Part of the Cambridge University Press's Introductions to Chinese Culture series, this overview of Peking Opera describes both the origins of the tradition and the modern-day incarnation of the opera. Illustrations of the traditional costumes, makeup, and staging are included.

Mitter, Rana, *Modern China: A Very Short Introduction*, Oxford University Press, 2008.

Part of Oxford's Very Short Introduction series, this slim, 144-page volume provides an excellent overview of the forces that have shaped contemporary China, including its leaders, controversies, and current economy.

Osnos, Evan, *Age of Ambition: Chasing Fortune, Truth and Faith in the New China*, Farrar, Straus and Giroux, 2014.

> Osnos, the Beijing correspondent for the *New Yorker*, gives a vivid and colorful description of life, society, and politics in contemporary China. He paints a portrait of a country in contradiction: the individual continues to gain more importance, but the Communist Party continues to clamp down on self-expression. The book won the National Book Award for nonfiction in 2014.

Spence, Jonathan, *Mao Zedong: A Life*, Penguin Books, 2006.

> Spence's biography tells how Chairman Mao rose from humble beginnings in rural China to become the leader of the Chinese Communist Party. Spence takes a thorough look at Mao's early years, spending less time on the latter part of his life and career. At less than two hundred pages, the book provides a good, readable introduction to Mao's life.

SUGGESTED SEARCH TERMS

Yiyun Li

The Princess of Nebraska AND Li

A Thousand Years of Good Prayers

Peking Opera

Nan Dan AND Peking Opera

Peking Opera schools

Mao Zedong

Yiyun Li AND Mao Zedong

Mao Zedong AND Cultural Revolution

Rappaccini's Daughter

NATHANIEL HAWTHORNE

1844

"Rappaccini's Daughter," a short story written by American author Nathaniel Hawthorne, first appeared in the *United States Magazine* and *Democratic Review* in December 1844. Its first book publication was in 1846 as part of Hawthorne's collection of stories and sketches *Mosses from an Old Manse*—a title derived from "Old Manse," the name of the home in Concord, Massachusetts, where Hawthorne lived from 1842 to 1845. (*Manse* can refer generally to a stately residence or more specifically to a Protestant cleric's current or former residence.) "Rappaccini's Daughter" tells the story of Beatrice Rappaccini, the daughter of a mad physician and medical researcher in Renaissance Italy, who cultivates and nurtures her father's garden of poisonous plants. In the process she becomes resistant to the poisons but poisonous to others, including a young medical student who is drawn to her mysterious beauty. The story is in many ways typical of Hawthorne's work because of its ominous, allegorical atmosphere and themes: in many of his novels and short stories, Hawthorne creates allegories of the dark, irredeemable human condition, a point of view most likely traceable to his New England Puritan roots.

Hawthorne, who remains best known for his classic 1850 novel *The Scarlet Letter*, was a major figure in the American romantic movement and is often regarded as a writer in the tradition of "dark romanticism." This is a subgenre of

American novelist Nathaniel Hawthorne
(© Everett Historical / ShutterStock.com)

romantic literature that includes, among other elements, social outcasts; the belief that the world is a place of darkness and mystery; and the conviction that humans are sinful, if not evil. At the extreme, the dark romantics, among them Edgar Allan Poe, Mary Shelley, and Herman Melville, feature in their works vampires, ghouls, and manifestations of Satan. "Rappaccini's Daughter," with its satanic garden, its isolated heroine, its mad scientist, and its atmosphere of poison and death, is consistent with the tradition of dark romanticism. "Rappaccini's Daughter" is widely available in anthologies of nineteenth-century American literature and collections of Hawthorne's short stories, including *Nathaniel Hawthorne: Tales and Sketches*, published by the Library of America in 1982.

AUTHOR BIOGRAPHY

Hawthorne was born on July 4, 1804, in Salem, Massachusetts, the second of three children of Nathaniel and Elizabeth Manning Hathorne; Hawthorne added the *w* to his name sometime after 1830 as a way of distancing himself from relatives he found embarrassing. His father,

a sea captain, died in 1808, leaving the family in poverty. He was raised in Salem and in Raymond, Maine, before attending Bowdoin College in Maine from 1821 to 1825, where, according to his own description, he was an idle student. After graduation, he returned to Salem to live with his mother and sister and tried to launch a writing career. One of his earliest efforts was an 1828 novel, *Fanshawe*, which he later considered a failure, so much so that he tried to collect and burn all copies of the book—and received help from a warehouse fire that destroyed the book's remaining unsold copies. He had more success with short stories, several of which were published in literary journals during these years, and his first collection of short stories, *Twice-Told Tales*, was published in 1837. He worked at the Boston Custom House from 1839 to 1841, and in 1841 he lived at (and was a founding member of) Brook Farm in Massachusetts, an experimental utopian community founded that year. By the early 1840s his income from writing was ample enough that he could marry Sophia Peabody in 1842. After his marriage, the couple moved into a house called Old Manse in Concord, Massachusetts, giving rise to the title of his 1846 collection, *Mosses from an Old Manse*, which includes "Rappaccini's Daughter." Sophia, a painter, illustrator, and writer, studied and spoke Italian and collaborated with her husband on names for characters in the story.

Hawthorne was connected with the American transcendentalist movement and counted among his friends such figures as Ralph Waldo Emerson, Henry David Thoreau, Bronson Alcott, and others, some of whom were his neighbors in Concord. (Transcendentalism was a cultural and literary reformist movement that rejected orthodoxy and conformity and urged its followers to find an original relationship with creation, often through the natural world.) Because of growing debts, he and his family moved back to Salem, where in 1846 he took a position as a custom house surveyor (an official charged with collecting taxes on imported and exported goods). He lost this job in 1849, but in 1850 he published his major novel, *The Scarlet Letter*, bringing him some measure of fame and financial security. He followed this novel with *The House of the Seven Gables* in 1851, *The Blithedale Romance* in 1852 (a novel based on his disillusionment with Brook Farm), and *The Marble Faun* (1860), which shares an Italian setting with "Rappaccini's Daughter." Meanwhile, he produced dozens of short stories that are considered classics of American literature: "My Kinsman, Major Molineux," "Roger Malvin's Burial," the witchcraft story "Young Goodman Brown," "Ethan Brand," "The Minister's Black Veil," "The Birth-Mark," and many others. He also wrote literature for children, including *A Wonder Book for Girls and Boys* (1851) and its sequel, *Tanglewood Tales for Girls and Boys* (1853).

In 1853 Hawthorne was appointed to the position of American consul in Liverpool, England, by his old college friend and classmate, President Franklin Pierce. After the position was eliminated in 1857, he toured Italy before returning home. He died in his sleep of undetermined causes on May 19, 1864, in Plymouth, New Hampshire.

PLOT SUMMARY

The story begins with a brief tongue-in-cheek prologue in which Hawthorne claims that the story is a translation of one written by a Frenchman, Monsieur de'Aubépine; Aubépine is the French word for "hawthorn," referring to the medicinal plant.

As the story opens, Giovanni Guasconti arrives from Naples to begin his medical studies at the University of Padua. He takes an apartment on the upper floor of a mansion that at one time belonged to a family of nobles. Giovanni finds his chamber dreary, and he is uneasy about being away from home, occasioning a heavy sigh from him. His elderly housekeeper, Lisabetta, responds by suggesting that he look out the window at the sunshine. When he follows her advice, he sees a garden below. Lisabetta informs him that the garden belongs to the famous physician Giacomo Rappaccini, who grows plants out of which he makes medicines. As Giovanni observes the garden's various features, including a decayed marble fountain and a statue of Vertumnus, a tall, sickly looking man dressed in black appears. He examines the plants, but he avoids smelling or touching them without heavy gloves. When he examines a shrub with purple blossoms, he covers his mouth and nose with a mask.

The man summons his beautiful daughter, Beatrice, and tells her that if he approaches the shrub, it could cost him his life, so he consigns the plant to her sole care. Beatrice gladly accepts, speaking to the flower and calling it "sister." In exchange for her care, the plant is to allow Beatrice to inhale its fragrance without her having to wear a mask or gloves. Evening approaches, and Giovanni fancies that the woman and the garden are fraught with peril. In the morning, however, Giovanni is more buoyant and considers himself lucky to live in a room with a view of such beauty.

At the university, Giovanni presents a letter of introduction to Dr. Pietro Baglioni, a highly admired medical professor. Giovanni asks the professor whether he knows Rappaccini. Baglioni responds by saying that Rappaccini is widely respected for his skills, but he adds that he is troubled by the doctor's ethics: In Baglioni's view, Rappaccini is coldly scientific and regards his patients as experimental subjects rather than human beings. He also points out that Rappaccini, his bitter rival for medical preeminence in Italy, makes deadly poisons from his plants, which he distills into cures for illness, some of which he admits are effective. Baglioni makes clear that he regards Rappaccini's experiments as dangerous and unethical.

On his way back to the mansion, Giovanni buys a bouquet of flowers. When he arrives at his room, he goes to the window, where he sees Beatrice enter the garden and embrace the shrub with the purple flowers. After she picks one of the flowers, he notices a chameleon on the walkway near the shrub. A drop of moisture from the flower's broken stem falls on the chameleon, which promptly dies. The same fate befalls a winged insect that hovers near Beatrice, who has placed the flower in the collar of her dress. After Beatrice sees Giovanni at the window, he tosses the bouquet of flowers to her. As she hurries back into her house, Giovanni notices that the flowers are withering.

After the passage of several days, Giovanni encounters Baglioni on the street. As they chat, Rappaccini appears, but before moving on, he stares momentarily at Giovanni. Baglioni implies that Rappaccini's daughter is helping her father study Giovanni with a view to ensnaring him as a partner for her. Giovanni grows angry and stalks away. Baglioni decides that out of friendship for the young man's father, he will do what he can to thwart Rappaccini's plans.

MEDIA ADAPTATIONS

- An operatic version of "Rappaccini's Daughter" under the title *The Garden of Mystery*, written by Charles Wakefield Cadman and Nelle Richmond Eberhart, premiered at Carnegie Hall in New York City in 1925.

- NBC's *The Weird Circle* broadcast a radio play based on "Rappaccini's Daughter." The play can be accessed at the Internet Archive at http://ia600508.us.archive.org/6/items/Weird_Circle_otr/Weird_Circle_-_441126_-_52_-_Rapacinis_Daughter_-_32-22_25m09s_5897.mp3.

- In 1963, Vincent Price starred in the film *Twice-Told Tales*, which included "Rappaccini's Daughter" as one of its three segments. (Note, however, that the story was not part of Hawthorne's *Twice-Told Tales*.)

- PBS's *American Short Story* series produced "Rappaccini's Daughter," starring Kristoffer Tabori, Kathleen Beller, and Leonardo Cimino, in 1980. Running time is fifty-six minutes.

- In 1983, Margaret Garwood's operatic version of "Rappaccini's Daughter" premiered at the Pennsylvania Opera Theater.

- Yet another operatic version of "Rappaccini's Daughter" was created by Ellen S. Bender, with libretto by Robert Di Domenica. It was first performed as a New England Conservatory recital piece in 1992.

- In Mexico, *La hija de Rappaccini* by Daniel Catán, an opera based on a play by the same name written by Octavio Paz in 1956, premiered in 1994. Highlights are available from Naxos recordings as MP3 downloads.

- An audio version of "Rappaccini's Daughter" is included on *The Nathaniel Hawthorne Audio Collection* from Harper Audio, released in 2004. The story is narrated by James Naughton.

- In 2014, the 26th Annual Festival of New Musicals presented *Beautiful Poison* (music by Brendan Milburn, lyrics by Valerie Vagoda, book by Duane Poole). The story is set in steamy New Orleans, where a rock star singer is booked at a New Orleans nightclub. Upon arriving, he meets a beautiful, mysterious woman held captive by her father, Dr. Rappaccini, in a garden of unusual and exotic plants.

After Giovanni arrives at his rooms, Lisabetta shows him a secret door into the garden. Giovanni enters the garden and scrutinizes the plants, concluding that they look almost artificial. Beatrice enters, but she does not question him about his presence and denies having any special horticultural knowledge. As the two walk through the garden, Beatrice questions Giovanni about his home, his family, the city, and his friends, asking questions that suggest she has never been outside the garden. Giovanni reaches out his hand to pluck one of the purple flowers, but Beatrice seizes his hand and warns him that touching the flowers is fatal.

Returning to his room, Giovanni puts aside his suspicions about Beatrice, concluding that she is gentle and lovable. The following morning, however, he awakens with pain in his right hand where Beatrice gripped it. He sees a purple imprint of her fingers, but he fails to connect the marks with Beatrice. From then on, he frequents the garden, and although Beatrice comes out of her house to be with him, she keeps her distance; the two never touch or kiss.

Baglioni visits Giovanni and tells him a story about Porus, an Indian ruler who presented Alexander the Great with a beautiful woman whose breath was like a rich perfume and who had been nurtured on poisons. He observes that Beatrice is like the woman in the story. Although Giovanni pronounces the tale nonsense, his misgivings about Beatrice are reawakened. Baglioni insists that her father exploits her in his experiments and wants to do the same with Giovanni. Believing it may not be too late to save Beatrice, Baglioni gives Giovanni a silver phial containing what he claims is an antidote that can counteract the poison in her system. Giovanni is uncertain what to do: he regards Beatrice as normal, despite the evidence of his senses, but he worries that she is indeed poisonous. He decides to conduct an experiment of his own: He buys a bouquet of flowers, intending to give them to Beatrice, but after he gets back to his rooms, he notices that the flowers are beginning to die. He then breathes on a spider, which convulses and dies. Giovanni gathers that he has been imbued with Beatrice's poison.

Giovanni confronts Beatrice in the garden. When she explains that the purple flower sprang from the earth when she was born and that she has lived an isolated life, Giovanni accuses her of luring him into the garden and filling his veins with poison solely to relieve her own solitude, turning him into a loathsome, deadly creature. Giovanni conducts a demonstration, breathing on garden insects, which then fall dead. Beatrice denies having done anything to change Giovanni and blames her father. Giovanni, his anger subsiding, produces the phial that Baglioni gave him, and Beatrice drinks the liquid it contains. When Rappaccini enters the garden, his daughter turns on him and tells him that rather being a creature of science, feared by others, she would rather have been loved. Beatrice knows that she is dying (raising the question of whether Baglioni has perhaps murdered her to thwart Rappaccini), and with her last words she tells Giovanni that he too has poison in his nature. As she dies, Baglioni, who entered Giovanni's apartment, stands at the window and calls out what is in effect an accusation that Rappaccini has killed his own daughter through his experiments.

CHARACTERS

Dr. Pietro Baglioni

Baglioni is a prominent physician at the University of Padua, and as such he is a bitter rival to Rappaccini for medical preeminence in Italy. Giovanni's father is a friend of the professor, and it is to him that Giovanni reports with a letter of introduction when he arrives in Padua.

Baglioni informs Giovanni that Rappaccini distills medicinal poisons from plants, and he indicates that he regards Rappaccini's experiments as ethically suspect. He later gives Giovanni a phial that contains a potion that he says will counteract Beatrice's poison; it is an open question whether he was trying to help the son of his friend or rather trying to thwart his rival by murdering his daughter.

Giovanni Guasconti

Giovanni is a young student from southern Italy who comes to Padua to study medicine. He takes an apartment in an old mansion that looks out over the garden kept by Dr. Rappaccini and his daughter, Beatrice. From his window, he sees Beatrice, and eventually he falls in love with her—or at least grows infatuated by her beauty and mysterious allure. He becomes suspicious, however, because he sees phenomena he cannot explain that suggest that Beatrice is in some manner deadly. Ultimately, he confronts her with the suspicion that she has infected him with the same deadly poison that fills her veins. Looking for a way to counteract the poison, he gives her a phial of liquid that Baglioni supplied as an antidote. Throughout, Giovanni is depicted as somewhat naive and immature, and he vacillates in his feelings for Beatrice.

Lisabetta

Lisabetta is the aged housekeeper in the mansion in which Giovanni rents an apartment. She conducts Giovanni through corridors that lead to a secret entrance to Rappaccini's garden.

Beatrice Rappaccini

Throughout her life, Beatrice has been exposed to the poisons in the plants and flowers that her father cultivates in his garden as part of his medical experiments. Although she has become poisonous, like the plants and flowers, she herself is immune to the poison. Her life is one of complete isolation until Giovanni moves into the apartment overlooking the garden and the two become acquainted and seem to fall in love. As Beatrice comes to understand what has happened to her, she turns against her father, telling him that she would rather have been loved than feared. She drinks a phial of liquid that Giovanni gives her in an effort to counteract the poison in her system, resulting in her death. Throughout, the narration makes clear that while Beatrice's body is corrupted by poison, her soul is pure and innocent. Ironically, the name Beatrice derives from the Latin for "she who brings happiness."

Dr. Giacomo Rappaccini
Rappaccini is a renowned physician at the University of Padua. In a garden attached to his house, he cultivates poisonous plants with the assistance of his daughter, Beatrice. He tries to extract medicinal cures from the poisons, but in the process of conducting his experiments, he has allowed his daughter to become poisonous. By keeping her isolated in the garden and house, he protects her from the outside world. Rappaccini can be thought of as an example of the "mad scientist" theme in literature—as one who explores the mysteries of science without regard to the effects of his experiments on others.

THEMES

Corruption
A central theme in "Rappaccini's Daughter" is corruption, although Hawthorne's treatment of the theme is ambiguous and subject to differing interpretations. Generally, it is thought that Hawthorne, in what is perhaps a reflection of his Puritan New England roots, uses the story to explore the notion of the corruption and sinfulness of humanity after the Fall of Adam and Eve in the Garden of Eden. The theme first emerges when Giovanni, observing the garden for the first time, notices that some of the plants "crept serpent-like along the ground," suggesting the serpent in the Garden of Eden. When Dr. Rappaccini appears in the garden, the narration states that "the man's demeanor was that of one walking among malignant influences, such as savage beasts, or deadly snakes, or evil spirits, which, should he allow them one moment of license, would wreak upon him some terrible fatality." According to one reading of the story, Rappaccini's soul is corrupt because he is guilty of the cardinal sin of pride: he defies God and nature to boost his reputation through medical experimentation that transforms his garden into a corrupt Eden. In the process, he corrupts his own body, which has become frail and sickly, and he corrupts his own innocent daughter, turning her into a poisonous "sister" to the lethal flowers in the garden. He may very well have corrupted even Lisabetta, using her as an agent to lure Giovanni

into the garden so that Beatrice can charm him and in this way entangle the young man in his schemes.

When she shows him the secret door to the garden, Giovanni has this thought: "This interposition of old Lisabetta might perchance be connected with the intrigue, whatever were its nature, in which the Professor [Baglioni] seemed to suppose that Doctor Rappaccini was involving him [Giovanni]." Despite his suspicions, Giovanni frequents the garden, forms a relationship with Beatrice, and in time absorbs the poisons that corrupt his body. Angry, he accuses Beatrice of corrupting him: "Thou hast filled my veins with poison! Thou hast made me as hateful, as ugly, as loathsome and deadly a creature as thyself,—a world's wonder of hideous monstrosity! Now—if our breath be happily as fatal to ourselves as to all others—let us join our lips in one kiss of unutterable hatred, and so die!"

The theme of corruption may extend to Professor Baglioni. He provides Giovanni with a phial of liquid that he claims is an antidote that will restore Beatrice to a normal state, but when she drinks it, she dies. One reading of the story is that his purpose is to protect Giovanni, the son of a friend, and that her death is the result of a fatal war in her system between poison and the antidote. An alternate reading is to see his actions as flowing from his bitter animosity toward Rappaccini. In this interpretation, he acts out of professional jealousy and ambition. Rappaccini and Baglioni despise each other, and it may be the case that to thwart Rappaccini, Baglioni deliberately poisons Beatrice; at one point he says to himself: "This daughter of his! It shall be looked to. Perchance, most learned Rappaccini, I may foil you where you little dream of it!" Thus, Baglioni has been corrupted by his own professional jealousy.

Ethics
Dr. Rappaccini is often thought of as an example of the "mad scientist" whose ethics are suspect in his quest to push back the boundaries of knowledge. This theme is voiced most prominently by Rappaccini's professional rival, Professor Baglioni, who says to Giovanni:

> But as for Rappaccini, it is said of him—and I, who know the man well, can answer for its truth—that he cares infinitely more for science than for mankind. His patients are interesting

TOPICS FOR FURTHER STUDY

- Among the characters in Theodora Goss's *The Mad Scientist's Daughter* (2010) is Beatrice Rappaccini. Goss's story is available at the Strange Horizons website (http://www.strangehorizons.com/2010/20100118/daughter-f.shtml). Read the story, then write a brief essay in which you explain the role Beatrice plays in the development of Goss's themes.

- Cassandra Rose Clarke is the author of a young-adult novel also titled *The Mad Scientist's Daughter* (2013). Write a review of the novel reflecting the opinion you think Hawthorne might have held of it were he alive to read it.

- A recurring DC Comics character is a "femme fatale" named Poison Ivy. Poison Ivy first appeared in *Batman* #181 in June 1966, and she has since appeared in various DC Comics series and in Batman television shows and movies. Locate any one of Poison Ivy's manifestations; one possibility would be the 1997 film *Batman and Robin* starring Uma Thurman as Poison Ivy. Using a technical tool such as EDpuzzle, prepare a presentation for your classmates illustrating the debt the creators of Poison Ivy owe to Hawthorne and "Rappaccini's Daughter."

- As an alternative, a recurring character in the Marvel comics universe is Monica Rappaccini, who first appeared in *Amazing Fantasy* #7 in 2005. Again, using a tool such as EDpuzzle, prepare a class presentation illustrating what her creators owe to Hawthorne and "Rappaccini's Daughter."

- "Rappaccini's Daughter" is often compared to an 1861 novel by Oliver Wendell Holmes Sr. titled *Elsie Venner*, which tells the story of a medical professor, a student, and a disturbed young woman whose mother was bitten by a rattlesnake while pregnant, making her daughter half-woman, half-snake. Read the novel, then prepare a written report on its similarities to Hawthorne's short story.

- Trace the historical roots of "Rappaccini's Daughter." Scholars cite several sources, including the biblical book of Genesis (the story of Adam and Eve); the *Geste Romanorum* (or "Deeds of the Romans") "Of the Poison of Sin"; the story told by Baglioni about the Indian prince, Porus, who presented Alexander the Great with a beautiful woman with poisonous breath (found in Sir Thomas Browne's 1646 *Vulgar Errors*); and the Bower of Bliss in book II, canto XII of Edmund Spenser's Renaissance poem *The Fairie Queene*. Trace these and other sources you can find and prepare a report on the connections between the sources and the story.

- The connection between poisons and medicine is ancient. Conduct research on this connection. What poisons have been thought to have medical benefits? How did physicians, especially in the past, use poisons to treat patients? Do contemporary physicians use substances that are thought of as poisons? Present the results of your research in a written report.

- Imagine that you are a journalist. Conduct an interview of Baglioni or of Giovanni for your local newspaper recounting his reactions to those events. Post your interview on your social networking site and invite your classmates to comment.

---

to him only as subjects for some new experiment. He would sacrifice human life, his own among the rest, or whatever else was dearest to him, for the sake of adding so much as a grain of mustard-seed to the great heap of his accumulated knowledge.

The story takes place at an unspecified historical time in Padua, Italy. (© *Tom Roche / ShutterStock.com*)

Rappaccini has sacrificed his own daughter to his quest for knowledge; at the very best, he has used his knowledge to protect her from the world. He has raised her in the isolation of his poisonous garden, thereby corrupting her with the poisons he distills for his own purposes. Some readers conclude that his intention is to ensnare Giovanni in his experiments through the agency of his charming and lovely daughter.

Love

On one level, "Rappaccini's Daughter" is a kind of perverse love story. Rappaccini has corrupted the body of his daughter, but her soul remains pure; she is gentle, naive, and innocent, even heavenly. It appears that after meeting Giovanni, she falls in love with him. When Giovanni produces Baglioni's phial as an antidote for the poisons in their bodies, she seizes it from him and insists on drinking the liquid first so that Giovanni can see the result; perhaps she suspects that she is the target of foul play and wants to test the antidote and thereby protect Giovanni. It remains an open question as to what extent Giovanni's love for Beatrice matches hers for him. For some readers, Giovanni is merely infatuated by Beatrice's beauty. When he concludes that she has deliberately corrupted him, he curses her, suggesting that his love for her is superficial; she, on the other hand, says to him: "It is my father's fatal science! No, no, Giovanni; it was not I! Never, never! I dreamed only to love thee, and be with thee a little time . . . . though my body be nourished with poison, my spirit is God's creature, and craves love as its daily food." In the end, Beatrice turns against her father, saying to him: "I would fain have been loved, not feared."

STYLE

Symbolism

"Rappaccini's Daughter" makes use of numerous symbols. One of the first is the ruin of the marble fountain in the center of the garden:

> There was the ruin of a marble fountain in the centre, sculptured with rare art, but so wofully shattered that it was impossible to trace the

original design from the chaos of remaining fragments. The water, however, continued to gush and sparkle into the sunbeams as cheerfully as ever. A little gurgling sound ascended to the young man's window, and made him feel as if a fountain were an immortal spirit, that sung its song unceasingly, and without heeding the vicissitudes around it.

The fountain and its gurgling water can be thought of as symbolic of physical corruption and purity of soul; in this regard it symbolizes Beatrice and her mixture of innocence and corruption. The poisonous plant from which Beatrice draws life represents the corrupting force of nature. The garden, referred to as a Garden of Eden, suggests the Fall of humanity at the hands of Satan—in this case, the satanic Rappaccini, whose black clothing is symbolic of evil. Finally, Beatrice herself is a symbolic character. She represents feminine beauty, purity, and goodness, and although her father has corrupted her body with his poisonous plants, her soul remains pure, like untainted water:

> Her spirit gushed out before him like a fresh rill, that was just catching its first glimpse of the sunlight, and wondering at the reflections of earth and sky which were flung into its bosom. There came thoughts, too, from a deep source, and fantasies of a gem-like brilliancy, as if diamonds and rubies sparkled upward among the bubbles of the fountain.

Indeterminate Setting

"Rappaccini's Daughter" is set at an indeterminate time in the past, although the first sentence of the story indicates a time "very long ago." Some of the references in the story suggest that it takes place during the Italian Renaissance, perhaps in the 1500s. The action occurs in Padua, a university city in northern Italy. Most of the action is set in the garden cultivated by Giacomo Rappaccini, a lush and luxurious garden filled with poisonous plants he uses to distill medicines. Further scenes are in the apartment overlooking the garden occupied by Giovanni Guasconti, a young medical student. The apartment, a "high and gloomy chamber," is in an old mansion that strikes Giovanni and the reader as sinister and mysterious, especially because it was once owned by a now extinct noble family. He imagines the family as having been depicted in Dante's *Inferno* (the first book of the *Divine Comedy*) suffering the agonies of hell, a detail that foreshadows the theological themes of the story. Also giving the mansion

a mysterious, gothic atmosphere is the secret door that leads to Rappaccini's garden.

Allusions

Hawthorne enriches the reader's understanding of the story through numerous allusions, that is, references to familiar characters, real persons, events, or concepts, used to make an idea more readily understood. Many of the allusions are biblical. The garden is compared to the Garden of Eden in the biblical book of Genesis, suggesting that Beatrice is a kind of Eve opposite Giovanni's Adam. Rappaccini, then, with his efforts to play God with other people's lives, is a false god, indeed a Satan. Although the parallels are not exact, the overall references to Heaven, Eden, sin, corruption, serpents, and the like allude to the story of Adam and Eve in Genesis, suggesting that at some level the story is an allegory about the Fall of humanity through original sin.

Additionally, the story alludes to the *Divine Comedy*, the immense epic poem written by Dante Alighieri early in the fourteenth century. One of the poet's guides in the poem is named Beatrice, and when Giovanni moves into his apartment, he recalls that one of the ancestors of the family that owned the mansion was depicted by Dante as having undergone the agonies of hell. These links to the *Divine Comedy* draw the reader's attention to the spiritual significance of the story. Finally, as Baglioni gives Giovanni the phial containing the supposed antidote to the poisons in Beatrice's system, he suggests that his antidote would have neutralized the most virulent poisons of the Borgias. His allusion is to the corrupt Borgia family, which produced two popes and dominated political and church intrigues in fifteenth- and sixteenth-century Italy.

HISTORICAL CONTEXT

Hawthorne is somewhat vague about the historical context of "Rappaccini's Daughter." Early on, the narration tells us that the events of the story take place in the distant past. A fixture of the story is the University of Padua's medical school, which was established in 1250, so clearly the story is set after that date. Further, the story makes reference to Giovanni's having read and studied Dante's *Divine*

COMPARE & CONTRAST

- **Renaissance:** Under the heading of "natural philosophy," the first stirrings of advances toward more modern science take place in such fields as astronomy, anatomy, physiology, and medicine.

  1844: New, more modern sciences have developed, spurred by advances in such fields as organic chemistry, physiology, geology, and physics; the word *scientist* was coined by William Whewell in 1833. The transcendentalist movement is expressing skepticism about traditional religious beliefs and urging a closer relationship with the natural order.

  Today: The scientific method is firmly entrenched, with formally trained medical researchers and scientists conducting controlled experiments with strict ethical requirements and submitting their results for publication and peer review.

- **Renaissance:** Universities with structured curricula emerged in Europe in the late Middle Ages, becoming established in the Renaissance. Medicine has become a standard part of the curriculum, typically offered as a field of study after a student has completed a master's degree.

  1844: Medicine as a science, or scientific medicine, is the result of advances in theory and practice on the part of European physicians.

  Today: Since 1999, European medical schools have striven to enhance the cross-border mobility of medical students.

- **Renaissance:** Medicinal plants are widely used by physicians to treat a range of disorders.

  1844: The Botanical Garden of Padua, affiliated with the university, continues to focus on medicinal plants and natural remedies. One of its collections includes poisonous plants.

  Today: In 2013, the New York Botanical Garden presents an exhibit called "Wild Medicine: Healing Plants around the World." The exhibit is a recreation of a sixteenth-century botanical garden from Padua.

Comedy, which was written in the early fourteenth century, and an allusion is made to Benvenuto Cellini, a famed Italian sculptor in the 1500s. These details suggest that the reader is to imagine the events of the story as having occurred in the Italian Renaissance of the late 1500s or perhaps even as late as the 1600s.

The question arises: Why did Hawthorne choose to set his story in Renaissance Italy rather than in nineteenth-century New England? One possible answer to this question is that during the nineteenth century, Italy was widely regarded by North Americans and northern Europeans as an exotic locale, one that was infused with the rich history of the Western world. The European Renaissance in large part was launched in Italy, and much of the West's cultural inheritance, from the classic authors of ancient Rome through the old masters of the visual arts, came from the Italian peninsula. For many authors and readers, Italy was inherently interesting. Its warm and sunny climate, combined with its aesthetic sensibilities (in contrast to dour Puritan New England, which in Hawthorne's mind lacked any kind of history worth consideration), sparked the imagination of authors, including Hawthorne, whose novel *The Marble Faun* was inspired by his extended travels in Italy late in his life. Numerous nineteenth-century American and British authors, including James Fenimore Cooper, Henry Wadsworth Longfellow, Harriet Beecher Stowe, Edgar Allan Poe, George Eliot, Robert Browning, and Henry James, found inspiration in the Italian experience and used it as a backdrop for novels, poems, and short

Beatrice is always in the garden, where poisonous plants grow. (© *AN NGUYEN | ShutterStock.com*)

stories. Still today, books and movies such as Frances Mayes's *Under the Tuscan Sun* (1996) attest to the sensuous allure of Italy.

Italy was also known as a place of political machinations. The Borgia family played key roles in the tortuous political and religious politics of Renaissance Italy, and various members of the family, including two popes and the infamous femme fatale Lucrezia Borgia, were guilty of assorted crimes, including adultery, incest, theft, bribery, murder—even, as Baglioni points out, murder by poison. Among nineteenth-century American Protestants, the Catholicism of Italy—its corrupt popes, its crafty and cunning Jesuit priests, its sensuous rituals, its incense and bells, its elaborate churches and cathedrals—rendered Italy a place of duplicity and decadence. Although an element of cultural stereotyping was at work, for a New Englander of the nineteenth century, Italy, with its lush sensuousness and its reputation for intrigue, would have been an appropriate setting not only for Rappaccini's garden but also for the sinister aims of Rappaccini and the political jousting of Rappaccini and Baglioni. At a more

practical level, the University of Padua was one of the leading universities in Europe. Its highly regarded medical school would have been the perfect home for a figure such as Rappaccini, and readers familiar with the Botanical Garden of Padua and its collection of poisonous plants would have recognized this.

It is also possible that Hawthorne wanted thematically to capture the struggle between faith and reason that was current in his own day in the conflict between the transcendentalists and those who favored a more common-sense approach to the pursuit of truth. This struggle mirrors a similar struggle that persisted throughout the Renaissance at the University of Padua. This controversy centered on the philosophical position called "fideism," which held that truth is dual, that is, that truths about *matter* are within the purview of philosophy (i.e., natural philosophy, or science) and can be arrived at through the use of reason, but that matters of the *spirit* lie within the purview of theology and can be arrived at only through faith. This conflict was replayed in Hawthorne's New England, where his transcendentalist neighbors, led by

Ralph Waldo Emerson, were skeptical about the Protestant religious beliefs they had inherited and urged a relationship with the divine through the natural order. Their writings on these matters provoked sharp controversy, especially at Harvard University, whose prominent divinity school urged the primacy of faith. This conflict between faith and skepticism mirrored the debates between faith and reason that occurred at the University of Padua and that are embodied in the character of Giovanni in "Rappaccini's Daughter." Throughout the story, Giovanni vacillates between faith in Beatrice's goodness and innocence and skepticism about her fundamental nature as expressed by Baglioni. It is perhaps his own uncertainty and lack of commitment to a belief in Beatrice's underlying goodness that ends up destroying her and denying him the love he seems to crave.

CRITICAL OVERVIEW

Many critics commenting on "Rappaccini's Daughter" call attention to the interpretive difficulties the story presents. Richard Harter Fogle, for example, writing in *Hawthorne's Fiction: The Light and the Dark*, calls it "the most difficult of Hawthorne's stories." Fogle goes on to state that "upon consideration, the difficulty seems to have two causes: the symbolism of Beatrice Rappaccini is puzzling, and the theme of the tale is double rather than single." Elaborating, Fogle says about Beatrice: "Symbolically she should represent . . . a contrast between outward beauty and inner ugliness and evil. . . . Instead, however, she is essentially simple and good." With regard to the themes, Fogle writes: "The real theme arises from Beatrice and Giovanni and concludes with a demonstration of Beatrice's spiritual superiority after both have undergone the severest possible trial. The theme of Rappaccini [as the mad scientist] is secondary but encroaches upon the first from the importance and complexity of its issues."

Also emphasizing the story's ability to baffle interpretation is Lea Bertani Vozar Newman, who writes in *A Reader's Guide to the Short Stories of Nathaniel Hawthorne*: "Each of the four main characters has been seen alternately as admirable or reprehensible, heroic or villainous, or as fancifully ideal or ironically grotesque." Newman explains:

Rappaccini is a tragic hero intent on defending God's estate and protecting his daughter. Or he is a devil whose lust for power drives him to supersede God's creation. Baglioni is a well-intentioned benevolent friend and the voice of the "normal conscience." Or he is a diabolical, malevolent murderer, at best a bungler whose motives are seriously suspect.

This comment emphasizes that different readers respond to the characters in markedly differing ways. Beverly Haviland, in "The Sin of Synecdoche: Hawthorne's Allegory against Symbolism in 'Rappaccini's Daughter,'" sums up the problem of conflicting interpretations in this way:

By provoking us to disagree with each other about what the story means, about what its sources are, about whether it is allegory at all, Hawthorne has produced a critical discourse in which differences must be preserved because there is no possibility of agreement.

Haviland concludes: "Accepting ambivalence and disagreement as inevitable, perhaps one is then fit to be a member of the audience Hawthorne imagined."

In his book *Nathaniel Hawthorne: The Man, His Tales and Romances*, Edward Wagenknecht briefly summarizes the "standard" interpretation of "Rappaccini's Daughter":

The point has often been made that though Rappaccini's garden inevitably suggests Eden, it is Eden after the Fall. Beatrice, then, lives, as we all do, in a "fallen" world, but her soul, like the pure water of the fountain, sings its song "unceasingly and without heeding the vicissitudes around it."

Thus, as Wagenknecht notes, the story invites a biblical, allegorical interpretation. Wagenknecht goes on to point out what many critics have noticed: the sexually charged nature of the story. He comments that Beatrice "is far from being a sexless creature, and the garden itself is drenched in sexual suggestiveness." In a similar vein, Frederick C. Crews, in *The Sins of the Father*, remarks:

If Beatrice's "poisonousness" accounts for [Giovanni's] characteristically ambivalent reaction, then that poisonousness may stand for her sexuality as it affects his contrary impulses. Hope and dread wage continual warfare in Giovanni's breast because he fears exactly what he desires. His sexual ambition triggers his fits of revulsion, for the closer he comes to Beatrice, the more he is appalled by her implied sexual power.

From there, numerous critics take a feminist reading of the story. Leland S. Person, for example, in *The Cambridge Introduction to Nathaniel Hawthorne*, comments:

> "Rappaccini's Daughter" is remarkable for the way it traces the operations of a man's imagination in the presence of a challenging woman. Hawthorne carefully delineates the process in which Beatrice is victimized by a man who cannot overcome his fears of woman. Giovanni cannot move beyond an essential narcissism—his assumption that Beatrice's role is to reflect an image of him.

Richard Brenzo, in "Beatrice Rappaccini: A Victim of Male Love and Horror," comments again on the interpretive difficulties the story poses, noting: "Critics have been fascinated by Nathaniel Hawthorne's 'Rappaccini's Daughter,' a tale which has proved as elusive, ambiguous, symbolic, and intimidating as Beatrice Rappaccini is in the eyes of Giovanni Guasconti." He then cites as an example Roy R. Male, who "sees the story as an allegory, rich in ambiguity, about a conflict between 'idealistic' faith and 'materialistic skepticism.'" He further notes that "other scholars view the tale as an allegory of corrupted and pure nature, or emphasize the attack on single-minded scientific inquiry." Brenzo goes on to offer his own alternative: "However, what I find striking is the story's concern with the relationship of three men to a woman, who, though she never deliberately harms any of them, and though the men profess to have her good in mind, is nevertheless destroyed by them."

Terence Martin, in his book *Nathaniel Hawthorne*, examines the story from more of a structural perspective:

> The structure of the tale involves two mutually dependent stories—one contained and given fuller meaning by the dimensions of the other. Though his focus is on Beatrice as she is seen by Giovanni, Hawthorne's story of this young man and woman is folded within the contours of Baglioni's rivalry with Rappaccini.

In commenting on how Giovanni sees Beatrice, Martin sounds a common theme in responses to his character:

> Giovanni, in short, lacks the depth of heart necessary to tender to Beatrice the love to which her spirit could respond. He vacillates between faith and doubt, between the promptings of the heart and those of the fancy—and his alternating moods comprise the essential dramatic movement of the tale.

In this respect, a reader can regard Giovanni rather than Beatrice as the central character in the story.

CRITICISM

Michael J. O'Neal

O'Neal holds a PhD in English. In the following essay, he examines Hawthorne's use of imagery in "Rappaccini's Daughter."

It could be argued, with only slight exaggeration, that the difference between literature and various forms of nonfictional writing—history texts provide a good example—is that the focus of literature is the *particular* while that of history is the *general*. History appeals largely to the intellect. It relies on the denotations of language to identify and record concepts and events. It strives to avoid ambiguity by providing a precise, semantically based meeting ground for the author and the reader, and its language serves as a means to that end. Literary language, in contrast, is not a means to an end. It is the end itself, for it is through the particulars of the language that authors create, rather than record, the particulars of the experience they want to evoke.

Authors have numerous tools to achieve their aesthetic ends: symbolism, metaphor and simile, personification. Poets, and even fiction writers, often rely on alliteration, assonance, and consonance to achieve aesthetic effects. A principal tool, however, is imagery, which underlines the fact that readers experience the world through their senses. Imagery, then, refers to literary language that calls up those sensory experiences. The word *imagery* implies that the technique is limited to language that captures visual experience, but imagery more broadly can encompass sound, smell, touch, texture, taste, movement, and even such sensations as hunger. Imagery is the tribute literature pays to other artistic forms, such as painting, sculpture, and music. It should be acknowledged that effective nonfiction writers often use imagery and other literary techniques to make their writing more vivid, but generally their focus remains on conveying an unambiguous semantic meaning.

"Rappaccini's Daughter" relies heavily on imagery, and it stands out from many other literary works by its reliance not just on visual

'RAPPACCINI'S DAUGHTER' EXISTS THROUGH ITS PROMISCUOUS WEALTH OF SENSORY DETAIL. NEARLY EVERY PARAGRAPH IS REPLETE WITH IMAGES THAT DRAW THE READER INTO THE EXPERIENCE OF THE STORY."

images but on other sorts of images as well. The fundamental "meaning" of the story is ambiguous, for its allegorical and symbolic elements invite various interpretations. But the story is not an essay on human corruption, or on the Fall of mankind in the Garden of Eden, or on the exploitation of people for the ends of science, or on the inability of an unsophisticated, repressed young man to commit himself to the love of a sexually alluring and therefore frightening woman. The story is about all of these and more, but "Rappaccini's Daughter" exists through its promiscuous wealth of sensory detail. Nearly every paragraph is replete with images that draw the reader into the experience of the story.

One set of images could be described as those of "entanglement." These images not only suggest the luxuriance of the garden but also suggest, thematically, the concept of the intermixture of spirit and flesh, good and evil, beauty and decay, health and death, innocence and corruption. Additionally, they add to the sexually charged nature of the garden, where Giovanni feels the threat of entrapment. Numerous passages contain these kinds of images. As Giovanni explores the garden and its plants, the narration comments:

> Some were placed in urns, rich with old carving, and others in common garden-pots; some crept serpent-like along the ground, or climbed on high, using whatever means of ascent was offered them. One plant had wreathed itself round a statue of Vertumnus, which was thus quite veiled and shrouded in a drapery of hanging foliage, so happily arranged that it might have served a sculptor for a study.

The narration elsewhere notes of the plants:

> Several, also, would have shocked a delicate instinct by an appearance of artificialness, indicating that there had been such commixture,

and, as it were, adultery of various vegetable species, that the production was no longer of God's making, but the monstrous offspring of man's depraved fancy, glowing with only an evil mockery of beauty. They were probably the result of experiment, which, in one or two cases, had succeeded in mingling plants individually lovely into a compound possessing the questionable and ominous character that distinguished the whole growth of the garden.

Beatrice is implicated in this ominous "commixture" and "mingling," which borders on the incestuous:

> Approaching the shrub, she threw open her arms, as with a passionate ardor, and drew its branches into an intimate embrace; so intimate, that her features were hidden in its leafy bosom, and her glistening ringlets all intermingled with the flowers.

Another set of images has to do with jewels and gems, along with language that suggests bright, glittering surfaces. These images point to the duality of the universe Beatrice and Giovanni inhabit, which, on the one hand, consists of a lush, gorgeous surface that glimmers and glistens but, on the other, is also corrupt, poisonous, and fatal. Reference, for example, is made to the garden's "gem-like flowers." The plant with the purple flowers that seems particularly poisonous is described in this way: "There was one shrub in particular, set in a marble vase in the midst of the pool, that bore a profusion of purple blossoms, each of which had the lustre and richness of a gem." It made a "show so resplendent that it seemed enough to illuminate the garden." These images are sustained in Giovanni's response to Beatrice, whose "glistening ringlets" have already been noted:

> Her spirit gushed out before him like a fresh rill, that was just catching its first glimpse of the sunlight, and wondering at the reflections of earth and sky which were flung into its bosom. There came thoughts, too, from a deep source, and fantasies of a gem-like brilliancy, as if diamonds and rubies sparkled upward among the bubbles of the fountain.

At another point, Giovanni observes that Beatrice "glowed amid the sunlight and . . . positively illuminated the more shadowy intervals of the garden path."

Yet other sets of images capture color and smell, the latter often suggested by breath:

> "Give me thy breath, my sister," exclaimed Beatrice; "for I am faint with common air!

WHAT DO I READ NEXT?

- Hawthorne's major work is his 1850 novel *The Scarlet Letter*, an allegorical tale of sin, guilt, and redemption set in early colonial America.

- Hawthorne's "The Birth-Mark," first published in 1843, was included in *Mosses from an Old Manse*. It tells the story of a scientist obsessed with an imperfection on the face of his beautiful young wife—a small birthmark in the shape of a hand. He tries to remove the birthmark, with tragic results.

- William G. Rothstein surveys the history of nineteenth-century American medicine, as both science and social science, in *American Physicians in the Nineteenth Century: From Sects to Science* (1992).

- A classic novel about the arrogance of attempts to control creation that has been enjoyed by generations of young adults is Mary Shelley's *Frankenstein* (1818).

- *The Island of Dr. Moreau* (1896), by H. G. Wells, often seen as a young-adult novel, is one of the earliest science-fiction novels to explore the topic of a deranged scientist who is more concerned with what he *can* do than with what he *should* do.

- *Wonders and the Order of Nature, 1150–1750* (2001), by Lorraine J. Daston and Katharine Park, surveys the topic of natural inquiry and the history of "wonders in the order of nature" in the late Middle Ages, the Renaissance, and beyond. The book would provide insight into the scientific passions of a character like Dr. Rappaccini.

- The Eastern roots of Western medicine and the cultural inheritance that might have affected a physician in Renaissance Italy is explored in *Medieval Islamic Medicine* (2007), by Peter E. Pormann and Emilie Savage-Smith.

- Philip Pullman is the author of *His Dark Materials*, an epic/fantasy trilogy for young adults consisting of *Northern Lights* (1995, published in North America as *The Golden Compass*), *The Subtle Knife* (1997), and *The Amber Spyglass* (2000). The trilogy embraces several themes and motifs found in "Rappaccini's Daughter," including a (possibly) mad scientist (in a world in which scientists are referred to as "theologians"), dangerous and unethical experimentation, an emphasis on the Fall of man in the biblical account of Adam and Eve in the Garden of Eden (a lead character is regarded as the new "Eve"), and original sin.

And give me this flower of thine, which
I separate with gentlest fingers from the stem,
and place it close beside my heart."

When Giovanni first hears Beatrice speak, he hears "a voice as rich as a tropical sunset, . . . which made Giovanni, though he knew not why, think of deep hues of purple or crimson, and of perfumes heavily delectable." The color purple, which plays a prominent role in the story, carries its own wealth of connotations. Because purple is a hybrid color, it occurs rarely in nature, so it has traditionally been thought to have a spiritual meaning, and purple flowers are often considered precious and delicate. The color is often associated with royalty and nobility and thus with luxury, ambition, power, wealth, extravagance, and grandeur, along with magic and mystery. Purple is thought to have various effects on people: it encourages the imagination and creativity, it boosts nurturing tendencies, and it enhances a feeling of the sacred. Purple is also often associated with feminine energy and power. All of these associations can come into play as Beatrice nurtures the plant with purple flowers, which she addresses as her "sister."

Giovanni unwittingly kills Beatrice when he brings an antidote, intending to rid her body of the poisons. *(© Rynio Productions / ShutterStock.com)*

When Giovanni meets with Beatrice in the garden,

> there was a fragrance in the atmosphere around her, rich and delightful, though evanescent, yet which the young man, from an indefinable reluctance, scarcely dared to draw into his lungs. It might be the odor of the flowers. Could it be Beatrice's breath, which thus embalmed her words with a strange richness, as if by steeping them in her heart?

This emphasis on breath, exhalations, and fragrances enhances the reader's sense of the redolence and sensuousness of the garden as well as its latent sexuality (which is often triggered by fragrances, as perfume manufacturers

know). What should also be observed are the auditory images in many of these passages. The reader is invited to hear the gush of water from the ruined fountain and, through the combination of visual and auditory images, feel the tension between ruin and salvation, between corruption and innocence.

The attentive reader can locate additional image patterns in the story: snakes and serpents, warmth and cold, sunshine and shadow, white and black. The reader's immersion in these images turns "Rappaccini's Daughter" into a lush, sensory experience and transforms its theological abstractions into the immediacy and tangibility of art.

> FOR EXAMPLE, THE BIBLICAL ANALOGUE PROPOSES BEATRICE AS THE TEMPTRESS EVE WHO LEADS GIOVANNI TO HIS FALL; THE DANTEAN MODEL MAKES HER THE ITALIAN, IDEALIZED BEATRICE WHO LEADS HER BELOVED TO PARADISE; AND THE OVIDIAN MYTH SUGGESTS THAT GIOVANNI AS VERTUMNUS WILL RESCUE HER INSTEAD."

Source: Michael J. O'Neal, Critical Essay on "Rappaccini's Daughter," in *Short Stories for Students*, Gale, Cengage Learning, 2016.

Lea Bertani Vozar Newman

In the following excerpt, Newman points out that "Rappaccini's Daughter" is a complex story, leading reviewers to conflicting conclusions about its meaning.

. . . "The most difficult of Hawthorne's stories"—such is Fogle's assessment of "Rappaccini's Daughter," and few of the circa seventy other readers whose interpretations are reflected in this review would disagree. Their very number attests to the complexities in the story, while their conflicting conclusions complicate the situation further. Each of the four main characters has been seen alternately as admirable or reprehensible, heroic or villainous, or as fancifully ideal or ironically grotesque. Rappaccini is a tragic hero intent on defending God's estate and protecting his daughter. Or he is a devil whose lust for power drives him to supersede God's creation. Baglioni is a well-intentioned benevolent friend and the voice of the "normal conscience." Or he is a diabolical, malevolent murderer, at best a bungler whose motives are seriously suspect. Even the star-crossed lovers, who emerge in most readings with Beatrice as the pure and selfless innocent victim and Giovanni as the inadequate, shallow, faithless lover, occasionally reverse roles with one reader giving precedence to Beatrice's poisonousness, another to Giovanni's good "common sense."

Several typically Hawthornian attributes contribute to and help to explain such a paradoxical array of responses. The first, and most crucial, is his handling of point of view; the second, and most apparent, is his unique kind of symbolic allegory; and the third, and most pervasive, is his ambivalence, a vacillation firmly rooted in a basic psychological and philosophical duality.

Point of view is listed as the first of these factors because it is in this fundamental aspect of form, in a subtle yet highly significant shift in perspective, that many of the interpretative problems lie. In the opening sentence of the tale proper, Giovanni is established as the subject of the story, and it is from his viewpoint that the garden and the other characters are initially described and the incidents in the plot are developed. The reader is presented with some objective facts that help to shape and assess Giovanni's character, but primarily the reader's sensibilities parallel Giovanni's and change, with his, between accepting the sensory evidence of Beatrice's poisonousness and the intuitive feeling that she is pure and good. The dilemma is a valid one for the first thirty pages of the thirty-seven-page story, but at this point, in the middle of a paragraph that reviews Giovanni's "dark surmises," the perspective shifts to an authoritative, omniscient point of view that informs the reader, but not Giovanni, that it would be a mistake to trust one's senses. The authorial voice unequivocally states, "There is something truer and more real, than what we can see with the eyes, and touch with the finger." Two pages later this authority verifies beyond doubt that "the real Beatrice was a heavenly angel." The uninitiated reader could easily overlook the actual source of the confirmation and assume that Giovanni shares the benefit of this insight. Those readers who have identified and analyzed the manipulation of the narrative structure have not approved of it. McCabe considers the abandonment of Giovanni's mediating consciousness as the "one unsatisfactory element" in an otherwise "compelling work of art," while Ross calls the intrusion of an outside superior knowledge "a serious flaw" that undercuts the reader's identification with Giovanni and makes for an inept resolution of the conflict. Waggoner, without specifically referring to point of view, assesses the plot as a series of controlled revelations of Beatrice's full character. Hawthorne's shift may be a part of this "controlled revelation," or it may be an arbitrary change inserted after he had decided to make Beatrice an angel and not a devil. (His indecision is discussed under circumstances of composition, above.) In either case, the reader who is aware of the privileged communication between author and reader will be better able to grasp Giovanni's dilemma.

The author's sleight of hand with viewpoint is significant in another way as well. It demonstrates and confirms one of the story's dominant themes—the unreliability of sensory perceptions. Several readers have discussed Giovanni's "quick fancy," a phrase Hawthorne uses to denote the faculty that receives and combines sense impressions. Most have condemned Giovanni for not being able to transcend his physical senses, but Franklin points out that the issue of whether Giovanni perceives Beatrice accurately is ultimately irrelevant. Giovanni's perception is a trick intended to momentarily delude the reader in the same way that Baglioni's and Rappaccini's "science" deludes all three men in the story. They "mistake the actual for the real." Without the authorial intercessions, the reader would too. If the narrative is directly calculated to "egregiously deceive," as Franklin claims, the change in point of view may not be a blunder but a case of the form skillfully echoing the content and reinforcing one of the themes.

The second factor that contributes to this story's interpretative difficulties is the allegorical "meaning" that it embodies. For the reader who defines allegory as a consistent set of symbols used to signify a second series of referents with exact correspondence, "Rappaccini's Daughter" is hopelessly "inconsistent" and finally unsatisfactory as "pure allegory." Such a rigid allegorical formula cannot be made to fit the multitude of conflicting literary allusions with which the story abounds. Each legend that it invokes suggests a different set of identifying symbols and a corresponding reversal in role assignments. For example, the biblical analogue proposes Beatrice as the temptress Eve who leads Giovanni to his fall; the Dantean model makes her the Italian, idealized Beatrice who leads her beloved to Paradise; and the Ovidian myth suggests that Giovanni as Vertumnus will rescue her instead. (See sources and influences, above.) These kinds of contradictions pose no problem for another set of readers who accept a broader definition of allegory. For them, allegory is a symbolic mode that thrives on irony and enigma. One such reader claims that "the confusion in the symbolism" aids this kind of fiction. Another commends Hawthorne for integrating a continuum of legendary allusions. Honig believes Baglioni's mixed motives add a dimension lacking in the antecedent legends and enhance the ironic character portrayals throughout the story. One explanation for Hawthorne's ambiguous allegory is that he could no longer accept the firm beliefs on which Spenser and Bunyan based their "allegory of certainty"; in following their manner but not their convictions, Hawthorne produces an "allegory of doubt."

Unbelief provides a shaky foundation for allegory, but readers have nevertheless attempted allegorical approaches to "Rappaccini's Daughter." Edenic parallels are the most common, undoubtedly because the story itself asks, "Was this garden, then, the Eden of the present world?—and this man [Rappaccini], was he the Adam?" The rhetorical question has been answered in diverse ways. Rappaccini could be the old Adam (Beatrice, like Eve, is created from him and for him); this would make Baglioni the serpent, who seduces and betrays, and Giovanni a second Adam who falls again. Giovanni's sin would be directly linked to his inability to accept Beatrice as a postlapsarian Eve. Or Rappaccini could be not Adam, but a kind of false God wielding his power over a perversely re-created Adam and Eve in an unnatural Paradise of his own making. If Giovanni is Adam, his offering Beatrice the antidote could be interpreted as the temptation of the apple, a situation that reverses the Miltonic emphasis on Eve as temptress. Or Giovanni might simply be Adam after the fall in a "lost Eden Paradise" that he cannot redeem because of his un-Christian selfishness.

Two other allegorical schemes have also been applied, one involving folklore, the other science. The former centers on the principals in the fairy tale—a prince and princess, a good fairy and an evil one. Like the counterparts in the biblical versions, the identities reverse and confuse their roles. Beatrice is the bewitched Princess-in-Distress, but she is not rescued by the Knight-Errant (Giovanni) because he fails the test (the poison); Rappaccini is the Wicked Enchanter, but he is partially good; and Baglioni, who tries to counteract the spell with a magic potion (the antidote), is as much an Evil Counselor as a good fairy. The self-contradictions, once more, underscore Hawthorne's ironic intent by forcing the reader to reshape his original expectations. As an allegory of science, the story yields, in one reading, a more clearly defined series of correspondences. Rappaccini is the experimental scientist, the garden is his laboratory. Beatrice is the new scientific generation; Giovanni, traditional education; and Baglioni, conservative science. This neatly assigned scheme has been severely criticized as arbitrary and irrelevent. One reader completely rules out the notion that the doctors in the story are meant to represent science because they display none of the objectivity associated with the medical profession even in Hawthorne's day.

Perhaps the most telling commentary on "Rappaccini's Daughter" as allegory is Hawthorne's own reaction in 1854, ten years after he had written it. In preparing the *Mosses* collection for a new edition, Hawthorne writes to his publisher, James T. Fields: "Upon my honor, I am not quite sure that I entirely comprehend my own meaning in some of these blasted allegories." Since reinsertion of the preface to "Rappaccini's Daughter" is one of the changes Hawthorne specifically mentions in this letter, and since the preface refers to "an inveterate love of allegory" as part of the author's problem, we can rightfully assume that this story is one of the "blasted allegories" that confuses its author as it docs many of its readers. . . .

Source: Lea Bertani Vozar Newman, "Rappaccini's Daughter," in *A Reader's Guide to the Short Stories of Nathaniel Hawthorne*, G. K. Hall, 1979, pp. 263–67.

SOURCES

Adler, Margot, "'Renaissance Garden' Highlights Medicinal Plants," NPR website, August 07, 2013, http://www.npr.org/2013/08/07/209909027/renaissance-garden-highlights-medicinal-plants (April 6, 2015).

Amesbury, Richard, "Fideism," in *Stanford Encyclopedia of Philosophy*, 2012, http://plato.stanford.edu/entries/fideism/ (accessed January 29, 2015).

Benigni, Umberto, "University of Padua," in *Catholic Encyclopedia*, Vol. 11, Robert Appleton, 1911, p. 17.

Bloom, Harold, ed., *Nathaniel Hawthorne*, Chelsea House, 2000, pp. 11, 223–24.

Borleffs, Jan C. C., and Eckhart G. Hahn, "Medical Education in Europe," NCBI website, April 22, 2010, http://www.ncbi.nlm.nih.gov/pmc/articles/PMC3140355/ (accessed April 6, 2015).

Botanical Garden of Padua (Orto Botanico Università di Padova) website, http://www.ortobotanicopd.it/en/ (accessed January 20, 2015).

Brenzo, Richard, "Beatrice Rappaccini: A Victim of Male Love and Horror," in *Nathaniel Hawthorne*, edited by Harold Bloom, Chelsea House, 1986, p. 141; originally published in *American Literature*, Vol. 48, No. 2, May 1976.

Crews, Frederick C., *The Sins of the Fathers: Hawthorne's Psychological Themes*, University of California Press, 1966, p. 119.

Fogle, Richard Harter, *Hawthorne's Fiction: The Light and the Dark*, University of Oklahoma Press, 1952, p. 91.

Goodman, Russell, "Transcendentalism," in *Stanford Encyclopedia of Philosophy*, 2011, http://plato.stanford.edu/entries/transcendentalism/ (accessed January 29, 2015).

Haviland, Beverly, "The Sin of Synecdoche: Hawthorne's Allegory against Symbolism in 'Rappaccini's Daughter'," in *Texas Studies in Literature and Language*, Vol. 29, 1987, p. 297; quoted by Bunge, Nancy, *Nathaniel Hawthorne: A Study of the Short Fiction*, Twayne, 1993, p. 71.

"Hawthorne, Nathaniel," *Merriam-Webster's Encyclopedia of Literature*, Merriam-Webster, 1995, p. 523.

Hawthorne, Nathaniel, "Rappaccini's Daughter," in *Nathaniel Hawthorne: Tales and Sketches*, edited by Roy Harvey Pearce, Library of America, 1982, pp. 975–1005.

"Health History—19th Century Medicine," Online Healthcare Degrees website, http://www.onlinehealthcaredegrees.com/resources/health-history-19th-century-medicine/ (accessed April 6, 2015).

Martin, Terence, *Nathaniel Hawthorne*, Twayne, 1983, pp. 87, 89.

Medieval Medicine website, http://www.maggietron.com/med/sources.php (accessed January 20, 2015).

Miller, John N., "Fideism vs. Allegory in 'Rappaccini's Daughter'," in *Nineteenth-Century Literature*, Vol. 46, No. 2, 1991, pp. 223–44.

Newman, Lea Bertani Vozar, *A Reader's Guide to the Short Stories of Nathaniel Hawthorne*, G. K. Hall, 1979, pp. 263–64.

Pearce, Roy Harvey, "Chronology," in *Nathaniel Hawthorne: Tales and Sketches*, Library of America, 1982, pp. 1471–76.

Person, Leland S., *The Cambridge Introduction to Nathaniel Hawthorne*, Cambridge University Press, 2007, p. 62.

Rothstein, "Opera: 'Rappaccini' Opens," in *New York Times*, May 14, 1983.

Snyder, Laura J., "William Whewell," in *Stanford Encyclopedia of Philosophy*, 2012, http://plato.stanford.edu/entries/whewell/ (accessed January 31, 2015).

Wagenknecht, Edward, *Nathaniel Hawthorne: The Man, His Tales and Romances*, Continuum, 1989, p. 55.

FURTHER READING

Gale, Robert L., *A Nathaniel Hawthorne Encyclopedia*, Greenwood Press, 1991.

> This volume includes roughly 1,500 entries on all aspects of Hawthorne's life and works: characters, plots, poetry, nonfiction prose, family members, friends, and associates. It includes a chronological listing of the events in his life, chronicles his personal relationships, and documents his experiences as reflected in his stories, reviews, poems, letters, and notebooks.

Kincaid, Paul, "American Fantasy: 1820–1950," in *The Cambridge Companion to Fantasy Literature*, edited by Edward James and Farah Mendlesohn, Cambridge University Press, 2012.

> Readers interested in the development of American fantasy literature will find this essay informative. The book as a whole includes essays on a wide range of topics having to do with fantasy literature.

Leeming, David Adams, and Kathleen Morgan Drowne, *Encyclopedia of Allegorical Literature*, ABC-CLIO, 1996.

> Readers interested in allegorical literature will find in this volume discussion of all aspects of allegory in the Western tradition, from parts of the Bible to modern fiction. It also includes discussion of works from Africa, the Middle East, South America, and other cultures.

Meltzer, Milton, *Nathaniel Hawthorne: A Biography*, Twenty-First Century Books, 2006.

> This volume is a biography of Hawthorne written for young adults. The biography explores the drama and tragedy of Hawthorne's life and is made more appealing by its use of drawings, paintings, and photographs.

Miller, Edwin Haviland, *Salem Is My Dwelling Place: Life of Nathaniel Hawthorne*, University of Iowa Press, 1992.

> Readers interested in a more comprehensive, scholarly biography of Hawthorne will find this entry satisfying. While steering clear of psychological jargon, the biography explores the suppression and anguish that marked much of Hawthorne's life.

Porte, Joel, *In Respect to Egotism: Studies in American Romanticism*, Cambridge University Press, 2009.

> This volume is a wide-ranging study of American romanticism and places Hawthorne in the context of other American romantics, including Edgar Allan Poe, Walt Whitman, Herman Melville, Emily Dickinson, and others. Hawthorne is discussed in chapter 5, "Hawthorne: 'The Obscurest Man of Letters in America.'"

Wright, Sarah Bird, *Critical Companion to Nathaniel Hawthorne: A Literary Reference to His Life and Work*, Facts on File, 2006.

> This volume constitutes a comprehensive guide to all things having to do with Hawthorne and his work. It includes critical entries on his novels, short stories, travel writing, and criticism. Additional entries examine his major characters, his family, friends, publishers, critics, and the periodicals in which his work appeared. It also contains full texts of reviews written by his contemporaries.

SUGGESTED SEARCH TERMS

Nathaniel Hawthorne

Rappaccini's Daughter AND Nathaniel Hawthorne

Nathaniel Hawthorne AND Twice-Told Tales

femme fatale

American romanticism

dark romanticism

Garden of Eden

mad scientist

Mosses from an Old Manse

nineteenth century AND American medicine

Puritanism AND America

University of Padua

Seventeen Syllables

HISAYE YAMAMOTO

1988

Hisaye Yamamoto's short story "Seventeen Syllables," first published in 1949, is considered the defining work of her career. Featuring themes of alienation between generations, the difficulty of cross-cultural understanding, and the fragility of human connection, "Seventeen Syllables" contains incredible emotional depth within a small package, not unlike the haiku poems featured prominently in the short story. Rosie Hayashi, a young Japanese American, comes of age amid a violent quarrel between her short-tempered father and artistic mother. Caught between the Japanese and the English language, her new love for a boy and the terrible truth of her mother's past, Rosie is a true Nisei—an American born to Japanese immigrant parents—straddling worlds that are as incongruous as they are complex. Yamamoto's narrative brilliance shines through a story at once comic, tragic, and absolutely unforgettable. The story is included in *Seventeen Syllables and Other Stories* (1998).

AUTHOR BIOGRAPHY

Yamamoto was born on August 23, 1921, in Redondo Beach, California. Her parents, Japanese immigrants to America from Kumamoto, Japan, owned and operated a strawberry farm. An enthusiastic reader from an early age,

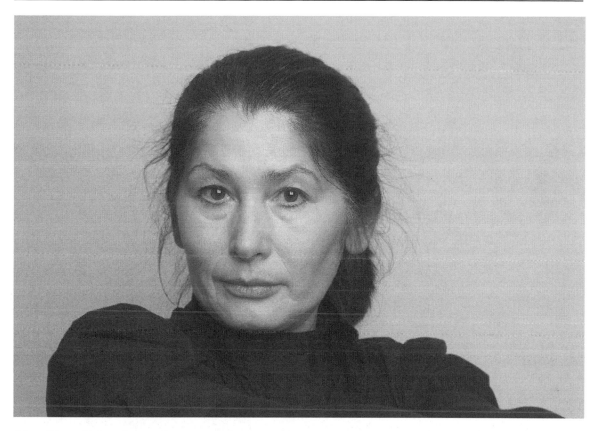

Mrs. Hayashi is unhappy but uncomplaining. (© *Vladimir Volodin | ShutterStock.com*)

Yamamoto submitted stories to Japanese American newspapers as a teenager. She was first published at the age of fourteen, writing under the pen name "Napoleon." Attending Compton College, she earned an associate of the arts degree.

During World War II, Yamamoto was forced to relocate to an internment camp in Poston, Arizona. Fear of a homegrown Japanese attack led the United States to intern innocent Japanese American citizens. For Yamamoto, the three years she spent at Poston left deep scars. She wrote for the camp newspaper, the *Poston Chronicle*, which also published her serialized mystery "Death Rides the Rails." She left camp to work in Springfield, Massachusetts, as a cook but returned to Poston after word reached her family of her brother's death. He had been fighting in Italy as a member of the US Army's 442nd Regimental Combat Team.

In 1945, the war ended and the Japanese American detainees were released. Yamamoto took a position as a reporter for the *Los Angeles Tribune*, covering racism against African Americans. Blaming herself for the arson death of a family after she had written an article in which she downplayed the threats against them from their white neighbors, Yamamoto left the paper in 1948 to travel across the country by bus and train.

When she arrived back in Los Angeles, it was with a new focus. Her short story "The High-Heeled Shoes: A Memoir," was published in the *Partisan Review* in 1948. The next year, Yamamoto received a John Hay Whitney Foundation Opportunity Fellowship. "Seventeen Syllables" was first published in 1949. In 1952, Yamamoto's short story "Yoneko's Earthquake" (1951) was included in *The Best American Short Stories: 1952*.

Yamamoto spent the early 1950s with her adopted son, Paul, working on Staten Island, New York, as a volunteer on a Catholic Worker Movement rehabilitation farm. She was married in 1955 to Anthony DeSoto, returning to Los Angeles to start a family. She was the mother of four children and grandmother of seven.

Yamamoto achieved great success in the postwar years as an author. Four of her stories were listed in Martha Foley's "Distinctive Short Stories" (a list included in the *Best American Short Stories* anthologies): "Seventeen Syllables," "The Brown House" (1951), "Yoneko's Earthquake," and "Epithalamium" (1960). This recognition was a notable achievement, considering the culture of distrust and racism that still existed toward Japanese Americans after the war. In 1986, she was awarded the American Book Award for Lifetime Achievement from the Before Columbus Foundation. Selected short stories and a few essays were collected in *Seventeen Syllables and Other Stories* in 1988. The book won the Award for Literature from the Association of Asian American Studies. After experiencing declining health following a stroke, Yamamoto died on January 30, 2011, in her sleep.

PLOT SUMMARY

"Seventeen Syllables" begins when Rosie Hayashi, a first-generation Japanese American, discovers that her mother has developed a passion for writing haiku poems. The first haiku her mother shares with Rosie is about cats. Rosie pretends to understand its depth and meaning, hoping to hide her lack of education in Japanese language and culture from her mother. She attends Japanese school one to two days a week but pretends her grasp of her mother's language is stronger than it is. She finds it easier to lie than to admit to her confusion. She is a lazy girl when it comes to language, preferring to use English because it requires less effort for her to remember the correct words and form phrases. Regardless of Rosie's false claim of understanding, her mother explains the subtleties of the haiku she has written while Rosie remembers a funny haiku she read in English. She reflects on the difficult gap created by language between herself and her mother.

Her mother submits haiku regularly to a newspaper in San Francisco, the *Mainichi Simbun*, though the family lives closer to Los Angeles. She writes under the pen name Ume Hanazono. Her real name is Tome Hayashi,

and she is a housewife as well as a tomato farmer alongside her husband and daughter. Absorbed in her new hobby, she writes after dinnertime every night, leaving her husband and Rosie to their own devices. Rosie's mother entertains guests of the family who also write haiku enthusiastically. Nonpoets are left to the company of Rosie's father. With a trace of foreboding, the narrator notes that the life span of Tome Hayashi's alter ego, Ume Hanazono, was only three months.

The Hayashi family visits their friends the Hayano family, who have four beautiful daughters, each named after a season of the year: Haru (Spring), Natsu (Summer), Aki (Autumn), and Fuyu (Winter). Their mother, Mrs. Hayano, is the opposite of her pretty, active daughters. She moves painfully for a woman her age, always trembling. She was the prettiest girl in her home village in Japan, and Mr. Hayano is quite attractive himself, but since the birth of her first daughter Mrs. Hayano has been a broken woman.

Haru shows off her new coat to Rosie while Mr. Hayano and Rosie's mother compare haiku notes. Rosie's father reads a magazine. When he speaks to Mrs. Hayano, it is too loudly, as if he thinks she is hard of hearing. Abruptly, he announces it is time to leave, pulling a disappointed Rosie and her embarrassed mother from their socializing. In the car, Rosie's mother says he must be tired and apologizes for letting her interest in haiku distract her from the lateness of the hour. Mr. Hayashi only grunts in response. Rosie decides she hates them both and wishes the car would crash. She regrets her wish immediately, imagining the wreckage and her family—including herself—dead.

Rosie is grateful for the arrival of her Aunt Taka and Uncle Gimpachi—relatives on her mother's side—as it provides her with the distraction needed to sneak away to meet Jesus Carrasco—a boy two grades above her at Cleveland High School, where he will be a senior in the fall. He and his parents work for the Hayashi family, helping them harvest their tomato crop. Jesus and Rosie have grown close working together in the fields. They like to race to finish picking rows and trade jokes. Jesus asks her to meet him in the packing shed, away from their parents, so that he can tell her a secret. Rosie demands to know the secret right away, but Jesus will not tell her and insists they meet that night. Until her aunt and uncle arrived she had not been sure she would meet him, but after dinner she pretends to go to the outhouse but races to the shed instead.

Jesus waits there for her, nervously asking if she regrets coming. She finds a passable unpacked tomato and eats it, wondering at the strange new power she has over Jesus. They kiss. Overwhelmed, Rosie runs to hide in the outhouse, waiting for her breathing to slow. When she returns to the house, her mother, aunt, and uncle are discussing haiku. Her father is in the bathhouse. Passing Rosie on his way out, he rudely refuses her request to help her scrub her back. She shouts at him, asking what she has done wrong. Alone, she takes a very loud bath, singing at the top of her lungs. She decides that noise will drown out her swimming thoughts. When she returns once more to the parlor, her mother, aunt, and uncle are still discussing haiku. Her father is not with them.

Rosie, wild with energy brought on by the kiss, acts out at Japanese school the next day, doing a repertoire of impressions of different accents and famous personalities for her friend Chizuko. At noon her father picks her up from school. It is the hottest day of the year and the tomatoes must be harvested in a hurry. Rosie works steadily until the approach of Jesus, who is driving the truck to pick up the first load of tomatoes for the packing shed, causes her to panic. She runs to the outhouse and watches Jesus through a hole in the wood. To her satisfaction, he looks around for her when she is not in the field where he expects her to be.

On her way back, a stylish black car pulls into the driveway. An attractive man asks in very elegant Japanese if this is the Hayashi residence. The man, in a fine suit and carrying a large package, follows Rosie to the tomato field where her mother works. He reveals to Rosie's mother that he is the haiku editor of *Mainichi Simbun* and has stopped on his way to Los Angeles to deliver the first prize from the newspaper's haiku contest to her.

Rosie's mother, effortlessly adopting the polished style of the editor, Mr. Kuroda, humbly accepts the prize as an honor. She asks if she may open it immediately, and Mr. Kuroda insists that she does. The prize is a beautiful print by the painting master Hiroshige, set in a thick, gold frame. Rosie's mother is delighted and offers Mr. Kuroda tea, which he accepts. Rosie and her father stay in the field and continue to work. Rosie's father calls her mother crazy, which disturbs Rosie, and then he tells Rosie to go fetch her mother so that she can continue harvesting.

Rosie finds Mr. Kuroda eating a rice cake with his suit jacket off, explaining a complex theory of haiku to her enraptured mother. Rosie, too shy to interrupt such an impressive man, waits for her mother to acknowledge her before speaking. Mimicking Mr. Kuroda's fancy language, she tells Rosie she will be only a minute. Rosie relays the message to her father. "They worked again in silence. But suddenly, her father uttered an incredible noise, exactly like the cork of a bottle popping." He rushes toward the house with Rosie trailing behind, calling after him. He shouts at her to stay behind.

She stands, frozen to the spot, watching as Mr. Kuroda flees the house shortly after her father enters. He backs out of the driveway and disappears. Her father emerges with her mother's haiku prize—the beautiful painting in the fine frame—and hacks it with an axe before setting it on fire atop the woodpile.

Rosie runs to the house, concerned for her mother. She finds her watching the fire silently. Rosie and her mother watch the prize burn until the fire dies out. Her mother asks if Rosie knows why she married her father. Rosie says no, terrified of the implications of the question. She wishes her mother would not tell her, since she is already overwhelmed by the events of the traumatic day.

Her mother tells her that, as a young woman, she fell in love with the first son of a wealthy family in Japan. She became pregnant. His family could not learn of the affair, as he was promised to another woman. Her family was too poor for her to be considered a suitable match for her love, and when they discovered her pregnancy she was shamed but not thrown out of the house. She gave birth to a stillborn boy. Desperate, she wrote to Aunt Taka, who lived in the United States, threatening to commit suicide unless she could escape her situation in Japan. Aunt Taka arranged her marriage to Rosie's father, a simple man who knew nothing of her past trouble.

Her mother recites the story of her past with no emotion in her voice. Rosie asks about her half-brother who died, refusing to think about the other grim details. Her mother kneels beside her and grabs Rosie's wrists, begging her to promise never to marry. Rosie thinks of Jesus but says yes, she will promise. Her mother, recognizing her tone as the false agreement she uses when cornered, calls her a fool. Rosie begins to cry, "and the embrace and consoling hand came much later than she expected."

CHARACTERS

Jesus Carrasco

Jesus Carrasco is a field worker for the Hayashi family. He attends Cleveland High School along with Rosie. He befriends her as they work in the fields together over the summer, exchanging jokes. He kisses her in the tomato-packing shed.

Chizuko

Chizuko is Rosie's friend at Japanese school, who loves Rosie's impressions. She laughs until she cries, telling Rosie she should be an actress.

Uncle Gimpachi

Uncle Gimpachi is Rosie's uncle on her mother's side. He married Tome Hayashi's favorite sister, Aunt Taka, and the couple helped Tome immigrate to the United States.

Ume Hanazono

Ume Hanazono is Tome Hayashi's pen name. She writes and submits haiku under this name.

Aki Hayano

Aki Hayano is the third daughter of Mr. and Mrs. Hayano. Her name means "Autumn."

Fuyu Hayano

Fuyu Hayano is the youngest daughter of Mr. and Mrs. Hayano. Her name means "Winter." She is eight years old.

Haru Hayano

Haru Hayano is the eldest daughter of Mr. and Mrs. Hayano. Her name means "Spring." Haru is boisterous and eager to impress Rosie with her new coat. She begs Mr. Hayashi to let Rosie stay the night, but Rosie's father tells her no.

Mr. Hayano

Mr. Hayano is an attractive man, married to Mrs. Hayano and father to four daughters. He shares an interest in haiku with Rosie's mother.

Mrs. Hayano

Mrs. Hayano, though once considered a beauty in Japan, is a shell of her former self. She developed many physical ailments after the birth of the first of her four daughters, including trembling and difficulty walking. She is married to Mr. Hayano.

Natsu Hayano

Natsu Hayano is the second daughter of Mr. and Mrs. Hayano. Her name means "Summer." Natsu is shy by nature and jealous of Hatsu's new coat.

Mr. Hayashi

Mr. Hayashi is the father of Rosie. He is a simple-minded tomato farmer. He married Tome Hayashi without knowing of her past in Japan. He is uncomfortable as well as resentful of his wife's sudden passion for haiku. He does not care for the time she spends writing or the intense discussions she has with other haiku enthusiasts. When Mr. Kuroda and his wife have tea after he presents her with a fine present for winning a haiku contest, Mr. Hayashi frightens Mr. Kuroda away. He smashes the Hiroshige print with an axe before burning it in a jealous rage.

Rosie Hayashi

Rosie Hayashi is the daughter of Mr. and Mrs. Hayashi. She lives with them on their tomato farm outside Los Angeles. She attends a typical

American high school as well as Japanese school, but she finds English the easier language to master. She is a jokester, entertaining her friends with impressions. Over the summer she becomes friends with Jesus Carrasco, sharing her first kiss with him in the packing shed. An observer of the tension between her parents over her mother's newfound love of haiku, Rosie is traumatized by her father's destruction of the prize and her mother's revelation of her past in Japan. She promises her mother she will not marry but does not take the promise seriously. After her mother sees through her false promise, Rosie cries.

Tome Hayashi

Tome Hayashi is the mother of Rosie and wife of Mr. Hayashi. She works in the tomato fields alongside her husband. Her alter ego, Ume Hanazono, is a talented writer of haiku poems. Tome navigates with difficulty the gap between her role as a submissive homemaker for her traditional husband and her writing career. After receiving the great honor of a personal visit from the haiku editor of the newspaper to award her the first prize in a haiku contest, she watches her husband destroy her reward in a fire. When her daughter joins her, she reveals that she married her husband only as an alternative to suicide. He provided a way out of Japan for her when she was desperate to escape. She became pregnant with the child of the son of a wealthy family who would not accept her as a potential bride. The baby was stillborn, but the scandal left her despised by her family in Japan. In a fit of desperation, Tome grabs hold of her daughter's wrists tightly and begs her never to marry. When Rosie begins to cry, Tome does not comfort her right away.

Mr. Kuroda

Mr. Kuroda is the haiku editor of the San Francisco newspaper *Mainichi Simbun*, where Rosie's mother submits her haiku. On the way to Los Angeles, he stops by the farm to present a shocked Tome Hayashi with the first prize from the haiku contest. He is attractive, dressing and speaking elegantly. He happily shares his thoughts on haiku with Rosie's mother over tea, before leaving in the face of Rosie's father's outrage.

Rosie's Father

See Mr. Hayashi

Rosie's Mother

See Tome Hayashi

Aunt Taka

Aunt Taka lives in the United States with her husband, Uncle Gimpachi. She is Tome Hayashi's best-loved sister. When Tome writes to her, threatening suicide, Aunt Taka swiftly arranges her marriage to Mr. Hayashi, granting her an escape from her situation in Japan.

THEMES

Coming of Age

"Seventeen Syllables" is a coming-of-age story, as Rosie grows in maturity as a result of the events of the summer. With Jesus, she experiences her first kiss, an experience so monumental that she finds her vocabulary reduced drastically to "yes," "no," and "oh." Rosie's crush on Jesus—her imaginary conversations with him, avoidance of him, giddiness at the sight of him—is the main concern of her narration. However, the activities of her parents frequently interrupt and overpower the first-love narrative in progress. As Rosie is maturing from girl to woman, her mother feels the wrath of her husband due to her interests outside the scope of their small farm.

The battle over her haiku, fought silently until the brutal end, does not concern Rosie. She senses the tension in the car ride home from the Hayanos, hating both her parents for their individual weakness, but she does not know why her father is upset in the washroom when Aunt Taka and Uncle Gimpachi come to visit. When her father calls her mother crazy as he sweats in the field while Tome serves the haiku editor tea, Rosie is extremely uncomfortable. Her discomfort grows exponentially as she is sent as messenger: her father demands, and her mother denies; her father snaps and stalks into the house. Rosie witnesses the shocking scene of violence, fleeing to her mother's side only to find her mother stiff and silent. Though Rosie wishes wistfully that she not hear the tale—having seen enough to understand that she will be traumatized by whatever her mother says—she hears it, and her maturation is complete. She now knows the secret of her mother's adult world. When her mother urges her never to marry, it is an acknowledgment of Rosie's

TOPICS FOR FURTHER STUDY

- Read Ronald Takaki's history of Japanese Americans for young adults: *Issei and Nisei: The Settling of Japanese America* (1994). Write an essay in which you explain how the history of Japanese immigrants presented in Takaki's history helps shed light on the family dynamics at work in "Seventeen Syllables." Find three facts about Japanese immigration from *Issei and Nisei* that are illustrated in fictional form in "Seventeen Syllables" to include in your essay.

- Visualize the differences between the Issei and Nisei generations of the Hayashis by creating an infographic that compares their social lives in "Seventeen Syllables." First, make a list of each of the three family members' friends or connections. For example: Rosie is friends with Chizuko and Jesus, and her mother has tea with Mr. Kuroda and discusses haiku with Aunt Taka and Uncle Gimpachi. Then choose an infographic you feel would best compare the information. Who is the most isolated Hayashi and why? Who is the most social and why? What conclusions can you draw about the Issei and Nisei generations from "Seventeen Syllables?" Go to the Easel.ly website and choose from the available infographic templates.

- Write five haiku poems, using five words chosen from "Seventeen Syllables" as your inspiration. Before composing your poems, visit the Haiku for People website at http://www.toyomasu.com/haiku/#howtowritehaiku and learn the guidelines for writing haiku.

- Choose another story by Yamamoto to read. How do the themes of the work relate to or differ from those of "Seventeen Syllables"? Do you notice other stylistic similarities between the two stories? Write an essay in which you compare and contrast the stories, including a brief summary of the story you chose.

adulthood. Rosie, fresh from childhood, has not considered marriage. The word conjures the image of Jesus rather than the scene of violence between spouses that she has just witnessed. Rosie's mother, recognizing that her daughter does not truly understand her desolate perspective on love, calls her a fool, failing to comfort Rosie immediately when she starts to cry. Thus the final scene shows how Rosie's mother now sees Rosie as a bearer of the burden of womanhood, a foolish idealist, and a grown-up capable of drying her own tears. Compared with the first scene of the story, in which Rosie's mother does not believe Rosie has a mind deep enough to understand the complexities of haiku, the final scene is a cold shock of adulthood for a carefree girl. Though the tale is at first couched in the innocent story of Rosie and Jesus, the conflict between spouses rams through the middle of the summer romance, bringing darkness and harsh reality with it that will mark Rosie's maturation into womanhood.

Generation Gap

The first generation of Japanese immigrants to America (the Issei) differ radically from their children, born American citizens (the Nisei). "Seventeen Syllables" features such a family, in which the reticent Issei parents are a mystery to their boisterous Nisei child. The generation gap between Rosie and Tome is large enough to be lost in. This is immediately shown in the first scene, as neither can reach across the gap to make themselves understood. Rosie, though raised by her Japanese parents to be quiet and respectful, interprets this in a lazy fashion to simply lie and pretend to understand even when she does not; "to say yes, yes," in order to escape further confusion. This impulse to agree returns in the final scene, as a shaken Rosie says yes to her mother's panicked request that she never marry. But her mother recognizes the lie, realizing that—as with haiku—she cannot force her daughter to understand the depth of the matter. The generation gap between Issei mother and Nisei daughter is aggravated by language, custom, and culture, but Yamamoto deftly shows how passionate, impulsive Rosie resembles her mother, whose passion and impulsivity nearly led to her suicide in Japan.

Rosie's budding romance worries her mother. *(© Rock and Wasp / ShutterStock.com)*

Multiculturalism

Rosie, a Japanese American girl, falls for Jesus, a Mexican American boy. Each attends Cleveland High School, a typically American school outside Los Angeles. Rosie also attends Japanese school, where she learns the language and culture of her parents. Jesus's family works for the Hayashis as field laborers. Mr. and Mrs. Hayashi are Japanese American immigrants. Mr. Hayashi moved to the United States alone, while Mrs. Hayashi did so to escape the limitations of her life in Japan, where she had dishonored herself with a child out of marriage by a man too wealthy to marry down to her station.

More comfortable with the Japanese language than with English, Tome Hayashi writes beautiful haiku poetry thick with meaning. Her daughter, more comfortable with English than with Japanese, entertains her friends at Japanese school with impressions of American celebrities. The multiculturalism of "Seventeen Syllables" is perfectly exemplified in the first scene, in which mother and daughter struggle to make their meaning clear to each other across three languages: Japanese, English, and French. The freedom of exchange between cultures is helped by love, openness, and humor (Jesus and Rosie) and hurt by rigidity, tradition, and lack of communication (Mr. and Mrs. Hayashi). In this way, Yamamoto allows some hope for future generations of multicultural Americans, who might learn to overlook differences in favor of similarities.

STYLE

Episodic Narrative

"Seventeen Syllables" is an episodic narrative, meaning that it is told in a series of episodes that are connected by the overarching themes. The first episode introduces Tome Hayashi and Rosie's failure to connect through language, as they struggle separately to communicate their thoughts on haiku. The next episode takes place at the Hayanos, introducing Mr. Hayashi's disapproval of his wife's activities. The third episode introduces Jesus Carrasco, and so on until the final episode—the death of Ume Hanazono, the poet's alter ego, at the hands of Mr. Hayashi. The episodic nature of the story reflects Rosie's carefree, youthful outlook as the narration flits from scene to scene with a light touch, leaving the work of connecting seemingly disparate parts for the reader. The episodes also serve to allow for the tension to build in the growing but silent conflict between Mr. and Mrs. Hayashi. With each jump forward in time, the string of Mr. Hayashi's resentment has tightened, threatening to break. Meanwhile, each episode finds Mrs. Hayashi comparing notes with a seemingly endless supply of fellow haiku enthusiasts, as her passion, like the fire, is fed. Only in the final scene do the episodes fall into place as a set: Rosie and her mother's lack of understanding is thrown into relief as Tome reveals her past, Mr. Hayashi—like a corked bottle—pops, and the artistic fire becomes a real one, as the haiku artist is sacrificed, leaving behind an unhappy housewife begging her smitten daughter never to marry.

Foil

A foil is a character in fiction whose qualities contrast with those of the protagonist. For example, Tome Hayashi is a foil to her daughter, Rosie. Just as Rosie is experiencing the first blush of love with Jesus, her mother's distrust of men and marriage has never been more concrete. Throughout "Seventeen Syllables," Rosie's naïveté is contrasted with Tome's ennui.

Rosie's happiness is pitted against her mother's depression. Tome begs Rosie never to marry. Rosie daydreams of Jesus even as her mother clutches her wrists. This deliberate contrast on Yamamoto's part serves to emphasize the large gap between mother and daughter caused by age, experience, language, and culture. The Issei mother struggles alone to express herself freely using a traditional Japanese art form as her Nisei daughter performs freewheeling impressions of famous Americans for her peers. Tome's desperate plea at the end of the story for Rosie to renounce marriage is her attempt to prevent her lighthearted daughter from becoming a broken woman like herself—denied a voice by a man she does not truly love. Thus the two major plots of the story—Rosie's meeting with Jesus and Tome's divisive passion for haiku—work in opposition. Rosie finds love, while Tome loses it through her artistic death in the fire.

Third-Person Limited Point of View

Third-person limited point of view, also known as third person limited, is a narrative technique in which the narrator is an inactive participant in the story who knows only the thoughts and feelings of a single character. In the case of "Seventeen Syllables," the narrator is limited to Rosie's mind. The reader can see only what she sees and know only what she knows. This is particularly significant to the plot, as Rosie—distracted by her changing relationship with Jesus—is not fully cognizant of the discord between her parents over her mother's new-found love of haiku. She is aware of the tension to an extent and has witnessed her father's outburst at the Hayanos as well as her mother's apology in the car afterward. But because she is young and inexperienced, she does not understand the depth of the divide until the day of the harvest, when the conflict turns violent. Because the reader is given only the information that Rosie has access to, the spousal tension must be gleaned through inference and context clues. The reader knows, for example, that Mr. Hayashi snaps at his daughter in the bathhouse because he is upset at his wife, who is once again talking haiku with guests, but Rosie assumes he is displeased with her, which shows she has no insight into the tension between the adults at the moment. The third person limited emphasizes Rosie's gradual loss of innocence as she progressively grasps more of the situation

COMPARE & CONTRAST

- **1949:** With the end of World War II in 1945, Japanese Americans are rebuilding their lives after forced internment. Many return home to discover their houses have been looted, vandalized, or destroyed in their absence.

  Today: Restitution payments begin to those interned during World War II after the passing of the Civil Liberties Act of 1988. In 2001, ten of the internment campsites are declared historical landmarks in honor of those wrongly imprisoned. Additionally, California celebrates the first annual Fred Korematsu Day of Civil Liberties and the Constitution on January 30, 2011, the first celebration of its kind honoring a Japanese American—one who fought a Supreme Court battle for the civil rights of the interned during World War II in *Korematsu v. United States.*

- **1949:** The Issei are outnumbered by the Nisei in America, creating a sense of isolation in the older generation as the younger

  are absorbed more easily into the American culture in which they were born.

  Today: Not only are there Issei and Nisei but also Sansei (third generation), Yonsei (fourth generation), and Gosei (fifth generation) Japanese Americans. They make up an integral and invaluable part of the American cultural landscape.

- **1949:** Yamamoto's writing career is successful in spite of her Japanese American heritage. Even after World War II, suspicions of and racism against Japanese Americans are widespread.

  Today: Japanese American literature is studied as an aspect of American literature. It is often classified as a part of Asian American literature, but it is also understood to possess its own distinct set of common themes and styles. Celebrated Japanese American writers include David Mura, John Okada, Kimiko Hahn, Lawson Fusao Inada, and Ruth Ozeki, among many others.

---

between her mother and father until, faced with learning the dark truth about the history of their marriage, she wishes she could learn no more.

HISTORICAL CONTEXT

Issei and Nisei

The Issei and Nisei are the first and second generations, respectively, of Japanese Americans. Issei, meaning "first," are those who immigrated to the United States from Japan. In the story, Mr. and Mrs. Hayashi, therefore, are Issei. Rosie is Nisei, meaning "second": an American born to Japanese immigrant parents. Issei first came to the United States between 1885 and 1924. In 1924, the Asian Exclusion

Act was passed, enacting harsh restrictions on Japanese immigration that lasted until the end of World War II. Issei were not given the right to become naturalized US citizens until 1952. The Nisei were generally born between 1915 and 1935. Citizens of the United States by birthright, they nevertheless were interned in camps during World War II along with the Issei, suspected without evidence of sympathizing with the enemy.

Issei typically spoke Japanese at home, while Nisei learned English in school. This created the divide in language that so frustrates Rosie and her mother in the first scene of "Seventeen Syllables." Literary groups typical of the Japanese writing community survived the journey to America, with magazines and newspapers devoted to various traditional Japanese

Mrs. Hayashi discovers that she has a passion and a talent for writing haikus.
(© Xiaojiao Wang | ShutterStock.com)

poetic and narrative forms published in Los Angeles and San Francisco. Like Tome Hayashi, Yamamoto—a Nisei—contributed to these publications frequently. Issei followed Japanese custom more closely than Nisei, having had firsthand experience of it in their homeland. The expected submission of Tome to her husband's will and the lack of verbal communication between spouses over their conflict are the behaviors of a traditional Japanese couple, who would avoid open argument at all costs. As King-Kok Cheung notes in *Articulate Silences*, "Nonverbal communication and indirect speech remain quite pervasive in traditional Japanese American families, at least among the first two generations." Likewise, Rosie's mix of the Japanese values of her parents and the American values she learns among her peers

is a trait of the Nisei, who must constantly navigate between two cultures.

Haiku

Haiku is a type of traditional Japanese poetry derived from an ancient form called a haika. A haika is a long chain of verses with a hokku, or "starting verse," at the beginning to set the tone. The modern haiku poem is a derivative of these hokku verses, popularized in the 1890s by Masaoka Shiki. Haiku are poems only three lines long. The first line has five syllables, the second has seven, and the third has five, for a total of seventeen (thus the significance of the name "Seventeen Syllables" for a short story about haiku). Despite the short length of a haiku, the haiku poet imbues the poem with meaning by the inclusion of symbols. For example, when Rosie hears her mother's haiku, she assumes it is simply "about cats." Rosie's mother explains that "she had tried to capture the charm of a kitten, as well as comment on the superstition that owning a cat of three colors meant good luck." In this way, haiku can be unpacked for meaning by one familiar with the cultural references and significance of certain words. In Japan, haiku was a hobby of the wealthy: a luxurious way to spend idle time. In America, a farmwife's obsession with haiku is troublesome for a husband rushing to bring the harvest in on time.

CRITICAL OVERVIEW

In her obituary of Yamamoto for the *Los Angeles Times*, Elaine Woo writes that Yamamoto was one of "the first Asian American writers to earn literary distinction after World War II with highly polished short stories that illuminated a world circumscribed by culture and brutal strokes of history."

King-Kok Cheung writes in the introduction to *Seventeen Syllables and Other Stories* that "having lived among both whites and non-whites, Yamamoto captures both the tension and the rapport among people from diverse ethnic backgrounds." Her broad appeal certainly helped her overcome the racism against Japanese Americans in the 1950s.

"Seventeen Syllables" is widely considered to be the most illustrative of Yamamoto's personal writing style and artistic skill. In her entry on Yamamoto for the *Densho Encyclopedia*, Nancy Matsumoto summarizes that style, noting that Yamamoto's short stories are "oblique, often deadpan in delivery and told with quiet humor and bracing candor. They reveal the love affairs madness, psychic and physical brutality that lay beneath . . . Issei and Nisei life."

While the majority of critics find Mr. Hayashi at fault for the violence that erupts the day of the harvest, Ming L. Cheng in "The Unrepentant Fire: Tragic Limitations in Hisaye Yamamoto's 'Seventeen Syllables'" finds both husband and wife are the victims of the limitations pressed upon them by their culture. The stoic husband works for the family's economic survival, a survival which Tome's misplaced upper-class obsession with haiku threatens: "The increasing extravagance of the wife builds as a powerful counterforce, deeply affecting the Hayashis's existence." Cheng, like many others, praises the unreliability of the third-person limited narration: "The narrative is composed by a reluctant witness whose life has been leveled, in Rosie's own words, 'to the very ground.'" In her introduction to Yamamoto's stories, Cheung offers high praise of the author's capricious narrative voice, calling it "a voice that is at once compassionate and ironic, gentle and probing, one that can elicit in rapid succession anger and pity, laughter and tears." This is certainly the voice found in "Seventeen Syllables."

CRITICISM

Amy L. Miller

Miller is a graduate of the University of Cincinnati, and she currently resides in New Orleans, Louisiana. In the following essay, she examines each member of the Hayashi family and the roles they play in the explosive final scene of "Seventeen Syllables."

The two plots of "Seventeen Syllables" crash together in the final scene of the story, causing the death of the alter ego of the quiet, haiku-writing housewife Tome Hayashi and scattering the survivors. This death of Ume Hanazono—the pen name used by the poet—has been foreshadowed in the story's first scene when the narrator explains that Ume Hanazono lived for only three months. Yet the reader, like Rosie, is an unwilling witness to the violence that destroys her mother's artistic life.

CERTAINLY TOME HAYASHI HAD INTERPRETED THE SIGNS OF HER HUSBAND'S DISAPPROVAL, BUT WHETHER OR NOT SHE EXPECTED SUCH A VIOLENT END IS UNKNOWN. HER SILENCE SEEMS RESIGNED, AS IF, WHETHER HAVING EXPECTED IT OR NOT, SHE KNOWS SHE IS ONCE AGAIN POWERLESS IN HER OWN DESTRUCTION."

Yamamoto accomplishes this grim surprise through the use of the third-person limited point of view. As King-Kok Cheung writes in *Articulate Silences*: "By playing the naive nisei point of view against the pregnant silence of the issei . . . Yamamoto constructs hidden plots and deflects attention from unsettling messages." Those messages—dark, adult mysteries of control and despair—seem a world away from Rosie's summer romance, until the violent collision on the day of the harvest bring mother and daughter together to watch the burning of Tome's haiku prize. By the story's end Mr. Hayashi is back in the field, satisfied that his troubles have ended, and Tome stands aloof as her terrified daughter cries. The similarities to Rosie's imagined car crash scenario after the disastrous night at the Hayanos—three bloody figures lying on the side of the road—will be apparent to the reader, considering the gulf that has opened up between each of the Hayashis as a result of the fateful day of the harvest.

The three members of the Hayashi family represent the Issei and Nisei generations of Japanese Americans, but other divisions are present between them as well. Gender divides the family, as does education. Language forms a barrier, disrupting easy communication. No one is more isolated than Mr. Hayashi. Man among women, Issei in America, uneducated among poetry lovers, he stands alone for rigid structure, old values, and respect for authority. Yet his adherence to tradition prevents a fluid adaptation to changing circumstances. He cannot cope with his wife's new hobby. When he stands at the Hayanos to leave after a night spent flipping through magazines, Ming L. Cheng writes, "the abruptness of his actions,

WHAT
DO I READ
NEXT?

- Toshio Mori's *Yokohoma, California* (1949) is a collection of short stories set in a Japanese American farming community in California. As Yamamoto does in "Seventeen Syllables," Mori captures the heart of the immigrant experience of Japanese Americans.

- In Yamamoto's "Yoneko's Earthquake" (1951), published in *Seventeen Syllables and Other Stories*, a Japanese American wife betrays her husband with a farmhand. Told through the eyes of the Nisei daughter of the couple, "Yoneko's Earthquake" is concerned with racism among minorities, domestic violence, and the limitations of tradition.

- In the young-adult novel *Black Mirror*, by Nancy Werlin (2003), a half-Japanese, half-Jewish prep school student must unravel the mystery behind her brother's suicide by infiltrating the seemingly innocent charity club Unity, of which he was a passionate member.

- Ryunosuke Akutagawa's *Kappa* (2009) is a satire of Japanese society and traditions told through the eyes of a man in a mental institution who journeys to Kappaland, a magical realm where creatures from ancient Japanese folklore roam.

- *White Teeth* (2000), by Zadie Smith, features two families, two generations, and a riotous mix of cultures set in London, England. Archie Jones and Samad Iqbal are veterans of World War II, struggling to forge their own paths amid the chaos of their growing families, while their children navigate a London shaped by diversity and danger.

- Bill Hosokawa's *Nisei: The Quiet Americans* (1969) is a dazzling nonfiction account of the struggles and triumphs of the Issei and Nisei generations of Japanese Americans, covering the years of heavy immigration leading up to World War II, the horror of the internment camps, and postwar reconciliation and rebirth.

- Monica Sone's memoir, *Nisei Daughter* (1952), follows the life of a Japanese American girl living in Seattle, Washington, whose young life is upturned by the enforced internment of Japanese Americans during World War II.

- *A Tale for the Time Being: A Novel* (2013), by Ruth Ozeki, tells the story of Nao, a sixteen-year-old girl living in Tokyo who has decided to record the history of her grandmother, as well as her own struggles at school, in a diary. When a woman named Ruth finds the diary washed up on the shore on the other side of the Pacific following the 2011 tsunami, Ruth struggles to discover more about Nao, a lonely, brilliant girl, and her fate across the wide ocean.

---

in a culture where even the smallest gestures are of great consequence, sends a clear signal." His wife, comparing haiku notes with the attractive Mr. Hayano, has upset the balance of power in their family. In a traditional home, the men and women would socialize separately, yet, as Cheng points out, art supercedes gender when it comes to haiku in "Seventeen Syllables." Mr. Hayashi is forced to spend the evening in the company of Mrs. Hayano, a woman whose broken body foreshadows the interior desolation later revealed in Tome. Mrs. Hayano, like Tome Hayashi, has been shattered by childbirth. In her case the affliction manifests physically in trembles and painful steps. For Tome, the pain of her stillborn son is a psychic burden relieved through haiku. Mr. Hayashi suffers silently, because he is expected to be a laconic figure as head of the household. His masculine power should lie in his brooding presence. Unfortunately, as Cheung writes in *Articulate Silences*, "Daughter and mother pay little, if any, attention to Mr. Hayashi's moodiness. They are absorbed alike in self-discovery, preoccupied with love or art." As the Japanese culture of the family is diluted by American influence, so does Mr. Hayashi lose some of the control he has been raised to expect from his family.

In fact, when Mr. Hayashi snaps at Rosie as he is coming from the baths, she has the audacity to snap back: "What have I done now?" This is an act of defiance typical of an American teenager, but an unthinkably disrespectful action for a Japanese girl toward her hardworking father. Rosie occupies the liminal space between cultures, however, a mix of Japanese and American that is entirely original to herself. Elaine Woo's summary of Rosie's part in the plot is particularly apt. She writes, "A nisei girl's blooming romance with a Mexican American classmate offers an achingly innocent counterpoint to her issei mother's arranged marriage." Independent of the tension between her parents, Rosie's romance is indeed a sweet, fragile thing, embarked upon without a clear destination in mind, only curiosity, as Rosie follows Jesus to the shed without guessing the nature of his "secret." In the field the day of the harvest, Rosie's mind wanders continuously to Jesus, so much so that when he does appear she runs away in nervous excitement. Even after Mr. Kuroda's appearance, Rosie is thinking of Jesus, not her father's disapproval of the situation: "She had emptied six lugs when he broke into an imaginary conversation with Jesus to tell her to go and remind her mother of the tomatoes." Not until the violence breaks out does Rosie's awareness snap away from her young love. Fearful of her mother's fate in the house, she runs to her side. But her mother's startling display of desperation sends Rosie's thoughts, in alarm, back to the safety of Jesus.

Woo writes of Yamamoto, "Among her most powerful characters are women who struggle to nurture their romantic or creative selves despite the constraints of gender, racism, and tradition." Though the reader is closely attached through the third-person limited narration to Rosie, Tome Hayashi is the force of change in the story. Rosie is a precocious girl,

Mr. Hayashi a gruff farmer. These are expected characteristics, but Tome defies expectation with her artist's soul. She is, Cheng writes, "a woman with passions which consume, who ignores the limits imposed by societal mores and the norms of behavior indicated by traditional gender roles." Far from the scribblings of a bored housewife tinkering with poetry, Tome's haiku win first prize, draw the San Francisco editor off course to meet her in person, and keep her friends up late with fascinating discussions. As noted by Cheung in *Articulate Silences*, the seventeen syllables of the haiku correspond to the age her stillborn son would have been had he lived. It is as if, for these three brief months, he is alive through her creative process. It is a birth that, rather than bringing her misfortune and shame, brings attention and reward. Until, of course, the moment her husband has had enough. When Rosie finds Tome alone in the house, silently watching the Hiroshige print burn, Cheung writes in her introduction to *Seventeen Syllables and Other Stories*, "the external calmness of the mother, almost frightening at this point, seems only to suggest the depth of her anguish." She has lost another creation. Like her son, Ume Hanazono is dead. Certainly Tome Hayashi had interpreted the signs of her husband's disapproval, but whether or not she expected such a violent end is unknown. Her silence seems resigned, as if, whether having expected it or not, she knows she is once again powerless in her own destruction.

She tells her story to her daughter, who is unwilling to hear, to have her Nisei fantasies of freedom and love destroyed by Issei history. But for Tome, there is no choice but to burden her daughter. Cheung writes in her introduction to Yamamoto's stories, "Deserted by her lover in Japan and stifled by her husband in America, Mrs. Hayashi has abandoned all hopes. . . . She can only try to prevent her daughter from repeating her mistakes." In the story's first scene, Tome seems unsure that Rosie has the capacity to understand the meaning of her haiku. Yet now she reveals to Rosie a past fraught with heartbreak and cruelty, in which Tome could not follow her dream owing to her family's poverty, in which a brother Rosie would have liked to meet dies, in which the family too poor to be worthy of her lover ostracizes Tome as unworthy of their support. Rosie tries to keep out the implications of her parents' arranged marriage, of her father's ignorance of her mother's past. But she has heard every word and will not escape the scar of knowing, however hard she tries to push back "the illumination which threatened all that darkness that had hitherto been merely mysterious or even glamorous." Then, her story complete, her mother drops to the floor at Rosie's feet, begging her without shame to renounce the possibility of love.

Critics like Cheng and Cheung have noted the similarity of Tome Hayashi's position kneeling on the floor, grasping her daughter's hands, to that of a marriage proposal. The deep irony of a mother assuming this position in order to beg her daughter never to marry is characteristic of Yamamoto's brilliant subtlety. As she has spent the story misdirecting her reader toward the young, silly love between Rosie and Jesus, she now plays with the reader's subconscious, corrupting the absolute pinnacle of romantic acts into a display of defiance against a system that has crushed Tome's passion, twice over. In her introduction, Cheung writes in praise of Yamamoto's undeniable skill: "Reminiscent of the verbal economy of haiku, in which the poet 'must pack all her meaning into seventeen syllables only,' Yamamoto's stories exemplify precision and restraint." In "Seventeen Syllables," Yamamoto restricts her narration to that of a carefree child named Rosie, and then proceeds to tell a story of such depth and hopelessness that by the end, after only a few short pages, Rosie is a child no more.

Source: Amy L. Miller, Critical Essay on "Seventeen Syllables," in *Short Stories for Students*, Gale, Cengage Learning, 2016.

Anne N. Thalheimer

In the following review, Thalheimer asserts that Yamamoto's short stories require multiple readings to reveal all their complexities.

Originally published by Kitchen Table: Women of Color Press in 1988, *Seventeen Syllables and Other Stories* was honored with the Award for Literature from the Association for Asian American Studies the year it was published. That edition is currently out of print, and has been replaced by this Rutgers University Press collection of Hisaye Yamamoto's short stories, which, like the original edition, contains fifteen short stories spanning Yamamoto's

Rosie's father seems to resent his wife's success.
(© leungchopan | ShutterStock.com)

lengthy writing career. The collection begins with her first breakthrough publication, 1948's "The High-Heeled Shoes, A Memoir," which is, in part, about varying forms of sexual harassment, and covers a span of four decades before ending with the more recent "Reading and Writing," a short story about the unique friendship between two very different women, published in Hokubei Mainishi in early January 1988.

Hisaye Yamamoto's most widely anthologized short story, the haunting "Seventeen Syllables," which juxtaposes the anguish of an Issei mother trapped in a difficult, loveless marriage with the bittersweet sexual awakening of her teenager daughter Rosie, is included in this book, along with the three other stories that earned places on the "Distinctive Short Stories" list, which lists the contents of the yearly volume of *Best American Short Stories*. As testimony to Yamamoto's storytelling skill, "Seventeen Syllables" made the list in 1949, "The Brown House" and "Yoneko's Earthquake" in 1951, and "Epithalamium" in 1960.

Yamamoto, who in 1986 won the Before Columbus Foundation's American Book Award for Lifetime Achievement, often composes stories informed by not only by her own history, and Japanese-American history generally—which includes her internment in Poston, Arizona during World War Two—but also issues that relate to gender, race, and ethnicity (with an emphasis on residual suspicion of Japanese-Americans after World War Two, shown in "Wilshire Bus"), and the difficulties and frustrations of family life and marriage (often arranged) in immigrant families.

Each of the fifteen stories details, in some way, the particular anguish of Japanese and Japanese-American women, from things as seemingly simple as a loveless arranged marriage in "Seventeen Syllables," or a strained union such as Henry and Marge Kusumoto's marriage in "My Father Can Beat Muhammad Ali," to severe mentally instability, possibly as a result of camp life or an inattentive ascetic father ("The Legend of Miss Sasagawara"). Some stories go further into the detail of women's lives but do so only through relying upon the reader to interpret what Yamamoto implies. For example, "Yoneko's Earthquake" tells the story of Yoneko Hosoume, who waits in vain for God to answer her prayers to end the aftershocks of an earthquake. She does not seem to fully comprehend the events around her, though their meaning becomes clear to the careful reader.

It is a credit to Yamamoto that the voice of her ten-year-old narrator in "Yoneko's Earthquake" is entirely convincing, a skill which establishes Yamamoto as the clear predecessor of current female Japanese-American writers, such as Lois-Ann Yamanaka, who create vivid female characters. Yoneko narrates the events of her own life in detail, while making only passing reference to those things—such as a sudden and mysterious mid-week trip to a city hospital and the simultaneous abrupt departure of Marpo, their Filipino farmhand—happening around her. The astute reader quickly pieces the hidden narrative together, aided by Yamamoto's masterful control of detailed depiction, and realizes that despair runs deep not just in Yoneko, but far more poignantly and tragically in her mother.

"The Brown House" and "Epithalamium" also deal with women who make choices—in the former, a wife who becomes resigned to her husband's gambling problem, and in the latter, a woman who chooses to marry an alcoholic who is intoxicated even as they recite their vows—and cast, like "Seventeen Syllables," a dim view over marriage and male-female relationships, as well as over men in general. Fathers (and father figures) do not fare well in these short stories, but that is not to say that Yamamoto passes judgment upon them, for she is skilled at making a character's vice his virtue, and never portraying anything as one single thing. Like haiku, a character in and of itself in "Seventeen Syllables," Yamamoto's short stories are layered in metaphor, imagery and irony, but never wordy or given to digression.

The introduction by King-Kok Cheung, Professor of English and Asian American Studies at UCLA, provides an excellent introduction to Yamamoto's work, especially to the reader unfamiliar with either Yamamoto herself or Japanese-American history. Cheung, who has written extensively on Hisaye Yamamoto's life and work, along with other Asian American authors such as Maxine Hong Kingston and Joy Kogawa, provides an efficient and interesting overview of Yamamoto's work, including a series of notes which place Yamamoto's work within a continuum of Issei (Japanese immigrants), Nisei (second generation Japanese-Americans), and Sansei (third generation) writers and scholarship.

Her introduction also provides the reader with a brief but sufficient synopsis of Japanese-American history, enough so that the connection between history and its appearance in Yamamoto's work is clear, but the history lesson is spare enough so that those interested in the topic are encouraged to read more, aided, in part, by the carefully compiled bibliography. A selected bibliography of both primary sources (listing where and when Yamamoto's stories originally appeared) and secondary sources (including scholarship of interest to both readers interested in Asian American literature and those more specialized in Japanese-American writing) is included.

The only complaint about the introduction is that, perhaps, it should have concluded the book rather than opening it. So many of Hisaye Yamamoto's short stories—for the first-time reader, anyway—possess a sort of power, an element of surprise seen in some of Flannery O'Connor's short stories, and rely on the reader to first wonder, then suspect, and then finally understand the hidden part of the story. King-Kok Cheung's analysis of Yamamoto's short stories is by all accounts first-rate but gives away the so-called "secrets" of the short stories. So, for those readers who have not yet had the fortune of reading any of Hisaye Yamamoto's works, the introduction should certainly be read, but only after reading the collection. On the other hand, Hisaye Yamamoto's short stories, like this collection, and like King-Kok Cheung's introduction, all merit multiple readings.

Source: Anne N. Thalheimer, Review of *Seventeen Syllables and Other Stories*, in *MELUS*, Vol. 24, No. 4, Winter 1999, p. 177.

SOURCES

Cheng, Ming L., "The Unrepentant Fire: Tragic Limitations in Hisaye Yamamoto's 'Seventeen Syllables,'" in *MELUS*, Vol. 19, No. 4, 1994, pp. 91–107.

Cheung, King-Kok, Introduction to *Seventeen Syllables and Other Stories*, Rutgers University Press, 1998, pp. ix–xxiii.

———, "Reading Between the Syllables: Hisaye Yamamoto's 'Seventeen Syllables' and Other Stories," in *Teaching American Ethnic Literatures: Nineteen Essays*, University of New Mexico Press, 1996, pp. 313–25.

———, "Rhetorical Silence: 'Seventeen Syllables,' 'Yoneko's Earthquake,' and 'The Legend of Miss Sasagawara,'" in *Articulate Silences*, Cornell University Press, 1993, pp. 27–42.

Ho, Pui-Ching, "Dear Miss Breed: Letters from Camp FAQ," Japanese American National Museum website, http://www.janm.org/exhibits/breed/gloss_t.htm (accessed February 18, 2015).

"Japanese American Relocation," in *History.com*, 2009, http://www.history.com/topics/world-war-ii/japanese-american-relocation (accessed February 18, 2015).

Matsumoto, Nancy, "Hisaye Yamamoto," in *Densho Encyclopedia*, October 26, 2013, http://encyclopedia.densho.org/Hisaye%20Yamamoto (accessed February 18, 2015).

Toyomasu, Kei Grieg, "What Is Haiku?," in *Haiku for People*, January 10, 2001, http://www.toyomasu.com/haiku/#whatishaiku (accessed February 18, 2015).

Woo, Elaine, "Hisaye Yamamoto Dies at 89: Writer of Japanese American Stories," in *Los Angeles Times*, February 13, 2011, http://articles.latimes.com/2011/feb/13/local/la-me-hisaye-yamamoto-20110213 (accessed February 18, 2015).

Yamamoto, Hisaye, "Seventeen Syllables," in *Seventeen Syllables and Other Stories*, Rutgers University Press, 1998, pp. 8–19.

FURTHER READING

Bowers, Faubion, *The Classic Tradition of Haiku: An Anthology*, Dover Publications, 1996.

Bowers gathers a short collection of the undisputed masters of the haiku form of poetry, highlighting the beauty, economy, and depth of the form. Each of the two hundred poems is presented in both Japanese and English.

Lee, Shelley Sang-Hee, *A New History of Asian America*, Routledge, 2013.

Lee's history of Asian Americans begins in the 1700s and leads to the present day, examining Asian Americans' effect on and participation in US history, as well as chronicling the watershed moments in Asian American culture.

Matsumoto, Valerie J., *City Girls: The Nisei Social World in Los Angeles, 1920–1950*, Oxford University Press, 2014.

Like Rosie in "Seventeen Syllables," the Asian American women of Matsumoto's *City Girls* are caught between the culture and language of their immigrant parents—the Issei generation—and their own American upbringing. Despite being born as US citizens, the women of *City Girls* face significant discrimination owing to their race.

Wong, Sau-ling Cynthia, *Reading Asian American Literature*, Princeton University Press, 1993.

Wong teaches readers new to Asian American literature the defining characteristics, common themes, history, issues and points of contention in this rapidly growing segment of American literature, focusing on how Asian American literature fits beneath the larger umbrella of American literature, as well as how the works interact with each other within the subdivision.

SUGGESTED SEARCH TERMS

Hisaye Yamamoto

Seventeen Syllables AND Yamamoto

Hisaye Yamamoto AND Seventeen Syllables AND short story

Japanese American AND Hisaye Yamamoto

Seventeen Syllables AND Rosie

Hiyase Yamamoto AND haiku

Seventeen Syllables AND King-Kok Cheung

Issei AND Nisei

Japanese American internment AND World War II

haiku

The Willows

ALGERNON BLACKWOOD
1907

"The Willows" is a story by twentieth-century British author Algernon Blackwood, who is known for his tales of the supernatural. The story was first published in Blackwood's *The Listener and Other Stories* in 1907 and was reprinted in several later collections. It is available in *Ancient Sorceries and Other Weird Stories* (2002) in the Penguin Classics series. "The Willows" is based on a canoeing trip that Blackwood made in the summer of 1900 with a friend down the Danube river between Vienna and Budapest. In the story, the two men land on a tiny island in the Danube. The river is rising, and the wind is howling. On the island, they soon begin to feel uneasy, and the narrator associates this feeling with the eerie presence of the willows. Strange events start to accumulate, and the men become increasingly afraid, even terrified. They believe they are in the presence of beings from another dimension, and they fear for their lives. "The Willows" has been acclaimed by a number of commentators as one of the finest supernatural stories ever written.

AUTHOR BIOGRAPHY

Blackwood was born on March 14, 1869, in Shooters Hill, Kent, England, to Sir Stevenson Arthur Blackwood, a senior civil servant, and Harriet Sydney Dobbs. The wealthy, aristocratic

Algernon Blackwood, one of the most prolific authors in the ghost story genre
(© Hulton-Deutsch Collection | Corbis)

family moved to Crayford, Kent, two years later and then to Beckenham, in the same county, in 1881. Blackwood was educated at Wellington College in Berkshire and then spent two years at a school in Germany. From 1888 to 1889, he attended Edinburgh University. Blackwood rejected the evangelical Christianity of his family and instead became interested in Eastern religions, theosophy, and the occult. His first published story was "A Mysterious House," a ghost story, in 1889.

Blackwood never felt called to pursue a particular career. He preferred to work at odd jobs and pursue a few business opportunities. From 1890 to 1892, he lived in Canada, working for a while for the Canadian Pacific Railway. He moved to New York City in 1892 and worked as a journalist before returning to England seven years later. Pursuing his esoteric interests, Blackwood became a member of the Theosophical Society, and in 1900 he joined the Hermetic Order of the Golden Dawn. In 1906, he published his first book, *The Empty House and Other Ghost Stories*,

which was soon followed by *The Listener and Other Stories* (1907), which contained "The Willows." In 1908, Blackwood published *John Silence: Physician Extraordinary* (1908), which contains five related stories. The book was a best seller and allowed Blackwood to devote himself full time to writing.

Blackwood moved to Switzerland in 1909, where he lived until he returned to England in 1915. While in Switzerland, he published *The Lost Valley and Other Stories* (1910), the novels *The Human Chord* (1910) and *The Centaur* (1911), *Pan's Garden: A Volume of Nature Stories* (1912), *Ten Minute Stories* (1914), and *Incredible Adventures* (1914). Several more books followed during World War I, including *Julius Le Vallon: An Episode* (1916), *The Wave: An Egyptian Aftermath* (1916), and *The Garden of Survival* (1918), as well as the short-story collection *Day and Night Stories* (1917). For a period of six months starting in late 1916, Blackwood was recruited by the British government as a secret agent, and he returned to Switzerland to pursue this war work, coming back to England in June 1917.

Blackwood continued to publish at a prolific rate in the 1920s. His work included the novel *The Bright Messenger* (1921) and another short-story collection, *Tongues of Fire and Other Sketches* (1924). He also wrote plays, including *The Crossing* (1920); an autobiography, *Episodes Before Thirty* (1923); and several books for children, including the novel *Sambo and Snitch* (1927). He also wrote many articles and reviews. In the 1930s and 1940s, he often gave talks and read stories on BBC radio and appeared as a guest on television programs. In 1936, he undertook a walking tour of Europe, during which he visited Austria, Italy, France, and Spain. In 1940, during World War II, his nephew's house in Hampstead, London, where he was living at the time, was hit by a German bomb. Blackwood was not in the house at the time, but many of his papers were destroyed. During the 1940s, Blackwood continued to write stories. In 1949 he was made a Commander of the British Empire, a high honor in Britain, and in 1951 he became a Fellow of the Royal Society of Literature.

Blackwood died in London on December 10, 1951, of cerebral thrombosis and arteriosclerosis.

PLOT SUMMARY

1

In mid-July, the narrator and his friend, referred to only as the Swede, take a canoeing trip down the Danube river. They started in the Black Forest, and when the story begins, they have left Vienna and are proceeding into Hungary in the direction of Budapest. They enter a region remote from civilization. The river is flooded, and it is windy. With some difficulty they land on an island, where there is an abundance of willow bushes on all sides. It is late afternoon. The island is no more than an acre, standing two or three feet above the river. As he explores the island, the narrator is in awe of the vast elemental forces at work in water and wind, and he also feels uneasy, an emotion he traces to the willows, which are seemingly everywhere, as far as the eye can reach. They seem to embody a power that is not friendly to the two travelers. The narrator feels that they may have entered an alien world where they are not welcome and may encounter great risks.

They pitch a tent. The Swede then points to the river and says there is a man's body floating down it. In fact, it is a living otter, which for a moment looked like a drowned man. Then they do see, at some distance, a man, who is in a boat on the river, steering with an oar. The man looks them, gesticulating and shouting, although they cannot hear what he says. He makes the sign of the cross before disappearing out of sight.

The men collect driftwood, start a fire, cook food, and talk. They are both struck by the "beauty and loneliness of the place." Under the light of a full moon, the narrator hunts for firewood and explores the island further. He finds the sound the willows make in the wind alarming. They seem to him like "a host of beings from another plane of life." He thinks of them as like an army, surrounding their camp and ready to attack. The Swede joins him, having wondered what was taking him so long. They both have a feeling of unease, as if disaster might strike them. They go into the tent to sleep, while the wind continues to rage.

2

The narrator wakes at midnight. Feeling uneasy, he crawls out of the tent. He sees the willow bushes swaying in the wind. They seem

to form huge shapes that make them look as if they are living beings that are constantly shifting. He is filled with awe and thinks he is seeing "the personified elemental forces of this haunted and primeval region." He thinks that they have been stirred up because he and his friend have disturbed them by entering their realm. He tries to convince himself that it is only his imagination at work, but as he creeps back into his tent, he feels fearful.

3

He is awakened again from sleep by the sound of "multitudinous little patterings." He is terrified but then thinks the sound must be from the leaves from a fallen branch brushing against the tent. He goes outside, but there is no fallen branch. The river is still rising and the wind howling. He is again filled with unease at the sight of all the willows. For a moment he is terrified by the wind, which seems to be like a living, walking presence. After calming down, he is again filled with alarm when he observes from his standpoint in the middle of the island that during the night the willows have moved closer to the tent. He is terrified by what he thinks is the hostility and menace of the willows. Then he tries to convince himself that such an idea is absurd. It is dawn, and he returns to the tent. The Swede is still asleep.

The narrator tries to convince himself that his feelings of alarm are due only to an overheated imagination. He falls asleep, still feeling uneasy and even a sense of dread.

4

In late morning, the Swede awakens the narrator. He is cooking breakfast. He says the river is still rising, and the island is smaller than it was. The narrator bathes in the river under a hot sun. As they talk over breakfast, the narrator gets the impression that his friend is frightened. They agree that they must leave within the hour, but the Swede is worried about the elemental powers in the place and whether they will let the men leave. He says that the steering paddle has disappeared and there is a tear in the bottom of the canoe. He points out the tear to the narrator, saying it was not there last night. The narrator says they must have scratched it on a stone as they landed, although he realizes this is an impossible explanation. The Swede then shows him the remaining paddle, which has been scraped down until it is very thin. The narrator attempts a natural explanation, but even he does not believe it, and neither does the Swede.

The narrator finds that deep hollows have formed in the sand, which he attributes to the wind. The Swede says the hollows are all over the island, and he does not believe the narrator's explanation.

The Swede repairs the canoe expertly. As they talk, they review the strange events of the previous day, and the Swede wonders whether the otter was in fact a dead man after all. Also, the Swede wonders whether the man they saw in the boat was indeed a man or something else. The narrator refutes both these suggestions, but the Swede tells him he is deceiving himself. The narrator accepts this and from then on starts to feel increasing fear.

By late afternoon, the wind has dropped, making the sounds of the river more prominent. The narrator experiences this as the "music of doom." It becomes cloudy, and with the loss of sunlight the atmosphere grows more sinister, as the narrator experiences it. He sees the willows seemingly moving independently like living creatures, and he feels they are grotesque and hostile. He dreads the coming of darkness.

The narrator cooks dinner but is called away to the riverbank by the Swede. Together, they listen to an unusual sound, like a gong in the sky. The Swede says he has been hearing it all day but cannot place its location. It seems to move around. He suggests it has been there all along, masked by the sound of the wind. He seems to think it is a cry made by the elemental forces of the region, but the narrator rushes back to his cooking, not giving him a chance to fully articulate his thought.

As they prepare their meal, they discover that all the bread they had in a sack has disappeared. The narrator explains this by saying he forgot to buy a loaf when they were in Pressburg. After a gloomy meal they sit mostly silent. The narrator can still hear the gong-like sound, seemingly coming from everywhere at once. The Swede says it is a nonhuman sound from what he calls the fourth dimension, and the narrator believes this too. He has a sense of dread because he fears they have stumbled upon the frontiers of an unknown world and may become victims, a kind of sacrifice to the powers that dwell there. He fears that their minds will be overcome by the unearthly powers that inhabit this region.

Both men are now frightened by the situation they find themselves in, although neither admits it directly. Then the narrator confesses that he is in a "blue funk," but the Swede remains outwardly calm. He says they must not try to run away but just sit and wait and keep still. Then the powerful forces he knows are present may not attack them. He thinks they have not yet located precisely where the two men are. He says they must stay in control of their own minds, since it is their minds that the alien forces feel. They must not get taken over by these forces, for that would be worse than death. He explains further that he has always been aware of a different kind of world than the one humans live in; the forces that inhabit it "deal directly with the soul" and have "nothing to do with mankind." However, he and the narrator happen to have stumbled on a place where this alien world intersects with their own. He says that their only hope is that some other being is sacrificed as a victim. This will distract the alien forces and allow the two men to escape. He thinks that if they can survive another night, they may be able to get away in the morning undiscovered.

As they talk further, the Swede says the sound of the gong, which they can still hear, is the sound of the other world that threatens them. The sound is in the willows, he says. His plan is that he and the narrator just act normally and go to bed; they are to pretend that nothing untoward is happening; that way their minds will not create the very reality they fear. The narrator then chances to think back to a mundane incident in London when he was fitted for a shoe; the sheer ordinariness of the situation has the effect of banishing his fear. He laughs, but at that moment the fear returns. They hear a strange cry above them; it is as if his laughter has attracted attention. The Swede, frightened, says they must leave right now, but the narrator, thinking that would be rash and unwise, given that it is dark, the river is flooding, and they have only one paddle, insists that they stay one more night and then leave at sunrise. The Swede acquiesces.

They go to collect wood but then see something moving near their campfire. The figure is neither human nor animal; the Swede thinks it is a group of willow bushes. Then the figure starts to come toward them, and the Swede exclaims that they have been discovered. They fall together to the sand. The Swede grips the narrator's arm hard, and the pain drives from his mind all thought of the strange creature or creatures, which has the effect of concealing him from them. The Swede loses consciousness, which has the same effect.

After a while they climb out of a bunch of willow branches. The Swede thinks the frightening presences have left and are pursuing a false trail somewhere. The humming has stopped. They return to their tent, which has collapsed. They find "deep funnel-shaped hollows in the sand" similar to ones they had observed earlier, but bigger. They enter the tent and fall asleep, realizing that that is the safest thing they can do.

5

The narrator wakes up in the night with the feeling that the tent is surrounded. He finds to his alarm that the Swede is not in the tent. Alarmed, he goes outside, where the humming sound has returned. He sees the Swede by the river, about to jump in. It seems that his mind has been taken over by the alien force, and he is about to commit suicide. The narrator drags him back to the tent. He calms down and goes to sleep, after saying that the danger has passed

because another victim has been found. He awakes several hours later remembering nothing of the incident. They bathe and prepare breakfast. There is no wind and no humming. The Swede says he feels safe again. Together they go down to the riverbank, where they find the dead body of a man, a peasant who must have been drowned a few hours earlier. They go to collect the body for burial but slip on the bank and fall onto the corpse. At that moment the humming returns, rising up from the corpse, "as though we had disturbed some living yet invisible creatures at work." They also notice that the body is indented with the same hollows that they had seen in the sand all over the island. The Swede says it is the mark made by the strange creatures. Just at that moment the body is swept away in the current and disappears.

CHARACTERS

The Narrator

The narrator provides no details about himself, not even his name. He is likely a young man, because the canoeing expedition on which he ventures requires some physical strength, skill, and endurance. He has made many similar trips before with his friend the Swede, although this appears to be their first trip down the Danube.

The narrator thinks of his companion as being without any imagination, from which it might be inferred that he, the narrator, regards himself as somewhat the opposite. This seems to be confirmed early on, before the feeling of unease takes hold, when he personifies the Danube as a living creature. He seems to have an imaginative, even poetic, response to his environment, and he has an eye for detail. Significantly, it is he, rather than the Swede, who first feels uneasy when they land on the island. Later, however, their roles change somewhat, as the Swede becomes convinced that strange things are happening, while the narrator tries to explain them away rationally. In his heart, though, he knows that the Swede is right. In the end, it is the narrator, supposedly the imaginative one, who keeps a firmer control on his mind than the Swede, and he is therefore able to prevent the Swede from drowning himself.

The Swede

The Swede is the narrator's friend who accompanies him on the canoe trip. He is an experienced canoeist, and the narrator is glad to have him along, regarding him as a "delightful and charming travelling companion." The Swede is a man of a "stolid, practical nature" in the eyes of the narrator. He is "imperturbable" and also very efficient, skilled, and dependable:

> He could steer down rapids like a red Indian, shoot dangerous bridges and whirlpools better than any white man I ever saw in a canoe. He was a great fellow for an adventurous trip, a tower of strength when untoward things happened.

Not surprisingly, the Swede is the one who mends the torn canoe, and he does so "with the skill and address of a red Indian."

The narrator also regards his companion as a man without imagination. He "never made remarks that suggested more than they said." However, the narrator does notice that the Swede seems more sensitive than usual about his environment after they land on the island. Like the narrator, he seems aware of the beauty and loneliness there; it becomes apparent that he is not just a practical man limited to what he can perceive through his five senses. After he sees the first two strange sights—the otter and the man in the boat—the Swede seems to become frightened, and from that point on, it seems that he is even more convinced than the narrator that they are in the presence of hostile, possibly supernatural powers. Their roles seem to become reversed, with the narrator—despite his own feelings of dread—trying to offer rational, reasonable explanations for what is happening, only to have the Swede dismiss them all out of hand. It seems that the Swede is able to articulate what the narrator is thinking but does not want to openly acknowledge. The Swede also reveals—surprisingly for a man who is supposedly practical and unimaginative—that all his life he has been "conscious of another region—not far removed from our own world in one sense, yet wholly different in kind."

THEMES

Supernatural

The story is imbued with a sense of the supernatural. The supernatural refers to something that exists beyond nature; a supernatural event

TOPICS FOR FURTHER STUDY

- Write your own weird tale. Bear in mind Blackwood's description of the moment of terror or beauty that can push even an average individual into some kind of experience that is completely beyond the normal. What is that experience going to be like in your story, and how will your characters react to it? What will the consequences be?

- As of 2015, no movie has been made of "The Willows" or any other Blackwood story. However, in 2008 filmmaker Wayne Spitzer told Buried.com that he was working on a screenplay for the story. You can read his comments at http://www.buried.com/interviews/horror.php?id=209. Do you think "The Willows" could be effectively adapted for film? How would you go about it? Write a detailed outline that explains your vision of what form such a movie might take. Post your outline to your blog, and invite classmates to comment on it.

- R. L. Stine's *Nightmare Hour: Time for Terror* (1999), is a collection of ten horror stories written for young-adult readers. Read some of these stories, and write an essay in which you compare Stine's technique to that of Blackwood in "The Willows." How do the two writers create and sustain the feeling of terror? How do they differ?

- Read several of Blackwood's stories and make a class presentation about his work as a whole, based on what you have read. Is "The Willows" typical of his work? How do other stories compare to it in subject matter and style? Which of the stories do you like best, and why?

would be something for which no rational explanation can be found in the laws of nature as they are known. Understood as a plane of existence beyond the earthly realm, the supernatural is a dimension in which beings, such as gods or spirits or ghosts, may dwell. Such a realm is normally invisible to human sight, but sometimes people may sense supernatural events or perceive something that seems supernatural, in which case they may be filled with awe—as a religious person might feel experiencing the presence of the divine—alarm, or even terror, depending on the kind of manifestation they are observing. The term *occult* is sometimes used to refer to such supernatural powers or forces. In literature, the supernatural is often related to horror, and supernatural stories are also sometimes known as "weird" tales.

In this story, at first the atmosphere is merely disquieting and somewhat eerie. Initially, allusions to the supernatural are raised only to be dismissed. For example, after the sighting of the otter that looked like a dead man and the boatman making the sign of the cross, the Swede comments that the man was probably scared by seeing them there, since he thinks that the locals probably believe in "fairies and elementals, possibly demons too." He comments disparagingly about how they had been told by a shopkeeper at Pressburg that the part of the river where they were now "belonged to some sort of beings outside man's world." The narrator, not as skeptical as the Swede, says that if they had any imagination, the locals would say the place was inhabited by the old Roman gods, as the Romans themselves must have done. Having sounded this note, the hints of the supernatural come quite steadily. The region the travelers have entered lies "on the frontier of another world, an alien world," and the seemingly alive willow bushes put the narrator in mind of "a host of beings from another plane of life, another evolution altogether." They are in a "haunted region," he decides at the end of the story's second section.

As the strange events continue to build up—in addition to the otter and the boatman, there is the loss of a paddle, the inexplicable tear in the canoe, and the strange sound of the gong—the Swede is unnerved, and it is he who fully articulates a theory of what is going on. The sound of the gong, he says, comes from a "fourth dimension." Further, he theorizes that in this desolate and lonely place they are at the border of two worlds, where the three-dimensional world in which humans live intersects with another universe altogether that exists in a fourth dimension. The beings that inhabit that realm are hostile because the two travelers have intruded on their realm. The narrator comes to believe that this is "a new order of experience" for him, one that is "in the true sense of the word *unearthly*." This eerie sense of the supernatural, having been firmly and repeatedly established, is then maintained throughout the remainder of the story.

Imagination

The events of the story may be supernatural and terrifying for the narrator and the Swede, but the question of whether they are objectively real or merely a subjective creation of the imagination is constantly brought to the fore. Are the two characters merely hallucinating the entire episode? The word "imagination" is used twelve times in the story; "imaginative" is used five times, and "imagine" is used three times. Early on, when they are first struck by the wonder of the remote world they have entered, the men agree that it contained "unwritten warnings to trespassers for those who had the imagination to discover them." The implication about the role the imagination is to play is clear. A little later, as the narrator looks out on the vastness of the Danube and thinks of the "great elemental forces" at work, he notes that "the sight appealed to the imagination." When he first connects his feelings of unease to the willow bushes, he sees them as "attacking the mind . . . and contriving in some way or other to represent to the imagination a new and mighty power, a power, moreover, not altogether friendly to us." After he sees the willows as huge, moving, nonhuman creatures, he struggles, not entirely successfully, to dismiss the experience as being merely a product of his imagination:

> The moonlight and the branches combined to work out these pictures upon the mirror of my imagination, and for some reason I projected them outwards and made them appear objective. I knew this must be the case, of course. I took courage, and began to move forward across the open patches of sand. By Jove, though, was it all hallucination? Was it merely subjective? Did not my reason argue in the old futile way from the little standard of the known?

The story opens peacefully with two men canoeing on the Danube River. (© *Vladimir Daragan | ShutterStock.com*)

The same question returns after he has been terrified by the sound of "little patterings" outside the tent and been out to investigate. After he returns to his tent he again seeks a rational explanation of the strange events: "With the daylight I could persuade myself that it was all a subjective hallucination, a fantasy of the night, a projection of the excited imagination."

The narrator is never fully convinced by his own arguments, however, and he soon accepts the supernatural explanations put forth by the Swede. Significantly, the narrator has always viewed the Swede as a man quite without imagination, so the fact that the Swede appears to believe in the objective reality of what is taking place suggests that it may indeed be so. However, the Swede also emphasizes that there is a strong subjective element involved. The supernatural beings will be able to locate and harm them only if they, the two men, entertain thoughts about them in their minds, especially fear. If they do not think of them, they will not attract them into their minds, where they could play havoc. "It is a question wholly of the mind, and the less we think about them the better our chance of escape," the Swede says, which again raises the matter of the degree to which the mind and the imagination are creating the entire experience the men have on the island. Even at the end of the story, the question is left open, since there might be a completely rational explanation for the small hollows they see in the flesh of the drowned man. These indentations seem to them to be exactly like the hollows in the sand that are all over the island, and they believe they are the mark of the alien forces. The two men are in a highly excitable and suggestible state at this point, however, and may well be predisposed to make this connection when none in fact exists.

COMPARE & CONTRAST

- **1907:** In addition to Blackwood, writers such as M. R. James, in *Ghost Stories of an Antiquary* (1904) and other works, contribute to a continuing tradition of horror and supernatural fiction.

  Today: The horror genre is alive and well in literature, film, and television. Supernatural and weird fiction is popular in the work of authors such as Laird Barron, Caitlín R. Kiernan, T. E. D. Klein, Thomas Ligotti, and Jeff VanderMeer.

- **1907:** Pressburg, where the two travelers in "The Willows" buy supplies, is a city in Hungary through which the Danube river flows.

  Today: Pressburg is now known as Bratislava. It has been the capital city of Slovakia since Czechoslovakia split into two independent nations, Slovakia and the Czech Republic, in 1993.

- **1907:** The Danube river flows through seven nations: Germany, Austria, Hungary, Serbia, Bulgaria, Romania, and Russia.

  Today: The Danube river flows through ten countries: Germany, Austria, Slovakia, Hungary, Croatia (which was under Austrian rule in 1907), Serbia, Bulgaria, Romania, Moldova, and Ukraine (the last two nations having become independent following the breakup of the Soviet Union in 1991).

STYLE

Personification

The narrator has a habit of personifying the natural forces that he and his companion encounter on their trip. Personification is a literary trope in which human qualities or emotions are attributed to inanimate things or those things are presented as if they are alive. For example, early in the story, when the travelers land on the island, the narrator observes the willow bushes "shining with spray and clapping their thousand little hands as though to applaud the success of our efforts." He also personifies the Danube river as a "Great Personage" and describes it thus:

> Sleepy at first, but later developing violent desires as it became conscious of its deep soul, it rolled, like some huge fluid being, through all the countries we had passed, holding our little craft on its mighty shoulders, playing roughly with us sometimes, yet always friendly and well-meaning.

Like a living being, the river sings and shouts and laughs. The narrator even gives it a personal history as an individual, when it was forming itself before humans were there to observe it, referring to "those early days of its irresponsible youth." Later, it becomes "grown-up."

This prepares the way for the sense of aliveness that animates the entire natural environment that the narrator and the Swede finds themselves in. The wind, for example, is also personified; it "was simply enjoying itself" as it blew wildly as if playing a game. Also, in the story, the willows are personified in a simile as being "like a herd of monstrous antediluvian creatures"; they talk among themselves, they laugh, they cry out, they sigh. The literary device of personification plays an important role in establishing the atmosphere of the story and making the supernatural events believable for the reader.

Point of View

Point of view refers to the method of narration. This story is told from a first-person point of view, that of the narrator himself, who never identifies himself by name. He is the "I" of the story. In a first-person narration, the reader is given direct insight only into the mind of the narrator, who may describe his or her own thoughts and feelings. The narrative must be

A storm traps the canoers on an island. (© *Markus Gann | ShutterStock.com*)

limited to what the narrator knows or has experienced directly or has been told about. Other characters can be revealed only through how they act and what they say. Thus, in this story, the other character, the Swede, is seen only through the narrator's eyes. The reader knows this character only through what the narrator says about him (and his view changes during the course of the story) and what he does.

HISTORICAL CONTEXT

Supernatural and Weird Fiction

"The Willows" belongs in the tradition of supernatural fiction, sometimes also called weird fiction. The latter term was defined by American author H. P. Lovecraft in his book *Supernatural Horror in Literature*. He distinguishes such tales from stories that merely evoke fear or are gruesome:

> The true weird tale has something more than secret murder, bloody bones, or a sheeted form clanking chains according to rule. A certain atmosphere of breathless and unexplainable dread of outer, unknown forces must be present; and there must be a hint, expressed with a seriousness and portentousness becoming its subject, of that most terrible

conception of the human brain—a malign and particular suspension or defeat of those fixed laws of Nature which are our only safeguard against the assaults of chaos and the daemons of unplumbed space.

The essence of "The Willows" could hardly be described in a better way. Lovecraft associates such stories with "a literature of cosmic fear" and states that it has existed as long as literature has. Examples can be found in the "most archaic ballads, chronicles, and sacred writings." Lovecraft finds it in the Old English epic *Beowulf* and in medieval authors from Dante to Edmund Spenser and Sir Thomas Malory. It surfaced again in gothic fiction in England beginning with Horace Walpole's novel *The Castle of Otranto* in 1764 and continuing with the work of Ann Radcliffe and Matthew Gregory Lewis, who published one of the most famous gothic novels, *The Monk*, in 1796. In the nineteenth century, the tradition of horror fiction continued. Mary Shelley's *Frankenstein; or, The Modern Prometheus* (1817) is a notable example. Sir Walter Scott incorporated many elements of the weird into his novels and poems; Charles Dickens wrote "several eerie narratives," and in the United States, the short stories of Nathaniel Hawthorne and especially Edgar Allan Poe belong in the same category, as does Henry James's story *The Turn of the Screw* (1898).

Blackwood was therefore drawing on a long tradition in his work. Lovecraft, writing in the 1920s, includes Blackwood in his chapter on the "modern masters." He comments that modern horror stories "possess a naturalness, convincingness, artistic smoothness, and skilful intensity of appeal" that is far superior to the gothic fiction of the previous century. Lovecraft names Blackwood's contemporary the Welsh writer Arthur Machen as one of these modern masters, particularly in his novella *The Great God Pan* (1894). Lovecraft notes "the cumulative suspense and ultimate horror with which every paragraph abounds" in this work. He also singles out Machen's novel *The Three Imposters* (1895) and his short story "The White People" (1904) as worthy of note. In addition to Blackwood and Machen, Lovecraft considers the Irish writer Edward Plunkett, the eighteenth baron of Dunsany, who published stories and plays under the name Lord Dunsany, to be a third modern master in this genre. A fourth such figure is M. R. James, who according to Lovecraft has "an almost diabolic power of calling horror by gentle steps from the midst of prosaic general life."

CRITICAL OVERVIEW

"The Willows" has long been admired by critics as well as readers, although the critical literature on Blackwood's work remains limited. One of the earliest critics to praise the story was the American author of horror fiction H. P. Lovecraft, in *Supernatural Horror in Literature*, an essay that was first published in 1927, revised in 1939, and published in book form in 1945. Lovecraft writes that in "The Willows," "art and restraint in narrative reach their very highest development, and an impression of lasting poignancy is produced without a single strained passage or a single false note." Jack Sullivan, in *Elegant Nightmares: The English Ghost Story from Le Fanu to Blackwood*, calls the story "unforgettable." He writes, "The elusive forces which besiege the campers on a Danube island also besiege the reader; they emerge as a deeply felt experience of 'bewildering beauty' and escalating terror."

In his book, *Seven Masters of Supernatural Fiction*, Edward Wagenknecht comments that

although "The Willows" is not a conventional ghost story,

> there is still a sense in which it represents the ultimate development of the ghost story. The threat embodied in a malignant departed spirit confined to a particular room or house is one thing, but when the world haunts its helpless victim, what is he to do?

For Mike Ashley, in *Starlight Man: The Extraordinary Life of Algernon Blackwood*, "Blackwood focuses on the power and psychology of a single location and suggests what would happen if this place, isolated and far away from civilization, had become a frontier between our world and another." The power of the story, according to Ashley, is due to the fact that "Blackwood could draw it from life. He lived and breathed that story because he was there, and had experienced such otherworldliness."

In his October 2014 blog entry, "Happy Halloween! Algernon Blackwood's 'The Willows,'" Charles May, professor emeritus in the English Department at California State University, who has published extensively on the short-story genre, writes that "The basic problem" in reading the story "is to determine whether the events take place in a realm of reality other than the natural world or whether all is a function of hallucination." May concludes that

> the entire story is an hallucination in which the imagination is projected both on the external world and on the minds of the characters .
> . . . We come to the story, just as the characters come to the island, with the willows already transformed by Blackwood into symbols. Inside the tale, the narrator sustains the plot by "thinking" the thoughts the Swede expresses and thinking into existence the actions of the mysterious willows. The story ends when a "real event" outside the thought processes of the narrator occurs and breaks up the projected illusion of the story itself.

CRITICISM

Bryan Aubrey

Aubrey holds a PhD in English. In the following essay, he discusses Blackwood's own views of the essential elements of the weird tale and analyzes how Blackwood incorporates these elements in "The Willows."

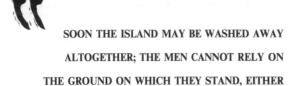

SOON THE ISLAND MAY BE WASHED AWAY
ALTOGETHER; THE MEN CANNOT RELY ON
THE GROUND ON WHICH THEY STAND, EITHER
LITERALLY OR FIGURATIVELY."

The origins of "The Willows" lay in a canoe trip down the Danube river that Blackwood took with his friend Wilfred Wilson in the summer of 1900. According to the account given by Mike Ashley, in *Starlight Man: The Extraordinary Life of Algernon Blackwood*, it seems to have been a challenging trip, with the two men successfully negotiating rapids and whirlpools in a slender canoe. Then, as they were about to leave Vienna, the canoe was swept away in the current with all their provisions. It crashed into a barge and was recovered with the aid of some local people. The canoe was repaired, and they set off again into Hungary and beyond Pressburg (present-day Bratislava). The river was flooded, and in addition to avoiding being swept into side channels and lagoons, "they also had to avoid many low, sandy, willow-strewn islands, some of which the water almost covered. The power of the water was so strong that Blackwood expected the islands to be swept away."

In his preface to *Selected Tales of Algernon Blackwood*, Blackwood offered his own reflections of the origins of some of the stories contained in the book. He recalls that on the trip down the Danube "the willows seemed to suffocate us"; then about a year or so later, when they made a trip down the river in a barge, "we found a dead body caught by a root, its decayed mass dangling against the sandy shore of the very same island my story describes." He adds, as if with a knowing wink, "A coincidence, of course!" Blackwood also describes the origins of the psychological component in his stories: "An emotion of a very possessive kind produced each tale," he writes, and he notes that he "felt shivers down the spine . . . as the horror of that Willows island crept over the imagination." Experiencing something like this type of feeling was essential for an authentic horror

story to emerge, Blackwood believed. He thought that any person might find in such a feeling a gateway into some realm beyond the normal, an "extra-sensory experience." All it needed was the sudden stimulation by means of a "dynamic flash of terror or beauty." That experience would then mesh with the kind of primitive superstition that modern man has certainly not outgrown, and out of that, a writer of the weird could produce his tale:

> The true "other-worldly" story should issue from that core of superstition which lies in every mother's son of us, and we are still close enough to primitive days with their terror of the dark for Reason to abdicate without too violent resistance.

Another key component in the "The Willows," it should be noted, is an appreciation of nature and close observation of it. The story unfolds in a leisurely manner, almost like a travelogue, with plenty of descriptions of the changing environment the two men find themselves in as they proceed down the river. For example, right at the beginning, the narrator offers this detailed piece of scene painting:

> In high flood this great acreage of sand, shingle-beds, and willow-grown islands is almost topped by the water, but in normal seasons the bushes bend and rustle in the free winds, showing their silver leaves to the sunshine in an ever-moving plain of bewildering beauty. These willows never attain to the dignity of trees; they have no rigid trunks; they remain humble bushes, with rounded tops and soft outline, swaying on slender stems that answer to the least pressure of the wind; supple as grasses, and so continually shifting that they somehow give the impression that the entire plain is moving and *alive*. For the wind sends waves rising and falling over the whole surface, waves of leaves instead of waves of water, green swells like the sea, too, until the branches turn and lift, and then silvery white as their under-side turns to the sun.

This is actually a little more than just a description of nature. Blackwood never loses sight of his purpose; it is the very aliveness of the willows, mentioned apparently innocuously here, that will form the core of the weird as it unfolds in the story. As the story progresses, the descriptions of nature become more overtly laced with menace, as if some unknown and hostile force is manifesting itself through the natural phenomena of water, wind, and willows. It is not only that the events themselves—the sight of the drowned man that

WHAT DO I READ NEXT?

- *Ancient Sorceries and Other Weird Stories* (2002), edited and with an introduction by S. T. Joshi, is a collection of nine of Blackwood's best stories.

- *The Complete John Silence Stories* (2011), edited and with an introduction by S. T. Joshi, contains six Blackwood stories that feature the psychic detective John Silence. Five of these stories were first published in one volume in 1908. Silence is called in to investigate strange cases in which people encounter mysterious forces.

- *The Weird: A Compendium of Strange and Dark Stories* (2012), edited by Jeff VanderMeer and Ann VanderMeer, is a huge (over a thousand pages) anthology of more than one hundred weird tales by twentieth- and twenty-first-century authors. H. P. Lovecraft, Franz Kafka, Rabindranath Tagore, Ryunosuke Akutagawa, Jorge Luis Borges, William Gibson, Stephen King, Angela Carter, M. R. James, Neil Gaiman, Mervyn Peake, and Michael Chabon are among the writers represented. This collection won the 2012 World Fantasy Award for Best Anthology.

- Neil Gaiman's *The Graveyard Book* (2010) is a horror novel for young-adult readers. It won the Newbery Medal and the Carnegie Medal. The story is about a boy who has been raised by ghosts.

- *Unutterable Horror: A History of Supernatural Fiction* (in two volumes), by S. T. Joshi (2014), is a comprehensive history of weird fiction from ancient times to the twenty-first century. Blackwood's work is covered in volume 2.

- Tananarive Due is an African American author of weird fiction. An award-winning writer of twelve novels and many short stories, Due's novella "Ghost Summer," published in an anthology in 2008, won a Kindred Award from the Carl Brandon Society. *Ghost Summer: Stories*, to be released in June 2015, is her first collection of short fiction.

turns out to be an otter (or is it really a drowned man?) and the boatman who makes the sign of the cross, for example—are disquieting, but they are made even more alarming by how the narrator and his companion react to them. In this respect, Blackwood does not mind piling up many repetitions of words that express alarm or fright, just to make sure that the reader is fully drawn into the mental and emotional world of the men. For example, the words "terror," "terrors," or "terrifying" occur fifteen times in the story. In section 2, at one point "terror" occurs five times in the space of six paragraphs. The word "alarm" or "alarming" occurs six times; "fear" occurs thirteen times, "frightened" five times, "disquieting" or "disquietude" four times, "distress" or "distressing" six times, and "dread" or variants such as "dreaded" or "dreadful" fourteen times. This may not be subtle or sophisticated storytelling, but it does ensure that the reader gets the point.

More subtle are the many other ways that Blackwood uses to create the otherworldly effect he desires, from the strange behavior of the willows as apparently conscious, moving entities, to the little pattering sounds in the night, the small hollows in the sand that start to appear all over the island, and the ominous sound made by the river, like the "music of doom"—to name only a few. The normal world that these two men are so used to inhabiting is changing, becoming undermined by forces they do not understand, and this is also nicely conveyed by the fact that the island they have landed on is shrinking, as the flood continues to wear away at it. Soon the island may be washed away altogether; the men cannot rely on the ground on which they stand, either literally or figuratively.

Particularly effective in conveying the eeriness of it all is the unusual sound they hear that resembles the striking of a gong. Blackwood waits until two-thirds of the way through his story before he introduces this sound, which comes like a crowning manifestation of the otherworldly, fourth-dimensional presence. The narrator describes it as

> a peculiar sound—something like the humming of a distant gong. It seemed to come across to us in the darkness from the waste of swamps and willows opposite. It was repeated at regular intervals, but it was certainly neither the sound of a bell nor the hooting of a distant steamer. I can liken it to

The fierce winds whip the willow trees until they release terrifying shadows. (© *3D Agentur* / *ShutterStock.com*)

nothing so much as to the sound of an immense gong, suspended far up in the sky, repeating incessantly its muffled metallic note, soft and musical, as it was repeatedly struck.

From that point on, the gong-like sound forms an omnipresent backdrop on the island as the story nears its climax:

> The curious sound I have likened to the note of a gong became now almost incessant, and filled the stillness of the night with a faint, continuous ringing rather than a series of distinct notes. At one time it was behind and at another time in front of us. Sometimes I fancied it came from the bushes on our left, and then again from the clumps on our right. More often it hovered directly overhead like the whirring of wings. It was really everywhere at once, behind, in front, at our sides and over our heads, completely surrounding us.

The Swede declares it is a sound that does not reach him through his ears; it is in this sense not part of the human, three-dimensional, five-sense world; its "vibrations," he believes, are a "fourth-dimensional sound."

Blackwood's use of this gong-like sound is interesting. In his preface to *Selected Tales of*

Algernon Blackwood, he writes that he has always been interested in what he calls "the Extension of Human Faculty," meaning "extended or expanded consciousness"—which is one thing that the use of gongs in religious ceremony, worship, and meditation is said to accomplish. The use of gongs has a long tradition in eastern religions, such as Buddhism; the vibrations that are set in motion when the gong is struck are thought to have the power to transform the consciousness of the listener, producing a state of calm and also cultivating wisdom. Since Blackwood was a member of the Toronto branch of the Theosophical Society, and that esoteric philosophy was deeply imbued with the spiritual wisdom of the East, he may well have known of this use of gongs.

Of course, in "The Willows" Blackwood has no interest in using the sound of a gong in a traditional way; instead, he uses it creatively for his own purposes, so the sound heard by the narrator and the Swede is not a harmonizing vibration that can aid in human betterment but an alien sound that seeps into human consciousness in this one wild, deserted spot as an

PERHAPS IT ARISES FROM THOSE MOMENTS
OF EPIPHANY WHEN WE INTUIT SOMETHING
GREATER THAN WHAT IS SHOWN IN THE WORLD.
IN BLACKWOOD THIS HAPPENS IN NATURE, IN
A PLACE OUTSIDE OF THE CONSTRUCTED WORLD
OF CITIES AND TOWNS."

ominous messenger from a strange, previously unknown, fourth-dimensional world that has nothing in common with the normal human world. The eerie effect created by his descriptions of the gong-like sound adds immensely to the atmosphere of the tale and is instrumental in bringing it to its climax. Using his natural gift for storytelling, thus did Blackwood, building on incidents and events in his own life and embellishing them with ghostly intimations from a realm of existence beyond the human, create a story that over one hundred years after its first publication still has the power to send a chill down the reader's spine.

Source: Bryan Aubrey, Critical Essay on "The Willows," in *Short Stories for Students*, Gale, Cengage Learning, 2016.

James Goho

In the following excerpt, Goho discusses how Blackwood's views on nature were influenced by his time in the Canadian wilderness.

In "The Wendigo" (1910), Algernon Blackwood (1869–1951) portrays the character Simpson alone in the great northern Ontario forest. Simpson hears footsteps and whispering voices in the woods. He sees figures "crouching behind trees and boulders." The murmur of the wind surrounds him, and "the shadows of the woods" threaten. Within this haunted wood, "nameless doom lurked." It is a "world of wizardry and horror." Yet in the forest, "untrodden by foot of man," Simpson is "enchanted by its austere beauty." And "his heart drank in the sense of freedom and great spaces." The wilderness is a grand otherness of hope and awe in Blackwood's stories, along with the counterpoint: the woods are a Gothic space.

The Canadian wilderness was a powerful force in the life of Algernon Blackwood. John Robert Colombo writes, "the forests and mountains have a Canadian cast" in Blackwood's fiction. Colombo also contends, "Imaginatively Canada would come to him [Blackwood] repeatedly during . . . his active, writing life." David Punter observes that Blackwood set "some of his best-known stories" in Canada. Greg Gatenby asserts. "Canadian imagery haunted Blackwood's writing," and Jeff Gardiner sees Blackwood's travels in Canada as "a great influence on him."

As a young man, Blackwood toured across Canada in 1887 with his father, Sir Arthur Blackwood. From 1890 to 1892, prior to moving to New York City, Algernon Blackwood lived in Canada, primarily in Toronto and then on an island in the Muskoka Lakes area of Ontario. From April to October in 1894, Blackwood returned to Canada to pursue a mining venture and spent six weeks in the Rainy River district in Ontario. His journeys there and back seemed more fruitful for him than the venture, which came to naught. On the journey, Blackwood rhapsodized, "Out of New York City into this primaeval wilderness produced intoxication. No more cities of dreadful night for me!" Mike Ashley suggests Blackwood was in the Muskoka Lakes area in the summer of 1896. He was back in Canada moose hunting in 1898.

Blackwood's experiences in Canada helped cast his sense of wonder with nature. His travels across Canada and his time in the forests aroused a feeling for the vastness of the country and the unbearable stretch of the wilderness. In *Episodes before Thirty* (1923), Blackwood exalted the island in the Muskoka area and his joy in the natural setting. His rhapsody in Nature is at the core of his life and his works. S. T. Joshi points out the deep significance of Nature for Blackwood. At times Nature is a Garden of Eden full of awe and wonder. In *Episodes before Thirty*, Blackwood stated that Nature "offered an actual sense of companionship no human intercourse could possibly provide." He experienced "a strange sense of oneness with nature." In his fiction, sometimes Nature is an escape, as in "The Camp of the Dog" (1908). The narrator rejoices as the campers head into the wilderness: "the horror of trains and houses was far behind us, the fever of men and cities, the weariness of streets and

Short Stories for Students, Volume 42   *2 9 1*

confined spaces." At times Blackwood writes of reconciliation within Nature, as William Blake depicted in "Night" when the lion says, "And now besides thee, bleating lamb, / I can lie down and sleep." In Blackwood's *The Centaur* (1911), Terence O'Malley speaks of "the call to childhood, the true, pure, vital childhood of the Earth—the Golden Age—before men tasted of the Tree and knew themselves separate; when the lion and the lamb lay down together and a little child could lead them." However, this idyllic vision of Nature is not always shown in Blackwood's short stories. In some, the natural world is at best indifferent and in others menacing. Gatenby believes "it was in Canada that he [Blackwood] best became aware of the often hostile power of Nature."

There is a mix of awe, loneliness, wonder, and fear in the wild. In "The Wendigo," Simpson feels "the forest pressed round him with its encircling wall: the nearer tree-stems like bronze in the firelight: beyond that—blackness, and, so far as he could tell, a silence of death." On the other hand, "the vigorous air of the wilderness brought its own powers of healing." Is a forest sinister in itself or is it our estrangement from Nature? Is it our alien presence that provokes the terror? Or is it that the wilderness in the Canadian stories is Nature infested by men who cannot understand it, who are cut off from the grand "stream of a Consciousness far bigger" than they? Peter Penzoldt suggests that "Blackwood's idea is that nature is good, beautiful, right and healing." Indeed, a substantial body of research supports Blackwood's notion of the healing power of Nature. David Punter sees "a kind of euphoria, a kind of rapture, in the visions which conclude many of Blackwood's stories."

Blackwood's Canadian stories conjure both visions. And this perspective of the wood pervades Blackwood's work. There is an ambiguity about the wilderness: it is foreign yet familiar; it is dangerous but beautiful; it is uncanny. This chapter explores Blackwood's Canadian stories to help understand the tension between these two views of Nature and perhaps to contribute to an understanding of how Blackwood's Canadian experience shaped his literary perspective on the wilderness and our place in that dark but glorious space.

Blackwood seemed to have had an idiosyncratic mythology of Nature. The Canadian wilderness may have been a key element in the elaboration of that myth. Karen Armstrong states that myth "looks into the heart of a great silence." That great silence is the unknown, or what at first we have no words to express. She contends that mythology is not opting out of the world; rather, it enables us to live more intensely within it. Blackwood seemed to believe that our perception limits our experience of the world. There is more to the world than we normally experience. But to achieve transcendence, which is a key to the myth, there is a harrowing journey. It is as if one must find a way to leap over the ontological ravine between humans and the rest of Nature. As Armstrong argues, myth is about going beyond our ordinary experience. For Blackwood, "an expansion of normal consciousness" will bring the numinous vision of nature.

Joshi argues that this is what Blackwood sought. Perhaps it arises from those moments of epiphany when we intuit something greater than what is shown in the world. In Blackwood this happens in Nature, in a place outside of the constructed world of cities and towns. Out there in the wilderness all things seem more bound up together, not always in peace, often in conflict, but composed of the same substance, of the same spirit.

. . . H. P. Lovecraft assessed Blackwood a "master of weird atmosphere." He revered "The Willows" as perhaps the finest supernatural tale in all literature. E. F. Bleiler concludes that the suspense of the story "is hard to match anywhere." The narrator and his companion are canoeing down the Danube. The companion is referred to as the Swede throughout the tale and is compared to a "red Indian" for his prowess in steering the canoe and in mending their torn tent, one of several attacks on their island encampment. The Swede is playing a role similar to that played by indigenous people in Blackwood's Canadian tales. Beyond the cities and towns they enter "the wilderness . . . the land of the willows." It is "the land of desolation." But it is also a "kingdom of wonder and magic," similar to what is expressed in "The Wendigo." Right away the landscape is animate with "the shouting willows." The river seems to sing and laugh. From their Canadian canoe they spy wildlife on the banks of the river, very much like in his Canadian stories. In a way "The Willows" is a companion piece to those stories, with the natural environment even more distant, even more uninterested in the lives of humans. The grandeur seems more menacing. Roger B. Salomon argues the "wonders are awful, the magic black" in the story. But there is "awe and wonder" as the narrator is enraptured by huge columns of figures flowing from the island into the sky, like animated aurora.

At first the narrator feels the healing of Nature; he lies "peaceful in the bath of the elements—water, wind, sand and the great fire of the sun." However, the island, "untrodden by man," turns out to be "an alien world" where the campers "are interlopers." They have passed a frontier into a "beyond region" of "disorder, disintegration, destruction." The island of willows is not like a forest. The narrator ruminates: "the mystery of great forests exercises a spell peculiarly its own. . . . They tend on the whole to exalt." The willows are different, the awe is infused with terror; the willows are like "silver spears," and they seem to crowd closer, purposefully, toward their tent. And this terror creeps closer throughout the story. So much so that the narrator fears being "drawn across the frontier into *their* world." This other world is called forth through a series of impressions. There is a sound like a "gong" or "the whirring of wings" or "muffled humming" or "a swarm of invisible bees," all seemingly like an attempt to describe the indescribable.

The marsh, the deadly willows, and odd sand-funnels set the stage for an encounter. The men see something moving. The impressions are different for the two campers. The narrator sees it "through a veil," and it seems like "several large animals grouped together." The Swede sees it "like a clump of willow bushes" and "coiling itself like smoke." They are groping for a reality within an unreal environment. Lovecraft noted the artistic craft in the "manner in which certain footprints tell certain unbelievable things" in "The Wendigo." But these enigmatic footprints are transformed in "The Willows" into titanic impressions of nameless things from an unknown, perhaps unknowable world. . . .

Source: James Goho, "The Haunted Wood: Algernon Blackwood's Canadian Stories," in *Journeys into Darkness: Critical Essays on Gothic Horror*, Rowman & Littlefield, 2014, pp. 79–81, 90–91.

> REACTING AGAINST VICTORIAN SCIENTISM AND TECHNOLOGY, HIS CHARACTERS ARE CONSTANTLY INDICTING THE OUTER WORLD AND PLUNGING INTO INNER VISION."

Jack Sullivan

In the following excerpt, Sullivan compares Blackwood to horror writers H. P. Lovecraft and Sheridan Le Fanu.

. . . It would be schematically easy simply to classify Blackwood as the master of the outdoor ghost story; he not only wrote more of them than anyone else, but he managed to create at least two authentic masterpieces, "The Willows" and "The Wendigo." But Blackwood also wrote more than a few claustrophobic haunted house tales, some of them (such as "The Listener") worthy to stand beside Le Fanu's "Strange Disturbances in Aungier Street" and Wakefield's "Blind Man's Buff." In addition, he wrote intermediary tales such as "A Haunted Island" which move in and out between the freedom of nature and the oppressiveness of old houses.

What binds Blackwood's work together is not a common setting, but a distinctive use of language and a distinctive vision. The vision is peculiar in that it is announced decisively but is undermined by the structure of the stories until it seems strangely unsure of itself. This ambivalence adds tension and intellectual credibility to the stories, which would be impossibly dull were they as programmatically "mystical" as they pretend to be.

Unlike the mundane characters of Le Fanu and James, Blackwood's heroes are visionaries who feel oppressed by everyday reality and who deliberately seek out other worlds. What they discover usually encompasses both ecstasy and horror, though sometimes only horror. In either case, the "other" reality is as unmanageable as the first, and the character often spends the rest of the tale desperately negotiating a re-entrance into what was renounced in the first place. Rarely, however, is there the slightest verbal retraction of the initial renunciation. Because most of Blackwood's heroes do make it back, he has been seen to be an uncharacteristically "positive" writer for this genre. There are few upbeat endings in Wakefield, M. R. James, or Hartley, and almost none in Le Fanu. On the other hand, Blackwood's characters, while they live to tell the tale, usually end where they started; the stories read like unresolved circles.

Blackwood's fiction is part of an intensively subjectivist tendency in modern British fiction. Reacting against Victorian scientism and technology, his characters are constantly indicting the outer world and plunging into inner vision. As we have seen, M. R. James also expresses an alienation from the modern world, but more through implication than authorial statement. Blackwood belongs to a more didactic tradition of ghost story writers which includes Yeats, Arthur Machen, Oliver Onions, E. F. Benson, and (somewhat ambiguously) Walter de la Mare. The writers in this group are quite individual, but they do have a few things in common. One is an earnestness of tone, an unease with irony, a desire to be taken with intense seriousness. For this reason, Walter de la Mare—even though his stories are permeated with rarefied visions—does not fit comfortably in this visionary company. His tone has too much fluidity, too much capacity for irony and conscious self-parody. Nevertheless, de la Mare's meticulously crafted stories do express the common desire of these writers to be rid of the modern world. In Machen's "The Great God Pan" and "The Inmost Light," the desire creates a sense of strain, a tendency toward stagey exposition and heavy-handed occultist dialogue. But Machen is redeemed by his empathy with the outdoors, his ability to make landscapes come alive with singing prose. "The White People," his masterpiece, has an almost trance-like lyricism and spontaneity: "I had seen something very amazing and very lovely, and I knew a story, and if I had really seen it, and not made it up out of the dark, and the black bough, and the bright shining that was mounting up to the sky from over the great round hill, but had really seen it in truth, then there were all kinds of wonderful and lovely and terrible things to think of, so I longed and trembled, and I burned and got cold." As is always the case with Machen's best work, beauty and horror ring out at precisely the same moment.

Benson strikes a similar dissonance in "The Man who Went too Far" and other nature stories, but within a consonant framework that allows for the comfort and balance of human relationships. Benson's descriptive prose is also more conventional than Machen's—less magical and surreal, more inclined toward standard late-romantic nature tropes. Though not a very sophisticated stylist, Benson has a sneaky way with contrast: his stories have a healthy out-of-doors quality, an aggressive prettiness, that suddenly becomes stained with the onslaught of vampires ("Mrs. Amworth"), giant slugs ("Caterpillars"), or mummies ("Monkeys"). Gruesome and horrifying in an abrupt modulation at the end, Onions's "The Beckoning Fair One" works the same way.

The visionary writers are not as cohesively linked as the antiquaries of the M. R. James school. Different in style, characterization, and setting, they resemble each other only in their pushy tone, their obsession with subjectivism, and their bitterness toward the grayness and ugliness of the modern world. Blackwood comes closest to being representative of this impulse in that he is thematically consistent (Benson and Onions are not) and remarkably prolific.

Indeed, Blackwood is probably the most prolific of all ghost story writers. During his long life (1869–1951), he published twelve collections of ghost stories and several forgotten fantasy novels. He seemed to possess an endlessly fertile imagination, creating more conceptual variations than any of his rivals. Though his fiction lacks the unity of Machen, Chambers, or Lovecraft (writers who use a central, organizing mythos), it has far greater variety. Like Poe's Roderick Usher, who speaks of "the sentience of all vegetable matter," Blackwood envisions a world in which everything is alive and anything can be a ghost: trees, bushes, earth, snow, even the wind (which in "The Wendigo" becomes one of his most unusual demons). His indoor apparitions are also nicely varied: the old gentleman from the eighteenth century in "The Other Wing," who has a gracious smile and impeccable manners; the leprous thing in "The Listener," who has very poor manners, leaving putrid odors wherever he appears; the Satan figure in "Secret Worship," who appears in a haunted monastery; the emaciated spectre in "Keeping His Promise," who, having starved himself to death, returns to haunt a kitchen, stuffing himself with endless amounts of food. Though Blackwood's human characters behave in predictable patterns, his ghostly characters do not.

Unlike his admirers, who view his work with a kind of religious awe, Blackwood is not unaware of the element of farce in these stories. His characters are often tuned into it as well: the narrator of "With Intent to Steal" speaks of the "element of the ludicrous" in the ghostly experience, an element which produces "empty laughter." Laughter is empty because it attempts, unsuccessfully, to exorcise the absurdly grim situation which provoked it in the first place (in this case, the situation of being trapped in an old barn with a ghost whose sole function is inducing people to commit suicide). Blackwood's humor is more closely akin to Le Fanu than to M. R. James. Lacking James's understated wit, Blackwood relies on outright farce. The grotesque silliness of "The Strange Adventures of a Private Secretary in New York" is a case in point. Mr. Garvey (who turns out to be a werewolf) explains why his Igor-like servant so often disappears:

> "He has a horrible predilection for vacuums," Garvey went on presently in a still lower voice and thrusting his face farther forward under the lamp.
> "Vacuums!" exclaimed the secretary in spite of himself. "What in the world do you mean?"
> "What I say of course. He's always tumbling into them, so that I can't find him or get at him. He hides there for hours at a time, and for the life of me I can't make out what he does there."

Given Mr. Garvey's habit of turning into a famished wolf, his servant's "predilection for vacuums" is not altogether surprising.

Blackwood's contribution to the ghost story did not go entirely unrecognized. Derek Hudson has pointed out that several of Blackwood's collections—*The Empty House, John Silence, The Human Chord, The Centaur, Jimbo,* and *The Education of Uncle Paul,*—received highly favorable reviews when they first appeared. E. F. Bleiler, editor of the *Checklist of Fantastic Literature,* recently made this summary evaluation: "With the work of Blackwood, it seems safe to say, the ghost story was finally recognized as a legitimate, respectable literary form." This is an exaggeration, ignoring

as it does the civilizing, "legitimizing" influence of M. R. James (to say nothing of Henry James). It also fails to note that Blackwood's audience, though enthusiastic, was always small. According to Hudson, Blackwood himself felt a keen sense of disappointment at not reaching a larger readership.

Blackwood's life resembles Le Fanu's in that it neatly parallels his work. He was very much like the mystical but vigorously active persona in his fiction. Though he returned to England in his old age to narrate ghost stories for the B. B. C., he spent most of his years attempting to live the life of the archetypal lone wanderer, continually seeking new places, experiences, and visions. He rebelled against his ruling-class parents (Sir Arthur Blackwood and the dowager duchess of Manchester) by steeping himself in occultism, eventually branching out into Buddhism and Rosecrucianism. In contrast to Yeats, with whom he became acquainted during their membership in the Order of the Golden Dawn, his rebellion was against Calvinism rather than atheism. He was educated in the Black Forest (which became, in "The Willows," his most memorable setting) at the Moravian school and later at the University of Edinburgh. His parents sent him away to Canada as a young man (where he again assimilated one of his more convincing settings, this time for "The Wendigo"), but he moved to New York, where he sustained a period of poverty later recounted in *Episodes Before Thirty.* Even after fleeing New York, he did not settle down, but alternated between England and Switzerland. Among other occupations, he worked as a businessman, a bartender, a journalist, a model, a milk-farmer, and a private secretary. Like the campers in "The Camp of the Dog," his life was apparently a consistent attempt to "shed" the "disguises required by the conventions of civilization." He never married and was considered "fundamentally solitary" by his friends, who also assert that "he was a happy man and the best of company." Even when renouncing convention, he displayed none of the spectacularly neurotic inwardness of Le Fanu or Lovecraft. . . .

Source: Jack Sullivan, "The Visionary Ghost Story: Algernon Blackwood," in *Elegant Nightmares: The English Ghost Story from Le Fanu to Blackwood,* Ohio University Press, 1978, pp. 113–17.

SOURCES

Ashley, Mike, *Starlight Man: The Extraordinary Life of Algernon Blackwood*, Constable, 2001, pp. 107–109.

Blackwood, Algernon, "Author's Preface," in *Selected Tales of Algernon Blackwood*, John Baker, 1964, pp. 8–12.

———, "The Willows," in *Selected Tales of Algernon Blackwood*, John Baker, 1964, pp. 13–66.

Harris-Fain, Darren, "Algernon Blackwood," in *Dictionary of Literary Biography*, Vol. 178, *British Fantasy and Science-Fiction Writers before World War I*, edited by Darren Harris-Fain, The Gale Group, 1997, pp. 35–44.

Lovecraft, Howard Phillips, *Supernatural Horror in Literature*, Dover Publications, 1973, pp. 15, 17, 87, 90, 96, 100.

May, Charles, "Happy Halloween! Algernon Blackwood's 'The Willows,'" Reading the Short Story website, October 28, 2014, http://may-on-the-short-story.blogspot.com/2014/10/happy-halloween-algernon-blackwoods.html (accessed January 25, 2015).

Sullivan, *Elegant Nightmares: The English Ghost Story from Le Fanu to Blackwood*, Ohio University Press, 1978, p. 120.

Wagenknecht, Edward, *Seven Masters of Supernatural Fiction*, Greenwood Press, 1991, p. 77.

FURTHER READING

Bleiler, Everett F., *The Guide to Supernatural Fiction*, Kent State University Press, 1983.
    This is a comprehensive work, arranged alphabetically by author, that covers all aspects of weird fiction, including supernatural, ghost, horror, and similar stories. It describes almost two thousand books published between 1750 and 1960. Blackwood is allocated eight pages (pp. 51–59).

Cavaliero, Glen, *The Supernatural and English Fiction*, Oxford University Press, 1995.
    Cavaliero discusses all the most important English writers of supernatural fiction, from Horace Walpole to Peter Ackroyd, including Ann Radcliffe, M. R. James, Rudyard Kipling, John Cowper Powys, James Hogg, Henry James, William Golding, Iris Murdoch, and Muriel Spark, as well as Blackwood.

Hay, Simon, *A History of the Modern British Ghost Story*, Palgrave Macmillan, 2011.
    Hay examines ghost stories in British literature from Sir Walter Scott and Charles Dickens through to the end of the twentieth century. He includes a reading of Blackwood's "The Willows."

Joshi, S. T., *The Weird Tale: Arthur Machen, Lord Dunsany, Algernon Blackwood, M. R. James, Ambrose Bierce, H. P. Lovecraft*, University of Texas Press, 1990.
    Joshi has written extensively about supernatural fiction. In this book, he examines the work of five of the early masters of the genre.

SUGGESTED SEARCH TERMS

The Willows AND Blackwood

Algernon Blackwood

supernatural fiction

horror fiction

weird fiction

ghost story AND Blackwood

weird AND Blackwood

H. P. Lovecraft

Glossary of Literary Terms

A

Aestheticism: A literary and artistic movement of the nineteenth century. Followers of the movement believed that art should not be mixed with social, political, or moral teaching. The statement "art for art's sake" is a good summary of aestheticism. The movement had its roots in France, but it gained widespread importance in England in the last half of the nineteenth century, where it helped change the Victorian practice of including moral lessons in literature. Oscar Wilde and Edgar Allan Poe are two of the best-known "aesthetes" of the late nineteenth century.

Allegory: A narrative technique in which characters representing things or abstract ideas are used to convey a message or teach a lesson. Allegory is typically used to teach moral, ethical, or religious lessons but is sometimes used for satiric or political purposes. Many fairy tales are allegories.

Allusion: A reference to a familiar literary or historical person or event, used to make an idea more easily understood. Joyce Carol Oates's story "Where Are You Going, Where Have You Been?" exhibits several allusions to popular music.

Analogy: A comparison of two things made to explain something unfamiliar through its similarities to something familiar, or to prove one point based on the acceptance of another. Similes and metaphors are types of analogies.

Antagonist: The major character in a narrative or drama who works against the hero or protagonist. The Misfit in Flannery O'Connor's story "A Good Man Is Hard to Find" serves as the antagonist for the Grandmother.

Anthology: A collection of similar works of literature, art, or music. Zora Neale Hurston's "The Eatonville Anthology" is a collection of stories that take place in the same town.

Anthropomorphism: The presentation of animals or objects in human shape or with human characteristics. The term is derived from the Greek word for "human form." The fur necklet in Katherine Mansfield's story "Miss Brill" has anthropomorphic characteristics.

Anti-hero: A central character in a work of literature who lacks traditional heroic qualities such as courage, physical prowess, and fortitude. Anti-heroes typically distrust conventional values and are unable to commit themselves to any ideals. They generally feel helpless in a world over which they have no control. Anti-heroes usually accept, and often celebrate, their positions as social outcasts. A well-known anti-hero is Walter Mitty in James Thurber's story "The Secret Life of Walter Mitty."

Archetype: The word archetype is commonly used to describe an original pattern or model from which all other things of the same kind are made. Archetypes are the literary images that grow out of the "collective unconscious," a theory proposed by psychologist Carl Jung. They appear in literature as incidents and plots that repeat basic patterns of life. They may also appear as stereotyped characters. The "schlemiel" of Yiddish literature is an archetype.

Autobiography: A narrative in which an individual tells his or her life story. Examples include Benjamin Franklin's *Autobiography* and Amy Hempel's story "In the Cemetery Where Al Jolson Is Buried," which has autobiographical characteristics even though it is a work of fiction.

Avant-garde: A literary term that describes new writing that rejects traditional approaches to literature in favor of innovations in style or content. Twentieth-century examples of the literary avant-garde include the modernists and the minimalists.

B

Belles-lettres: A French term meaning "fine letters" or" beautiful writing." It is often used as a synonym for literature, typically referring to imaginative and artistic rather than scientific or expository writing. Current usage sometimes restricts the meaning to light or humorous writing and appreciative essays about literature. Lewis Carroll's *Alice in Wonderland* epitomizes the realm of belles-lettres.

Bildungsroman: A German word meaning "novel of development." The *bildungsroman* is a study of the maturation of a youthful character, typically brought about through a series of social or sexual encounters that lead to self-awareness. J. D. Salinger's *Catcher in the Rye* is a *bildungsroman*, and Doris Lessing's story "Through the Tunnel" exhibits characteristics of a *bildungsroman* as well.

Black Aesthetic Movement: A period of artistic and literary development among African Americans in the 1960s and early 1970s. This was the first major African-American artistic movement since the Harlem Renaissance and was closely paralleled by the civil rights and black power movements. The black aesthetic writers attempted to produce works of art that would be meaningful to the black masses. Key figures in black aesthetics included one of its founders, poet and playwright Amiri Baraka, formerly known as Le Roi Jones; poet and essayist Haki R. Madhubuti, formerly Don L. Lee; poet and playwright Sonia Sanchez; and dramatist Ed Bullins. Works representative of the Black Aesthetic Movement include Amiri Baraka's play *Dutchman*, a 1964 Obie award-winner.

Black Humor: Writing that places grotesque elements side by side with humorous ones in an attempt to shock the reader, forcing him or her to laugh at the horrifying reality of a disordered world. "Lamb to the Slaughter," by Roald Dahl, in which a placid housewife murders her husband and serves the murder weapon to the investigating policemen, is an example of black humor.

C

Catharsis: The release or purging of unwanted emotions—specifically fear and pity—brought about by exposure to art. The term was first used by the Greek philosopher Aristotle in his *Poetics* to refer to the desired effect of tragedy on spectators.

Character: Broadly speaking, a person in a literary work. The actions of characters are what constitute the plot of a story, novel, or poem. There are numerous types of characters, ranging from simple, stereotypical figures to intricate, multifaceted ones. "Characterization" is the process by which an author creates vivid, believable characters in a work of art. This may be done in a variety of ways, including (1) direct description of the character by the narrator; (2) the direct presentation of the speech, thoughts, or actions of the character; and (3) the responses of other characters to the character. The term "character" also refers to a form originated by the ancient Greek writer Theophrastus that later became popular in the seventeenth and eighteenth centuries. It is a short essay or sketch of a person who prominently displays a specific attribute or quality, such as miserliness or ambition. "Miss Brill," a story by Katherine Mansfield, is an example of a character sketch.

Classical: In its strictest definition in literary criticism, classicism refers to works of ancient Greek or Roman literature. The term may also be used to describe a literary work of recognized importance (a "classic") from any time period or literature that exhibits the traits of classicism. Examples of later works and authors now described as classical include French literature of the seventeenth century, Western novels of the nineteenth century, and American fiction of the mid-nineteenth century such as that written by James Fenimore Cooper and Mark Twain.

Climax: The turning point in a narrative, the moment when the conflict is at its most intense. Typically, the structure of stories, novels, and plays is one of rising action, in which tension builds to the climax, followed by falling action, in which tension lessens as the story moves to its conclusion.

Comedy: One of two major types of drama, the other being tragedy. Its aim is to amuse, and it typically ends happily. Comedy assumes many forms, such as farce and burlesque, and uses a variety of techniques, from parody to satire. In a restricted sense the term comedy refers only to dramatic presentations, but in general usage it is commonly applied to nondramatic works as well.

Comic Relief: The use of humor to lighten the mood of a serious or tragic story, especially in plays. The technique is very common in Elizabethan works, and can be an integral part of the plot or simply a brief event designed to break the tension of the scene.

Conflict: The conflict in a work of fiction is the issue to be resolved in the story. It usually occurs between two characters, the protagonist and the antagonist, or between the protagonist and society or the protagonist and himself or herself. The conflict in Washington Irving's story "The Devil and Tom Walker" is that the Devil wants Tom Walker's soul but Tom does not want to go to hell.

Criticism: The systematic study and evaluation of literary works, usually based on a specific method or set of principles. An important part of literary studies since ancient times, the practice of criticism has given rise to numerous theories, methods, and "schools," sometimes producing conflicting, even contradictory, interpretations of literature in general as well as of individual works. Even such basic issues as what constitutes a poem or a novel have been the subject of much criticism over the centuries. Seminal texts of literary criticism include Plato's *Republic,* Aristotle's *Poetics,* Sir Philip Sidney's *The Defence of Poesie,* and John Dryden's *Of Dramatic Poesie.* Contemporary schools of criticism include deconstruction, feminist, psychoanalytic, poststructuralist, new historicist, postcolonialist, and reader-response.

D

Deconstruction: A method of literary criticism characterized by multiple conflicting interpretations of a given work. Deconstructionists consider the impact of the language of a work and suggest that the true meaning of the work is not necessarily the meaning that the author intended.

Deduction: The process of reaching a conclusion through reasoning from general premises to a specific premise. Arthur Conan Doyle's character Sherlock Holmes often used deductive reasoning to solve mysteries.

Denotation: The definition of a word, apart from the impressions or feelings it creates in the reader. The word "apartheid" denotes a political and economic policy of segregation by race, but its connotations—oppression, slavery, inequality—are numerous.

Denouement: A French word meaning "the unknotting." In literature, it denotes the resolution of conflict in fiction or drama. The *denouement* follows the climax and provides an outcome to the primary plot situation as well as an explanation of secondary plot complications. A well-known example of *denouement* is the last scene of the play *As You Like It* by William Shakespeare, in which couples are married, an evildoer repents, the identities of two disguised characters are revealed, and a ruler is restored to power. Also known as "falling action."

Detective Story: A narrative about the solution of a mystery or the identification of a criminal. The conventions of the detective story include the detective's scrupulous use of logic in solving the mystery; incompetent or ineffectual police; a suspect who appears guilty at first but is later proved innocent; and the detective's friend or confidant—often the narrator—whose slowness in interpreting clues emphasizes by contrast the detective's brilliance. Edgar Allan Poe's "Murders in the Rue Morgue" is commonly regarded as the earliest example of this type of story. Other practitioners are Arthur Conan

Doyle, Dashiell Hammett, and Agatha Christie.

Dialogue: Dialogue is conversation between people in a literary work. In its most restricted sense, it refers specifically to the speech of characters in a drama. As a specific literary genre, a "dialogue" is a composition in which characters debate an issue or idea.

Didactic: A term used to describe works of literature that aim to teach a moral, religious, political, or practical lesson. Although didactic elements are often found inartistically pleasing works, the term "didactic" usually refers to literature in which the message is more important than the form. The term may also be used to criticize a work that the critic finds "overly didactic," that is, heavy-handed in its delivery of a lesson. An example of didactic literature is John Bunyan's *Pilgrim's Progress*.

Dramatic Irony: Occurs when the reader of a work of literature knows something that a character in the work itself does not know. The irony is in the contrast between the intended meaning of the statements or actions of a character and the additional information understood by the audience.

Dystopia: An imaginary place in a work of fiction where the characters lead dehumanized, fearful lives. George Orwell's *Nineteen Eighty-four,* and Margaret Atwood's *Handmaid's Tale* portray versions of dystopia.

E

Edwardian: Describes cultural conventions identified with the period of the reign of Edward VII of England (1901–1910). Writers of the Edwardian Age typically displayed a strong reaction against the propriety and conservatism of the Victorian Age. Their work often exhibits distrust of authority in religion, politics, and art and expresses strong doubts about the soundness of conventional values. Writers of this era include E. M. Forster, H. G. Wells, and Joseph Conrad.

Empathy: A sense of shared experience, including emotional and physical feelings, with someone or something other than oneself. Empathy is often used to describe the response of a reader to a literary character.

Epilogue: A concluding statement or section of a literary work. In dramas, particularly those of the seventeenth and eighteenth centuries, the epilogue is a closing speech, often in verse, delivered by an actor at the end of a play and spoken directly to the audience.

Epiphany: A sudden revelation of truth inspired by a seemingly trivial incident. The term was widely used by James Joyce in his critical writings, and the stories in Joyce's *Dubliners* are commonly called "epiphanies."

Epistolary Novel: A novel in the form of letters. The form was particularly popular in the eighteenth century. The form can also be applied to short stories, as in Edwidge Danticat's "Children of the Sea."

Epithet: A word or phrase, often disparaging or abusive, that expresses a character trait of someone or something. "The Napoleon of crime" is an epithet applied to Professor Moriarty, arch-rival of Sherlock Holmes in Arthur Conan Doyle's series of detective stories.

Existentialism: A predominantly twentieth-century philosophy concerned with the nature and perception of human existence. There are two major strains of existentialist thought: atheistic and Christian. Followers of atheistic existentialism believe that the individual is alone in a godless universe and that the basic human condition is one of suffering and loneliness. Nevertheless, because there are no fixed values, individuals can create their own characters—indeed, they can shape themselves—through the exercise of free will. The atheistic strain culminates in and is popularly associated with the works of Jean-Paul Sartre. The Christian existentialists, on the other hand, believe that only in God may people find freedom from life's anguish. The two strains hold certain beliefs in common: that existence cannot be fully understood or described through empirical effort; that anguish is a universal element of life; that individuals must bear responsibility for their actions; and that there is no common standard of behavior or perception for religious and ethical matters. Existentialist thought figures prominently in the works of such authors as Franz Kafka, Fyodor Dostoyevsky, and Albert Camus.

Expatriatism: The practice of leaving one's country to live for an extended period in another country. Literary expatriates include Irish author James Joyce who moved to Italy and

France, American writers James Baldwin, Ernest Hemingway, Gertrude Stein, and F. Scott Fitzgerald who lived and wrote in Paris, and Polish novelist Joseph Conrad in England.

Exposition: Writing intended to explain the nature of an idea, thing, or theme. Expository writing is often combined with description, narration, or argument.

Expressionism: An indistinct literary term, originally used to describe an early twentieth-century school of German painting. The term applies to almost any mode of unconventional, highly subjective writing that distorts reality in some way. Advocates of Expressionism include Federico Garcia Lorca, Eugene O'Neill, Franz Kafka, and James Joyce.

F

Fable: A prose or verse narrative intended to convey amoral. Animals or inanimate objects with human characteristics often serve as characters in fables. A famous fable is Aesop's "The Tortoise and the Hare."

Fantasy: A literary form related to mythology and folklore. Fantasy literature is typically set in non-existent realms and features supernatural beings. Notable examples of literature with elements of fantasy are Gabriel Gárcia Márquez's story "The Handsomest Drowned Man in the World" and Ursula K. Le Guin's "The Ones Who Walk Away from Omelas."

Farce: A type of comedy characterized by broad humor, outlandish incidents, and often vulgar subject matter. Much of the comedy in film and television could more accurately be described as farce.

Fiction: Any story that is the product of imagination rather than a documentation of fact. Characters and events in such narratives may be based in real life but their ultimate form and configuration is a creation of the author.

Figurative Language: A technique in which an author uses figures of speech such as hyperbole, irony, metaphor, or simile for a particular effect. Figurative language is the opposite of literal language, in which every word is truthful, accurate, and free of exaggeration or embellishment.

Flashback: A device used in literature to present action that occurred before the beginning of the story. Flashbacks are often introduced as the dreams or recollections of one or more characters.

Foil: A character in a work of literature whose physical or psychological qualities contrast strongly with, and therefore highlight, the corresponding qualities of another character. In his Sherlock Holmes stories, Arthur Conan Doyle portrayed Dr. Watson as a man of normal habits and intelligence, making him a foil for the eccentric and unusually perceptive Sherlock Holmes.

Folklore: Traditions and myths preserved in a culture or group of people. Typically, these are passed on by word of mouth in various forms—such as legends, songs, and proverbs—or preserved in customs and ceremonies. Washington Irving, in "The Devil and Tom Walker" and many of his other stories, incorporates many elements of the folklore of New England and Germany.

Folktale: A story originating in oral tradition. Folk tales fall into a variety of categories, including legends, ghost stories, fairy tales, fables, and anecdotes based on historical figures and events.

Foreshadowing: A device used in literature to create expectation or to set up an explanation of later developments. Edgar Allan Poe uses foreshadowing to create suspense in "The Fall of the House of Usher" when the narrator comments on the crumbling state of disrepair in which he finds the house.

G

Genre: A category of literary work. Genre may refer to both the content of a given work—tragedy, comedy, horror, science fiction—and to its form, such as poetry, novel, or drama.

Gilded Age: A period in American history during the 1870s and after characterized by political corruption and materialism. A number of important novels of social and political criticism were written during this time. Henry James and Kate Chopin are two writers who were prominent during the Gilded Age.

Gothicism: In literature, works characterized by a taste for medieval or morbid characters and situations. A gothic novel prominently features elements of horror, the supernatural, gloom, and violence: clanking chains, terror, ghosts, medieval castles, and unexplained phenomena. The term "gothic novel" is also applied to novels that lack elements of the traditional Gothic setting but that create a similar atmosphere of terror or dread. The term can also be applied to stories, plays, and poems. Mary Shelley's *Frankenstein* and Joyce Carol Oates's *Bellefleur* are both gothic novels.

Grotesque: In literature, a work that is characterized by exaggeration, deformity, freakishness, and disorder. The grotesque often includes an element of comic absurdity. Examples of the grotesque can be found in the works of Edgar Allan Poe, Flannery O'Connor, Joseph Heller, and Shirley Jackson.

H

Harlem Renaissance: The Harlem Renaissance of the 1920s is generally considered the first significant movement of black writers and artists in the United States. During this period, new and established black writers, many of whom lived in the region of New York City known as Harlem, published more fiction and poetry than ever before, the first influential black literary journals were established, and black authors and artists received their first widespread recognition and serious critical appraisal. Among the major writers associated with this period are Countee Cullen, Langston Hughes, Arna Bontemps, and Zora Neale Hurston.

Hero/Heroine: The principal sympathetic character in a literary work. Heroes and heroines typically exhibit admirable traits: idealism, courage, and integrity, for example. Famous heroes and heroines of literature include Charles Dickens's Oliver Twist, Margaret Mitchell's Scarlett O'Hara, and the anonymous narrator in Ralph Ellison's *Invisible Man*.

Hyperbole: Deliberate exaggeration used to achieve an effect. In William Shakespeare's *Macbeth*, Lady Macbeth hyperbolizes when she says, "All the perfumes of Arabia could not sweeten this little hand."

I

Image: A concrete representation of an object or sensory experience. Typically, such a representation helps evoke the feelings associated with the object or experience itself. Images are either "literal" or "figurative." Literal images are especially concrete and involve little or no extension of the obvious meaning of the words used to express them. Figurative images do not follow the literal meaning of the words exactly. Images in literature are usually visual, but the term "image" can also refer to the representation of any sensory experience.

Imagery: The array of images in a literary work. Also used to convey the author's overall use of figurative language in a work.

In medias res: A Latin term meaning "in the middle of things." It refers to the technique of beginning a story at its midpoint and then using various flashback devices to reveal previous action. This technique originated in such epics as Virgil's *Aeneid*.

Interior Monologue: A narrative technique in which characters' thoughts are revealed in a way that appears to be uncontrolled by the author. The interior monologue typically aims to reveal the inner self of a character. It portrays emotional experiences as they occur at both a conscious and unconscious level. One of the best-known interior monologues in English is the Molly Bloom section at the close of James Joyce's *Ulysses*. Katherine Anne Porter's "The Jilting of Granny Weatherall" is also told in the form of an interior monologue.

Irony: In literary criticism, the effect of language in which the intended meaning is the opposite of what is stated. The title of Jonathan Swift's "A Modest Proposal" is ironic because what Swift proposes in this essay is cannibalism—hardly "modest."

J

Jargon: Language that is used or understood only by a select group of people. Jargon may refer to terminology used in a certain profession, such as computer jargon, or it may refer to any nonsensical language that is not understood by most people. Anthony Burgess's *A Clockwork Orange* and James Thurber's "The Secret Life of Walter Mitty" both use jargon.

K

Knickerbocker Group: An indistinct group of New York writers of the first half of the nineteenth century. Members of the group were linked only by location and a common theme: New York life. Two famous members of the Knickerbocker Group were Washington Irving and William Cullen Bryant. The group's name derives from Irving's *Knickerbocker's History of New York.*

L

Literal Language: An author uses literal language when he or she writes without exaggerating or embellishing the subject matter and without any tools of figurative language. To say "He ran very quickly down the street" is to use literal language, whereas to say "He ran like a hare down the street" would be using figurative language.

Literature: Literature is broadly defined as any written or spoken material, but the term most often refers to creative works. Literature includes poetry, drama, fiction, and many kinds of nonfiction writing, as well as oral, dramatic, and broadcast compositions not necessarily preserved in a written format, such as films and television programs.

Lost Generation: A term first used by Gertrude Stein to describe the post-World War I generation of American writers: men and women haunted by a sense of betrayal and emptiness brought about by the destructiveness of the war. The term is commonly applied to Hart Crane, Ernest Hemingway, F. Scott Fitzgerald, and others.

M

Magic Realism: A form of literature that incorporates fantasy elements or supernatural occurrences into the narrative and accepts them as truth. Gabriel Gárcia Márquez and Laura Esquivel are two writers known for their works of magic realism.

Metaphor: A figure of speech that expresses an idea through the image of another object. Metaphors suggest the essence of the first object by identifying it with certain qualities of the second object. An example is "But soft, what light through yonder window breaks? / It is the east, and Juliet is the sun" in William Shakespeare's *Romeo and Juliet.*

Here, Juliet, the first object, is identified with qualities of the second object, the sun.

Minimalism: A literary style characterized by spare, simple prose with few elaborations. In minimalism, the main theme of the work is often never discussed directly. Amy Hempel and Ernest Hemingway are two writers known for their works of minimalism.

Modernism: Modern literary practices. Also, the principles of a literary school that lasted from roughly the beginning of the twentieth century until the end of World War II. Modernism is defined by its rejection of the literary conventions of the nineteenth century and by its opposition to conventional morality, taste, traditions, and economic values. Many writers are associated with the concepts of modernism, including Albert Camus, D. H. Lawrence, Ernest Hemingway, William Faulkner, Eugene O'Neill, and James Joyce.

Monologue: A composition, written or oral, by a single individual. More specifically, a speech given by a single individual in a drama or other public entertainment. It has no set length, although it is usually several or more lines long. "I Stand Here Ironing" by Tillie Olsen is an example of a story written in the form of a monologue.

Mood: The prevailing emotions of a work or of the author in his or her creation of the work. The mood of a work is not always what might be expected based on its subject matter.

Motif: A theme, character type, image, metaphor, or other verbal element that recurs throughout a single work of literature or occurs in a number of different works over a period of time. For example, the color white in Herman Melville's *Moby Dick* is a "specific" motif, while the trials of star-crossed lovers is a "conventional" motif from the literature of all periods.

N

Narration: The telling of a series of events, real or invented. A narration may be either a simple narrative, in which the events are recounted chronologically, or a narrative with a plot, in which the account is given in a style reflecting the author's artistic concept of the story. Narration is sometimes used as a synonym for "storyline."

Narrative: A verse or prose accounting of an event or sequence of events, real or invented. The term is also used as an adjective in the sense "method of narration." For example, in literary criticism, the expression "narrative technique" usually refers to the way the author structures and presents his or her story. Different narrative forms include diaries, travelogues, novels, ballads, epics, short stories, and other fictional forms.

Narrator: The teller of a story. The narrator may be the author or a character in the story through whom the author speaks. Huckleberry Finn is the narrator of Mark Twain's *The Adventures of Huckleberry Finn.*

Novella: An Italian term meaning "story." This term has been especially used to describe fourteenth-century Italian tales, but it also refers to modern short novels. Modern novellas include Leo Tolstoy's *The Death of Ivan Ilich,* Fyodor Dostoyevsky's *Notes from the Underground,* and Joseph Conrad's *Heart of Darkness.*

O

Oedipus Complex: A son's romantic obsession with his mother. The phrase is derived from the story of the ancient Theban hero Oedipus, who unknowingly killed his father and married his mother, and was popularized by Sigmund Freud's theory of psychoanalysis. Literary occurrences of the Oedipus complex include Sophocles' *Oedipus Rex* and D. H. Lawrence's "The Rocking-Horse Winner."

Onomatopoeia: The use of words whose sounds express or suggest their meaning. In its simplest sense, onomatopoeia may be represented by words that mimic the sounds they denote such as "hiss" or "meow." At a more subtle level, the pattern and rhythm of sounds and rhymes of a line or poem may be onomatopoeic.

Oral Tradition: A process by which songs, ballads, folklore, and other material are transmitted by word of mouth. The tradition of oral transmission predates the written record systems of literate society. Oral transmission preserves material sometimes over generations, although often with variations. Memory plays a large part in the recitation and preservation of orally transmitted material. Native American myths and legends, and African folktales told by plantation slaves are examples of orally transmitted literature.

P

Parable: A story intended to teach a moral lesson or answer an ethical question. Examples of parables are the stories told by Jesus Christ in the New Testament, notably "The Prodigal Son," but parables also are used in Sufism, rabbinic literature, Hasidism, and Zen Buddhism. Isaac Bashevis Singer's story "Gimpel the Fool" exhibits characteristics of a parable.

Paradox: A statement that appears illogical or contradictory at first, but may actually point to an underlying truth. A literary example of a paradox is George Orwell's statement "All animals are equal, but some animals are more equal than others" in *Animal Farm.*

Parody: In literature, this term refers to an imitation of a serious literary work or the signature style of a particular author in a ridiculous manner. A typical parody adopts the style of the original and applies it to an inappropriate subject for humorous effect. Parody is a form of satire and could be considered the literary equivalent of a caricature or cartoon. Henry Fielding's *Shamela* is a parody of Samuel Richardson's *Pamela.*

Persona: A Latin term meaning "mask." Personae are the characters in a fictional work of literature. The persona generally functions as a mask through which the author tells a story in a voice other than his or her own. A persona is usually either a character in a story who acts as a narrator or an "implied author," a voice created by the author to act as the narrator for himself or herself. The persona in Charlotte Perkins Gilman's story "The Yellow Wallpaper" is the unnamed young mother experiencing a mental breakdown.

Personification: A figure of speech that gives human qualities to abstract ideas, animals, and inanimate objects. To say that "the sun is smiling" is to personify the sun.

Plot: The pattern of events in a narrative or drama. In its simplest sense, the plot guides the author in composing the work and helps the reader follow the work. Typically, plots exhibit causality and unity and have a beginning, a middle, and an end. Sometimes, however, a plot may consist of a series of disconnected events, in which case it is known as an "episodic plot."

Poetic Justice: An outcome in a literary work, not necessarily a poem, in which the good are rewarded and the evil are punished, especially in ways that particularly fit their virtues or crimes. For example, a murderer may himself be murdered, or a thief will find himself penniless.

Poetic License: Distortions of fact and literary convention made by a writer—not always a poet—for the sake of the effect gained. Poetic license is closely related to the concept of "artistic freedom." An author exercises poetic license by saying that a pile of money "reaches as high as a mountain" when the pile is actually only a foot or two high.

Point of View: The narrative perspective from which a literary work is presented to the reader. There are four traditional points of view. The "third person omniscient" gives the reader a "godlike" perspective, unrestricted by time or place, from which to see actions and look into the minds of characters. This allows the author to comment openly on characters and events in the work. The "third person" point of view presents the events of the story from outside of any single character's perception, much like the omniscient point of view, but the reader must understand the action as it takes place and without any special insight into characters' minds or motivations. The "first person" or "personal" point of view relates events as they are perceived by a single character. The main character "tells" the story and may offer opinions about the action and characters which differ from those of the author. Much less common than omniscient, third person, and first person is the "second person" point of view, wherein the author tells the story as if it is happening to the reader. James Thurber employs the omniscient point of view in his short story "The Secret Life of Walter Mitty." Ernest Hemingway's "A Clean, Well-Lighted Place" is a short story told from the third person point of view. Mark Twain's novel *Huckleberry Finn* is presented from the first person viewpoint. Jay McInerney's *Bright Lights, Big City* is an example of a novel which uses the second person point of view.

Pornography: Writing intended to provoke feelings of lust in the reader. Such works are often condemned by critics and teachers, but those which can be shown to have literary value are viewed less harshly. Literary works that have been described as pornographic include D. H. Lawrence's *Lady Chatterley's Lover* and James Joyce's *Ulysses.*

Post-Aesthetic Movement: An artistic response made by African Americans to the black aesthetic movement of the 1960s and early 1970s. Writers since that time have adopted a somewhat different tone in their work, with less emphasis placed on the disparity between black and white in the United States. In the words of post-aesthetic authors such as Toni Morrison, John Edgar Wideman, and Kristin Hunter, African Americans are portrayed as looking inward for answers to their own questions, rather than always looking to the outside world. Two well-known examples of works produced as part of the post-aesthetic movement are the Pulitzer Prize–winning novels *The Color Purple* by Alice Walker and *Beloved* by Toni Morrison.

Postmodernism: Writing from the 1960s forward characterized by experimentation and application of modernist elements, which include existentialism and alienation. Postmodernists have gone a step further in the rejection of tradition begun with the modernists by also rejecting traditional forms, preferring the anti-novel over the novel and the anti-hero over the hero. Postmodern writers include Thomas Pynchon, Margaret Drabble, and Gabriel Gárcia Márquez.

Prologue: An introductory section of a literary work. It often contains information establishing the situation of the characters or presents information about the setting, time period, or action. In drama, the prologue is spoken by a chorus or by one of the principal characters.

Prose: A literary medium that attempts to mirror the language of everyday speech. It is distinguished from poetry by its use of unmetered, unrhymed language consisting of logically related sentences. Prose is usually grouped into paragraphs that form a cohesive whole such as an essay or a novel. The term is sometimes used to mean an author's general writing.

Protagonist: The central character of a story who serves as a focus for its themes and incidents and as the principal rationale for its development. The protagonist is sometimes referred to in discussions of modern literature as the hero or anti-hero. Well-known protagonists are Hamlet in William Shakespeare's *Hamlet* and Jay Gatsby in F. Scott Fitzgerald's *The Great Gatsby*.

R

Realism: A nineteenth-century European literary movement that sought to portray familiar characters, situations, and settings in a realistic manner. This was done primarily by using an objective narrative point of view and through the buildup of accurate detail. The standard for success of any realistic work depends on how faithfully it transfers common experience into fictional forms. The realistic method may be altered or extended, as in stream of consciousness writing, to record highly subjective experience. Contemporary authors who often write in a realistic way include Nadine Gordimer and Grace Paley.

Resolution: The portion of a story following the climax, in which the conflict is resolved. The resolution of Jane Austen's *Northanger Abbey* is neatly summed up in the following sentence: "Henry and Catherine were married, the bells rang and every body smiled."

Rising Action: The part of a drama where the plot becomes increasingly complicated. Rising action leads up to the climax, or turning point, of a drama. The final "chase scene" of an action film is generally the rising action which culminates in the film's climax.

Roman a clef: A French phrase meaning "novel with a key." It refers to a narrative in which real persons are portrayed under fictitious names. Jack Kerouac, for example, portrayed various friends under fictitious names in the novel *On the Road*. D. H. Lawrence based "The Rocking-Horse Winner" on a family he knew.

Romanticism: This term has two widely accepted meanings. In historical criticism, it refers to a European intellectual and artistic movement of the late eighteenth and early nineteenth centuries that sought greater freedom of personal expression than that allowed by the strict rules of literary form and logic of the eighteenth-century neoclassicists. The Romantics preferred emotional and imagi-

native expression to rational analysis. They considered the individual to be at the center of all experience and so placed him or her at the center of their art. The Romantics believed that the creative imagination reveals nobler truths—unique feelings and attitudes—than those that could be discovered by logic or by scientific examination. "Romanticism" is also used as a general term to refer to a type of sensibility found in all periods of literary history and usually considered to be in opposition to the principles of classicism. In this sense, Romanticism signifies any work or philosophy in which the exotic or dreamlike figure strongly, or that is devoted to individualistic expression, self-analysis, or a pursuit of a higher realm of knowledge than can be discovered by human reason. Prominent Romantics include Jean-Jacques Rousseau, William Wordsworth, John Keats, Lord Byron, and Johann Wolfgang von Goethe.

S

Satire: A work that uses ridicule, humor, and wit to criticize and provoke change in human nature and institutions. Voltaire's novella *Candide* and Jonathan Swift's essay "A Modest Proposal" are both satires. Flannery O'Connor's portrayal of the family in "A Good Man Is Hard to Find" is a satire of a modern, Southern, American family.

Science Fiction: A type of narrative based upon real or imagined scientific theories and technology. Science fiction is often peopled with alien creatures and set on other planets or in different dimensions. Popular writers of science fiction are Isaac Asimov, Karel Capek, Ray Bradbury, and Ursula K. Le Guin.

Setting: The time, place, and culture in which the action of a narrative takes place. The elements of setting may include geographic location, characters's physical and mental environments, prevailing cultural attitudes, or the historical time in which the action takes place.

Short Story: A fictional prose narrative shorter and more focused than a novella. The short story usually deals with a single episode and often a single character. The "tone," the author's attitude toward his or her subject and audience, is uniform throughout. The short story frequently also lacks *denouement*, ending instead at its climax.

Signifying Monkey: A popular trickster figure in black folklore, with hundreds of tales about this character documented since the 19th century. Henry Louis Gates Jr. examines the history of the signifying monkey in *The Signifying Monkey: Towards a Theory of Afro-American Literary Criticism,* published in 1988.

Simile: A comparison, usually using "like" or "as," of two essentially dissimilar things, as in "coffee as cold as ice" or "He sounded like a broken record." The title of Ernest Hemingway's "Hills Like White Elephants" contains a simile.

Socialist Realism: The Socialist Realism school of literary theory was proposed by Maxim Gorky and established as a dogma by the first Soviet Congress of Writers. It demanded adherence to a communist worldview in works of literature. Its doctrines required an objective viewpoint comprehensible to the working classes and themes of social struggle featuring strong proletarian heroes. Gabriel Gárcia Márquez's stories exhibit some characteristics of Socialist Realism.

Stereotype: A stereotype was originally the name for a duplication made during the printing process; this led to its modern definition as a person or thing that is (or is assumed to be) the same as all others of its type. Common stereotypical characters include the absent-minded professor, the nagging wife, the troublemaking teenager, and the kind-hearted grandmother.

Stream of Consciousness: A narrative technique for rendering the inward experience of a character. This technique is designed to give the impression of an ever-changing series of thoughts, emotions, images, and memories in the spontaneous and seemingly illogical order that they occur in life. The textbook example of stream of consciousness is the last section of James Joyce's *Ulysses.*

Structure: The form taken by a piece of literature. The structure may be made obvious for ease of understanding, as in nonfiction works, or may obscured for artistic purposes, as in some poetry or seemingly "unstructured" prose.

Style: A writer's distinctive manner of arranging words to suit his or her ideas and purpose in writing. The unique imprint of the author's personality upon his or her writing, style is the product of an author's way of arranging ideas and his or her use of diction, different sentence structures, rhythm, figures of speech, rhetorical principles, and other elements of composition.

Suspense: A literary device in which the author maintains the audience's attention through the buildup of events, the outcome of which will soon be revealed. Suspense in William Shakespeare's *Hamlet* is sustained throughout by the question of whether or not the Prince will achieve what he has been instructed to do and of what he intends to do.

Symbol: Something that suggests or stands for something else without losing its original identity. In literature, symbols combine their literal meaning with the suggestion of an abstract concept. Literary symbols are of two types: those that carry complex associations of meaning no matter what their contexts, and those that derive their suggestive meaning from their functions in specific literary works. Examples of symbols are sunshine suggesting happiness, rain suggesting sorrow, and storm clouds suggesting despair.

T

Tale: A story told by a narrator with a simple plot and little character development. Tales are usually relatively short and often carry a simple message. Examples of tales can be found in the works of Saki, Anton Chekhov, Guy de Maupassant, and O. Henry.

Tall Tale: A humorous tale told in a straightforward, credible tone but relating absolutely impossible events or feats of the characters. Such tales were commonly told of frontier adventures during the settlement of the west in the United States. Literary use of tall tales can be found in Washington Irving's *History of New York*, Mark Twain's *Life on the Mississippi*, and in the German R. F. Raspe's *Baron Munchausen's Narratives of His Marvellous Travels and Campaigns in Russia*.

Theme: The main point of a work of literature. The term is used interchangeably with thesis. Many works have multiple themes. One of the themes of Nathaniel Hawthorne's "Young Goodman Brown" is loss of faith.

Tone: The author's attitude toward his or her audience maybe deduced from the tone of the work. A formal tone may create distance or convey politeness, while an informal tone may encourage a friendly, intimate, or intrusive feeling in the reader. The author's attitude toward his or her subject matter may also be deduced from the tone of the words he or she uses in discussing it. The tone of John F. Kennedy's speech which included the appeal to "ask not what your country can do for you" was intended to instill feelings of camaraderie and national pride in listeners.

Tragedy: A drama in prose or poetry about a noble, courageous hero of excellent character who, because of some tragic character flaw, brings ruin upon him- or herself. Tragedy treats its subjects in a dignified and serious manner, using poetic language to help evoke pity and fear and bring about catharsis, a purging of these emotions. The tragic form was practiced extensively by the ancient Greeks. The classical form of tragedy was revived in the sixteenth century; it flourished especially on the Elizabethan stage. In modern times, dramatists have attempted to adapt the form to the needs of modern society by drawing their heroes from the ranks of ordinary men and women and defining the nobility of these heroes in terms of spirit rather than exalted social standing. Some contemporary works that are thought of as tragedies include *The Great Gatsby* by F. Scott Fitzgerald, and *The Sound and the Fury* by William Faulkner.

Tragic Flaw: In a tragedy, the quality within the hero or heroine which leads to his or her downfall. Examples of the tragic flaw include Othello's jealousy and Hamlet's indecisiveness, although most great tragedies defy such simple interpretation.

U

Utopia: A fictional perfect place, such as "paradise" or "heaven." An early literary utopia was described in Plato's *Republic,* and in modern literature, Ursula K. Le Guin depicts a utopia in "The Ones Who Walk Away from Omelas."

V

Victorian: Refers broadly to the reign of Queen Victoria of England (1837-1901) and to anything with qualities typical of that era. For example, the qualities of smug narrow-mindedness, bourgeois materialism, faith in social progress, and priggish morality are often considered Victorian. In literature, the Victorian Period was the great age of the English novel, and the latter part of the era saw the rise of movements such as decadence and symbolism.

Cumulative Author/Title Index

Cumulative
Nationality/Ethnicity Index

African American

Baldwin, James
  The Rockpile: V18
  Sonny's Blues: V2
Bambara, Toni Cade
  Blues Ain't No Mockin Bird: V4
  Geraldine Moore the Poet: V40
  Gorilla, My Love: V21
  The Lesson: V12
  Raymond's Run: V7
  The War of the Wall: V39
Brooks, Gwendolyn
  Home: V35
Butler, Octavia
  Bloodchild: V6
Chesnutt, Charles Waddell
  The Goophered Grapevine: V26
  The Sheriff's Children: V11
Clifton, Lucille
  The Lucky Stone: V34
Collier, Eugenia W.
  Marigolds: V28
  Sweet Potato Pie: V30
Ellison, Ralph
  King of the Bingo Game: V1
Hughes, Langston
  The Blues I'm Playing: V7
  Slave on the Block: V4
  Thank You Ma'm: V29
Hurston, Zora Neale
  Conscience of the Court: V21
  Drenched in Light: V42
  The Eatonville Anthology: V1
  The Gilded Six-Bits: V11
  Spunk: V6
  Sweat: V19

Lee, Andrea
  New African: V37
Marshall, Paule
  To Da-duh, in Memoriam: V15
McPherson, James Alan
  Elbow Room: V23
Myers, Walter Dean
  The Treasure of Lemon Brown:
    V31
Toomer, Jean
  Blood-Burning Moon: V5
Walker, Alice
  Everyday Use: V2
  Roselily: V11
Wideman, John Edgar
  The Beginning of Homewood: V12
  Fever: V6
  What We Cannot Speak About We
    Must Pass Over in Silence: V24
Wright, Richard
  Big Black Good Man: V20
  Bright and Morning Star: V15
  The Man Who Lived Underground:
    V3
  The Man Who Was Almost a Man:
    V9

American

Adams, Alice
  Greyhound People: V21
  The Last Lovely City: V14
Agüeros, Jack
  Dominoes: V13
Aiken, Conrad
  Impulse: V34
  Silent Snow, Secret Snow: V8

Aiken, Joan
  Lob's Girl: V38
  Sonata for Harp and Bicycle: V33
Alcott, Louisa May
  Back Windows: V41
Alexie, Sherman
  Because My Father Always Said
    He Was the Only Indian Who
    Saw Jimi Hendrix Play "The
    Star-Spangled Banner" at
    Woodstock: V18
Allen, Woody
  The Kugelmass Episode: V21
Alvarez, Julia
  Daughter of Invention: V31
  Liberty: V27
Anaya, Rudolfo
  In Search of Epifano: V38
Anderson, Sherwood
  Death in the Woods: V10
  The Egg: V37
  Hands: V11
  Sophistication: V4
Asimov, Isaac
  The Machine That Won the War:
    V33
  Nightfall: V17
Baida, Peter
  A Nurse's Story: V25
Baldwin, James
  The Rockpile: V18
  Sonny's Blues: V2
Bambara, Toni Cade
  Blues Ain't No Mockin Bird: V4
  Geraldine Moore the Poet: V40
  Gorilla, My Love: V21
  The Lesson: V12

Subject/Theme Index

Subject/Theme Index